AMERICAN NIGHT

Publication of this book was supported in part by a generous gift from Ruth and Tom Green.

© 2012 The University of North Carolina Press
All rights reserved
Designed by Jacquline Johnson
Set in Minion Pro
by Tseng Information Systems, Inc.
Manufactured in the United States of America

The paper in this book meets the guidelines for permanence and durability of the Committee on Production Guidelines for Book Longevity of the Council on Library Resources.

The University of North Carolina Press has been a member of the Green Press Initiative since 2003.

Library of Congress Cataloging-in-Publication Data
Wald, Alan M., 1946–
American night : the literary left in the era of the Cold War / Alan M. Wald.
p. cm.
Includes bibliographical references and index.
ISBN 978-0-8078-3586-9 (cloth : alk. paper)
ISBN 978-1-4696-1881-4 (pbk. : alk. paper)
1. American literature—20th century—History and criticism.
2. Communism and literature—United States—History—20th century. 3. Socialism and literature—United States—History—20th century. 4. Right and left (Political science) in literature.
I. Title.
PS228.C6W34 2012
810.9′358—dc23

2012012540

A portion of chapter 4 originally appeared as "The Great Outsider: On the Centennial of Richard Wright, 1908–1960," *Against the Current* 138 (January–February 2009): 15–19. Used with permission.

cloth   16 15 14 13 12   5 4 3 2 1
paper 18 17 16 15 14   5 4 3 2 1

THIS BOOK WAS DIGITALLY PRINTED.

AMERICAN NIGHT

The Literary Left in the Era of the Cold War

ALAN M. WALD

The University of
North Carolina Press
Chapel Hill

TO ANGELA

A glistening emerald drop hangs
from the end of a straight stem.
BORIS PASTERNAK

Blacklisted by trade unions we once had suffered to build,
Shot down under a bust of Plato by HUAC *and* AAUP.
Perhaps the commune must fail in the filth of the American
  night—
Fail for a time . . .
But all time is redeemed by the single man—
Who remembers and resurrects.
And I remember.
I keep
The winter count.
—THOMAS MCGRATH, *Letter to an Imaginary Friend*, 1962

Fog over the river, fog over Dock Street, the street that ran alongside the river. He heard the chug-chug of Jubine's motorcycle, way down on Franklin Avenue, going slowly, visualized him, head bent forward, peering, trying to see both sides of the street at once for fear he'd miss something . . .
—ANN PETRY, *The Narrows*, 1953

May the passion, the experience, and even the faults of my fighting generation have some small power to illumine the way forward.
—VICTOR SERGE, *Memoirs of a Revolutionary*, 1963
  (written 1943)

Contents

Preface xi

INTRODUCTION Late Antifascism 1

CHAPTER ONE Postwar 22
 The Culture Wars of Kenneth Fearing 22
 The Mask of Irony 27
 Rage against the Machine 33
 Study in Fundamentals 37
 The Virtue of Intentions 41

CHAPTER TWO Scenes from a Class Struggle 49
 Somewhere beyond Proletarianism 49
 The Intellectual under Fire 55
 The Making of Zhdanovists 60
 Grand Illusions 70
 Humboldt's Gift 75

CHAPTER THREE The Cult of Reason 84
 Coming Home 84
 After the Popular Front 92
 The Sublime Saxton 98
 The Ruins of Memory 103
 Gender and the Crisis of Form 107

CHAPTER FOUR The "Homintern" Reconsidered 117
 Butterfly Friends 117
 The Closeted Past 127
 The Double Life of Harry Dana 134

Tough Guys 139
Mama's Boys 144

CHAPTER FIVE Lonely Crusaders, Part I 150
The Great Outsider 150
"I Tried to Be a Communist" 156
Personal History 163
American Pages 169
The Radical Stranger 174

CHAPTER SIX Lonely Crusaders, Part II 179
Melville in Old Saybrook 179
Contingencies of Gender 184
The Fog 190
The Etiology of Mourning 195
Red, Black, and Gay 201
Exile and Its Discontents 208

CHAPTER SEVEN Jews without Judaism 216
Deconversion and Disavowal 216
Friends of the Unconscious 225
Analytical Realism 230
The Book of Memory 238
A Novel of Emotions 243

CHAPTER EIGHT Off Modernity's Grid 250
The Strange Career of People's Poetry 250
Imaginary Friends 256
Memories of the Future 265
Socialist Surrealism 271
Auden in Brooklyn 281

CONCLUSION The Sense of an Ending 292
The Afterlife of Literary Communism 292
The Indeterminacy of Art 296
The Presence of an Absence 304

A Note on Methodology 319
Notes 325
Acknowledgments 391
Index 397

Illustrations

Howard Fast 4, 5
Kenneth Fearing 23
Budd Schulberg 53
Samuel Sillen 62
Charles Humboldt 76
Dr. Annette T. Rubinstein 81
Sam Ross 90
Lloyd Brown 91
James Neugass 95
Alexander Saxton 99
Vera Caspary 110
Lillian Barnard Gilkes 122
Naomi Replansky 123
Rebecca Pitts 125
Henry Wadsworth Longfellow Dana 135
Richard Wright 157
Ann Petry 180
Harry Slochower 199
Willard Motley 202
Abraham Polonsky 226
Katya and Bert Gilden 232
Aaron Kramer 251
Thomas McGrath 258, 259
Gene Frumkin and Alvaro Cardona-Hine 269
Walter Lowenfels (1) 273

Walter Lowenfels (2) 275
Sarah Wright and Lucy Smith 277
David McElvey White 283
Don Gordon 289
Carlos Bulosan 299
Earl Conrad 308
Milton Meltzer 309
Ira Wallach 310
Edward Newhouse 312

Preface

The ingenuity of literary history does not belong to documents but to the queries posed: To what extent is a "Communist presence" to be found in the mainstream as well as in the tributaries of U.S. letters after the mid-1940s? What are the criteria for measuring the magnitude and merit of this presence? Does this literature speak to us any longer? In the political culture of the era, is the designation "Progressive" simply a code word for "Communist"? And when and how did it become so tricky to say for sure what political terms such as "Communist" and "Progressive" really meant? Although events of the past have never been so contested as they are about the Cold War and political amnesia is habitually deplored by critics of contemporary society, extant literary histories are oblique about such large-bore issues. The answers to these questions require detective work like that of a picture restorer with a badly damaged canvas. What we have at the moment is principally the mute present of a deficient postwar archaeological dig.

American Night: The Literary Left in the Era of the Cold War is the finale of a trilogy written in hot pursuit of the eternally elusive "black box" of truth about the passage of writers in the United States through the most violent and repressive three decades of the mid-twentieth century. *Exiles from a Future Time: The Forging of the Mid-Twentieth-Century Literary Left* (2002) probed the paradoxes of art consecrated to Marxist political commitment in the early years of the Great Depression. *Trinity of Passion: The Literary Left and the Antifascist Crusade* (2007) chronicled the careers of those who devoted their resources—physically, emotionally, and creatively—to combating fascism in Spain and on the domestic and other international fronts of World War II. This volume turns to the lives and works of writers grounded in the sensational events of the transition from postwar to the McCarthy era.

Between 1945 and the late 1950s, the socialist vision fashioned in the 1930s became the target of a nonstop "culture war," the term used today for a political polarization exploding in the public sphere around hot-button issues indicative of a divide between Right and Left. The outcome, induced by unprecedented domestic and international changes, was a species of "memory crisis" in respect to the political and cultural inheritance of the 1930s Left. Such "enforced forgetting" produced a hostile transformation in meanings and concepts that disrupted the forward movement of literary radicalism, a mode of politico-cultural activism largely bound up in the tacit identity of writers with the Communist movement.[1]

In the late 1940s, "Communism" was successfully established as a trigger word by its opponents, who fired off rounds to hit people with the labels of disloyalty and deceit. Such inflammatory characterizations of individuals in the vanguard of racial justice, working-class organization, and anticolonialism pushed the potential targets among writers toward hasty self-editing of political autobiographies and slippery disclaimers of affiliation. Forgetting was necessary. Due to the absence of an open space for candid political discussion, many of the unknowns of Communist identity have been preserved as if in amber. Sixty-five years later, even the language used by the literary Left comes across as a reified procession of terms and phrases uprooted from contexts, shards of thought uncoupled from the past that constituted meaning.

To speak to this wrenching episode, *American Night*, a work of social literary history, brings into play a conceptual frame proposing imaginative literature as a communal autobiography of several generations of writers committed to the 1930s vision of advancing a new society. The vision reformulated national patriotism into world citizenship and demanded an economy democratically controlled by the producers.[2]

Into this mix came Soviet Communism, a Janus-faced juggernaut that heroically fought against fascism and colonialism while defending a police state. In the associative mental architecture of the Communist movement, this meant that the worthy vision of the 1930s became synonymous with the safekeeping of an egregiously idealized Soviet Union. The moral hazards of such a false positive were harvested as "Communist" took on a compound meaning, one that embodied a simultaneity of paradoxical experiences, a beguiling alloy of sacrifice and delusion, humanitarian ideals, and ruthless realpolitik.

The writers treated in *American Night* are mostly gifted and dedicated to humane politics, but Communism always had many faces. Wherever one was caught up in a moral certainty about a state regime, East or West, there were certain circles of hell that could not be squared. Some intelligent and honest individuals even traveled about the Soviet Union and returned to write true reports of the untruth that they lived.

The nationalization of the Soviet economy and the anti-imperialism of its foreign policy beget an amalgam of benefits and shams still in dispute. I personally believe that, early on, the movement known as "Stalinism" lost the moral compass and quality of critical reason necessary to socialism. Yet the story told of writers in *American Night* is meant to remind us that one can have perfectly good incentives for talking oneself into downing a potent cocktail of beliefs while still being wrong. I presuppose this twofold standpoint ubiquitously, although it is tedious to cite it at every conceivable opportunity.

My study departs from all earlier inquiries into the literary Left in being more about structures of feeling than the dramatization of formal ideology. Literary texts are selected for scrutiny to exemplify the psychological state of the adherents of the 1930s vision, charting the span of what amounts to an alter-tradition in various cultural strata. Archival research, oral history, and literary theory and criticism are conjoined to explore characteristic responses through an assortment of intimate portraits and close readings. While this compilation is tied to a range of ideological and personal mutations that have rarely received a searching examination, the incentive for *American Night* is not merely the fascination of a gone world or to carve out an overlooked moment. To be alive in the early twenty-first century is to live in the residue of mixed inheritances of the postwar era; we do not have the option to be unentangled in this lost time.

Entrenched as it is in the archaeology of historical and biographical research, *American Night* is nonetheless far from a conventional study of artistic achievement in the Cold War. In some measure, I was goaded into writing this midrash of literary Communism by a yearning to probe the inscrutability of what I call Communist literary modernism. This is an intentionally ironic category, formulated to describe qualities I have come to admire in left-wing U.S. writing in the 1940s and 1950s, and in some of its afterlife. The phrase combines a dissident Marxism—a chastened, more "contingent," less "positivist" historical sensibility still attuned to class and racial oppression—with explorations of subjectivity informed by insights echoing psychoanalysis and existentialism. Writers like Kenneth Fearing, Ann Petry, Richard Wright, Thomas McGrath, and Carlos Bulosan lure us into such an Orphic underworld even as the authors retain a Marxian notion that the social order dominates individuals and molds them to those purposes that effectively contribute to the preservation of a class system. The finest of this haunted fiction and poetry is marked by cognitive originality and a sweep of consciousness.

In the 1950s, it is several modernist-like hidden narratives—not any realist or naturalist storylines of explicit radical activism—that recount the labyrinth of Left history, one too often simplified as the straight line of a single continuing tradition from the 1930s to the 1960s.

The radical ideas in works such as Petry's *The Narrows* (1953) are not expressed at the level at which they were ordinarily adjudicated in classic Left fiction such as *The Grapes of Wrath* (1939). They are now refashioned by the exigencies of a postwar imagination, suggested by a quotation from *The Narrows* serving as an epigraph to this book; the novel's political-artistic protagonist, the photojournalist Jubine, tries to see both sides of the road at once through a fog. In Petry, it is the deepening aporia, not the rise of the agitator, that signals the political agenda. Steinbeck deftly wove symbol and myth into his novel, but Petry's contradictions of meaning demolish the illusion of fiction as a copy of reality; she creates disquieting literary truths for her era with which it may be more difficult to wrestle. As early as Fearing's *The Big Clock* (1946), certain novelists were departing the 1930s tradition of forward motion toward a discernible goal of a targeted upheaval against economic injustice; they were becoming permanent insurrectionists against more unfathomable dominions of authority.

Kenneth Fearing and Alexander Saxton (author of *The Great Midland*, 1948) variously prefigure those writers who several years later would commit deicide against the competing hegemonies of Cold War polarization even while remaining loyal to the guiding principles of the vision of the 1930s. The writings analyzed at length in *American Night* show evidence of a resolute willingness to enter spaces of contradiction and deep disturbance, symptomatic of a frame of mind akin to Theodor Adorno's *Minima Moralia: Reflections from Damaged Life* (1951). Among the many reasons that the postwar Communist presence is central to mid-twentieth-century letters is that, due to a piercing emotional acuity and an atmosphere of cosmic dissent in writings expressive of the new contingency, the tradition became a facilitator of the acceptance of the existentialism and psychoanalysis now commonly identified with the era.

The Communist literary presence after World War II is discernible in the cultural work of several hundred writers who at the time were pro-Communist by inclination and sometimes by Party affiliation. Postwar Communism itself is reminiscent of the famous optical illusion of a rabbit and a duck that can only be seen at any one moment as one or the other, and writers' passions were molded long after in ways that they did not fully understand. In my choosing to treat Communism more as a verb than a noun, the narrative of a Communist presence in *American Night* alters over time and in setting. There are no cookbook recipes for identifying commitments and creative practice. Once reformulated into an examination of the affective rather than merely the political response to Communism, the scope of this topic for postwar culture is so large that a single volume, even the last of a trilogy, cannot pretend to provide a comprehensive canvas of its manifestations.

Like its predecessors, *American Night* limits its choices of careers, literary works, and characteristic problems to clarify the social, historical, and personal conditions that fashioned the writers' disparate achievements. A complete accounting of literary lives on the Left would require an encyclopedia, not a narrative. In regard to the investigation of imaginative literature, one must be unavoidably selective rather than exhaustive, offering not a survey but a sampling in which the tips of many icebergs are encountered. The aim is not to overthrow or institute a canon but to unbolt the gateway to insights about how lived, remembered, and imagined experience pushes against the particulars of literary representation.

The account provided in *American Night* climaxes in the late 1950s with the crumbling of the core of the mid-twentieth-century literary Left, the organized Communist movement. The immediate cause was the excruciating crisis that followed Premier Nikita Khrushchev's disclosures about criminal aspects of Stalin's rule in a February 1956 secret speech to the Twentieth Congress of the Communist Party of the Soviet Union. This involved episode will hereafter be referred to in shorthand as the "Khrushchev Revelations." The resulting internal disintegration of the Communist movement, not total but sufficient to permanently fragment the pro-Communist cultural tradition, was rooted in earlier incongruities between the ideals and actuality of Stalinist Communism.[3] What came next provided only the blurred sense of an ending; broken apart, the pieces of the tradition thereafter constructed themselves in a fashion that resists being reduced to a story.

For the decades following the Khrushchev Revelations, the impact of Literary Communism continues as an "afterlife" in the manner observed by historian Robin D. G. Kelley: "The collapse of an organization does not necessarily signify the destruction of a movement or the eradication of traditions of radicalism."[4] Throughout *American Night*, abundant articulations of this afterlife are cited, some of the finest providing elegiac inscriptions of a historical trace. Such references to future literary developments are included chiefly as gestures toward scholarly projects yet to come, although more wily readers may suspect that this is the trilogy of an author who has difficulty counting only to three.

The structure of the volume is straightforward. An introduction, "Late Antifascism," engages the problematical meanings for literature of the prevailing political strategy of the pro-Communist Left. Chapter 1 considers the effort of the poet and novelist Kenneth Fearing to fashion literary forms appropriate to the postwar mood, ones especially responsive to his recognition of new historical contingencies. Chapter 2 deliberates the fortunes of the postwar proletarian tradition in criticism and the synthetic intellectual world of Communist literary critics, primarily Samuel Sillen and Charles Humboldt. Chapter 3 examines the post–Popular Front record in fiction, Alexander Saxton's *The Great Midland*, and women writers of the 1940s. *American Night* then devotes four chapters to tracking the postwar transit of "outsider" presences within the Left—gays and lesbians, African Americans, and Jewish Americans. The book moves on to a study of the fate of postwar Left poetry and a conclusion that recapitulates the argument of the book by examining the afterlife of Literary Communism and the concept of Communist literary modernism as an expression of Theodor Adorno's "negative dialectics," a term that came to embody the Frankfurt School theorist's method as it evolved after the 1930s.

Adorno professed no expertise in U.S. literature, but his observations are particularly suggestive for thinking about aspects of the Communist literary presence. Like several of the writers featured in *American Night*, Adorno was not unsympathetic to the concerns motivating the postwar phenomenological turn. A focus on the structures of consciousness led to thinking, in theory as well as in art, about a problematic subjectivity as one that fails to recognize the contradictions between categories and specificities. Yet for Adorno as well as for postwar cultural workers, political assimilation to the capitalist order remained impossible, even repulsive. There was in Adorno as well as in postwar cultural workers a parallel contemplation of the fate of the lost opportunity of the vision of the 1930s and a sense that writing might be a substitute for unavailable political activities. Negative dialectics as well as Communist literary modernism expressed a vexing ambiguity: Are these writings intended to be entrées to the pessimism of a historical impasse, or the beginning of a new theory and praxis around the transformation of consciousness?

The following are the framing concepts of *American Night*, the leitmotifs that serve as guiding threads throughout the narrative outlined above:

—Even prior to the unambiguous advent of a Cold War in 1946–47, a domestic culture war in partnership with the consolidation of a "Consumers' Republic" was underway, a mixture that induced a variety of memory crises apropos the legacy of the radical vision of the 1930s.[5]
—The writing of the late 1940s and 1950s increasingly took on a palimp-

sestic character as the fading 1930s vision was refurbished under unanticipated circumstances and articulated in new literary forms.
— The "Cultural Cold War,"[6] congruent with neither the domestic, antiradical culture war emerging after World War II nor the Cold War beginning in 1946, was largely a debate between two compromised factions of liberalism, each handcuffed to a Great Power, both behaving in a manner at odds with their professed principles and as a consequence respectively guilty of double-bookkeeping.
— Left poetry of the postwar period, in the aftermath of the noteworthy anthology *Seven Poets in Search of an Answer* (1944), was wedged between an "official" demand by Left critics for simplicity and optimism and the more prevailing forms that expressed postwar isolation and generated imaginary friends, secret selves, and sometimes a "socialist surrealism" as it recaptured an oblique ancestry in modernism.
— Due to the 1950s "converso" culture of deradicalization (the result of a surface conversion, like the fourteenth-century switch to Catholicism of Spanish and Portuguese Jews, under pressure and with indeterminate results), the most distinguished works in the Left tradition brought to the fore the writers' covert agonies, often in disguised form: Cold War paranoia, doppelgängers of homeless radicals, and Melvillian stoicism of those who recognized that the dream of a better world had been stillborn.[7]
— Although Cold War ideology was officially bifurcated between West and East, the postwar struggle against colonialism emerged as the third element to create a "triangulated" global topography (what Michael Denning calls the "Age of Three Worlds") in ways that complicated the political choices of writers of the time, especially those with Marxist views and of non-European ancestry.[8]
— Writers of the "High" Cold War faced a crisis of conscience as many broke in various degrees with the legend of the Soviet Union, although a number adhered to an unspoken convention of silence, declining to make public declarations of disaffiliation as long as McCarthyism was at fever pitch.
— Under the coercion of governmental persecution and blacklisting, a small number of writers and other cultural workers testified against their former comrades; in the most extreme instances of naïveté or delusion, a handful had earlier participated in unwitting or willful acts associated with espionage.
— In more characteristic trajectories, writers withdrew from Communist Party–led institutions and sought surrogate radical commitments—

ranging from the burgeoning civil rights and Black Power movements to utopian projects such as Synanon (an alternative community in Santa Monica, California).

While *American Night* is the successor to and culmination of the earlier two volumes, the politico-literary sensibility under scrutiny differs in vital ways. Writers at the core of volume 1 were "exiles from a future time," but now they are more accurately "exiles from their own time," longing for a rebirth of the social vision and movements that distinguished the Great Depression decade. Moreover, the antifascism that was given such a high priority by writers examined in *Trinity of Passion* returns after 1946 in a second manifestation, a "late antifascism." This was a dangerously overstated (although not baseless) perception of U.S. foreign and domestic policy as the analogue to European fascism, hence appearing to require the reconstruction of a dubious version of the antifascist politics of the pre–World War II and wartime Popular Front. The greatest disservice of this approach was to make the new anti-Nazism dependent on misguided pro-Sovietism.

To be a pro-Communist writer after World War II was indeed a complex fate. *American Night* begins at a moment of peripeteia. How did men and women who passionately hated fascism become ever more likened to fascists (sometimes even called "Red Fascists") by the government, media, and population?[9] Why did artists who yearned to hone their craft for the liberation of humanity become identified as crude propagandists on behalf of cultural dictatorship? The picture of Communist writers prevailing after 1945 was the reverse of what they imagined themselves to be. Like protagonists in the Hollywood noir films of the post–World War II and Cold War era, writers who were Communists or who had pro-Communist pasts felt increasingly trapped, betrayed by all sides, and fearful of revealing the truth of their lives. To what extent was the fault of this turn-of-events in their stars, due to their inadequate selves, or the result of the malice of their enemies?

AMERICAN NIGHT

Introduction

Late Antifascism

Sidney Greenspan (1915–44) was a small, skinny, myopic Jew with sloping shoulders, a prominent nose, and thin brown hair. He died brutally in Carano, Italy, during World War II's "Operation Shingle." His death occurred two days after Allied forces carried out an amphibious landing on Anzio Beach to outflank the German troops and facilitate an attack on Rome. On 24 January 1944, Sidney, serving as a medic, was hit by machine-gun fire that first shattered his right hip and then splintered his left forearm. Sidney continued caring for the wounded, hauling them to safety until he bled to death. In recognition of his acts, the T-4 (Technician Fourth Grade) wrote Sidney up for an appropriate citation. But when Sidney's name was proposed for a Congressional Medal of Honor, there was an investigation of his past and the proposal was dropped. Sidney Greenspan was a Red.

Sidney had joined the Young Communist League in 1934 at the age of nineteen, close to the time he had participated in a big demonstration in Manhattan against inadequate relief and lack of jobs. In early 1937, Sidney arrived in Spain as part of the Abraham Lincoln Brigade of U.S. volunteers supporting the loyalist government. For the next sixteen months, he associated with notable soldiers in the International Brigades such as Dave Doran (1910–38), John Gates (1913–92), Milton Wolff (1915–2008), Robert Merriman (1908–38), James Lardner (1914–38), and Vernon Shelby (1902–38). In Spain, Sidney displayed surprising strength; he singlehandedly carried two wounded brigade members, Smith and Goldstein, across the Ebro River following a defeat and after that swam back to rescue more comrades.

Throughout his brief life, Sidney's diminutive body endured relentless brutality. His afflictions began with the poverty of his youth—his brother fell to his death under a truck in the street at the age of seven; his sister died of inadequate care of an infection of her mastoid bone; his mother, thin and dispirited, passed away when he was seventeen; and Sidney himself was beaten as a youth by anti-Semites in the vicinity of the Washington Heights tenement where he lived. In a student demonstration at the City College of New York in the early 1930s, Sidney's jaw was fractured; shortly afterward he required seven stitches when clubbed by a policeman at Union Square. In Spain, he received two shrapnel wounds. The cruelest suffering occurred when he was captured in September 1938 by Franco's Moorish troops. They broke all his fingers and then turned him over to the Nazis, who tortured him in a standing cell for months before he managed to escape.

Following Franco's victory in Spain, Sidney rejoined his wife, Jane Albertson, in New York City. He underwent an operation on his hand, recuperated for three months in the countryside, and then went south to organize African American sharecroppers. From October 1940 to December 1941, he dodged the bullets of the Ku Klux Klan. Following the news of Pearl Harbor, he convinced a doctor in New Jersey to falsely attest to his physical fitness for army enlistment, although the lingering effects of his torture caused him to be placed in the medical corps. Word leaked out to officers that Sidney had been a volunteer in Spain, and his efforts to switch to the infantry were met by red-baiting. He was then assigned combat duty as a medic and served the final months of his life in North Africa, Sicily, and, finally, on the west coast of Italy.

Sidney was buried overseas, but his close friends and comrades in New York felt that he deserved some kind of written tribute. They gathered massive amounts of material—old letters that Sidney had written from Spain, oral interviews with surviving family and associates, newspaper articles, research about the historical events that had fashioned his life, everything that was known and remembered of Sidney. Yet, in the end, his friends abandoned the idea of an elaborate tribute. The research, despite its quantity, did not fit together in a way that explained the meaning of Sidney's life. Instead, after reading a number of obituaries in the *Daily Worker*, his friends and comrades decided upon just one word that satisfactorily served to make clear what they called the "fabric" of Sidney. It was not "Jew," not "Communist," not "Progressive," not "antiracist," not "proletarian internationalist," not "husband," not "son"—it was "antifascist." To that they added: "who fell in the people's struggle..."[1]

Was Sidney Greenspan an actual person? There is no easy answer to this question. He was conceived as the title character of a much-discussed and debated 1947 short story by Howard Fast (1914–2003), first published in the pro-Communist *Jewish Life* magazine and later reprinted in *Departure and Other Stories* (1949), called "An Epitaph for Sidney." Yet readers insisted that they knew Sidney personally. Morris Schappes (1907–2004), the editor of *Jewish*

Life, declared: "You know Sidney; I know Sidney. Maybe the Sidneys I know are not named Greenspan. The ones I know are Chaikin and Mendelson and Ziegler. The ones you know have other names. They are all our friends and comrades who died fighting fascism. . . . Let Sidney be their first names."[2]

Indeed, Sidney is a composite of tens of thousands of young people—not just Jews and not just men—pulled toward the ideals of the Left from the onset of the Depression through the close of World War II. Scholarly books, oral histories, collections of letters of Abraham Lincoln Brigade volunteers first from Spain and later on from service on the battlefields of World War II, historical novels, and memoirs are overflowing with cases of pro-Communists who underwent at least one and often several of the experiences depicted by Fast. Prototypes of Sidney were attacked in student demonstrations at City College, clubbed at Union Square, inspired to fight on the front lines for the Spanish Republic, eager to risk their lives organizing in the South, and among the first to sign up for active service in World War II. They were the targets of discriminatory red-baiting in the army and were killed in combat along with other Spanish Civil War veterans—in France, Germany, and Northern India or on the Murmansk Run and in the South Pacific.

Fast's method was to dramatize the telling of specific personal details that rendered Sidney recognizable to his likely readership—largely left-wing New Yorkers who were principally secular Jews. Fast tells us about Sidney's marriage to a taller non-Jewish woman of "old American stock"; his attendance at New York City schools and various jobs in grocery stores and warehouses; and his father's timid temperament and fears that Sidney's radicalism would get him in trouble.[3] Such minutiae reminded readers of themselves and of people with whom they had associated; the heartstrings of sentimentality were pulled to elicit a nostalgia for the decade that had just passed. Zelig-like, Sidney is inserted into events in the collective memory of the Left such as the Union Square demonstration, the Spanish Civil War, labor organizing in the South, and the Italian campaign during World War II. Sidney's multiple acts of quiet heroism, perhaps in aggregate pushing the boundaries of believability, nonetheless remained embedded in firsthand memories of readers and likely emerged from Fast's gathering of anecdotes about actual militants.

Yet, Sidney Greenspan, in the pages of *Jewish Life*, was in point of fact a liminal creation, as mythical as genuine. Every individual facet of Sidney's tale rings true, but collectively the events coalesce into a fable that hides essential and compromising aspects of his prototypes. The fictionalized Sidney provides a sanitized version of the Communist experience from the early 1930s through the wartime Popular Front even as he honors genuine martyrs. The narrator of "An Epitaph for Sidney," who is nameless but evokes Joseph

Two portraits of Howard Fast, author of "An Epitaph for Sidney," published in the January 1947 issue of *Jewish Life*. Fast led a double life as a best-selling historical novelist and major spokesperson for Literary Communism from 1943 until 1956. (Courtesy of Rare Book and Manuscript Library, University of Pennsylvania)

Conrad's Charles Marlow, describes himself as a companion of Sidney's; his meandering account has the aura of talking to a group of like-minded comrades. In contrast to Marlow's reminiscences of Lord Jim, Kurtz, and other of Conrad's protagonists, however, the background data about the narrator's friend Sidney is acquired through the efforts of a number of people and then handed to the narrator, who at this point feels a need to justify the group's decision to produce his one-line epitaph.

Tellingly, the narrator indicates that the saga behind the choice of the epitaph is not solely Sidney's; it is a lament for an era that produced a certain phase of Communist activism: "In those days . . . it seemed that the world we lived in could not go on; and indeed that world is dead today, washed out in the blood of thirty million souls, even if the fight is not over."[4] The Communism of the prewar era produced Sidneys who were commonly labeled "troublemakers" rather than subversives; even Sidney's father grumbles, "Wherever you look, those Communists make trouble."[5] Sidney, despite a mild demeanor, was of a generation of men and women whose anger expressed the communal response of millions to class oppression. Sidney's hatred "of the things that pervert and destroy human beings" was transformed into a vitality that made him "a prow rather than a rudder."[6] In Sidney's world, one had no choice but to act in concert with others, and collective action was its own reward. When a judge demanded to know the reason for the young radical's participation in a protest, Sidney proudly responded: "Could I make you hear a million voices?" He then held out an empty hand and added: "I get paid in my own coin."[7]

By 1947, the times had altered from the Great Depression's steady march to the Left; the war was over and a new national atmosphere was being introduced. Symptomatic was the creation of the Americans for Democratic Action after the electoral defeat of the New Deal Democrats in the midterm elections in 1946, a setback partly due to the Republican accusation that Truman had been too gentle with the Soviet Union. An aim of the new organization was to purge former allies who were pro-Communists from positions of influence in the Democratic Party, the labor movement, and intellectual life. The electoral defeat also revitalized the House Committee on Un-American Activities, which, in October 1947, issued summons to forty-three Hollywood Leftists to testify in Washington, D.C., about Communist subversion in the film industry.

The narrator of "An Epitaph for Sidney" remarks at the story's onset: "Sidney was not the stuff of which heroes are made, at least in the conception of heroes which is most popular in America today."[8] Later the narrator is even more explicit: "The papers, the magazines, the press of the whole nation explain why people like Sidney Greenspan are corrupt, selfish, and enemies of mankind, and to that they devote countless words."[9] Yet the narrator insists that the truth about Sidney is that "there was no rest for him so long as one man was enslaved, oppressed, or exploited by another."[10] Thus, in light of the growing hysteria about Communist subversion, a new post–World War II strategy for continuing "the people's struggle" was being born.

The resurrection theme is clear in the concluding phase of Sidney's life. When he becomes a private first class in the medical department of the army, he is transformed from activist to prophet. His most heroic exploits took place in Spain, but, even as he was promoted from lieutenant to captain in the Lincoln Battalion, he was not singled out as being uncommon. It is only afterward, during his time on the frontlines in World War II, that Sidney becomes a "legend." Curiously, the myth of Sidney is not due to his fighting skills, or even his medical aptitude, but to his moral certainty about the antifascist cause: "There had been no legend from the work he did in Spain and in the States, but now in Italy there was emerging a quality of calm and certainty for men who had no certainty, many of whom didn't know where they were going or what they were fighting for."[11] For his fellow soldiers, "Sidney Greenspan was something out of another world and another struggle. He had an answer that no one else could give them."[12]

By having Sidney Greenspan killed in his story, Howard Fast creates an effective martyr to the cause of 1930s radicalism. But I believe that in the "moral certainty" of Sidney Greenspan about his antifascist "answers" resides a political and cultural riddle that has shadowed the legacy of the cultural Left. This enigma of the evolving meaning of "antifascism" came to a crisis under the contradictions of the early Cold War, but its inheritance echoes in culture wars even today. The mystery of that political trope is flawlessly captured in the story perhaps because Howard Fast's own biography blends pre- and postwar pro-Communism. Fast was not known as a Communist or Leftist in the 1930s, when he published his first historical novel at age eighteen, although he was undoubtedly sympathetic. In 1946, at the time he was writing of Sidney, he had been a Communist Party member for three years. With the passion of one who had been for too long yearning to shout out his convictions, he became very much the left-wing cultural worker transforming the outlook and sensibility of prewar Communism into a more serviceable form for the postwar era—into a politico-cultural posture that I designate "late antifascism," politically murkier than the earlier opposition to Franco and to what had happened at Munich.

What was the genealogy of the Left cultural worker prior to the time of late antifascism? The scholarship on this subject is now enormous and perhaps unending because of the difficulty of pushing headstrong and evolving individual writers into categories. Moreover, in the background is a sequence of practices promoted in the Soviet Union that were inconsistently exported to and then echoed among U.S. writers and critics on the Left. Official Soviet policies included socialist realism, codified and authorized between 1932 and 1934 to develop socialist consciousness within an evolving socialist state, and Zhdanovism (named for cultural spokesman Andrei Zhdanov, 1896–1948), most famously expressed in decrees in 1946 and 1948 that demanded ever stricter adherence to the Soviet government policy and opposition to alleged individualism and formalism. Where there seems to be agreement is that the radical writer was not a Soviet clone but emerged in the early Depression from the nineteenth-century social realist tradition, using techniques of panorama and documentary, often adapting modernist techniques (to which some had been loyal in the 1920s) to address economic and racial injustice in urban plebeian and regional settings.

He or she was commonly an ideological Communist (strict membership was often irrelevant) and said to be an exponent of some version of "proletarian culture," a term variously defined to mean producing texts expressive of working-class life or from a "revolutionary" perspective (according to the Communist interpretation of Marx and Lenin). The political program was for the United States to follow the example of the USSR.[13] Then, with the first Popular Front from mid-1935 to 1939, and again with the wartime alliance from 1941 to 1945, the Left cultural worker was primarily advocating a "people's culture," battling for "democracy," and ultimately championing an anti-Axis "victory."[14] What was good for the United States was also good for the Soviet Union, and vice versa. Communists had always felt a loyalty to populations of all countries, but now a concurrent allegiance to the two governments appeared feasible.

Initially, the post-1935 Communist cultural workers, those in the Party as well as those in the broader movement led by the Party, aimed to be in an alliance with "Progressives." The term meant Left liberals and socialists who more or less shared the Communists' pro-labor and antiracist outlook and who also downplayed criticisms of the Soviet government. Some Progressives felt a genuine attraction to the regime, while others wished mainly to promote the partnership of the Soviet Union and the West against fascism. In due course, however, a monumental confusion was created as many pro-Communists, especially those who did not work openly for the Party and had a professional position or reputation, began to refer to *themselves* as Progressives. A new category of "progressive culture" was in the meantime expanded backward to include nineteenth-century writers—Walt Whitman, Mark Twain—now seen as part of a "Great Tradition" of writers who engaged the social and political issues of their time from a perspective interpreted as consistent with Progressives (and Communists) of the second half of the 1930s and after.[15] Ever afterward, the term "Progressive" had the capacity to function as a weasel word; it was coyly useful subterfuge at the time for deflecting red-baiters and unifying forces without too many questions asked, but subsequently obscured political identities desired by anyone trying to ascertain the degree of importance to attach to Communist organization and leadership. For the remainder of this book, the use of the terms "social realism," "proletarian literature," "socialist realism," "Zhdanovism," "Progressive," and "people's culture" are built on the scaffolding provided in this introduction.

In the latter Depression, and during the alliance of the United States with the Soviet Union, there was an alluring simplicity to this post-1935, Progressive stance—politically, intellectually, culturally, ethically—as there is in all war against one great evil. Troubling concerns that a liberal might have had about the behavior of one's Communist and Soviet allies were understandably put up on the shelf; one would have to wait to solve them until after the primary menace of fascism had been addressed. On the other side, pro-Communists, always under the threat of red-baiting, could use the label Progressive to achieve protective coloration. After all, the political identity of a Progressive is never precisely clear, unless the Progressive individual identifies himself or herself as a "Communist." For a cultural worker to describe himself or herself as a "true New Dealer" in the antifascist era was not inaccurate—even as he or she might also be, beyond that, a Communist Party member or fellow traveler. To say that one is a Republican in 2011 does not rule out that one may also be a Tea Party activist. A Catholic may identify himself or herself as a Christian and not go further, especially when there are bigots around who may hold that there is a contradiction.

In other words, outside of the eighteen months of the Hitler-Stalin Pact, which will be discussed below, a Communist identifying himself or herself as a Progressive was telling the truth and lying at the same time, a state of mind that could be habit-forming. The person was leaving something "more" out of the picture, personal information that might be used by red-baiting demagogues to break up antifascist unity. And this Popular Front unity was hard to disentangle, making it difficult to assess the degree of a Communist presence and the manner in which it was manifest. A Progressive might well explain that he or she was a non-Communist, leaving ambiguous the matter of whether this really only meant that he or she did not hold formal membership in the Communist Party. Or, if a Progressive explicitly stated nonaffiliation with the Party, there was still the possibility (indeed, likelihood) of there being very warm feelings about the leadership of the Soviet Union. No doubt there were large numbers of bona fide Left liberals in the Popular Front—individuals with more questions than certainties about the Soviet Union, and perhaps minor worries that Communists were too dogmatic—but primarily focused on the enemies to their Right. The distinction between Communists and Progressive liberals was difficult to determine due to legitimate political hybridism and evolving positions, even as clear lines between them and Communists were sometimes intentionally obscured.[16] Yet the presence of these two elements is required, as are both liquid and gas in producing H₂O. There could not have been a Popular Front without pro-Communists, who provided not merely political slogans but crucial energy and much of the networking among labor, civil rights, student, and professional organizations.

This fuzziness of political labeling was surely assisted by the history of the designation "Progressive," which always had multiple meanings.[17] It originally referred to supporters of the imperialist Theodore Roosevelt as well as of the radical Robert La Follette; to those for and against intervention in World War I; and to Farmer-Labor Party advocates, Musteites ("The Conference for Progressive Political Action"), and isolationists in the Midwest. In the postwar era, "Progressive" was the term of choice for those claiming the New Deal mantle who were also convinced that emergent Cold War liberalism was a new form of reaction evidenced by its suspicion of the Soviet Union and Communists. Yet, as documentary evidence piles up in archives, it seems probable that most of the key activists among Progressive cultural workers were in some sense Communists or fellow travelers (in the United States, usually meaning close allies of the Communist Party but not official members).

This is less the case with narrowly political Progressives. Henry Wallace was weirdly anticapitalist (for a "people's capitalism"), and perhaps naive about the USSR, but not a Communist. Dr. Frederick Schuman, the Dean of Canterbury, Eddie Rickenbacker, Joseph Davies, and Harlow Shapley — these public figures were possibly not even socialists but during World War II and the early postwar years considered themselves at least temporarily part of the Progressive movement.[18] Surely a small number of genuinely non-Communist liberals, and maybe even oddball conservatives like Rickenbacker, also existed in more strictly cultural circles, but they are harder to find.

Among the names of now-major writers once supportive of Popular Front progressive culture — Lillian Hellman, Arthur Miller, Dashiell Hammett, Lorraine Hansberry, Norman Mailer, Ralph Ellison — no serious scholar believes today that they were not, in pre- or postwar years, or in both if old enough, pro-Communist ideologically in some significant way. In literary culture, Communism was part of the mainstream, even if it came in shades and degrees. And there is little doubt that the major postwar Progressive organizations in which writers participated — such as the National Council of the Arts, Sciences and Professions and the Committee for the Negro in the Arts — were decisively influenced by pro-Communists. In the register of sponsors for the 1949 Cultural and Scientific Conference for World Peace organized by the National Council of the Arts, Sciences and Professions, one finds many individuals for whom a Communist identity seems unlikely. Yet, if one isolates the names of creative writers from the United States, those with some sort of Communist affiliation in the recent past make up nearly the entire list.[19] It would be unsurprising if future archival research, with fair-minded definitions, provided convincing evidence that even some of those cultural and intellectual figures currently regarded as Progressives might just as readily be described as pro-Communists.

What, then, was the exact meaning of Progressive in the years after the breakup of the alliance between the United States and the Soviet Union, when there was increasing two-dimensional polarization? From the Communist Party's point of view, there was merely a division of labor between those identifying themselves as Progressives and those calling themselves Communists. The former were to fight for the rights of labor, African Americans, and cultural workers and for peaceful responses to any Communist actions abroad; they would expose the various corrupting influences of monopoly capitalism and denounce anti-Communists and alleged enemies of the Soviet Union. Communist intellectuals, in distinction, had the "positive work of creating new values and showing how they can be realized in the struggle for socialism."[20] This definition meant that it was still uncomplicated for Communists to call themselves Progressives and put forward most of the Party program for a Progressive movement; only a select number, such as Howard Fast and *New Yorker* profile writer Richard O. Boyer (1903–73), went further in publically declaiming Communist allegiance.[21]

Arguably, for Party supporters, "Progressive" could function as a code word, especially as anti-Communism became a national obsession. To designate individuals or a group as Progressive signaled to pro-Communists that friends of Communists were involved. At the same time, the label ensured that, at least momentarily, activists normally disinclined to follow an avowed Communist leadership might be enticed to join the organization; perhaps they would moderate their views about Communists as they subsequently discovered that the hardest working members of the organization were Party members or allies. The term "Progressive" as well offered some relatively safe space for those who knew and liked Communists but did not want to confront the complexity of the situation of aligning with the Soviet Union or having to defend *Daily Worker* dogma; one could simply deflect the charge of being responsible for Soviet atrocities by switching political discussion over to issues of international peace and friendship. Finally, being a Progressive was a logical place for one who had close friends or relatives in the Communist Party or who had drifted away from a prior affiliation without becoming overly critical.

American Night draws attention to the constructedness of this hard-to-pin-down variety of postwar Progressivism. Whatever its original autonomy in the Depression, postwar Progressivism was a project significantly kept alive postwar by the pro-Communist presence, and among creative writers and critics Progressivism became a space ever more populated by Party loyalists. More generally in U.S. history, mid-twentieth-century Progressivism became with time treated as a radical-liberal politics based exclusively on the uncontroversial ideals of Popular Front-era antifascism. But the story that Progressivism was a self-governing liberalism aimed at maintaining the authentic policies of the New Deal is an oversimplified fable. The term "Progressive" mostly captured a desired emotional truth—the hope that core Communist values were actually in the mainstream and thus compatible with Left liberalism. The passion, talent, and ardent belief of the writers studied in *American Night* assured the term "Progressive" a surprising degree of circulation and longevity. By the time that the fable of Progressivism lost its targeted audience of the 1940s and 1950s, it had become a commonplace term and is still often used as a substitute for careful analysis.[22]

Thus it was a Popular Front version of antifascism that was the crucible in which Sidney Greenspan's "answers," his "calm," his moral certainty, were forged. It was the point of reference in the phrases "another world" (the Soviet Union) and "another struggle" (Spain) that Sidney was said by the narrator of Howard Fast's story to have brought to the Italian front in 1944.[23] Whether or not Sidney was at that point still a member of the Communist Party is extraneous.[24] Sidney's state of mind exemplified a subspecies of what the Italian political philosopher Giambattista Vico designated in *The New Science* (1725), where he asserted that each age has its own lens through which people see the world. For the cultural Left of the 1930s-1950s, Popular Front antifascism was a close approximation of that phenomenon, roughly a platitude of the times. This antifascist optic persisted in various incarnations, increasingly constructed, for over several decades, albeit specific Popular Front tactics varied from country to country.[25]

Yet such an outlook, when redeployed in 1946 as the moral certainty of late antifascism, was already circumscribed by limits going back to the 1930s. Earlier, in 1922, antifascism was inaugurated among Italian American radicals after Mussolini's seizure of power, and it became a cause that united socialists, Communists, anarchists, and Industrial Syndicalists (IWW) in coalitions. With Stalin's consolidation of authority in 1928-29, however, Communist policy changed.[26] In 1933, when Hitler seized power, U.S. Communists held the view that socialists were actually "social fascists" (the twin of fascism). Communists in the early 1930s attacked, verbally and sometimes physically, the anti-Nazi protests that they did not control.

Then, after the 1935 announcement of the Popular Front, Communists took the lead in developing what we now call antifascism. They gave it, according to historian Paul Buhle, a "defining purpose and distinctive rhetoric."[27] Not only did defense of the Spanish Republic become the Communists' central international cause, but U.S. Communists linked the domestic phenomena of anti-Black racism, anti-Semitism, anti-immigrant sentiments, and anti-labor policies to the growing fascist threat. At the same time, Buhle points out, this new antifascism undermined the earlier widespread mobilizations against war itself, such as the sensational "Oxford Pledge" demonstrations of students, which had focused on war-profiteer capitalists and the capitalist system that made them possible. This was a sentiment that the Left in the late 1940s would find difficult to resurrect. Antifascism, in practice, also had what Buhle calls the liability of "aim[ing] at preservation of the Western democracies in a world of non-whites still largely oppressed by colonialism and neo-colonialism."[28] The result was a downgrading (although not disappearance) of anti-imperialist and independent African American initiatives, increasingly treated as potential obstacles to broader unity.[29] Popular Front antifascism tended toward the eradication of the "necessity for socialist transformation from Communist plans and rhetoric."[30]

Antifascism during the Great Depression was a politics of hope yet paradoxically glued to the Soviet Union's underside of purge trials and repression of Left rivals in Spain. Sidney Greenspan's "calm" and "answers" made up a "moral certainty" about an antifascism that was authentic and heartfelt yet part of this larger, treacherous political framework. In affiliating with this incongruous kind of endeavor, the antifascist Popular Front increasingly detached the answers of Marxism from their customary function. The long-term socialist vision, attractive to liberals as well as Communists in the 1930s, was intended to arise from the results of continual scrutiny and reevaluation of the intricacies of class struggle on the ground. Now, under frightening conditions such as Nazi violence, that vision was simply "guaranteed" by assigning a benign and necessary leading position for the Soviet regime. Protecting the Soviet state and giving the benefit of the doubt to the Stalin leadership were conclusions that hit one like a shot of triple espresso, a *coup de foudre*; these became "moral truths" of the genre depicted by psychologist Jonathan Haidt in his much-cited 2001 study, "The Emotional Dog and Its Rational Tail."[31]

Continual deference to these two commitments in promoting Popular Front antifascism could certainly be buttressed by intellectual arguments. But it was also a political reflex or habit of mind that could be carried out with a minimum of ratiocination and reflection; only an unequivocal about-face for the Soviet Union, such as the 1939 pact with the Nazis, caused a layer of Progressive liberals and even some pro-Communists to pull back. Howard Fast fittingly declines to provide any insight into Sidney Greenspan's thought processes, reading, or political discussion, thus depicting his type of "moral certainty" as in harmony with Jonathan Haidt's, an intuition in which "one just sees without argument that they [these political positions] are and must be true."[32] Popular Front antifascism encouraged among its advocates a near-intuitive assumption that, if the USSR was promoting a policy, it must be good for workers throughout the world. An equally hazardous corollary was that those who objected to such practices and policies must be ill-motivated and subjectively or objectively aiding reaction. The result was a movement held together by a beguiling alchemy of courageous human solidarity and thoughtless compliance. It would be another nine years after the publication of "An Epitaph for Sidney," not until 1956, before Stalinist politics would fall on Howard Fast's head like a collapsing roof.

To further parse this development: 1930s antifascism benefited humanity by educating a generation to militantly oppose the greatest threat of the first half of the twentieth century, Nazism; this inaugurates the idea of antifascism as the core of a justifiable moral certainty, one reconfirmed by historical research decade after decade. But the 1939 advent of the war in Europe produced a qualitative change for the worse in terms of trying to unravel the eternal teaser of the degree to which Popular Front antifascism was a viable independent political stance for the Left, or whether there were actually hidden strings attached that rendered it a tactical maneuver subordinate to Soviet foreign policy, imagined as the assurance of social justice. First, the 1939–41 Hitler-Stalin Pact meant that pro-Communists and their Progressive allies halted their organized anti-Nazi agitation in the United States for eighteen months.[33] Then, after the Soviet Union was attacked by Germany (Operation Barbarossa), Phase II or wartime antifascism returned with a vengeance, with part of its fire aimed at segments of the Left. In the United States, the Communists launched a domestic campaign against alleged "Fifth Column Saboteurs." This was a category that amalgamated genuine right-wing elements and isolationists with Left critics of the U.S. war policy. The last included those who opposed Japanese American internment and labor's No-Strike Pledge, both of which were courses of action that the Communists felt were needed to win the war.[34]

The race policies of the wartime Popular Front are particularly distressing, since antiracism was a centerpiece of the pro-Communist Left. Although individual Party supporters may have looked in the other direction or even waffled, the Communist press characterized the 1943 Black and Latino domestic rebellions in Harlem, Detroit, and Los Angeles (the Zoot Suit Riots) one-sidedly and simplistically; rather than reflective of domestic racism exacerbated by the war, they were depicted as a Nazi-engineered "invasion" to advance Hitler's objectives.[35] Arguments about the need to prioritize unity in the war effort were used to oppose both A. Philip Randolph's March on Washington to desegregate the military and the NAACP's "Double V" campaign.[36] The long-term aims of Party members here were admirable; the flaw lay in the "moral certainty" that locked such motives within the shocking tactics of this Popular Front antifascist framework. The low point for this heartbreaking calculus was the Communists' active support of the use of the Smith Act to imprison the leaders of the Trotskyist movement for their Marxist ideas. This set the precedent under which Communists would themselves be victimized in less than a decade. Even for those who disbelieved the charges made by other radicals about Soviet deception in Spain and the fraudulent character of the Moscow Trials, or for those who brushed aside the questionable wartime behavior of the West (such as the firebombing of civilian populations in Japan and Germany, and then the dropping of the atomic bomb), there were more than enough reasons in the records of the West and the Soviet Union to put under scrutiny any moral certainties about the Popular Front variety of antifascism.

Can one be "anti" fascism without being "for" something—and what is the political, economic, and social reality of the thing that one is for? The conundrum is similar for those who try to organize movements as "anti-Stalinist," "anti-Zionist," or, more recently, "anti-Mubarak." What comes next? How to conceptualize a struggle against world fascism under the excruciating conditions of the 1930s and 1940s is not so simple. In the effort to answer this question, one sees more clearly the reason why Stuart Hall wrote in such an impassioned manner in 2010 about the import of the standpoint of the "first" New Left that was born in 1956: "a conjuncture—not just a year—bounded on one side by the suppression of the Hungarian Revolution by Soviet tanks and on the other by the British and French invasion of the Suez Canal zone. These two events, whose dramatic impact was heightened by the fact that they occurred within days of each other, unmasked the underlying violence and aggression latent in the two systems that dominated political life at the time—Western imperialism and Stalinism.... In a deeper sense, they defined for people of my generation the boundaries and limits of tolerable politics."[37] Fifteen years earlier, these were also the "boundaries" of "tolerable politics," but they were harder to see due to the aggressive actions by Germany and Japan, and it was much more difficult to know what to do.

In 1939, to be "for" the West against fascism was to ally with a system of colonialism and class oppression, one that had its own virulent white supremacism, tolerated if not abetted the rise of Nazism, and would, postwar, support all manner of dictatorships that acceded to its imperial policies. To be pro-Soviet meant to blind oneself to a near-Nazi-like variety of police state that had malformed the most promising revolutionary outcome of World War I, the 1917 Russian Revolution, and specialized in the execution of outstanding Communists, writers, and artists. It seems, then, that the blanket phrase "antifascism" can cover over conflicts as unfathomable as twentieth-century political life itself. And "moral certainty," Aristotle's notion of intuitive probability sufficient for action, is also rather impenetrable. The pro-Soviet kind of antifascist conviction that gave Sidney Greenspan his beacon, originating in emotions and experiences of the 1930s, was by the 1940s a kind of intuitive cognition that led in several directions. The more catastrophic ones were carefully omitted from Howard Fast's "An Epitaph for Sidney."

By 1946, when Howard Fast was drafting his story, a late antifascism was becoming resurrected as yet another phase in the development of antifascism, but this one would turn out to be the last stage of the political chess game for the postwar cultural Left. In 1949, surveying the national political scene in the United States, Fast articulated a frightening perspective: "Fifteen years ago [1934] . . . this same pattern of fascist terror and intimidation unfolded in Germany"; intellectuals were deluded if they imagined that "the rising tide of American fascism will, like all bad dreams, come to an inevitable and natural end."[38] Alarm about right-wing developments was justified, but Fast aimed to re-create the mentality of the 1930s when an uncritical embrace of the Soviet Union seemed obligatory under desperate conditions.

A year earlier, Fast's line of thought was codified in the first issue (March 1948) of the newly combined *Masses & Mainstream* (which fused the *New Masses*, a political and cultural journal, with *Mainstream*, a short-lived literary publication). It was a well-designed issue that featured Picasso's 1933 etching *Bull-Headed Sphinx* on the cover, and on the inside were additional drawings by Picasso, Hananiah Harari (1912–2000), Al Blaustein (b. 1924), Robert Gwathmey (1903–88), Ben-Zion (1895–1987), and others. The *Masses & Mainstream* editorial escalated valid apprehensions in a crudely fearmongering manner: "We appear at a grave hour. The arsenal of reaction has become the arsenal of world reaction, servicing every scoundrel from Chiang Kai-shek and the Mufti to Tsaldaris and De Gaulle. An arrogant government of bankers and generals presses a bipartisan policy of world conquest. Preparations for war against the Soviet Union and the new people's democracies of Europe have passed the stage of hypocritical concealment. And the architects of this desperate strategy, the rulers of a decaying capitalism, are redesigning the land of the free as a land of witch-hunts where the FBI inherits the functions of the Gestapo and the Un-American Activities Committee checks our thoughts by the anti-Communist tests of *Mein Kampf.*"[39]

What followed was the now-standard rhetoric of late antifascism, characterizing the era as one of a "war of Wall Street against the American people and the peaceful people of other lands" and rallying forces to a "fight on the cultural front, in the battle of ideas," against the "book-burners" who "prepare a barbed-wire camp for American art." The answer of *Masses & Mainstream* was "a progressive culture" where the people "sing our own songs" against the "cash-register culture" and produced writing that "identified with the working class and progressive people's movement."[40] Late antifascism appealed to values dear to all radicals but rarely missed an occasion to simplify and exaggerate.

McCarthyism truly had the stink of fascism; U.S. foreign policy was unabashed about overthrowing popular regimes to institute dictatorships; detention camps for domestic dissidents were designated; and class war remained in progress. One can also recognize that different segments of the U.S. population experienced the Cold War in contrasting ways, with those among the racially oppressed and in the front lines of social struggle feeling particularly targeted. Exactly how far the United States had gone toward reaction was a legitimate matter of dispute. Yet the mental picture of the United States as a nation past the halfway mark of becoming Nazi Germany was as outrageous as the contemporary claims of Tea Party activists who variously decry the presidency of Barack Obama as inaugurating Communism, socialism, and fascism. Late antifascism promoted a particular *blend* of ideas that was responsible for a profound disorientation.

Unrealistic Communist Party positions, based on such overstated beliefs about the situation in the United States, intensified a self-willed blindness about the Soviet Union. The Communist-led movement was thus impelled toward a fatal collision with the fracturing Stalinist realities of the Tito-Stalin split (1949), the East German workers' uprising (1953), Khrushchev's secret speech to the Twentieth Congress of the Communist Party of the Soviet Union (early 1956), and the Hungarian Revolution (late 1956).[41] The belief that the United States was well en route to fascism produced hysterical, crude propaganda in the Communist press and internal witch hunts in the Party (against alleged FBI agents and "white chauvinists").[42] The mentality of late antifascism logically led to calamity. It was as if U.S. Communists had promised themselves a midlife crisis and refused to be denied one.

Julius and Ethel Rosenberg were executed in 1953 for conspiracy to commit espionage in time of war. Although they were subject to sensational allegations by federal prosecutors, the press, and the judge and to false testimony (by David Greenglass against his sister, Ethel), Julius did indeed engage in passing to representatives of the Soviet Union classified information, at least about aviation and engineering technology. Ethel was most likely aware of this behavior. Comporting themselves in a manner that would have been exemplary if they had been antifascists living in Germany in the 1930s, the Jewish American couple went to their deaths denying all and implicating no one. Their execution was abominable, but there may have been no way out for Julius other than naming names of individuals he had recruited to his activities years earlier, to him an unthinkable act of personal betrayal.

Yet awe for the Rosenbergs' courage cannot be unscrambled from shock at the enormity of their miscalculations about the society in which they were living and the regime that they sought to aid. The Rosenbergs' political activities did not occur in the fascist tyranny they imagined. Yes, the United States was unquestionably experiencing a decade of ugly repression and Joseph McCarthy might have been a U.S. version of a fascist. But the Rosenberg execution was less than two years away from the Montgomery Bus Boycott that inaugurated a whole era of revolt against segregation, massive student protests, and a social upheaval inducing millions to go into the streets to stop an unjust war.

In her autobiography, onetime Communist leader Dorothy Healey (1914–2006) recalls how a group of California Party members meeting to defend themselves against the Smith Act in 1951 came to realize the dangerous flaws in a political strategy based on the claim that "an all-out war with the Soviet Union and the onset of domestic fascism were all but inevitable": "While it was true that the Party was under attack (we could hardly forget that, given the circumstances under which we were meeting), that did not add up to a convincing parallel with Germany in 1933 or Italy in the early 1920s. To speak about the onset of 'fascism'—when our Party offices were still open, when our Party press was still publishing, when the labor movement was able to function legally, and there were the first stirrings of what would become the civil rights movement—seemed a perverse and inaccurate characterization. This was a time of hysteria when civil liberties were at risk, but we had lived through such times before."[43]

Even more heartbreaking, the Rosenbergs, devoted Communists, had sacrificed all while having faith in, and working to strengthen, a society that replicated fascism's most repressive political features. If they are to be honored appropriately for their bravery, something more is required beyond the obvious first step of the safeguarding of civil liberties from fearmongers; there needs to be a forthright understanding of the causes of (and remedies for) the moral and intellectual catastrophe that assisted the destruction of aspiring political idealists.[44] The Rosenberg espionage case lives on in public debate, but it is also a suitable subject for interrogation in imaginative literature, as it has been, because it is a human story of ideals merged with delusions that cannot be convincingly decoded into simplified narratives: either a lurid horror story of disloyal traitors to the American people, or a fable of two Jews cynically framed up by anti-Semites to falsely appear to be pro-Communists and teammates in espionage.[45]

In late antifascism, Communists were necessarily leading more convoluted dual or multiple lives. In public, and often still identifying as "Progressives," they fought to save the New Deal heritage. In private, and increasingly in semi-clandestine, security-conscious Communist Party activity, they steeled themselves to resist — underground, if necessary — what they surmised to be a burgeoning fascism in the United States. In both manifestations, Progressive and Communist, they professed to be waging a battle for "peace" against a looming Third World War, a war that was allegedly the underlying objective of Truman's "containment" policy. Although Howard Fast's story, "An Epitaph for Sidney," omits any reference to the Soviet Union, late antifascism was more unswervingly bound than ever to the Soviet regime and its expanding sphere of influence. Much like the United States–led "Free World," it had become a "camp" to be defended at all costs.

This is why "An Epitaph for Sidney," in which the selection of the commemorative phrase "antifascist" conceals as much as it reveals, and the background details omit specificity about Communism, epitomizes the principal context and many of the challenges that need to be taken up in studying the culture of the postwar era. But taken up not to remove us all back to a place where the Cold War never ended, not to merely keep the past alive as an academic industry. Rather, taken up to resolve the debilitating persistence of the past; to round out the picture of what happened to those hundreds of cultural workers pledged to the internationalist, antiracist, pro-labor vision of the 1930s; to further clarify what went wrong, as well as right, and why and how; to do more explaining and understanding, and less judging and condemning.

Michael Denning's *The Cultural Front: The Laboring of American Culture in the Twentieth Century* (1996) is superb in successfully knocking off the old paradigm of the cultural Left as a mere 1930s aberration, created and delimited by exceptional conditions. The cameo theory of literary radicalism — that Left writers made a dramatic entry in the 1930s, remained momentarily on the stage, and then faded out as the main story of U.S. literature resumed — is dealt its decisive blow. Denning shows cultural radicalism's profound roots in the rise of the organized industrial working-class movement, expressed in the finest hopes of the social unionism of the Congress of Industrial Organizations. Other scholars had begun this process back in the 1980s, while only Denning had the extraordinary multidisciplinary synthetic vision to carry it through.

Nevertheless, this crucial historical contextualization must now be joined by critique. The next step is to embrace and clarify, not downplay, the contradictory aspects of the Popular Front and late antifascism, which require closer attentiveness to the intricacy of the Communist presence. Although Denning's view of Stalinism is similar to my own, his method is to sideline the organizational and ideological presence of Communism due to a reasonable concern that the larger phenomenon of Popular Front culture might otherwise be perceived as a Communist exercise in manipulation. Yet this strategy results in some simplifications about Communism's mixed legacy in politics and cultural achievement for the postwar era that I aim to remedy in this book.

Postwar radical literature exhibits no easy generic affiliation that enables identification, although the noir-inflected title of *American Night* pays tribute to a late-1940s aura of the darkness and gloom that especially marks novels and films—a significant divergence from the 1930s penchant for using the glare of searchlights to expose the naked oppression of the social order. Inasmuch as scores of authors had in 1939 stepped back from their liaison with the Communist Party and drifted away after the 1945–46 campaign against literary Browderism that culminated in the public censure of novelist Albert Maltz,[46] or quietly disaffiliated for other reasons, the postwar bond between Left writers and Communist political doctrine is more tenuous than that of their prewar counterparts. Yet formulaic and rigid links between writers and the Party were never the main point for the scholars aspiring to clarify the cultural activity of the era.

In what follows, I am less concerned with affixing a label or establishing comparative rankings than I am with exploring a set of relationships among subjective political commitments, literary forms and themes, and what historians have been learning about the tangible postwar environment. What may be brought in the open is a counter-narrative to the previous narrower histories of the postwar era that operate through hyper-canonization of writers such as Saul Bellow, J. D. Salinger, and Flannery O'Conner; my aim is not to unseat such canonical writers but to provide a basis for seeing new points of contact in a process of tracking the circuitous fate of the 1930s marriage of imaginative literature and radical social commentary. The alternative reading of literary history presented in *American Night* aspires to address postwar memory loss by disturbing the imagined community of the Consumers' Republic, not just by indexing individualistic discontent in the manner of Bellow, Salinger, and others but by probing the costs of the socioeconomic foundations of the 1940s and 1950s for "the way we live now." The phrase was originally used by Anthony Trollope as the title of his 1875 satirical novel but meaningfully reappropriated by former Communist Party member Warren Miller (1921–66) for his 1958 best seller of life in a Consumers' Republic, *The Way We Live Now*.

In an "An Epitaph for Sidney," Howard Fast remains opaque about the details of the protagonist's organizational affiliations after his 1934 membership in the Young Communist League. Too many veterans of the experience, along with friends and relatives, have followed suit. Defenses of this sort against the perceived defamation that can result from identifying one as a Communist may be well meaning but are about as helpful to intellectual clarity about cultural history as using rollers to paint a miniature. Similarly, one could write a Talmud in reply to the oceans of confusion generated by anti-Communist zealots who reinforce this historical mistake of relying on generalities but from the opposing side, by characterizing Communist commitment using the language of fronts, dupes, useful idiots, devious secret Party members, and disloyal un-Americans. Starting with its first chapter, *American Night* aspires to present an up-front, evenhanded, fact-checked version of the Communist literary experience following World War II.

Chapter One

Postwar

THE CULTURE WARS OF KENNETH FEARING

In March 1944, as World War II peaked ferociously in Europe, the *New York Times Book Review* gently registered the premonitory rumblings of a new chapter in the history of the novel in the United States. *Dangling Man*, the first published volume of fiction by future Nobel Prize winner Saul Bellow (1915–2005), was the subject of "Man Versus Man," a canny appraisal by Depression-era celebrity poet Kenneth Fearing (1902–61). "In this curious interim between two ages," Fearing announced, "when history has dropped the curtain upon one of them but seems in no hurry to give the next one its shape and color, Saul Bellow's *Dangling Man* swings aimlessly about in space and searches his soul."[1] This crisscrossing of writers of dissimilar generations—the twenty-something Bellow asserting his aloofness from prior convictions; the middle-aged Fearing wary of an out-and-out breach with the Left culture of the 1930s—is indicative of the ironic intricacy involved in assessing any shift in the literary climate. Postwar, many species of novels were generated; few writers were anointed for canonization.

Fearing, at this moment, was the established big name, his career far from finished and in many respects on a roll, issuing a book of poetry or prose published by Random House every year between 1938 and 1943. Bellow was still the unproven apprentice, testing his artistic wings with fiction in the guise of a narcissistic diary. Fearing's own first novel, *The Hospital* (1939), with its quick-paced vignettes of patients and doctors during a power outage, straightaway sold over 6,000 copies; *Dangling Man* garnered perhaps 1,500 in sales. That was similar in number to Fearing's *Clark Gifford's Body* (1942), a surreal soaring of the imagination about the revolutionary seizure of a radio station (in manuscript originally titled "The Attack at WLEX") reported by thirty narrators. It was regarded by editor Bennett Cerf as a sales fiasco.[2]

Kenneth Fearing, foremost Communist poet of the Great Depression, forged a new radical sensibility in the following decade with his noir thrillers such as *The Big Clock* (1946). (Courtesy of Library of Congress)

Following his review of Bellow's first novel, Fearing, in August 1944, commenced a hiatus of fourteen months to complete *The Big Clock*, his most commercially successful work. A psychosexual *roman noir* stressing the sinister effect of market segmentation in the publishing industry, *The Big Clock* sold lucratively to general applause from critics, then swiftly capitalized on the very mass-market venues that the book derided. Within a year of the appearance of the hardback edition published by Harcourt Brace, Fearing issued a shortened magazine version under the title "The Judas Picture" and a Bantam paperback selling for twenty-five cents with a classic pulp cover.³ Next came an Armed Services edition in 1947, then a Grosset and Dunlap reprint that tied in with the 1948 film based on the book starring Ray Milland and Charles Laughton. The novel has remained in print ever since.⁴

No writer is an island, including longtime Communists, and Fearing, who came to literary maturity in the Marxist maelstrom of the 1930s, drew nourishment much as Bellow did from a bookshelf of eclectic affinities. At the University of Wisconsin, he studied French and German. According to the poet Horace Gregory (1898–1982), Fearing's emotional and intellectual attitudes progressively crystallized around a triumvirate of Marx, Dashiell Hammett, and H. L. Mencken after his 1924 arrival in New York City.⁵ Fearing himself named poets Walt Whitman, François Villon, and John Keats as his chief influences, along with the impressionist composer Maurice Ravel and the painter George Grosz.⁶ The novelist Edward Dahlberg (1900–1977), in his introduction to the self-announced "proletarian volume" of Fearing's 1935 *Poems*, linked him with French Symbolists such as Tristan Corbière, albeit "with Marxian insight."⁷

By the 1940s, Fearing was drawing upon George Gissing's *New Grub Street* (1891) for his depiction of hack writers and literary back-biting in *Dagger of the Mind* (1941) and *The Big Clock* (whose protagonist is named "George"), Mary Shelley's *Frankenstein* (1818) and myriad works by H. G. Wells for his technology-obsessed writings culminating in *The Loneliest Girl in the World* (1951),⁸ and Wilkie Collins's *The Woman in White* (1859) and Edgar Lee Masters's *Spoon River Anthology* (1915) for his application of sequential dramatic monologues as the narrative device in most of his poetry and prose. Nearly forgotten pulp masters such as his friend Vincent Starrett (1886–1973) and Harry Stephen Keeler (1890–1967) were among those he customarily read. Methodologically, Fearing's fiction poses multiple challenges. Fearing was not a radical novelist in the tradition of putting forward a broad panorama of postwar U.S. society or depicting events that generate an empathy with the economic underclass. At the same time, there is modest introspection in his work as he uses a style that in the end curbs lyrical expression of the personal.

The seven novels that Fearing published from 1939 to 1960 are weirdly imaginative. Often called "thrillers," they boldly flout any genre. The louche plots approximate high-wire performances while his characters let loose bravado soliloquies, an effect both glib and aestheticizing. Quirky details in *Dagger of the Mind* (1941; reprinted as *Cry Killer!*, 1958) and *Loneliest Girl in the World* (reprinted as *The Sound of Murder*, 1952) often provide an idiosyncratic richness, although fresh energy is unsustained and there are moments in *The Generous Heart* (1954) and *The Crozart Story* (1960) when Fearing appears to be merely mapping out scenes. Like circles in a Venn diagram, his novels incompletely overlap the taut colloquial elegance of the poetic oeuvre that Fearing assembled in seven volumes between 1929 and 1956.[9] The stanzas of *Angel Arms* (1929), *Poems, Dead Reckoning* (1938), *Afternoon of a Pawnbroker* (1943), *Stranger at Coney Island* (1948), and others of his verse collections are customarily remembered for vernacular images wrapped in popular culture. Both his poetry and prose are a blend of the demotic avant-garde with hardboiled Marxism, breaching the boundary between art and daily experience. These strange books should almost certainly be filed under "F" for "Fearing" rather than "M" for "Modernist" or "P" for "Proletarian."

In the 1940s, Fearing's suspense fiction fashioned a new kind of criminal, an "executive type" adumbrated in his 1930s poetry, which emerged from the institutions of the U.S. media and advertising.[10] At their finest, his narratives of murder and suicide can be hypnotic, generating as a forceful emotional waterfall a main character's life while evidencing only slight anxiety about linear chronology. Fearing's limited writing style renders his novels mostly an acquired taste; his wide intellectual range is channeled into a narrower artistic one. *The Big Clock* is the exception, a virtuoso performance in syncopated, urban poetic-prose. In a plot stretched tight, Fearing conveys the manic, gothic-like loneliness and subterranean terror of the rising middle class. Through a sequence of inspired dramatic monologues, in which major and minor characters compulsively rationalize and calculate each step of their lives, the reader is pulled into a vision of an affluent urban and suburban dreadful night. America is reimagined as a new civilization in which the ascendant forms of mass communication are ready-made for propaganda purposes, with the population well en route to a loss of agency and individuation. In concert with his melancholy verse of the same decade, Fearing's novel teeters dangerously close to the precipice of desolate cynicism, restrained only by eruptions of a madcap sense of humor.

At the core of Fearing's postwar America, revealed in his provocative genre-deformations of the novel, is a frightening and fragmentary hollowness redolent of T. S. Eliot's "The Waste Land" (1922). *The Big Clock*, however, is neither a Lost Generation narrative of the decline of Western civilization nor an ex-radical's segue to an accommodation with "Our Country and Our Culture."[11] The menacing ambience of dislocation that permeates *The Big Clock* is structurally and symbolically rendered as industrial capitalism, a socioeconomic order in which the avenues of communication, especially publishing and the airwaves, are evolving into a science of planned manipulation designed to ensure profitability. Well-paid deceivers, together with the naively deceived, are imprisoned as cogs in the apparatus of private enterprise's modern institutions. Even after the novel's climax, one hears the ticking of pitiless doom and is haunted by the cast of coded characters who, although not always quite believable, suggest a buried symbolic scheme, one difficult to decipher but intimating a margin of hope. Two years after the novel's publication, at a 1948 writers' conference at the University of Illinois, Fearing emphasized the allegorical basis of his art: "Literature is a means for crystallizing the myths under which society lives."[12] The genius of *The Big Clock* is its previsioning of the manifold mythological dimensions of a "Consumers' Republic" that would typify the era.[13]

The historic postwar transformation of mass consciousness generated a memory crisis, one resisted by writers such as Fearing, as the stirring social unity of the Great Depression transformed into the quest for the fulfillment of private material wants in the late 1940s. It was the conservative side of a culture war orchestrated in support of the superficially innocuous belief that mass consumption served the national interest, which unsurprisingly harmonized with the imperial implications of publisher Henry Luce's 1941 pro-interventionist announcement of "The American Century." The result was a devastating blow to the remnants of what historians call the "New Deal Order," itself a political regime of compromise. The setback was effected in political life by taming vestiges of the previously obstreperous social movements, an endeavor shared by Democratic and Republican leaders of business, government, labor, and civic groups. This new civilization redefined citizenship as being an integral part of consumerism and recast the function of trade unions from being a vanguard of social justice into a competing interest group. It preceded but later interlocked with the Cold War and its polarizing ideological battles.

Fearing's *The Big Clock* is the strange story of George Stroud, a writer-for-hire in the 1940s. Stroud is an investigative journalist unaccountably obsessed with the paintings of Louise Patterson, a forgotten New Deal artist. The tale told of the potential assassination of Stroud by his bosses, a murder deflected by his ability to mask the location of Patterson's Works Projects Administration (WPA) art, is an imaginative correlative for precisely the coming rout of the precious radical achievements of the 1930s. It expresses the reversal of the internationalism, social unionism, antiracism, and collective social responsibility that emerged during the Great Depression. Ten years after the publication of the novel, in the 1956 foreword to *New and Selected Poems*, Fearing alluded to *The Big Clock* as having been written on the cusp of the "terrible drama of the past decade," 1946–56, "in which a long phase of our society died."[14]

Kenneth Fearing and Saul Bellow were thus, in that mid-1940s illusory "interim," responsive in their respective ways to the wartime transition in national temperament, a quietly creeping culture war veiled by the officially sanctioned posture of patriotic unity. But Fearing, always more fox than hedgehog, was in cultural predilection no mere throwback to 1930s social realism. His book review unequivocally endorses the self-criticism of Bellow's isolated antihero Joseph ("I had not done well alone"), then confesses his own similitude: "The author has outlined what must seem to many others an uncannily accurate delineation of themselves."[15] In mood, at any rate, both writers partook of the great alteration in literary intonation that distinguishes the sharpness of Depression realism from the gloom of postwar noir. Yet, owing to the choices that followed, the career paths of the two wordsmiths were to be fixed forever in discordant cultural epochs, one diminishing and the other mounting. What, then, was the distinction between the fiction of the ascending younger writer and the still-evolving veteran? What was Bellow discarding at his moment of embarkation on a journey that would so conspicuously refashion the U.S. novel in the "shape and color" of the 1950s and the years beyond?

THE MASK OF IRONY

The asymmetry of the literary arcs of Bellow and Fearing are somewhat derived from their oddly overlapping early biographies. Notwithstanding a thirteen-year age difference and divergent appreciations of their Jewish identity, both spent their formative days in Chicago, attended the University of Wisconsin for a brief time, worked on the Federal Writers Project during the late Depression, won Guggenheim Fellowships in their early thirties, and were idiosyncratically committed to factions of the Marxist Left until the onset of the war. Otherwise, Bellow would outdistance Fearing in virtually every respect, not only by winning the Pulitzer Prize (1975, for *Humboldt's Gift*), the Nobel Prize for Literature (1976), the National Book Award (three times), and the National Medal of Arts (1988), but also in number of marriages (Bellow destroyed his first four; Fearing managed to wreck only two), years lived (Bellow reached ninety; Fearing died at fifty-nine), and ultimate renown. Even Bellow's capacity to write long novels was superior: Fearing would peter out after 200 pages, while Bellow frequently surpassed 500 or 600 pages. Where Fearing was surely the champ was in drinking; his sensational alcohol addiction was evident from his college days, recorded in memoirs and the diary entries of his friends over forty years, a prevailing feature of autobiographical characters in his novels, and confirmed by his autopsy.[16]

Kenneth Fearing's inner life was a dungeon of secrets, and his art was no less baffling. An anticipation of looming calamity had been lodged in his psyche since his college years; it promptly produced a craving for alcohol and cigarettes that sent his lungs and liver on a deadly race to destruction. The majority of the poems he offered to the *New Yorker*, the publication with which his name was most coupled in the 1940s, were rejected for reasons of incomprehensibility.[17] Sometimes Fearing was his own bewildering landscape. A recurrent character in his writing was the artist as a killer, most graphically depicted in his 1928 poem "John Standish, Artist" and in his 1943 mystery *Dagger of the Mind*, originally titled "Kill That Guy!"[18] In his 1948 "Stranger at Coney Island," the avatar of death — "perhaps sprawled beneath a striped umbrella, asleep in the sand" — is the one who "alone . . . can solve these many riddles we have found so difficult."[19]

Only in fiction by others has Fearing's quirky personality been given a measure of justice. In 1927, W. L. (customarily called "Les") River (1903–81) published an experimental psychological novel, *Death of a Young Man*; Fearing wrote the flattering review of it in the *New Masses* and in both the 1930s and 1950s praised the novel as an accurate literary rendering of himself.[20] River's novel purports to be the diary of David Bloch, convinced that his doctor has told him that he has only a short time to live. In his diary, Bloch endeavors to observe himself dispassionately. Always intrigued by criminal instincts, Bloch obsessively dwells on the idea of committing a murder. In a semi-hallucinogenic episode, Bloch believes that he has strangled one of the two girls he loves but learns otherwise; later, he jumps off the back of a train and imagines that the second girl had followed him to her death. In the end, Bloch commits suicide.

As psychohistory, these events have a rough correlation with Fearing's tumultuous love affair with Margery Latimer (1899–1932). In Latimer's autobiographical novel, *This Is My Body* (1930), the young Fearing is portrayed as twenty-one-year-old Ronald Chardon and Latimer as Megan Foster. Other characters are modeled on River, Carl Rakosi (1903–2004), Leon Serabian Herald (1894–1976), and the poet William Ellery Leonard (1876–1944), an agoraphobic socialist "Man of Letters" on the University of Wisconsin faculty who was an inspiration to them all. The lovers meet at a college poetry reading where Chardon is to be the star performer. He arrives in classic Fearing style: "Suddenly a boy tumbled into the room as if from a tree, nodded, tripped over the sofa and landed in a chair."[21] Chardon then goes into a corner, pulls some dirty paper from his pocket, and reads his lines "as quick as pistol shots."[22] The English instructor hosting the event pompously proclaims: "Chardon, I see the influence of [Edwin Arlington] Robinson in your stuff." In his laconic reply, one hears Fearing's low, willfully unpretentious voice: "Sure. I suppose so. . . . I like him all right. Read him a lot. Sure."[23] Initially enthralled by Chardon's sarcasm, Megan is desperate to own him, but she is disenchanted by his callous rejoinder to her talk of love: "It's in bad taste to mention it unless you're joking." After Chardon is expelled by a dean for his nonconformist editing of the college literary magazine, the couple moves to New York City. Megan discovers that Chardon is willing to marry her, but only grudgingly. He protests: "You want me to love you differently—I can't—I love you as much as I'm capable of loving anyone."[24] Following an abortion and the discovery of Chardon's infidelity, Megan realizes that Chardon will never allow himself to be happy; the relationship is painfully ended.

This Is My Body omits any reference to the botched suicide attempt by Fearing that was fictionally consummated in *Death of a Young Man*. The biographical incident was revealed forty years after the fact in Horace Gregory's 1972 memoir, *The House on Jefferson Street*. According to Gregory, Fearing failed to show up for a scheduled late afternoon coffee with him; he and Latimer then rushed to the rooming house where Fearing lived to discover him in bed unconscious. An unlit gas heater had been turned on full blast. They shook him back to life, making a silent pact to never again refer to the incident.[25] Suicide, however, is a recurrent theme in Fearing's work, featured in both his last novel, *The Crozart Story*, and his final, most disturbing piece of published fiction, "Champagne and Bitters."[26]

Fearing's friends River and Latimer undertook the literary project that he himself apparently eschewed, the dramatization of a thinly veiled biography. Unlike the work of his contemporaries James T. Farrell, Henry Roth, Tillie Olsen, and Richard Wright, there cannot be found in Fearing's oeuvre a fictionalized version of the traumas and ordeals of his youth or young manhood. Yet Fearing's personality, captured in the 1935 painting of the charismatic poet with a skeleton in his heart by Alice Neel (1900–1984), is nonetheless primary in his manic-compulsive art. A profound inner turmoil, a dense energy that pooled deeply, encouraged him to use ordinary scenes and invest them with feeling and mystery so that literary images and personal life are tangled. When sketching city streets in prose and poetry in the 1920s and 1930s, Fearing reveals a landscape of the mind more than one of place. His post-Depression novels might initially evoke the "entertainments" of Graham Greene and the mysteries of C. Day Lewis (written as "Nicholas Blake") inasmuch as all three novelists write in a singularly inventive manner, beyond potboilers, and borrow thriller techniques to attract a broader range of readers. But Fearing is alone in affording glimpses of a netherworld of defeat and confusion, a revelation fused, as in his poetry, with acidic portraits evoking Edgar Lee Masters and Edwin Arlington Robinson. Even as he focuses increasingly on institutions, his target is the false front of a corrupt society, embodied in the illusions of romantic love, education, and freedom.

The malignancy in Fearing's ghostly cosmos, his continual crime and punishment theme, is transmuted through portentous literary tableaux of fear, anguish, and frustrated desire. Such a beguiling, sulfurous pessimism may be explainable by the story of his life. Troubled feelings about his Jewishness indisputably played a part. His Jewish mother had abandoned him, while his tolerant father expressed anti-Semitic opinions; a familiar kind of Jewish humor is evoked in Fearing's flippancy connected to darkness. Less solvable is the extent to which escapist anodynes of drink and drugs—in Fearing's case, the opium he smoked with his 1930s Communist friend Kenneth Waldron Doolittle (1903–78, the lover of painter Alice Neel)—were inspirational or detrimental to his writing.[27] To what degree did the genesis of Fearing's animatronic characters and social settings rapidly shifting from parlor games to blood sport, and the armed and dangerous zingers shot from the mouths of protagonists, lie in the twisted perceptions and judgment induced by alcoholism? Addiction may account for the unfulfilled promise of Fearing's career. His most exalted poems are his early ones, and his final novel, *The Crozart Story*, reads like an unfinished scenario for what less-damaged powers of concentration might have revised into his greatest book.

Fearing was also a curiously committed Communist for most of the 1930s: by day, a dependable writer of verse, reviews, and fiction for the *New Masses* and a muse for the avant-garde Marxist poets of *Dynamo* magazine; by night, a notorious sex pulp author primarily known as "Kirk Wolfe," churning out several narratives a month for Street and Smith's *Snappy Stories* and *Spicy Stories*, as well as *Bedtime Stories* ("For Grown-Ups Only") and *Ten Story Book* (sold under the counter and featuring female nudes). Politically, it might be said of Fearing's sort of less-disciplined, bohemian-type revolutionaries that they launched a crusade against injustice as depicted in a Victor Hugo novel. To be sure, the loose, "Communist" writers of his political cohort anticipated the misconstruing of their motives by enemies, as well as likely personal sacrifice; but vindication would undoubtedly follow, as it did for Jean Valjean. Ten years later, the Left's nineteenth-century fiction of romance ripened under the national security state into pure Kafka. In the 1950s, writers still clinging to the chimera of the Soviet Union found themselves, like characters in the classic Maupassant story "The Necklace," psychologically manacled to a ruinous illusion.

Fearing, however, at all times cleaved closest to the Kafka mode. Marya Zaturenska (1902–82), married to fellow poet Horace Gregory, even believed that the thin, dark-haired and dark-skinned Fearing, who spoke in a Humphrey Bogart–like gravelly voice but with a gentle lisp, bore "a resemblance to the portrait of Kafka—a weaker, less tragic Kafka."[28] Fearing had a penchant for dark suits; rumor had it that his first wife, Rachel Meltzer, a medical social worker at the Montefiore Hospital in the Bronx, filched them from a storage room for the cheap but respectable clothing in which impecunious terminal patients were buried.[29] His other well-known traits included bushy hair falling low over his forehead, small eyes behind owlish horn-rimmed glasses, messy personal habits, and chronically immature behavior—all of which accented Fearing's little-boy appeal, which had a surefire aphrodisiacal effect on beautiful young women.

By 1928, Fearing was frequently talking to Communists, having written for the *New Masses* since 1926. Young militants with literary ambitions, such as Nathan Adler (1913–94), later an eminent San Francisco Bay Area clinical psychologist, saw Fearing as an earnest revolutionary despite his "Yellow Book" aura that recalled the decadent poet Ernest Dowson.[30] Perhaps declaring for the Communist Party was a way of shedding a privileged class background that to him felt shameful; more likely, the outcast status of the Communist Party made it attractive to one who was himself an outcast. In 1929 Fearing became a founding member of the Communist Party–led John Reed Club and in 1930 commenced three years as a contributing editor of the *New Masses*. Undisciplined, scarcely an activist, unwilling to sacrifice his time or take personal risks, and far from exclusively focused on social suffering and injustice, he was never seen at such normal activities as a picket line.[31] His organizational commitments during the Depression were limited to select pro-Communist literary venues, especially ones that allowed him to sidestep intellectual conformity. First came the John Reed Club, where he served (at least in name) on the executive committee and the editorial board of its journal, *Partisan Review*. After 1935, he was among the initiators of the League of American Writers where for the first year he worked for its national council. In 1939 he taught poetry technique as a faculty member of its New York Writers School.

Fearing was paradoxically an outsider to Communist Party institutions while recklessly wearing his Communist politics on his sleeve. The *New York Times* nonchalantly described his 1935 *Poems* as "the second book of a 33-year-old Communist from Chicago."[32] Horace Gregory and Marya Zaturenska diplomatically noted in their 1946 *History of American Poetry* that "Fearing veered in the direction of Stalinist Marxism."[33] Novelist Jerre Mangione (1909–98), who attended meetings of the New York chapter of the John Reed Club with Fearing and later knew him on the Federal Writers Project, entertained no doubts that Fearing "was clearly identified with the Stalinist faction."[34] Starting in 1931, Fearing signed a range of fervently pro-Soviet declarations, culminating in the notorious "Open Letter of the 400" that appeared in August 1939, defending Stalin's regime in glowing terms.[35]

Such politics do not provide an explanation of Fearing's basic poetic or literary talent. Yet his Marxist period becomes critical to the electrifying verse that made him an irreplaceable and inimitable icon in Depression literary history. His trajectory might be periodized: Following his move to Manhattan, Fearing's anti-romantic skepticism was soon informed by a rudimentary appreciation of capitalist economics. After the stock market crash, his penchant for satire began to reverberate with the imagery of class division and misery of the dispossessed, an unfolding perspective evident in the progression of his verse from *Angel Arms* to *Poems*. In the latter he tapped purposefully into the Depression's atmosphere of crisis and its appeal for a day of reckoning, attracting an appreciative and growing audience. In 1938, Fearing explained to the *Daily Worker*: "I've not tried deliberately to be a Marxist in poetry.... Marxism is valuable in literature only to the extent that the writer assimilates it. Consequently its principles become a part of the writer's background, the way he thinks and feels and interprets it."[36] A year later he was harnessing the same sensibility to his wacky psycho-thrillers, where implied social commentary was painlessly integrated with whirling action.

Even with such limitations, "Comrade Fearing" was an oxymoron to some. Lurking beneath his occasionally playful literary persona was a fearsome nihilism, one that made the troubled open-mindedness and uncertainty of Keats's "negative capability" look like joyous sanguinity. The poet Carl Rakosi remembered Fearing's trademark conversation as "cruelty wrapped in wit."[37] In a 1937 personal letter to Nathan Adler, the poet Sol Funaroff (1911–42) described Fearing's mordant disposition as a "mask of irony" shielding "a man hurt and embittered by life."[38] A small number of those who knew him, such as novelist Albert Halper (1904–84), fictionalizing Fearing as the cynical poet "Jason Wheeler" in *Union Square* (1933), wrote off Fearing's Marxist avowals even in the 1930s. In 1942 Fearing submitted a puzzling reply to a questionnaire for a literary reference book: "Political convictions: a mystery to me."[39]

In all probability, he was conceding the emotional basis of his earlier attraction to Communism, yet his fudging made it feasible for others to follow Halper in swearing that Fearing's revolutionary political posture was merely a pose or joke.[40]

RAGE AGAINST THE MACHINE

Fearing conspicuously did not conform to the canons of political commitment to which more fervent Communists subscribed. *Partisan Review* editor William Phillips (1907–2002) depicted Fearing as "a cynical figure, who managed to act as if there were no constraints on him even while supporting the Communists."[41] All his life Fearing gave the impression of being principally engaged in a sardonic war against an inscrutable universe, with no hope of improving society by rational means. His temperament, a mistrust of all political premises and a disbelief in all ameliorative options, ran contrary to any connection with a large organization that demanded ideological conformity and an activist commitment. Probably his Communist Party membership, if it existed, was a one-meeting affair. Yet there was entrenched in Fearing's psyche and his art an undying mutiny against the conventions of a society based on profit, commodities, and exploitation. His was a deep-rooted radicalism that at the onset was derivative of his revulsion against World War I.

In this respect, Fearing was somewhat typical of mid-twentieth-century U.S. Leftists; disgust with the international slaughter of 1914–18 set the stage for a Marxist assessment of power and profits, one Fearing never discarded. His first presidential ballot was cast for the Progressive Party in 1924, whose candidate, "Fighting Bob" La Follette, was most noted for his anti-interventionist views. In 1932 Fearing voted for the Communist William Z. Foster, but during the Popular Front he simply stopped voting; he did not cast a ballot for Roosevelt at any time or, in 1948, for the Progressive Party presidential candidate Henry Wallace.[42] Cynicism must have been part of the reason, but there is also abundant evidence that Fearing held a systematically distrustful view of the liberal state. Why would a mere cynic bother to compose precise political declarations, as Fearing did in 1939 and 1940, about the challenge of World War II to writers and governments?[43] Why did he persist, against the advice of his editors, in publishing a full-length novel, *Clark Gifford's Body*, approvingly depicting an enigmatic guerrilla struggle against war in the midst of a war?[44] T. C. (Theodore Carl) Wilson (1912–50), a poet and Communist fellow traveler who was close to Horace Gregory, observed astutely in the April 1939 issue of *Poetry* that the central theme for Fearing "was always war and threat of war."[45] This unbroken strain of continuity provided a basis for Fearing's post–World War II rebellion; a mutation of his 1930s radicalism, it was less ideological than in the fibers of the self and functioned as a counterpoint to the principal wave of disenchantment marked by Bellow-like individualistic rejuvenation.

Whatever the vagueness of Fearing's affiliation with the Communist Party—he was regarded as a fellow member by the *New Masses* editor A. B. Magil (1905–2003)—personal bonds between himself and several Communists ran deep.[46] His closest friend at Oak Park–River Forest High School was Les River. After Fearing left the University of Wisconsin in 1924, River and Fearing moved to Manhattan, where they shared an apartment for several years. Fearing dedicated the poem "Saturday Night" to River; it appeared first in the *Menorah Journal* (1928) and was subsequently reprinted in *Angel Arms* and *Collected Poems* (1940). By the mid-1930s, River had emerged as a leading figure in the Communist cultural movement—as a novelist, screenwriter, and activist—and remained so until he was blacklisted in Hollywood in 1951.[47]

Beginning with his undergraduate days, Fearing was an eccentric literary guru and inveterate bohemian who fostered an entourage on campus and later in Greenwich Village that always included musicians, painters, pulp writers, and hangers-on; these worked their way into his fiction and poetry, as did newspaper articles, films, cartoons, and a spectrum of his reading.[48] Yet those en route to the Communist movement were at all times at the center of his life. These included his most intimate male associates at the University of Wisconsin, the poets Leon Serabian Herald, Carl Rakosi, and Horace Gregory.[49] All were idealistic socialists and pro-Soviet Union in the 1920s; Herald subsequently became a leader of the John Reed Club in New York, joined the Communist Party, and induced Rakosi to join the Party in 1935. Although Rakosi drifted away organizationally from the Party before the Cold War, both he and Herald remained sympathetic to Communist ideas into the 1960s.[50]

From his earliest days in New York until his death, Fearing's most intimate companion was Harry Ross (dates unknown). Fearing dedicated the poem "Evening Song" to Ross, which appeared in *Transition* in 1927 and was reprinted in *Angel Arms* and *Collected Poems*. Fearing also wrote an early novel about Ross, which he was unable to publish. Ross was a Communist Party member and journalist who worked episodically for the *Daily Worker* and for the WPA in the 1930s, as a stringer for TASS (Telegraph Agency of the Soviet Union, which collected U.S. news for all media in the Soviet Union) in the 1940s, and as an editor in the field of medical journalism during the 1950s.[51] They shared many of the same friends on the Left, especially poets and Communists. Ross took up Fearing's literary career as something of a personal cause.

In a 1938 *Daily Worker* interview, Fearing would claim that he first learned about socialism in Madison through fellow undergraduate Sender Garlin (1902-99), an admirer of the radical economist Scott Nearing (1883-1983).[52] The two reconnected in New York City, where Garlin was writing for the *Daily Worker*. This led to Fearing's friendship with Harry Freeman (1906-78), then also a *Daily Worker* writer who soon became a lifelong employee of TASS.[53] In the 1920s, Freeman wrote poetry, like his older brother Joseph Freeman (1897-1965), to whom Harry had introduced Fearing in 1927. The older Freeman socialized with Fearing in the 1950s and was the first to make an effort to salvage Fearing's papers after his death.

Fearing's love life was also bound up with the Communist political and cultural milieu. His lover in the 1920s was Margery Latimer, who introduced him to the *New Masses* and tried to drag him to picket lines at Communist-backed strikes. His first wife, Rachel Meltzer, whom Fearing met in 1931 on a blind date, was a Communist who described herself as "politically engaged and active in left-wing causes."[54] After they broke up, Rachel married Edward Landon (1911-84), himself a noted left-wing painter.[55] Fearing's second wife, Nan Lurie (1908-88), was a participant in Communist-led art circles who worked for the Federal Arts Project and specialized in prints and lithographs; while she paralleled Fearing in her mix of social realism and surrealism, she was a more conventional Leftist in her focus on poverty and African Americans.[56] His last girlfriend, in the late 1950s, was remembered by Joseph Freeman as a true believer in the Communist Party and financial supporter of the Fair Play for Cuba Committee.[57]

At the zenith of the Cold War, the Communist literary journal *Masses & Mainstream* tried to reprint a recent essay by Fearing (Fearing's objection to the reissuing was tactical; that this Communist venue would be used by reactionaries to discredit his ideas) and featured Alice Neel's painting of him on its cover when he died.[58] The week of Fearing's final hospitalization, he had been scheduled to attend a dinner with writer Meridel Le Sueur (1900-1996), herself still a Communist Party member. Pro-Communists formed a coterie at his funeral, and some even walked out under the leadership of Lillian Hellman (1905-84) when *Sports Illustrated* editor and onetime-proletarian novelist Robert Cantwell (1908-78), reputedly an informer, rose to make remarks.[59]

Fearing's rupture with the institutions of the Communist Party was, nonetheless, quite real and predated all of his novels except *The Hospital*. In the second half of the 1930s, while still retaining a public posture of pro-Communism, Fearing began to harbor corrosive doubts. Factionalism was not in his blood. As a staff member of the Federal Writers Project, he was unique in that his all-around amiable relations with others included Trotskyists.[60] Then, starting in 1937, his literary and political friend Alfred Hayes (1911–85) regaled him in person and by mail with warnings about the travesty of the Moscow Purge Trials and the ruses of Soviet policy in Spain.[61] The last-minute switch of the title of Fearing's 1939 collection of poetry from "X-Ray" to *Dead Reckoning*, denoting "guesswork" without predictive instruments, conceivably portends a future without the certainties of the Third International as a political guide, which was apparently the situation until that time.[62] Although the League of American Writers voted *Dead Reckoning* the outstanding book of 1939 after Steinbeck's *The Grapes of Wrath*, the *Daily Worker* review by Communist Party–supporter Nelson Algren (1909–81) identified warning signs of Fearing's priorities. The collection, Algren noted, was more antiwar than antifascist and more anti–George Babbitt (the title character in Sinclair Lewis's novel) than anti–Martin Dies (the reactionary Texas congressman).[63] When Fearing agreed to contribute to the summer 1939 symposium on "The Situation of American Writing" sponsored by the semi-Trotskyist *Partisan Review*, he was flaunting his unorthodox readiness to dialogue with those labeled renegades by his Communist comrades.[64]

Fearing overtly broke ranks with the Communist Party at the very moment when a tightening of the party line was required—following the August 1939 proclamation of the Hitler-Stalin Pact—by means of his *New Yorker* poem "Pact." The reference to Ezra Pound's 1913 "The Pact" and specific language may have been cryptic to outsiders, but Fearing's call for "another dream" and a fresh fight for a better world was unmistakable heresy to his Communist Party allies.[65] This political breech was irreconcilably deepened by his anger at the subsequent invasion of Finland by the Soviet Union.[66] By relinquishing once and for all the fable of the Soviet Union as the liberator of the world's oppressed, Fearing put himself into a distinct category as a post-Communist radical. No mercy was shown to Fearing by his former comrades; he was denounced as a renegade in the *New Masses* by poet Alexander F. Bergman (born Alexander Frankel, 1912–41),[67] who disparaged his latest work for "the confusion and pessimism of an ironic insight undirected by political foresight." Bombastically, Bergman labeled Fearing's newest poems "a surrender and a contribution to the propaganda of the press and radio, to their deliberately cultivated fatalism designed to rob the people of the spirit of resistance against the fascist offensive.... They constitute a cancellation of his identification with the progressive forces among the people." Bergman's conclusion exemplified the arrogant fanaticism that corrupted so much Communist critical discourse: "It may seem harsh and ungrateful to push aside a poet whose contributions were lately so highly valued.... But the people owe no debt of gratitude for sympathies rendered."[68]

Afterward, Fearing never again referred to the Soviet Union favorably; several of his indirect comments tended to equate it with the United States.[69] Reviews of Fearing's work in the Communist press became scarce. A few barbs were saved for the *New Masses* review of *Clark Gifford's Body*, which was criticized as an attempt to present an alternative to the Communist Party's view of the war: "Mr. Fearing tells his tale in a series of news flashes and first person narratives that jumble time, space, and events into an almost senseless confusion.... The result, of course, is horrible. Seen from the ivory tower of those who will still neither understand nor cooperate, the war becomes a meaningless morass of pain, cruelty, fanaticism and death, which no person—and here lies the morale-sapping danger of *Clark Gifford's Body*—would do anything but flee from."[70] Since 1940, Fearing had been noting parallels between the Soviet Union and Nazi Germany; in due course, he would shift toward holding a convergence theory of the Soviet and the U.S. empires, even indulging in the belief in the early 1950s that the Korean War was fought for the benefit of both.[71]

STUDY IN FUNDAMENTALS

Soviet Communism provided a temporary vision that allowed Fearing to work out an idiosyncratic Marxist standpoint that lived on without being grounded in a party or a country. His ongoing misanthropy rivaled but never quite trumped his internationalist antiwar convictions; repudiation of capitalism remained the stance from which he would never retreat. His need of a political perspective regarding art appeared satisfied by his summer 1939 declaration that the writer must "tell the truth as he sees it" because "the literature of today controls at least some of the guns of tomorrow ... any writer who promotes freedom of thought and action for larger and still larger masses of the people is loyal to the democratic idea."[72]

Once Fearing had lost his confidence in his imagined community of a workers' world, his writing more starkly conveyed a sense of the inexorable march of events toward a likely disaster. All of his adult life, Fearing had been breaking free of imprisoning allegiances; in the late 1930s, he projected an alter ego in his frantic prose in the form of a "resigned agent" spiraling through a nightmarish civilization.[73] This dark apparition implied but did not capitulate to a fatalism; his characters navigated a convoluted and opaque system, a machine but not one that produced events mindlessly and randomly. In *The Big Clock*, he simply locates his metaphor of the indecipherability of history, a "big clock," side-by-side with a work of art signifying a lingering filament of 1930s culture, *Study in Fundamentals*. The protagonist, George Stroud, is chary of the menace of the imagined specter of an eternal clock but gains a measure of self-control and autonomy based on his unarticulated bond with an anticapitalist painter's rendition of two hands exchanging money.

If the new fiction of the postwar era was, as is so often said, an intricate investigation of disillusionment, Fearing's *The Big Clock* does not quite qualify; from the onset, George Stroud has no illusions to lose. Moreover, a trope of salvation is present: the *Study in Fundamentals* canvas by a nonconformist female painter associated with New Deal art. Indeed, an essential thread of Fearing's novel can be traced to a now-iconic moment in art history— March–April 1944, when *Time*, *Life*, and *Newsweek* ran simultaneous articles describing how thousands of water-stained and mildewed Federal Arts Project canvases had been purchased en masse from a New York City junk dealer and were now on sale for cheap prices at a bric-a-brac shop on Canal Street. Among the artists who rushed to salvage some of their 1930s work was Fearing's friend and portraitist, the by-then-neglected WPA painter Alice Neel. Neel is fictionalized as Louise Patterson in the novel, which reenacts the episode in the antique shop where her painting *Study in Fundamentals* is given a new name by the doomed Pauline Delos, *The Temptation of Judas*; the painting is insistently purchased by Stroud for his collection of Patterson's art. Stroud, a well-paid executive of the Consumers' Republic, has an uncontainable need for ostensibly worthless paintings of the early 1930s, emblematic of the very culture that is being erased and trivialized right before his eyes.

Patterson's *Study in Fundamentals* depicts two individuals exchanging coins. The implication is that society's solvable problems are more deeply rooted in capitalist economic relations than in the existentialist "Big Clock," whose imaginary mechanical hands Stroud is obsessed with dodging. (Fearing vigorously objected to *The Big Clock* as a title; he preferred "The Temptation of St. Judas.")[74] One can append that Earl Janoth's abrupt defenestration at the conclusion of the novel recalls capitalist stockbrokers jumping out of office windows in 1929. Stroud, evidently, is facing intimations of mortality, a personal midlife crisis and, by implication, a midcentury crisis of American culture; his hair is turning gray, his family is growing, and he is not living where he wants to reside in the hierarchy of suburban neighborhoods. The only discernible resolution in Stroud's reified world is a greater salary.

Dereification apparently resides somewhere in the realm of the novel's two "free women," although the expression "free women" must be used in the same manner as the bitter sarcasm of Anna Wulf in Doris Lessing's *The Golden*

Notebook (1962). These two women are Pauline Delos, the ice-cold bisexual blond mistress of the Henry Luce–like publishing tycoon Earl Janoth, and Louise Patterson, the dark-haired rebel artist, an unmarried, erstwhile 1930s painter who boasts of children by various men. To document the realities of the new social order, Fearing takes advantage of noir techniques; he creates the look, the mood, the feel of the mid-1940s in the United States and especially its moral and emotional life—indeed, its very dream-life. His ostensible crime plot of a commercial writer, a specialist in lost persons, assigned to stalk himself as a stand-in who takes the rap for a murder committed by his capitalist boss intimates harmonics with subterranean meanings.

The saga of Janoth Enterprises is plainly built on the publishing empire of Henry Luce (1898–1967), where Fearing was employed as a writer for six months in 1942. The intrigue at the top of the operation refers back to events of the late 1920s. Luce had launched his career with a partner and rival, Britton Hadden (1889–1929), and together they founded *Time* magazine in 1923.[75] Although the two men took turns serving as president of the corporation, Hadden was considered the presiding genius and Luce the sidekick. In December 1928, Hadden was stricken with a terminal illness. He deliberately left his shares of *Time* to his family, out of Luce's reach, when he died early the next year. Luce, however, managed to gain control of these crucial stocks, then erased Hadden's name from the masthead of *Time* and the official memory of the company. Luce even managed to secure Hadden's papers and house them at Time, Inc., inaccessible to the public. Afterward, Luce launched *Fortune* in 1930 and *Life* in 1936, creating the network of publications that is depicted in *The Big Clock*.[76]

Fearing reworks this betrayal of Hadden by Luce, re-created as Steve Hagen and Earl Janoth, while also attributing menacing homosexual overtones to their relationship. The names of the protagonists are selected for mythological associations to boost the symbolic significance of the triangles of power and desire beyond the specific relationships of the plot: Janoth's name suggests the Roman god Janus; Hagen, the murderer of Siegfried (the warrior god of Germanic epics); and Delos, the Greek island where the oracle of Apollo lived.[77] The incentive for the homicide in *The Big Clock* is supposedly sexual. Janoth and Pauline Delos trade accusations of what appear to be uncontrolled sexual activity coded as deviancy. Janoth, in a jealous rage, reminds Pauline not only of past male lovers but more pointedly of lesbian affairs. Pauline, in turn, accuses Janoth of being a repressed homosexual and of camping (flaunting one's homosexuality) with his intimate friend Hagen, whom she describes as "a fairy gorilla."[78] These insults escalate suddenly to incite violence. The murder episode of Delos, however, is literally ripped from the headlines. It derives significantly from Fearing's reliance for aspects of his plot on the Lonergan murder case, a notorious criminal trial that was extensively reported by *Time* and most New York City papers in the months before Fearing began to write his novel.

On 24 October 1943, Wayne Lonergan, a Canadian aircraftsman in the Royal Canadian Air Force, murdered his wife, a socialite New Yorker whose maiden name was Patricia Burton, with a night-table candelabra. The news coverage was on the front page of the *New York Times* for six days, dispensing details of the crime as well as the personal lives of husband and wife. Witnesses came forward to attest to Wayne's homosexuality and Patricia's infidelity. As in *The Big Clock*, the killing of Patricia Lonergan was provoked by exchanges of sexual taunts, and Wayne Lonergan calmly departed the scene afterward by a taxi to attend a party. The case motivated a widespread public discussion of the nature of homosexuality and its possible connection to mental illness.[79]

Fearing, of course, changes the candelabra to a phallic decanter, but other details are identical. He adds the information that Janoth learns of a looming financial catastrophe for his company just prior to his rendezvous with Delos. This disturbing knowledge suggests that his masculine power was threatened preceding the fatal confrontation; it may explain why Pauline's hints about her sexual autonomy, combined with jibes about Janoth's personal connection to Hagen, are so incendiary. But there is no question that the id, in the general sense of unconscious drives animated by sexual desire and unresolved conflicts, is a central component of Fearing's semi-naturalist vision.

For sexual ecstasy with Pauline, George Stroud has already risked not only the marriage and family that he desires to maintain but his job and physical security as well. He comes close to calling the thrill of sex, not love, the very purpose of life. Before having sexual intercourse with Pauline the first time, Stroud declares her "the mystery," "the last, final, beautiful, ultimate enigma." On consummation, he announces, "I found out again why we are on this earth. I think."[80] Likewise, Janoth, at the instant of the murder, succumbs to a moment of transport; he finds himself being taken over by a giant a hundred feet tall who manipulates his hands so that he ends up clobbering Pauline to death. The role of the unconscious in determining his behavior is underscored by his declaration that "all of my life had led to this strange dream."[81] Without declaring his intention to later deny the crime, Janoth semiconsciously wipes off his fingerprints and flees by taxi to Hagen's apartment, and it is Hagen who gives voice to Janoth's subconscious plan. If Janoth is id, Hagen is ego (in the sense of a reality principle). In defiance of the Freudian schema, a superego is absent.

Yet there is a third component of what amounts to an unholy male trinity in the novel; Bill (who has no last name) is a combination chauffeur and thug-for-hire, available to Janoth and Hagen as the agent of death. His nickname "Billy" echoes the phallic billy club and the randy billy goat, suggesting that he supplies conventional masculinity to the sexually dysfunctional male duo of Janoth and Hagen at the head of the corporation. As with additional postwar novels, there are strong intimations that the life of the organization man in the gray flannel suit is one provoking a crisis of masculinity. In *The Big Clock*, this is joined by added prescient postwar themes of the framing of one's associates, informing for pay, misleading investigating committees, and covering up one's links with the radical culture of the 1930s. Like John Proctor in Arthur Miller's *The Crucible* (1953), George Stroud knows that he is guilty of sexual bad behavior, although not of the particular crime with which he has been charged.

The Big Clock is a noir nightmare, where no one can be trusted in its atmosphere of anxiety and paranoia; where there is no stability on the battleground of claustrophobic urban space; where a blond femme fatale lures the half-willing protagonist to cross moral and legal lines; and where crime bosses in business suits aided by a silent but deadly thug, Bill, who was previously a strike-breaker, lie constantly in wait. Fearing is gazing at an evolving social structure and readily takes the pulse of the rising new middle class from the inside. Like Adorno in the postwar years, he sees the recent past as the last sign of hope.

THE VIRTUE OF INTENTIONS

At the start of *The Big Clock*, the idea of social revolution is twisted into a cynical joke; Stroud makes a quick analogy between the Afro-Caribbean struggle that overthrew white supremacy in Haiti and the fantasy of an uprising of himself and fellow writers to escape from the fate of a life at the Janoth magazine *Crimeways*. This is central to *The Big Clock*'s ironic perspective, consisting mostly of witty incongruities, which initially appear to be Fearing's only strategy of resistance to compulsory consensus and rose-tinted conformity. But Stroud's gesture intentionally fails to dismiss the issue of social transformation.

Fearing's genus of irony does not approximate the detachment of a Stephen Crane, a writer much admired by Fearing in college. It reverberates with an ominous tone, insinuating, even in some of its Marx Brothers moments, that a disturbing alternate universe of gangster capitalism lurks under the halcyon exterior of postwar consumer wealth. To wit, beneath Fearing's bizarre humor of naming George's wife "Georgette" and his daughter "Georgia," and of all three calling each other "George," is his "Stepford wife" suggestion of the growing loss of personal identity in the nascent white-bread culture of the male-dependent suburban nuclear family. And spurring this drift is the growing supremacy of big media in determining identity and ethics. The irony and tension propelling *The Big Clock* was aimed at affecting consciousness: The 1930s may be over but History is yet flashing in a moment of danger. People are still living in a state of emergency. They have to fight back. Fearing's is an irony that has the virtue of good intentions.

Contemporary critics allowed the noir, mystery, psycho-thriller marketing niche, into which *The Big Clock* so comfortably fits, to obfuscate the main show. Due to a failure of the imagination, they missed seeing that Fearing's drama of domination and vulnerability is unmistakably performed in a theater of society and economics.[82] The relations between Fearing's people are power relations indicative of the semi-invisible culture wars starting to be waged on the home front in the 1940s—the very wars that progressively redefined every sphere of human activity to bolster the needs of the growing Consumers' Republic. They were not open class or race wars but battles of gradually more mechanized forces that encroached on the private lives of citizens. Fearing's characters in the 1940s and 1950s are socially privileged, but his fiction still illuminates, as did his poetry in the 1930s, the stifled sensibilities of a larger public. His political understanding became increasingly inchoate, but in his mind the achievements of the social vision of the Depression were blended into idealized memories of the New Deal.

In the novel, unlike the 1948 film, there is no genuine "Big Clock." The phrase is only George Stroud's compelling metaphor for an unseen adversary that rises above individuals in society. Yet the referent of the "Big Clock" is not quite a metaphysical one. It is an image of the mystified reification of social and biological fate in the urban capitalist environment; the giant hands of this slowly moving but relentless imaginary machine threaten all the characters in the novel. Earl Janoth himself is insufficiently powerful to defy this self-propelled system, somehow created by the intrigues of humans but given sovereignty even over those who are at the top of the heap. George Stroud ends the novel by predicting that his evasion of the deadly power of the clock was but a temporary respite.

What stands against the "Big Clock" is art, primarily *Study in Fundamentals*, now called *The Temptation of Judas*. Stroud's abrupt decision to retain Patterson's painting, even at great risk to himself, results in his choice to defy the "Big Clock" and Janoth—which he successfully does. Thus the narrative, expressed through monologues of seven characters, is structured between warring antitheses: *The Temptation of Judas*, a truth-telling act of the imagination that can bind generations, and the "Big Clock," a mental image of the postwar social order and the culture wars of the Consumers' Republic for which it stands.

There are other sites of artistic practice in the novel beyond the Patterson paintings. Gil's tavern, among George Stroud's favorite hangouts, is the home of a "personal museum" behind the bar that is used in a game where the winner gets a free drink.[83] This kind of non-elitist culture on display in Gil's is something of a popular art alternative to the Janoth corporation itself, which as a culture industry crudely produces pre-digested ideas in its magazines for a profit. The publishing enterprise additionally serves as a home for would-be artists; their employment conveys the notion that the reader is witnessing an exceptional moment in history when writers are being sucked into emergent corporations and other institutions to be eviscerated of their independence. Stroud is among those who unhappily conform to this fatal cultural machine, at one point even called "The Big Gadget" (the term for the atomic bomb during its testing period).[84] Other allusions to the ambiguities of art and creativity in *The Big Clock* include Stroud's taking Pauline to attend a studio production of his favorite radio show, the escapist *Ranger of the Sky*, and the stories Stroud crafts each morning to entertain his daughter, Georgia, pedagogically aimed at inducing her to eat breakfast.[85] But it is only the painting of the bohemian-radical Louise Patterson that Fearing associates with a possible defiance of the cultural drift of the postwar society. Stroud becomes at risk of being found guilty of a falsely attributed crime, the murder of Pauline, if it can be proven that he favors Patterson's particular kind of art, one coming unexpectedly out of the past. Hence he is tempted to destroy her paintings.

Louise Patterson is an emblem of the radical background of the Great Depression; although her reputation has faded, her glory days as an artist were those spent in association with the 1930s WPA, a haven for left-wing cultural activity that Fearing wants to recoup.[86] She also has the name of a famous Black Communist cultural leader, Louise Patterson (1901–99), an associate of Langston Hughes's married to William L. Patterson (1891–1980), the African American attorney who supervised the International Labor Defense during the Scottsboro case. Fearing depicts Patterson as a garrulous eccentric full of Neel's famous "non-stop stream of racy stories, politics, and philosophical musings" and other unconventional, free-love, and even proto-feminist behavior associated with the painter.[87] Patterson has "love children" by many different "husbands," which she freely declares; adamantly insists on being called "Miss"; announces that she rejects all long-term or marriage relationships because men have tried to destroy her; and, at the novel's end, becomes a potential future lover for Stroud as he clandestinely enters her name in his telephone address book.[88]

The art of Louise Patterson is difficult to grasp for those imprisoned by the culture of the postwar world. Steve Hagen, for example, is incapable of identifying as a Patterson the characteristic painting, *Study in Fury*, that hangs in George Stroud's office in the Janoth building. In the sixteenth chapter (the novel is divided into sections according to monologues attributed to each main character), Stroud describes himself and Hagen examining a photograph of a Patterson exhibition from nine years earlier, presumably 1935 or 1936, capturing five of her canvases. The paintings on the left and in the center are unnamed. Between the two is *Study in Fundamentals*, the work depicting the betrayal of human brotherhood through the exchange of money. On the far right is the painting hanging in Stroud's workplace on the floor immediately below, *Study in Fury*, evocative of Earl Janoth's sexual rage produced by the desire for domination, control, and ownership when faced with independence and autonomy. Stroud is astounded at Hagen's inability to connect the painting in the photograph with the one he has seen many times in the office of the man he is trying to entrap. Such blindness as to the import of art in unexpected places may also apply to the initial misapprehension by critics of Fearing's stratagem of converting a psycho-thriller into the repository of an acute appraisal of the very culture that gave *The Big Clock* exalted status in the market.

This returns us to Fearing's peculiar place in our effort to gain a perspective on the fate of 1930s radicalism in the creation of the new postwar canon exemplified by the advance of Saul Bellow. Although Fearing's worldview should be treated as a way of thinking and not a meticulous philosophy, *The Big Clock*, his biggest success, was a development of the vision of the 1930s and not a repudiation. Fearing, however, did see the postwar moment as one bringing a crisis in meanings, and his goal was to deepen the radical's sense of historical continuity that was in danger of erasure if one over-adjusted to the new world system of Luce's American Century. After their brief encounter in the pages of the *New York Times Book Review* in March 1944, in the interval between "two ages," Bellow retooled in quest of survival and what amounted to accommodation, while Fearing, in *The Big Clock* and succeeding works, marched off in a quixotic war to prevent the fall of the New Deal Order.

The homologous origins of Saul Bellow and Kenneth Fearing as Depression Leftists must be acknowledged but not overstated in appreciating such postwar cultural configurations. Bellow's connections to a Left cultural legacy were genuine; they included his advantageous links to radical writers and journals of the 1930s, the urbane political education he attained as a young

Trotskyist, and the raw material from his personal life that he worked into future narratives. Yet Bellow's chief growth spurt came after the Red Decade, principally when articulating in fiction the death of the social realist legacy in the Dostoevskian cerebrality of *The Victim* (1947) and the Dickensian picaresque of *The Adventures of Augie March* (1953). A mood of deadening suffocation may be found in the former and one of buoyant celebration in the latter; these were Bellow's inspired literary strategies for his postwar realignment away from the social and toward the personal. Although he fluctuated in preferred literary forms, his novels share a thesis: The agonies of persecution as well as the enigmas of identity, rather than comprehensible and rectifiable social arrangements, are indicative of psychological infirmities and metaphysical puzzles.[89]

Fearing's work anticipates the peaking in the next decade of Communist literary modernism, an invention of postwar conditions in the sense that different periods in art are the unique product of consciousness of that time. Fearing and contemporaries such as Paul Bowles (1910–90) held that using the novel form to primarily replicate society in realist simulacra was not to create an authentic art responding to the new conjuncture. Like Hegel and Marx, they held that only through contradiction could the real be comprehended in its totality; in a Consumers' Republic, one needed oblique ways to provoke such experience.

Fearing's existentialist-like mask of irony and cynical veneer are actually protective coloration for an allegorical secular project whose goal is the liberation of the fully human, an evolution of social realism in certain respects but also very much part of the avant-garde trend within modernism. Of course, when discussing form and sensibility in this era in terms of modernism, one must be wary of the undiscriminating capaciousness of this category; much recent scholarship has made modernism virtually ubiquitous. One may reject one-way elitist models of what the term means while still favoring strong over weak definitions of the concept. Fearing and others who would create this postwar presence of Communist literary modernism are not employing their literature to express that there is nothing to express; it is only that their literature returns no answer to those in search of a ratification of social myth. Their art was not an attempt to open up modernism in new ways, a feature of much other 1950s writing, because the Leftists simply were not coming at modernism from the inside.

Fearing's post-1939 writing surely embodies criticisms of Marxism, but sympathetic ones. His bitter mockery of human self-delusion never presents caricatures of the Left through a pretense of an objectivity in service of Cold War liberalism. Nor do Fearing's near-nihilist forays into a world of masks and disguises indicate that he is above the fray. What is imperative is that his writing safeguards the essential ambiguity of experiences that suggest that one cannot simply use what is deemed to be enlightened reason, regardless of the source, to subject the universe to one's will. The cultural history of the era of *The Big Clock* is paramount in Fearing, and it enters the narrative by assorted routes—ones sometimes not that different from writings of his explicit pro-Communist past. The setting of the novel is approximately 1945, although there is no plain reference to World War II or its aftermath. Much imaginative literature of the Great Depression aimed to provide a rich social picture, but Fearing's work always resisted characters fixed by forces of memory and attachment.

One finds some historical and topical references in Fearing's poetry and fiction but rarely religion, ethnicity, and nation. In his novels of the 1940s and 1950s, his fictionalized characters similarly lack depth. Yet they are unmistakably embedded in the texture of society, the product of a recognizable culture and economic system. Even when the manipulations of experimental fiction are evident in Fearing's routines of paradox and pastiche, the reader never has the sense that there can be a mere interchangeability of experience among the protagonists. In *The Big Clock*, Fearing allocates little personal history to the CEO duo (Earl Janoth and Steve Hagen) or the leading women (Pauline Delos, Georgette Stroud, Louise Patterson), but they are all evocatively distinctive, suggestive of competing psychosexual male drives and believable female identities for the era. Fearing, like any Marxist, would agree that the individual is never self-constituted.

Where the social references of *The Big Clock* are distinct from Great Depression work such as *The Hospital* is mainly because there is a change in the kind of institution under examination. In his postwar writing, Fearing concentrates obsessively on the mores of the growing middle class. From *The Big Clock* onward, all of Fearing's novels and most of his poems illustrate personal crises distinctive of a culture in which there has occurred an increasing consolidation of economic power and estrangement from the political process. From a historical perspective, one can see his postwar project revealing itself as the depiction of social victims of a new type, working in institutions of advertising, fund-raising, technology, and media. Lacking the examples of Depression-era collective power in action, these materially privileged individuals are thrown back on themselves with disastrous or at best limited results.

To construct a mental map on which novels such as *The Big Clock* can be plotted, one must appreciate that writers such as Fearing, with a record of pro-Communism followed by a stubborn refusal to condemn the Soviet Union in public, were not fanatically committed to what is now judged to be totalitarianism. Their commitment was to the achievement of world equality and peace, an attainment that would come through Communism. By conflating Communism with totalitarianism, one cannot grasp the level of personal pain and self-effacement these writers tolerated, which would presently become the matrix of Communist literary modernism. Fearing had truly hitched his somewhat nihilist wagon to the star of a Communist dream in a manner fraught with risk. But doubts had been gnawing away at him since the Moscow Trials so that the evaporation of his loyalty in 1939 was not as harrowing for his artistic productivity and quality as it might have been. Moreover, the credence he had given the Communist Party and its worldview was never the main point for his art; this was propelled forward by his capacity to blend the persona of a strange, lost child with that of a world-weary Greenwich Village bohemian.

Whether or not formal ideologies determine outcomes in artistic production is a complex matter. What we know is that one's connection to a movement can involve inspiration as well as a fear of negative judgments from one's allies. Confusion around the composite meanings of Communist identity is a reason for the misreading of so many writers and also explains why a force that altered the course of U.S. literature remains strangely obscure. Those who equate Literary Communism with a declared membership or formal literary characteristics suggest the drunk in the famous bar story who looked for lost keys under a lamppost because "that is where the light is." One way or another, the core values of Fearing's 1930s vision remained intact into the 1950s; in his writing, class war continued by other means. For Fearing, the socialist dream was not over, but it had to be sharply redrawn. In *The Big Clock*, this Communist poet turned author of thrillers secretly practices his revolutionary faith by using a murder mystery to narrate the attempted destruction and ultimate rescue of a cache of New Deal art.

How, then, does one connect the postwar political and cultural dots? Art may be individualist in expression, but Fearing's is at the same time the product of the culture within which he lived. Two of the features that link Fearing to a tradition going forward may be the "unfinishedness" of his life and writing and the sincere irony of his message. In his own way, Fearing attempted to discover the historical and social forces at work to leave a message to a new Left, but his legacy is a body of fiction and some poetry standing consciously against the kind of simplifications that treat ideas as merely social forces in disguise. The irony in Fearing's writing was generated by the identification of contradictions or antinomies that emerge inevitably from any character's erroneous account of the relation of consciousness to reality, especially if reason and rationality are not understood as Janus-faced. That element of perception remained consistent, but enlarging especially after 1939 until his death. Irony of this type is easily misread as banging one's head against an obdurate wall of illusions, but the reconstruction of his art in context demonstrates what I've described as a virtue of intentions.

In the next two chapters, we will investigate the literary criticism and fiction of the postwar Communist presence, especially of those writers closer to the social realist forms associated with the Great Depression. A focus on addressing this Communist presence—refusing either reductive or evasive approaches to a writer's political history—is not an endorsement of any notion of Communism as a recipe for high-quality writing. The outsider status of pro-Communist writers potentially gave artists a critical space within literature representing an alternative reality independent of the state and prevailing conformities, but not everyone took advantage of this opportunity to contribute to a secular re-enchantment of literature as socialist contingency along the lines of Fearing. It is still the art and not the political background with which one must end to get the full measure of what these postwar writers accomplished. But to distinguish the art, one must consider the emotional as well as the moral, social, and psychological aspects of pro-Communist writers—the inner life of people too often treated as if they had none.

Chapter Two

Scenes from a Class Struggle

SOMEWHERE BEYOND PROLETARIANISM

In *The Decay of Living* (1889), Oscar Wilde famously reversed mimesis: "Life imitates art far more than art imitates life."[1] Pro-Communist writers in the postwar years, fashioning both their art and literary criticism in a tradition variously identified as proletarian literature, socialist realism, democratic culture, and people's art, faced a parallel tussle between their personal visions, growing out of psychology and experience, and the succession of models and doctrines exalted by the international Communist movement.[2] How does a creative writer express subjectivity, or a critic provide assessments, when facing the beckoning call of a social aesthetic? Proletarianism, in many ways the most original and permanent contribution of the literary Left in the United States, persisted after the early 1930s not by maintaining doctrinal purity but by amalgamation with other facets of social realism, modernism, mass culture, ethnic consciousness, and regionalism.

Proletarian literature resists precise definition. Debates of the early 1930s described it as literature expressing a revolutionary view, or else dramatizing working-class experience or even authored by workers, and appealing to a working-class audience.[3] Yet the prior tradition of social realism, depicting hardship and injustice, is also often regarded as pro–working class in perspective, and there are stylistic affinities hard to disentangle from Great Depression proletarianism. The chief difference between social realist and proletarian literature may simply be the presence of the Communist Party in the worldview of an increasing number of writers after the 1920s, an organization that proclaimed itself the arbiter of working-class interests. Ardent Communist cultural critics, as well as some critics hostile to proletarian literature, as a result took the category of proletarian literature to be a euphemism for promoting the Communist point of view. In practice, however, many works of fiction and poetry, even by those writers active in Communist political organizations, enacted a Marxist sensibility of a loose type while tacitly rejecting the rigidity of any Soviet or U.S. Communist-inspired aesthetics. This remained the state of affairs even after the demand for socialist realism became an official Soviet doctrine in 1932 and migrated to U.S. literary discussions in 1934.

The reason for this frequent disjuncture between formal Communist doctrine and creative literature lies in the imaginative process itself. Writings by avowed Leftists aimed to tackle questions of race, ethnicity, gender, and the ambiguities of experience that were not containable within the narrow structures of form or thought emanating from an official ideology. This record of subtlety can be hard to appreciate for anyone looking at the proletarian tradition through the prism of the preconceptions that unsympathetic critics have promoted to suggest that left-wing writing is tantamount to industrial soap opera.[4] Communist spokespersons, sometimes self-appointed, only added to the confusion by anointing or excommunicating various writers in language suggesting that there is a clear standard of proletarian aesthetic rectitude. Reviews in the Communist press could echo straitlaced, middlebrow cultural criticism at its most pernicious, treating certain writings as if threatening to the moral health of the working class.[5] Too often, writers were celebrated on sentimental grounds, praised for displaying a "deep and abiding love for people."[6] Proletarian fiction, in certain respects, shaped itself according to those who made use of the category or were identified as having done so by others.

The cultural workers who created the Communist presence after World War II, best comprehended as consisting of several layers of novice and maturing writers transformed by a Marxist sense of mission, reassigned their radical sensibility mainly through reference and indirection. Postwar, one was no longer talking only of how inspiring Communist ideas and norms shaped literary projects and styles but also about the consequences of a period of palpable change in the fortunes of the Left. After Pearl Harbor, the historical context metamorphosed into a deceptive national unity followed by phases of insurgence, fear, and isolation. Writing that emerged from a Left literary sensibility into this ambience did not necessarily replicate 1930s proletarianism yet still exhibited the tone, mood, and point of view of those who knew the score in regard to class oppression and often made use of the documentary impulse of the Depression by going to the source.

Some writers worked with an ideology of attendant implications reflective of the Progressive, antifascist outlook, while others principally wrote in the literary afterglow of the Depression. But proletarianism per se was never repudiated outright or subject to censorious or even searching criticism by the Communist movement; it endured for decades and regularly resurfaced with more flexible definitions as an available option for literary praise from the Left.[7] In 1939, when John Steinbeck's *The Grapes of Wrath* was published at the height of the Popular Front, the *Daily Worker* carried the headline "*The Grapes of Wrath* is a Great Proletarian Novel."[8] A few weeks later, the *New Masses* published a matching judgment by Granville Hicks (1901–82): "Hitherto, whenever anybody asked us what we meant by proletarian literature, we had to say, 'Well, it ought to have this quality that you find in so-and-so's work, and that quality so exemplified by the other fellow, and such-and-such found in somebody else.' . . . We shan't have to offer that kind of composite illustration any more. We can now say, 'Proletarian literature? Oh, that means a book like John Steinbeck's *The Grapes of Wrath*.'"[9] Yet the same novel was an icon of people's and progressive culture, and Steinbeck did not embrace the term.

Even during the months of the Hitler-Stalin Pact, people's literature and proletarian literature remained acceptable options, although the state of affairs in regard to praising works was complicated by the sometimes hair-trigger political evaluations of where a particular writer was thought to stand politically. One famously bewildering episode, the cause of some mythmaking, began in April 1941, just on the eve of Operation Barbarossa, the German invasion of the Soviet Union, and the formation of the Allies to fight Germany. The literary editor of the *New Masses* since 1937, Samuel Sillen (1911–73), published a lead review commending "two excellent novels," *What Makes Sammy Run* (1941), by Budd Schulberg (born Seymour Wilson Schulberg, 1914–2009), and *Out of This Furnace* (1941), by Thomas Bell (born Adalbert Thomas Belejcak, 1903–61). Sillen titled his essay "Sammy Glick and Johnny Dobrejack," the names of the protagonists in each book. His review articulated the tone for the era that more or less evolved after 1935 by championing both novels as "alternate ways of hitting back at a social order which staggers along on topsy-turvy standards, cynically indifferent to human values." While the two shared "a deep core of identity" in their political principles, Schulberg's book used "ironic detachment" and other devices "borrowed from the 'hard-boiled' school of [James M.] Cain and [John] O'Hara," while Bell's "places the lives of workers in a historical perspective" to produce "an excellent proletarian novel." Both avenues would remain open to pro-Communist writers throughout the war years and into the postwar era. But there was an undeclared axiom: Sillen fused the two novels in his review because he assumed that the two authors, both pro-Communists, were loyal to "the common men and women who alone have the stamina and bravery and eagerness to inherit this earth."[10]

It was customarily the case, in the Communist-led cultural movement, that politics in the end trumped aesthetics. But to see Sillen's review as merely the establishment of a "line" on two novels by "The Party" is only a half-truth. The half that is true is indeed vital: The Communist leadership assumed that it had the entitlement, competence, and even duty to lead a literary movement; critics such as Sillen vied to formulate judgments to further that end. Still, a caveat is obligatory because, within the circles of official Communist cultural policymakers, there were now and then contradictory and unforeseen appraisals. Even when infected by pomposity and a dogmatic certainty of judgment, failings by no means restricted to Communist critics, literary reviews by Communist Party cultural leaders could express a range similar to those found in the popular press. On this occasion, the *New Masses*, beginning on 29 April 1941, consistently championed Schulberg's *What Makes Sammy Run* as a fit companion for more classical proletarian fiction, despite knowing that the West Coast Communist paper, the *People's Daily World*, had earlier in the month performed an about-face on its own prior positive assessment. How did this twofold evaluation occur? An exclusive focus by cultural historians on the negative treatment of Schulberg's novel has produced a simplified legend worth correcting if the Communist presence in post-1930s literature is to be grasped.

On 7 April, Charles Glenn (dates unknown), a columnist for the *People's Daily World* and a recent recruit to its Los Angeles staff from the Midwest, published a rave review of *What Makes Sammy Run*, based on page proofs given to him by Schulberg.[11] Glenn revealed thirty years afterwards to a researcher that the Hollywood cultural leader John Howard Lawson (1894–1977) immediately summoned him to an hour-and-a-half-long meeting. Here Lawson browbeat Glenn into writing a second review, one that chastised Schulberg for failing to accurately represent the role of Communists and ordinary working people in the progressive movement in Hollywood and for putting too much emphasis on characters who could fuel anti-Semitism.[12] This second review was published in two parts, on 23 and 24 April, a week before the *New Masses*' high praise of Schulberg's novel appeared.

A decade later, Schulberg published his own account of the background of Glenn's second review, which he recalled in connection with his 1951 cooperation with the House Un-American Activities Committee (HUAC) in providing the names of individuals who had once been in the Communist Party.[13] His version of the reversal of judgment on the novel begins in March 1939, when he, a Communist Party member, submitted a proposal to a writers' clinic

Budd Schulberg in military uniform during World War II. The controversy over his novel *What Makes Sammy Run* (1941) became an issue in his congressional testimony during the Cold War.

sponsored by the Hollywood Communist Party; Schulberg hoped to gain counsel about reworking his magazine stories depicting a character called Sammy Glick into a novel. The reaction of Communist Party members John Howard Lawson and Richard Collins (b. 1914) was negative, but Schulberg nonetheless relocated in Vermont to write the novel. Following a return to Hollywood in March 1940, Schulberg had more discussions about his novel-in-progress, in this instance with Lawson and V. J. Jerome (born Jerome Isaac Romain, 1896–1965), the chairman of the Communist Party Cultural Commission, who was visiting from New York. At this point, Schulberg supposedly proclaimed to them his discomfort with the Hitler-Stalin Pact and resigned from the Communist organization. According to Schulberg's account, he would have been acutely at odds with the Party during the entire year leading up to the publication of his novel.

Yet the *New Masses*, in commending *What Makes Sammy Run* as a model of fiction for the post–Popular Front moment, was unruffled at this turmoil on the West Coast. The editors must have been aware of the uproar in Southern California because the *Daily Worker* in New York had already reprinted both the positive and negative reviews from the *People's Daily World*, and Jerome (a Lawson ally) surely trumped Samuel Sillen in political authority. The *New Masses*, however, published no letters to the editor or other indications of disagreement with the *New Masses'* laudatory assessment of *What Makes Sammy Run*, nor was Sillen required to make a self-criticism. Moreover, in the 29 July 1941 issue of the *New Masses*, Schulberg was one of ten prominent individuals invited by the editors to give a statement in a symposium called "How I Feel about the War," which principally presented arguments for aiding the Soviet Union in its fight with Germany following the five-week-old disintegration of the Hitler-Stalin Pact. Every other cultural figure in the symposium was a staunch pro-Communist, and Schulberg used the occasion to praise Soviet ambassador Maxim Litvinov as a political leader far superior to those of England and France.[14]

Plainly, Schulberg was not as disaffected as he later claimed, and a divided opinion on Schulberg's novel remained. The *New Masses'* July 1941 invitation to make a statement for the symposium was a public sign that he was still welcome in the Communist movement, a prompt of the magazine's earlier endorsement of *What Makes Sammy Run*, one serving as a counterweight to Glenn's appalling second review in the *People's Daily World*. Schulberg's name, one of the few in the symposium featured on the cover, was even listed as the first among those contributing statements about the war. Moreover, from April until at least the end of 1941, both before and after the Communist Party's *volte-face* regarding the war in Europe, *What Makes Sammy Run* was featured in a special-offer advertisement in virtually every issue of the *New Masses*; it was one of a handful of books by pro-Communist writers such as Earl Browder, Bruce Minton, and Theodore Dreiser available through the magazine's office at a discount with a year's subscription. Although the *Clipper*, edited largely by Communist Party members in Los Angeles, ran an article by W. L. River critical of *What Makes Sammy Run*, the East Coast *Di-*

rection magazine published one poles apart by longtime Communist reviewer Edwin Seaver (1900–1987) urging that the novel be nominated for the Pulitzer Prize![15]

Schulberg in his 1951 HUAC testimony both inflated and simplified his March 1940 rupture with the Communist Party. There was actually a split decision about the content of his novel, mirroring the response in the mainstream press, and whatever doubts Schulberg had about the Party and the Hitler-Stalin Pact did not lead to a clear break; the doubts were assuaged by the new pro–World War II position. His name even appears with Lawson's as a sponsor of the 1949 Cultural and Scientific Conference for World Peace, a list that includes no writers who spoke out against the Stalin regime and mostly those close to the Party. But Schulberg's 1951 slippery reconstruction of his political biography has led to the view, depicted in work of historians unfriendly to the Hollywood Left, that Schulberg was the victim and not the victimizer of the Communist Party writers whose names he provided, such as Glenn and Lawson.[16] One can recover a sufficient number of comparable episodes to demonstrate that the Communist cultural movement was never as stage-managed as some of the lazy stereotypes suggest.

THE INTELLECTUAL UNDER FIRE

As the Schulberg imbroglio points out, adjudicating the authority of book reviews in Communist Party publications requires a discernment of the force field operating amid assorted constituents. The tradition of proletarian literature was also affected by socialist realist doctrine exerting an oblique but commanding pressure on Communists in capitalist countries such as the United States to adhere to its requirement that a writer present a correct discrimination of the progress of history, especially the presence of the Soviet Union—"the central social reality of our time."[17] Establishing that a writer in the non-socialist United States was properly creating an instantiation of socialist realism's telos, or how skillfully this was being accomplished, could be a byzantine undertaking. The years following the 1939 advent of the war in Europe created quandaries for deducing the politics of fiction due to Moscow's rapid tactical and strategic shifts bringing new pressures and demands. At the end of the day, assent to Soviet foreign policy was the deal breaker in assessing the work of living novelists; it was rare for a literary critic associated with the Party to duck the enforcement of this requirement.

If Schulberg or Thomas Bell had made anti-Soviet statements, *What Makes Sammy Run* and *Out of This Furnace* could not have been championed as exemplary, regardless of their literary quality. Political obligation, however, did not rule out oddities in literary appraisals in regard to contradictory reviewing of Schulberg, Steinbeck, Henry Roth, and others. On occasion, they arose simply because of the complex personalities of critics; personal animus and coterie vendettas are quite real in critical judgments, and score-settling is omnipresent in a book such as Howard Fast's *Literature and Reality* (1950). But the mutations of proletarianism as a cultural orientation were mostly the result of the unpredicted changes in political circumstances. This is apparent if one reexamines, from another angle, the contortions in the Communist press around the assessment of *What Makes Sammy Run* in the spring of 1941, when intellectuals were very much "under fire" from the guns of a complicated war. The judgments by Party critics that refer to the general tasks of the writer in relation to war and class struggle were surely a result of the Communist Party's shift on foreign policy. Pro-war "renegades" in June, with whom Budd Schulberg might have been linked by Lawson for his reasonable doubts about the Pact, were abruptly transformed into potential allies in July, hence destabilizing the literary judgments once linked to real or imagined political attitudes.

The apparent disorder was associated with a transition in cultural policy away from and then back to a variation of the Popular Front. Its wider significance for the proletarian tradition was apparent on 6 June 1941 when, in the last two weeks of the Hitler-Stalin Pact, Mike Gold (born Itztok Isaac Granich, 1893–1967) emerged from nearly four years in the literary shadows to address the Fourth American Writers Congress with "An Evaluation of Proletarian Literature of the 1930s."[18] His remarks could not be published immediately as revisions were required, and in the interim, on 21 June, the Soviet Union was attacked by Germany. So categorical and intemperate was Gold's 6 June denunciation of literary supporters of military intervention against Hitler (he branded them fascists, in line with the earlier Hitler-Stalin Pact orientation) that his address was immediately rendered obsolete. The manuscript was then consigned to the archives of the League of American Writers and did not appear in print until it was posthumously published three decades later. Nonetheless, if one passes over the personal smears, there is an authority in Gold's 6 June assessment of proletarianism as a necessary stage in the triumph of "the democratic renaissance of the 1930s"; this view was noncontroversial and is a better statement of the longer-term coherence in Communist Party literary policies than acknowledged in histories that solely deride the switches.[19]

A point of view comparable to Gold's was presented by Samuel Sillen in his address to the same Fourth American Writers Congress. Since Sillen's remarks were in publishable form, his text was slipped into the 24 June issue of the *New Masses*, typeset just a day or two before the Soviet-mandated policy change. Under the title "The Intellectual under Fire: Reason Shall Be Enthroned Again," Sillen argued, in a slightly more restrained manner than Gold, that the war hysteria must be resisted and that "the only truly creative force in society is the working class and its allies in the middle classes." His line of reasoning was buttressed by the method of using ugly innuendos commonly found in the *New Masses*: Deviations from the Communist perspective on literary engagement were said to be motivated by a hope of gaining financial privileges, while political backsliding (W. H. Auden and Stephen Spender were accused of both sins) was coupled with allegations of sexual impropriety (flirtatious behavior toward the rich and powerful and even homosexual inclinations). Invoking three familiar literary icons of the Communist-led movement during the eighteen months of the Hitler-Stalin Pact—Carl Sandburg, John Steinbeck, and Richard Wright—Sillen reiterated the Communist Party catechism that the Soviet Union constituted "a world in which there is no racism or national discrimination, no oppression of man by man, no bitterness and futility and despair." In the United States, "Reason" demanded an antiwar stance and the unqualified right of workers to strike, positions that were at that very moment being redefined by the Communist Party to become the hallmarks of an alleged pro-Hitler Fifth Column.[20]

Although political policy had changed, Gold's assessment of proletarian literature was unambiguously endorsed by Sillen a few weeks later in "Sharpen the Arrows: The Social Base for a Resurgent Proletarian Literature." This was a feature article in the *New Masses*' "Special War Issue" that was quickly assembled for publication on 1 July. Sillen's article uniquely documents a passing but instructive moment of cultural militancy amid the confusion of the Communist Party's new international position; Sillen insisted that proletarian literature was in a revival and posited that the fate of such literature was tied to the struggle of the working class, a fight that could not be deferred simply because of the requirements of the war. By September 1942, in "Too Quiet on the Western Front," Sillen's emphasis had switched to the logic of cultural policy following political necessity for which "reason" could always provide validation. He was now demanding that literature during wartime be focused exclusively on the needs of the war; culture must be mobilized in a manner analogous to what had happened in industry and the military.

Delighted that there was no significant opposition to the war among writers, Sillen bent the stick in the opposite direction of the tradition of revolutionary socialists during and after World War I. To accept the war was not enough—writers needed to be affirmatively on a pro-war offensive.[21] Sillen's rudimentary theorizing was backed up by the book, theater, and film reviews of Alvah

Bessie (1904–85), who selected writings (all by Communists, although they were not so identified) expressive of the need to articulate an appropriate state of mind to fight a war. Bessie praised the novel *Telegram from Heaven* (1942) by Arnold Manoff (1914–65), later a blacklisted television writer who used the name "Joel Carpenter," and the play *Winter Soldiers* (1942) by Daniel James (1911–88), later also a blacklisted writer using the name "Daniel Hyatt" and achieving notoriety in the 1980s as "Danny Santiago."[22]

Sillen brought his writings for the year to a conclusion with a December 1942 essay, "Trends in War Writing," which deepened his call for writers to abandon an isolated conception of their craft and become involved in the common purpose of participating in a "fighting literature." The phrase meant writing that not only depicted "how" the war was going but "why" people were fighting.[23] By the end of the following year, just after the late 1943 Teheran Conference, Communist Party leader Earl Browder, who was putting all references to socialism on the back burner, announced that the Party would no longer counterpoise any critical slogans to the ideology of "Free Enterprise"; he pledged to help make capitalism work even in the postwar era.[24] A few months later, in yet another special "War Issue" (16 May 1944) of the *New Masses*, Sillen's embrace of Browder's strategy of unity with the Roosevelt administration at all costs was effusively put on display. His essay, "The Challenge of Change," explained that 1930s proletarian literature was a narrow movement that failed to unreservedly celebrate the deeply progressive nature of Roosevelt's New Deal. What the wartime situation required was not a literature of resistance and opposition but one that was boldly positive.[25] Ironically, in less than a year, the pendulum would start swinging in the opposite direction as part of a disastrous Left turn culminating in an American version of Zhdanovism (see introduction) on the part of Sillen and his fellow Communist Party critics.

Even during the closing days of the 1940s, when the frame of mind of late antifascism was at its summit, proletarian literature never regained its pre-1935 eminence as the supreme category of literary achievement, although it remained on the radar screen of most pro-Communist writers. The Popular Front had created a permanent space for other varieties of fiction, unsurprisingly grouped under the rubric of "Progressive," as long as Communist Party critics did not discern adverse political implications about the Soviet Union in a text or become aware of an author's public statements that might be inconsistent with shifting Soviet policies. Judgments by individual cultural critics in the Communist Party press were given some leeway, but with mixed results. Most predictably, the Communist Party's wartime political stance encouraged Alvah Bessie to embellish the importance of mediocre writing by Arnold

Manoff and Daniel James. But Samuel Sillen's earlier commendation of Budd Schulberg and Thomas Bell as exemplars for the new era was a sound literary estimate, one that illustrated the excellence of many novelists drawn to Communism. Schulberg and Bell had produced superb, benchmark works in the respective genres of writing about Hollywood and the proletarian novel.

Of course, the career of the two novelists in the aftermath of the *New Masses'* endorsement also says something about the significance and legacy of the pro-Communist literary tradition. Both remained variously on the Left to the end of their lives but also gravitated toward the two main trends among intellectuals. Bell, a milder personality who suffered serious physical ailments beginning in 1932 that would eventually combine with cancer to kill him at the age of fifty-eight, was organizationally peripheral to the Communist Party but identified with the Communist movement as early as 1934. Thirteen years later, in 1947, he contributed a short story to the Communist Party's new journal *Mainstream*.[26] Two of his novels in the 1940s, *Till I Come Back to You* (1943) and *There Comes a Time* (1946), were modest achievements; the latter made use of his political contacts to dramatize the organizing efforts of the Office and Professional Workers Union, which was expelled from the CIO in 1949 as Communist-led. In 1949, Bell was also an endorser of the Cultural and Scientific Conference for World Peace, an event strongly associated with pro-Communist intellectuals. Around 1950, Bell developed a writer's block, which drove him into a long period of psychoanalysis and reduced his literary output to one or two lightweight love stories per year. His final work was a posthumously published notebook of his fight with terminal cancer, *In the Midst of Life* (1961).

Schulberg continued to function in the Hollywood chapter of the League of American Writers and taught at its writers' school until 1942. Like Bell, he supported Henry Wallace's Progressive Party presidential campaign in 1948. Schulberg's *The Harder They Fall* (1947) remains a hard-boiled boxing classic, and *The Disenchanted* (1950) is a haunting novel suggestive of the final years of F. Scott Fitzgerald. Schulberg's decision to inform before HUAC as a friendly witness created much anguish as it was not motivated by a belief in the guilt of those against whom he testified; he collaborated only out of a fear that he himself would be blacklisted or indicted. As he explained in a letter to Fitzgerald's biographer Arthur Mizener, the activities of his former associates in the Communist Party could be considered as criminal only if pulled out of historic context.[27] Although Schulberg wrote a major screenplay affirming his Left-liberal politics while justifying informing, *On the Waterfront* (1954), neither he nor Bell ever repeated their 1941 successes in fiction. Schulberg's ethical standing was damaged considerably by subjecting his former friends and comrades to persecution in 1951. Bell remained unconscionably silent about the Stalinist horror he had once supported. The dualism between the two writers recapitulates, more or less, the predicament of pro-Communists who made the transition into the 1940s and 1950s.

THE MAKING OF ZHDANOVISTS

At the onset of *The Making of Americans* (1925), Gertrude Stein remarks: "It is hard living down the tempers we are born with."[28] The postwar tradition of Communist literary criticism, like the evolution of the radical novel, was not piloted by anonymous forces channeling Moscow through writing for the *New Masses* and *Daily Worker*. In regard to Party publications, it was fashioned by a group of principally Jewish American men (perhaps four-fifths) of uneven talent and sometimes capricious personalities who yoked their specific cultural sensibilities to a war against injustice that voluntarily looked to the Soviet Union for direction. Samuel Sillen, Isidor Schneider (1896–1977), and Charles Humboldt (born Clarence Weinstock, 1910–64) supplanted Mike Gold, Joseph Freeman, and Granville Hicks by assuming crucial Communist Party editorial posts from the late 1930s to the late 1950s. These three and others came forward after 1934, when Communism's Third Period sectarianism was being replaced by a mounting latitudinarianism that fed into the first Popular Front from mid-1935 to mid-1939.

By the early Cold War, the application of politico-critical tenets in the Communist Party press devolved precipitously to a stilted and arrogant dogmatism that few of these World War II-time writers could long endure. A growing percentage of the *New Masses* and *Daily Worker* reviews and literary columns became devoted to killing non-Communist writers' reputations by amalgamating them with fascists, elitists, and opportunists. Outstanding literary scholars close to or briefly members of the Party or Young Communist League—such as Kenneth Burke (1897–1993), Newton Arvin (1900–1963), and Stanley Edgar Hyman (1919–70)—were quietly moving away. Pro-Communists trying to maintain academic careers in literature departments—for instance, Edwin Berry Burgum (1894–1979), Margaret Schlauch (1898–1986), and Harry Slochower (1900–1991)—shifted their publishing venue almost exclusively to *Science & Society*, a scholarly quarterly founded in 1936 by pro-Communists but not directly under Communist Party control.

Like Guy and Bruno, the deluded doubles in *Strangers on a Train* (1950), by former Communist Patricia Highsmith (born Mary Patricia Plangman, 1921–95), the salaried Communist Party critics half-consciously found themselves collaborating with their associates in "crisscross" murders (albeit only on paper) that inexorably led to one "frenemy" Communist critic becoming the other's victim.[29] In 1946, Samuel Sillen censured Isidor Schneider for trying to liberalize the *New Masses'* literary section and by 1948 was himself editor-in-chief of its successor, *Masses & Mainstream*, with a circulation of about 10,000. Then, in 1956, Sillen pulled out of *Masses & Mainstream* in shock after the Khrushchev Revelations, his editorial job immediately assumed by Charles Humboldt, who managed to keep the circulation at about 4,000 internationally. In 1961, Humboldt, after a literary dispute over his decision to publish a poem, was supplanted by Yale University American studies graduate student Robert Forrey (b. 1933).

Apart from congenital ideological rottweilers like V. J. Jerome, who joined the Communist Party in 1924, the customary trajectory of Popular Front–era Communist literary men (and several women) commenced in the neighborhood of free-spirited literary and artistic bohemianism, above all for Schneider and Humboldt. Critics were initially drawn to Communism more by the ideals of the movement than by the often pompous and crude prose of reviews in the Party press. When twenty-five-year-old Samuel Sillen arrived in New York City in the spring of 1935 to wrap up the last chapter of his University of Wisconsin doctoral dissertation while teaching summer classes at New York University and living at home, he actually detested the prevailing literary criticism of the *New Masses* and the *Daily Worker*.[30]

What roiled Sillen above all were the swift applications of defamatory political labels, a perfunctory Marxism that squeezed out any room for indispensable artistic detachment, the pileup of clichés of revolutionary jargon, and a tendency to extravagantly extol the Communist Party's own claque of Communist writers.[31] But a decade later, in the winter of 1946, the same Sillen emerged at the head of the pack in the gang-up of Communist Party intellectuals on novelist Albert Maltz (1908–85), who had questioned the efficacy of the slogan "Art as a Weapon."[32] In a series of six *Daily Worker* columns that astounded even his closest friends, the mild-mannered Sillen committed every one of the repugnant offenses about which he had formerly complained. For this reason, a man who authored some original pieces of scholarship, including a forerunner of 1960s feminist history called *Women against Slavery* (1955), earned a place in U.S. literary history as a loathsome hatchet man.[33] In March 1948, Sillen was perhaps at his most discredited in publishing a fawning essay in praise of V. J. Jerome in *Political Affairs*.[34]

Sillen's descending narrative, a downhill slide after World War II, epitomizes the tribulations of late antifascism in literary criticism. Sam, as he was always called, was the first-born son of Jewish immigrants from Vilna, Lithuania.[35] His father immigrated to New York City at the age of fourteen in 1903,

Samuel Sillen held a doctorate in English from the University of Wisconsin. After World War II, he served as literary editor of the Communist *Daily Worker* and then as the editor of *Masses & Mainstream* until he quit the Party in 1956. (Courtesy of Janet Sillen)

shortening a longer family name (of which there is no record) to "Sillen," and immediately began working as a tailor; Sam's mother arrived about the same time. Sillen's parents were self-educated, and a source of pride for them was obtaining a piano and lessons for Sam and his brother, Louis. The Sillens lived in the Crown Heights section of Brooklyn, with occasional trips to and summers in Connecticut. Recognized as a special child, Sam was bright and his grades were outstanding at school. He was fascinated by current events and world affairs. Exceedingly affable, he established a five-piece band, the Rainbow-Chasers, with a theme song, "I'm Always Chasing Rainbows." The group performed on radio, at weddings and parties, and in restaurants. Sillen entered New York University at the age of sixteen, supporting himself by piano performances and scholarships. During the summers, the Rainbow-Chasers played in the Adirondacks. Upon graduation from New York University, Sillen won a teaching fellowship in English literature to the University of Wisconsin. There he completed a doctoral dissertation in 1935 on Sir Leslie Stephen (1832–1904), a British biographer and critic and the father of Virginia Woolf, with whom Sillen carried on a correspondence.[36] Sillen's attraction to Stephen, whose work engaged the ethical and philosophical dimensions of literature, began at New York University, where he initially encountered Professor Edwin Berry Burgum, always called "Berry" in person, and Burgum's graduate student William Phillips, who later became a founding editor of *Partisan Review*.

In late 1934, Sillen first laid eyes on Janet Feder, an undergraduate at the University of Wisconsin. By December they had drawn close and, starting in the New Year, realized that they were madly in love. But there was a dilemma. Janet was extremely active in the Young Communist League and a talented organizer, yet she was far from a theoretician, and by her own admission she did not know very much. She had also been arrested in a protest about the same time that the Wisconsin state senate launched an antiradical investigation of sociology professor E. A. Ross and others alleged to be sympathetic to Communism. From that moment on, Sillen became acutely aware of the threat to academic freedom posed by right-wing persecution and was revolted by the thought of having to participate in an ordeal similar to Ross's. Incongruously, Sillen was attracted to Janet for her fiery spirit and single-mindedness. A woman with an aggressive and abrasive manner, Janet was continually on the go.

Sillen's own disposition was the polar opposite. He was friendly, pleasant, and slow to anger. A clean-shaven young man with hair and eyes that were dark brown to the point of being nearly black, he wanted to read and play the piano. Sillen loved libraries, was sedentary, and had a passion for collecting old editions of the *Spectator*, the weekly British magazine of politics and culture that had begun in the 1820s. Through family upbringing, he was a committed socialist but was neither aggressively outspoken nor an activist; the purpose of Marxism, in his view, was to make people cool and thoughtful.[37] Sillen expressed himself in writing with far more confidence and ability than verbally and was above all anxious to avoid any kind of altercations, especially ones that were publicly broadcast. Sam's favorite poem, which he often quoted, was Emily Dickinson's "I'm nobody! Who are you?," indicative of his desire to stay in the background.[38] His greatest fear was that Janet's commitment to Communism would pull her away from him, since he could not participate as a militant.

During the winter of 1935, the pro-Soviet journalist Anna Louise Strong (1885–1970) spoke in Madison on a lecture tour and suggested that Janet raise money to travel to the Soviet Union to write a book on students there.[39] To both Sam and Janet, this appeared to be an opportunity for Janet to see firsthand the actuality of the Soviet Union and also allow for a cooling-off period while Sam finished his dissertation and moved back home with his family in New York City. Janet's book did not get written, partly because the university she was to visit closed down, so she went on a tour of regions of the Soviet Union. Any hope that Sillen had that an exposure to Soviet reality would put a brake on Janet's Communist enthusiasms was dashed. Her Soviet experiences were refracted through familiar bifocals; blinded by a vision of the glorious socialist future, she easily discounted the appalling destitution, bureaucracy, and political repression all around her. Returning to the United States that fall, Janet was assigned by the Communist Party to go to Milwaukee and to work in the National Student League. She had no chance of rejoining Sam until December 1935.

In the meantime, Sillen finished his dissertation and was offered an instructorship in New York University's English department beginning in September 1935. But being alone during the spring and summer had been a terrible ordeal for him. He felt he could not live without Janet, even though Janet's Soviet sojourn had rendered her even more politically intransigent; by mail she was demanding that he join the Communist Party and take an active part in workers' struggles. In his letters replying to her, sent at least daily, Sillen argued against what he saw as the Soviet chauvinism of the Party and its refusal to acknowledge the ethical basis of Marxism. He complained that the Party came down like a ton of bricks on any dissenter and that it evidenced the insanity of zealotry by lumping socialists (like himself and his father) together with reactionaries such as William Randolph Hearst.[40] Allergic to any organized political activity, he far preferred to be undisciplined than straitjacketed.

Although Sillen had no sympathy for Trotskyism, he met with friends in the Trotskyist Workers Party of the United States (a fusion of the Communist League of America and the American Workers Party) to discuss their views, and he occasionally read their newspaper.[41] He thought that Stalin was fine for the Soviet Union but that American workers had to formulate their own policies. He acknowledged that his interest in the Communist Party was mainly due to Janet. In literary matters, he was in favor of Marxist writing but unenthusiastic about the poetry of Kenneth Fearing, then all the rage among the pro-Communist critics. In 1934 he had reviewed Jack Conroy's *The Disinherited*, a celebrated proletarian novel that in his assessment was a modest achievement at best; what was most hopeful about Conroy's work was in its signs of craftsmanship. An artist needed both detachment and experience.[42] When it came to literary criticism, Sillen favored the Marxist upstarts William Phillips and Philip Rahv (1908–73) by far over *New Masses* icon Granville Hicks.[43]

Sillen's emotions followed a standard pattern, perhaps redolent of the conversion experience of the Protestant Reformation. After declaring his heartfelt objections to the Communist movement in a letter to Janet, Sillen subjected himself to convulsions of self-loathing even before receiving a reply. This would be followed by the resuscitating influx of deliverance as he announced in a follow-up communication (usually that same day or evening) that his first missive had erroneously exaggerated his political concerns and that at this point he held to the certainty that their love would triumph over everything. But following the arrival of more letters from Janet, in which she reaffirmed a commitment to the Communist cause that was for her thoroughly identified with the Soviet motherland, Sillen's tranquillity and conviction that he was accurate in his confidence about their romantic relationship was succeeded by a mental explosion of misgiving that he described as a kind of madness.[44] At last Janet agreed in late 1935 to forsake her political work in Wisconsin to build a new life with him in Manhattan. By early 1936, Sillen's crisis was over, and his whole personal and political universe fell into a new pattern. He now had an answer to all his questions: He would be a Communist but not a Communist Party member, and he would participate in the workers' struggle by writing for the *New Masses* and being active in the American Federation of Teachers.

Sillen's psychological need for an accommodation with Janet is far from the sole explanation for the transformation of his attitude toward the Communist Party, but it was a precondition. Sillen was also aware, beginning on

21 July 1935, that the Communist International's political orientation was becoming transformed by the decisions of the Seventh Congress of the Comintern in Moscow, which ended a month later. Sillen saw his criticisms of Communist sectarianism echoed by top leaders of the international Communist movement and adopted by the U.S. Communist Party.[45] Prior to the Seventh Congress, Sillen's insistence that the Communist Party cease its vituperative attacks on the Socialist Party fell on deaf ears, but now it was official policy.

A second development influencing his views about the Communist Party was his association with a substantial number of pro-Communist professors at New York University, whom he had half-humorously referred to as the "Stalinists."[46] Berry Burgum and Eda Lou Walton (1896–1962) proved exceptionally congenial, and Margaret Schlauch was not only a top-ranked philologist but one who lived comfortably. All were exceedingly active in the New York Teachers Union (AFT), one of the few organizations in which Sillen felt that he could function. Finally, through his friendship with Walton and her live-in partner, Henry Roth (1906–95), Sillen found himself being drawn into the *New Masses* circle.

First, at a dinner at Walton's, he met Richard Bransten (1906–55) and Louise Rosenberg Bransten (1908–77), a wealthy couple from the San Francisco Bay Area who were connected with the Communist Party leadership. Sillen found the thin, self-effacing Richard (who used the Party name "Bruce Minton") to be appealing as a person; he also noted that, while committed revolutionaries, the Branstens managed to have a first-rate apartment and a new car.[47] Richard suggested that Sillen stop by the office of the *New Masses* and introduce himself to the staff. When he did so, shortly thereafter, he met Isidor Schneider and discovered that Schneider was not the mad sectarian that he had imagined from reading Schneider's essays, especially a 1 October 1935 piece about Karl Radek that Sam despised.

The book reviews that Sillen started to submit to Schneider even before Janet's move were well received, and he was asked to write more, including work on editorials. In the meantime, reviews by Sillen were being accepted by the *New Republic*, the *Nation*, and the *New York Herald Tribune*. Inasmuch as a number of New York University English professors were appearing in the Communist press under their own names, Sillen discussed the situation with Schneider and decided to use the pseudonym "Walter Ralston" for his *New Masses* work.[48] In December 1935, he and Janet were married.

After that, Sillen rose progressively through the ranks of the Communist literary apparatus as openings became available. Following the 1936 departure for Europe of Schneider (one of several pro-Communists who won Guggenheims in the mid-1930s), F. W. Dupee (1904–79) stepped in to handle reviews.

But Dupee, an active Communist Party member, fell under the influence of Phillip Rahv and William Phillips, both of whom felt marginalized by the Popular Front and bristled at what they perceived as the Communist Party's new opportunism in promoting writers who fit the new ethos. Consequently, Dupee became embroiled with Sillen in a dispute about the works of John Steinbeck, regarded by many Communist Party cultural activists as a close ally even if individualistic.[49]

As "Walter Ralston," Sillen had written an enthusiastic review of Steinbeck's *In Dubious Battle* in early 1936, whereas Mary McCarthy (1912–89), already gravitating away from the Communists and toward the Phillips-Rahv milieu, had savaged it in the *Nation*.[50] Dupee, who like McCarthy saw sympathy for Steinbeck as an example of the Communists' poor literary taste, then arranged for Rahv to write the *New Masses* evaluation of Steinbeck's *Of Mice and Men*. Rahv's straight-out attack on the book elicited protests from readers.[51] This controversy became a stepping-stone in the departure of Dupee from the magazine. In December, Dupee appeared as one of the editors of the newly independent *Partisan Review*, a journal that was still revolutionary and Leninist but hostile to Stalin's regime and unabashedly sympathetic to literary modernism. With Dupee's departure, the door was open for Sillen to assume the post of *New Masses*' literary editor. There would never be, in his case, Communist Party assignments beyond writing and occasionally attending conferences in the United States and abroad.

In Communist Party publications, Sillen's specialty became U.S. literature and literary history, but he wrote on many other subjects, including theater and politics. He continued teaching at New York University, where signs of a mounting repression were present from the moment that he had begun his job. Some of the New York University administrators were blowing like pliant reeds in the increasingly virulent anti-Communist wind.[52] By the late 1930s, Berry Burgum and the other pro-Communist faculty were advised not to mention Communism in the classroom, accepting this warning as a rule of the game.[53] The Moscow Purge Trials began in 1936, but Sillen was already immersed in the world of Communism through his association with faculty friends, his primary literary interests, and his marriage. Janet insisted that the Moscow Trials were justified; Sam agreed *sur-le-champ*, then joined the Communist Party.

When the Hitler-Stalin Pact was announced in 1939, Sillen instantly applauded the Soviets' decision to sign it. Sillen later wrote admiringly about Alexei Tolstoi's *Road to Calvary* (1922–42), a trilogy depicting the Russian intelligentsia's route in support of the Soviet Union, regarded as a fight against dead values and an attempt to achieve a new sense of purpose of life.[54] The book nicely captured Sillen's 1936 reorientation. Even as his literary criticism waxed more arrogant, he maintained his friendly disposition and was frequently in demand to play the piano at left-wing social gatherings. Nonassertive, he never held or desired a membership slot on the Communist Party's national committee, despite his growing emergence as an "influential." He participated somewhat in his local Communist Party branch life, but mainly he just wanted to write.

Prior to 1939, Sillen found that his teaching activities meshed well with working on the *New Masses*. He soon stopped submitting writings to other publications and dropped his pseudonym. He next wrote to Granville Hicks about a public meeting where Communist Party leaders argued inspiringly that the first job of professionals was to excel in their own fields.[55] In other letters to Hicks, he anxiously tracked the movement of intellectuals toward the *New Masses* or toward the rival *Partisan Review*. Newton Arvin, for example, was scheduled to talk to Van Wyck Brooks (1886–1966) about Brooks's relationship to the Communist movement. Harvard professor Harry Levin (1912–94), Sillen reported, was by no means in the grip of the *Partisan Review* and should still be regarded as a friend. Sidney Alexander (1912?–99), then a Communist poet but who during the Cold War became a leading Renaissance scholar living in Florence, played a crucial role in selecting poems to be published in an issue of the *New Masses*.[56] Joseph Freeman, already moving out of the Communist movement under a cloud of political suspicion, had been too much of a freelancer and had allowed Horace Gregory to think that he was sole master of the *New Masses'* poetry selections. Rumors of a somewhat independent albeit pro-Communist new literary magazine were in the air, but its projected editors seemed an untrustworthy bunch—Alan Calmer (a pseudonym for Abraham Klein, dates unknown), Edward Newhouse (born Ede Ujhazi, 1911–2002), and Muriel Rukeyser (1913–80).[57] Mike Gold's writing struck Sillen as impressionistic and slap-dash. He thought that John Steinbeck, Erskine Caldwell, and Albert Maltz should be regarded as potential sources for *New Masses* fiction, since they were on board politically and had other outlets that they could exploit to earn money.[58]

Although Sillen was concerned that political material might crowd out literary coverage, he found that the Communist Party organizationally did not exert much pressure or have a direct influence on the *New Masses* staff members. Party discipline was almost entirely self-willed by editors and contributors, whether or not one held formal membership in the Party. He was pleased to report to Hicks that he had recently participated in a meeting with Communist Party general secretary Earl Browder in which Browder had pledged that the Party would begin selling an increased number of issues and that Browder personally would hold weekly consultations with the magazine's staff.[59] As Sillen assumed liaison work with Hicks, who maintained communication with the office from his home in upstate New York, he found himself agreeing that party-line political thinking was not incompatible with aesthetic analysis. Smugness grew early on as Sillen began to see himself moralistically as a hard-working, self-sacrificing non-careerist inside the radical movement, much in contrast to people like the *New Republic*'s Malcolm Cowley and the *New York Times*' John Chamberlain who were free to criticize Communist matters from a comfortable chair. Just before the Hitler-Stalin Pact, Sillen was given the important task of summing up the history of the League of American Writers, which he published as a feature accompanied by a portrait of John Steinbeck, elected a vice president, also including a special note about the successful expulsion of Trotskyists from the organization.[60]

In the 1940s, as Sillen became a father of two sons, Thomas and Robert, the situation at New York University grew increasingly tense. Anti-Stalinists in the philosophy department, Sidney Hook and James Burnham, who were morphing from the Left to the Right, had become increasingly obsessed with eliminating Communist influence on the campus. Sillen's position at New York University as a lecturer teaching composition had never been secure, and the thought of an eventual public confrontation was more than he could bear.[61] In the fall of 1944, he simply resigned his teaching position and took a full-time job as the literary editor of the *Daily Worker*. In 1947, the Communist Party founded *Mainstream: A Literary Quarterly* and appointed Sillen its editor. In 1948, *Mainstream* merged with the *New Masses* to become *Masses & Mainstream*, of which Sillen was the editor until 1956.

Sillen's rise in the Communist literary movement may not have been conventionally careerist, but there are elements of a jockeying for power. In 1942, there was a new altercation about Steinbeck (the first was in 1936) where Sillen defended *The Moon Is Down* against those who thought it was insufficiently antifascist.[62] Shortly after, he began to work with V. J. Jerome, and from there he moved step-by-step up the Communist Party's literary hierarchy. With the Communist Party's International Publishers, he encountered no problems in bringing out anything he wanted published; he submitted proposals to edit and introduce *Walt Whitman: Poet of American Democracy: Selections from His Poetry and Prose* (1944) and *William Cullen Bryant: Selections from His Poetry and Prose* (1945). Later, he wrote the prefaces for other volumes issued by Communist Party–connected publishers: *Julius Fuchik: Notes from the Gallows* (1948), *Pablo Neruda: Let the Rail Splitter Awake and Other Poems* (1950), and *Poems of Nazim Hikmet* (1954). The last complete book he produced as a Communist was a collective biography of Black and white female abolitionists, *Women against Slavery*. Sillen's dedications in these volumes were always to his immediate family members, but in the public sphere, he was the voice of Communism's view of fiction and criticism. In 1945, his collection of Whitman was singled out for an essay-length polemical criticism in the *Nation* by Lionel Trilling, who made an influential case for the impoverished vision of the Communist critic.[63] One ought to do criticism with everything that one has, but Sillen focused on writers who could be selectively exploited to advance art according to the Party's current political needs, or else he rapped knuckles when a writer fell short of expectations. The result was arrogance on paper; Sillen wrote as if his self-satisfaction as the spokesman of late anti-fascism was an epistemic advantage instead of a risk factor. As usual, pride goeth before a fall.

GRAND ILLUSIONS

There is a grim, tragic undertone to stories such as Sillen's, and it is hard to find a comic counterweight anywhere except in a few yarns about V. J. Jerome's pompous zealotry.[64] The squandering of talent apparent in the Communist saga of postwar "Marxist" literary criticism in this manner surely implies a form of "corruption." This was different in brand from a bribery induced by money. As a group, Communist literati cannot be fit into the boxes constructed either by their hostile antagonists, as power-hungry neurotics, or by soft-headed apologists, as tender idealists merely erring about certain facts. In *The Captive Mind* (1953), Czeslaw Milosz rejects the simple notion that Stalinist writers "sold themselves" but adds an enigmatic caveat: "Consciousness does not help them to shed their bonds; on the contrary, it forges them."[65] Possibly Milosz intended to indicate that Stalinist corruption was a dance of ideals and deceptions that invited the writers—mostly hard-working and self-sacrificing types like Sillen—to gradually remake themselves into the very martinets they had at the outset reviled.

The cultural wing of the Communist movement was a particular ideological location or configuration that exercised a shaping power on whatever happened within it. In this process, Jerome was both a master and a symptom of the cultural circumstances, the malign impresario of ultra-orthodoxy who was uniquely adept at skillful positioning in order to preserve himself. Under Jerome's tutelage, even those who may have joked about him behind his back were drawn into a fantasy world about the prospects of Communism in the

United States. One example is when the weekly *New Masses* collapsed due to lack of support in early 1948, subsequently fusing with the short-lived literary journal *Mainstream* to become a monthly called *Masses & Mainstream*. The palpable setback was feted as a great advance, calling to mind the dictator who "fixed" his stalled train by lowering the blinds and pretending it was moving.[66] In his polemical writing, Jerome, who seemed untroubled by the brutal necessities of factional struggle, was a magician in invoking a climate of scientific objectivity as he unleashed the fires of hatred mixed with tart nuggets of truth about racism and fascism.[67]

Literary critics may reveal more about the thinking of the Communist cultural movement than poets, fiction writers, or dramatists, inasmuch as the reviewer's techniques of analytical investigation required the direct scrutiny of the artistic re-creation of life, and specific judgments were required of such commentators. But no discussion of the work of the major Communist critics can occur without addressing the alternate reality of the larger culture of the Communist Party, even if one is unsure about the extent to which all the critics lived within it. To become a full-time Communist Party worker over a period of years as a rule meant to become a core member with a special mentality, one who assured the constancy of the Communist Party through all its alterations in line and leadership. Sillen was atypical in that he had a fourteen-year university teaching career prior to serving ten years as a Communist Party full-timer. But once Sillen departed academe to work entirely for the Party, he was for the most part living in a synthetic intellectual world.

For Sillen and others, hallowed meanings were fused together, especially the values of the Left and pro-Sovietism. Whatever the false reality of the ideas in which Sillen lived, his experience had a genuineness that allowed him to voluntarily keep adding block after block to fit together in a way that ultimately tolerated no spaces or windows; he thereby sealed himself within the entire edifice that was his special universe. As Gordon Allport remarked, convictions about political economy run a close second to religious certainties.[68] Sillen became aware of all the well-known psychological benefits one obtains by belonging to an elite group, especially an organization claiming moral superiority and special knowledge. Once Sillen found a niche for himself in the Communist Party publication network, he also began to get that warm feeling that evolves from the notion that one is serving a cause that rises above one's self-centeredness. A contemporary Marxist might be appalled that the Communist Party in the United States never knowingly said or did anything different from or contrary to Moscow's wishes, but Sillen acquired a sensation of superiority from his daydream that he was an internationalist living in a larger universe than the insulated box of the academic that he had once occupied. Tasks that might otherwise be routine and emotionally unrewarding took on new meaning and ethical importance.

In the postwar era, Sillen saw the Soviet Union as an expression of fraternity and peaceful intentions, even believing there was voluntary support among its citizens for the regime. Resistance to alternative interpretations was less a conscious taboo than an inability to think in any other way, especially to understand other Leftists who saw Stalin's regime as a departure from socialism. For example, on 17 June 1945, after Germany had surrendered but before the atomic bomb was dropped on Japan, Sillen claimed in the *Daily Worker* that to be antifascist one had to be pro-Soviet; after all, rooting out fascism required the friendship of the United States with the Soviet Union, and to be critical of the Soviet Union might unleash forces that could prevent a total antifascist victory.[69] Back in January 1945, Sillen simply stated that the mark of a good fascist was that he or she hated Communists; ergo, anyone opposed to Stalin's rule was a fascist.[70]

Further clouding Sillen's judgment were his understandable feelings of resentment about his own personal sacrifice, risk, and relative economic deprivation in becoming a public Communist full-timer. Combined with those feelings was the memory of his rationalizations for the maltreatment of comrades who had earlier questioned Party policy, such as Hicks, Maltz, and Bransten, thus making it harder for Sillen to admit that he had also misjudged Stalin and the Soviet Union. Yet, in the imaginary world of his thinking, Sillen was not a supporter of repression of dissent or of the arts. This core belief was demonstrated in 1956, when Sillen realized that the critics of Stalinism were mostly accurate. He was finally forced to appreciate that the desirability of socialism and the benignity of the Soviet regime were two separate and independent propositions that required different sorts of supporting evidence and reasoning. Once Sillen actually came to believe that atrocities had happened in the Soviet Union—such as the execution of Jewish cultural figures in 1952—he could no longer defend the Soviet regime, even if he would refuse to criticize it in public out of fear of encouraging reaction. Sillen had carried loyally on for twenty years, but now the emotional bank account of Communism became overdrawn and the depository found to be bankrupt. He was gone in a flash.[71]

As word of the Twentieth Congress swept through the Communist Party membership, Janet also quit, going into a period of intense rage against her past illusions and those who had encouraged them. However, the departure of the Sillens from movement life was an occurrence not completely unwelcomed by the couple. Sam had hated working under Jerome and frequently complained about doing so. Although he sounded opinionated in his writing, Sillen was revolted by the notion of actually being a commissar and dreaded the responsibility that came with his position and influence. His discomfort about the 1946 Albert Maltz debate haunted him. At the time he felt that his private angst was not due to a disagreement with Party orthodoxy but mainly because he did not want to be in a position where Jerome gave him orders. Now he knew he was utterly wrong. In the Party, Sillen did not have young disciples, but he was part of a circle of Communist male intimates that included *Masses & Mainstream* contributors such as Joseph Bernstein (1908–75), Richard O. Boyer, Lloyd Brown (1913–2003), and Sender Garlin. They continued to meet during the 1950s and 1960s, but Sillen's demeanor was mostly melancholy.

Janet had worked full-time for the American Youth Congress (AYC) during her first six years in the Communist Party and became close to Eleanor Roosevelt. With the demise of the AYC in 1941, she continued to be active and was perceived as a stalwart, but an unhappiness began to surface. By the 1950s, she was pursuing a career in market research, where she rose to the position of vice president of her company, then worked for the New York Guild for the Blind, the Geriatric Evaluation and Service Unit of the Bellevue Hospital Center, and finally as executive secretary of Bellevue's Geriatrics Project from 1968 to 1970. Alongside Gerda Lerner (b. 1921), a friend from her Communist days, Janet became active in the feminist movement, the anti-nuclear weapons movement, and the movement against U.S. intervention in Nicaragua. She even began an autobiography.

The Sillens were living in Croton-on-Hudson at the time they departed the Party, and Sam went to work for a left-wing publishing house, Citadel Press. From 1963 to 1968, he was employed as a senior editor of *Medical World News*, a weekly magazine for members of the medical profession. He then put his literary skills to good use by writing a successful commercial book, *The Standard Handbook of Style* (1963). Serving as associate editor of *Annual Progress in Child Psychology and Child Development*, he pursued medical research prior to writing *Racism and Psychology* (1972), coauthored with Alexander Thomas, which continues in print.

Sam remained a radical, supporting the anti–Vietnam War protests, but he was not active. He resisted the appeals of friends who wanted him to criticize the Soviet Union in publications such as the *New York Times*. His view, like many former Communists, was that, if one wanted to build a peace movement, one should not make any statement in public that would increase anti-Soviet feelings, although it was all right to express such views in private. In 1959, some fourteen years before his death, he was diagnosed with bladder cancer and forced to use a urostomy bag. His father had endured the same illness, but it was lymphoma that killed Sam at the age of sixty-two in 1973.

As a leading Communist Party critic from the late 1930s to the mid-1950s, Sillen produced no critical analyses that are prominent today, and his work was not revived in the late twentieth century when the search for Marxist literary ancestors was at its summit. Sillen's early book reviews were often sympathetic to writers, even if never uncritical. After the 1930s, his style became increasingly schoolmasterly and polemical at the same time, although he always resisted using recherché terms and references. A characteristic passage is his celebration of Walt Whitman in dreary rhetoric: "Whitman is cherished by Marxists, as by all other supporters of democracy, because he is an implacable foe of human oppression in any form. Men of socialist vision have always responded to the great strivings of the poet for a better world."[72] There are undoubtedly book reviews and columns by Sillen that offered original and useful insights into the craft of writing, less so about dispensing the political requirements for achieving success in such an endeavor. In 1945, Sillen issued an appreciation of William Cullen Bryant that deftly combined multiple facets of his literary achievement as poet and journalist, albeit the climax was predictable: "With learning and eloquence he devoted a rich lifetime to the fight for freedom and democracy."[73]

The quantity of material authored by Sillen is overwhelming, yet there are not many sentences worth quotation. After he began his *Daily Worker* column and fell under the shadow of V. J. Jerome, he never really acquired his own voice. The postwar situation accelerated even further the latent tendentiousness and formulaic phrases Sillen had earlier resisted; sometimes it seemed as if his columns were merely a charge sheet dictated by rhetorical posturing. Too often he was placed in the role of being the prosecutor rather than the judge, pouring scorn on alleged pretensions and refighting old battles in a new key. His style combined Marxist and economic criticism with a tincture of nineteenth-century moralism. His writing could be somewhat pedantic but only captious when politically motivated. His best longer essays progressively assumed the weakening air of derivation from models such as Van Wyck Brooks, with whom he maintained a correspondence. These can be pleasantly written but are often tedious recitations. What was missing was a curiosity capable of overstepping familiar categories to open up fresh perspectives. He presents well-chosen and amusing anecdotes, sidelines, and vignettes in fluent and readable prose accessible to a general reader. Mike Gold threw his sentences like punches, but the industrious Sillen seemed to write on automatic pilot to the point of becoming something of a recycled soul. Perhaps his ambitions never exceeded his range.

HUMBOLDT'S GIFT

Although Charles Humboldt, the literary and political pseudonym of Clarence Weinstock, published only essays, reviews, and a few poems, the postwar legacy of the Communist cultural movement cannot be measured without taking into account his charismatic presence. Annette T. Rubinstein called Humboldt "the only real Socialist man [I] ever knew."[74] At the age of twenty, he emerged as an extraordinarily confident and assertive reviewer in the pages of *Poetry*.[75] His essays as a Communist showcased critical acumen as well as a ferocious style; he seemed to know everything, as if he were one of the last great generalists before the age of specialization definitely set in. Humboldt possessed an ironic dueling wit that could grow short-tempered even with friends. In contrast to Sillen, he also represented a semi-secret opposition to the worst excesses of socialist realism, seeing a margin of hope in the work of Communist artists such as Picasso and Neruda.

Humboldt was born the only child of a wealthy German Jewish conservative family headed by Abraham Weinstock in New York City's Washington Heights.[76] In 1925, after a lonely and repressed childhood, he dropped out of high school at the age of fifteen in rebellion against his parents' orders that he attend the private, elite Townsend Harris High School. Humboldt then hitchhiked to California to meet his literary idol, Robinson Jeffers. Next he hoboed around the United States and Western Europe for nine years, first studying art in Paris and then living among Pueblo Indians in New Mexico and spending a year holding a Zona Gale creative writing scholarship at the University of Illinois. By 1929, Humboldt was bringing out poetry and literary reviews in little literary magazines and was known by the literary nickname of "Shelley,"[77] although he published under his birth name, Clarence Weinstock. The verse was usually on classical themes, such as a sequence in the May 1930 issue of *Poetry* called "Romans." This particular series included sections with the headings "Caesar," "Petronius," "Julian the Apostate Dying in Persia," and "Saint Augustine Meditates."[78] In 1934, returning after a long sojourn in Europe, he disembarked in New York. Sporting his trademark cape, he immediately jumped into a picket line of WPA artists. Thomas McGrath (1916–90) later quipped that once Humboldt joined that picket line, he never left.[79]

Humboldt quickly came to wide notice as a central editor of *Art Front* (1934–37), producing scintillating essays (also under the name Weinstock) on the form and aesthetics of painting that are still reprinted in anthologies.[80] His friends thought him brilliant, charming, and lovable. Eventually he became managing editor of the journal and personal friends with many of the contributors, who included Max Weber, Stuart Davis, Ben Shahn, Raphael

Charles Humboldt, charismatic art critic, poet, and literary essayist. He was the true genius of the Communist cultural movement in the 1940s and 1950s. (Courtesy of Annette T. Rubinstein)

and Moses Soyer, Jack Levine, Philip Evergood, Arshile Gorky, and Willem de Kooning.[81] By the late 1930s, he was writing (as Weinstock) for the *New Masses* on topics such as Brecht and in the 1940s became a member of the editorial board of the *New Masses* as "Charles Humboldt," after which he was rarely referred to in the Communist press by any other name.[82]

In World War II, Humboldt served on the Italian front as a cryptographer, breaking codes, and then in Information and Education, preparing bulletins and booklets on the progress of the war. As a returning veteran, Humboldt resumed his visible role in Communist literary publications and supported himself with odd jobs rewriting and editing translations on scientific, technical, and literary subjects for drug firms and publishing houses. He also worked for the left-wing Citadel Press as an editor of books on literary and political history and for the Palestine Foundation Fund, where he prepared texts and assembled graphic material for an exhibit at Radio City Music Hall that ran for over a year. Then he spent 1952–53 in Mexico, making use of benefits from the G.I. Bill.

Ostensibly, Humboldt was there to study the Mexican muralists, about whom he wrote several essays later on, and to learn Spanish. But he also claimed in a job résumé a few years afterwards that he was part of a group of anthropologists responsible for the relocation of a number of Indian villages that were to be inundated by the waters of a newly built artificial lake.[83] More likely, his time in Mexico was a formal political assignment or perhaps motivated by a feeling that he needed to evade the repressive political situation in the United States. Humboldt was accompanied by his first wife, Elizabeth Timberman (called "Timmy," 1908–88), a dancer, former *Life* magazine photographer, and activist associated with the Film and Photo League.

Once he returned to New York, Humboldt covered medical conferences and wrote special features for a weekly in the medical field called *Scope*; he also prepared scripts and exhibits for pharmaceutical companies. Humboldt was one of those for whom the Khrushchev Revelations came like a bolt from the blue; his first reaction was a declaration that he would simply not write any more. Then his conviction returned that a "real" socialism would produce a new kind of people.[84] After the departure of Sillen from *Masses & Mainstream*, Humboldt returned to full-time work as editor of the new *Mainstream* from 1956 to 1960. By this time, he was married to Miriam Robbins Haas (known as "Mimi," 1920–2005), a painter and collagist whom he had first met in Mexico. Following his resignation from *Mainstream* as well as his separation from the Communist Party due to an eruption of a long-simmering controversy about his editorial policy, Humboldt served as a staff member of the left-wing *National Guardian* from the fall of 1960 until his death in 1964.

Humboldt was a natural when it came to appreciating visual art, poems, and fiction; scores of draft manuscripts passed through his hands, and he seemed indefatigable as a correspondent. His range shows an exceptional mastery of many precincts of culture: major and minor novelists, poets of various countries, literary criticism, art and aesthetics, contemporary politics, history. Encompassing a bristling arsenal of allusions, his essays of the late 1940s and 1950s are most consistently impressive regarding the art of fiction addressed to novelists and short story writers. In the fall of 1947, while serving as the literary editor of the *New Masses*, he published a marvelously original theoretical essay, "The Novel of Action," in the new Party-sponsored *Mainstream*. In it he offered a grand perspective by which to scrutinize contemporary Left writers such as Ira Wolfert (1908-97), Barbara Giles (1906-86), and Howard Fast.[85]

Although always assuming the posture of an orthodox political Communist, he had the skill of a Georg Lukács in giving plausibility and sophistication to a potentially crude set of propositions. His subsequent piece "The Lost Cause of Robert Penn Warren," in the newly fused publication of *Masses & Mainstream*, deftly probes the political ironies beneath the three novels by Warren, a Southern Agrarian becoming associated with the New Critics.[86] In 1949, Humboldt published a long study called "Communists in Novels" in two issues of the same journal, providing original research and a perspective that remain fresh to this day.[87] Whether the writer was major or minor, Humboldt devoted full attention and inventive critique to his cacophony of subjects of follow-up reviews: Carl Marzani, Boris Pasternak, Aleksandr Solzhenitsyn, Steinbeck, Robert Penn Warren, Norman Mailer, James Baldwin, Philip Bonosky, Isidor Schneider.

As an editor and occasionally practicing poet, Humboldt brought a younger generation of writers into the pages of *Mainstream*. Among the most skillful in their acute and varied angles of vision were two poets nurtured by Thomas McGrath in California: Gene Frumkin (1928-2007) and Alvaro Cardona-Hine (b. 1926). George Hitchcock (1914-2010), an older Communist militant, began to hone his surrealist imagination in its pages. Humboldt also remained a critical figure among a range of New York writers, many of whom gathered at the apartment of Dr. Annette T. Rubinstein. Their association began in the Writers and Publishers Division of the National Council of the Arts, Sciences and Professions (often referred to as simply Arts, Sciences and Professions), which periodically issued a journal called the *Contemporary Reader*. When the organization collapsed in the mid-1950s, an informal discussion group continued with monthly meetings that usually focused on literary criticism.[88] Other signs of literary life connected with this circle appeared fleetingly around the magazine *Venture*, launched in 1955 as one of the last efforts of the Writers Workshop of the Arts, Sciences and Professions, and the *Promethean Review*, issued by the Liberty Book Club run by pro-Communists Carl Marzani (1912–94) and Angus Cameron (1908–2002).

The *Mainstream* controversy came to a head three years after the Khrushchev Revelations when Humboldt published a love poem, a short verse called "Morning Departure" by Hershel Horn (a pseudonym for Sid Gershgoren, b. 1937). McGrath had been visiting in New York and helped out with the selection.[89] This was a minor piece but elicited a major blast from Mike Gold in his August "Change the World" column in the *Worker*: "[This] poem appeared in the July issue of *Mainstream*, the only magazine in our backward country that is dedicated to Marxist culture. . . . Should a Marxist pauper magazine devote some of its precious space to spreading this 'new' abstract poetry, this unintelligible, irrational, deathly stuff, the metaphysics of an aspiring class that no longer knows how to face reality?"[90] Zhdanovism had indigenous roots.

Humboldt had a brilliant ally, the poet and playwright Ettore Rella (1907–88), who used the pseudonym John Condell to reply to Gold. His fine rebuttal, "Hands Off the Imagination," begins: "Why is Michael Gold so enraged and scornful and destructive when a poet in *Mainstream* shows evidence of some freedom of the imagination?" Rella then aimed directly at the well-known downside of the Communist legacy: "Down through the years, there has been an effort to organize the tastes of the Left toward a poetry that is off the top of the head—toward the immediately intelligible, romantically proletarian, utterly optimistic mass commodity." Rella's summary was magisterial: "The Left should know better. . . . There is no broad, straight, super-highway for the imagination. The expression of the imagination is infinitely diverse, explorative, unpredictable. And it is these characteristics which give the imagination its essential humanity."[91]

The *Mainstream* debate was highly controlled but indicative of quandaries of cultural policy deeply embedded in unresolved matters stemming from 1956. The texts of various communications speak for themselves. A letter to the editor that appeared in the same issue of *Mainstream*, from "a San Francisco Reader," declared: "It is high time that some discussion is brought forth about the only progressive literary magazine in this country. . . . Michael Gold brought out only one aspect, poetry. It is very sad that this modern drivel has made its way into all forms of art. . . . The paintings very often reflect the same drivel. Lines and blotches may have a meaning to Freud, but they do not communicate with me."[92] Mike Newberry (a pseudonym for Stan Steiner, 1925–87) jumped in by way of his column on the arts in the *Daily Worker*: "Mike

Gold and *Mainstream* have been at loggerheads over the style and contents of a poem by Hershel Horn.... The question, which has been politely skirted, is one that arises, I think, on the part of many readers over the character of *Mainstream* itself. Not over this poem, or that story ... but rather the basic aim of the publication."[93] History was not repeating itself, but it was rhyming with earlier disputes over *Partisan Review* and Albert Maltz.

At the beginning of 1960, Annette T. Rubinstein, a contributing editor to *Mainstream* and another Humboldt ally, protested to the *Daily Worker* that other Marxist publications available in English may overlap with *Mainstream*, "but today there is no other periodical in the United States directed to that very, very large audience interested in literature, which is not basically ... anti-Marxist [or] anti-social or reactionary." In her cross-country lecturing trip of the previous year, Rubinstein "found it was precisely the special literary quality of *Mainstream* that attracted both graduate and undergraduate students, and that it was the only periodical in its Marxist orbit which many of them found at all interesting or convincing."[94] Newberry rebutted Rubinstein in the same issue of the paper: "Annette Rubinstein, one of the editors of *Mainstream*, writes that she believes the Left magazine is ... for a ... specialized audience.... To me, this sort of attitude merely perpetuates the literary isolationism that has, in part at least, emasculated the artists." Newberry saw *Mainstream*'s purpose as the opposite: "On principle, such an approach severs the very bonds to working class life, the very 'connection,' that Marxists should offer the already too rarefied and too specialized art worlds."[95]

In August 1960, Charles Humboldt's name disappeared from *Mainstream*, and a new board of editors was listed without explanation. In November 1960, also missing from the roster of contributing editors of *Mainstream* were Annette T. Rubinstein, Thomas McGrath, and Barbara Giles. A letter appeared in a box on page 47 of the issue: "Dear Friends: I've been telling everyone how much I've enjoyed the September issue of *Mainstream*.... For the first time in too, too long, I've felt a deep satisfaction, and pride, in reading our magazine. It's on my level, it's humane, related to people and material that has real meaning to me.... Sincerely, A Friend."[96] There is little doubt that Humboldt published "Morning Departure" as a smack to the face of what he saw as the deadening solemnity of Communist culture in the United States. He judged this grave earnestness as an obstacle to linking up with the rising poetic currents such as the Beats and the San Francisco Renaissance, where he saw a hopeful cultural radicalization. He surely meant to invoke Baudelaire's animus against the poetry of edifying intentions, although he did not go so far as to embrace William Carlos Williams's "no ideas but in things."[97]

His goals are made explicit in his voluminous personal correspondence.

Dr. Annette T. Rubinstein, a secret member of the Communist Party until 1952, played a leading role as an educator in Marxist literary criticism. This photograph was taken in 1953 as she completed reading the page proofs of her two-volume *The Great Tradition in English Literature: From Shakespeare to Shaw*. (Courtesy of Annette T. Rubinstein)

On 4 May 1956, as the new *Mainstream* editor, Humboldt wrote to Kenneth Rexroth (1905–82), a former Communist who had become a leader of the San Francisco Renaissance in American poetry: "Dear Kenneth Rexroth: It may surprise you... to hear from us, but many new things have happened in the last few weeks that are forcing us to reconsider our relations with writers throughout the country. We're also examining the causes of our separation, often not of our own choosing but just as often through errors on our part, from people like yourself." His humility was atypical for a Communist cultural leader: "I don't think it's necessary in this feeling-out note to go into the mistakes of yesterday, and we don't flatter ourselves that we have shaken them off so that the duck's back is dry. But we're trying. Might we then ask you whether you'd consider sending us any poems from time to time, or writing about anything else that interests you?"[98] That October, Humboldt expressed himself more fully in a twenty-four-page essay in *Mainstream*, "The Salt of Freedom," that is worth quoting at length:

> Since our editorial invitation to discussion did not exclude the editors themselves, I should like to take advantage of the implicit permission to comment on the article by "Timon" [a pseudonym for Abraham Polonsky, 1910–99] which appeared in our August number. The issue raised therein—based on a consideration of Simone de Beauvoir's *The Mandarins*—is one of the most crucial of our time. . . . *Is intellectual freedom compatible with social commitment?* The question has a somewhat indirect but pertinent corollary; to what degree is personal liberty nullified by the exercise of authority over the individual? . . . What is unique, as it is related to *The Mandarins*, is the subject of the discussion: the nature of the [Russian] revolution toward which some intellectuals looked with hope and love and others with fear and even hate. (And still others with hope and fear) . . .[99]

Humboldt longed to confront such hard questions, although he never got very far in the Communist movement and was afterward in a state of recovery that was cut short by a heart attack.[100]

After he left the Communist Party, Humboldt published a fine essay in the *Massachusetts Review* on the art of Ingmar Bergman, putting on display the dialectics of his aesthetic vision: "The belying of his [Bergman's] theory by his own performance illustrates the continual interplay of a classical and romantic trend within his mind, the one controlling, the other enriching the creative process."[101] Found on his desk when he died was a manuscript-in-progress on Jean Genet. His essay two years earlier in *Trace* on Kenneth Fearing, "The Voice Persisted until Death," was at least in part his own literary testament. It was a breakthrough reading of the work of the poet and novelist, in a vivid prose style that resonated with the achievement of a generation.[102] Fearing and Humboldt lived contrasting lives as far as their political activism was concerned, but Humboldt's Marxist sense of modernity had become so expansive that he fully understood, without a shred of condemnation, Fearing's elegant asperities and mordant antipathies.

Humboldt also struggled in verse to communicate socialist politics in an emotional texture of life and art. This sensibility is evident in "The Fifth Season," a 1959 love poem Humboldt wrote to his wife, Mimi. "The Fifth Season" had a double meaning for him, denoting both personal/erotic love and socialism. The final stanza climaxes:

In that fifth season
when the snow
Flares in an ecstasy of change
And from the hot horns of the deer
Grows the green forest
where we range.[103]

Despite such inner intensity and passion, Humboldt was primarily and demonstrably an opinionated, tenacious, and tendentious critic.[104]

Charles Humboldt's essays are too scattered to allow more than impressions of a latent genius in the history of the literary Left. He was capable of crafting lines that seemed like a bracing blast of clean, cool air in a musty room. He could radiate hauteur and moral outrage and be snarky and irascible, but he rarely stooped to haranguing in the manner of a V. J. Jerome.[105] A reader may dispute Humboldt's judgments, but many are articulated in tersely fastidious, finely parsed phrases that are sharply etched in tropes of exquisite finesse. As novelist Jose Yglesias recalled, Charles Humboldt was "no one's patron and no one's protégé."[106]

Taking up cudgels against real and imagined renegades in the 1940s, Humboldt could write with the fury of a caged animal, and he even put his name to a foolish apology for Zhdanov.[107] More often, as a new radicalism broke through during the late 1950s, he wrote with the grace of an angel. In his 1962 appreciation of Kenneth Fearing, Humboldt moves from discussing the "lyrical irony" of the poems to "the fantasy of critical estrangement" that characterizes the novels. His conclusion encapsulates the paradoxes of his own aesthetic: "Isn't it presumptuous to ask that a work out of a certain mold do more than its form requires? Particularly when, as in Fearing, the alien implies its opposite and the yearning for a better world is imbedded in the hard dark of the present like a seed in rock?"[108] A painter and poet in every fiber of his being, Humboldt's finest artistic creation was himself.

Chapter Three

The Cult of Reason

COMING HOME

The world the novel makes proposes its own causality and contingency. To treat post–World War II Marxist fiction solely as a declension narrative, due to the ultimate disaster of the Communist movement in 1956, is to miss one of U.S. culture's most significant streams. Customary accounts of the "Long Retreat" of literary radicalism obviously contain some truth, and there are sound reasons why the political parable of the clean sweep of Cold War liberalism in fiction has had its remarkable run.¹ But scores of novelists once affiliated with or newly drawn to the pro-Communist Left would be a forceful presence in every cultural register even in the worst of times. Others worked quietly in the margins and in a few cases experienced rehabilitation in the 1960s. Novels of this era cannot be assessed en bloc from a single aesthetic viewpoint; they must be broken up and reassembled in multiple contexts as a Cubist portrait renders objects from contradictory angles. This chapter tells their story.

The prevailing radical climate of the 1930s depicted socialism as both inscribed in the historical process and requiring a literary defense. The latter came through the adherence of hundreds of writers to an underlying rational order expressed in the paradigms of social realism. This "Cult of Reason," essential to both the proletarian and people's culture varieties of novels, evokes the atheistic belief system of the French Revolution that went by that name. It was plain in the calls to reason in the literary criticism of Samuel Sillen and frequently evidenced through writers' fidelity to an official mode of Communist rationality based on a "category thinking" about history, class, and the functions of art. Only in the late 1940s would there take root the heretical notion that reason was not so well served by this Communist variety of Marxist positivism, thereby giving rise to the contingent thinking that was a precursor of Communist literary modernism. Although they did not theorize reason as Janus-faced as did Adorno, radical novelists began to search for a deepened sense of the idea of experience, an investigation that gave rise to the need for new strategies to transform sensibility. Kenneth Fearing's *The Big Clock* might stand for this postwar reintroduction of a "new contingency," a critical rationality posed in opposition to the positivist one that was promoted by Communism. Afterward came works by Ann Petry (1908–97), Jo Sinclair (born Ruth Seid, 1919–65), and John Sanford (born Julian Lawrence Shapiro, 1904–2003), exceptional art with an even more vigorous interest in the terms of its own creation.

Most radical writers of the 1940s, emerging from a preoccupation with fighting fascism abroad and still stuck on the memory of the left-wing vision of the 1930s, were only dimly conscious that their latest novels, social realist or reaching beyond, were already part of the formation of a countertrend to the newly evolving Cold War reconstrual of the past. Fearing leaped ahead of the pack with his visionary insight that the advent of a Consumers' Republic created an unforeseen challenge to the procedures of artistic representation. In his pursuit of a literary form adequate for the truly radical imagination, Fearing discerned the disorientation underway owing to the new era's amplification of commercialization and commodification, even though the Cold War's "enforced forgetting," a revision of national collective memory, would require several more years to reach a climax and was hardly the consequence of consumerism alone.

Like all novelists, Fearing arranged constellations of characters and events to reveal his ideas, but there was a distinguishing sensibility. For Fearing and those veterans of Marxism drawn increasingly toward the new contingency and away from the Cult of Reason, the meaning of new experiences could not emerge through old categories unable to absorb the particularity of unanticipated postwar phenomena. Their art began to search for forms and dramatic events to express the new notions, such as the idea that the import of any phenomenon could come into sight only when configured with other phenomena. What Fearing still shared with the social realists was the view that society strives to preserve and reproduce itself through the activities of individuals, the very conduct through which persons maintain a class structure that is fundamentally antagonistic to their needs. But his writing after 1939 increasingly suggested that positivist rationality could no longer be regarded as having established categories of understanding and alternatives a priori.

This quasi-Marxian new contingency came into view gradually and erratically among diverse writers belonging to the same mental collective structure as Fearing. It can be found in a wide range of artistic expressions, even if one must focus on a small number of examples. Moreover, a visibly nonconformist Marxism such as Fearing's, sometimes unrecognized for what it was, was not a prerequisite to effectively expressing the major literary project of the Left, a linking of an aesthetics of responsibility to an ethics of witness and testimony. Some notable books were published by writers who still held fast to the old prophecies of a Party-led revolt against capitalism, judging their uncertain times as but a new gyre, a transition before an assured annunciation. What was achieved in the postwar left-wing novel as a whole, by those resisting as well as embracing the new contingency, was far from negligible, a literary legacy more sinned against than sinning. Writers were trying to create art in a tradition of which the very premises were being overturned by world events. Faced with the pangs of disconfirmation, they were trapped in the dissidence between inherited, paradigmatic forms and uncertain realities. But the era began on a political upswing.

As World War II drew to a close, a radical frame of mind was unmistakable; the Left was determined that the momentum of the antifascist crusade not be lost. The post-Liberation upsurge in Western Europe and the march of the Chinese Revolution toward victory were underway. The Communist movement in the United States was itself reviving. Party membership stood at 63,000 in mid-1945, with another 10,000 on leave due to military service. Half of these were trade union members, and 10 percent were African American. Two Communist Party–aligned publishing houses, International Publishers and New Century, sold more than 2 million books and pamphlets a year. Tens of thousands were attending classes in Communist Party–led schools in cities across the country, and a quarter of the CIO unions were Communist-led.[2] What was then known as the "Cultural Division" of the Party was a component of its Industrial Department and divided mainly between New York and Los Angeles. In the former there were over 1,000 members separated into sections: writers, theater, music, art, and advertising.[3] The principal work of these sections was in the appropriate unions, such as Actors' Equity, the American Federation of Musicians, the Screen Actors Guild, and the Screen Writers Guild. But pro-Communists played a decisive part in organizations such as the National Council of the Arts, Sciences and Professions (NCASP, which evolved in 1948 from the Independent Citizens' Committee of the Arts, Sciences and Professions that was formed in 1945 to support liberal candidates) and the Committee for the Negro in the Arts (CNA, founded in 1947).[4] At specific points, "fractions" of Party members and close allies were established to discuss practical work in different fields, especially in the case of New York's People's Songs, a labor and folk music organization established in 1945, and in activities generated by the Party's Writers Unit.[5]

Much popular fiction, now forgotten, addressed the new political temper of domestic antifascism, as in *Coming Home* (1945) by Lester Cohen (1901–63). Cohen, whose career had begun earlier as a successful novelist (*Sweepings*, 1926) and screenwriter (*Of Human Bondage*, 1934), was not a Communist Party member but was visibly active in the pro-Communist cultural movement from 1931 to 1941 or 1942.[6] By the time late antifascism was fully established, his associations with the Left would be buried.

Through the eyes of Cohen's Joe Drew, a returning Marine veteran of Guadalcanal, the reader observes Drew's once-familiar world of Pittsburgh transformed into an alien landscape, the fabric of its prewar society torn asunder by massive social and economic change. Reactionary forces have gained control of the city, and Joe must rely on his own resources to restore his former life. The threat of yet another international war, this one to be entirely automated, looms as the novel closes. *Coming Home* was not a highly imaginative fiction, and it was composed in traditional, if popularized, social realist form. This was the means by which it successfully ratified the confidence of the Cult of Reason, the belief that one has genuine access to the world by focusing the rational powers of one's own consciousness.

Reviewing *Coming Home* in the *New York Times Book Review*, Kenneth Fearing aptly branded the novel a call to arms: "As Lester Cohen tells it, the Pacific battles were almost mild compared to the home-front campaign of this veteran who had to realize in a literal sense the things for which he had been fighting in the abstract."[7] Fearing, whose own direction in fiction was already veering toward a quest myth where one never wins, must have approved the political sentiment, but he managed to give it an antiwar twist. A review in the *Boston Globe*, by a former Marine combat correspondent, was more orthodox Leftist, claiming that the novel "shows how fascism is in existence in this country" and is "a stirring warning to the American people of what may happen when servicemen return from combat and discover that things haven't been very pleasant for their friends and families."[8] Late antifascism was now in the air, even if its Cold War matrix was not fully formed.

When the anti-Communist campaign began shortly thereafter, the literary Left had a range of options between the approaches of Cohen's and Fearing's. In novels over the next four or five years, an uncertainty of political outcomes mingled with evolving opportunities to unbolt horizons of expectation; the novels were animated by the inspirational efforts of writers to remake and reimagine the relations of past, present, and future. The assembled multiplicity of ingredients in the novels—popular, modernist, neonaturalist, romance, historical, existentialist, proletarian, ethnic, feminist—forces one to reassess all previous categories by which critics have attempted to regularize this complexly variegated terrain of politics and aesthetic expression. Marxist themes were already at hand in pulp and detective fiction stories, and careers were under way among science fiction authors nurtured by Communist beliefs prior to the war—Isaac Asimov (1920-92), Cyril Kornbluth (1923-58), John B. Michel (1917-69, whose Communist literary views were called "Michelism"), Fredrik Pohl (b. 1919), and Donald A. Wollheim (1914-90). Entering the Cold War years, novelists themselves necessarily created a literary landscape that eluded critical efforts to contain it. The kernels of multiculturalism, feminism, and other future developments, planted by the Left in the 1930s, continued to develop under changed conditions that cloaked their eventual import.

The early years of the postwar speedup of the Consumers' Republic were disproportionately strewn with these new forms. Each subgenre is worthy of a research monograph, but to get a quick sense of the radical presence, one can turn to a landmark literary anthology called *Cross Section*. It was published from 1945 to 1948, edited by Edwin Seaver, and featured previously unpublished writing in several genres. The names of many of its authors are still recognizable, including Nelson Algren, Gwendolyn Brooks, Robert Hayden, Arthur Miller, Ralph Ellison, William Gibson, Norman Mailer, Thomas McGrath, Ann Petry, and Richard Wright. Fully three-quarters of the contributors to *Cross Section*, counting the editor and all of the above-cited authors, were recent or current pro-Communists. Radicals were reaching out for new points of contact among literary schools that had once been viewed separately; they were not just reiterating Marxist ideas but were involving themselves in the late 1940s dialogue about the advancement of literary techniques.

The Big Clock was published the year after Lester Cohen's *Coming Home*, along with a notable range of other radical approaches to culture and society, but what is extraordinary is how many authors had a Communist Party association of one sort or another. Their books include Thomas Bell's *There Comes a Time*, Robert Carse's *Deep Six*, Carlos Bulosan's *America Is in the Heart*, Robert Coates's *The Bitter Season*, Howard Fast's *The American*, Mark Harris's *Trumpet to the World*, Alfred Hayes's *All Thy Conquests*, Carson McCullers's *The Member of the Wedding*, Ann Petry's *The Street*, Jo Sinclair's *Wasteland*, and Jim Thompson's *Heed the Thunder*. Also appearing were unabashed mystery thrillers, such as Robert Finnegan's *The Bandaged Nude*, William Lindsay Gresham's *Nightmare Alley*, and Roy Huggins's *The Double Take*.

Novels written by similar authors out of the pro-Communist Left that had comparably inventive forms and uneven quality appeared in the subsequent year (1947), such as Stuart Engstrand's *The Sling and the Arrow*, Barbara Giles's *The Gentle Bush*, Josephine Herbst's *Somewhere the Tempest Fell*, Chester Himes's *The Lonely Crusade*, Willard Motley's *Knock on Any Door*, Budd

Schulberg's *The Harder They Fall*, George Sklar's *The Two Worlds of Johnny Truro*, and an increasing number of mysteries such as Sam Ross's *He Ran All the Way*, Edwin Lanham's *Politics Is Murder*, James Norman's *The Nightwalkers*, and Julius Fast's *Walk in Shadow*. The year 1948 was even more auspicious for such Left fiction, with widespread recognition of Howard Fast's *My Glorious Brothers*, Stefan Heym's *The Crusaders*, Norman Mailer's *The Naked and the Dead*, Irwin Shaw's *The Young Lions*, and William Gardner Smith's *The Last of the Conquerors*. A signal year for literary radicals with formal ingenuity and distinction was 1949, with the publication of Nelson Algren's award-winning *The Man with the Golden Arm* and Paul Bowles's best-selling *The Sheltering Sky*. In contrast, 1950 was a defining moment; far fewer novels by radicals appeared as a beleaguered tradition moved into the shadows of the American night and Communist literary modernism flowered in a subterranean existence. (Novels from after 1950 will be discussed in later chapters.)

The postwar geographical reach of pro-Communist writers—beyond the traditional centers of New York and Chicago—deserves particular notice, especially as it was sustained for some fifteen years. Radical fiction appeared from coast to coast and waypoints in between. Such efforts were prefigured in the Left's early encounter with regionalism in Gastonia, North Carolina, the scene of the great 1929 textile strike.[9] After World War II was over, Pittsburgh and western Pennsylvania were the settings for Alfred Hayes's *Shadow of Heaven* (1947), Lloyd Brown's *Iron City* (1951), Stefan Heym's *Goldsborough* (1953), and Phillip Bonosky's *Burning Valley* (1953) and *The Magic Fern* (1961).[10] Gallup, New Mexico, was the location for four novels that Phillip Stevenson (1896–1965) published under the name "Lars Lawrence," *Morning, Noon, and Night* (1954), *Out of the Dust* (1956), *Old Father Antic* (1961), and *The Hoax* (1961). The radical literary tradition of the South was kept alive in the region through the career of Stetson Kennedy (1916–2011) and novels such as Fielding Burke's *Sons of the Stranger* (1947) and Alfred Maund's *The Big Boxcar* (1957).[11] Jim Thompson (1906–77) explored the rural and small-town wastelands of Nebraska and Texas in *Heed the Thunder* (1946) and *The Killer Inside Me* (1952). Although not a novelist at that time, Meridel Le Sueur became an icon of regionalism in Minnesota.[12]

This was a regionalism at odds with both backward-looking romanticism and the growing urban-existentialist mood, even if stylistically the modern advances of Faulkner and Hemingway tended to be overlooked. The pro-Communists writing of western Pennsylvania and New Mexico, relying on bulk and sprawl, sought to speak of the power of a place without erasing the often brutal history that was covering up the politically impoverished present. By focusing on race, poverty, and land ownership and using new sources of

Sam Ross, briefly a member and a longtime sympathizer of the Communist Party, was the author of *He Ran All the Way* (1947), one of the many novels by radical writers launching careers after World War II. (Courtesy of Sam Ross)

Lloyd Brown, a Communist editor of the *New Masses* after World War II and then of *Masses & Mainstream* until 1954, published the novel *Iron City* (1951), about a Black prisoner in Pittsburgh. (Courtesy of Lloyd Brown)

evidence in community and oral traditions, writers on the Left asked disturbing questions about relationships between ordinary people and their communities, history, and literature. Such works, educating readers by dramatization and historicization, fomented a revolution in self-representation as writers looked at the way in which class was imagined in the 1940s and 1950s. Many loyal to Communism considered themselves internationalists even as they were for the most part firmly situated within their respective regions. To its credit, the Communist vision of American reality saw urban literature as a kind of region, too, with ghettos of various cities—Chicago, in particular—functioning as an integral part of the scene in this "urban regionalism."

Those novels that adhered closest to the social realist tradition (not to be confused with Soviet socialist realism) after World War II were singular in their aim of recounting the extent to which class explains the experience of people in the United States. They might even be looked upon as precious in literary history because class was so obfuscated in much of the national cultural discourse. Yet the promise of these novels could also be frustrated because such narratives were informed by a complex of largely unspoken axioms inherited from the same Left tradition that spawned them. It is easy to separate books into the sheep and goats division of great and not great, but an evenhanded discussion of the latter can be quite challenging. None of these postwar social realist novels can be dismissed out-of-hand for simply imitating the looking-glass world of much Soviet socialist realist art. More exactly, the pro-Communists peered through the fog of class war in different registers.

AFTER THE POPULAR FRONT

In contrast to Oscar Wilde, George Santayana wrote that "art is a delayed echo."[13] This was a facet of the dilemma of those novelists who persisted in building on the vision of the 1930s in the postwar years. They looked to models in art, but the models themselves seemed to embody the reality of the Great Depression that produced them. From the more obscure 1930s efforts of writers such as Robert Cantwell to the celebrated works of John Steinbeck, the postwar writers inherited images of Depression proletarianism hard to cast off: Art should be pertinent and comprehensible to working people, feature scenes of everyday life, aspire to realism in the representational sense, and move the reader emotionally and intellectually toward the goal of socialism.

Steinbeck's *The Grapes of Wrath* popularized numerous conventions of the American labor narrative, many already present. One was the use of hardboiled characters, another a sequence of unveilings of hitherto masked relations by which class society was apprehended through moments of symbolic disclosure and at times through violent shock and rupture. His writing featured the Left's standard utilization of older mentors and martyrs and the creation of a radical political community as a substitute family. Additional strategies of proletarian fiction that appeared in the 1930s and continued in the postwar years included profiling a character who attains social consciousness but is beset by bourgeois weaknesses that affect his or her motives. A violent social upheaval might appear to some characters as a naturalist vision of cosmic forces yet contain signals to the reader that such explosions are based on incompatible class relations. Beyond the feted models emerging from the United States, several writers in the Soviet Union and Europe were revered by Communists, including Maxim Gorky (1868–1936), Mikhail Sholokhov (1905–84), and Martin Andersen Nexø (1869–1954).[14]

This kind of Great Depression Marxism, even when watered down by the Popular Front, came with certain costs. The proletarian writers were once part of a vital vanguard, spreading the new gospel of the 1930s; ten years later, a writer might feel trapped in a tradition that did not allow a pleasing freedom of improvisation to create not just memorable passages but characters that live their own lives. Marxist-influenced writers walked an aesthetic tightrope, shuttling back and forth between describing what was and suggesting what ought to be. Fictions of the Left were created by both present-oriented and future-oriented writers. It was a paradox, raised originally by Aristotle, sometimes productive and other times paralyzing.

Fashioning novels in this framework produced troubling impediments for those writers who aspired to go beyond the borders of subjects and styles that could win praise from the pro-Communist press. Nonconformists ran the risk of offending those who might impute allegedly sordid political implications to the imaginative work of writers suspected of deviation. Much art approved by Soviet critics notoriously glorified the poor, encouraging its sentimental practitioners to produce allegories of proletarian virtue. Such versions of the pastoral and romantic ran up against the desire of many Communist writers, such as the Chicagoans Nelson Algren and Richard Wright, to view the impoverished through unillusioned eyes.

A hard question was being posed in all this: How should the explosive and volatile history of class struggle, a history in the making, be represented in fiction without lapsing into the impoverished aesthetic of didacticism? One problem the writers faced in their efforts to commit literary acts of political solidarity is that fiction deals in stories that require looseness and even irresponsibility toward that which has not occurred. Another conundrum is whether narrative strategy is ideologically neutral as opposed to being a product of history, impregnated with subliminal cultural nuances. Communism put pressure on one to construct narratives that would resolve the haziness and uncertainties of a world that the Left believed could be clarified by the a priori categories of class struggle; the omniscient narrator of social realism, authoritative and promising a degree of closure, was the most tempting way to go.

The regional novels by Communists such as Stevenson, Giles, and Bonosky (b. 1916) had many strengths. One can admire the vision behind the writing: class struggle comes on the scene to prevent a vigorous local regeneration of exploitation and discrimination, expressing an implicit utopia of a future reconciliation of economic, gender, and racial antagonism. Usually there is a plot action carefully organized to guide the reader toward the significance of the main act. But if one lacks prior interest in the material, some of these novels move with the pace of mules across an endless prairie; occasional flashes of power are insufficient to sustain stretches of flat monotony.

This accounts in part for a wide splay of opinions about the radical tradition in the U.S. novel. On an average day, much of the lesser-known Left writing, like forgotten fiction in general, was typified by earnest mediocrity, portraits of dozens of characters with hardly any vividly remembered. Many of the pro-Communist novelists were highly skilled, but a painterly eye is not a transformative one. Art must involve the alteration of materials under aesthetic heat. An author such as Philip Stevenson was a writer of prose rather than blank verse.[15] In his multivolume chronicle of a famous mid-1930s miners' strike in New Mexico, he produced an ethnographic study as well as a literary exploration into the racial heterogeneity of the Southwest. One can convert ethnography into fiction, but Stevenson could not. James Neugass (1905–49) drew with a steady hand a warty profile of the viperous playground of the New Orleans elite in *Rain of Ashes* (1949).[16] His highly mannered, ornamental style brings occasional flashes of power, but some sections flow like glue up a hill; the result is an unconvincing tragedy of family disintegration. Other writers, such as Barbara Giles, simply lack dramatic force; a fictional world can be full but not teeming.[17] Phillip Bonosky's novels have real power yet grind forward like armed and unstoppable Sherman tanks. One would not be far off in sensing that such writers are as interested in the political agenda of epiphanic moments as in tapping into elusive consciousness.

The novels by Stevenson, Giles, and Bonosky attempt to create a short period in the history of humanity on an epic scale while simultaneously producing a realist novel of contemporary life; several tell the story of a particular person at a particular moment. Such books can have passages of courageous beauty without quite becoming a vibrantly coherent creation. Yet one does

James Neugass was a Lost Generation poet who joined the Communist Party in the mid-1930s and drove an ambulance for the Republicans during the Spanish Civil War. In the year of his death, he published the novel *Rain of Ashes* (1949), satirizing his New Orleans family. (Courtesy of Myra Neugass)

not need go to exertions to make a cause célèbre out of ephemeral, minor, or commercial fluff to find distinction in this "not great" part of the postwar Left legacy. Jim Thompson is without equal in his tales of another America, a pastoral hell of greed ruled by violent primitives. John Sanford exhibits a Flaubertian precision of detail refracted through a cinematic lens. The novels of William J. Blake (born William Blech, 1894–68) are compendious and expansive, as rich in specificity as Dickens and Balzac. Howard Fast had the ability to construct an easily absorbed but nonetheless complex plot while also outlining an array of well-developed characters.

The most unsatisfactory facet of these novels is a recurrent lack of psychological dimension in their major and minor protagonists. Without candid explorations of the psyche, the suspense created by the inner oscillations is less convincing. Several authors fail to place psychology persuasively at the hub of the work, carefully interwoven with the ideas ultimately responsible for one's redemption or fatal transgression. Lacking emotional depth, documentation of the plight of the dispossessed is restricted in literature. Was this merely a technical failing of particular cultural workers, or was it the consequence of a view of the world that is at bottom both positivist and moralist?

Even an Émile Zola could imagine contradictions in virtuous and reasonable people. But in too many Left novels, a neonaturalism, said to be realism, takes the reader into a dualistic world in which virtue and villainy, eternally distinct from one another, are everlastingly locked in combat. Novels by no means capitulated entirely to such simplicities, and a discerning reader may detect the perhaps unconscious markings of psychic complexities. Yet one senses a tilt in the direction of crafting protagonists beholden to a Cult of Reason; the weapon of righteousness is wielded on behalf of communal welfare with the aim of achieving justice. Some writers may have even strategized an absence of authorial intervention to suggest that the reader is free to extract his or her own conclusions, but such efforts seem insincere when the conclusion preferred by the author is abundantly clear.

The Communist Party press treated proletarian and people's art as citadels to be defended; all through the postwar years, the *Daily Worker* and *New Masses* maintained the pressure of constant admonitions against literary narcissism, soul-searching, and vaguely defined perversion, frequently suggesting that those who deviated from the (changing) Communist line craved security and status. Enemies were to be found everywhere, especially among former allies, as was demonstrated in the Party-published booklet by Roger Garaudy (b. 1913), *Literature of the Graveyard: Jean Paul Sartre, François Mauriac, André Malraux, Arthur Koestler* (1948). Reviews in the *Daily Worker* and *New Masses* relentlessly reinforced the notion that genuine pro-Communist writers should be opposed to foregrounding in their texts the personal fears, sexual obsessions, and psychological analyses that allegedly dominated bourgeois and petit-bourgeois literature. At the least, such scolding could freeze the imagination, inhibiting authors from tapping into the emotional complexities of their own selves in the manner of a Dostoyevsky.

A forthright admission of the recurrent literary shortcomings of postwar Left writers mentioned above, especially the diminished psychological development of characters, is inescapable. The enticement of melodramatic simplification was always tempting for radicals, as it was for other novelists, and the outlook of late antifascism decisively amplified this lure. Pro-Communist writers were superbly alert, early on, to the dangers of Mussolini and Hitler; but the Nazi experience presented them with unforeseen varieties of oppression that provoked some into giving greater weight to a Manichean view in their novels describing class warfare and the brutalization of humanity by power-hungry profiteers, anti-trade unionists, and racial elites. Such sentiments were quite consistent with the familiar radical plot—as rehearsed in *The Grapes of Wrath*—of a protagonist who moves toward an enlightened consciousness in which he or she comes to understand that public and private life are inseparable. In short, with the emergence of Hitlerism, a fire-breathing, monstrous creature out of Teutonic mythology materialized on earth, and dragon slayers were necessary in order to kill it. In one wartime *New Masses* cartoon, the dragon sported a Hitler-like mustache and the armed warrior opposing it wore a Red Army uniform.[18]

Yet the problem must be larger, for one finds analogous failures to those of explicit class war narratives in historically and autobiographically based plots. What sporadically reverses this drift are the increasingly melancholic meditations of Left writers in the postwar era, to some degree prefigured by *The Heart Is a Lonely Hunter* (1940), by Carson McCullers (1917–67), written as the author was emerging from her Communist moment. In such literature, there is an increasing distance, mostly unacknowledged, between the Communist rhetoric that once swayed these writers and the reality that they lived—which was becoming too excruciating to endure. Although subliminally felt at first, the youthful confidence and compelling ideology that had originally recharted their identity was moving toward an uncertainty that was never fully resolved. The prospect that social realism might be the incubator of the new contingency, a critical realism beyond the positivist one, is suggested in the work of Alexander Saxton (b. 1919). A devoted Communist Party member from late 1941 to 1959, Saxton envisioned the entire decade of the 1930s and the generation that led its battles as a site of memory to be revivified under postwar conditions. In *The Great Midland*, he endeavored to re-create the previous era of revolutionary hope with a closeness and complexity of life worthy of a Theodore Dreiser.

THE SUBLIME SAXTON

Primarily writing his novel while at sea in the merchant marine, Alexander Saxton returned in his mind and memory to 1930s Chicago to give birth in his novel to a forceful vision of politics, culture, and commitment that he deemed essential in the postwar era. The plot, unpromising in its bare-bones version for those outside the Left, re-creates the late 1930s experiences of Communist David Spaas, a U.S. volunteer in the Spanish Republican cause, who returns to Chicago to organize railway workers and attend to the collapse of his marriage. The result in the imaginative world of *The Great Midland* is a dramatic rendition of the class struggle in a fashion bold for its time, or any time, which aimed to embrace all of life.

Although his refusal to use the neo-modernist forms and temper of the late 1940s cost Saxton the serious attention of those literary critics looking for new postwar voices, one never feels in his novel that social forces are everything or characters mere instruments of biology and environment. In a novel that should be esteemed as a singular, surprising work of the early Cold War and a high point in the radical literary tradition, there is an intensity of feeling and a rightness of language in nearly every episode of the book. By taking direct action in opposition to a Consumers' Republic, through a remonstration against the waning of historical consciousness, Saxton demonstrates that complexity and nuance need not negate a passionate commitment to social justice. While it is reasonable to question an assertion in his autobiographical writings that he emerged from the Stalinist era with a guiltless conscience, his novel, like his life as a union militant and a Marxist scholar, was an act of sublime defiance.[19]

Kenneth Fearing aimed at discovery by using an oddball, pyrotechnical mixing of inherited genres. His characters evidence representative qualities but are without a full social portrait or biography. Saxton aspired to reinhabit and enlarge a tradition that already existed, roughly following the reverse route of Fearing by returning to the theme of oppression as expressed through a narrative of social injustice. Together the two authors, a generation apart even though their novels were written virtually simultaneously, can suggest the perimeters of radical resistance to a Consumers' Republic through outstanding fiction suggesting parallel movement from social realism to the new contingency, the transition to 1950s Communist literary modernism. Both crafted versions of the left-wing novel that carried forward and transformed

Alexander Saxton, a member of the Communist Party for nearly two decades, published a cutting-edge work of social realism in *The Great Midland* (1948) and later became an eminent historian. (Courtesy of Alexander Saxton)

the vision of the 1930s, artistically blossoming briefly under the impact of an unanticipated crisis.

Saxton's Chicago novel rises higher than its contemporaries, and above many novels of the previous decade, for the artistry of its narration and its trenchant psychological depiction of character. There are episodes in which nearly every detail and every sentence carry significance. Unusually poignant are the intimate exchanges between Ann Spaas, the mother of Communist protagonist Dave Spaas, and her daughter-in-law, Stephanie Kovniak, about men—Ann's late husband, Joe; her brother-in-law, Eddie; and her son, Dave (Stephanie's husband). One can appreciate the intricacy of the ache and density in the tragedy of Ann's imprisonment in a patriarchal family without having to endure the slightest bit of authorial lecturing.[20] Ann's warning about Dave is palpable for her daughter-in-law, another grim ingredient to be factored into the mental anguish already in progress; Stephanie, a working-class woman who has become a graduate student, is suffering an emotional war set off by an inability to reconcile her scientific materialism with Marxist utopianism.

Should Stephanie stave off a fear of death by accruing gratifying experiences as the opportunity arises, or subordinate conventional comfort to activity on behalf of a vision of a just society? Just as one comprehends the organic connections of a cell in an intricate structure, so one may discern the magnitude of the many tiny but dense building blocks in Saxton's novel: his vignettes of the 1919 race riot; the steps by which the former Wobbly militant Uncle Jennison degenerates into bigotry and then opposition to union democracy; and Dave's compulsion to act first and face the consequences later. *The Great Midland* ingeniously balances a sovereign, restrained, historically omniscient overview with rhapsodic passages bordering on frenzied indiscipline.

Saxton's piercing insights into personal emotions chiefly revolve around the struggle to seize control of one's destiny, although the novel is far from a Freudian offensive against the unconscious. Both Fearing and Saxton depict individuals with emblematic values, reflecting types of the era, but Saxton's characters are more capacious in their emotional candor. Willfully crafted to stand for kinds of people, Saxton's workers, union bureaucrats, graduate students, and others are concurrently tangible individuals, suggesting that Saxton was well grounded in the English realism of Defoe and Fielding. *The Great Midland* corroborates that proletarian and radical literature, even in the late 1940s, was not a phenomenon separate from the mainstream literary tradition but grew out of earlier as well as contemporaneous cultural developments. The structural innovations pioneered by John Dos Passos and the colloquial, hard-boiled dialogue of Ernest Hemingway are apparent. Saxton did not introduce new language and forms so much as give force and nuance to previous models, perhaps even gleaned from Balzac and Zola.

Saxton's unquestionable debt to a writer like Joseph Conrad might correspond to that "anxiety of influence" famously postulated by Harold Bloom as the major link between literary masters and disciples, had not Saxton also developed the measured classic tone of Conrad's writing in new directions.[21] Most surprising is Saxton's decentered historical framework. Ostensibly organized around international wars—the First World War, the Spanish Civil War, the Second World War—the battles in *The Great Midland* are overwhelmingly those of domestic U.S. class and race wars and those in the psyches of his protagonists. The literal time is set in the year or so after Dave Spaas's return from combat in Spain in 1939, but many of the novel's crucial events occur in 1933 (the beginning of the relationship between Dave and Stephanie) and 1934 (Dave's decisive turn to Marxist politics).

History is relentless in *The Great Midland*. But the hard facts of the local and international class struggle are never so systematic and insistent as to drive out the haunting atmosphere central to the novel's mood—the erstwhile Wobbly Eddie Spaas's increasingly mournful theme song, "The Preacher and the Slave"; the incessant coming and going of trains, suggesting the as-yet-unharnessed power of the ubiquitous radical notion (attributed to Hegel, Marx, and Lenin, among others) of the revolution as the locomotive of history; the aura of inevitable death and mutilation that comes to the fore in the troubled graduate student Marguerite Strauss's translation of the medieval *Danse Macabre*, then bursts explosively with the agonizing demise of Roman Koviak and the brutal killing of Pledger McAdams.

It was Saxton's wholly unconscious identification with Stephanie, the trope of existentialist doubt, and not Dave's stubborn Cult of Reason, that rendered *The Great Midland*, decades after its publication, a model of the new contingency in a manner rare among social realist novels of the Left at the time.[22] This female protagonist, likely suspect among Communist troglodytes due to her sexual infidelity and awe of university culture, expressed by her behavior and philosophic questioning the challenge of critical rationality to a positivism that in the end can betray reason. Throughout the novel, Stephanie is trapped between two men of certainty. One is her Communist husband, Dave, and the other is her conservative lover, a graduate student in philosophy, Martin. In relation to Stephanie, these dogmatic males are somewhat parallel, perhaps more than Saxton originally intended. Dave's admirability in plowing ahead is compromised by his limited understanding, even in the face of skeptical queries about Communist Party policy from a union activist called "Red." Stephanie, who wonders more circumspectly about the relationship between the logic of science and the redemptive possibilities of collective struggle, is in her uncertainty the herald of critical socialist hope in the novel. This was missed entirely by the Communist reviewers, especially Howard Fast, who celebrated the novel but described Stephanie as corrupted by a longing for middle-class comfort.[23]

Saxton, even more than Fearing, came of intellectual age in tandem with the vision of the 1930s. Beginning as an idealist and pacifist as a Harvard College student and after transferring to the University of Chicago, he absorbed from the radical movement principles of human solidarity that cut across national, regional, cultural, ethnic, and racial borders. When he drew closer to the Communists, he learned how labor was to be prized for its contribution to humanity. As the decade ended, he was absorbed by the threat of fascism as both a foreign and domestic danger; he reluctantly realized that an international war, while an unacceptable solution, would have to be waged.

Saxton's reading of Marx deepened his view that commodification and commercialization needed to be brought under democratic management by producers; there would have to be an emancipation of urban space for living and recreation through government intervention. Saxton's Communism was premised on a preventative literary and political revolt that never materialized and went down in a grueling defeat. He did not anticipate that, postwar, a Consumers' Republic would seal the victory of a commercial civilization, in which a public civic life would be replaced by rewards of purchasing personal material products, where the well-to-do would escape to suburbs and accept poverty in the midst of plenty for urban and rural indigents. By the mid-1950s it became obvious to Saxton that "the Stalinist dictatorship" had itself "murdered socialism in the name of socialism,"[24] and he saw how a Consumers' Republic patriotism arose victoriously through its subordination of the struggles for the liberation of labor and minorities during the Cold War. This brutal climate was both the cause and result of the unleashing of a New Right that, in an appalling bloc with a faction of liberals, used anti-Communism as a wedge to divide social victims both at home and abroad.

Fearing and Saxton were radical writers who went beyond the issues of only one period; Fearing focused on the cultural consequences of the postwar transformation in communications, Saxton on the enduring riddles of race, class, and commitment. In retrospect, both represent the post–World War II dilemma of the Left in expressing the profoundly unfinished character of the moment. Their shared inheritance, like other writers discussed in *American Night*, was fidelity to the unique form of social consciousness galvanized during the Depression in which the Communist Party played a crucial role.

Postwar, the two sprang outward from the 1930s tradition and traversed the range of possibilities from the unabashed Marxism of Saxton to the radicalism drenched in bleak existentialism of Fearing. What may be true of both men at the time that *The Big Clock* and *The Great Midland* appeared is that they were perhaps living in the ideal historical moment for the nature of their art. In the afterglow of the powerful cultural ethos of the 1930s past, but not yet in the grip of the 1950s future, they both diversely took advantage of their freedom to display their ability to absorb technical features of other writers and appropriate them as their own.

THE RUINS OF MEMORY

Alexander Saxton unveiled rare poise and ingenuity in *The Great Midland*'s reanimation of older, realist literary forms, while Kenneth Fearing mined popular genres. What about postwar women writers on the Left, equally opposed to any notion of a consumer-based politics of liberation? Many appeared comparatively irresolute about the strategies by which fiction might give voice to a desire to see sweeping changes in society. In several instances, insecurity about a literary vision at times intermingled with qualms concerning the legacy bequeathed by Stalinism as a shifting political landscape prepared the ground for the incongruities of late antifascism. Several gifted women novelists were among the stratum of pro-Communist cultural veterans who, unlike Saxton in the 1940s, recalled the proceedings of the late 1930s with considerable disquiet. Their misgivings were not over Soviet pacts and alliances per se, nor were they yet at the point of a total recoil from the cruelty of Stalin's regime. More expressly, they chafed at the repeated and robotic subordination of Communist Party policies in the United States to the unpredictable strategic needs of the Soviet Union.

Women such as Fielding Burke (born Olive Tilford Dargan, 1869–1968), Vera Caspary (1899–1987), Josephine Herbst (1892–1969), Grace Lumpkin (1891–1980), Myra Page (born Dorothy Page Gary, 1910–90), Mary Heaton Vorse (1874–1976), and Leane Zugsmith (1903–69) had come into their own as novelists during the Depression; they now found the postwar Consumers' Republic a complex moment in which to conduct a search for structures, characters, and themes by which to mange their assorted feelings of loss, disenchantment, frustration, injury, and longing. From 1941 to 1944, liberals and Communists had participated in a sustained political bloc that limited the goals of the Communist-led Left to the framework of the status quo. In the war years, praise for Communist Party general secretary Earl Browder, soon to be an Ozymandias, and the Soviet Union emanated from Communist Party circles as mechanically as a believer counts beads. This was poor preparation for the events of the late 1940s.

Pondering what she came to recognize as the postwar dislodgment of literary forms associated with the 1930s, Josephine Herbst published "The Ruins of Memory" in the *Nation* in 1956, the same year that Kenneth Fearing decreed the death of "a long phase of our society."[25] In Herbst's terminology, what had been lost in the postwar era was "a sense of the world." Literature in the late 1940s had been colonized by an introspective view of people as "isolated moral atoms." The postwar era when critics adulated Kafka, Hawthorne, Melville, and James operated as a "genteel retreat from a period too complicated to confront easily"; postwar novels, correspondingly, detached themselves from the tumultuous past to become "a kind of smokescreen to conceal the present dilemma, and the ruins." What might have been only a passing phase in literature was subsequently "frozen by the Cold War." Paradoxically, Herbst insisted that to see humanity in 1956 "in relation to the 'actual world' — in the tradition of Austen, Flaubert, and Tolstoy," was a literary stance that had now become "avant garde." Still, the ruins of the tradition that had existed prior to the postwar zeitgeist "can be as good a point of departure as any." The veteran international correspondent concluded: "There is usually new life in the ruins as anyone who ever saw a population react from a bombing can testify." The obligatory bridge from the Depression to the 1950s should be a continuous affirmation of the 1930s "new dynamic" of a prevailing pattern in fiction, one that prevented characters from becoming merely "case histories."[26]

It is for that reason curious that Herbst's own major fiction of the 1940s, *Satan's Sergeants* (1941), published on the cusp of U.S. entry into the war, and *Somewhere the Tempest Fell* (1946), emerging after the close of hostilities, progressively took on a facade of shapeless rumination. The architecture of emotions in these novels, and Herbst's heat-seeking eye for a character's telling reflection or action, portend art at the zenith of a career; her writing had been tempered by successive engagements during the two eras she deemed most fertile, the 1920s and the 1930s. Instead, the two novels were weirdly stillborn. Her confidence of a few years earlier, almost bordering on arrogance, must have been sapped from her literary vision.

Especially in *Somewhere the Tempest Fell*, where the autobiographical allusions cry out for some kind of electrifying connection to the reader, one probes the isolated episodes as if feeling for cranial bumps, but a diagnosis fails to jell. The novel's events occur in Chicago in the final week of August 1943, alternating primarily between the habitués of two households. One is the home of the demoralized writer Adam Snow, and in the other lives the bustling bohemian divorcée Ada Brady, suggesting symbolic sites of decay and renewal. The half-dozen chief protagonists who come and go from these residences, too numerous and internally undeveloped, are rapidly overwhelmed by legions of half-baked secondary and tertiary characters. If Herbst had been a more attentive student of her own growth as a writer, she might have recognized that the otiose ruins of form that she agonizingly toiled to put into place were in these latest two novels more analogous to shells or perhaps carcasses.

A year prior to the events in the novel, in May 1942, Herbst was summarily fired from her job of writing pro-war propaganda at the German desk of the Office of the Co-ordinator of Information (known as the Donovan Committee), an independent intelligence agency in Washington partly under federal government supervision through the Office of Facts and Figures. She was not informed of the grounds for her dismissal, but the FBI suspected her of Communist sympathies and perhaps of taking secret documents from the office; incongruously, the FBI also suggested that she might be profascist. Biographical scholarship to date has revealed that Herbst was not a formal member of the Communist Party but since 1931 had been something of a dues-cheater. She had, however, pulled back from her illusions about Stalinism even before the Hitler-Stalin Pact and had not been reenergized by the Nazi attack on the Soviet Union. Only with the U.S. entrance into the fighting in late 1941 did she return to activism by assisting the war effort.[27] Her opinions and experiences may be found in the culminating sections of *Somewhere the Tempest Fell*; they are attributed to the male character Harry Light.

Light is brought to a party in the basement of Ada Brady's home by the aspiring writer Bart Short. Light describes himself as a character in a Russian novel and immediately starts to act out a drama in which he plays two male parts. One has messy hair and the other has his hair combed down; the former is accused of being a "Red" and the latter of being a "Fascist."[28] Light proceeds to have an argument with Short, who reads a "Letter to the President" demanding the opening of a second front in the war. Bart declares that the intention of the Allies is "to let the Russians bleed white and when the Germans were sufficiently weakened, they would crash in and claim all the glory." Harry replies that his own experiences with the government show that the opinions of civilians are irrelevant, and, besides, "the Russians would like to see the allies bled white," after which he makes "a comical face." The next day, Bart and Harry return to Ada's house and again quarrel about politics. When Bart accuses Harry of being a do-nothing, Harry retorts: "I'm sick of grand bloated schemes. . . . I was in the thick of them in Washington and couldn't make head or tail of them. I learned my lesson." Bart gets apoplectic: "This is a people's war. . . . They are on the march." Harry replies: "I'm afraid that's true, but do they know where they are going? ... If it's democracy you want, you better first define it, then fight for it, in every house, every street, every inch of ground and you can begin with yourselves."[29]

This is good advice, but what is one to make of its inclusion? If Herbst is using Light as surrogate for herself, she is indulging in a sanitization and trivialization of her political past to the point of corrupting the integrity of the novel. Moreover, Herbst can be found in parts of other characters, especially men. One of the most obvious is Ralph Johns, an author of some forgotten fiction and once a journalist on the Republican side in the Spanish Civil War.[30] The character of Adam Snow as well exhibits hesitancies about political action but introduces an overriding preoccupation with guilt.[31] *Somewhere the Tempest Fell* certainly suggests political allegory through its characters and their relationship to each other and to Herbst's own life. Yet artistry failed her, and the analogies never come to fruition. What happened?

In her Lost Generation days, Herbst wrote *Nothing Is Sacred* (1928) and *Money for Love* (1929) about the mystifying collapse of traditional values that necessitated one's adaptation to circumstances devoid of a feeling of purpose. Her method, then, was to reveal the inner consciousnesses of multiple narrators unsentimentally, skillfully honing the mode of authorial detachment popularly referred to as the "Hemingway School."[32] In the Depression, Herbst's well-constructed family-saga trilogy (*Pity Is Not Enough*, 1933; *The Executioner Waits*, 1934; and *Rope of Gold*, 1939) carefully staged its theme of middle-class decay and proletarian emergence. At that time, she employed structural devices evoking the contemporaneous novels of John Dos Passos. But just two years later, *Satan's Sergeants*, in its contrasting the oddly crisscrossing lives of rich and poor in an imaginary rural Pennsylvania community, "Merlin," offers a slighter reach and stumbling trajectory. The drama is wedged obscurely between the pressures of class and a fallen fate common to all. The postlude to the crises of the novel is a stock resolution featuring the departure of one of several female protagonists, the fifty-nine-year-old Mrs. Willard; readers may be left a tad mystified.

Then came *Somewhere the Tempest Fell*, a novel that imparts a dream message behind a dream work, even though its referent, in some murky manner, is tantalizingly close to Herbst's personal Communist history. In lieu of a unity of narrative, Herbst principally tracks the mental and physical meandering of Adam Snow, her middle-aged, self-inventorying author of popular detective stories and avatar of angst, not unlike a character out of Kenneth Fearing. It is a fool's errand to parse fact from fiction, but Herbst sowed her plot with unrelenting pleas for the reader to do so, and it is hard to resist. Throughout *Somewhere the Tempest Fell*, events on loan from Herbst's recent life come forward in puzzling fashion. In some sense, without engaging specific issues, it aspires to be a novel about political life itself, her meditation on the cost of living with political principles. Herbst might have written the *Orlando* of Communism—a work both coded and revealing, erotic and censored—but the necessity of subterfuge pushed her into some darkness further than self-recognition, and she thereby bungled her art.

Herbst still retained extraordinary literary skill, as would be confirmed in her 1954 novella *Hunter of Doves*, which points to some of the involvedness of personal revelation. But she lacked the vision to realize a novel. The facts of her intimate and political life could not be frankly addressed in a repressive culture, and allegories failed her.

Thinking about the enigma of addressing a "cost" buried in Herbst's *Somewhere the Tempest Fell* may be a clue to unraveling the mystery of left-wing women novelists in the postwar era. In the 1930s, female novelists were a gathering storm. The Great Depression is now the source of many reprints of novels and several iconic proto-feminist literary figures (not only Herbst but also Tillie Olsen and Meridel Le Sueur); the era also supplies nearly all the material for the standard chapters in reference books that address women, proletarianism, and class.[33] In dissimilarity, the 1940s is conceivably the missing decade in the recorded chronicle of women's fiction; the most memorable postwar novel by a female author of American radicalism is likely *Letty Fox, Her Luck* (1946), by Australian Christina Stead (1902–83).[34]

GENDER AND THE CRISIS OF FORM

Little appeared in print in the 1940s from the talented pens of several famous writers who got their start earlier, such as Katherine Anne Porter (1890–1980) and Djuna Barnes (1892–1982). But in the fits and starts of the struggling careers of radical writers, one finds much minor fiction attending to matters such as women's agency, the exploration of gender asymmetry, and the theorizing of the specificity of women's writing and spaces. It will take some time for historians and critics to sort out the eventual meaning of this record, but it is the weakening in the distinction of the work by those emergent from the 1930s, like Josephine Herbst, that perhaps accounts for the inattention to women's postwar novels. The evolution of Josephine Johnson (1910–90) is not unlike that of Herbst's. Johnson had blended socialist hope with lyricism in *Now in November* (1934) and reverted to more conventional social protest in *Jordanstown* (1937), but she found her next novel unpublishable due to its absence of plot. Readers' reports agreed that nothing much happens except a continual torrent of words.[35] Six years later, Johnson published the despairing novel *Wildwood* (1945). Replete with themes of mental collapse and suicide, its form is weakened by excessive literary (especially biblical) quotations and a melodramatic, self-pitying narration.

Mari Sandoz (1886–1966) had climaxed the 1930s with a rousing proletarian novel, *Capitol City* (1939), but her only fiction produced in the 1940s was *The Tom-Walker* (1947), an obscure populist-themed narrative of a wounded civil war veteran. Kay Boyle (1902–92) published four novels now dismissed by most critics — *Primer for Combat* (1942), *Avalanche* (1944), *A Frenchman Must Die* (1946), and *1939* (1948). Pearl Buck (1892–73), of course, produced a novel a year, sometimes under the name "John Sedges," but the sole survivor is *Dragon Seed* (1942), a frankly propagandistic political work about the Japanese invasion and occupation of China. Only Martha Gellhorn (1908–98) somewhat reversed the trend. She ended the 1930s with *A Stricken Field* (1940), a pedestrian historical novel of Czechoslovakia's fall to fascism, but returned a few years later with the more evocative narrative of interracial sex and power, *Liana* (1944), and the unnerving story of a Jewish soldier who confronts Nazi sadism, *The Wine of Astonishment* (1948).

Four of the more celebrated and productive women connected with the Communist movement stumbled and fell in the postwar period. Olive Dargan, who published her novels as Fielding Burke, began *Sons of the Stranger* in the early 1940s but agonized over its size, shape, and structure until its unsuccessful publication in 1947.[36] Mary Heaton Vorse, a dissident and nonorganizational Communist since the late 1920s, stopped writing novels altogether in the 1940s.[37] Leane Zugsmith, whose achievement in fiction in the 1930s was robust, turned to publishing glib tales in *Collier's* and the *New Yorker* during the war years and then to largely fruitless collaborations with her husband, journalist Carl Randau.[38] Myra Page remained supportive of the Communist Party until her death but abandoned her membership in the early 1950s after years of feeling compelled to take stances with which she felt uneasy. In the 1940s, Page published no fiction.[39] Her final novel, initially called *With Sun in Our Blood* (1950), was in point of fact drafted in the mid-1930s when she had transcribed the oral history of Dolly Hawkins, a Tennessee-born woman whom Page encountered while doing political organizing in Arkansas. In 1946, Page began to rework her Hawkins material into a skillful narrative that juxtaposed ideology and experience in the making of a working-class woman's subjectivity. The outcome, appearing after four years in novel form from the radical Citadel Press, was reissued by the Feminist Press in 1986 to wider appreciation as *Daughter of the Hills*.[40]

Even among the truly gifted writers, most of whom experienced a less-protracted association with the Left than Page, there are chasms and gorges after the Depression decade collided with the Consumers' Republic. Often there are texts showing the potential of talents never fully realized in chosen forms, with some writers going into a tailspin. Carson McCullers ended the 1930s by writing *Reflections in a Golden Eye* in 1939 (published in 1941) and *The Heart Is a Lonely Hunter*. She began the next decade with work on *The Member of the Wedding* in 1941, but the novella did not appear until 1946. Thirteen years passed between *Mountain Path* (1936) and *Hunter's Horn* (1949) by Harriette Simpson Arnow (born Harriette Louisa Simpson, 1908–86). Other radical women managed only one novel for the entire decade: Jane Bowles's *Two Serious Ladies* (1943), Lillian Smith's *Strange Fruit* (1944), Jo Sinclair's *Wasteland* (1946), Eudora Welty's *Delta Wedding* (1946), and Laura Z. Hobson's *Gentleman's Agreement* (1947). Jean Stafford, married to poet Robert Lowell from 1940 to 1948, published two novels, *Boston Adventure* (1944) and *The Mountain Lion* (1947), but her reputation is based on her short stories. Elizabeth Hardwick, a former Communist, also married to Robert Lowell from 1949 to 1972, published *The Ghostly Lover* in 1945 but is admired mainly as a literary critic.

Some varieties of literary permutation are better seen from a distance. The disjuncture between the promise of social realist form at the climax of the Depression and the sensation of losing ground in the 1940s is unmistakable in the trajectory of one noted Communist woman novelist who in the late 1930s sat down to write an urban psycho-thriller, *Laura* (drafted in 1939, published in 1943). Vera Caspary, a Sephardic Jew born in Chicago, was committed to the Communist movement longer than her public statements divulge, some ten to fifteen years. In a distinct way, she recognized that aesthetic representation is a vital political weapon in the social battle for female self-expression, and her own work was often preoccupied with the struggle between men's objectification of the female and women's struggles for self-control.

For Caspary, gender functioned as a primary category of social identity and was under inspection in *Laura*, a novel famous for its disruption of conventional detective story motifs through the strategies by which she unriddles the ostensible murder of the heroine. Caspary was always attentive to combat between the sexes and making female identity visible, a set of concerns resonating with the present-day view that the novel is the literary form that women found best suited to their self-representations. Certainly *Laura*'s brilliant disclosure of the threat of the feminine is distant from the sort of domestic novels that portray identity as natural so that the operation of social power is veiled to the reader. The novel emerged in a late 1930s moment of political crisis, which turns out to have been a productive space. Caspary was at the same moment doubting the Communist movement but had not yet entered

Vera Caspary, author of *Laura* (1942), was a Communist Party member in the late 1930s and a sympathizer in the 1940s. Here she is shown in 1956 with performers in her play *Wedding in Paris*. (Courtesy of Wisconsin Center for Film and Theater Research)

a full-scale repudiation of the doctrine itself (and would eventually lie about her political history rather than inform against comrades).[41] She unexpectedly rotated to ostensibly nonpolitical subjects that she knew well, and these in turn became the settings for displacements of anxiety about personal betrayal, social pressure, the price of romantic illusions, and the need to marshal one's own resources to regain footing for stamina and advance. The work, foregrounding female desire and confined to action within a limited time span enhanced by memories and flashbacks, is outright optimistic about the possibility of a woman's transcending subordinate status.

Vera Caspary was an inexhaustible novelist, film writer, playwright, and journalist who progressed from writing popularized social realist fiction in the early Depression era—*The White Girl* (1929), *Music in the Street* (1930), *Thicker Than Water* (1932)—to a single dazzling success, *Laura*, in the early years of World War II. After the Consumers' Republic hit full blast, Caspary continued to write fiction on the theme of women's quest for identity, but only in a minor vein.[42] While much of Caspary's life remains relatively unexplored by scholars, the circumstances of her writing *Laura* are recorded in her autobiography, *The Secrets of Grown-Ups* (1979).[43] Caspary acknowledged being a formal Communist Party member for three years during the late 1930s, including the period of an April 1939 tour that she took to the Soviet Union. Several months later, she was stunned by the Hitler-Stalin Pact.

During that fall of 1939, Caspary tried to extricate herself from Communist Party membership in Connecticut but found that her comrades were reluctant to let her go. In January 1940, she was besieged by a visit from John Howard Lawson (who had initially recruited her) and ended up agreeing to an arrangement that allowed her to quietly drift over to the status of a fellow traveler. But it was during that interim of crisis about her Party status that she tried to escape political discussion by writing a mystery play that eventually became *Laura*. After relocating to Hollywood in the winter of 1940, Caspary became active as a nonmember in Communist circles and smoothly made the 1941 transition to a pro-war position after the German attack on the USSR. By that autumn, however, she was feeling secure but unfulfilled following a recent spate of successful Hollywood studio script-writing jobs. She then came across the 1939 mystery play and felt a sudden desire to develop it into a fuller narrative with a stronger villain. After a friend suggested that she study the techniques of British novelist Wilkie Collins, she completed the novel *Laura* by Christmas of 1942.[44]

The life of Caspary's protagonist, Laura Hunt, parallels Caspary's own background as a female from the Midwest seeking a career at a time when women were primarily channeled toward conventional domesticity. The theme is a peculiar kind of death and rebirth. Laura is believed by her friends and the police to have been murdered, most likely by her loser fiancé or by an ex-boyfriend, while she had actually traveled to the country for the weekend to burn her youthful diaries and meditate on her forthcoming marriage. On a whim, Laura had also loaned her apartment to a working-class woman-turned-model, Diane Redfern. Redfern was killed in Laura's place by a shotgun blast to the face while wearing Laura's robe; this is the reason why she is mistaken for Laura by the murderer as well as by those who later identify the body.

The novel was intended to supply a dose of reality to the naive heroine about the evil that men do while at the same time serving as a proto-feminist report on the status of sexual politics in the early 1940s. It is furthermore a narrative about personal betrayal but with political resonances expressed by means of men of different political valences pressing Laura to behave as they desire. At the core are overlapping love triangles. Thirty and unmarried, the stylish advertising writer Laura Hunt is engaged to Shelby Carpenter, a gorgeous but weak and childlike scion of a southern family. He has financial reasons for pursuing Laura but is simultaneously conducting an affair with Diane Redfern. Laura is also being stalked by her onetime mentor, the obese but ultra-sophisticated cultural entrepreneur Waldo Lydecker. Lydecker sports a walking cane that serves as a secret shotgun. It is in fact Lydecker who, in a fit of rage over Laura's impending marriage, fires this weapon directly into a face when the door to Laura's apartment opens. He does not realize that Redfern had taken Laura's place.

Following the discovery of the ostensible murder of Laura and prior to her surprise return to New York, a proletarian detective assigned to the case, the autodidact Mark McPherson, becomes enthralled with the aura of Laura's apartment and a portrait of her that hangs within. In life and now in her presumed death, Laura has been betrayed by her male admirers, Carpenter and Lydecker; it remains to be seen if McPherson will follow the same route. The detective is characterized as a political "Progressive," one who has undergone a period of reading and reflection after he received a leg wound as a result of a police battle with gangsters. Whether Mark has achieved sufficient maturity to appreciate Laura is cast into doubt by his initial behavior when he offers uninformed, flippant, and condescending judgments about her character. Moreover, in the course of the novel, each male is tagged with a phrase suggesting a failure in relation to manhood: Shelby is referred to as a baby and Lydecker as an old woman, and the once wounded McPherson walks with "the tortured gait of Oedipus."[45]

Carpenter is the simplest to parse: a handsome romantic illusion who had been two-timing Laura with Diane (even giving Diane the gold cigarette case that was a gift from Laura) and otherwise sponging off Laura's successful career as an advertising writer. After Laura reappears and he learns that Diane was the murder victim, Carpenter flatters himself by acting arrogantly certain that Laura was the killer and believes that she must have been motivated by irrepressible jealousy over the narcissistic hunk's affair with Diane. In a mock-heroic gesture, Carpenter declares that his manly responsibility is to lie to McPherson on Laura's behalf so as to afford her protection. When that strategy blows up in his face, he becomes worried that suspicion might fall on himself and quickly transforms into a witness for the state and finally an informer against Laura.

Lydecker is the more fascinating figure. He is largely modeled on Alexander Woollcott (1887–1943), a drama critic of caustic wit who was captivated by murder mysteries, host of a CBS radio show, author of a best seller, and perhaps the most quoted cultural commentator of his generation. Millions have seen Woollcott depicted as the radio wit Sheridan Whiteside in the 1939 play and 1942 film *The Man Who Came to Dinner*. Woollcott was also politically minded; a close friend of the pro-Soviet *New York Times* correspondent Walter Duranty (1884–1957), a now discredited journalist who provided a pro-Soviet slant on the 1932–33 famine in the Ukraine and the Moscow Purge Trials, as well as an intimate of Soviet foreign minister Maxim Litvinov.[46] In *Laura*, Lydecker imagines himself the designated heir to the Western literary tradition but is by the same token the embodiment of the cynicism underlying the capitalist commercialization of culture. Laura has been too easily swayed by others because her fear about "world conditions" has produced a sense of responsibility troubled by her own commercial career; the result is a "guilt complex."[47] There is an example of this in the novel regarding Diane Redfern, a Polish American proletarian who has changed her identity (her name was originally "Jennie Swobodo"). Laura's blind act of kindness facilitates a murder.[48] By taking critical distance from all this, now that she has come back from the "dead" and is assuming a new outlook apropos her prior beliefs and behavior, Laura is depicted as advancing to a state of maturity appropriate to the era of war and post-Depression.

The ingenious plot of *Laura*, which features an adored murder victim arriving from the grave only to be looked upon by the police as the possible murderer, accentuates the impression that the male protagonists are variously complicit in forms of necrophilia. In life, Carpenter and Lydecker sought to manage Laura for their own ends; the latter carried the desire for domination to the extreme of masculine rage by blowing off what he imagined to be her face with pellets from his phallic cane-and-gun device. When Laura comes back to New York City and the two men realize that she is not the murder victim, control is pursued even more fanatically. Carpenter, assuming that the police are accurate in suspecting Laura as the murderer, casts Laura in the role of jealous avenger of his affair with Diane, essentially a means of extricating himself from suspicion, and Lydecker is compulsively driven to make certain that Laura remains a corpse by attempting a repeat of his crime. When McPherson first comes on the scene to solve the case, he dismisses Laura as a bimbo, then falls steadily in love with the presumably dead woman, creating his own image of her character and appearance. For Carpenter and Lydecker, the ingredient of necrophilia is generated by their own poor self-esteem; the former is a ne'er-do-well, the latter grotesquely fat and impotent. The logic of their demand for total control guarantees there can be no rejection by the beloved.

McPherson, in contrast, transcends the necrophilia experienced alone in Laura's apartment; as he meets the real Laura, he comes to love the woman she actually is. His simplified image of her as a romantic icon is eradicated by his learning her version of the details of her relation to Carpenter and Lydecker, as well as by her obstinate behavior during the police investigation. As the novel progresses through a series of first-person narratives penned in sequence by Lydecker, Laura, and McPherson, the latter two are depicted as emerging from the traps of prewar gender ideology to a new kind of realism that might form the basis of a companionate marriage of mutual understanding. Such a reposition is reinforced by the novel's ingenuity in form; the return of the dead female is reflected in the startling appearance of Laura as one of the three main narrators of the novel. This proves an effective device for knocking off-balance the conventional male discourse of closure and linear momentum, one strongly present in the opening section narrated by Lydecker and suitable to the customs of the mystery genre. What works here is the powerful joining of social vision and formal strategies that express the displaced anxieties of the late 1930s. But Caspary's subsequent efforts at duplication failed as the clarity of social vision disintegrated.

In 1946, Caspary published *Stranger Than Truth*, also a blend of mystery and romance making use of multiple points of view. Its subject was a promising one for the postwar era. As in *The Big Clock*, *Stranger Than Truth* is a story of the culture industry that re-creates a memorable and high-ranking figure in the business. Bernarr Macfadden (1868–1955) was a physical culture fanatic who fashioned a network of magazines such as *Physical Culture*, *True Story*, *True Romance*, *Dream World*, and the *New York Graphic*. He is reimagined in the novel by Caspary as Noble Barnes, the messiah of self-help psychology. But *Stranger Than Truth* is neither aimed at the 1940s nor intended to interrogate a changing society; it revisits the 1920s and a minor personal experience when Caspary worked on Macfadden's *Dance* magazine. At that time, Caspary's assistant was Macfadden's daughter, Eleanor Macfadden, a woman dominated by her father's quack theories to the point where her health became endangered. She appears in the novel as Eleanor Barnes, the daughter of Noble Barnes, and suspects her publisher parent of murder and plagiarism.

In *Stranger Than Truth*, Caspary fails to achieve a blend of compelling structure and characterization to match the novelty of *Laura*. Her subsequent novels are frequently more effective for a vivid evocation of setting and sometimes an expert manipulation of tension. On occasion, Caspary's skill at characterization returned to the extent that one or two of her books after *Stranger Than Truth* developed a following as character studies. But the intricate plotting that marked the formal achievement of *Laura* evaded her for the next three decades. The writing of *Laura* had been energized by an emotional crisis that was nonetheless within a still workable social vision. *Laura* served as a means for steering clear of immediate political conflicts, and Caspary managed to relocate her concerns in the creative space afforded by genres of the bildungsroman and mystery novels. These were areas allowing the imagination to operate beyond the debates ranging around her, but the resulting novel nonetheless bore the imprint of the circumstances of its creation. The triumph of this variety of displacement is shown by the confidence, precision, and expertise of Caspary's disruptive narrative form.

It is awkward to set apart fiction of the 1930s and 1940s in terms of gender because novelists such as Caspary were still writing under the shadow of the usage, going back to the nineteenth century, by many literary critics of the expression "women's literature" as a pejorative term. Yet her novel adds to the up-to-date analysis that female patterns of living have produced a different point of view. A somewhat earlier novel by a Communist woman, Grace Lumkpin's *The Wedding* (1939), is a more classic feminist work in the sense that it confronts the powerlessness of those who are economically subordinated, trying to understand ostensible passivity. *Laura* is more in the modern vein in that Laura Hunt has achieved financial independence but not intellectual autonomy. Both novels address the victimization and betrayal of female protagonists in a social context with a vibrant grasp of the psychology of women aspiring to move from object to subject. They express the strength of the trend in the 1930s that inspired women to reach for forms of fiction aimed at a totalizing vision of the world, not to be satisfied with impressionistic immediacy. If fictions of the 1930s were goaded by feelings of linear notions of progress, movement, and hope, then the crisis in form that came to a head in the next decade might be understood as the reverse. It was the collective product of the new failure of the imagination rooted in the postwar mounting defeat of the 1930s social aspiration that had previously cultivated and fueled these earlier, more successful forms. The national imagination was changing.

Left writers were critics not just of society but of its premises. Herbst, Caspary, and their contemporaries could not develop new imaginative structures to fit the content of disintegrating visions. Under such conditions of the dead weight of uninspired literary strategies, a mechanical form may strangle content or squeeze it back into triviality. This might have been a pardonable eccentricity if not so widespread. *Laura*, earlier, escaped that fate. In the Depression catastrophe of the late 1930s, Caspary momentarily found a new vision of experience as well as its expression. She mingled fiction and autobiography to intensify emotion and forge compound literary strategies to newly dramatize female experience.

In *Laura*, women's consciousness puts on the fabulous forms of double and disruptive narratives before it can speak fully and openly. This is a novel superficially about a mysterious murder, but something more is being said about which we feel a profound frisson because it is masked behind the external verbal forms, communicating oblique messages underneath highly wrought structures. A decade later there would be compelling novels by and about women—Arnow's *The Dollmaker*, Page's *Daughter of the Hills*—but they rarely addressed feminist issues as did Caspary. What they provided instead was a steady, unromantic concentration on the immediate lived experience of working-class females, one reinforced in short fiction by writers such as Meridel Le Sueur and Irene Paull (1908–81). The 1940s labor of dissidence around gender and the attending mourning of the decline of social vision might have opened up new literary spaces to competing voices of a new feminism, one working against the painful legacy of fossilized Stalinist memories. But in a postwar era when "Rosie the Riveter" was being forced back into the kitchen, many women novelists had a will to perfection without a compelling unifying idea.

Chapter Four

The "Homintern" Reconsidered

BUTTERFLY FRIENDS

By 1951, much of the leadership of the Communist Party was convinced of the inescapability of a war between the Soviet Union and the United States. For that reason, instructions were sent from the Communist Party's national office to district organizers such as Junius Irving Scales (1920–2002), who supervised North and South Carolina, to interview each member during the annual registration. Scales's mandate was to seek out weak links who might compromise the Party if it was outlawed and its adherents required to go underground; he was told to interrogate members about their intimate affairs but write nothing down. One of the questions he was to ask was, "Are you either homosexual or bisexual?," presumably reflecting a concern that such individuals might be blackmailed by the FBI into becoming informers.[1]

Scales had long assumed that several of his young comrades were homosexual, but throughout the interview process, he was nonetheless taken aback by the sheer number of members who answered yes to his question about same-sex activity. These members were "young and old, men and women, Negro and white, married and single, workers and students." Among those who answered affirmatively were two of the Party's leading African American trade unionists, several outstanding student leaders, "and others exceptional in their ability and activity." When Scales followed up with personal visits, he encountered several members who expressed guilt that they were not heterosexual and who told him that they would make a "switch" in their choice of sexual partners. The loyalty to and trust in the Communist Party that Scales saw exhibited was sufficient to convince him that they would stand up to threats of blackmail about their sexual activities; he concluded that the Communist Party's security concerns were essentially a cover for sexual bigotry. Satisfied with his comrades' pledges of "discretion" in their behavior, Scales simply ignored the Party's directive to drop their membership, although his counterparts in other regions did not act similarly.[2]

This episode in Communist Party history suggests why obtaining a precise appraisal of the sexual orientation of participants in the postwar literary Left can be a convoluted affair. Secrecy about personal life and the Communist Party's complicity in homophobia immensely complicate the already daunting uncertainties about identifying a writer as "Communist" or "gay," let alone both. If the evolution of sexual radicalism in the United States is understood as occurring in three large waves—the turn-of-the-century sexual reform advocates, the lesbian and gay liberation movements in the 1960s, and the "queer" activist current of the 1990s—the decade of the postwar Consumers' Republic falls well between the cracks.[3] The Depression is considered an intermediary age of reaction against several decades of more visible gay activity when people were not as starkly divided into homosexuals and heterosexuals.[4] In the notoriously repressive 1940s and 1950s, there was an understandable unwillingness of individuals to take the risk of openly embracing a stigmatized, nonconformist sexual identity.

With both gays and lesbians, there is more often than not a lack of records that can be used to responsibly determine one's same-sex erotic orientation; often there are only speculations based upon one's appearance (such as hairstyle and apparel), marital status, or even rumors. Disagreement about definitions and terminology continues to impede a clear resolution of methodological challenges. What does a cultural historian do when a writer has destroyed all "compromising" sexual and political evidence, or when family members and friends of a deceased writer are engaged in what they believe to be posthumous protection of a writer's reputation by denying that he or she was a Communist or homosexual, or both?

Moreover, the Communist Party's policy since the 1930s had purportedly been to prohibit gay people from joining it, associating homosexuality with social decadence.[5] In *A Very Good Land to Fall With* (1987), a fictionalized autobiography in short scenes interspersed with pieces commenting on U.S. history, novelist John Sanford re-creates an emotional June 1945 reunion between himself and the gay left-wing Cherokee writer Lynn Riggs (1899–1954). It occurs at Sanford's home in Encino, a hilly neighborhood of Los Angeles, where Sanford and his wife, the screenwriter Marguerite Roberts (1905–89), both Communists at the time, were living. Riggs, an independent radical poet and playwright occasionally employed as a screenwriter for Paramount and Universal, indicates that he, too, wishes to be a member of the Party.

Sanford feels compelled to reveal to Riggs, in words that would haunt him for the next forty years, that he was interrogated about their friendship at the time he was first recruited to the Communist Party. A Party leader had confided: "We've been debating about you for some time. We'd like you to be one of us, but, frankly, we're leery of the company you keep.... Specifically, Lynn Riggs and his butterfly friends." When Sanford protested this intrusion into Riggs's personal life, he was told that "the butterfly preference" opened a person to a threat of public exposure and he or she might "cave in and turn informer." "I was considered a risk, then," Riggs replies. "Along with—I'm sorry to say—drunks and addicts," answers Sanford. Riggs responds, "But, John, suppose I hoped to find another preference." Sanford gloomily says that any effort to change the state of affairs would be futile. After an affectionate farewell, the two men never see each other again.[6]

Nevertheless, the rule for recruitment to the Communist Party that Sanford revealed was not in writing and exceptions were made, especially if the individuals could "pass" as heterosexuals or did not draw attention to themselves (for example, by being arrested) or if they were famous and of unquestionable political zeal, as was the composer Marc Blitzstein (born Marcus Blitzstein, 1905–64).[7] In some instances, it is unclear whether a gay pro-Communist was formally prohibited from joining the Party or decided on his or her own that membership would be a bad idea. Irwin Silber (1925–2010), a former Communist and editor of the left-wing folk music magazine *Sing Out!*, recalled that the folksinger and detective fiction writer Lee Hays (1914–81) was a non-Party Communist but is not sure why Hays never joined: "He may have stayed out—or been kept out—because of his homosexuality."[8] The situation seems similar with playwright and stage director Arthur Laurents (1918–2011), who reworked many of his friendships and political experiences into the film *The Way We Were* (1973; originally a novel, 1972). In his autobiography, *Original Story By: A Memoir of Broadway and Hollywood* (2000), Laurents says that, as a "Jew and a homosexual," he felt drawn to left-wing activists who were "friends to the outsider," but he had one difficulty: "Much as I wanted these leftist friends . . . I was uncomfortable with them because I had to be deceitful; I had to be deceitful because the Communist Party didn't sanction homosexuality. . . . I pretended to be straight and made the problem mine, not theirs."[9] Other gay Jewish cultural figures, such as Lincoln Kirstein (1907–96), Leonard Bernstein (1918–90), and Aaron Copland (1900–1990) were similarly pulled toward the Communist Party but appear not to have taken the step of joining it, although Jerome Robbins (born Jerome Wilson Rabinowitz, 1918–98) acknowledged his membership from 1943 to 1947.[10]

With discretion valued about politics and sexuality, pro-Communists—especially those in the public eye such as teachers, journalists, and writers—remained quiet about their sexuality or confided only in trustworthy friends.

A rare document is by Arthur D. Kahn (b. 1920), the Peace Crusade organizer and Progressive Party activist, who was also the Communist author of the novel *Brownstone* (1953), about urban loneliness in a 1950s multiethnic Manhattan rooming house. Late in life he published an autobiography where he described his decision to reveal his homosexual activities to his Communist friend, the journalist and photographer Albert E. Kahn (1912–79). Sympathetic but naive, Albert (an older mentor but no relation) assured Arthur that his "problem" would disappear once he met the "right" woman.[11] Correspondingly, the pro-Communist poet T. C. Wilson left personal correspondence describing his own same-sex attractions that indicates that he had taken the poetically and politically allied Horace Gregory into confidence.[12]

In the context of the late 1940s and 1950s, a writer who might today be regarded as pro-Communist and gay was more likely to use the term "progressive writer" rather than define himself or herself on the basis of an explicit political ideology or sexual activity. Moreover, it was not uncommon for gay people to be married to partners of the opposite sex; this was true in the cases of male homosexual, bisexual, and lesbian Communist Party members such as Marc Blitzstein, Willard Maas (1911–71), Harry Hay (1910–2004), Paul Peters (born Harbor Allen, dates unknown), Paul and Jane Bowles (born Jane Sydney Auer, 1917–73), and Lorraine Hansberry (1930–65).[13] Unlike the twenty-first century, when one is not particularly surprised to read in the *New York Times* about the lives of married bisexuals, each partner with his or her own same-sex lovers, this mode of relationship before the 1960s was usually acknowledged only to the couple's closest friends.[14] Yet the explanation for the absence of people overtly embracing gay identities is not due exclusively to prudence in the face of compulsory heterosexuality and anti-Communist repression. Left writers were multifaceted personalities alert to the instability of any identity, bristling at the notion of being put in boxes by others and often attuned to the complexity of their own simultaneous embeddedness in class, sexual, ethnic, and racial associations.

The expression "homintern" was quietly circulated on the eve of World War II. The reference was to a milieu of gay men that was at one time pro-Communist, and the term was intended to suggest a humorous parallel between international networks of homosexuals and of Communists.[15] In contrast, the term "invisibility" is frequently associated with lesbians throughout all postwar decades, suggesting that it can be particularly difficult to know how to address their lives. To be sure, there were scores of intimate relationships among literary women in and around the Communist movement, and often there was a closeness recalling nineteenth-century modes of female companionship between well-regarded unmarried women. A number of pro-

Communist women exchanged letters expressing love, now and then using romantic language. Several women lived together but with no public indication of an erotic element in their relationship; it is simply not known whether their associations crossed the border of genital sexuality.[16] But some of their manifestations of love of each other were probably not dissimilar from what many scholars of recent decades describe as lesbianism.

One well-known female couple on the literary Left was made up of Columbia University professor Dorothy Brewster (1883–1979), a Virginia Woolf specialist, and New York University professor Lillian Barnard Gilkes (1900–1976), a Stephen Crane specialist. They often lived and traveled together, and some correspondents addressed letters to them jointly. But the subject of naming their sexuality is hard to get hold of. In autobiographical statements and letters, Brewster and Gilkes revealed nothing about physical intimacy in their lives. They wrote on independent women—Brewster's *Virginia Woolf's London* (1959) is a classic study, and Gilkes's *Cora Crane: A Biography of Mrs. Stephen Crane* (1960) is the definitive life history—but avoid matters such as same-sex relations. They may well have considered themselves different from the heterosexual majority but in their day could honestly reject popular "lesbian" representations as being unlike themselves.

The indistinct political documentation regarding Brewster and Gilkes mirrors the sexual ambiguity. Public records provide evidence of nearly four decades of sympathy for the Soviet Union and association with Communist Party–led cultural activities, but there are no elaborations of their beliefs that categorically classify them as "Communists" as opposed to "Progressives." Both were friends and correspondents with accused Soviet agent Martha Dodd (1908–90), a capable novelist who was later on the target of salacious demolition jobs, as well as New York University professor Margaret Schlauch, who was definitely a Communist and was perhaps the hub of their circle of closest friends.[17] Schlauch, in turn, was the mentor of Annette T. Rubinstein, a single woman living with her mother who had intimate female friendships. Rubinstein was a secret Communist Party member until 1952 and a close Party ally for another eight years. Yet women intellectuals in the Communist Party were encouraged to be tough, independent of conventions, and sexually liberated from double standards. This culture may have provided a safe space for lesbians, but the specifics of a lesbian presence in the Communist movement remains awkward to recognize and address.

A few literary women with pro-Communist associations have directly or indirectly identified themselves as lesbians: Rebecca Pitts (1905–83), Naomi Replansky (b. 1918), Audre Lorde (1934–92), Lorraine Hansberry, Jane Bowles, Eleanor Flexner (1908–95), Patricia Highsmith, and Jo Sinclair.[18] Pitts, in par-

Lillian Barnard Gilkes (shown here) and her close friend Dorothy Brewster were literature teachers at New York University and Columbia University. Gilkes was a specialist on Stephen Crane and Brewster on Virginia Woolf. Both had long associations with the Communist movement. (Courtesy of Syracuse University Library)

Naomi Replansky started publishing poetry in New York City in the late 1930s and was associated with the Communist movement into the early Cold War. (Courtesy of Naomi Replansky)

ticular, left some documentation of her life as both a literary Communist and lesbian, much of it through letters to Josephine Herbst.[19] Pitts also spent the last six years of her life preparing a volume of elegantly melancholy verse, *Brief Authority: Fragments of One Woman's Testament* (1986). This is a sophisticated but quietly agonized collection showing a talent for arresting formulations that evidence the traces of Communist literary modernism, marks left by the postwar expulsion and exile of one woman from the left-wing cultural center and the certainties of positivist realism.

Pitts was born in Indianapolis to Quakers. She was the older sister of Robert Franklin Pitts (1908–77), eventually a world authority on renal physiology. As can be seen by the medical references that suffuse her poetry, she shared many of his scientific proclivities. Their parents, John and Estelle Pitts, educated the children in the puritan virtues of industry and careful planning, but only Robert took to it. From a young age, Rebecca was conscious of being "different," mainly in the sense of resisting her parents' notion that her life should be focused on marriage and children. Instead, she tenaciously clung to the idea of becoming a writer and was attracted to Communism by age twenty-five.[20] Pitts was also fascinated by Henry James and graduated from the University of Chicago in 1930 with an M.A. degree and wrote a thesis on characters in James's work.[21] Pitts promptly became active in the John Reed Club in Chicago. She then returned to her family in Indianapolis, where she threw herself into the local John Reed Club and helped to edit its journal, *Midland Left*.

In 1935, Pitts was present at the founding Congress of the League of American Writers and was engaged in publishing a series of significant essays on women for the *New Masses* between 1934 and 1936.[22] In the middle of this productive period, the summer of 1935, Pitts had an affair with Richard Wright.[23] She had included his poem "Rise and Live" in the January–February 1935 issue of *Midland Left* and planned to publish selections of his prose until it was determined that the magazine would be terminated with the Party turn to the Popular Front. Pitts probably influenced Wright to give special importance in his thinking to what Communists called the "Woman Question," a subject that preoccupied Wright, although he rarely addressed it with success.[24] Pitts then spent three years writing and editing the *Federal Writers Project Guidebook: A Guide to the Hoosier State* (1941), after which she temporarily relocated to Washington, D.C., seeking national employment with the WPA. Research into the Indiana Writers Project shows that as regional editor, she was the outstanding thinker, writer, and organizer.[25]

Pitts next moved to New York City, where she aimed to become a freelance writer. She briefly worked as an editor for the antifascist *Decision Magazine* (1941–42), associating with the internationalist literary group surrounding the publication—Klaus Mann (1906–49), Carson McCullers, Muriel Rukeyser, and Horace Gregory. However, after serving as managing editor for an issue, she and Rukeyser staged a walkout over administrative and manuscript selection issues. Pitts then reviewed for the *New York Times* and *New Republic*, edited for Doubleday Doran, wrote some documentary film scripts, and was employed by Pearl Buck's East and West Association. She befriended novelist Somerset Maugham, and a manuscript of her own, called "The Valley of Decision," apparently a study of art and democracy, was announced but never appeared. In 1943, she was invited for the first of several visits to Yaddo writers' community, where the untamed personal behavior of herself and Carson McCullers scandalized novelist Katherine Anne Porter.[26]

In the fall of 1944, Pitts was living in Bucks County, Pennsylvania, at the rambling home of one of her lovers, Josephine Herbst, but soon had to return to Indianapolis due to family illness. In 1946, Pitts landed a position on the English faculty of Butler University, which her brother had attended, but in 1948 she was accused of being a Communist by a fellow member of the English department and fired.[27] After a few years of misery, she was engaged as a lecturer at a small-town extension of Purdue University. In 1955,

Rebecca Pitts in 1925. An ardent Communist in the 1930s and 1940s, Pitts published noteworthy essays on the status of women and traveled in Left literary circles throughout the World War II years. During the Cold War she taught literature in Indianapolis, publishing essays on religion and existentialism. (Courtesy of Annette T. Rubinstein)

Pitts was appointed to a part-time post at Indiana University's Extension University, teaching as well at Indiana University–Purdue University Indianapolis. She published in literary journals, on subjects from Shakespeare to Jean-Paul Sartre, and assisted her scholarly friend Allegra Stewart in writing *Gertrude Stein and the Present* (1967). Muriel Rukeyser occasionally visited, and Josephine Herbst kept in touch by mail. Pitts retired in 1976 as an associate professor.

In the 1950s, Pitts took her political persecution personally and associated it with her sense of sexual difference. For a period, she became profoundly religious in an existentialist mode, taking a journey inward guided by the writings of Martin Buber. She stayed essentially underground in Indianapolis, still seething about injustice but glad to be away from people whom she felt had betrayed the ideals once shared. She was mostly teaching six days a week and lived in relative poverty while taking care of her ailing father. Gradually she became loved and respected by women intellectuals in the city, and her university profile blossomed as well. In 1973, she partnered with the philosopher Lawrence Lampert to found *Genesis*, a student literary magazine. She also founded her department's English Club and the Accolade Honorary Society for women. Posthumously, the Department of English would offer two annual awards in her honor, the Rebecca Pitts Poetry and Fiction Award and the Rebecca E. Pitts Scholarship.

When the younger generation of female students brought feminism to Indianapolis in the 1970s, Pitts passionately became involved. She helped start *Womankind*, a feminist journal, where she played an irreplaceable part due to her prior experience in producing left-wing literary magazines. Her intellectual path expanded yet again. She had started in the Depression with the *New Masses* publication of "Something to Believe In," a 1934 testament of Marxist faith, and moved on after World War II to "Prayer and the Incarnation," a 1953 meditation in a theological journal on the possibilities of religion. Now she published "Are We 'Our Own Worst Enemies'?," a manifesto in *Womankind*.[28] Pitts's feminist reawakening inspired her to outline an entire book on radical feminism, but then she was diagnosed with terminal cancer. Six months before her death, Pitts spoke at a public library on women poets; she adapted the title from Emily Dickinson, "A Loaded Gun."[29]

Upon retirement from teaching at Butler University, Pitts had destroyed all of her previous writings. Unable or unwilling to present a sequential or historical body of her work to document the stages of her belief, she chose instead to bequeath a group of poems that used flashing insights to reconstruct her life. These would offer what she called an "unfinished interpretation" of "an invisible text."[30] The collection that appeared posthumously, *Brief Au-*

thority: Fragments of One Woman's Testament, recasts her utopian hopes in abstract language such as the following:

There were roads not taken
not this unending
ever-widening asphalt
but roads wandering away from
all this desert
into a green freedom
half wilderness[31]

The volume, moving but minor, is an offshoot of a Communist literary modernism to which she never gave adequate expression. Pitts retrospectively reflects on the "dream of meaning" in the 1930s and watches the crumbling of the "House of the Real" in the 1940s.[32] Her feminist-environmentalist and to some extent mystical meditations on the contingencies of experience combine with coded references to her intimate life that she aptly calls her "haunted perspectives."[33] She had also organized a citywide feminist study group in Indianapolis that bore a striking resemblance to the old John Reed Club; this association continued for fifteen years after her passing, and the memory of Pitts reverberated much longer among the young women of the city inspired by the bridge she built between the 1930s and the new feminism.[34]

THE CLOSETED PAST

Some future Leftists, homosexual and heterosexual, wrote novels with homosexual characters distinctly prior to any Marxist commitments. In 1933, Parker Tyler (born Harrison Parker Tyler, 1924–96) coauthored with Charles Henri Ford (1913–2002) *The Young and the Evil*. This was a humorous novel about gay life in New York City in the early 1930s that shows the stylistic influence of Gertrude Stein and Djuna Barnes. Tyler was not visibly involved in any Left activities until 1938, when he began contributing to the Socialist Workers Party's magazine *New International* and associating with cultural figures in the *Partisan Review* circle.[35] From 1940 to 1947, he was assistant editor of *View*, a Left surrealist-influenced magazine, and then wrote reviews for the socialist *New Leader* and books of film criticism, including the classic *Screening the Sexes* (1972).

In 1934, Lew Levenson (1898–?), subsequently an influential staff writer for the *Daily Worker*, published the outrageously homophobic *Butterfly Man*, about a high school athlete who succumbs to homosexual decadence and dies a drunken death.[36] Levenson was born in Rochester, New York, the son of a lady's barber, and attended the Columbia University School of Journalism. Fluent in French, he joined the U.S. Army during World War I as an interpreter, then married and settled in New York City, where he was employed as the press agent for Rogers and Hart musicals produced at the Vanderbilt Theater. In 1932, he was hired by Columbia Pictures and moved his growing family to the West Coast; they were living in Laguna Beach when his job ran out in 1934. Levenson was then drawn to the Communist Party and became active in organizing Mexican and Mexican American beet workers in the Imperial Valley and contributing to the *Nation*.[37]

In 1936, Levenson returned to New York City to write for the *Daily Worker*, where he was regarded as a journalistic whiz.[38] Soon, however, he somewhat mysteriously became deputy head of the local Federal Writers Project, only to be quickly named as a Communist Party member by an informer during the hearings of the House Appropriations Subcommittee investigating the administration of federal relief.[39] To evade a subpoena, he hid out in the home of a sportswriter friend in New Hampshire until the situation calmed down. After that experience, Levenson became a sportswriter himself, often writing under other names, at first publishing in *Collier's*, the *Saturday Evening Post*, and the *Sports Digest*, then writing a radio show for baseball star Frankie Frisch and a biography of Roy Campanella.[40]

Unlike Parker and Levenson, who moved left, some novelists dropped their radical associations just prior to or soon after publishing novels on gay and lesbian themes and later appear to be apolitical. Gale Wilhelm (1901–91), a contributor of poetry to the *New Masses* when it was in its early "proletarian" phase, subsequently published two lesbian-themed novels, *We Too Are Drifting* (1935) and *Torchlight to Valhalla* (1938), as well as several ostensibly heterosexual-themed works.[41] An even more prolific writer was Myron Brinig (1900–1991), who traveled in radical circles in the 1920s and early 1930s, publishing two substantial prolabor novels, the successful *Wide Open Town* (1931) and *The Sun Sets in the West* (1935). In 1932, Brinig wrote a novel about two gay sons, *This Man Is My Brother*, a sequel to his earlier Jewish American immigrant classic, *Singerman* (1929). Brinig was publically closeted but bequeathed an archive of personal letters detailing his gay life. He published a total of twenty-one novels, most of which avoided direct references to homosexuality, and there is no evidence of his having left-wing connections after the mid-1930s.[42]

The pattern of launching oneself as a Leftist around Communism but dropping associations when addressing gay themes was to some extent replicated in the later careers of John Cheever (1912–82), Carson McCullers, Paul Bowles,

Jane Bowles, Stuart Engstrand (1904–55), Truman Capote (1924–84), and of course James Baldwin (1924–87).[43] Paul Bowles was dissimilar in having had a twelve-year association with Communism prior to his joining the Communist Party in the fall of 1938, a year before the Hitler-Stalin Pact, and resigning from the Communist Party in the spring of 1941, when the Party called upon the United States to join the war effort.[44] Jane was a member of the Party for the same period, although it appears that she did not have Paul's earlier political background. By going into permanent exile in Tangiers in 1947 (Paul) and 1948 (Jane), the Bowleses seemed to have stepped outside the Cold War, thereby avoiding any subsequent need to affirm or repudiate their politics.[45]

The other writers mentioned primarily had youthful associations with Communism, its cursory appeal becoming merely residual after the United States entered World War II. The postwar "Lavender Scare" made an acknowledgment of any linkage to or between sexual and political nonconformity even less alluring than it had been before.[46] As a consequence, these writers' connections to pro-Communism have all but vanished from historical memory. John Cheever, for example, was mainly sympathetic to Communism during the Depression, when he got his start contributing to little proletarian magazines such as the *Left* (in which a story called "Fall River" appeared in August 1931), working for the WPA, and associating with pro-Communist writers and artists. His literary agent, beginning in 1935 and enduring into the 1940s, was the Communist Maxim Lieber (1897–1993), who led a secret life as a collaborator of Whittaker Chambers's in espionage. Cheever married Lieber's secretary, Mary Winternitz, whom he met at Lieber's office in November 1939 and who retained her association with Lieber into the war years.[47] Carson McCullers declared her Communist commitment when initially submitting her fiction to *Story* magazine in December 1936. In 1940–41, she was part of a left-wing bohemian group living at 7 Middagh Street in Brooklyn, a brownstone that served as a communal living quarters as well as a salon.[48] Other radical residents included George Davis, Gypsy Rose Lee, Paul and Jane Bowles, W. H. Auden, and the composer Benjamin Britten.

The most unexpected association of gay writer with the Communist Left is that of Truman Capote, who regularly contributed a humor column, "Kaleidoscope," to *Reader's Scope*, from its launch in early 1944 until mid-1946. The magazine, combining reprints and fresh material, prominently featured Communist writers such as Howard Fast, Ella Winter, Dyson Carter, Albert E. Kahn, William S. Cunningham, Helen Kay, Lew Levenson (writing as Charles Dexter), and Earl Browder, as well as many others from the Communist Party milieu such as Harry F. Ward, Franz Weiskopf, Johannes Steel,

Norman Corwin, and Philip Van Doren Stern. The editor of *Reader's Scope*, Leverett ("Lev") Gleason (1898–1971), was a famed publisher of comics such as *Daredevil* in the 1940s and early 1950s.[49]

Not much is known about Capote's political thinking in 1944, but in June 1946 he began a romantic relationship with Smith College professor Newton Arvin, to whom *Other Voices, Other Rooms* (1948) was dedicated. If Capote had been gravitating toward the Left, or was simply naive about the political orientation of a magazine that offered to pay for his writing, it is possible that Arvin, a pro-Communist in the 1930s but increasingly disenchanted in the 1940s, persuaded him to keep his distance.[50] Arvin was too political to remain silent on the subject with his lover. On the other hand, Capote may have left *Reader's Scope* simply because his career as a fiction writer began to take off in the spring of 1945 with the publication of his short story "Miriam" and an invitation to stay at the Yaddo the following year. A more durable link with Lev Gleason was perhaps evidenced in Capote's choice of subject and approach in his nonfiction novel *In Cold Blood* (1966). One suspects the influence of Gleason's long-running "true crime" comic series, *Crime Does Not Pay* (1942–55), whose artists and writers sometimes met with criminals to obtain material.

A disquieting case among writers moving from a Left milieu to writing on gay subject matter is the rise and fall of Stuart Engstrand, a mass market author whose pulp paperback sales during the Cold War were phenomenal and whose early novels won high praise in the mainstream press. Originally an activist in the John Reed Club chapter in Chicago, a regular participant in the Marxist literary salon of novelist Lawrence Lipton (1898–1975), and an associate of Communists who worked on the Federal Writers Project and in the League of American Writers, Engstrand seems to have quietly discarded his organized Leftist interests after 1938.[51] In 1935, with a reputation as a "hypersensitive person whose life was deeply involved with his fiction writing," he married another aspiring novelist, Sophia Belzer (1908–?), and quickly produced a series of radical novels with proletarian, utopian socialist, and antifascist themes: *The Invaders* (1937), *They Sought for Paradise* (1939), and *Spring 1940* (1941).[52] The first was hailed by a leading Communist critic, Edwin Berry Burgum, as "the finest proletarian novel that has yet appeared in the United States," while *Spring 1940* was described as comparable to Steinbeck's *The Moon Is Down*.[53]

Then came a mysterious hiatus during which Engstrand and his family moved to Los Angeles. There Engstrand immersed himself in the work of psychologist Wilhelm Stekel (1868–1940), and his career took a dramatic turn with the publication of *The Sling and the Arrow* (1947), a notorious and controversial best seller that shot through five printings. Although it was at the time treated as an appraisal of the plight of a homosexual, the novel is more accurately a misguided Freudian study in transsexuality.[54] The protagonist, Herbert Dawes, is a fashion designer who has suppressed his desire to be female since childhood. In a benevolent review in the *New Leader*, James Baldwin, expressing concerns that may have contributed to *Giovanni's Room* (1956), identified personally with Dawes's "terrible sense of guilt," "the compulsion to be accepted," and "his helplessness in the face of the war within him." Baldwin observed that "the contemporary sexual attitudes constitute a rock against which many of us flounder all our lives long" and complained that Engstrand had erred in accepting the popular opinions. *The Sling and the Arrow* should have presented "a personality" and "not an abnormal psychology, not a study of human helplessness, but a carefully embroidered case history."[55]

Engstrand's subsequent fiction continued to address psychosexual themes, often depicting a male with an inadequate sense of his masculinity, and included *Beyond the Forest* (1948, which was the basis for a 1949 movie starring Bette Davis), *Son of the Giant* (1950), *Husband in the House* (1952), *The Scattered Seed* (1953), and *More Deaths Than One* (1955). Engstrand's last novel appeared shortly before his suicide, committed by walking into MacArthur Park Lake, earning him a chapter in Mark Seinfelt's *Final Drafts: Suicides of World-Famous Authors* (1999). The death swayed at least one scholar of gay fiction to the view that Engstrand suffered "anguish over a failed marriage and latent homosexuality."[56]

James Baldwin's 1947 *New Leader* commentary on Engstrand is usually cited as an early moment in Baldwin's socialist and gay consciousness. But it should be coupled with a never-mentioned poem that Baldwin published a year earlier, "Nursery Rhyme," featured in a quartet of verses by men that appeared in the 21 May 1946 issue of the *New Masses*. Baldwin's vision of a new world is depicted as the rising of a "sunless dawn." "Nursery Rhyme" concludes:

These days are watching the world grow sick
The dead lie rotting. Come, Jack, pick
Your way past the dead, the dead lie thick.
Jack be nimble, Jack be quick.[57]

The poem, paired with a cartoon depicting the horrors of "Free Enterprise" on the facing page, seems to call for forbearance in the face of capitalist misery until the inevitable moment of revolution.

Baldwin's poem appears in an issue of the *New Masses* that reflects the post-

Browder Leftist lurch; the cover article is titled "Why I Joined the Communist Party," and the effects of the controversy about Albert Maltz's challenge to the slogan "Art as a Weapon" are registered by the precipitous disappearance from the *New Masses* editorial board of two of Maltz's sympathizers, Isidor Schneider and Arthur Miller.[58] Alongside Baldwin's poem is one by Ray Smith (1915–94), who had recently written *No Eclipse* (1945) and was a frequent contributor to the Communist press. Smith's poem "The Journey" also seems a paean to a socialist future.[59] Following Smith, Bernard Evslin (1922–93), later a playwright, screenwriter, and authority on mythology, contributed "Renegade," a faithful reiteration of the Communist Party's view of sellouts. The fourth poem is by Paul Eluard (1895–1952), a founder of the surrealist movement in France who joined the Communist Party and became a celebrated admirer of Stalin; his "Pardon Peddlers" demands full vengeance against the defeated Nazis.

Biographical research about James Baldwin in the mid-1940s is murky, usually emphasizing in some hazy way his connection with members of the Young People's Socialist League (at that time affiliated to the Socialist Party), Trotskyists such as Stan Weir (1921–2001), and the editors of the anti-Stalinist magazines *New Leader*, *Partisan Review*, and *Commentary*.[60] These associations of Baldwin's, however, were toward the end of the decade; Baldwin did not appear in the *New Leader* until the spring of 1947. Ten years earlier, as a teenager living in Harlem, Baldwin had marched in a May Day parade as a convinced fellow traveler of the Communist Party and was a student of recognized talent in a course on the short story taught by the Communist Mary Elting at the Writers' School of the League of American Writers.[61] In 1945, a quartet of Baldwin's close friends, who dreamed of forming a commune, included Saville Sax (1924–80), later accused of being a Soviet agent at the very time that he knew Baldwin.[62]

Baldwin's radicalism was unconventional but Far Left. Stan Weir, then a member of the (Trotskyist) Workers Party, recalled in a memoir that three years earlier, in 1942, he had felt sufficiently at ease with Baldwin's politics to ask him to join his Leninist group, the Workers Party, a recent (1940) breakaway from the official Trotskyist movement, based on their shared revolutionary opposition to U.S. intervention in World War II.[63] It appears, then, that for much of the 1940s, Baldwin was still comfortable roaming around various currents of Marxism, although he increasingly concentrated on gaining acceptance of his sexual orientation. He would feel sufficiently liberated to address the matter in the pages of the *New Leader*. No political novice in 1946, he was in some sense an anti-Stalinist, yet the Communist Party was insufficiently toxic in his eyes to preclude him from appearing in the pages of the *New Masses*.

What about the political and erotic dimensions of the poem itself? Do its lyrics trace some of the ways in which same-sex desire and unconventional notions of masculinity and femininity in general have been manifest in individuals who do not conform to the heterosexual norms of their time? What apparently escaped the *New Masses* editors, a wary and watchful bunch who ordinarily had sharp eyes for heresy, is Baldwin's peculiar use of "Until sunless dawn arise" as the symbol of the revolutionary moment for which one waits.[64] While the phrase at first glance recalls left-wing expressions such as a "Red Dawn" and "Arise Ye Workers," one wonders how the absence of the sun (which customarily connotes enlightenment) at dawn signifies a Marxist vision of revolution. "Sunless dawn" seems more probably an anti-Communist representation of a revolution betrayed, which produced dark totalitarianism. But the phrase "sunless dawn" has its likely source in a famous essay in *Studies in the History of the Renaissance* (1873) by Walter Pater, a critic usually regarded as one who expressed a homosexual sensibility in his aesthetics. Pater's reference is to a work by the Florentine artist Sandro Botticelli, whose homosexuality had come to controversial attention of art history specialists in the 1930s. There is evidence that Baldwin may have been introduced to both Botticelli and Pater by the gay African American painter Beauford Delaney (1901–79), whom Baldwin had met in 1940; Baldwin specifically recalled that Delaney taught him about the role of light in painting and that it was Delaney who "caused me to begin to see."[65]

Pater applies the term "sunless dawn" to Botticelli's painting of Venus rising from the sea, conceiving the goddess of pleasure as radiating a sadness due to the great erotic power she holds over the lives of humanity. Pater describes the "cold light" of the painting as a "sunless dawn" that permits a superior vision, one that he associates with the Greek temper and Hellenic spirit. In Baldwin's poem, the "sunless dawn" is positioned as an emblem of hope for a postrevolutionary world, but if associated with Pater's rendering of Botticelli's Venus, it brings to mind much more; sexuality may be liberated from its ruling-class chains, but the wisdom of experience reminds one that other sources of despair reside in the unpredictable and sometimes overwhelming powers of desire. Baldwin's imagery also re-creates something of Pater's notion of the dreariness of the modern city ("Snatch at the tabloid, catch the train, / Reel through the infinite inane, / Silence the roaring brain").[66] Other metaphors and similes in "Nursery Rhyme" may also be read autobiographically, such as the censorious father who treats the poet like a "cripple" and the misery of the poet trapped in a dying world where he is forced to "stare at the wormwood in the cup / And drink it up." Yet "Sunless Dawn," which plausibly expresses the tensions of being gay in a straight society, was published in the *New Masses* as an ostensibly asexual radical poem.

THE DOUBLE LIFE OF HARRY DANA

Among pro-Communist literary academics of the era, some were secretive about their homosexuality, such as Newton Arvin, but others were less cautious, as was F. O. Matthiessen.[67] At least one Marxist critic with impeccable Harvard University credentials was for four decades hounded as being gay and a Communist, both of which were true.[68] Henry Wadsworth Longfellow Dana Jr. (1881–1950), called Harry, had the personality of a thoroughgoing dissenter, although his writings were never read, analyzed, or remembered as part of a gay tradition. Harry was even arrested on a "morals charge" — a euphemism for suspected homosexual activity — in Boston in 1935, an event that generated unwanted publicity in national newspapers such as the *New York Times*.[69] But the harassment failed to terminate Dana's stature as a leading fellow traveler of the Communist Party. Well-known by the mid-1930s as an authoritative and prolific critic of Soviet theater, Dana was doubly famous due to his family history and his role in maintaining ancestral archives; he was the grandson of both the nineteenth-century poet Henry Wadsworth Longfellow and the novelist Richard Henry Dana (author of the 1840 classic *Two Years Before the Mast*). Dana was also honored for his martyrdom as a victim of political repression in World War I when he had been fired at Columbia University.[70]

Perhaps in an unintentional double entendre, the law professor and first amendment scholar Zechariah Chafe began his obituary of Dana for a Harvard University class report as follows: "The best word describing Harry as boy and young man is 'gay.'"[71] Born in Boston, Dana received his B.S., M.A., and Ph.D. from Harvard, having written a dissertation titled "Medieval Visions of the Other World." As a youth, Dana's appearance was remarkable for his keen blue eyes and curly light hair. After several years traveling in Europe, Dana became an instructor in English and comparative literature at Columbia University in 1912. Two years later, having witnessed massive antiwar protests in Berlin, Paris, and London, Dana began to devote himself to antimilitarist activities at Columbia. Although Dana was promoted to assistant professor in June 1917, Columbia University president Nicholas Murray Butler gave his approval for an investigation of a pacifist society that Dana had helped organize. No violations of the law or specific charges were filed, but Dana was

Henry Wadsworth Longfellow Dana, Communist fellow traveler and authority on drama in the Soviet Union, dressed as a Cossack on the porch of the Longfellow home in Cambridge, Massachusetts. (Courtesy National Park Service, Longfellow National Historic Site)

ordered to resign. After refusing to do so, he was dismissed. Columbia University professor of history Charles A. Beard resigned his own position in an act of solidarity.[72]

Dana's political activities continued to escalate, taking on an increasingly socialist and then Communist character. After his dismissal from Columbia, he gave lectures at the Rand School of Social Sciences on social forces in literature and civilizations at war, and became a leader of the Intercollegiate Socialist Society and an editor of the *Socialist Review*. He then devoted himself to working-class education and drafted a proposal for a labor college in Boston, where he later taught literature and became a charter member of the Greater Boston Federation of Teachers. His support for the anarchists Sacco and Vanzetti was so intense that he visited Vanzetti's family in Italy and remained in correspondence with Vanzetti until he was executed. During that time, when Dana was in his late thirties, with a strong teaching background but a still undistinguished scholarly record, he moved permanently back to his Cambridge residence and settled into a suite of rooms in the historic family home, known as Longfellow House. Recalled for his humor and good nature, Dana was described in Zechariah Chafe's obituary as "an off-horse, but being perpetually out of harness he sometimes got among queer companions and into bad trouble." What he did not say was that Dana was ridiculed behind his back by Leftists as well as others for his allegedly fussy, effeminate behavior. As he aged, he began to resemble the comedian Jack Benny and was sometimes called "Mrs. Dana."[73]

Dana was a perpetual news story. After making headlines with his Columbia dismissal, he attracted notoriety again in 1922 when he was cut out of the will of his father's brother because of his socialist activities.[74] He also seemed to be embattled within the Left. Correspondence in November 1925 indicates that Dana had been removed from the executive committee of the Workers Education Bureau, a subcommittee of the radical American Fund for Public Service. Dana protested to civil liberties activist Roger Baldwin (1884–1981) that workers' education is "the cause to which I am devoting all my active work," describing himself as "one without a country, without a party, and rapidly becoming almost without a friend." He also urged more tolerance toward the Soviet Union.[75] In the meantime, he continued to live a double life, having been attracted to a gay underground culture during his Paris years; his personal papers contain numerous love letters from men, evidence of a long-term affair with a Yale professor, many blackmail threats, and a full-frontal photograph of himself in the nude.[76] John Cheever habitually told an anecdote about when in the mid-1930s Dana invited him to a theater performance and then a lavish dinner at the Longfellow mansion (sometimes called

"Craigie Castle"), after which the fifty-year-old man disrobed and propositioned him.[77]

Dana's growing association with the Communist movement is evidenced by a 1921 letter to him from J. Louis Engdahl, of the Workers Council of the United States, asking for his help in establishing the Workers Party National Convention, intended to unify all elements who accepted the leadership of the Third International.[78] In June 1926, Dana received a letter from Communist Party organizer Bert Miller (a pseudonym for Benjamin Mandel, later an infamous informer) asking to chat with him about working to bring about a labor party meeting.[79] His correspondence with Communist leader James P. Cannon documents Dana's active involvement in supporting the International Labor Defense in the region.[80] By 1933, he received a letter requesting that he officially join the Communist Party unless he had already made an arrangement "with those in higher authority" to pay special dues, or if he thought he could be more effective outside the Party. The letter stated that the decision was up to Dana, but it recommended that he make unrecorded cash payments to the Communist Party's sustaining fund.[81] As a Communist, Dana was active in the theater group of the John Reed Club of Boston, and his literary contributions to pro-Communist publications were constant.[82] He also organized a public meeting of the John Reed Club for the Black writer Dorothy West (1907–98) after she returned from the Soviet Union.[83]

Starting in the late 1920s, Dana took his own extensive trips to the Soviet Union; he lived there from 1927 to 1928 and had gone back four more times by 1935. In the Soviet Union he met with leading writers, actors, and directors of both theater and film. E. E. Cummings's *EIMI* (1933), a memoir of his Soviet travels that he assembled from journals after returning from a 1931 trip, refers to Dana, said to be a man with deep-set eyes and sagging jowls, as the author's "Virgil," due to his role as a personal guide. Cummings then describes how he became disillusioned with his mentor and finally broke with him over Dana's pro-Soviet political stridency. Nevertheless, the Soviet visits gave Dana a new career. He claimed to have witnessed over 600 stage plays, resulting eventually in a series of minor but noteworthy volumes: *Handbook on Soviet Drama* (1938), a guide and bibliography; *Drama in Wartime Russia* (1943), an illustrated account of Soviet theater and music as part of the resistance to the Nazi invasion; and *Seven Soviet Plays* (1946), an anthology for which Dana wrote the introductions. During World War II, he was nationally known for his activity on behalf of Russian War Relief and the Council on American-Soviet Friendship.

As a Harvard University alumnus, Dana became particularly energetic toward the mid-1930s in a project with the pro-Soviet philanthropist Corliss

Lamont (1902–75) and others to honor the revolutionary journalist John Reed. This produced the backdrop to an episode when Dana's political and sexual nonconformity were brought jointly under attack. The centerpiece of the commemoration was a painted portrait of Reed by Robert Hallowell obtained as a gift to Harvard to celebrate the twenty-fifth year of Reed's graduation. On 5 April 1935, as the date of the unveiling of the painting approached, three young men were arrested in Boston for speeding. They were then charged with stealing the automobile of Allston Dana, a Harvard Law School student and cousin of Harry's. One of them, a sixteen-year-old Cambridge boy named Constant Aviza, immediately made a counter-accusation that resulted in Cambridge police coming forth with a morals charge against Dana, referred to in the papers as a "former Harvard and Columbia instructor widely known for radical activities."[84] The next month, Dana was acquitted, but the notoriety caused him to be temporarily turned out of his home a year later by the Longfellow House Trust, which hoped to avoid future embarrassment through an unsuccessful bid to sell the famed Longfellow residence to Radcliffe College. When Dana came back, he continued to scandalize the Boston elite by entertaining African Americans (such as Paul Robeson, when he appeared at the Brattle Theater), hosting endless gatherings of Harvard students and other young men (sometimes just for literary soirees), and parading around the veranda of Longfellow House in a striking Cossack's uniform that he had brought home from the USSR.

During the ordeal of the morals charge, Dana received some explicit support from friends in the Communist movement. Granville Hicks sent a letter mentioning that the Boston-based African American Communist writer Eugene Gordon (1891–1974) had reported to Hicks at the 1935 Writers Congress "that the outrageous charges being brought against you, having served their political purpose, would probably not be pressed. The whole business is an infuriating example of the lengths to which the ruling class will go."[85] A few weeks later, Corliss Lamont wrote: "That whole business has made not the slightest difference in my own feeling toward you."[86] Lamont urged Dana to remain as a member of the John Reed Memorial Committee but agreed with Dana's suggestion that he stay out of the committee's public activities. That month Harvard accepted and placed in Adams House the portrait of John Reed.

Dana's connection with the efforts to honor Reed continued during the rest of that decade and into the next. Hicks, writing a biography of Reed, asked Dana to bring back with him items from the Soviet Union, a mission he accomplished in early 1936.[87] In April 1941, the young composer Leonard Bernstein invited Dana to speak at Harvard on the Soviet Union for the John

Reed Society.⁸⁸ In the summer of 1941, Communist journalist Joseph North asked Dana to address a 12 October public meeting about John Reed sponsored by the *New Masses*, together with Corliss Lamont, Robert Minor, and John Stuart, who had collaborated with Granville Hicks in researching *John Reed: The Making of a Revolutionary* (1936).⁸⁹ In 1944, Dana taught at the Communist Party–led Sam Adams People's School for Social Studies in Boston. Starting in 1945, he was active with the Independent Citizens Committee for the Arts, Sciences and Professions. In May 1946, Dana suffered a physical breakdown and depression, which he believed to be related to unspecified political developments.⁹⁰ Having lived alone in Longfellow House since his aunt Alice Longfellow passed away in 1928, Dana struggled for the next four years to maintain his regimen of contributing to pro-Soviet publications and speaking at Communist-organized events celebrating the Russian Revolution. He died suddenly of a heart attack at the age of sixty-nine in 1950.

TOUGH GUYS

In addition to his family tradition of involvement in political reform and the impact of world upheavals, Dana's ambiguous relation to society as a gay man no doubt encouraged him to question received ideas about society and develop insights into the arbitrariness and injustice of prevailing political forms and institutions. His kinship with other gay pro-Communists was primarily through his deep commitment to being a social critic, which for him was a less tangible literary presence than can be found in the contributions of fiction writers such as William "Bill" Rollins Jr. (1897–1950). Rollins was born into a comfortable middle-class home in Belmont, Massachusetts, and was enrolled for a while at Boston University. His activities during and after World War I, perhaps embellished by his love of storytelling, included service in the Morgan-Harjes Unit of the American Ambulance Corps in France, a period in the French Foreign Legion, and work as a newspaperman in Boston. He was popular among the expatriates and was mentioned in letters written by John Dos Passos, who joked about Rollins's neuroses and psychological pain, quipping: "I wish he'd take to whoring or get married. That's probably what's the matter with him."⁹¹ The two remained friends until Dos Passos dramatically broke with the Communist movement in 1936–37. Other of Rollins's intimates from the era included Harold Loeb, Malcolm Cowley, Susan Jenkins (married to William Slater Brown), Kay Boyle, Josephine Baker, and Ernest Hemingway, whose character Bill Gorton in *The Sun Also Rises* (1926) has a sense of humor that recalls Rollins's. A special female friend of Bill's was Peggy Cowley (born Marguerite Frances Baird, 1890–1970), a suffragist and artist who had been married to pro-Communists Orrick Johns and Malcolm Cowley. She was traveling with Hart Crane at the time that he committed suicide in 1932.[92]

Rollins's first commercially successful writing included tough-guy short stories published in *The Black Mask*,[93] leading to a friendship with Dashiell Hammett, and a novel called *Midnight Treasure* (1929), a mystery narrated by a neglected orphan. An autobiographical novel of adolescence, *The Obelisk* (1930), a portion of which drew notice when it appeared in the third annual *American Caravan* in 1929, was enthusiastically reviewed for its Joycean technique. Today it might be read as a lightly coded gay-themed work. The novel chronicles the late adolescence and early manhood of the introspective Lewis Raey. Rollins's narrative proceeds from Raey's first year at school, when he is still painfully self-conscious and fearful of the powers of his vivid imagination, to age twenty-five, when he judges himself to be craven, undistinguished, and unsound. As in Oscar Wilde's *The Picture of Dorian Gray* (1891), Raey's "vices" are never particularized. Raey's longing for a new life takes the form of a fantasy in which he takes a road leading from an imagined obelisk in the middle of the forest of the Fontainebleau in France, but nothing in his own experience suggests such an option; he is convinced that there is no escaping his sense of futility. The theme of *The Obelisk* recalls Willa Cather's "Paul's Case" (1905) in its depiction of a homosexual victim who is guilty of contributing to his own misfortune.[94]

Given Rollins's ironic view of life, one might have deduced that he was an anarchist. His legendary drinking made him seem an unlikely candidate for discipline of any kind. Yet he became stanchly pro-Communist in the very early 1930s and remained so until his death at the age of fifty-three in 1950. The height of his Left political commitment was expressed in two timely works, the strike novel *The Shadow Before* (1934), issued in the Soviet Union in 1935, and a Spanish civil war novel, *The Wall of Men* (1938), praised by Richard Wright as a triumphant amalgamation of pulp fiction and Left politics.[95] At the onset of his proletarian phase, Rollins used the pseudonym "Stacy O'Conner" when he published *Murder at Cyprus Hall* (1933), a mystery novel narrated by its leading character; it was dedicated to a mysterious "Urann Thayer," apparently another pseudonym used by Rollins when writing ghost stories. In 1947, Rollins returned to the mystery genre under his own name with *The Ring and the Lamp*, a whodunit set in France after World War I that involves a secretive business cartel.

Like Kenneth Fearing, Rollins's organized Communist activities were minimal and confined mostly to literary venues. He was a stalwart of the

League of American Writers, signing the initial call for the pre–Popular Front American Writers Congress in 1935 and serving on the league's national council. In an early issue of the *Partisan Review*, under the title of "The Collective Novel," Rollins published a piece on the translation of Mikhail Sholokhov's *And Quiet Flows the Don*, in which he argued for a greater breadth in U.S. fiction.[96] A year later he contributed a statement on the proletarian novel to the *New Masses*, and an excerpt from *The Shadow Before* appeared in International Publishers' *Proletarian Literature in the United States* (1935).[97] Out of the country for a period after 1937, he returned to teach a course on writing detective stories in the fall of 1940 at the Writers' School of the League of American Writers in New York City and signed the 1941 call for the Fourth Writers Congress.[98] In the early World War II years, he contributed a number of propaganda pieces to *Soviet Russia Today*.[99]

During the Depression, while working on *The Shadow Before*, Rollins lived in a Greenwich Village rooming house near the Cooper Union Library on Washington Square South that was dubbed "the House of Genius" because of its legendary former inhabitants, which included Stephen Crane and Theodore Dreiser. Jerre Mangione (1909–98), an Italian American writer and former editor for the Federal Writers Project, recalled Rollins as a man with "rapid-fire talk bristling with sharp and funny nuances." He seemed to be perpetually broke, living on hackwork and the tolerance of his landlady who liked his good looks and fluency in French.[100] Certain about Rollins's pro-Soviet political devotion, Mangione summed him up as a character out of a Hemingway novel, "an idealist with a sardonic sense of humor."[101]

During the first part of the 1930s, Mangione shared not only an apartment with Rollins but much of his politics as well. Mangione belonged to the John Reed Club and published in the Communist press under two pseudonyms, "Mario Michele" and "Jay Gerlando."[102] Although he moved to Washington, D.C., in 1937, Mangione remained in touch with Rollins until his death. Was Rollins gay? Mangione was convinced that Rollins was "bi-sexually inclined"; more specifically, Mangione assumed that Rollins's relationship with a former Syracuse University student he knew, Vernon Smith, called "Smithie," was a homosexual one. Rollins lived with Smithie during the late 1930s and first part of the 1940s. After borrowing money from Smithie, Rollins repaid it by inviting him to live in the Soviet Union on the royalties from *The Shadow Before*. Although Rollins claimed that he had an invitation to remain in the Soviet Union as long as he wished, the two men stayed there just a little over a year. Rollins's personality appeared to Mangione as neither ultra-masculine nor effeminate. He mainly aspired to an acute objectivity, which produced an overly keen awareness of his own failings. He expertly used humor as a weapon of self-defense.[103] Mangione also believed that Rollins suffered from "the guilt he derived from his homosexuality," which was the cause of his "suicidal" drinking, although he was not himself suicidal.[104]

According to Mangione, it was Edmund Wilson who suggested that McBride Publishers bring out Rollins's *The Shadow Before*. Although sales were only about 2,000 copies, Rollins got a $500 advance and a contract for a few weeks' work in Hollywood; however, the Soviet edition turned out to be so popular that he was able to cover his round-trip travel expenses. *The Shadow Before* received what now seems to be inordinately high praise, although mainly from critics who shared Rollins's political sympathies—Louis Kronenberger, Horace Gregory, John Dos Passos, Robert Cantwell, and others.[105] The plot involves the events leading up to and following a strike of thousands of textile workers in a large mill town; it was set at Jones Mill in Fullerton, New England, an imaginary location, but was inspired by what occurred in New Bedford, Massachusetts, in 1928 and Gastonia, North Carolina, in 1929. Rollins's structure seems adapted from the John Dos Passos strategy; it involves the progressive linking of detached stories about individualized characters that commence separately, and the narrative is interspersed with songs, newspaper headlines, fragments of speech, court transcripts, play scenes, and Communist Party slogans.

Rollins's protagonist is Harry Baumann, a young Jew whose family owns the mill. After anti-Semitic incidents cause Bauman to become self-conscious of his "race," he turns against his family and supports the strike. But his motivations are not political; they flow from a psychopathic, neurotic hatred. Eventually Baumann becomes criminally insane and commits suicide. A contrasting character is Larry Marvin, probably modeled after Gastonia strike leader Fred Beal, a closeted gay man originally from New England.[106] A true Communist, the tall, sandy-haired Marvin is the product of genuine convictions, although he is also puritanical, confiscating dirty postcards that belong to workers and moralizing. Another character is Ramon Vieira, a Portuguese immigrant worker who ultimately scabs on the strike. Mickey Bonner, a tough Irish woman, loves Ramon but breaks with him over the matter of class loyalty. When Mickey finally has a baby (whose paternity is ambiguous), the child is named after Lenin. There is also a homosexual episode; Olsen, an effeminate Swedish bobbin boy with a lisp, is savagely beaten because of the frank homoerotic love he expresses for the alcoholic Frenchman Drouet.

The Shadow Before almost effortlessly lends itself to interpretation as a gay novel in which the conventional equations between politics and gender are disputed. The chief challenge to what Rollins certainly anticipated as predictable Left opinions comes in his contrast between Ramon and Mickey. The former is a worker, from an immigrant group noted for its militancy in trade union actions, and is traditionally handsome in a masculine way. Ramon would seem to be ready-made as the hero of a proletarian novel, yet he identifies with his class enemy. It is Mickey, in contrast, who is the strongest character in the book: a nontraditional woman with what was at the time a classical male Irish first name (it is derived from Michael, which is also a popular Irish term for a penis). Mickey chooses her own lovers and comes to embody the spirit of the strike. What's more, the girlish Olsen and the drunk Drouet, in all probability projections of Rollins's critical self-image and on the surface unfit for the Communist movement, are redeemed in his narrative because they remain faithful partisans of the strike.[107] Baumann is used to show not so much the inherent treachery of the bourgeoisie as the futility of confusing one's personal rebellion with a political obligation. His need for retaliation against his family takes precedence over class solidarity, and his suicide echoes the fate of hedonist bohemians of the 1920s, such as Harry Crosby and Hart Crane, who perhaps could not resolve inner conflicts through a commitment to the working class. In the end, Rollins presents an orthodox viewpoint—judge by politics above all, not appearances—even if heterosexist stereotyping is his target.

From Washington, D.C., Mangione kept in touch with Rollins, witnessing a drastic decline in his morale after the 1930s—drinking more and writing less. With metronomic regularity, debts multiplied and friends were lost as Rollins fell into literary anonymity and grew vocally sour about the poor sales of his work. Vernon Smith and Rollins remained friends, but Smith could not bear the ugly situation and moved out. Rollins's loneliness became even more palpable. Desperate for an income, he arranged various job interviews, which he seemed to self-sabotage, and made a few efforts at radio script-writing. Just before his fatal illness, he secured work at Fawcett Publishers, reading and rewriting manuscripts while immersed in the dream of a comeback. When he was diagnosed with terminal throat cancer, he was told by his doctor that it was only an obstruction, so he forged ahead with plans to write a novel about the U.S. Congress. His illusion at having a second chance at life was enhanced by a miraculous outpouring of visits from old friends, including John Dos Passos, although these acquaintances were motivated to go to him by the news of his impending death. After he insisted on returning home to tend his garden, he soon developed pneumonia and was taken to the Montefiore Hospital. There his old companion Smithie was able to see him just before he died.

MAMA'S BOYS

Rollins's personal life and the substance of his novels supply an uncommonly clear-cut basis for exploring the presence of a gay writer in Left culture. Yet Rollins was by no means an archetype; homosexuals, whether Communist or not, are far too diverse to share a single sensibility that permits sweeping generalizations. Henry Myers (1893–1975), born in Chicago, exemplifies a very dissimilar pro-Communist, gender-nonconforming writer. If Bill Rollins cloaked his personal pain in tough-guy cynicism, Myers was a whimsical, funny man, a dandy, boulevardier, and self-educated litterateur in the manner of Oscar Wilde. He was a brilliant, marvelous, and exciting personality whose writings reflected a lyric gift and a droll, probing skepticism. With triangular eyebrows, Myers occasionally came across as a puckish toff. As a young man, he sported a long, wavy musician's hairstyle and sideburns and conveyed the etiquette of a British aristocrat. Later he took to wearing a monocle, which fostered a Prussian officer look, dressing in elegantly sporty clothes, including a Prince de Galles tweed jacket that made him appear years younger. When introduced to the man who became his longtime collaborator, Dimitri Tiomkin (1894–1979), the film score composer and conductor, Tiomkin's very first words were: "Henry, are you a fairy?"[108]

An unathletic-looking man of average build, Myers conjured himself larger as a fierce figure on the sometimes violent picket lines during the 1945 Hollywood Conference of Studio Unions strike. Lame from childhood polio, he carried a walking cane that he "wielded like a sword at the goons"; a few years later, he shook it menacingly at anyone who mentioned the emissaries from the House Committee on Un-American Activities who were arriving in Hollywood.[109] He was as serious about his Marxist politics as he was distant from the masculinist proletarianism fostered by the Communist movement. Myers's preferred tastes were those of upper-class culture, the opera and theater, and it never occurred to him to contribute to the *New Masses* or submit any of his writing to the Communist Party's Hollywood Writers Clinic, like brother-in-law Ben Barzman (1910–1989) did. When he wrote fiction or comedy, his primary concern was not how it related to Marxism but whether it worked dramatically. A collector of first editions and rare books on witchcraft, which had been a hobby of his mother's, Myers wrote novels about the Children's Crusade and explorer Leif Ericson. He was a Communist who surely did not echo the gravity of the writers who led the cultural Left. To Myers, everything was a joke, and he made jokes about everything. He liked to think of himself as cultivating the illusion of being a mama's boy while he was secretly planning to pull a fast one. His addiction to gambling, poker, and roulette was legendary, but friends and comrades, charmed by his wit and his outré personality, went out of their way to find jobs for him and give him money when he needed it.[110]

What is known about Myers's sexuality is less definite than that of Bill Rollins's. His first cousin, Norma Barzman (born Norma Levor, 1920), twenty-seven years younger, considered Myers the love of her life and had an affair with him beginning at the age of twelve that continued throughout the 1930s.[111] She speculates that Myers had sexual relations with men as well as women and was part of a circle of left-wing bisexual men in Hollywood that included his collaborator Mortimer Offner (1900–1965) and the British writer John Collier (1901–80).[112] Barzman, however, did not look upon Myers as bisexual, believing his sexuality to be primarily a reflection of his weird childhood. Even before his birth, during his mother's pregnancy, he had been abandoned by his father; yet Myers later cryptically told people that his father had died. At the age of one, Myers and his mother ("Muzzy") moved to New York City, where polio weakened one of his legs and he fell under the complete domination of the strong-willed woman. Muzzy was difficult; she tried to isolate Henry from his friends and had two more brief marriages that failed. Although a German Jew, Muzzy had a special animus against other Jews. Henry, who never had a bar mitzvah, seemed shocked by this but nonetheless followed some of her proclivities. He became a devotee of German high culture and idealized females who were blue-blood WASPs. In the 1930s, however, he expressed solidarity with Jews through his activism in the Hollywood Anti-Nazi League and, after 1942, through his fund-raising on behalf of the Jewish Anti-Fascist Committee.

Myers's childhood in New York was privileged, due to money Muzzy's family had made by ownership of a pincushion and comforter factory. He attended Townsend Harris High School, the Columbia University School of Music, and the Damrosch Music School. Muzzy and son lived together in Greenwich Village until Myers was in his mid-thirties. At Muzzy's insistence, Myers pursued a career as a musician and composer, despite his longstanding clandestine desire to write. He formulated a compromise goal of composing Wagnerian-style librettos, and his mother allowed him to return to Columbia University to study playwriting. Still without a college degree, he launched a new career in New York, urged on by his mother, as a playwright, lyricist, and performer. He mainly lived as a gentleman and an artist but eventually supported himself as a press agent. Myers's greatest success was his drama *The First Fifty Years* (1922), but he also saw five other of his plays produced: *The Checkerboard* (1920), *Me* (1925), *Bare Facts of 1926* (1926), *Good Boy* (1928), and *Garrick Gaieties* (1930).

In 1930, after composing forty-five plays and three grand operas and making an effort to write short stories, Myer suddenly shifted from being a playwright to a motion picture scenarist. He took a train to Hollywood, where he was briefly on his own for the first time—at the age of thirty-seven. Soon he was joined by his mother, who lived there with him for the next fifteen years. When Norma Barzman was initially brought by her mother to Hollywood to visit her cousin—both women equally were enchanted by Henry—she was startled at how this handsome man could have no girlfriends. Instead of dating, he took the preteen Norma everywhere, and a year later he began fondling her, which eventually led to intercourse. Henry's charm, when he was not being mean, was his Byronic gaze, romantic limp, and theatrical declarations about Norma being his one and only true love. Norma and Henry's excitement was further spiced by their breaking the double taboo of their age difference (nearly three decades) and their blood relationship.

Norma married the screenwriter Ben Barzman in 1942, but by that time several other women were already in Henry's picture and her recollections of them are the only source. While in New York during the 1920s, Henry fell for an older actress from the South, Marion Trabue. They had met while Henry was doing the piano accompaniment for her sister, Virginia Trabue, an aspiring opera singer whose career was derailed by stage fright. Thinking that she could do better, Marion rejected Henry. In Hollywood during the Depression, while still pining for Marion, Henry turned part of his attention to his screenwriting partner, Gertrude Purcell, recalled by Norma Barzman as a very masculine, funny, and hard-drinking woman. In the mid-1940s, Myers was briefly married to the pro-Communist political activist Barbara Alexander, whom Norma Barzman remembered as cruel, manipulative, cold, and perhaps even violent. After Henry and Barbara divorced, Marion Trabue had an accident on an ocean liner while crossing the Atlantic that made her change her mind about Henry; she craved the security and devotion that Henry could provide. This led to Henry's strange second marriage, to the tall and slim Marion, which also brought along the bulky, heavy sister Virginia. Both women acted the part of Henry's wives, and they were known as a trio. Two of Myers's novels, *The Utmost Island* (1950) and *The Signorina* (1956), were jointly dedicated: "For Marion and Virginia." When Marion died in the late 1950s, Virginia stayed on with Henry, and the two became the couple.[113]

Myers had arrived in California as an apolitical artist with a capital A but in 1932 felt a magnetic pull to support Roosevelt's campaign. By 1934, he was a militant organizing the Screen Writers Guild in Hollywood. Soon he was reading Marx and Lenin, attending Communist classes and political meetings, and accepting the pro-Soviet point of view. His most visible Left political activity was in the Hollywood chapter of the League of American Writers in the late 1930s and early 1940s. He served on the executive committee in 1939 and was elected vice president in 1940, at the time of the Hitler-Stalin Pact, and again in 1942. He taught at the Hollywood Writers' School in 1940 and 1941. Barzman believed that, in Los Angeles and later in New York, Myers bore all the signs of being an organized Communist Party member, although she never knew this technical affiliation for certain. Even when she and her husband angrily broke with the Communist movement in 1968—because of the Soviet Union's invasion of Czechoslovakia and the French Communist Party's conservative role in the 1968 student uprising in France—Henry remained unmoved. So far as Norma Barzman was aware, Henry never criticized the Soviet Union or the Communist Party. His final book, a satirical confessional monologue, centered on the idea that only cockroaches could survive a nuclear war, was called *The Winner of World War III* (1966). It was put out by an East German publishing house, Seven Seas.

Myers is principally recalled for writing films and fiction. But during the 1930s and 1940s, he invested—sometimes with money won by gambling—in New York productions of plays that he wrote, including the drama *The Other One* (1932), the three-act comedy *Hallowe'en* (1936), and the operetta *Gypsy Lady* (1946). He also penned the lyrics for a political satire, *Meet the People*, successfully staged in Hollywood and New York in 1940 and 1941 and filmed in 1944. His film-writing career, spanning twenty years, brought him in contact with numerous stars ranging from Marlene Dietrich and James Stewart to Boris Karloff and Jack Benny. The pinnacle of his career in cinema was the authorship of the film *Destry Rides Again* (1939), where his Popular Front politics are evident in its antifascist and antiwar themes, as well as in the transformation of a misunderstood Russian immigrant into an all-American cowboy. Other films written by Myers include *Her Wedding Night* (1930), *Million Dollar Legs* (1932), *Diplomaniacs* (1933), *Father Brown, Detective* (1935), *The Black Room* (1935), *The Luckiest Girl in the World* (1936), *College Holiday* (1936), *Merry-Go-Round of 1938* (1937), *Hey, Rookie* (1944), and *Alice in Wonderland* (1950). At the end of his profitable cinematic run, Myers was being named before investigating committees as a Communist Party member. He moved to Europe at the end of the 1940s. It was while living in Switzerland that he completed his last film and the draft of *The Utmost Island*.

Our Lives Have Just Begun (1939), Myers's first novel, re-creates the lost cause of the Children's Crusade in eleventh-century Europe. He provides a sardonic account of the expedition of the 10,000 young people who were led to the Holy Land, only to be betrayed and sold into slavery. *The Utmost Island*, of which the title refers to an ancient poet's name for Iceland, was a Book of the Month Club selection in October 1951. Myers presents an implicit comparison of the world of 977 to his present world in the sense that both were on the brink of tremendous changes in political regimes and faiths. Once again, Myers takes a dim view of Christianity. With *O King, Live Forever* (1953), the account of a New Yorker named Paul Gibbs, born in England, Myers promotes surprisingly affirmative values in a vision of life as an incalculable blessing to be extended to the outermost horizon. Although Gibbs has a poor constitution, he has a will to survive, and, recalling George Bernard Shaw's *Back to Methuselah* (1918–20), he lives to be a hundred. Myers's trademark anti-Christian theme is evident in the subplot featuring two clergymen with homicidal feelings toward each other.

Myers was also surprisingly modern in his sympathy for the women who are at the core of several of his stories, although Norma Barzman reports that decades later he exploded in a paranoid rant about manipulative females.[114] *The Signorina* is a fictionalized biography of Maria Malibran (1808–36), a nineteenth-century mezzo-soprano considered perhaps the greatest opera singer who ever lived. Malibran introduced Italian grand opera to the United States and then died at the age of twenty-eight of an accident. Myers re-creates her in the mold of the French novelist George Sand, who challenged the prevailing views of her time by resisting the subjection of women and altering the outlook of men.

Late in 1950, Myers returned to Manhattan and took a few jobs in television while he worked at writing these last several novels. But opportunities for commercial success increasingly dried up. He refused to ghostwrite or use pseudonyms and became dependent on friends for support. During much of the 1950s, Henry, his wife Marion, and her sister Virginia lived together at Fifth Avenue and 11th Street. They had little money, and the state of affairs grew worse. When Myers took a trip to Europe in 1973 in search of material for a new novel, it was funded by Norma and Ben Barzman. Back in New York, Myers rarely left the apartment except to attend the funerals of left-wing friends. Around 1975, he had a stroke and was placed at the Motion Picture Home in the San Fernando Valley. He could not speak or see and was kept in a wheelchair with the lower part of his face hidden behind a white sheet.

The careers of Henry Myers and William Rollins Jr. combine features of an avant-garde experimentalist, a mass market cultural worker, and a traditionalist storyteller; temperamentally, they were both connoisseurs of irony on one level while adhering with blind faith to the Communist politics on another. Yet Myers was far more accomplished and successful than Rollins, writing hit films, best-selling novels, popular plays, and innumerable lyrics. As an artist, Myers reveled in displaying withering powers of observation, working small details into a narrative with relentless clarity, and expressing exuberance and a vitality of perception. His writings have many clever twists and ironic viewpoints, which are often expressed in the voice of a European skeptic. His novels alone range over an extraordinary variety of genres using many forms. These earned him a reputation as a magpie experimenter who always discovered the precise idiosyncratic manner in which to present his offbeat material. In places, Myers's style may be forced, but the sheer range of his work makes Rollins by comparison a one-trick pony. What comes through politically in his fiction is that Myers was a militant atheist who maintained that human history would have been a lot more peaceful if it had not been for religion.

In Rollins's and Myers's fiction, there are intimations of a shadow world of double entendre and coded gesture; Rollins's suggests the closet and Myers's a masquerade. Norma Barzman suspects that Myers wrote historical novels and zany comedies because he could not write about himself; he could not face who he was sexually. It is obvious that Myers did not use homosexuality as an element of self-definition in the same way that Rollins did. Informing Myers's choices of characters and perspectives, there is perhaps a repressed homosexuality in attendance, but the tracking down of that possibility goes beyond the range of *American Night*. What is more readily evident behind the scenes is a Left political agenda. Myers's most triumphant novels are about power and belief systems, cleverly packaged in a remote past that obliquely calls to mind the immediate present.

Chapter Five

Lonely Crusaders, Part I

THE GREAT OUTSIDER

Life on the postwar Left for African American writers was overflowing with exiles among exiles. Willard Motley (1909–65), after publishing *We Fished All Night* (1951), his novel of Progressives, Communists, and the labor movement in late 1940s Chicago, withdrew to Mexico for the remainder of his life. James Baldwin, whose casual associations with Communism were evidenced in 1937 and 1946, took off for Paris and London in 1948, from where he published his first novel, *Go Tell It on the Mountain* (1953). William Gardner Smith (1927–74), a student of Communist philosopher Barrows Dunham (1905–95) and friend of Trotskyist C. L. R. James (1901–89), permanently quit the United States for Paris in 1951 after publishing his second radical novel, *Anger at Innocence* (1949). Richard Wright (1908–60) had moved there in 1947, and Chester Himes (1909–84) would arrive in 1953, as would Richard Gibson (b. 1931) in 1954. Ann Petry, veteran of a decade of Harlem activism in association with the Communist movement, withdrew to her hometown of Old Saybrook, Connecticut, in 1947 to nurse her masterpiece of the underside of a Consumers' Republic, *The Narrows*. Paule Marshall (born Valena Pauline Burke, 1929) was the daughter of recent emigrants from Barbados and grew up in a close-knit West Indian community in New York that distinctively marked her literary imagination.

Three African American writers of the Depression generation—Richard Wright, Ralph Ellison (1914–94), and Chester Himes—were particularly seared by their itinerary of gravitation toward and their revulsion against the Communist movement.[1] Their initial esteem for the commitment of Communist militants to racial equality was spectacularly eroded by the Communist Party's accommodation to the shifting needs of the Soviet regime. By the postwar years, the trio revisited the anguish of their Communist autobiographies in a weirdly symbolic triptych— *The Lonely Crusade* (1947), *Invisible Man* (1952), and *The Outsider* (1953). Fusing metonymic action with personal and political fixations, these three novels, depicting Black men repudiating the Party as an organization and defying the boundaries of Communist propriety in emotional and sexual candor, made an indelible contribution to the postwar renovation of the Black protest tradition. Ellison, more specifically, produced a work that proved serviceable to the post hoc construction of the Cold War liberal narrative in the novel. None, however, were intended to be anti-Communist, let alone anti-Marxist, novels at their inceptions. On the contrary, the documented record suggests that the three authors' conspicuous postwar disenchantment with Communist Party policies and political leaders was focused on the United States. All three were relatively slow in expressing politics hostile to Stalin's rule or repudiating the Soviet Union as a tyrannical state. Wright was well disposed to a variety of Marxism until the end of his life.

As scholar Barbara Foley argues in her unique study of the drafts of *Invisible Man*, Ellison's novel ought to be treated "from the standpoint of the many decisions that went into its making rather than as the product that resulted from those decisions, seemingly inevitable once enclosed between covers." She rejects the "circular practice" of reading such texts (and lives) through "the palimpsest supplied by Ellison's writings after 1952 and, more generally, by the cold war narrative that abridgingly shapes most discussions of American writers"; in contrast, one should "read forward to *Invisible Man*" from multiple drafts, outlines, and notes.[2] This is a method that ought to be applied to the entire generation of writers who separated from Communism in these years.

To parse the political evolution of Wright, Ellison, and Himes, one must note the uncomfortable truth that the zealous (and disgraceful) 1939–41 Communist Party policy in support of the Hitler-Stalin Pact was in their eyes a step forward. This break with Popular Front antifascism caused a reshuffling of political priorities that promised an aggressive campaign placing Black rights on center stage. All three were politically energized as never before and perhaps never again. Wright and Ellison sneered at alleged backsliders like Granville Hicks, who resigned from the Party at news of the pact, and cheered what they judged to be a Nazi onslaught to break the back of the British Empire.[3] Then all was altered by the entrance of the Soviet Union into the war and its growing demand for an alliance with the United States. By 1942, Wright and the others had arrived at a dissident consensus about the Communist Party.

But it was not one holding that Stalin had instituted a brutal tyranny or fostered a counter-revolution, the view of the *Partisan Review* writers after 1936 (and some as early as 1933).

Instead, the trio held throughout the 1940s that the leadership of the Soviet Union should be trusted to do whatever was necessary for its survival. What they expressed increasingly after 1942 was a rage against alleged liberal opportunism and the incompetence of both the white and Black leadership of the Communist Party in the United States; in pursuit of winning over New Dealers to support a joint war effort of the United States and the Soviet Union, the Communist Party had liquidated its vow to continue the battle for African American liberation, regardless of whose feathers got ruffled.[4] For Black literary Marxists, who were by no means immune from believing that they themselves constituted an elite Leninist vanguard, the primacy of class had to be tested by prioritizing antiracist actions.

The title and theme of Chester Himes's novel *The Lonely Crusade* dramatized the three writers' prevailing view through the end of World War II and for a while afterward. Black Marxists had to continue to be "lonely crusaders" on behalf of the interracial working class in spite of the Communist Party betrayal during the war. Five years later, Ralph Ellison's ideologically woollier *Invisible Man* signaled what would become his steady march toward an African American version of neoconservatism; *The Outsider* represented Wright's at-times-incoherent endeavor to develop a "Third Force" based on Black internationalism.

These three novelists are central in understanding the African American cultural Left because of their justified literary fame; their books are probably the most astute criticisms of the cultural malaise generated by the Communist Party during Stalin's "Second Period" (after 22 June 1941). Yet they are not fully representative of the postwar spectrum of Black radical thought; the personal situations, ages, and additional factors created assorted views about Communism among other artists and intellectuals. Langston Hughes (1902–67) pulled back from public support of the Communist Party but not necessarily from a private pro-Sovietism, while some of Wright's contemporaries—among them Theodore Ward (1902–83) and Frank Marshall Davis (1905–87)—seemed politically in step with wartime Browderism. Ann Petry and Willard Motley created their own versions of the "Lonely Crusade" without the particular venom of Wright and others toward the Communist Party. Paule Marshall experienced disillusionment with the white members of the Old Left as she was pulled in the direction of the early Black Arts movement. Lloyd Brown's views were indistinguishable from the intractable Stalinist elements associated with William Z. Foster and V. J. Jerome. Even more significant than Wright, Ellison, and Himes for the next wave of Black cultural radicalism were two African American cultural celebrities—Paul Robeson (1898-1976) and W. E. B. Du Bois (1868-1963)—who assembled ironclad rationales for fusing the cause of racial liberation in the United States to idolization of the Soviet Union.

Such an alarming calculus by Robeson and Du Bois, contingent on the international context of the history of racism in the United States, which led to an over-valuation of the Soviet Union's attractive anticolonialism, proved inspirational to a younger generation of Black cultural figures. Several of the younger writers were attracted to the youth organizations of the Communist Party, such as the American Youth for Democracy and Labor Youth League, and even to the Party itself. Pro-Communists initiated and kept alive the Council on African Affairs, the Committee for the Negro in the Arts, the Harlem Writers Club (then the Harlem Writers Guild, following a murky power struggle), and affiliated publications such as the *Harlem Quarterly*, *Freedom*, *New Africa*, and *Freedomways*. In the postwar decades, the outlook of Robeson and Du Bois was variously shared by John Oliver Killens (1916-87), Audre Lorde (1934-92), Paule Marshall, Alice Childress (1912-94), Lance Jeffers (1919-85), Julian Mayfield (1928-84), Lorraine Hansberry, Douglas Turner Ward (b. 1930), Loften Mitchell (1919-2001), John Henrik Clarke (1915-98), Shirley Graham (1896-1977), Rosa Guy (b. 1925), William Branch (b. 1927), Frank London Brown (1927-62), Theodore Ward (1902-83), and Sarah Wright (1928-2009).[5]

In the 1950s, African Americans published other political novels revitalizing the earlier protest tradition—William Gardner Smith's *Anger at Innocence* (1950), John Oliver Killens's *Youngblood* (1954), Frank London Brown's *Trumbull Park* (1959), and Julian Mayfield's *The Hit* (1957) and *The Long Night* (1958). These skillful and passionate authors, all variously influenced by Communism, were artistically outdistanced by Ann Petry, who, in tandem with Wright in *The Outsider*, was the supreme redactor of the postwar historical trauma of left-wing African Americans. In *The Narrows*, her innovative strategies to navigate the devastated landscape of the Consumers' Republic are on bravura display. Only Ellison's *Invisible Man* is on a par with Petry in bespeaking a political allegory that linked the ideological debates of their generation with the creative uncertainties of major art.

Wright's *The Outsider* and Petry's *The Narrows* were both published in 1953 with their principal action set in 1950-52. The books share a morbidity in their plots and events, careening toward melodramatic finales of murder and mayhem. They are alike in presenting images of an implacable male force and characters who have been reborn. Two of the protagonists, Wright's

Cross Damon and Petry's Link Williams, express a depressive mode of being that evidences a dread and melancholia associated with their biological and adopted mothers. Although framed as novels, a politically charged subtext for the both of them is visual art: abstract expressionism (called "non-objectivist art") in Wright and tabloid photos (urban documentary) in Petry. The two African American protagonists, Cross and Link, bond with nonconformist white men who are modeled on Jews—Wright's Ely Houston (based partly on psychiatrist Fredric Wertham, 1895–1981) and Petry's Jubine (a substantial re-creation of photojournalist Arthur Fellig, 1899–1968, known as Weegee). Damon and Williams are equally attracted to emotionally desolate white women, Eva Blount and Camilo Sheffield, whose fantasy lives are filled with noble images of the Black poor; both recall neurotic white females in Faulkner, such as Joanna Burden in *Light in August*, yet are treated with compassion. The men, Cross Damon and Link Williams, succumb to paranoia, go on self-destructive sprees making themselves obvious targets, and die of bullet wounds at the hands of assassins.

The novels of Wright and Petry rotate around love affairs between Black men and white women, a tactical mistake in the context of the limitations of Cold War cultural puritanism. For readers, reviewers, and marketers at the time, the novels became luridly typed for their interracial romance, promoting expectations of either sensationalized sex or realistic characters in a Dreiserian mold. Yet neither author aspired to such a limiting project as writing a novel to graphically depict or justify interracial sex; they aimed instead at more capacious, near-surrealistic, psychoanalytic, and philosophic revelations about history and politics. What impels the interracial couples in each novel toward each other and then tears them apart is not attributable to differences in their "race"; in both instances, the problem is mistaken identity. Link Williams perceives Camilo Sheffield as a Hollywood fantasy of beautiful innocence, not a lying, adulteress heiress; and Eva Blount is sure that Cross Damon is a hunted Black revolutionary, not a womanizing serial killer.

The Outsider and *The Narrows*, underrated by all but a few specialists and frequently the victims of oversimplified plot summaries, fell between the cracks of literary history. They also confounded the expectations of scholars after the 1960s who were seeking a Black radical tradition; the authors do not use fictional characters to exemplify civic virtue but to sort out basic moral problems and confront new emotional situations. Politically, Wright and Petry were trying to step outside the polarity of the Cold War but were ill equipped to do so because the third space between the Cold War antagonists of West and East had been undermined; among contemporaneous works, perhaps only Norman Mailer's *Barbary Shore* (1951) had an equivalent audacity. Sixty years later, as with Mailer's poorly received but now increasingly appreciated second novel, Wright's and Petry's critically unfashionable works of 1953 come across more vividly than the correct modernism of Gwendolyn Brooks's *Maud Martha* (1953) or the more conventional Black protest tradition of John Oliver Killens's *Youngblood*.

In technique, there is some similarity between *The Outsider* and *The Narrows*; this is ironic inasmuch as Petry's 1946 *The Street* was habitually (and mistakenly) regarded as being derivative of *Native Son* (1940). But in these 1953 novels, there is a correspondence noticeable in cryptic and repetitive dialogue, in which key phrases thread throughout the narrative, and also in the authors' rooting several strategic episodes in documentary sources, above all in a reliance on newspaper stories from past decades. The novels, too, trouble generic implications in analogous fashion because they initially seem realistic and naturalist, but their mood and plot are romantic, melodramatic, and modernist, exaggerated by shadowy, gothic imagery. Wright and Petry address the postwar crisis of the vision of the 1930s in relation to Black America, but the crisis is reenacted in the darker 1950s. What seemed providential plotting in the earlier novels *Native Son* and *The Street* has given way to uncertain resolutions; the two later novels are saturated with classic themes of the Cold War—existential uncertainty, dread of a looming total destruction of humanity, and a desolate futility regarding any efforts to remake the world. Yet an even closer look at the novels' styles, when one rotates the critical kaleidoscope another notch, shows that the Petry and Wright of 1953 are spectacular antipodes.

The Narrows is a version of postwar modernism, evolving from social realism. It is marked by rhythmically unrelenting prose that forges a sequence of five subjectivities. In shifting from person to person, the reader experiences the limited perspectives of a large number of characters, and the question is raised of whether or not it is actually possible to fully see and apprehend an "objective reality." In contrast, Wright uses a free, indirect discourse that reveals the wires and supports of his explosive psychic material. Like most of Wright's fiction after the scandalous novelty of *Native Son*, the far-more-audacious philosophical strategy of *The Outsider* backfired with poor reviews due to the anticipation of readers and critics that he was still in some sense aiming to fulfill the realist and naturalist expectations of a 1930s writer.

In *The Outsider*, Wright, like Himes and Ellison, wanted to depict people in the Communist Party as being in a world apart from the real one; but efforts to get inside heads and perceive the realities of others, to penetrate their minds, rarely work when one is enraged at one's subject. Knowing that, Wright had never intended to dramatize Communism through a use of the naturalist-inflected psychological realism by which he had vivified the inner world of Bigger Thomas; rather, he chose the technique of a sequence of expressionist noir episodes shaped by existentialist emotions. Despite a brief moment of mistaken identity due to *Native Son* in 1940, Wright was no Theodore Dreiser, moving forward like a freight train from *Jennie Gerhardt* (1911) to *An American Tragedy* (1925), one naturalist masterpiece becoming the building block for the next. *The Outsider* retained a naturalist veneer but was premised on a metaphysical leap more akin to Fyodor Dostoyevsky's frenzied passage from *Poor Folk* (1846) to *The Possessed* (1872).

"I TRIED TO BE A COMMUNIST"

In the spring of 1940, Wright's *Native Son* was published to such acclaim that the Black Trotskyist C. L. R. James decreed the novel "not only a literary but also a political event."[6] By means of a riveting naturalist fictional technique, depicting the world through the eyes and ears of the twenty-year-old unemployed African American Bigger Thomas, Wright evoked the volatile brutality of poverty and segregation on Chicago's South Side during the latter part of the Depression. In *Native Son*, the economic constraints and cultural claustrophobia were so crushing that it is only when Bigger is abruptly severed from his former life—by committing an accidental murder—that he acquires his first authentic glimmer of self-consciousness and insight into the conditions of his existence. The killing transpires when Bigger finds himself with the inebriated white woman Mary Dalton, alone in her bedroom. Mary is the daughter of a wealthy liberal family who offered Bigger employment as a chauffeur. When Mary's blind mother enters the room, Bigger becomes so terrified of being discovered that he suffocates Mary to silence her. The last third of the novel (which was 359 pages long in the first edition) features a sensational trial where Boris Max, a Jewish pro-Communist lawyer, battles in vain a racist prosecutor to save Bigger from the electric chair.

Wright's high-octane amalgamation of art and revolutionary politics vexed his reputation ever afterward. A driven, occasionally ham-fisted author and controversial left-wing activist, Wright was fascinated by the psychology of oppressed people, a subject he explored in manifold dimensions through his fiction, autobiography, historical documentaries, poetry, essays, travelogues, and radio dramas. Although Wright focused on the condition of African Americans in both the rural South and the urban North, his vision was grounded in the belief that displaced African Americans were a perilous prototype of the emerging condition of urbanized mass society on a world

Richard Wright in Paris, where he completed his philosophical novel about Communism, *The Outsider* (1953). (Courtesy of Yale University Library)

scale. Thus the scope of his writing progressively encompassed international dimensions.

His first novel, "Cesspool" (completed in 1935 and published posthumously as *Lawd Today* in 1963), blended proletarian material with a structure inspired by James Joyce's *Ulysses* (1922). By the mid-Depression, Wright acknowledged that he had passed through, and beyond, an attraction to Black nationalism and that he had a profound respect for African American folk culture in the South.[7] Yet he looked upon traditional Black culture as peasant-based and beneficial principally to the survival of African Americans in rural, agricultural settings; the mounting twentieth-century conditions of capitalist modernity and urban industrial life demanded that Black writers avail themselves of the most sophisticated attainments of the West. Wright's supreme curiosity about Black people's culture centered on religious strivings, which he had closely studied when he lived in Mississippi with his maternal grandmother, Margaret Wilson.[8] His observations about her ability to cope with the cruelty of Jim Crow by living in a supernatural world of religion profoundly affected his view of Black American life. Later, Wright came to see a resemblance to this religious function in the role of ideology in the Communist Party. Communists harnessed comparable emotional needs but claimed to gird their mental picture of a just society with a logical analysis aimed at secular ends.

Wright had allied with the Communist movement in 1932 and publicly departed the Party in 1944, albeit he was disaffected from it for the previous two years of his membership.[9] His rupture is habitually remembered in connection with "I Tried to Be a Communist," a memoir recounting his experiences in Chicago. This essay, initially intended to be part of his autobiographical *Black Boy* (1945), appeared in the *Atlantic* in 1944 but achieved wider currency in 1949 when it was republished in Richard Crossman's landmark Cold War anthology of autobiographies by former Communist intellectuals, *The God That Failed*. Wright gives a picture of Communists in the United States as narrow, arrogant, and intolerant fanatics, setting the stage for his 1953 novel, *The Outsider*, which further portrays them as power-hungry and murderous. Yet, in his political practice of the 1950s, Wright would defy the paradigm of the Cold War "anti-Communist." Instead of prioritizing Soviet aggression and subversion, he gave supreme consideration to his unyielding opposition to Western colonialism, which he identified with capitalism itself.

Wright had left Chicago for New York in 1937; in 1947, he departed the United States to reside in Paris. There he identified himself with the efforts of the French existentialist philosopher Jean-Paul Sartre, who had joined forces with the former Trotskyist David Rousset (1912–97)[10] to create the Rassemblement démocratique révolutionnaire (Revolutionary Democratic Assembly, RDR) as a political alternative to movements allied with either the Soviet Union or the West. In 1948, Wright threw himself into the new organization and delivered a major speech against both Western imperialism and Soviet totalitarianism that was extensively cited. However, a year later, in April 1949, Wright began to discern that Rousset was leading the organization into a de facto alliance with the United States. That summer, he and Sartre publicly resigned on the grounds that the RDR had become too exclusively anti-Soviet.[11]

In retrospect, it is now clear that Wright's relationship with the Communist Party was always fraught with potentially explosive tensions that stemmed from his view of himself as an artist. From the onset of his affiliation, Wright happily accepted the Marxist analysis of the nature of capitalism and the perspective of historical materialism. Yet he resisted, initially through waging a kind of guerrilla warfare, efforts to transform him into a Party worker that would force him to abandon or modify what he felt was his true calling as an artist. Among his worries was his conviction that, blinded by their ideals and oversimplified policies, Communists romanticized the condition of African Americans, minimizing the consequences of their oppression and the desperation of a people who longed for a full life as much as anyone else. Wright developed his most recognized character, Bigger Thomas, as a symptom of a racist and class-divided society, but he also saw Bigger as a means of confronting the Communist Party with a slice of the unvarnished reality to which he believed it was blind.

In the novel, Jan and Mary, a Communist Party member and sympathizer, try to befriend and recruit Bigger to the Party. Yet they end up as his victims, Mary dead and Jan falsely implicated as her kidnapper. This turn of events is partially the result of Mary and Jan's inability to grasp that, no matter what they may profess, Bigger regards them primarily as whites and therefore threatening. The more Mary and Jan cavalierly seek to establish a personal relationship with Bigger and involve him in their political projects, the more frightened and hostile he inwardly becomes. Mary's obliviousness to the danger she represents to Bigger as a white woman is a crucial ingredient in creating the fear that leads Bigger to smother her. Even the admirable defense attorney Boris Max cannot fathom how and why Bigger shockingly decides to accept responsibility for the crimes he has committed; he cannot grasp that such defiance allows Bigger a sense of power and freedom much more attractive than the role of a "victim of society" that Max has so eloquently portrayed to the judge. Only Jan, who has suffered the profound personal loss of his lover at Bigger's hands, has a possibility of reaching across the racial divide.

In his subsequent novel, *The Outsider*, Wright depicts Communists (white and Black) as titillated and filled with admiration because they believe that the protagonist, Cross Damon, has killed a white man in response to a racist incident and is hiding from the police. In truth, Damon had impulsively murdered a fellow Black postal worker whom Damon believed was blocking his efforts both to evade economic responsibility for his abandoned wife and children and to escape rape charges by a fifteen-year-old girl that Damon had impregnated and ditched. In sum, a vital function of Wright's literary and political mission, made clear by *Native Son*, was to desentimentalize the prevailing liberal and left-wing views of racist oppression as purely victimhood. More specifically, he argued that African American disenfranchisement from the fruits of industrial society was an intensified form of a process affecting a growing proportion of humanity and that a revolutionary change—the nature of which is never elaborated—was essential to avert the dire consequences of what was under way.

By the late 1940s, Wright finally came to see the Soviet Union as a brutal dictatorship and the Communist parties of the world its deluded servants. But unlike Trotskyists, with whom he might seem to have a kinship, Wright did not theorize the Soviet Union as a revolution in defeat. The Trotskyist view was that a once-inspiring upheaval of workers and peasants against the czarist autocracy had, through historical conditions of the 1920s, been transformed into a new kind of dictatorial system. This meant that Communists in the West, as well as those in the decolonizing world, were trapped in a complicated location; they were sandwiched between their legitimate impulses for social justice and their loyalty to the treacherous Soviet regime. The Trotskyists therefore aspired to propose an affirmative revolutionary socialist alternative to both capitalism and Stalinism. Wright's outlook ran along parallel lines to the Trotskyists, although he chose not to embrace their particular dual vision and placed greater hope in the elites of the Third World. But neither did he argue in support of the prevailing outlook of Cold War liberalism, which was that the horrific outcome of the Russian Revolution was inscribed from the outset, the logical result of the Bolsheviks' bid for power. He simply denounced what he thought the international Communist movement had become during the 1930s and afterward.

Using his critique, vividly embodied in *The Outsider*, Wright emphasized mainly the ease with which a hierarchical organization that demanded military-like discipline becomes a device of personal power. Aspiring leaders mask their will to dominate behind the altruistic long-term aims of the organization's ideology, deriving pleasure from the psychological perquisites of even a limited authority. Wright saw a telling feature of this dynamic in the drive to stamp out any potentially threatening subjectivity that might resist conformity with an organization's ideology, an ideology touted as being the objective interests of a class but for all intents and purposes the codification of a specific party's particular program, a program "interpreted" by individuals who benefited. Those who hesitated to conform and who raised questions were stigmatized as counter-revolutionaries, "Trotskyites," petit bourgeois, or various other kinds of heretics. The Communist Party cadre, leaders and devoted members, regarded ordinary people, including African Americans, as instruments to be deployed on behalf of policies that altered according to commands issued from the top of the Party. In Wright's opinion, African Americans were just as susceptible as others in investing their emotions in this Party-orchestrated zealotry, and perhaps even more so because Communism sincerely repudiated distinctions based on "race."

Wright's view of Communism, part of a fundamental break from the terms of ordinary life, was shaped by his growing convergence with the postwar existentialist philosophy that appealed to his fascination with ontology, the nature of being and existence. Such an affinity is apparent when comparing *Native Son* to *The Stranger*, a 1941 novel by Wright's future friend Albert Camus, the French Algerian author and former Communist. While it is documented that Wright read *The Stranger* in 1948, as he was completing *The Outsider*, there is no evidence that Camus had read *Native Son*. Yet both novels abound with thematic similarities and are focused on a semiconscious murder. In each instance, the protagonists, Bigger Thomas and Meursault, wander about in a reverie of immediate experiences and sensations until a combination of accident, the natural environment, and the social structure propels them into carrying out a killing.

After the murders, the significance of earlier incidents comes into play, and the two novels climax with the imprisonment of the protagonists after a titanic struggle between the respective lawyers for the defense and the prosecution. Each of the defenders argues that the killings were due to extenuating circumstances, while the legal representatives of the state attribute to the defendants a criminal mind and premeditation. Both novels end with the impending execution of the protagonists, during which time each man utters enigmatic remarks about his fate. Bigger Thomas and Meursault are without fathers from a young age, enmeshed in romantic relationships to which they (unlike the females involved) attach no significance, and deeply alienated from their mothers. Both violently reject Christian religious representatives who try to impart meaning in their plights. The settings of both novels are colonized situations (the internal colony of Chicago's Black ghetto and the French-owned Algeria), and racial fear and misunderstanding are factors in both murder situations. Neither Wright's Bigger Thomas nor Camus's

Meursault are put forward as positive role models; rather, they are individuals whose condition and fate illustrate a pitiless natural world and societies that foster myth, delusion, and persecution.

However, Wright's wacky blending of pulp fiction and comic strip episodes with eccentric philosophical conversations in the manner of Dostoyevsky and D. H. Lawrence is at the furthest remove from Camus's economical prose and deadpan descriptions. Wright required a somewhat fantastic form to communicate his passionate rage at the betrayal he felt that he, as an African American, had suffered at the hands of the Communist Party; a similar need was expressed in near-surreal techniques by Chester Himes in *The Lonely Crusade* and Ralph Ellison in *Invisible Man*. Yet the compulsively verbose emotionalism of *The Outsider* seems over-the-top if attributed to that necessity alone. What is now apparent and crucial to the emotional crisis enacted by the novel is that practically all of Wright's biographers prior to Hazel Rowley (*Richard Wright: The Life and Times*, 2001) misled the public and scholars about the condition of Wright's marriage to Ellen Poplar at the time of the novel's completion in 1951–52.

Poplar, born Freda Poplowitz, was a longtime Communist Party organizer who in France became a literary agent for writers such as Nelson Algren, Simone de Beauvoir, Eldridge Cleaver, and Violette Leduc. Perhaps to protect the image of an interracial marriage, controversial and in many states illegal in the United States, or in deference to the Wright family, biographers before Rowley made no mention of his marital problems, even though Ellen Wright moved alone with their daughters to England in 1959. In point of fact, the marriage was close to termination in 1950, and probably in trouble earlier due to Wright's incurable extramarital womanizing in which he had been engaged since the early 1940s.[12] Thus the fury and frenzy of the novel, with its theme of broken promises and emotional hard-heartedness, is as much an indictment of Wright's personal self-delusions and egotism as it is of the political betrayal of others. *The Outsider* can partly be read as the record of a world-class midlife crisis. Its wrenching confessional nature renders the calamitous events in the novel more poignant and human, even if they are sometimes hard to appreciate given the melodrama of five deaths for which the protagonist Cross Damon is directly or indirectly responsible.

When *The Outsider* first appeared, the majority of critics argued that, during his Paris sojourn, Wright had simply become an existentialist, even penning the first existentialist novel in U.S. literary history.[13] Today the estimation is more that he was drawn to existentialism through his own experiences and that he ultimately rejected versions of the philosophy that broached nihilism or discarded collective solutions to social existence.[14] Like Sartre, he retained

Marxism as his larger framework, seeking to find a means by which to participate in the centuries-old effort to abolish exploitation. In the passion of his politics, as well as his literary style, he departed from Camus, who declared his artistic commitments more central than political activism. Perhaps Wright during the Cold War years most closely followed Simone de Beauvoir's argument in *Art and Action* (1948) that the demand for freedom must necessarily be fleshed out in the arena of social action.[15] This is not to suggest that Wright was able to devise a viable roadmap for social change. Wright was battered considerably by his attempt to forge an independent position, and another of Hazel Rowley's disclosures is that he was plagued by paranoid episodes and on occasion collaborated with U.S. authorities in order to combat his pro-Communist African American rivals.[16]

In recent decades, Wright has gained enhanced consideration for his cosmopolitanism, one uniquely marked by a rethinking of Enlightenment rationality through a broad identification with people of color throughout the world.[17] In 2008, HarperCollins Publishers issued a single volume edition of Wright's *Black Power* (1954), *The Color Curtain* (1956), and *White Man, Listen!* (1957), with an introduction by Princeton University professor Cornel West. West restates the argument of these three works, emphasizing Wright's claim that "Europe missed the boat": "So now the spirit of the Enlightenment that made Europe great must be carried forward by courageous and compassionate rootless intellectuals of color like himself who must expose the lies of the West and East, speak the unpopular truths of our suffering world, and bear witness to justice for all."[18] This double view of rationalism is present in *The Outsider*, which makes a negative example of a character who, breaking out of a dream world, disastrously employs his newfound freedom only to imitate his adversaries and create new traps for himself. Wright's underlying analysis is that the industrializing world lacks a unifying set of values, thereby forcing all rebels against the old order—Communists, Fascists, and everyone in between—to cynically exploit ideology in the interests of personal supremacy.

PERSONAL HISTORY

Readers of Richard Wright are sometimes led off course about the biographical sources of his art due to the extraordinary facility with which he turned all manner of experience into imaginative prose. Although it seems as if nearly everything in his life was transformed into or by his writing, scholars and readers often operate as if his logically argued *Black Boy* and the material from earlier allegedly nonfiction essays reprinted in *American Hunger* (1977) tell the "true" story, while the frenzy and mayhem of his fiction does not. Yet

Wright was no different from many novelists in his propensity to rewrite his own personal history in both venues. In his ostensible autobiographical writings, he at minimum exaggerated episodes for effect and allowed his past to be shaped in accord with immediate needs, emotional and literary, at different stages in life.

In some instances, he no doubt believed that his semi-invented renditions were closer to the truth, but that seems highly unlikely in his handling of his chief literary friendships and activities in Chicago. In the section of *American Hunger* originally called "The Horror and the Glory," and published separately in many versions, the fundamentally vital South Side Writers Group is transformed satirically into "a Negro Literary Group on Chicago's South Side" and chronologically situated prior to rather than following his membership in the Communist Party. Instead of depicting pro-Communist artists and intellectuals of some ability—Margaret Walker, Edward Bland, Theodore Ward, among others—the reader is told about "boys and girls" with some "academic learning" who were "preoccupied with twisted sex problems."

Wright is obviously settling many old personal scores and revealing little of a factual nature when he writes that he was "encountering for the first time the full-fledged Negro Puritan invert—the emotionally sick—and I discovered that their ideas were excuses for sex, leads to sex, hints at sex, substitutes for sex."[19] Beneath this portrait of a clique of sex-crazed Black intellectuals are anxieties about his own personal association with Walker (who seems to have had designs on him), gossip about the possible bisexuality of Ward and himself, his thwarted romance with Marian Minus (1913–73) and her love relationship with Dorothy West (1907–98), and his brother Leon's rumored homosexuality.[20] Equally unexpected is that the redoubtable writing salon of Lawrence Lipton (1898–1975)—where around 1936 Wright was chairing meetings that involved Nelson Algren, Sam Ross, Stuart Engstrand, Stefan Heym (born Helmut Flieg, 1913–2001), and many more—is nowhere in his autobiography.[21]

Crucial, self-defining incidents in Wright's life are never directly discussed in his nonfiction, but some do appear symbolically and atmospherically in the hallucinatory text of *The Outsider*. One group of events concerns his direct dealings with the Communist Party in New York City from 1937 to 1945; they induced a decisive trauma, one deeply imprinted on Wright's imagination. Also woven into his fictional world are the bulk of his sexual relations with women, above all his adulterous liaisons and ones he had with Jews and lesbians. The relationship between the actual women in Wright's life and his fictional women is difficult to parse, but to explore such matters is not to subject Wright's life to any overarching accusation in need of a defense. To the contrary, it is a very "Wrightian" move; the genius of *The Outsider* is precisely in Wright's rendering of his characters' delusionary rhetoric about themselves when it comes to rationalizing selfish behavior.

In mid-November 1952, Wright replied from Paris to a letter he had received from the poet Naomi Replansky, his secret lover in New York. After Replansky reported that her passport application had been rejected due to her associations with the Communist Party, Wright expressed worry about his own passport renewal. He then turned to his forthcoming novel about the Communist Party: "It [*The Outsider*] is a hard book. It is full of blood, violence, betrayal, deception, murder. It is how I feel."[22] This admission acknowledged his need to present imaginary violence as a solution to real problems, now and later through the modus operandi of reproducing iconic visuals inspired by film noir.[23] His novel about his grief-stricken divorce from Communism, like those of Ellison and Himes, had an artistic and emotional, not literal, truth. Archival research—discussed in this chapter and the following—on the careers of Wright as well as the supremely secretive Ann Petry and Willard Motley discloses that even the most sensational characters and episodes of *The Outsider*, *The Narrows*, and *We Fished All Night* were imaginatively reconstructed memories and experiences of the authors. Among postwar Black novelists, the personal stories of Wright, Petry, and Motley, sexual and political, provide the context for and part of the explanation of the artistic achievements of the Lonely Crusaders. What Wright, Petry, and Motley share in common with Himes and Ellison is a profound sense of loss regarding the 1930s communal vision of social progress.

Eva Blount is the central female character in *The Outsider*; she is a composite of Wright's two Jewish wives and many white lovers, but as an artist also provides an emotionally charged self-revelation of Wright's personal feelings about his experience as a writer while a Communist Party member. The ethnic background of the Communist painter Eva is not disclosed, although her husband, the thirty-six-year-old Gil Blount, is unmasked as a Jew after he is murdered by Damon. Blount's real surname, "Bernstein," appears in the newspapers, and his prejudiced Jewish sister, Blanche Bernstein, attends the funeral.[24]

More important than her ethnicity are Eva's identity as an abstract expressionist artist (the term "non-objective art" was more frequently employed by the Communist Party and is used in the novel);[25] her infatuation with the mysterious Black intellectual Damon, to whom she attributes wholly undeserved emancipatory powers; her secret diary, detailing her tortured emotional life; and her spectacular suicide by jumping out of a window as a consequence of her dual disillusionment. Eva's disenchantment came, first, with the Communist Party, which had assigned its leading member Gil Blount to marry her, and, second, with the charismatic Cross Damon, who lied about his past and clandestinely read her diary. She is a victim but not just of men; the racism of her society caused her to fall in love with an imaginary redemptive stereotype.

The primary biographical models for Eva are almost certainly Ellen Poplar, Joyce Gourfain, and Dhimah Rose Meidman. Regarding Poplar, the novel is a literary confession of Wright's sexual betrayal of her from the first year of their marriage. The undercurrent of guilt is also because Wright had destroyed Ellen's Communist belief system, and the world in which she had gained respect and status, only to progressively abandon her in quest of satisfying his own egocentric desires. In *The Outsider*, Eva has an important standing in the Communist Party, somewhat like Wright's own position in the New York party, when he was judged a prize catch at the time of *Uncle Tom's Children* (1938; revised 1940) and *Native Son* and before he began to withdraw in 1942. In choosing to ally with Damon, who is pretending to be loyal to the Party, Eva completely abandons her identity as an artist, which had already become more secretive in her relationship with Gil Blount. She plans to devote her life to the Communist Party and to the memory of her allegedly martyred husband. But then she finds that Damon has also betrayed her, and she perceives his deceptions as similar to Gil's, who was actually in love with his secretary, Rose Lamkin.

"Ellen Poplar" was the Communist "Party name" of Freda Poplowitz, the daughter of Rose and Isador Poplowitz, who had moved to New York from Bremen in Germany in 1912, the year she was born. Freda left home in 1929 at the age of seventeen, joined the Communist Party, and was calling herself "Ellen Poplar" by 1930. Throughout much of the Depression, Poplar had a day job as a secretary in an insurance company and after hours worked closely with Israel Amter (1881–1954), a founding Communist leader known for his single-minded devotion to politics. A pianist who had given up his music entirely for Communist Party organizing, Amter was accordingly annoyed with writers or artists who demanded autonomy for their work, not hesitating to voice his objections in the *Daily Worker* to politically incorrect writing by Communist Party members.[26]

In the summer of 1939, Poplar, the leader of the Communist Party's Brooklyn branch headquartered on Fulton Street, achieved some notoriety when she was arrested for distributing leaflets in upstate New York. She was twenty-six when she met Wright during that same year; he was attending her branch and they were introduced by his onetime Chicago comrade Herbert Newton (the African American husband of Jane Newton, from a prominent Chicago family) after a meeting of the executive committee. Straight away smitten by Ellen, Wright proposed marriage so quickly that she turned him down; he later claimed that it was only to spite Ellen that he immediately proposed to Dhimah Meidman. When the Black/Jewish couple of Wright and Poplar finally came together, it caused a Poplowitz family crisis. Ellen's sister, Florence, broke relations with her, but her brother, Martin (Moe), supported her. The parents took a middle ground of not being happy but accepting the marriage.[27] As far as can be determined, Poplar, who subsequently called herself "Ellen Wright," assumed a parallel attitude of unhappy acceptance toward Wright's compulsive infidelity, which was soon evident and widely known.[28]

A conspicuous feature of the despondent character Eva is her yearning to share the hurt and shame that she imagines to be suffered by African Americans. This blend of condescension and stereotyping stems from Eva's feelings of inadequacy about her self-worth; it is expressed in its looniest form by her fantasy that the serial killer Damon is a man beloved by the masses of Harlem. Eva believes that the oppressed Black masses are uncorrupted by their horrible living conditions and that Damon's aura of anguish is due to his mulling over the past wrongs done to his people. This particular dimension of Eva's character is based in part on Wright's memories of his mid-1930s affair in Chicago with Joyce Gourfain, an artist and writer who was the wife of Wright's friend Edward Gourfain.[29] Joyce was Wright's first significant sexual relationship with a white woman, and the liaison thus parallels the situation between Damon and Eva, although Damon had experienced a brief sexual contact with the white prostitute Jenny. Wright was very close to the Gourfains, much as Damon becomes intimate with the Blounts; he even wore one of Ed's castoff suits inasmuch as he and Ed had the same small, slight build. Joyce Gourfain was a member of the executive committee of a Communist Party unit in Chicago and served as a Communist functionary as late as 1938. Ed was a Communist, too, but made good money in the field of advertising; he seems to have put up with the affair as long as his marriage stayed intact.

In the company of Wright, Joyce Gourfain attended the meetings of the writers' group that met at the home of Lawrence Lipton. She completed some fiction for which she was unable to find a market; her only success came in the early 1950s when she published *Punchy: The Cat Who Wanted to Be a Tiger* (1950) and *Dust under the Rug: Six Stories* (1952).[30] Like the character Eva, Joyce Gourfain was also a painter; she was employed by the Federal Arts Project in Chicago and mostly addressed the theme of interracial solidarity. Some of her work was published two decades later in *Negro History and Brotherhood: A Folio of Prints by Chicago Artists*, edited by pro-Communist Margaret Burroughs.[31] In *The Outsider*, Wright particularly drew on Gourfain's tendency to pour out her heart to him in letters, even though she warned him never to use her revelations of anguish in his writing, a trust he ostentatiously violated. In the novel, Damon discovers parallel outpourings in Eva's secret diary. Among Joyce's confessions, she told Wright that she had married a Jew (Edward Gourfain) due to her romantic streak, which Wright transformed in his depiction of Eva's romanticization of Blacks and her belief that her love for Damon might serve as a blow against the oppressive social system that produced her inner turmoil.[32]

In addition to the Gourfains, another couple who paired art and Communism helped to form the background of Wright's representation of Eva and Gil Blount: Lydia Gibson (1891–1964) and Robert Minor (1884–1952). Gibson was an artist who did illustrations for the *Masses* and for children's books, and Minor was a well-known political cartoonist who became a dogmatic Communist Party leader with a special interest in race issues. Gibson and Minor lived in Chicago in the 1920s and were known in Communist Party circles for hosting interracial gatherings. They encountered Wright in New York City where Minor, by then part of the central Communist Party leadership, wrote one of the most vicious attacks on Wright's apostasy, which appeared in the *Daily Worker* in 1944.[33]

The emergence of the artistic trend of abstract expressionism as a theme in *The Outsider* is most likely linked in some manner to Dhimah Rose Meidman, Wright's first wife, who had originally been a modern dancer but in due course turned to painting nonobjective art. A vivacious woman with an impish look, whom Wright married on 12 August 1939 with Ralph Ellison as his best man, Dhimah at first alleviated the stress in Wright's life by answering the letters and telephone calls that he received. Within a short time, her enigmatic, perhaps flaky, personality emerged, disconcerting him. Dhimah was of Russian Jewish origin but claimed that she had been born in a variety of places, such as Odessa, Russia, and Cairo, Egypt. She managed to keep her birth date a secret, but it was likely between 1900 and 1907.[34] Dhimah's first known dance recital was in May 1928 at the Guild Theater; she performed a ballet to poems based on the Koran. The Communist Left, during its revolutionary Third Period, had enthusiastically embraced modern dance in the United States, and by the mid-1930s Dhimah was featured in the pro-Communist journal *New Theater*. When she danced in Moscow, where traditional ballet was favored, she got varied reviews.[35] Dhimah was first married to an Englishman, Peter Wollman, and they had a son, also named Peter.

Dhimah's relationship with Wright deteriorated after the publication of *Native Son* and money began to pour in. In March 1940, distressed by the "Little Red Scare" of the post–Hitler-Stalin Pact months, the couple traveled to Mexico. Dhimah introduced Wright to members of a Spanish Civil War refugee colony there, some of whom he thought were Trotskyists. In Mexico, Wright met Herbert Kline (1909-99), a Communist once associated with Chicago's *Left Front* and now editor of New York City's *New Theater*. Kline introduced Wright to John Steinbeck, with whom Kline was collaborating on the film *The Forgotten Village* (1941).³⁶ Wright and Dhimah's marriage was surprisingly over by June, after which Wright returned to Chicago. He later refused to talk about Dhimah Meidman, except to say that she spent his money too freely and had failed to impart the worldly wisdom and sophistication that he had imagined her to possess. After their divorce, she married a man by the name of Goldsmith, and as "Dimah Goldsmith" she developed a small reputation as an abstract expressionist who painted oils on masonite, a number of which are called simply *Abstract*.³⁷

A half-dozen extramarital affairs fed into Wright's *The Outsider*. One was a mutually adulterous liaison in New York City in the early 1940s with Henrietta Weigel, frequently called "Henri." Weigel was a Leftist working in the book industry who wrote *Age of Noon: A Novel* (1947), about an unhappy romance in the 1930s, and self-published a book of poetry, *Paper Dolls Out of Rain* (1954).³⁸ Her correspondence with Wright refers to episodes reverberating in *The Outsider*: she urged that Wright get together with a left-wing psychiatrist; facilitated a meeting between Wright and Carson McCullers, whose *The Heart Is a Lonely Hunter* is echoed at times in *The Outsider*; and recommended that Wright read Kenneth Fearing's *Dagger of the Mind*, a noir novel resembling *The Outsider* in quoting directly from *Macbeth* and employing its theme of an irresistible murder undertaken in order to achieve power.³⁹

Three other Communist literary women were also among Wright's lovers: Rebecca Pitts in the mid-1930s; Naomi Replansky in the early 1940s and 1950s;⁴⁰ and Replansky's close friend Edith Anderson (born Edith Handlesman), married to the German Communist poet and editor Max Schroeder, in Paris in mid-November 1952. The first two were lesbians, and Anderson acknowledged that part of Wright's attraction to her stemmed from his fascination with her desire to write about love between women.⁴¹ But Wright did not craft a developed lesbian character, or Jewish female, in *The Outsider* or elsewhere in his work.⁴²

AMERICAN PAGES

Other developments in the 1940s profoundly shaped the themes and events in *The Outsider*, above all Wright's aborted preparation of a new publication, "American Pages." This was a projected magazine that Wright had first envisioned in 1944 and would later discuss with C. L. R. James and his wife, Constance Webb.[43] On the surface, Wright planned to clarify the personal and cultural problems of minority groups, using the "Negro Question" as a frame of reference to reflect on American civilization as a whole. Wright's actual agenda was to psychoanalyze the value assumptions, habits, and experiences of the white middle-class readership whom he aspired to reach. The magazine would explicitly reveal Wright's intentions but would hopefully render the reader conscious of false illusions about race and "subject" peoples, as well as about individual loves and "happiness and success formula[e]." Bringing together a team of white and Black writers, "American Pages" would explain the emotional cost of living in racist America. An eleven-page proposal for the publication is preserved among Wright's papers.[44]

Presenting itself as nonpolitical, "American Pages" would espouse no creed or ideology. Wright's view was that the condition of African Americans, and especially the antisocial behavior expressed by crime and violence, was a component of the overall problem of national culture. The roots of such behavior were in a lack of consciousness that produced the primitive expressions of individuals caught up in an industrial society, the demands of which went far beyond the emotional capacities of just that one group of oppressed people to resolve. For Wright, the issue of racial exploitation was not in the slightest restricted to justice or civil rights; it was conceptualized as a recognizable life problem shared to a degree by both majorities and minorities. What "American Pages" could do was to heighten an insight into these problems.

In no rush to bring out this magazine in 1944, Wright most likely intended it for a postwar world; he saw "American Pages" ideally being published at the moment when the public could sense both the broad outlines of the U.S. victory and the coming political reaction. "American Pages" would be vivid and entertaining, presenting material in a convincing manner and couched in a popular frame of reference. Wright saw it as an important publication, although not a "beautiful" one; the publishers would pay for all writing assignments but use cheap paper, in due course creating a product that would be judged to be in good taste. Included would be at least one crime story each month that would explore the motives that compelled some individual who crossed the legal line, Black or white, to engage in antisocial action for gratification or on impulse. Wright also wished to promote his theory that the growth of jazz music in the United States was driven by a sense of African Americans "not belonging." One can detect the many ways that *The Outsider* grew out of his vision for "American Pages."

One noteworthy difference between the prospectus for "American Pages" and the content of *The Outsider* is that, when Wright formulated his magazine project, the subject of Communism was not included in his scenario of literary topics, least of all in connection with his longstanding fascination with crime and antisocial behavior. These strands began to fuse after the fall 1944 killing in Chicago of Black labor leader Hank Johnson; Johnson's death became the critical bridge for Wright between Communism and antisocial conduct and the inspiration for the climactic assassination of Cross Damon in *The Outsider*.[45] Wright had known Hank Johnson in the mid-1930s in Chicago through their involvement in the National Negro Congress. At that time, Johnson was close to the Communist Party and was the leading African American figure in the Packing House Workers Organizing Committee; Arthell Shelton, the Black man who killed Johnson, nicknamed "Sweet Potato," was in similar circles and was close to Johnson.[46] By 1941, Johnson had switched his allegiance to the United Mine Workers (UMW), which meant breaking with the Communist Party. Shelton, apparently a zealot who supported anything that Johnson proposed, also switched to the UMW. But in 1944, Johnson and Shelton had a falling out over an internal dispute in District 50 of the UMW; Shelton charged Johnson with malfeasance and mismanagement of UMW funds. On 23 October 1944, Shelton shot Johnson during the union-organized trial of Johnson at the UMW's Chicago office. Two other union officials were wounded.

On 16 January 1945, the journalist Neil Scott, who had asked Wright to collaborate on a biography of Joe Louis, told Wright that the wife of Hank Johnson was in New York. Scott reported that Gladys Johnson was claiming that Hank had been murdered by Communists and that she had proof of it. Wright was shocked and wanted to hear all the details, although he realized that it was dangerous to get involved.[47] While it is uncertain whether Wright met personally with Gladys Johnson, the story that he seemed to believe was that her husband had been murdered on orders from the Communist Party because he had broken with the Party. In fact, there is no evidence that the Communist Party was connected with Johnson's murder. By the time of the murder, both Johnson and Shelton had strayed far from the Communist Party milieu and were closely associated with the UMW and its 1943–44 strikes, which were opposed by the Communist Party. Nothing was to be gained for Communists by such a murder, even if one believed that the Communist Party was capable of settling old scores in this fashion.[48] Wright, however, felt emotionally that the Communist Party's hatred of former members who had broken with it was tantamount to murder; in *The Outsider*, it is implied that Damon's killing is carried out by Communists, although the fact is not stated explicitly. Damon's assassination is implemented by a shadowy thug named "Hank," a coded reference to the Hank Johnson homicide. Damon's wife, like

Hank Johnson's, is named Gladys, and she, too, makes a desperate trip from Chicago to New York.

Damon is certainly a fictional character who has the charisma associated with Hank Johnson, but much more went into his making. In personal instability, Damon recalls Wright's friend in the Southside Writers Club, the literary critic Edward Bland (1908–45), a brilliant postal worker who had epic marital problems. Bland was an autodidact who lined the shelves of his Chicago apartment with thousands of used books. His essays influenced the young Ralph Ellison and Gwendolyn Brooks. His mother, Philomene, seems to have passed on her artistic talent and interests to her sons—another son was the novelist Alden Bland (1911–92)—and their children. After his fifth separation from his wife in the early 1940s, Edward Bland volunteered for the army. His son, Edward Bland Jr., reports that Edward put himself into increasingly perilous positions in combat that led to his death.[49]

To what extent does Damon's life also correlate to Wright's? The significant dissimilarity is that Wright was born in 1908 and Damon in 1924. Also different from Wright, Damon had never lived in the South. Otherwise, Wright and Damon are comparable in having intemperately religious mothers (Damon is named for the cross of Jesus) and absent fathers. It is probable that Damon's entanglements with Black females—Gladys, Dot, and the lesbian Myrtle—recall some of Wright's personal dealings with women in Chicago. Notwithstanding factual discrepancies, *The Outsider* gives the feel of Wright's 1937 relocation from Chicago to New York to begin a new personal and political life. Damon is said to marry Gladys in 1945, the same year in which Wright's diary was focused on such matters as the Hank Johnson murder and his increasing friction with the Communist movement.

Moving about in Chicago and New York, Damon's name continually changes from Cross Damon to Charles Webb to John Clark to Addison Jordan and finally to Lionel Lane. Casting aside his earlier family and social world to become an uprooted intellectual in New York City, Damon retains the physical appearance of a Black man while assuming some of the psychological features that are often associated with Jewish intellectuals, such as his urban alienation and deracinated cosmopolitanism. In Wright's worldview, a common political identity of Jews and Blacks as minority "races" was fused from his Chicago days forward, reinforced by his immersion in Communism. Wright defended the Hitler-Stalin Pact by claiming a U.S. entry into the war would definitely produce an increase of domestic anti-Black racism and anti-Semitism.[50] There was also much intended symbolism in his marriage to the Jewish Ellen Poplar. At the 12 March 1941 wedding ceremony, Wright was flanked by two Communists, the African American Ben Davis, a prominent figure in Harlem, and the Jewish Abe Aaron, who had recruited Wright to the John Reed Club in Chicago. Direct references to Jews in Wright's fiction are rare but revealing; Boris Max was partly a stand-in for Wright in *Native Son*, and other portraits of Jews alternate between vignettes of martyrs and people with stereotypical Jewish physical features.

The Outsider was plainly written as a revenge fantasy against the Communist Party. Damon knocks off not only a leading member of the Communist Party's Central Committee (after he steals his wife) but also an editor of the *Daily Worker*. Communists are subjected to many indignities. Comrade Blimmin's name is a variant of the expletive "blasted," "bloomin'" or "bloody," and Damon gives Blimmin a political lecture about power that makes the reader think of Bigger Thomas finally gaining a voice and turning the tables on Boris Max. In Damon's behavior as a secret manipulator, one sees an aggressive wish fulfillment on Wright's part; Wright is imagining that he had never really been the instrument of the Communist Party during membership but was in point of fact manipulating his comrades all the time, something probably true mainly during his final year or two in the Party.

The Outsider draws from Wright's biography in other ways. District Attorney Ely Houston's last name is borrowed from the Black attorney Charles Houston, who had a personal friendship with Wright going back to the 1930s when Houston was associated with the Scottsboro case. Houston, once dean of the Howard University Law School, defended Communist leader Eugene Dennis in the 1949 Smith Act case of *Dennis v. United States*, the first time in American history that an African American lawyer was asked to represent such a well-known political figure. But Ely Houston is more directly drawn from Jean-Paul Sartre and especially Fredric Wertham, the Jewish German American psychiatrist, yet another Leftist married to an artist, the sculptor Florence Hesketh (1902–81). Wertham is today remembered for protesting the supposedly harmful effects of mass culture on youth, especially comic books, in his study *Seduction of the Innocent* (1954).[51]

In 1946, however, Wertham, Wright, and other Leftists in Harlem launched the Lafargue Clinic, named in memory of Marx's son-in-law Dr. Paul Lafargue. This was a psychiatric hospital dedicated to understanding the realities of Black life. In *The Outsider*, Cross Damon and Ely Houston re-create the iconic Freudian pair, analyst and analysand. Damon is cursed with a wandering thought pattern, but with assistance from Houston he finds that his voice and his ideas start to thrive; their exchanges smooth the progress of a new form of thinking to which Damon becomes addicted. In Wright's fictional re-creation of the Lafargue clinic setting, Houston, like a midwife, facilitates an environment in which Damon can verbalize himself in the presence of another. He finds himself sharing secrets with Houston that, before surfacing, he had no idea existed. This deepens the psychoanalytic atmosphere in the novel, in which Damon's dreamlike adventures often occur inside and outside houses and apartments, an imagery suggestive of Freudian symbols.

The Communists in *The Outsider* are constructed of features from many intellectuals and cultural leaders with whom Wright crossed swords, especially during his 1944 break with the Communist Party. Gil Blount, as mentioned, resembles Robert Minor in his marriage to an artist and supposed expertise on matters of race. But Wright's portrait of Blount also takes a swipe at Isidor Schneider, who had written a mild criticism of *Black Boy* that had enraged Wright, and whose wife, Helen, had conducted a well-known affair with a Black Communist leader.[52] In the novel, there is an explicit reference to the Jewish Communist journalist Ben Burns (1913–2000), the editor of *Ebony*, with whom Wright had a falling out; Burns's birth name, like Blount's, was kept secret and was also "Bernstein."[53] The inscrutable John Hilton brings to mind Samuel Sillen, who had also been critical of *Black Boy*; like Hilton, Sillen was a former teacher who became a full-time staffer for the Communist Party paper.[54] In the power struggle between Blount and Hilton, one that had the prize of the nonobjective artist Eva at its center, Wright may have been alluding to the brutal controversy in the *New Masses* over the issue of "Art as a Weapon," in which the political domination of art was at stake.[55] The character Herbert Menti suggests the Communist Party historian Herbert Aptheker (1915–2003), who aspired to mentor African Americans in learning their own history. Wright's disdain for the African American leaders in the Communist Party was so great, however, that he didn't even bother to compose satiric portraits of them. Langley Herndon, the fascist owner of the Charles Street apartment, might be a cryptic reference not only to Langston Hughes but also to Angelo Herndon (1913–97), the former Black political prisoner and editor with Ralph Ellison of the pro-Communist *Negro Quarterly*. Herndon precipitously vanished from the Communist scene in the early 1940s. Bob Hunter, a Black Communist labor organizer treated unfairly by the Communist Party, may recall Oscar Hunter, a friend from Chicago who was active in the John Reed Club, the campaign to unionize meatpackers, and the Abraham Lincoln Brigade.[56]

THE RADICAL STRANGER

The Outsider also includes a compendium of incidents from the internal history of American Communism. The name "Damon" calls to mind the well-known Communist Party leader Anna Damon, who played a crucial role in the Scottsboro Defense Committee and in the defense of Angelo Herndon; like Eva, Anna Damon committed suicide by jumping out a window in 1944.[57] The crushing of Blount's skull by Cross Damon and the attempt to blame the death on the white fascist landlord Langley Herndon evoke the 1930 murder of Alfred Levy in Harlem, which was dramatically reported in several articles that Wright probably read in the *Chicago Defender* when he was becoming a radical during post office work in Chicago. Levy apparently had his head crushed by a brick thrown by a Black man in a fight between Communists and Black nationalist followers of Marcus Garvey, but the Communists blamed the murder on the police.[58] Wright was an equal-opportunity disseminator of political in-jokes, as evidenced by his choice of his characters' names, of which an extraordinarily high percentage are those of writers and activists with whom he likely interacted. The two policemen who appear at the end of *The Outsider* are named Farrell and Clark, a possible reference to the Trotskyist writers James T. Farrell and Eleanor Clark, who were intimately involved with the *Partisan Review* in the late 1930s and early 1940s.

Wright was obviously sensitive about the circumstances relating to his ownership of the home on 13 Charles Street, for which he believed he was being criticized by the Communist Party. He used the building's exact address in *The Outsider*, but then inverts in a bizarre manner most of the events that occurred there. In early 1945, to avoid a confrontation with the building's racist owners, Wright purchased the Greenwich Village house at 13 Charles Street, forming the Richelieu Realty Company by using his white lawyer as an intermediary. On 3 February 1945, Wright's diary reports that he had heard from Ralph Ellison that the Communist Party was spreading the story that Wright was buying up real estate in Greenwich Village; he subsequently claimed in his diary that the *Daily Worker* had run an article charging him with maltreatment of his tenants. This piece of journalism has never been located.[59]

Shortly afterward, Wright was stunned to learn that two Communist former friends of his, Franklin Folsom, executive secretary of the League of American Writers from 1937 to 1942, and Mary Elting (Folsom's wife), who had introduced Wright to his literary agent Paul Reynolds, were renting an apartment in the building and that a rent strike by other occupants was in progress. Franklin Folsom would later acknowledge that he and Wright never spoke when they passed in a hallway of the building, but he was adamant that the rent strike was called off as soon as it was learned that Wright was the building's owner.[60] In the novel, however, it is a fascist who owns the building at 13 Charles Street and who becomes outraged that his Communist tenant, Gil Blount, would invite a Black man to live in his home. This precipitates a violent fight in which the Communist Gil Blount kills the fascist Langley Herndon; then Cross Damon steps in to kill off Blount.

What can account for Wright's insistence on interpolating the biographical fact of the 13 Charles Street address into his novel along with the reversal of the ownership and tenancy? Wright was likely aiming at an allegorical use of the Charles Street property, drawing on his feelings about the place of people of color in relation to World War II and the Cold War. Ownership of the structure is actually in the hands of the Far Right (Herndon), and the Left (Blount) seeks to undermine that power by making use of an African American (Damon). Instead of allowing himself to be "used," Damon stands apart while Blount kills Herndon, then spontaneously steps in to finish the job and liberate himself. In the aftermath, attorney Houston observes the political affiliations of the two dead men and remarks: "It's the Russian-German war all over again, eh?"[61] Damon seems to escape suspicion at first because no one can devise a motive for the intervention of a third party. This would reflect Wright's thinking about the Communist-liberal betrayal of African Americans with the onset of World War II and the appropriate, independent stance of the Third World in the Cold War confrontation of East and West.

Wright's original conversion to Communism in Chicago was less about his being indoctrinated in a particular system of economic thought than it was a total dissent from his previous existence; becoming a Party member was experienced as a metaphysical transformation that made him, even in the Communist movement, a radical stranger in a strange land. Wright was drawn to the magic grandeur of human striving that elicited excitement about new possibilities and a sense of achieving a special inner life. As a Communist, and for perhaps a few years afterward, Wright stood firm with the Soviet Union, but primarily because no safe place existed in the United States in which he might ever invest his emotions; his embrace of an idealized party and a far-off country had not been a choice but a necessity. Afterward, in 1942, he felt as if he were a person not only without a party but without a country or even a family. Wright understood, however, that his commitments to both had been externalizations of his philosophical rebellion against the nature of life and a means of living more fully. Even in repudiating the Communist Party, and eventually the Soviet Union, and in choosing Paris as a new home, he never drew back from the metaphysical leap that he had made; his basic position remained not just a rebellion against capitalism but against the constraints of life.

Native Son, although expressive of a period before *The Outsider*, also aimed to indict something beyond simply racism; it depicted citizens negatively affected by a limited culture and by industrialization. Wright held that oppressed people turned to antisocial behavior to extend their personalities because they had no other means of expression available. The mark of an outsider would always be a restlessness, a refusal to accept limits. Wright set Cross Damon's story, even more than Bigger Thomas's, in a gaudy, urban, angst-ridden context of naked streets and a high body count. *The Outsider* is a world on the verge of disintegration, much like the point of view of Chester Himes's *The Lonely Crusade*, for which Wright wrote an introduction to the French translation.[62] Cross Damon is not out to redeem society; he lives by the code of a tough guy who thinks he can count on only one thing, himself.

As always, Wright's story moves with the swift precision of a well-planned robbery. But it could never achieve artistic acclaim due to its undisciplined prose. There is plenty of emotion presented, but perhaps too seldom recollected in tranquillity; some of Wright's monologues seem to be a love affair with his own opinions. At the worst, Damon's painfully self-lacerating monologues and soliloquies seem like emotionally unrestrained dancing in rhetorical muck. There are torpid moments, which leave the protagonist as well as the reader benumbed. But this is truly the object of *The Outsider*. Wright intends to offer no hope in the unfulfilled rage that drives Damon toward even greater atrocities in his thoughts (such as Damon's willingness to kill Bob and Sarah Hunter), ones that exceed his brutal actions. Damon's murders and manipulations are increasingly meaningless, and yet he keeps on going.

Despite his full abandonment of Communism by 1948, Wright's fiction is still saturated with a sense of mission as he portrays this sickening cruelty buried in the heart. *The Outsider* is a supreme act of rebellion in contradiction of the *New Masses*' admonitions against narcissism. Wright, of course, was always a fitful writer. Some of the speeches in *The Outsider* have a touch of unnaturalness, especially the longer ones, and the final scene is a disaster. Like Paul Bowles's Port Moseby in *The Sheltering Sky*, Damon has gone too far "outside" the framework of his culture and can't return. Moseby, however, dies without making an attempt to leave a message, and one wishes that Damon, instead of mouthing banalities, had done the same. But one can still respect such writing for its unadorned directness and earnest conviction. Damon emerges as a superbly murderous hero concealed behind a torrent of glib prattle, tormented beyond all reason with guilt regarding the death of Eva; and she is perfect as a ready-made victim imbued with racist paternalism, masquerading as a preposterous Lorelei who lures Damon to his final shipwreck.

The Outsider, along with *The Narrows*, is at its finest in depicting the claustrophobic tensions of everyday life in the urban postwar United States. For Wright, in contradistinction to Petry, there is some literary and political opportunism woven into the literary strategy. He seems to exploit the knowledge that a certain frisson is acquired by amalgamating high and low cultures; in this case, Wright mixes Søren Kierkegaard with Dashiell Hammett. Then there are the automatic headlines acquired when a noted intellectual publically renounces a former faith. Similar to Whittaker Chambers, whose *Witness* appeared a year later, Wright became a melodramatist of the moral life. Like St. Augustine, both former Communists inflated sins in order to enhance the drama of reform. Yet Wright's novel did not supply answers similar to the consolingly simple ones provided by Chambers, who told many truths about Soviet espionage but also helped consolidate a false view of Communist monolithicism that would continue to do its damage through the Vietnam War.

Wright, Petry, Himes, and Ellison all mobilized a veneer of realism while actually moving away from the artistic goal of social representation. In the vacuum of the postwar Communist experience, they couched their nonideological protagonists amid psychological trauma and irony. Shooting beyond Wright in artistic perfection, Ann Petry's *The Narrows* brought into play the lyricism of a Virginia Woolf to attain a mesmerizing fictional embrace of the morsels and fragments of human subsistence, which the author then wove into a spectacular narrative of disconcerting historical resonance.

Chapter Six

Lonely Crusaders, Part II

MELVILLE IN OLD SAYBROOK

Ann Petry's *The Narrows* unveils a panorama of Marxist stasis, closer to suspended animation than hypersleep.[1] The 1953 novel, depicting events from October 1951 to the spring of 1952, bequeaths a social vision like that in Melville's *Moby Dick*, according to the analysis published that same year by C. L. R. James. In *Mariners, Renegades, and Castaways: The Story of Herman Melville and the World We Live In*, James posits that, for the mid-nineteenth-century world of the *Pequod*'s doomed crew of international sailors, Melville sees change in social power as mandatory for survival; there must be a way to stop the *Pequod*'s Ahab and oppressive rule on other privately owned vessels and ships of state. The requisite agencies of change, however, are paralyzed by a global situation in which conditions have yet to mature for consolidating a successful revolt on the part of the *Pequod*'s laborers or officers.[2] Such immobility also characterizes the state of affairs in *The Narrows* in Monmouth, Connecticut, a hundred years later. An assorted group of Black and white protagonists of various classes are set against a background of multiethnic proletarians, some of whom are sailors hanging out in the Last Chance saloon at the dock and others employed by the Treadway munitions industry. Oppression, especially racial segregation, may be increasing, but there is "no exit" in Monmouth for the flux of contingent realities stifled by the immovable structures of the Cold War United States.

The pivotal figure in *The Narrows* is Lincoln (his moniker suggestively spelled "Link") Williams, a handsome, brilliant, athletic, Paul Robeson-like young African American named for the "Great Emancipator."[3] Link has returned from his post–World War II military duty, approximately 1946 to 1948, without a purpose or vision. The last straw seems to have been a Bartleby-like assignment in the U.S. Navy's version of a dead letter office, where he served

Ann Petry with her daughter, Elisabeth, at the time she began to write a masteriece of modern literature, *The Narrows* (1953). (Courtesy of Elisabeth Petry)

as a censor in an installation in Hawaii reading the wretched love missives of servicemen.[4] Had Link come into maturity in the radical 1930s or witnessed the immediate postwar upsurge at home, his talent might have flourished under the stimulation of vital social and political movements. Although fifteen years younger, Link is significantly modeled by Petry on two Black men who associated with the Left in the late 1930s and 1940s: George David Petry (her husband), a WPA writer who later worked as an advertising representative for the *People's Voice*, and Carl Ruthven Offord (1910–90), who wrote journalism and fiction for the *Daily Worker*, *New Masses*, and *Masses & Mainstream*. Petry's view was that both men held in common personalities that tended toward "more action than introspection."[5]

In the noirish 1950s, when *The Narrows* opens, Link is rudderless, caught between the amoral masculinity and Black nationalist pride of the local crime boss, Bill Hod, and the puritanical blindness of his middle-class adoptive mother, Abigail (always called "Abbie") Crunch. With nowhere to turn and emotionally gutted by traumatic memories of earlier lost and betrayed love, he falls under the enchantment of the beautiful white woman Camilla (always called "Camilo") Treadway Sheffield. Camilo is scarcely a person to Link; she is more aptly alluring as an effect of commodity fetishism. From his side, their relationship is exclusively mediated by values of beauty and female sexuality associated with film and fashion. Her legs in his eyes are immediately compared to Marlene Dietrich's, and he thinks that she dresses as if she walked out of the display window of a Fifth Avenue shop in New York City.[6] Link is fixated on Camilo's silky, soft hair; laughing, beautiful face; long neck; and incredibly blue eyes. He never asks about her personal life or activities but fantasizes about her "thin thin nightgown, pale pink stuff like gossamer," and her "feet perfect, toenails painted with a pale pink polish." Not once does he recall thoughtful observations or insights on her part, only how the couple walked up Fifth Avenue as she hunted for "dresses and shoes and jewelry," all the time giving off the impression "of absolute innocence, of laughing innocence."[7]

When Camilo proudly reveals that she holds a degree in literature from Barnard College and was judged so talented that she "was offered an instructorship in English once I got an M.A., preferably at Columbia University," Link laughs at her and says: "That I can't picture . . . that's funny."[8] He assesses her exclusively in Humphrey Bogart–like movie lingo, smirking to himself that she has "all the parts in the right place" and telling her, "You're much too beautiful to think."[9] In the novel, Camilo is also identified with a fairy tale told by Malcolm Prowther to his son, J. C., about a "princess with the golden hair"; the reference in point of fact is to a sensational short story of that same name by Edmund Wilson in *Memoirs of Hecate County* (published in 1946 and immediately banned) about a wealthy blond adulteress whose alluring tresses blind the narrator to her hollow character.[10] Camilo is, likewise, entirely the product of wealth and privilege, but Link learns of that only when it is too late. Closer to Flaubert's Emma Bovary than any "absolute innocence," Camilo gives to Link an odd false name; she calls herself Camilo Williams (the same surname as Link's) in order to cover up the fact that she is a munitions industry heiress married to a stockbroker, Captain William "Bunny" Sheffield. ("Bunny" was the well-known nickname of Edmund Wilson.)[11]

Link's world is a rather fantastic small town in Connecticut named Monmouth. Unlike Petry's hometown of Old Saybrook, Connecticut, to which she returned in 1947 following the end of World War II and the success of her novel *The Street*, the fictitious Monmouth has a thriving Black community confined to a strip of land called "the Narrows," or "Little Harlem."[12] Petry's imaginary Little Harlem, probably inspired by blending elements of Hartford, New London, and Bridgeport,[13] is populated with a strange cast of characters, some of whom were borrowed from the bona fide Harlem and New York City she had known in her years of radical activism in the 1930s and 1940s.[14] These denizens include the trickster crime boss, Bill Hod; his partner and the world's greatest Black chef, Weak Knees; a sexpot blues-singing adulteress, Mamie Prowther; a street artist prophet, Cesar the Writing Man; and the legless Black World War I veteran, Cat Jimmie. At least one character, Abbie's husband, Theodore Crunch (called "the Major"), has a family correlation for Petry; her grandfather was Theodore Lane, also called "the Major."[15] Petry also had an "Aunt Frank," who was a family friend named Frances Jackins or Jackson. In *The Narrows*, Frances or "Frank" Jackson is Abbie's close companion. Petry's Aunt Frank cooked for a widow who owned a rooming house, which is Abbie's situation.[16]

Petry's personal biography is tapped as a source for other details: Like Camilo, Petry felt herself to have been overweight as a child and later on loved to drive fast and took many short trips from Connecticut to New York.[17] Petry altered the spelling of her first name (from Anna to Ann) and was secretly wedded in New York for two years (1936–38) to the gorgeous George Petry, a mysterious and brilliant hunk with the shoulders of a football player who won a scholarship to Columbia University.[18] Soon after the clandestine marriage, in an episode reworked into *The Narrows*, Petry was the subject of a newspaper article in New York's *Amsterdam News*. Commenting on her visits to the theater in New York City, the item featured a striking photograph in which she was identified as "Anna H. Lane" and described as the daughter of "prominent" parents in Old Saybrook.[19]

Like Link, the young Petry was mortified by a teacher's demand to play the part of a Black servant character in an elementary school performance (Jupiter in Edgar Allan Poe's story "The Gold Bug"), skipped school in rebellion, and eventually fell under the spell of a white teacher who taught her about slavery (Harold White; Link's analogous mentor is named Robert Watson White).[20] Petry's obtaining of her first desk was as transformative to her as it is to Link.[21] An uncle of Petry's, Willis H. James, had witnessed the 1919 race riots, as did Bill Hod.[22] The name "Crunch" seems derivative of Mr. Cruncher, the character from Charles Dickens's *A Tale of Two Cities* (1859), about whom Petry wrote her first attention-getting piece of fiction in high school.[23] Like Abbie, Petry had an aversion to hard liquor, was a natural rhymer, had an "obsessive sense of propriety," and could seem at "emotional remove."[24]

Most critical to the novel's aesthetic angle is a radical white photojournalist, Jubine, whose noir photographs aim to expose the truth about race and class relations. In character traits, appearance, artistic temperament, and photographic style, Jubine is principally modeled on Weegee (Arthur Fellig), the legendary Manhattan author of *Naked City* (1945). Petry would have known Weegee through the New York left-wing newspaper *PM (Picture Magazine)*, financed by Chicago millionaire Marshall Field from 1940 to 1948, and she likely owned at least one of Weegee's books in Old Saybrook.[25] Weegee was *PM*'s leading photographer while Petry was a reporter and editor for the politically related *People's Voice* in Harlem. The *People's Voice* was printed on *PM*'s presses; Petry contributed a number of book reviews to *PM*, which published an interview with her.[26] Weegee as well as Jubine are identified by a single, peculiar name; specialize in street photography; sell their prints in the wee hours of the morning; and have a sixth sense for being first on the scene to secure a dramatic picture, often one connected with poverty and violence. Petry's physical description of Jubine, with "the face of a clown," certainly resembles Weegee's famous self-portraits in 1940, 1944, 1950, and later.[27] They are both cigar-smoking self-promoters who hang around nightclubs and know the city's underside. Jubine lacks only Weegee's police band short-wave radio and custom-built car outfitted with a darkroom.

Several of Weegee's celebrated photographs are adapted for dramatization in *The Narrows*. In *The Critic* (1943), Weegee places a scowling street woman next to two wealthy ladies emerging from the Metropolitan Opera. In *The Narrows*, Jubine stages a photograph by placing the legless World War I veteran Cat Jimmie in the center of the ritzy wedding party of the wealthy Treadway munitions industrialists.[28] In *Sudden Death for One . . . Sudden Shock for the Other* (1944), Weegee catches on camera the horrified expression of a well-dressed woman in a state of shock as she realizes that she has just killed a workman with her car. In *The Narrows*, Jubine is mysteriously on the scene to capture a photograph of Camilo, who, wearing a mink coat, stands stupefied by her golden Cadillac after running down a poor child in the streets of Monmouth.²⁹

Akin to a guerrilla fighter, Petry's Jubine is attired in old army fatigues and boots and put-puts about Monmouth late at night on his motorcycle along the River Wye in order to catch a crucial shot. Jubine has something of the aura of radical Columbia University sociologist C. Wright Mills in the early 1950s, who "came roaring into Morningside Heights on his BMW motorcycle, wearing plaid shirts, old jeans, and work boots, carrying his books in a duffle bag strapped across his broad back."³⁰ Described by Abbie as looking like "a Bolshevist" and repeatedly denounced by *Monmouth Chronicle* publisher Peter Bullock as a "communist,"³¹ Jubine is a remnant of the Old Left cultural movement, just as Weegee was associated with the radical Photo League during his *PM* days. This organization was originally formed in 1930 as the Workers' Camera League and until 1936 often called the Film and Photo League. It was placed on the U.S. attorney general's list of subversive organizations in 1947 and closed down in 1951.³² Neither Weegee nor Jubine can be regarded as ideological, but their activist photography, in its subject matter and calculated aspect, has more than a whiff of the Communist view of "Art as a Weapon."³³ Jubine is still fighting the war against class oppression and racism, although now insisting, unpersuasively, that his art is impartial: "Jubine watches. Jubine waits. Jubine records but Jubine never never interferes—."³⁴ He and the other characters are all ensnared, in the years 1951–52, in a permanent interval with no place to go. As if intuiting an observation of Hannah Arendt's— "Without repeating life in imagination you can never be fully alive"—Petry reinvented this teeming and magical urban world from compound sources of memory and emotion while raising her daughter in the relative seclusion of Old Saybrook.³⁵

CONTINGENCIES OF GENDER

Like Abraham Polonsky's *The World Above* (see chapter 7), Petry's novel tenders a coded critique of Marxism with a special emphasis on gender. But the questions Petry raises relate to the fiasco of Marxism and historical forecast, not psychoanalysis. Petry is more a witness to than a herald of fresh revelations. Link lives in a reified universe, but he seeks historical consciousness; problematically, the main frame of reference that he carries into the postwar world is the history of African American slavery, a major topic of study for himself in the 1930s and 1940s as it was also for Marxist historians such as W. E. B. Du Bois, James Allen, and Herbert Aptheker. In high school during the latter Depression and as a Dartmouth College student, Link had studied the mid-nineteenth century with an obsession. Now, in 1951–52, parallel to the mechanical Marxist who is unable to see the contemporary world in categories beyond those cast up by the Russian Revolution, Link schematizes his pre-1865 historical paradigm as the lens through which he views his personal predicament with Camilo. At the end of the affair, he thinks: "Maybe I know too much about the various hells the white people have been cooking up for the colored folk, ever since that Dutch man of warre landed at Jamestown in 1619 and sold twenty 'Negras' to the inhabitants."[36]

When Link learns, via Bill Hod's collection of old tabloid newspapers, Camilo's actual identity, he assumes that the reason for her fabrication is a mentality duplicating that of a slave master's wife about whom he had read. Being wealthy, like Camilo, this antebellum southern woman kept on hand a collection of muscular young Black men to service her sexual needs in secret. In truth, Camilo is unhappily married to the liberal but weak stockbroker Captain Sheffield, and she indisputably thinks that she loves only Link. The authenticity of this love is somewhat undermined for the reader, not by any evidence of a lustful slave-mistress mentality on the part of Camilo but through its origins in Camilo's personal disquiet and ignorance about "race."

Camilo's attraction to Link begins not in sexual desire but when he contradicts her preconceptions of the African American male. They first meet on the dock in the Narrows in an impenetrable fog. She is drawn there from curiosity after seeing Jubine's captivating photographs of the Black community. Terrified by the sound of an imperceptible Cat Jimmie rolling on his cart, Camilo is pulled toward Link's cultivated voice for comfort. When she comes to make out Link's color, once they are inside the Moonbeam bar, her mental image of the Black man, which had seemed terrifying, is profoundly challenged. She chooses to act secretively with Link about her private life, but the reason is not because he is one of her many Black boy-toys. Socially conditioned to a life of privilege, with an overbearing mother, Camilo feels too frail, and confused about what she wants, to risk the change in her public situation that would come from a divorce and the interracial marriage desired by Link.

Five months later, when Link, stunned by her lies, coldly and abruptly ends the affair without explanation, Camilo mistakenly comes to a conclusion about Link equivalent to his own misconception about her. She cannot imagine any reason for Link's change of heart other than his having become infatuated with another woman. Then, divulging a self-hatred for her whiteness and a fantasy of superior Black sexuality, Camilo imagines that Link must be in love with the voluptuous Mamie, a character distinctively African American in her blues singing but also coupled in the novel with the nude paintings of Peter Paul Rubens. Mutual misrecognition, associated with but not reducible to racism, is what this love affair is all about.

Link's fixation on an outdated historical model of African Americans as chattel also causes him to miss the intricacies of his immediate situation. Absorbed in the sexual-power dimensions of the slave economy, he is unaware that Camilo is the scion of the Treadway family's twentieth-century munitions empire, now headed by Camilo's demonic mother, which economically controls his community. It is a war-profiteering enterprise that Petry explicitly compares to the German Krupp family, the Nazi collaborators who survived postwar occupation and then the war crimes tribunals to thrive once more in the early 1950s.[37] The story of the Treadway gun, analogous to Krupp's "Big Bertha," is taught in the Monmouth public schools, one of which is named "Arsenal." Yet Link is so narcissistically fixated on his theory about Camilo's mentality that he is unmindful that the fundamental racist patterns that remain overt in the South are also at work behind the scenes in the North, a truth suggested by the tree called "the Hangman" that grows in Link's backyard.[38] When Camilo charges Link with rape in order to revenge her jealousy of Mamie, Link laughs at the notion that her accusation might be taken seriously by anyone in Monmouth. While he may be Black, he has a Dartmouth College degree and the police in Monmouth work on behalf of Bill Hod, his surrogate father. Yet Link's racial transgression, his winning the love of a rich white woman, runs so deep that, even in Monmouth, lynch law is simply carried out by substitute means.

Alternative and coexisting explanations, beyond racial reductionism, of the disaster that befalls Link and Camilo are present in *The Narrows* through a more totalizing scrutiny of the narrative. The most compelling motif is the intimation that any heterosexual pairings will lead to misfortune for Link if a surfeit of emotion is invested. One has only to note Abbie Crunch's maltreatment of Link following the death of her husband, the Major; Malcolm Prowther's betrayal of Link's identity to Mrs. Treadway because of his rage over his own wife's infidelities with Bill Hod; and Captain Sheffield's fury in response to his wife Camilo's adultery that leads to the murder of Link. In the background there is a stream of references to the horrors of married life, both white and Black: the Prowthers, the Bullards, the Orwells, the Valkills, and the Reverend Lord and his widow. The most functional human relationships among the main characters in *The Narrows* are the same-sex pairings:

the cook Weak Knees with the crime boss Bill Hod, and the widowed Abbie Crunch with the undertaker Frances ("Frank" or F. K.) Jackson.[39]

The novel is less a study of the interracial relationship of Link and Camilo and much more significantly the portrait of the implicitly lesbian couple of Abbie and Frances, one based on Petry's Columbia University writing teachers Mabel Louise Robinson (1874–1962) and Helen Hull (1888–1971).[40] These white women, recast as middle-class African Americans, Abbie the seamstress and Frances the undertaker, were well known to Petry from the time she was a student in the program in which they taught in the mid-1940s.[41] Robinson, closest to Petry, was the instructor in advanced fiction from 1919 to 1945 and part-time after that; she and Petry kept in touch in subsequent years. Sometimes this relationship was sustained by mail, but Petry also made visits to Robinson's class. Petry contributed essays to published collections edited by Hull and studied Robinson's stories and novels, reproducing in *The Narrows* some of the themes and concerns of Robinson's *Bright Island* (1938), *Island Noon* (1942), and *Bitter Forfeit* (1947). Petry and Robinson were also alike in their early infatuation with Louisa May Alcott, but the mature subjects of Petry's and Robinson's novels shared a fixation on isolation, loneliness, impossible marriages, and orphans. Petry's greatest tribute to Robinson was her transformation of personal and corporal features of Robinson and Hull into Abbie and Frances, buttressed by her decision to dedicate *The Narrows* to Robinson.[42] Moreover, "Abigail" was the name used by Robinson for the protagonist in her award-winning *Bright Island*.

One cannot take too lightly the centrality of Robinson as a literary influence on Petry's craft in *The Narrows*. In a letter that Petry mailed to Robinson from Old Saybrook in the postwar period, she explains that one visit to Robinson's Columbia writing class would serve as a yearlong inspiration.[43] Several pieces of advice that Petry received from Robinson about the art of fiction are fundamental in understanding the method of *The Narrows*: a writer must regard emotions as more revealing than facts; share other people's experiences; and get rid of all prejudices.[44] What may be most significant is that Robinson snapped Petry out of a writer's block in 1950 with some wise advice. She told Petry that her basic problem was that the earlier writings of her New York years were fueled by passions of anger and distress about how the world was run. Now, living more quietly in another era in beautiful New England, Petry needed new emotions to fuel her art.[45]

Fortunately, Petry did not try to find these emotions in a celebration of postwar America or in a Richard Wright–like rage about the betrayal of social idealism. Turning directly to brooding passions generated by the disintegration of the 1930s communal vision of social progress, she became productively engaged in creating a mode of narration enabling a meditative inquiry into the human experience of time in exile from historical consciousness. Abbie is obsessed with the belief that "the answer is in the past."[46] In *The Narrows*, the succession of what has been, what is, and by implication the possibility of what may be emerges from personal memories encountering obdurate realities.

To that end, Petry constructs a near-phenomenological novel centered on a postwar community undergoing increasing segregation and domination by big business and organized crime. Frances's assistant observes of the increasing racial separation that it will not be long until Monmouth will "be just like Georgia except for the climate."[47] It is, to be sure, a version of late antifascism in its recognition of diminished space for social action, a rigid class-based economic system, the isolation of the handful of rebel spirits (Jubine), and the loss of bearings by the young and able (Link). But there is no sign of the Communists' hysterical belief in the imminent triumph of complete reaction or their self-appointed status as the vanguard of redemption. While there are some references to Moscow, the Soviet Union is peripheral as an ambiguous fantasyland.[48] Moreover, Petry several times questions a character's use of the terms "Nazi" and "fascist" when they are casually thrown around.[49]

There are myriad facets to the narrative method of *The Narrows*, with passages that put on display Petry's background in painting and theater. At the outset of 1951, one encounters lengthy flashbacks in memory. *The Narrows* opens with Abbie walking near the dock by Dumble Street and sensing a fear of the River Wye. Then the reader is immediately taken back to 1933 when Abbie saw Link swimming under Bill Hod's guidance, which leads to further memories of her conversation with Frances at the time and of the events precipitating her loss of Link to Hod's authority. By page 4, Abbie is back in the present, but such recollections often go on much longer in the novel. On page 99, Link is eating his breakfast in 1951, but from page 101 to page 120, he is back in 1933. The transitions in space and place are usually indicated, but on page 416, Abbie is in her apartment and then alone on the street without a word of warning.

Petry employs a sequence of interior monologues to stage an inquiry into structures of consciousness lived through the first-person point of view of five characters: Abbie Crunch, Malcolm Prowther, Link Williams, Mamie Prowther, and Peter Bullock. The novel is also objectively rooted in a cluster of physical sites often with curiously significant names: #6 Dumble Street, the Hangman, the Last Chance, the Moonbeam, Treadway Hall, and so on. Each is worth a few paragraphs of analysis. The Moonbeam, for example, is the bar where Link and Camilo become aware of each other's color after meeting on the foggy dock. But a moonbeam is not a ray of light directly from the moon, only a diffuse reflection of sunlight. Link has assumed Camilo to be a light-skinned African American, "high yaller," but realizes that Camilo is white only due to the reaction of the waiter, Bug Eyes.[50] Unlike Link, Bug has lived in the South and learned, out of necessity, how to tell whether a woman is white or not by her behavior; in Camilo's case, there is a condescension in her voice.[51]

It is also in this chapter that Link recalls the story of the wife of Reverend Ananias Hill; she was a Black woman with skin so light that no one was certain of her family origins.[52] Such thoughts about determining racial identity and its meaning are linked to the phrase "When all candles bee out, all cats bee gray," repeated at least a half-dozen times in *The Narrows*.[53] The quotation is accurately attributed by Petry to poet John Heywood, and also to Ben Franklin, who cited it when praising his pastime of seducing older women. Link uses it to refer to his meeting with Camilo in the fog and alternately to question whether women are the same even if white, rich, and beautiful.

Another procedure of Petry's is to introduce subtle themes by indirection. In the instance of Mamie's adultery with Bill Hod, the reader may notice something peculiar about Malcolm Prowther's flinch and grimace when he is forced to answer Abbie's question about how he learned of her vacant room at #6 Dumble Street, explaining that it was "my wife's cousin told me."[54] Then there is Mamie Prowther's "anticipatory gleam" in her eyes when she learns that the apartment has "an outside back stairs."[55] Next there is the scene where Abbie is startled to find a man standing with Mamie by the clothesline and Mamie says casually, "Meet my cousin, Mr. Bill Hod."[56] Finally, when Abbie tells Link about the relationship, he is jolted and thinks: "Cousin.... Yah!"[57]

Of course, Mamie's adulterous behavior becomes crucial to the gender themes in the narrative as it progressively inflames Malcolm Prowther's paranoia in complex ways. Mamie's affair with Bill does not threaten the marriage directly, inasmuch as Bill is satisfied with sex alone and Mamie has no illusions that Bill might become her long-term alternative partner. Malcolm, however, believes that Link's ability to attract the beautiful white Camilo means that he can also take Mamie from him at will, which leads to his decision to betray Link—in an episode recalling both the biblical Cain and the informer Whittaker Chambers—to Mrs. Treadway, Captain Sheffield, and their henchmen.[58] Selecting which threads to follow becomes clearer as one notes configurations of repetition, including events that are retold from various points of view.

THE FOG

What is complicated is locating the sources in order to determine patterns and priorities. Petry relied not only on her subconscious but also on volumes of her diaries that she retained in order to revisit and then rewrite events from earlier years. She also drew upon the thousands of books that she owned as well as massive clipping files and pursued independent studies in philosophy, psychology, art, art history, music, anthropology, cinema, architecture, and current events.[59] Her fiction came out of bits and pieces of everything she read, creating a compound of talk therapy and the presentation of shards of a dream. One wonders if, when writing what must seem to a logical mind like a white-water ride, Petry was privately recalling James Joyce's quip to Max Eastman: "The demand I make of my reader is that he should devote his whole life to reading my work."[60]

Mabel Louise Robinson's teaching method involved a combination of careful analysis of the major works of Joseph Conrad, D. H. Lawrence, Virginia Woolf, and many other classics, with the careful parsing of rarer short stories.[61] In an interview published coincidentally with the appearance of *The Narrows*, Petry pointed to Flaubert's *Madame Bovary* and Tolstoy's *Anna Karenina* as "the two books she never really stops reading."[62] The weight of these masterworks is obvious in *The Narrows* beyond just the adultery theme. Camilo, like Emma Bovary, is overwhelmed by the emptiness of her life, and Bunny, like Charles Bovary, is adoring but lacks ambition and ability. The art is as much in details and hidden patterns as in the action. As in Tolstoy, themes of jealousy, hypocrisy, and carnal passion are pronounced, and the mood is very much that of a conduit between the social realist and modernist novel.

Yet Petry was far from Eurocentric; she had an extraordinary grounding in African American history and culture. She knew the standard artifacts but also knew the atmosphere of Black life to the extent that she could make unique contributions. One of the blues songs that Mamie sings, "Same Train," is a noted nineteenth-century spiritual; but Mamie's "Tell me what color an' I'll tell you / what road she took" is Petry's paraphrase of Blind Willie McTell's "Ticket Agent Blues," recorded for Columbia Records in April 1935.[63] The name spontaneously created by Camilo in coping with her unexpected discovery of herself in a Black environment, Camilo Williams, echoes that of Camilla Williams (1919–2012), the first African American opera singer to achieve acceptance in white society through her 1946 contract with the New York City Opera. Petry also does some rewriting of DuBose Heyward's *Porgy and Bess* (1926) in *The Narrows*, and then draws attention to the foolishness of seeing the world through such literary oversimplifications.[64] A 1949 letter by Petry to the *New York Times* sums up her view that nothing is too good or off-limits for the African American artist. Responding to an article in which members of a college drama group of Black actors were said to be "out of place" in "white" plays, Petry insisted that no Black performer should be "cheated out of the kind of varied acting experience which can only be gained by playing the big complicated roles to be found in Shakespeare, O'Neill, Ibsen, etc."[65]

The physical attributes of Abbie Crunch (short and plump) and Frances Jackson (tall and bony) recall Mabel Louise Robinson and Helen Hull, and the dynamic of their relationship is approximated. Frances (Hull), always described as masculine, is brainy and wishes to dominate. She is a Wellesley College graduate who aspired to be a doctor but was instead diverted into helping her father in an undertaking business.[66] The fictionalized couple is treated with warmth but also a Jamesian satirical edge. Frances is reminiscent of Olive Chancellor in *The Bostonians* (1886), while Abbie has middle-class (near-racist) prejudices and is an American "innocent" adrift in a dangerous world of hidden violence and eroticism.

Perhaps the most obvious instance of a Jamesian theme is Abbie's insistence on buying the brick house at #6 Dumble Street as an emblem of protection that she seeks due to her prudish proclivities; yet both floors of the house become the location of adulteries, with participants observed in flagrante delicto, resulting in out-of-control jealousies and violence. Frances, in contrast, assumes the male role in a heterosexual couple and even voices a nasty homophobia that is derogatory of the effeminate behavior of Howard Thomas, her hip-wiggling, gay assistant at the funeral parlor.[67] Absent from *The Narrows* is a sense of the political convictions of the two white women; while never Communists, Robinson and Hull were feminists active in the Heterodoxy Club in New York, a group of twenty-five self-described unorthodox females who met to seek psychic freedom.[68]

When one adds to the Abbie and Frances relationship the numerous descriptions of the domestic living arrangements of Bill Hod and Weak Knees, often corresponding to heteronormative roles of husband and wife, the centrality of gender issues in the novel eclipses political references. Communism, the Soviet Union, Bolshevism, Stalin, the atomic bomb, and even the Hiss-Chambers case are all brought up, but only incidentally, not translating into any explicit politics in the customary sense of the term.[69] Poverty is mentioned at many points but is subordinate to the essential argument that Link's crisis is deeply emotional and cultural. Anti-Communist harassment, such as the government's persecution of Paul Robeson, is cited but not investigated by Petry in a systematic mode; it is perhaps just one more result of the

"Great Absence" in the novel, a consequence of the demise of the 1930s social movements. For those like Petry who came to political consciousness with the vision of the 1930s, the passing away of the labor, antifascist, and antiracist social movements has produced an epistemological calamity, the detritus of which is dispersed throughout the pages of *The Narrows*.

The chronology of *The Narrows* is critical, but, as in Marcel Proust, one must read the novel first, then reread it to get a comprehension of the myriad ways in which everything in the novel is interlinked. Its narrative begins in October 1951, when Link is twenty-six and Abbie Crunch is seventy. Much of the account, however, reproduces Link's memories of the 1930s, when he was a preteen and Abbie was in her fifties. Link was born in 1925 and his biological parents are unknown. Theodore ("the Major"), a chauffeur, and Abbie Crunch, a former schoolteacher but now a seamstress and landlord, adopt Link. The circumstances are vague, although there are intimations that Bill Hod and the prostitute China, apparently a light-skinned African American woman, might be Link's biological parents. This would justify Hod's particularly brutal reaction to Link's sexual approaches to China and also the unexplained close personal connection between the Major and Hod.[70]

Link is eight years old when the Major dies of a stroke in 1933, an emotional turning point for him. Link is forgotten by the grief-stricken Abbie and concludes that he must be somehow to blame; he later wakes up late at night sobbing, "I didn't do it. I didn't do it."[71] Effortlessly and straightaway, Link is taken in by Bill Hod, hardly a family man in any respect. Hod resides across the street from Abbie's house at the Last Chance saloon, one of Bill's many properties. The traumatic nature of this calamity at age eight for Link underscores its roots in the oedipal stage. Link had fantasies of marrying Abbie, but his rival, the Major, inexplicably dies. Seeing Bill Hod naked, Link falls madly in love: "As long as he lived that picture of Bill Hod, naked, moving about as though he enjoyed having no clothes on, lingered in his memory."[72] Link's transference of affection and identity to a (surrogate) father is complete, although he later has problematical attractions to women (China, Mamie) whom he perceives as Bill Hod's private property.

In 1935, at the age of ten, now back with Abbie and under the co-supervision of Frances, Link is forced to attend church. But inasmuch as his love has decisively shifted to Hod, he sneaks back to the Last Chance saloon every Sunday night for a feast prepared by Weak Knees. This is also the year of the Arsenal Elementary School minstrel show, in which Link is pressured to perform by Miss Eleanora Dwight. Without fully apprehending the reasons, Link is revolted by Miss Dwight's assignment to him of the degrading role of Sambo;

he even interprets her apparent speech defect as a personal insult.⁷³ Falling ill on the date of the school event, he becomes further alienated by Abbie and Frank's middle-class talk about his responsibility to "the race." Instead, he is drawn to Hod and Weak Knees's stories about a Black woman (Ma Winters) who had armed herself during the 1919 Chicago race riot. The two men start to call him "Sonny," a practice later picked up by their photographer friend Jubine, whose flowery way of talking is adopted by Link.

The year 1935 is also the one in which Link notices that the white shoe repairman marks the shoes of African Americans with the word "negre." In 1936, Link, age eleven, wants to be a cook; a year later he gets a summer job working for Mr. Valkill, who is revealed to be a molester of young boys, a mode of behavior incomprehensible to the naive Abbie but quickly recognized by Frances and Bill.⁷⁴ In 1939, Link is fourteen but ignores girls and wants to study medicine like the family's Black pediatrician, Dr. Easter. In 1940, Link, now fifteen, reads and excels in athletics at Monmouth High School, where he is a star football player. Abbie attends a game and is shocked to hear the crowd yell "get the nigger," but Frances ignores the slur because she has already achieved immunity to the epithet by despising the Irish.⁷⁵

From October to January 1940, Link is encouraged by his white teacher, Robert White, to study U.S. slavery; he drops his previous interest in chemistry in favor of history as his major. Link wins a bet with Hod regarding his academic achievements and receives a new desk. In 1941, Link is sixteen and visits China's house of prostitution for the first time. China straightaway alerts Bill Hod of Link's presence; Hod appears on the scene and physically threatens the teenager. After a second attempt to see China, Link is nearly beaten to death with a rawhide whip by Bill, and the horrified Dr. Easter declares that the person who has done this to Link should be arrested. Link tries to shoot Bill with the gangster's own gun but cannot do it. He then gets a job hauling ice and steals Frances's gun in order to make a second attempt. Abruptly Link changes his mind and apologizes; he has concluded that Bill and Weak Knees balance the world of Abbie and Frances. Link enrolls at Dartmouth College, majoring in history and winning the support of one of his professors.

In 1942, at the age of seventeen, Link is home from Dartmouth for the summer and showing a clear-cut attraction to girls. In 1945, he completes his studies at Dartmouth and plans to be a historian of slavery. As graduation gifts, he receives the Major's diamond stickpin from Abbie and a Cadillac (nearly identical to the one that Camilo will later drive) from Bill; but two months later he is drafted into the postwar military. In June 1949, Link returns from his navy service in Hawaii, his assignment of censoring personal letters of servicemen, mostly about love, having fed a cynicism about women and indirectly sapping his intellectual ambition. He now lives with Abbie, who is taking in boarders on the second floor of her Dumble Street home, and works at the Last Chance saloon behind the bar. Abbie and Link quarrel about Link's spending Saturday nights playing cards with Jubine, Bill, and Weak Knees. Frances and Abbie try unsuccessfully to interest Link in Black middle-class "progressive," college-educated women who are concerned with housing problems and nostalgic for the wartime Grand Alliance of Roosevelt, Churchill, and Stalin.[76]

On a Saturday night in October 1951, Link meets Camilo Sheffield in the fog on the dock near the Last Chance saloon. Earlier that same afternoon, Jubine brought three photographs, ones that he shot at the same location, to the editor Peter Bullock of the *Monmouth News*. Jubine's images are of the footprints of a suicide who had jumped into the river. This connection of the encounter on the dock with the suicide photos is the first of two episodes prefiguring the disastrous demise of the affair and of Link; the other is Mamie's singing her death song ("Same Train") as Link dresses for his first date with Camilo.[77] On 25 December in New York City, Camilo gives Link as a Christmas present a diamond-studded cigarette case with his initials. He proposes marriage to her, and she replies with a phrase that will be repeated at crucial moments in Link's mind, "Come spring."[78]

Sometime in January 1952, the cigarette case—a popular World War II gift of women to servicemen, to protect their hearts—is taken from Link's room. The case in *The Narrows* resembles the one in Vera Caspary's *Laura*, given by Shelby Carpenter to Diane Redfern, and plays a similar part in turning up to identify clandestine lovers on the eve of a marriage thwarted by murder.[79] The culprit in the theft of Link's diamond case is J. C., one of the children of Mamie and Malcolm Prowther, the couple now living upstairs in the Crunch home. Malcolm is employed as the butler at the Treadway mansion, and Mamie is conducting a long-term affair with Bill Hod. But there are hints that J. C. is actually Hod's child with Mamie and possibly Link's half-brother.[80] About the same time, Camilo is caught sleeping in Link's bedroom by Abbie and thrown naked onto the street to be greeted by Mamie's laughter. In February, Link sees a year-old newspaper, from January 1951, intentionally left for him by Hod, which displays Camilo's photograph and her married name. Within the next few weeks, he breaks off his relationship with her and Camilo accuses him of rape. Sometime that spring, Link is kidnapped and executed by Camilo's husband, Captain Sheffield, in the company of several army buddies and under the direction of Camilo's mother.

THE ETIOLOGY OF MOURNING

Like much modernist literature in the 1950s, *The Narrows* echoes Freud's "Mourning and Melancholia" (1915, published 1917), an analysis that he developed during World War I but that was discussed a great deal during the post–World War II years. Abbie suffers emotional paralysis following the death of the Major; for months she mourns by exhibiting a total lack of interest in the outside world. This condition lingers as a profound melancholy for seventeen years as she feels frequent rage at herself and a humiliating sense of inferiority masked by her quick judgments about the propriety of others. Abbie, however, responds very differently to Link's murder. Following a brief period of mourning, she is able to sever any melancholic emotional attachment, and after the funeral she reinvests her psychic energy in a new object—the child J. C.[81] If there is an optimistic element in the novel, it comes from these final moments. Abbie had been psychologically stalked by secret guilt, producing melancholy, due to the events of 1933, which intensified the narrow-minded prejudices that cut her off from life. Both of these qualities come into play in her hatred of Weak Knees. She is offended when he openly expresses his own guilt, for the accidental death of a friend named Eddie, in his public gestures to ward off Eddie's spirit or ghost. Abbie also refuses to recognize Weak Knees's extraordinary culinary talent due to his curious disability, one that causes him to walk as if drunk. Abbie's narrow-mindedness reaches an all-time high when, discovering Camilo in Link's bedroom, she treats her as a prostitute. Even following Link's murder, Abbie persists in solely blaming Camilo. But subconsciously, she is absorbing certain new perceptions—"We all adopt each other" (Abbie thinking about Frances) and "It were everybody's fault" (Frances's housekeeper Doris's take on the murder).[82] Suddenly, Abbie has changed. Instead of repeating her behavior toward Link after the Major's death, she reaches out to J. C., who becomes a symbol of a possible new direction.[83] When Frances proposes that the two women live together, so Frances can take care of her, Abbie defers acceptance, preferring to be on her own for the first time. She also reverses her hatred of Camilo, deciding to become her defender when she learns that Bill Hod has plans to take revenge on her.

If Abbie has been in mourning, "melancholia" more aptly describes the condition of Link; he has long been grieving over the loss of his idealized notions of Abbie, who had abandoned him in her sorrow, and then Bill, who had mysteriously policed his sexuality with a whip. As a substitute for these vacated emotions, Link has a near-religious experience at the cinema, which imparts to him a sense that he can "conquer the world."[84] Camilo's appeal to him, mostly represented by body parts and clothes, is connected with the glamorous film images that he has absorbed; the pulp paperback edition of *The Narrows* even depicts Camilo as a Marilyn Monroe look-alike.[85] When Camilo expresses her rage at Link's behavior by calling him "a black bastard" and seems to betray once again the emotions that he had felt for Abbie and Bill, Link evidences melancholia in the form of internalized aggression.[86] The self-hatred he manifests with his self-destructive actions in February 1952 is really an expression of his hatred of the objects who betrayed his love and their continuing power over him. He violently breaks off the relationship with Camilo, disappears to ski slopes in Canada, and then engages in dangerous, suicidal behavior by taunting the armed Captain Sheffield and Mrs. Treadway about the interracial aspect of his affair with Camilo. In this last, he is redirecting toward himself the murderous impulses that he had formerly felt toward Hod and Camilo.[87]

A peculiar feature of *The Narrows* is that episodes in the novel are variously borrowed and adapted from a notorious historical event that occurred in 1932 known as the "Massie Trial" or the "Massie Affair," although, true to her sometimes cantankerous personality or perhaps a seriously faulty memory, Petry later denied it.[88] Nonetheless, in chapters 22–24 of *The Narrows*, many incidents recounted or remembered are little different from those of the murder and trial in Honolulu, Hawaii. These had been widely reported in the press and in subsequent books and films, always with attention to the racial dynamics.[89]

In the actual case, the wealthy white mother of Thalia Massie, Grace Fortesque, was charged with murdering a Hawaiian prizefighter, Joseph Kahahawai. She used the defense that her daughter, Thalia, had been raped. Like Camilo, Thalia was white and married to a white man, a naval lieutenant named Thomas ("Tommie") Massie, stationed at Pearl Harbor. The white population in Hawaii wanted a quick trial of the accused rapist, but the jury was deadlocked and a mistrial declared.[90] Thalia's mother grew impatient and talked Tommie and two enlisted men into kidnapping the boxer. Kahahawai was then shot and killed as Tommie's men and Thalia's mother were attempting to beat a confession out of him. Similar to the situation portrayed in *The Narrows*, Kahahawai's body was wrapped in a sheet and taken to a dumping ground. Exactly as in *The Narrows*, the blinds on the car were pulled down to hide its interior. A policeman on a motorcycle became suspicious of the blinds, pulled the car over, and arrested all four for murder.[91]

The Narrows, however, is not a historical novel but rather a landscape full of ruins representing an old and dying order. If there is a social center, it is a monopoly capitalism in which the munitions industry calls the shots and the public press has been bought out. Petry shows worlds experienced deeply but not consciously understood by the very people living within them, and it is far from clear that Petry even wants the readers to "decipher" her novel in relation to specific events such as the Massie Affair. Yet her underground streams of imagery are consistent with the dilemma of the African American cultural Left in the era of the Cold War. Even if Petry was never technically a member of the Communist Party, her experience of the ambience of the movement—the forward motion of the 1930s and the World War II era moving toward a climax that evaporated into stasis—remained at the core of her emotional biography well into the 1950s.

The effect is of Petry's writing in a borderland of sensibility, describing events from the standpoint of an observer, as in naturalism, while narrating from the standpoint of a participant, as in critical realism. In providentially opting for the experiments in subjectivity associated with the modernist novel, she was wisely seeking an artistic solution to the contrariness of time and memory through a literary tradition famous for transcending the formal methodologies of psychology, sociology, philosophy, and political science, even while carrying out comparable work. With a residual sympathy for unorthodox Marxism, Petry depicts protagonists as being without purpose or design, as if their experiences and existence were produced by accidental interrelationships of memory and circumstance.

Yet Petry's political biography is that of a woman of the Left engaged with social struggle into the mid-1940s. When Petry believed that Harlem was being "criminalized" in the pages of the *New York Daily News* during World War II, she used her role as a journalist for the *People's Voice* to interview Harlem women and report their distress, which included information on a boycott initiated by Petry's organization, Negro Women, Inc. When a similar journalistic criminalization of African Americans is described in *The Narrows*, set ten years later, there is simply no social movement available to fight back.[92] Thus Petry's novel serves as a paradoxical memory screen for the 1930s–1950s era; events and concerns of that era are recast in the frequently blind groping of individuals searching for meaning in their past lives that will meet their present needs. We learn that a sense of history operates through a nexus of ideas that one carries into the present but that these are sadly circumscribed by one's obsession with personal trauma in the world of Monmouth.[93] What other technique than those of a renovated modernist novel could adequately depict subjects rendered disoriented, silenced, evasive, and unnarratable amid the wreckage of so many lost passions and vacated promises as those that were suffered by the African American Left?

A later version of such Cold War themes—the gutting of political hope, the turn toward one's own resources—was published as "Brooklyn," a 1959 short story by Paule Marshall. Marshall's political background is something of a delayed rendition of Petry's. Marshall was born in Brooklyn to Barbadian parents and as a teenager came under the influence of both Garveyite nationalism and Communism. In an autobiographical memoir, she states that in 1946, at the age of seventeen, she briefly belonged to a group on the "Communist fringe," the American Youth for Democracy (AYD).⁹⁴ The AYD was the youth group of the Communist Party, which had changed its name from the Young Communist League in 1944 as part of the Browderite effort to "Americanize" the Communist Party's image and politically conciliate the Allies. In 1948, the AYD would dissolve briefly into the Young Progressives of America in order to support Henry Wallace's Progressive Party presidential campaign; a year later it reformed as the Communist youth organization Labor Youth League (LYL). The LYL was a magnet for several future African American cultural figures who were contemporaries of Paule Marshall—Lorraine Hansberry, Douglas Turner Ward (born Roosevelt Ward Jr., 1930), and Audre Lorde.

Details about Marshall's own bond to the Communist movement in those years remain vague. What is known is that during the 1950s, she traveled in the same circles as did John Oliver Killens's Harlem Writers Guild, an organization that maintained autonomy from the Communist movement while sharing many of its perspectives. By the late 1950s and early 1960s, Marshall and her colleagues also led the Association of Artists for Freedom, noted for its sharp attacks on the hypocrisy of white liberalism, a category that for them to some extent included the Communist movement and the Old Left milieu.⁹⁵ While "Brooklyn" is routinely cited as a depiction of sexual harassment, the issues of race, ethnicity, Communism, political repression, resistance, commitment, and the complexity of victimization all come into play in prophetic ways.⁹⁶

During the early 1950s, Marshall was a student at Brooklyn College. She took a literature course from Harry Slochower (1900–1991), an outstanding scholar of European literature who was a fellow traveler (and possibly a member) of the Communist Party in the 1930s and 1940s. His books included *Three Ways of Modern Man* (1937), *Thomas Mann's Joseph Story: An Interpretation* (1938), and *No Voice Is Wholly Lost* (1945). In 1952, Slochower refused to cooperate with a senate internal security subcommittee, taking the Fifth Amendment when asked about Communist Party affiliation, and was fired as associate professor of German and comparative literature, one year before Marshall graduated in 1953.⁹⁷ Slochower sued for reinstatement, and in 1956 the U.S. Supreme Court ruled that he had been denied due process. Although he was reinstated and given $40,000 in back pay, he was instantly suspended on the grounds that he had made false statements at the senate hearing. Slo-

Harry Slochower was a brilliant specialist in German literature at Brooklyn College who was fired in 1954 for invoking the Fifth Amendment about past Communist affiliations. He became the subject of a distinguished short story by Paule Marshall. (Courtesy of Annette T. Rubinstein)

chower then resigned and devoted himself full-time to the practice of psychoanalysis, teaching at the New School for Social Research from 1964 until 1989 and becoming editor of the psychoanalytic quarterly *American Imago* until his death.

The events in Marshall's short story, inspired by her classroom experience, are precipitated by her protagonist's writing for a college class an essay treating André Gide's *The Immoralist* (1902), a novel about a gay man's progressive discovery of his own sexuality. The author of the essay is Miss Williams, a returning African American female student taking a night course on modern European literature taught by a brilliant and engaging Jewish American professor, Max Berman. Berman, in his appearance and manner, is a likeness of Harry Slochower. Unlike Slochower, Berman originally taught at a small community college in the 1940s but was forced out after refusing to name the names of Communist associates in front of an investigating committee. By accident, he has obtained some temporary summer teaching at Brooklyn College, but he expects to be discovered and dismissed before long.

In Marshall's haunting portrait of the relationship between an African American student with literary aspirations and a blacklisted professor, Marshall refuses to be awestruck by and forgiving of the fact that Berman has the mantle of a hero-victim. In his sexual attraction to Miss Williams, Berman believes her to be exotic and fantasizes a submissiveness on her part; this affords him a fleeting sense of empowerment, even as he realizes that these are racist thoughts and he shuts them out. There are biographical references to Berman's personal history of having been rejected by his father due to his refusal to follow the Jewish faith. In contrast, Williams recalls being taught by her own parents never to trust whites. But when Williams confronts Berman at the story's end, she realizes that, by taking control of her emotions and behavior, she is the one with more power. Marshall does not suggest that Williams's character is free of ambiguity; her power over Berman is connected with her youth and sexual attractiveness, and his designs of sexual conquest are always undermined by his belief that he is too old to be attractive.

Considering its date of conception and publication, Marshall's story likely reflects the new nationalist disparagement in her circles of the traditional Communist Party by young militants in the 1950s. Max is certainly an avatar of the Old Left, down to his name, Max, echoing "Marx" as well as Boris Max, the elderly spokesman for Communist ideals in Richard Wright's *Native Son*. In a further evocative move, the narrative is similar to that in *Death in Venice* (1912) by Thomas Mann, the central figure in Harry Slochower's literary scholarship. In Mann's novella, the aging artist is fixated on a boy as a last-minute means of affirming life, whereas in "Brooklyn" the taboo object for the older professor is a young Black woman. Present, too, are several themes from Gide's *The Immoralist*—the journey of self-discovery and the notion that one must destroy another to see oneself. Williams has learned a great deal from Berman, intellectually and from his effort at paternalist domination (not unlinked to her reminding him of his own persecution); as with Petry's Abbie Crunch, Miss Williams ascertains how one's future must be under one's own control.

RED, BLACK, AND GAY

Once considered scandalous, Leslie Fiedler's contention in *Love and Death in the American Novel* (1960) that the "archetypal image" in the most beloved books in U.S. literature may be found in "a white and a colored American male" ("colored" referring to Native American and African American) escaping "from civilization into each other's arms" triggers a plausible question within the scope of this book: What was the relation of gays and lesbians of color, especially African Americans, to the anticapitalist and interracial utopia of the pro-Communist Left?[98] Hungering for something superior to a social order that rendered them double and triple outcasts, non-straight Black radicals sought a political and cultural theater in which to enact a common humanity beyond the predominant system's sanctioned normativities. This became detectable to them in the vaunted ideals of socialism combined with facets of the antiracist practice of the Communist movement.

In the first four decades following the Russian Revolution, many African American cultural workers, ones whose same-sex relationships were later claimed by scholars, participated variously in literary and political activities of the proudly interracial Communist movement: Robert Hayden (1913–80), Owen Dodson (1914–83), Langston Hughes, Alain Locke (1885–1954), Countee Cullen (1903–46), Claude McKay (1889–1948), James Baldwin, Chester Himes, Marian Minus, Dorothy West, Lorraine Hansberry, Audre Lorde, Bob Kaufman (born Robert Garnell Kaufman, 1925–86), and Willard Motley. The presence of such talent necessitates at least a preliminary investigation of how pro-Communists and Progressives concurrently inhabited color and gender in their imaginative writing. Although an individual cannot represent a group, the tale of the habitually overlooked Willard Motley is instructive for its relentless war against the "fixedness" of concepts of race and gender. An anti-essentialist avant la lettre, Motley saw such identities as constructions, not imprints, even though his translation of homosexual alterity into fiction was ultimately stunted.

As a mature man, Motley was probably exclusively a homosexual; he was

Willard Motley, second from left, carousing with friends in a Chicago bar during the late 1940s. The popular author of *Knock on Any Door* (1949), Motley went into permanent exile in Mexico in 1951. (Courtesy of Founders Memorial Library, Northern Illinois University)

attracted to darker and muscular men, mainly Latinos and Italian Americans.[99] His own behavior was performatively masculine in a conventional manner. All of his life he prided himself on his high school football career, during which, due to his small stature, he was called "The Little Iron Man." Beyond that, recollections of Motley's expressions of his homosexuality vary among four individuals who were later willing to be interviewed about this subject. Theodore "Ted" Pierce (1901–99), a gay African American friend whom Motley met in Madison, Wisconsin, in the mid-1930s, was adamant that Motley, like himself, had understood and accepted his sexual orientation at an early age. Both men had been eager participants in a milieu of midwestern gay culture that existed as if it were a "magic triangle" surrounding Chicago and reaching to Madison and beyond.[100]

Zev Braun (b. 1928) was a younger friend from a well-to-do Chicago Jewish business family who met Motley while attending Roosevelt University in the late 1940s. Braun was certain that Motley's first profound love was for a white female high school classmate.[101] She was, Braun insisted, a counterpart of the blond-haired, blue-eyed "dream shiksa" of every Jewish boy. The young woman was responsive, but the relationship was thwarted due to the social conventions of the day. Only afterward, Braun believed, did Motley acquire a gay identity. This seems confirmed by Motley's own diaries.[102] In the 1940s, Braun claims, contrary to Pierce, Motley kept his affairs exceedingly private, never frequenting gay bars or participating in the gay cultural scene.[103]

Alexander Saxton was a close friend of Motley's as well as acquainted with Dorothy Andrews (known as "Drews"), Motley's literary assistant going back to the Hull House days. Saxton served as a literary-political role model for both of them. Drews, a lesbian and aspiring novelist herself, urged that Motley use Saxton as the inspiration for Grant Holloway, the journalist hero of *Knock on Any Door*.[104] Saxton was also the first person thanked by Motley in the pages of the published novel. Saxton's recollection is that Motley was frequently in the company of young men and women who seemed to be gay and lesbian, but he simply did not speak of his sexual life.

Archibald Motley III, the son of painter Archibald Motley Jr. (1891–1981), the uncle of Willard, believed that the objects of Motley's affection were known and precise. Much of Willard Motley's love interest fixated on a handsome white bartender and aspiring actor, Morris Glen, who was married but bisexual and whose commitment to Willard was ambivalent. Later, Willard's affections focused on a young Mexican American man, Sammy Ramirez, a relative of his friend Matias Noriega, also the object of at least platonic adoration by Motley. These identifications are consistent with references that can be found throughout the correspondence in Motley's papers.

That Motley as a novelist was to any extent part of a postwar phenomenological turn associated with Communist literary modernism appears counterintuitive from the style and form of the best-selling novel with which he crashed into the literary scene.[105] *Knock on Any Door* (1947; film 1949) was the fictionalized case history of a poor Italian American boy, Nick Romano, driven to crime and murder, a narrative that climaxed in a thrilling trial. The three novels that came after— *We Fished All Night* (1951), *Let No Man Write My Epitaph* (1957; film 1960), and the posthumous *Let Noon Be Fair* (1966)— seem even less preoccupied with structures of consciousness; they mostly tend toward naturalism in the sense of aspiring to inclusiveness and an aura of scientific objectivity. Although all three were published while Motley lived in exile in Mexico, the first two re-created the tawdry urban-anxiety mood of *Knock on Any Door* and are set in the horror and beauty of industrial Chicago; the last delineates the effects of U.S. tourism on a Mexican resort town in the 1950s.

The bulk of this four-volume oeuvre is part proletarian literature and part suspense thriller, with the author relying alternately on a huge cast of characters and sometimes-pedestrian internal monologues. What the new postwar contingency meant for Motley was obviously not a break from the style of vigorous realism; the form of his fictional writings is analogous to the wrapping paper that must be undone to see the gift inside. Motley depicts central conflicts stemming from economic and political sources accepted by the Left, but his eye is on characters with disobedient gender identities; he simply refuses to allow a sense of social order to be achieved at the expense of psychosexual individuality and autonomy. This is the one matter in which Motley's literary imagination was poised on the fault line between the older techniques of the 1930s and the sensibility of the new contingency: the performative aspect of identity. Whatever the clumsiness of his articulations, he did not want a world in which people were divided up into heterosexual and homosexual any more than by race.

Motley additionally aimed to challenge his era's widespread contempt for gay people by showing the difficulties they faced in a nonaccepting society. Although Ted Pierce insisted that Motley's "roots were in the gay world," he was intellectually disaffiliated from what he believed to be the prevailing notions of "Negro" and homosexual behavior and psychology.[106] But was negation enough? His emotions are more difficult to fathom. Assorted personal inhibitions, rooted in gnawing family secrets, were determinant in preventing Motley's construction of a convincing Black and homosexual presence in his fiction. Motley the person is the key to the books, instead of vice versa; the constituent parts of much of his novels are rooted in his personal history. Of course, one cannot ignore the challenge of countenancing the obvious limitations of the conditions under which gay novelists were forced to negotiate with their publishers. What is surprising is that when one turns to Motley's unpublished manuscripts and chapters deleted by his editors, one finds the same curtailed efforts that limit the work in print: incomplete artistic formulations of circumstances and emotions that the author refuses to disclose.

Like Oscar Wilde, Motley yearned for an escape from moralistic prohibitionism, but unlike Wilde he would not turn victimization into martyrdom. In personal notes he kept for a planned book-length novel about homosexual culture in the postwar era, he explained that he did not want to write the kind of book later known as the "Homosexual Problem Novel"; he hated the ones he read such as Gore Vidal's *The Pillar and the City* (1946).[107] He also refused to depict a homosexual as a redemptive figure, as in James Baldwin's *Another Country* (1962). While Motley's rejection of the available racial and gender definitions makes sense in a pre-Stonewall age, the absence of an alternative turned into a no-win predicament. Rather than producing fiction that replaced settled forms of identity with processes embedded in class, national, ethnic, and personal contexts, Motley could generate only a disconcerting sequence of enigmas and stereotypes.

Hoist with his own petard of nondisclosure, Motley nonetheless partook, instinctively, of an "Adornian" dialectic through which his novels register a cognition of tension between concepts of race and gender and the nonconceptuality of the same. He merged with Petry and others in eroding prior categories, which in Petry's case created a narrative that promoted a dissolution of the 1930s idea of the novel as reflective of the material configuration of experience. But anyone seeking in Motley a nimble and buoyant presentation of such art will be disappointed. He aspired to panoramic volumes on a grand scale, and these are weighted with the deadly undertow of exhaustively researched sociological settings. Only a vigilant reader can discern how Motley's literary trajectory exhibits a process of paradoxical self-negation. Unlike Petry, there is no rematerializing logic to his texts through a vivid seizure of the imagination.

In the eyes of his FBI watchers, Willard Motley was simply a "Negro writer with Leftist and homosexual tendencies who has lived in Mexico for a number of years."[108] To understand more intricately what this redaction denoted, one needs to recover motives and meanings from Motley's intimate life. The central calamity of Motley's biography, and the source of the pain that drove him into seclusion and the bizarre behavior that precipitated his early death, stemmed from his mortification over the circumstances of his birth.[109] Throughout his career as a novelist, Motley avowed to have been born in 1912; he claimed that Mary ("Mae") Motley, a Chicago teacher, was his mother, and even dedicated his most successful work, *Knock on Any Door*, "To Mary, My Mother." He furthermore stated that Archibald Motley Sr., a Pullman porter, was his father; that Florence ("Flossie") Motley, fourteen years older, was his sister; that the famed painter Archibald Motley Jr., twenty years older, was his brother; and, later, that Sergio Lopez was his son, as written in his dedication to *Let No Man Write My Epitaph*, "For My Son, Sergio." None of this was true. Motley was actually born in 1909, and the name on his birth certificate read Willard Frances Bryant.[110] The Motley family attorney, Walter Roth, has no record of any adoptions of a son by Motley, and no adopted children have ever made any claims on his estate, although he had property in Mexico that could have been inherited.[111]

Bryant was the name of a thirty-six-year-old boarder in the Motley home in the Engelwood neighborhood in Chicago in 1909, who impregnated Mae Motley's fourteen-year-old daughter, Flossie. A hasty marriage, followed by a quick annulment, was arranged; this was engineered so that Willard would technically not be illegitimate. An agreement was then made for Willard's grandparents, Mae and Archibald Sr., to act as if they were Willard's parents and for his uncle and biological mother to pretend to be his brother and sister. The arrangement worked until Willard was twelve. At that time, Mae, in a fit of rage over some misbehavior by Willard, blurted out the truth; Willard burst into tears and was shaken to his roots. When he eventually confronted Flossie, she retaliated by claiming that Bryant the border had also been Mae's lover.

Willard never knew whether Flossie's accusation was true, but he thought it was possible when he later learned that his grandfather was a womanizer who contracted syphilis and was hospitalized at the time of Bryant's residence. Instead of personalizing his anger, his bitterness initially fueled an undying hatred of the pretensions of the African American middle class. He turned his back on the past, first by tramping around the United States for nearly a decade, then by moving in 1939 to the very slums from which middle-class people aspired to escape. Although he had published regularly in the *Chicago Defender* since childhood (he was the paper's original "Bud Billiken" columnist) and wrote on matters such as Black artists,[112] his associations were overwhelmingly Euro-American and Latino. Motley's dearest friend after 1939 was the man to whom *Let Noon Be Fair* would be dedicated: "For MATIAS NORIEGA: Friend, compadre, brother." Noriega was a "tough as nails" Chicano truck driver, World War II hero, and member of a Chicago gang that periodically executed drug dealers who tried to peddle narcotics in his neighborhood. Noriega was also a valuable insider source for many episodes in Motley's novels, as well as the inspiration for some of his hoodlum characters.[113]

Over the years, Willard maintained a relation with Flossie, who eventually married and had five more children; but he chafed bitterly at his biological mother's refusal to embrace him openly as her son. The pain was first masked and deflected by personal rage against the "Black bourgeoisie," then subsumed into his postwar career as a literary radical in Chicago, where he aimed to do penance for his apolitical youth by focusing on class oppression in relation to all ethnicities. In early 1947, however, he came to the conclusion that he needed to write a novel about his childhood trauma and sent a letter to his editor, Ted Purdy, detailing every last throbbing memory—although the events were couched as a work of fiction.[114] The project was deflected by his move to Mexico and then by the decision to continue the saga of Nick Romano, perhaps for commercial reasons, through a novel about Romano's son, *Let No Man Write My Epitaph.*

Motley felt a fervent identification with the celebrated final remarks of Irish nationalist Robert Emmett. Under indictment as a traitor in 1803, Emmett insisted that only the inhabitants of some future and more just society could explain his character and motives. For the time being, he said, "Let no man write my epitaph." Motley insisted, against his publisher's advice, that Emmett's remarks be both the title and epigraph of *Let No Man Write My Epitaph*. The theme is picked up throughout the book. In one critical incident, the journalist Grant Holloway—the white, well-to-do crusading radical in *Knock on Any Door* who reappears, albeit less centrally, in this third novel—sits in the Shillelagh, a bar that attracts many homosexuals. He ruminates: "To deny any is to deny yourself. Every human being is dignified. Or should be. Has something of quality. God! If you knew the life of any one of them here from cradle to this point. If you knew what brought them here. How can anybody judge anyone else? Not, at least, without knowing all of his life and that of his parents and his grandparents. It's easy to judge. It's hard to dig down into the solid rock of cause."[115] The reference to parents and grandparents is one of several allusions to phantoms enduring in Motley's own psyche and impairing artistic fulfillment.

In Mexican exile, Motley had to some extent tried to step outside his personal history yet instead found that his childhood memories were increasingly consolidated. Now he decided to embrace them, an utter reversal of his feelings in the early 1930s when he wrote in his diary: "I recognize no one in this damnable family as being related, regardless of how distantly, to me. I stand and am alone—alone—."[116] In Mexico, he felt closer than ever to Mae, acknowledging that her strength of personality had contributed to the artistic drive of himself and his uncle, Archibald Jr. But Motley also progressively fell into a psychological abyss, which came to a crisis following Mae's death at the end of the 1950s. After a period of mourning, he was momentarily unblocked on the subject and drafted detailed plans to write a three-volume novel about her life. It would be called "The Family" and required research trips such as one to New Orleans to make inquiries into her family history. There would also be a separate book-length volume about himself, called "The Grandson," and one about Archibald Motley Jr., called "The Brother."[117]

In a familiar pattern, Motley put off the next steps toward carrying out this emotionally grueling family project. As an alternative, he turned his writing in a completely new direction that, at least superficially, took up more immediate concerns. His last years were entirely devoted to nonfictional and fictional books about the effects of U.S. tourism on Mexico. Although friends and family who visited Motley from Chicago made appearances in some of this new work, his source materials were far from the personal and family experiences in the United States on which he had been meditating. The setting and historical events of his last writings came from what he had casually observed in Puerto Vallarta, where he lived, and Acapulco, where he visited. And yet Motley's childhood trauma still seemed to hamstring his creations of literary characters, none of whom are memorable. In the only book-length manuscript of his last decade that saw print, *Let Noon Be Fair*, the ghosts of this early psychological damage revisit in customary as well as in new shapes to create a demoralizing finale to his literary career.

EXILE AND ITS DISCONTENTS

Motley's writing was never about just homosexuals or African Americans; his gaze focused first of all on the skeins and rags of human existence, shaping them into narratives that layer one story inside another. Like Nelson Algren, Motley felt most comfortable with the very poor, the *lumpenproletariat* of bums, drug addicts, prostitutes, and hustlers. A growing distance from the 1930s did not mean for Motley a narrowing of social range; on this point, critically unfashionable novelists like Motley and Algren, hewing to the underclass that time forgot, came across as vividly as many who dominate the received memory of the literary 1950s. Motley wanted to use his characters, people on the bottom, to practice new emotional situations; the truth of Black or gay identity would not emerge from this writing like the prize figure in a nest of Russian dolls.

Motley was by no means reluctant to transform African American life into fiction; he just did it badly. In all four of his novels, there are many diverse Black characters; even more appear in writings that he was unable to get into print, including short stories, sections of his novels cut by editors, and plans for future projects. He could come up with striking titles, such as "I Discover I'm a Negro" (an unpublished essay, probably 1943–44) and "The Almost White Boy" (a story published in 1963). But the disclosures of African American life were disappointing when compared to the essays and fiction of the slightly younger up-and-coming James Baldwin. The problem was not that Motley was out to dramatize a clear-cut thesis in the manner of pro-Communist W. E. B. Du Bois (1868–1963), who intended in *The Black Flame* (1957–61), a massive and ungainly fictional trilogy, to make racism an international issue. Motley aspired only to set Black life in a broad class context, allowing multiethnic bridges to be built and alliances to emerge. African American culture, he seemed to say, was but one of many cultures to which he wanted access. As a foil, he opposed the use of Blackness as a narrow vantage point from which to assess the world. This led him to publish inflammatory articles in 1947 and 1963 claiming that Chester Himes and James Baldwin expressed a hatred of whites and were becoming what he disparaged as "Professional Negroes."[118]

One might wonder if there was a self-hatred of Motley's own African American background behind such unwise pronouncements. Motley's personal journals are filled with complex and contradictory emotions about his Blackness, complicated by his upbringing in a white middle-class neighborhood and the Roman Catholic faith. A typical passage reads: "This is the first time I've really hated being part a Negro. Other times it has been rather fun—like a game—as if I were the prince in a fairy story—under the spell of some evil witch."[119] The sum of these inconsistent feelings, alternately pride and shame about his color, are uncontainable by any label.[120] In contrast, in conversation and in many places in his fiction, Motley expressed simplistic views that seem to advocate "racelessness" and "color blindness." Some of his characteristic statements are attributed to a minor Black character, Dave Wilson, in his second novel, *We Fished All Night*. Dave is said by his white friend Milo to think that "people are just people" and to be uninterested in "just the Negro Problem."[121]

Such platitudes are open to a variety of interpretations, and one is that Dave is not denying race consciousness or solidarity but invoking a larger framework. When Motley himself declared that "my race is the human race," he seemed to think that he was not disavowing his Blackness but affirming his commonality with all the oppressed.[122] The expression recalls the closing lines of the socialist anthem "The Internationale": "The Internationale shall be the human race." "The Internationale" was a favorite of Motley's, and in a noted episode in the fall of 1951, Willard sang it on the terrace of the Bella Vista Hotel in Cuernavaca, after some white Texans were ejected for making racist remarks. The newspapers reported the incident as proof of Motley's Communism.[123]

Parallel questions about possible self-hate or shame on the part of Motley might be raised by the analogous manner that he used his novels to include gay and lesbian characters and the depiction of gay life. There are intimations in these writings that Motley believed anti-gay prejudice to be deeper than racism, yet he mocked other gay males as sissified, distancing himself from his gay characters. These figures often exhibited monolithic, stereotyped features, as in a description in *Let No Man Write My Epitaph* of a gay bar: "The men speak in high-pitched voices and laugh in girlish screams, even the old ones. They move their bodies petulantly and suggestively. The women broad-shoulder their way to the bar in their blue jeans, proud of their tattoos, of their somewhat muscled arms, their husky voices."[124] When Motley most plainly represents himself as Dave in *We Fished All Night*, all the reader can grasp is that he is quiet and modest. Dave is always in the company of other masculine figures of diverse ethnicities. He displays no effeminate characteristics and is devoid of sexual interests. In Motley's work, the most positive representation of homoerotic feelings comes through the quiet interracial camaraderie of young men.

Motley the Marxist was somewhat less mysterious in his self-definition than Motley the Black gay man. In the 1940s and early 1950s, he rapidly moved to a militant anticapitalism and became a fiercely independent revolutionary. These politics were never abandoned, but he deemphasized them in Mexico. A friend, William Goodwill (called "Sweet William" in several of Motley's writings), had briefly joined the Communist youth group AYD and met Motley through Progressive Party activities in Chicago. After staying with Motley for a while in Cuernavaca, Goodwill was interviewed by the FBI in California due to delinquency in regard to his draft board notice. His testimony, which seems credible, is that Motley was somewhat pro-Soviet and believed that the United States was at fault in the Korean War. Goodwill described Motley as a friend of U.S. Communists living in exile—Albert Maltz, John Bright—but not a Communist himself.[125]

Oddly, in the 1930s, when Motley spent much of eight years wandering around the country as a young man, he showed no political interests at all. Only in 1939, when he abandoned his family's white middle-class neighborhood and moved to an apartment in the Chicago slums at Fourteenth and Union Streets, did he begin to fall under the influence of the heterogeneous radicals who hung around Hull House, founded by Jane Addams. As a member of the Illinois Writers Project in the early 1940s, he grew close to pro-Communists Jack Conroy (1898–1990) and Nelson Algren.[126] In the next decade, he had periods of association with individuals and activities connected with both the Communist and the Trotskyist movements, climaxed by his wholehearted support of the Henry Wallace Progressive Party campaign in 1948. *We Fished All Night* retrospectively supported the Progressive Party movement, putting into fiction the view that the Democratic Party had been transformed into an instrument of the ruling elite. The novel was intended to go beyond even *Knock on Any Door* in announcing a complete break with class society and the apolitical illusions to which Motley had subscribed until the late 1930s. It's the only work of Motley's not dedicated to an individual person: "This book is for all the soldiers who fought for all the countries that failed them in the hope that they will never again have to fight for all the countries that will again fail them."[127]

Plot summaries can too easily annul the unique aspects of Motley's outlook, and no generalization can do justice to his varied imaginative world.

Motley's Marxism was of the "Which side are you on?" variety. Although strikes and unions are symbols for unity and justice in *We Fished All Night*, the industrial working class was not Motley's subject; he takes his distance from the Communist Party in a manner that accurately reflects his own skepticism following a period (1942–43) when he apparently toyed with the idea of joining. Motley's "pacificism" was akin to the internationalist opposition to World War I. Personal correspondence leaves no doubt about his political orientation to the Far Left, and the manner in which his novels dramatize episodes from his life communicates his feelings about politics.

A series of letters documents Motley's Marxist development. In September 1945, Motley received a query from his assistant Drews, requesting an explanation of how he could have been both a Marxist and a conscientious objector. His answer can be found earlier, in a 1943 correspondence with Alexander Saxton about Communism and pacifism. Motley explained that he would have fought with the Republicans in Spain and that he was willing to do armed battle against the capitalist McCormicks and Hearsts, as well as their European counterparts. But he saw no solutions through wars in which working people were pitted against each other, and he could not countenance what he saw as the lie that the United States was fighting for democracy when it insisted on segregating its own military.[128] In *We Fished All Night*, Eric, a Communist novelist (undoubtedly modeled on Alexander Saxton), struggles patiently to explain Communist Party policy on pacifism to the potential recruit Aaron Levin, but simply gives up in the face of the poet's reiteration of antiwar dogma: "Only the men who refuse to fight can stop war."[129] If he had any disagreements about the Soviet Union or other aspects of the Communist philosophy or program in the early 1940s, they were not expressed.

In the eight years between this correspondence with Saxton and the publication of *We Fished All Night*, Motley's Marxist commitment deepened. There was evidence of continued sympathy for the Communist Party but also indications that he was not held hostage to its politics. At the beginning of the war, his role models were avowedly Saxton and other Chicago Communists, such as Conrad Komorawski, whose association with Motley was noted by the FBI.[130] But Motley's experiences with courses at the Communist Party–led Abraham Lincoln School in Chicago brought mixed results, similar to the encounters of the Jewish poet Aaron Levin (probably modeled on his friend Harold Miller) in *We Fished All Night*, one of the three central protagonists of this complex narrative. The sense of purpose, idealism, and basic values of the Communist Party remained a magnet for Motley, but the Communist Party's insistence on a correct line, handed down from above, and often with an arrogant intolerance of those who saw things differently, was unendurable.

Support for the Progressive Party became Willard's means of achieving the same ends as the Communist Party, only without the narrow constraints of Communist Party doctrine and a constant monitoring by Communist Party leaders. Ted Pierce believed that Motley held Communist Party membership, while Saxton, who departed for the West Coast in 1942, finds that inconceivable.[131] Motley primarily functioned as an erratic fellow traveler. His activities were often with the National Council of the Arts, Sciences and Professions, essentially the successor of the League of American Writers, which mobilized support for the Progressive Party. Motley nevertheless demonstrated a genuine independence when he became active with the Trotskyist Socialist Workers Party in two political defense cases. The first was of James Hickman, a Black worker who had killed his Black landlord after a fire of suspicious origin had burned to death four of Hickman's children.[132] The second concerned James Kutcher, a Trotskyist and legless veteran of World War II who was fired from his Veterans Administration job for being an alleged subversive.[133] In 1949, Motley was a member of both the Communist-led National Non-partisan Committee to Defend the Rights of the 12 Communist Party Leaders and the Trotskyist-led Chicago Committee for James Kutcher. He was a one-man United Front.

When his literary reputation soared in the late 1940s, Willard Motley was a striking-looking, handsome man. He had hair that was cropped short, sculpted high cheekbones, a thin little mustache (like the actor Adolph Menjou), and a light skin color. His voice was flat but musical. His body was compact; he was five feet six or seven inches tall and weighed 135 pounds. He became bowlegged as he aged but remained trim and energetic, always walking up a couple of steps at a time. He was a gentle soul who rarely showed anger and responded to everyone with compassion. But he was increasingly beset by melancholy; by the late 1940s, he had become a very heavy drinker, a functional alcoholic, who began with beer in the morning, ate very little, and was always at least a bit tipsy. He frequently passed out in the evening.[134] When he moved to Mexico in 1951, he told his lawyer that it was just a temporary visit to avoid political subpoenas.[135] But traveling south of the border had already been attractive to him for a kind of sexual tourism, even though the details are vague, and a growing affinity with the nonindustrial culture. The exile became permanent, and Motley's return visits to the United States became less frequent. Throughout the 1950s, his circle of friends and visitors became smaller and his behavior less explicable. Saxton, who attempted to reestablish contact in these years, believes that Motley in Mexico became dependent on drugs, probably amphetamines, and others agree.[136] Years came to pass with laborious writing but increasingly fewer publications.

On the last day of February 1965, Zev Braun, by this time a thirty-seven-year-old award-winning film producer in Hollywood, received a panic-stricken phone call. Braun was stunned to hear the alarming news that Willard had been transported to a hospital in Mexico City by a young Mexican man, Sergio Lopez, who claimed to be the author's adopted son. As later reported in the press, the fifty-five-year-old Motley, having lived alone in exile from the United States for fourteen years, was suffering from a gangrenous infection.[137] The Mexican youth claimed that Motley's condition had existed for some time. Motley's friends would learn that, under the influence of a doctor with disreputable credentials, Motley had been administering his own penicillin and treating the infection in unconventional ways.

Instantaneously, Braun, in true Hollywood fashion, went on a campaign to mobilize everyone he could to save Willard's life. Braun's brother-in-law, a medical student studying hematology, supplied the name of a specialist. Braun then arranged to pay for Matias Noriega's airfare to Mexico. With several members of Motley's family, the two men went immediately upon arrival to the hospital in Mexico City, only to find Willard in a coma from which he would never awake. Braun and the others were crushed by the swiftness of these unexpected events. On 4 March 1965, Willard died. A hurried decision was made to bury him in Cuernavaca, in the Mexican earth whose beauty he so adored. As a lapsed Catholic, Willard had often said that no priest should officiate at his last rites. So members of the group turned to Braun to deliver the eulogy. Braun, however, was emotionally shattered and began choking up. All eyes then turned to Matias Noriega. Matias came forward, straddled Willard's grave, stared fiercely at the small gathering, and then blurted out enigmatically: "He was a man!"[138]

It is true that art does not necessarily gain from directness, but the shallow depictions of sexuality and ethnicity that can be discerned in Motley's later fiction have baffled most of his readers, encouraging misinterpretations and neglect of his work. His first two novels are landmarks of unsparing realism, but his inability to achieve an innovative negotiation of the difficult path to free himself from ideological and contextual traps about identity only doomed the articulation of a new vision. By the time of *Let Noon Be Fair* (drafted by Motley but cut and reorganized by his editor, Peter Israel), his view is mostly that sex of any kind only brutalizes people's sensibilities. This novel and a related unpublished manuscript of the same years, "My House Is Your House," uniquely comment on the export of racism from the United States to Mexico but present no vivid characters and little remarkable prose.[139] Painful childhood memories may have hacked away the roots of whatever beliefs he was trying to formulate about the possibilities of the human condition. There was something personal in his obsession with the idea of external corruption of a local environment on which he fixated in his two treatments of foreign sensation-seekers descending on small Mexican tourist towns. The frustration of his vision is dramatized at the climax of *Let Noon Be Fair*, a novel that camouflages the erotic component of Motley's own attraction to Mexico while providing an unforgiving if superficial critique of the sexual tourism of others.

Motley professed a love of Mexican indigenous culture, but he fails to vivify its traditions against the overpowering atmosphere of absence, loss, and exile that fill the book. As a writer always immersed in firsthand research about specific locales, he somehow evolved into a ghost without attachments or habitation. The final pages show the author's psyche invaded by repressed forces in the form of a grotesque Mexican child, Juana. Depicted by Motley as deformed and repulsive, Juana is the discarded daughter of a couple, Florencia and Silvio. She was given to a female servant to raise following the loss of her own child, an abandonment that at one remove reenacts Motley's own childhood of rejection by his biological mother. Juana is an emblem of Motley's internalized shame, self-hate, and revulsion—a feeble-minded creature, virtually homeless, who for years wanders the village in search of love. Now she has grown into a huge adolescent of several hundred pounds (nicknamed "La Luchadora," the wrestler) seething with lust. Juana enters the home of Tom Van Pelt, a writer who resembles the novelist Motley as he presented himself in public.

Although he is white, Van Pelt is from Chicago, an early discoverer of the pre-tourist town of La Casas, and a man ashamed of the predatory behavior of his countrymen. Van Pelt adheres to the literary creed often expressed by Motley: "The artist, the realistic writer, is involved with life as it is. . . . He explores the ugly, the miserable, the humble, to show the beauty and humanity in it."[140] As Van Pelt thinks these thoughts, Juana lies on the floor of his cottage, lifts her dress, and begins aggressively fingering her vagina while calling out to him. Van Pelt, still meditating about the duty of the realistic artist, mechanically puts on a condom, masturbates, and enters Juana with fantasies of "beautiful women, loves of times past."[141] The repressed and fractured selves of Motley are thus reimagined, pathetically (and, one hopes, satirically), in the sexual intercourse of the freakishly depicted Mexican orphan with the burned-out expatriate writer. Van Pelt's weary statement of an artistic calling in such banal thoughts, presented as if they were profundities, and his performing of an act of love while on automatic pilot are depressing markers of the obstructing psychic dynamics that blocked Motley's way to any forward-looking literary practice.

Motley is the odd man out in both radical and gay literary history. At its best, his early writing suggests the later Alfred Döblin (1878–1957), especially when comparing *Berlin Alexanderplatz* (1929) to *We Fished All Night*, the difficult work that holds the key to his oeuvre. The two authors created novels of the metropolis that juxtaposed workers' districts to the city of the bourgeoisie. As with Nelson Algren, Motley can powerfully dramatize the crisis of masculinity within men of the underclass, which usually culminates not in redemption but social suicide. In both writers, violence explodes out of the mix of the individualism of contemporary capitalism and the void left by the suppression of the collective alternative. But a conviction that one is in the truth-telling business is not enough; the quantity of details supplied in Motley's novels only tests the patience of readers when he fails to find a way to boldly embrace the enigmatic dialectics of identity. By the time of *Let Noon Be Fair*, the sole appeal of his work is in its status as a rare Cold War–era artifact that is disapproving of the decadent and racialized expatriatism of well-off people in an underdeveloped economy. Motley's trajectory from the rousing *Knock on Any Door* to the personal demoralization and even sexual self-ridicule of this last novel is a reminder of the impasse reached by some of those trapped between social realism and the new contingency. No generalization applies to the wide-ranging heritage of gay and lesbian pro-Communist writers, but Willard Motley stands as one writer who came back fighting from his own private war against the official propaganda of World War II, only to collapse in exile into the loneliness of the radical homosexual.

Chapter Seven

Jews without Judaism

DECONVERSION AND DISAVOWAL

The record of Jewish American cultural achievement in the postwar decades is extensive and irregular. Many of the emerging writers in the era, now treated as fomenting a "Jewish American Renaissance," had a background in Marxism, usually Communism, by personal or family association.¹ What is still visible of the left-wing reference points of this literary tradition resembles a disrupted itinerary, fractured but conveying information nonetheless. A few authors made open but laconic references to their political pasts in their writing, including Norman Mailer, Saul Bellow, Allen Ginsberg, Grace Paley, and Tillie Olsen. Others, such as Bernard Malamud, evaded the subject, and there are indications of radical pasts that biographers might pursue in respect to Karl Shapiro, Philip Roth, and even J. D. Salinger. Only recently, the more precise Communist personal histories of Leon Uris (1924–2003), inspired to write by Mike Gold's *Jews without Money* (1930) and William Blake's *The Copperheads* (1941), and Arthur Miller (1915–2005), whose enthusiasm for the movement began in 1935, have come to notice.²

Of the hundreds of lesser-known writers who were part of the broad Left anchored by the Communist movement, one can make exalted claims for only a few. Still, apart from literary distinction and whatever distance the authors did or did not take from their backgrounds in Marxism, the fiction and poetry of a good number function as a sort of dissident literature. This embedded protest may have been inspired by opposition to the commercialization of culture in the 1950s but was also tacitly against the stifling mentality generated by pro-Communists and Progressives under the spell of late antifascism.

Even prior to the 1950s, novels that were fragmented and convoluted, self-absorbed and bookish, constituted by definition a decided rebellion against most of the Soviet literary models. It was with a new consciousness regarding the terrain of the Consumers' Republic that one-time Leftists Bellow and Malamud reacted at least implicitly to the excesses embodied in Zhdanovism by promoting an ethical concern that valued individuality and creativity over mythologized heroics of self-sacrifice. Their best sellers, *The Adventures of Augie March* (1953) and *The Assistant* (1957), showcased the very interiority and idiosyncrasy of the private person that remained at odds with the two rival political forces pressing upon them from opposite sides: the ideologically saturated official culture of the Stalinist regime and its imitators in the United States, and the stifling constraints of McCarthyism and Cold War conformity. Limits were thus created that confined openly political articulations to a few outcast books, such as Norman Mailer's canny but roundly deplored *Barbary Shore* (1951).

Yet the labor of dissidence of even the restricted rebellion by Bellow and others won out. It came into view more effectively than the less discernible backdrop of the particular group of Jewish American novels that are the subject of this chapter, ones unmistakably expressing an attendant mourning for a lost sense of evolution toward a collective aim. Ironically, it was writers like the rightward-moving Bellow and the even more conservative Jack Kerouac (also a socialist in his youth) who eventually helped to release new literary space for a younger generation of radical political voices who returned in the 1960s to broader and often militant social criticism.

Walter Benjamin coined the phrase "Left Melancholia" in the early 1930s as an epithet criticizing a radical writer's backward-looking attachment to petrified sentiments and analysis.[3] It is an elusive concept when applied to literary practice, not to be reduced to the psychiatric definition, but augments the better-known "diaspora" (a community of people in exile), "trauma" (psychic injury), and the broader concept of Weberian "disenchantment" (eradication of traditions and emotions) as one of the critical categories by which to understand the 1945–60 unraveling of Jewish American Communism as a movement. In specifically literary matters, the joining of Left Melancholia with the terms "deconversion" and "disavowal" may create a productive perspective on the inner workings of Jewish American fiction of the long postwar era that emerges from the splintering political tradition of the previous decades.[4] The combination provides an idiom for translating the common structures of feeling of several superior but overlooked novels that register a crumbling worldview.

Taken in unison, these three concepts also allow a pointed contrast with the renowned Cold War, anti-Communist confessional autobiographies of Louis Budenz, Elizabeth Bentley, and Whittaker Chambers, a genre in which a surprisingly small number of Jewish Americans appear. In point of fact, Bentley's *Out of Bondage* (1951) and the others are more accurately narratives of "reconversion" than they are of deconversion; the informer turned memoirist ineluctably makes his or her way back to a lost freedom as a means to reaffirm religion or Americanism.[5] In most cases, the rebirth of Budenz and others is complemented by a ritualized obsession with monolithic "communism," a phenomenon well skewered in famous essays by Hannah Arendt and Isaac Deutscher.[6] Alternatively, the narrative fictions of disavowal and deconversion written by Jewish American Left authors are seldom works of explicit apostasy. Even less are they characteristic of the renegacy in which, as Arendt notes, the mind-set of a once-devoted Stalinist simply reverses the sides of an antinomian opposition. Among novelists, thoughts pertaining to Jewish pro-Communist affects and experiences revolve indecisively around a nostalgic hope; they rarely jell into support of the certainty of a new system or of a return to the old religion that was rejected at the outset.

In the absence of theology, then, what are the sources of the imagination for the Jewish American cultural Left? The intricate and multifaceted saga of the imbrication of Jews in the Communist movement in the United States emphasizes the prevailing allure of a dream of a cooperative society in which Jews in some manner function harmoniously with other ethnicities.[7] Such an image arose in part from the Jewish culture of exile, one sponsored in sundry ways by both Jews and gentiles, to be performed near-intuitively by the Jewish writer in the theater of American culture. In its secular radical manifestation, what is exceptional in exile is the emphasis on the aspect of homelessness. It is the expression of a writer's multiple alienations, a distancing not only from a direct or indirect persecution by anti-Semites but also estrangement from the backward and repressive lives of the old-world Jewish rabbi and shtetl merchant.[8] The internationalist universals that emerged as rivals to ethnic particularisms, and that typify the Jewish American radical novelist, were, perhaps cryptically and unconsciously, aimed at reconciling these specific tensions. They embody forms of Jewish presence and rootlessness, even in the Jewish American writers' efforts to imaginatively perform the lives of others, especially African Americans. The Jewish provenance of the postwar literary arc in Left fiction was entrenched not just in the universals of mutual causes and collective hopes for humankind but also in inherited commonalities of language, frames of reference, and hierarchies of value. Jews without Judaism offered a version of the "consent and descent" dilemma in U.S. culture.[9] Although their Communist past was mostly behind them, the Jewish novelists still remembered.

Internationalist ideals militated against special favors for the Jew. In the

Communist movement, one could receive an education in Jewish history that directly countered the notion of "chosenness," a contentious concept generally believed to be an essential idea in Jewish identity. The Left alternative, expressed in a recent memoir by literary scholar Eugene Goodheart, was a belief in "the need for the Jewish people to identify themselves with the suffering of other people, to insist on our common humanity."[10] Such an internationalist orientation was present even in novels where Jewishness might be unseen or functioning through a surrogate character by way of a disguised situation analogous to a Jewish situation. Tensions in this variety of novels may serve as metaphors, their power nourished by a writer's half-hidden politico-ethnic identity. Such efforts were occasionally aided by the writer's publishing under a neutral or non-Jewish name, which could be by choice (Jo Sinclair, John Sanford) or inheritance (Howard Fast, Arthur Miller).

Sometimes, in a novel or in autobiographical data released by a writer, there is a deafening silence about one's Jewish and Communist background. It may be that the biographical experience had truly receded or had never been that powerful. But in the Cold War, such reticence could also stem from a mixture of conscious strategizing and unconscious mental gymnastics in order to avoid real or imagined danger. Some version of this mix is suggested by the carefully controlled biographical material generated by the husband and wife team Katya Gilden (born Minnie Alpert, 1919–91) and Bert D. Gilden (1915–71), writing as "K. B. Gilden." They authored *Hurry Sundown* (1964), a best seller about the failure of postwar liberal ideals in the South, followed by *Between the Hills and the Sea* (1971), the premier labor novel of the 1950s Left. In the instance of the Gildens, a researcher can use personal letters and interviews to establish the political (Communist) and ethnic (Jewish) biographical facts critical to understanding their political and artistic aims, including the desire (never carried through) to fully present Communist characters.[11] Their aspiration to control their public image is reasonable, but the cost to literary memory is lamentable.

Even when a novel in the postwar Left tradition has no major Jewish characters, as is the case in the two books written by the Gildens, a writer's ethnic self is not necessarily dissolved. It may be enacted in background events, in atmosphere, or under another name. Several possible reasons come to mind. First, as with the Gildens, there could be a fear of political repression or of narrowing one's readership. Or perhaps one is immersed in genuine psychological denial about issues in one's background. But one could also gain freedom from self-censorship by switching the ethnicity of fictional persons resembling oneself or one's acquaintances; some writers desperately need characters and situations that address their plight in ways that are subtle and dramatic without being politically and ethnically explicit and obvious. Abraham Polonsky's *The World Above* (1951) is a similar example of a dramatization of Jewish American consciousness without Jewish American protagonists.

The novels by the Gildens and Polonsky illustrate that there is no necessary connection between a "true confession" of one's autobiographical references and the attaining of artistic quality, especially if one aims to depict contradictions and process, a worthy objective for these dialecticians of the imagination. A novel like Polonsky's that uses metaphor—psychoanalysis as a surrogate for Marxism, a German American for a Jewish American—may be technically "lying." But if carefully chosen, such substitutes provide a shape and structure fruitfully representing the self in the interstices of the unconscious mind and the conscious will. This is the special triumph of the Gildens and Polonsky, elevating their novels away from the pedestrianism that dominated so much radical regionalism and toward the Communist literary modernism of Ann Petry's *The Narrows*.

The memory of the Jewish Left is a gift that keeps on giving; it appears in myriad forms, over many generations. Most of the novels that might be associated with such a Left tradition in the decades after World War II emerged from heartfelt emotions about shared cultural moments and experiences that were generated by the pro-Soviet radical movement itself. The fate of Communism-cum-"Progressivism" was a more pervasive source for this subtext than was the Jewish religion or purely ethnic traits.[12] Such a diminishing apparition of hope and desire was addressed using sundry styles over a long stretch. Edward Newhouse wrote satirically of it in *The Hollow of the Wave* (1949), William Herrick sardonically in *The Itinerant* (1967), and Sam Ross breezily in *Windy City* (1979). Michael Blankfort used indirection in *The Juggler* (1952) and *The Strong Hand* (1956), as did Joy Davidman in *Weeping Bay* (1950), Dan Levin in *The Dream and the Flesh* (1953), Gordon Kahn in *A Long Way from Home* (written in the early 1950s, published in 1989), and Norman Rosten in *Neighborhood Tales* (1986). Some novelists re-created their emotions in settings before the Great Depression—Benjamin Appel in *A Time of Fortune* (1963), Louis Falstein in *Laughter on a Weekday* (1965), Ben Field in *Jacob's Son* (1971), and Jean Karsavina in *White Eagle, Dark Skies* (1974). Others addressed the 1930s by de-centering the U.S. Left—Yuri Suhl in *One Foot in America* (1950), Gerda Lerner in *No Farewell* (1955), and David Alman in *Generations* (1971). Helen Yglesias wrote of Communism earnestly in *How She Died* (1973) and John Sanford with relentless obsession in several of the five volumes of his *Scenes from the Life of an American Jew* (1985–91). What could never be restored, by any form of literary modus operandi, was authors' partaking in the purposeful and righteous community of which they had imagined themselves to be a part, however briefly or indirectly. The Golden Age of their memory corresponds to the time when these writers were drawn to the idealized actions and residual myths of believing Communists.

As the preceding analysis indicates, a number of postwar Jewish novelists were variously molded by a Communist background, but some are nearly invisible when a literary historian's searchlight seeks only authors self-identified as Jewish or whose novels offer an affirmative portrayal of Jewish characters and culture. Rarely parochial in their subject matter and points of view, Jewish American pro-Communist writers voluntarily embraced models of identity partially imported from the global Communist movement.[13] Communist belief systems and identity locations associated with that past, even for those who grew up speaking Yiddish, remain mostly outside the more ethnocentric models in the field, such as *The Rise of David Levinsky* (1917). Starting in the Depression, to be sure, there were some frank celebrations of Jewish culture, particularly Mike Gold's *Jews without Money*, but there were also harsh, if more artistically compelling, renunciations of this culture, as in Henry Roth's *Call It Sleep* (1934). Writing with a Communist sensibility, writers produced severe portraits of the insatiability of a Jewish climber, as did Budd Schulberg in *What Makes Sammy Run*, and the devastating effects of Jewish self-hatred, as did Jo Sinclair in *Wasteland*. The fiction of Nathanael West, who improbably moved toward Communism in the late 1930s, is demonstrative of a Jewish sensibility without conspicuous Jewish characters and references.

After World War II, the Jewish literary Left seemed to tolerate a reduced amount of free play in its treatment of Jewish matters. The revelation of Hitler's horrors understandably increased sensitivity about the capacity of white supremacists to exploit anti-Semitic stereotypes. Then the policy of the international Communist movement suddenly shifted to support of a Jewish state on the eve of Partition; this required a disturbing rote agreement with an abandonment of the Party's prior attempt to create an alternative to Zionism based on Palestinian Arabs and Jewish immigrants sharing dominion. With the growing propaganda about fascism in the West, the mood of the leadership of the cultural Left reverted more and more to its own witch-hunt mentality in order to censor what it perceived to be negative images of Jews.

The journal reflecting the Communist Party's outlook, *Jewish Life*, made formulaic parallels between the oppression of Jews and Blacks, with the magazine calling for a boycott of the film *Oliver Twist* (1948) as it had for *Gone with the Wind* (1939). Idealized stories about the Maccabees were published to encourage support for resistance against the West, and photographs of Nazi atrocities were frequently reproduced to remind readers what might happen again. A chief activity was *Jewish Life*'s initiation of a vocal campaign against what it saw as the re-Nazification of Germany, a line of attack that involved the dubious designation of any Jewish organizations or Jews hostile to Soviet Communism as a homegrown *Judenrat* (Jewish council that cooperated with the Nazis). *Jewish Life* also entirely denied the oppression of Jews in the Soviet Union and the anti-Semitic character of the 1952 Slansky Trial and the Doctor's Plot. For a diminishing number of readers, the magazine created a unique kind of cultural world based on interlocking beliefs, including the illusion that Birobidzhan, supposedly a Jewish autonomous region in the Soviet Union, was an ideal Jewish homeland to which Israel might hope to measure up.[14]

This shift had inhibiting consequences for art. One sign was Arthur Miller's statement in 1948 that he had turned away from using Jews as explicit subject matter because of the growth of anti-Semitism; even an innocent allusion to Jewish wrongdoing could inflame anti-Jewish sentiment, and, as an impassioned artist, Miller could not write about a subject while censoring his own imagination.[15] As if to prove Miller's point, *Jewish Life* subsequently published a stinging condemnation of *Bride of the Sabbath* (1951) by Samuel Ornitz (1890–1957); the piece was written by David Alman (b. 1919), who served as president of Contemporary Writers, a group close to the Communist Party after World War II. There appears to be no political or personal motivation for Alman's crude review; Ornitz's martyrdom as one of the "Hollywood Nine" (the tenth member, Edward Dmytryk, had already switched sides) was acknowledged by Alman, himself a skillful craftsman of fiction.[16] Ornitz was also one of the pro-Communist literary movement's best-known authors; his 1923 *Haunch, Paunch and Jowl* was a classic of immigrant life.

Only a righteous fanaticism that judges art by current political values could rationalize Alman's formulaic, prefabricated logic: "Although the novel [*Bride of the Sabbath*] deals with the East Side of pre–World War I, we cannot forget that it was written after World War II. . . . In spite of its frequent insights into anti-Semitism and resistance of Jews to oppression, *Bride of the Sabbath* does not show itself sufficiently aware of what impends today [World War III] and does not point itself in the direction of new paths of resistance."[17] In Alman's all-too-familiar expression of dogmatism gone wild, Ornitz was repudiated not only for his treatment of his Jewish American characters but for his treatment of African American ones as well. In the Ornitz affair, the Communist Party once again shot itself in the foot and blasted off a few Communist toes. Understandably, Ornitz was permanently alienated by this review. After his death, which occurred six years later, his friends still considered it inappropriate for the successor to *Jewish Life* to publish an obituary, which it never did.[18]

A set of embedded feelings about the relationship of Jewishness to Communism evolved during the postwar era. The upshot was that many masts of novels were displayed separately but shared the interconnected sail of a vessel en route to a memory crisis. Such literature did not necessarily enunciate Jewish Communist life patterns by addressing the subject with directness. When looking back at decades of literature in many cultural registers, the contemporary reader faces the pieces of a political mosaic. The Jewish American literary Left, far from homogeneous, at times conformed to the phenomenon, also seen in Hollywood films and the New York theater, of Jewish authors deleting Jews as well as Left politics from their own cultural sites. What sets three novels apart in respect to Communist literary modernity, however, is an acute awareness of interiority, an excess of memory rather than the excess of forgetting seen elsewhere. They were published at ten-year intervals: Abraham Polonsky's *The World Above* (1951), Jo Sinclair's *Anna Teller* (1960), and K. B. Gilden's *Between the Hills and the Sea* (1971). Expressive of the postwar crises of late antifascism that peaked in 1956, all exemplify elements of Communist literary modernism.

This quality of stamping the present with the seal of the anterior became even more apparent in 1985, when John Sanford unexpectedly brought into print the first volume of *Scenes from the Life of an American Jew*. His series turned out to be a captivating antidote to the danger of forgetting, a blend of history and the imagination that culminated brilliantly in two of the volumes affording a detailed re-creation of the postwar era to 1961. Writing in the second person, referring to himself as "you," Sanford expresses unremitting dismay at his earlier personality and behavior. He makes two exceptions: his late-1930s adherence to Marxist principles and his 1951 defiance of HUAC, both depicted as more ethical than ideological. Whereas Polonsky would exhibit Communist literary modernism through the manner in which he probed issues of intellectual commitment, and Bert and Katya Gilden in the way they explored the historical trajectory of the labor movement, Sanford's inquiry is an audacious shattering of the novel form itself that educates by allegory and parable; each telling detail illuminates a world of meaning, especially ones pertaining to his Jewish and Communist identities. His work is an inspired montage, far from what one might imagine from an individual who reveals himself throughout these pages to be a redoubtable eccentric, eminently argumentative, arrogant, condescending, humorless, and socially tone-deaf.

Scenes from the Life of an American Jew, launched with *The Color of the Air* (1985) and followed immediately by *The Waters of Darkness* (1986) and *A Very Good Land to Fall With* (1987), was conceived as a trilogy. These works covered Sanford's childhood, education, aborted law career, early adventures as a writer, transition to Hollywood, marriage to scenarist Marguerite Roberts (1905–89), and first activities in the Communist movement. But Sanford's reimagined and dramatized life in the fifteen years after World War II exploded into memory during his trancelike writing marathons to produce two more full-length volumes, *A Walk in the Fire* (1989) and *The Season, It Was Winter* (1991). Even then, Sanford was driven to continue on, albeit far less successfully, filling in gaps and making additions with *Maggie: A Love Story* (1993), *We Have a Little Sister* (1995), and *A Palace of Silver* (2003). This last consists of imaginary dialogues with his dead wife that occur in the cemetery where her ashes are buried.

The fictionalized memoirs reveal that Sanford is deeply bitter about the behavior of most local Communist Party leaders that he knew, and eventually of the Soviet leadership for its stupidity. But his letters in various archives, as well as late-life interviews, show that he remained in some curmudgeonly way a champion of an imagined Communism.[19] It is by relentlessly injecting his dialogical memoirs with deconstructive self-questionings and lacerating episodes of self-betrayal that Sanford instinctively transforms his life history from the earlier ideological and psychological positions of determination to one of doubt. His exterior topic may be regret over behavior toward his parents, or his allowing Marguerite (who was apparently less political) to join the Communist Party along with himself, but the larger emotional texture becomes an index of the loss of moral certainty. To be sure, there are scornful perspectives from which Sanford appears to be a nostalgic lifelong Stalinist and a self-indulgent serial autobiographer, but almost all of the work that poured out from him following his post-blacklist writer's block was exemplary of the ritualistic, substitutive practices prompted by melancholia.[20]

Sanford was always a novelist of sparseness, clarity, and precision. During the Popular Front he began to transgress boundaries of style and genre with informed speculations about history in *Seventy Times Seven* (1939) and even more centrally in *The People from Heaven* (1943). He published two radical novels in the Cold War before he was silenced by blacklisting and then a writer's block, *A Man without Shoes* (1951) and *The Land That Touches Mine* (1953). As he returned to publishing fiction in the 1960s, with *Every Island Fled Away* (1964) and *The $300 Man* (1967), he became increasingly interested in refining and hardening, not blurring and softening. Unlike other novelists with a background in film, Sanford knew how to splice his cuts so that he draws upon the past even as time is collapsed. *Scenes from the Life of an American Jew*, a strange blend of arrogance and humility, is written both within and at a remove from the periods recalled. It is nothing less than a love affair with memory, a literary-historical pastiche that can freeze the blood.

FRIENDS OF THE UNCONSCIOUS

When the distance between the Communist rhetoric that once had swayed them and the reality that they lived started to become too painful to bear, Abraham Polonsky, K. B. Gilden, and Jo Sinclair responded in different ways, diversely sharing their generation's increasingly melancholic meditations. Polonsky, best known now as a blacklisted film-writer and pioneer of noir, was born on the Lower East Side of New York and drawn to gangs, socialism, and literature as a teenager. He received a degree in English in 1932 from City College and then a law degree from Columbia in 1935. Already a Communist, he began employment as an attorney on behalf of the staff of a radio series, *The Goldbergs*, and soon began writing scripts and then attempting novels. By 1943, he was employed as a screenwriter in Hollywood at Paramount Studios but with the advent of the war he quickly took an assignment with the Office of Strategic Services in Europe. Returning to Hollywood in 1945, Polonsky became a behind-the-scenes figure on the Left, visible mainly as an editor of the left-wing *Hollywood Quarterly* and producing two successful films with fellow traveler John Garfield. In 1950, Polonsky was identified as a Communist Party member several times in HUAC hearings and in 1951 was himself summoned and declined to answer questions. Although he had earlier published a potboiler, *The Goose Is Cooked* (coauthored with Mitchell Wilson, 1943) and an adventure novel, *The Enemy Sea* (1943), the blacklist helped impel him to serious fiction.[21]

The World Above, his one masterpiece, is divided into four sections: The Crisis, The Search, The Battle, and The Trial. Although not the familiar Hegelian triad, these units appear to be stages in a process: a religious experience, a psychological transformation, and a rebirth. From this perspective, Polonsky's text is perfectly at home in the 1930s tradition of social realism. He provides the expected critique of false consciousness, followed by the development of a character who, through experience and ideological enlightenment, develops the capacity to de-reify the social environment and seek a better world. *The World Above* has many formal features of the classic left-wing narrative, energized by a vigorous, fast-paced, even racy style — one that flows out of a realist and naturalist tradition that Polonsky adapted to meet the needs of the broad audience he never reached. In content, however, Polonsky presents a complex challenge not only to a world order ruled by capitalism but to orthodox Marxism itself. When the protagonist declares, late in the novel, that he is organizing a group called "Friends of the Unconscious," he is describing not only Polonsky's project but that of the Gildens, John Sanford, and Jo Sinclair as well.[22]

226 Jews without Judaism

Abraham Polonsky, screenwriter and novelist, with his children in European exile in the 1950s. As the Hollywood blacklist descended, Communist Party member Polonsky moved to Cannes, where he finished his novel *The World Above* (1951). (Courtesy of Paul Buhle)

Polonsky's protagonist, Carl Meyer, is a surprisingly unsympathetic psychiatrist, self-centered and overconfident. His German American background and his name echo Karl Marx. Modeled on Polonsky's recently deceased college teacher, Morris Raphael Cohen (1880–1947), a passionate advocate of scientific reason, Carl has risen from his working-class background in the depths of the Depression to express his talents in laboratory research. Suddenly his funding is capriciously pulled, leaving him adrift in Vienna during the rise of fascism. Carl returns to the United States in the late 1930s, pledged to search for a new method of psychoanalysis, one based on scientific premises but not tied to purely biological criteria. Throughout his career, Carl is paired with an alter ego, Dr. Val Curtin.[23] Curtin seems destined for an achievement analogous to Carl's, but he is more rigidly bound to formal, biologically based scientific procedures. In a dramatic episode, the two men compete to cure a young woman, "Little Emily." Emily is lost to catatonia and is most likely the victim of a sexual abuse of which she cannot speak. Carl resorts to talk therapy and Curtin to insulin shock. Emily momentarily shows signs of recovery; then, to the dismay of both, dies at the age of twenty-one.

World War II sweeps Carl into its maelstrom, and he is assigned to serve as an army officer in England. There he reencounters his former friend David Seawithe, a New Deal lawyer from a wealthy family who has risen to a high post in the U.S. government. Like Carl, David has allegorical features; he personifies the spirit of the New Deal, which, during the course of the war, becomes transformed into a burgeoning imperial authority that seeks to replace the old colonial powers as the global guardian of an expanding capitalist system. David is also depicted as a repressed homosexual obsessed with capturing Carl's talents for his own purposes, even trafficking in women that pass between and bind the men. The association of Carl and David is meant to suggest the cross-class alliance of the New Deal. The upper class, embodied in David, attempts to co-opt the greatest talents that emerge from the proletariat, represented by Carl. But at the height of the war, Carl recognizes that David is a "wild revolutionary in favor of things as they are"—an assessment that also can be applied to the corrupted New Deal.[24] With the Axis powers crumbling in Europe, David darkly tries to enlist Carl in a plan that involves relocating to China, apparently part of an ill-fated strategy to keep the Chinese revolutionaries from coming to power. But Carl, still seeking scientific purity, returns to the United States and his partnership with Curtin.

Together, with government funding, Carl and Curtin launch an experimental psychoanalytic foundation in Los Angeles, the Sierra Institute, to treat war veterans who have returned home mentally fraught. The two psychiatrists continue to differ over methods, but Carl has been pushed toward a more historical approach to the problem of mental illness. A critical element in his transition is Carl's sudden reconnection with his estranged brother, Bill Meyer, who has become a leader of the left wing of the United Auto Workers Union (UAW). In a crucial event, on the eve of the war, Carl had been mistaken for Bill by a gang of antiunion thugs, who proceeded to carry out perhaps the most brutal beating found in the pages of American literature. Through this ultra-naturalist rendition of a death and rebirth sequence, Carl becomes physically introduced to the iron heel of capitalism, the barbaric flip side of the same system that rewards him with research funds to readapt the psychologically distraught to the prevailing social order. Thus Carl becomes increasingly dubious of the system; he now sees the mentally ill as being socially ill, mirroring the factual world. In a speech before a New York audience, he states: "Science is one of the social forces that must liberate the human spirit from its social prisons. But the spirit [of science] is a spirit of the flesh, the flesh of the society, and so in the end we are forced to act actively within that society as part of our system of cure."[25] Carl's alienation from the prevailing social order is further reinforced by the meaningless death of Bill in a military mishap in Germany.

The theme of creative science in *The World Above* comes to a climax as congressional investigators seek to grab headlines by questioning the unorthodox ideas implemented by Carl at the Sierra Institute. Val Curtin, who uses a more mechanical methodology, has reached a dead end; somewhat like David Seawithe, Curtin needs to harness Carl's talents for his own survival. Thus he urges Carl to say whatever he is required to say in order to retain his funding. Carl enters the congressional hearings with ambivalence, but his disgust with the demagoguery of the proceedings and the committee's demand that he forfeit intellectual independence incite Carl to declare his unorthodox principles in a forthright manner. In this instance, Carl's behavior at the hearing contrasts significantly with Polonsky's appearance before a Hollywood congressional hearing after his novel appeared. At that time, Polonsky entered the inquest proceedings with no doubts and simply took the Fifth.

If there is an episode in the novel paralleling Polonsky's testimony, it is almost certainly when Carl is confronted by the antiunion thugs who are after Bill. He could have simply said that he was not the man they wanted, but instead he kept silent to protect his brother.[26] The appearance of Carl before the congressional committee hearing is more closely modeled on the 1946 HUAC hearings during which the Hollywood Ten were interrogated; that was when the Ten attempted to make the First Amendment the ground of dispute. Moreover, Carl is a composite of the Hollywood Ten in certain other respects—he has the compact wrestler's build of Albert Maltz, the thin mustache of Dalton Trumbo (1905–76), and the principled tenacity of John Howard Lawson, and, like Ring Lardner Jr. (1915–2000), he marries the wife of a brother who was killed fighting fascism.

Politically, the novel, the personal and intellectual history of a psychiatrist from 1932 to 1950, champions unorthodox Marxism in its call for the creative use of Freudian psychoanalysis.[27] There had long been a Communist presence in the field of psychology, and in the late 1930s Marxists in the profession marched on May Day under slogans such as "Fascism Is the World's Worst Behavior Disorder" and "Don't Be Unconscious, Join Our Ranks." Immediately following World War II, pro-Communists taught both psychology and psychiatry at the Party-led Jefferson School of Social Science in New York and participated in forming a left-wing Benjamin Rush Society for physicians. Nevertheless, with the increasing dogmatism in the Communist movement in the era of late antifascism, combined with the impact of McCarthyism, the Communist presence disintegrated into sectarian polemics. Anti-Freud and pro-Pavlov campaigns were carried into U.S. Communist circles from the Soviet Union and European parties, triumphing by 1949. Polonsky's work evidences a notable challenge to that drift; his view is that Freud's theory of the unconscious can be read as exposing the social at work behind what is taken to be natural.[28]

Yet *The World Above* is uncomfortably silent on the larger question of Communism and the Soviet Union, even though its setting during World War II and its inclusion of substantial material about the maltreatment of the left wing in the UAW implicitly call for some kind of critical appraisal. Another disquieting feature is Polonsky's treatment of fascism, which is never much of an independent issue in *The World Above*. Fascism's defeat at the hands of the omnipotent United States seems a foregone conclusion, and Polonsky's focus is on the new domination of the world by a hegemonic United States. In the perspective that the dying fascism in Europe has simply been incorporated into the political project of the rulers of the United States, Polonsky is presenting a version of the Communist Party's late antifascism. What saves *The World Above* from being diverted into such political oversimplification is not only its neo-Freudianism but a decidedly existentialist shading. The questions tackled in Polonsky's novel are not actually debates about political strategy as late antifascism was put forward in the first issues of *Masses & Mainstream*; they probe the more fundamental matters of how one lives one's life beyond ideology, and how to find personal freedom and meaning in a world run by mad Ahabs on a collision course with destruction. There is more than a hint of (Henry) Jamesianism in Polonsky's depiction of character, consciousness, and the paradoxical freedom of taking responsibility for one's choices of action.

Through an effective literary strategy, the decisive background to the postwar years—the decade of the Great Depression—is brought into *The World Above*. Polonsky takes the reader along on Carl's pilgrimage of a return visit to his family, which is actually a non-ethnic version of Polonsky's own Jewish socialist environment and memories of his parents and the grandmother who so crucially influenced his development. Even as this formative context for Meyer as well as Polonsky is underscored, it is the imminent postwar world that is the subject of the novel, one that will be global and that must be based on human solidarity at every level. Perhaps Polonsky's most critical theme is his expression of familiar secular Jewish deracination—"there was no home and would be no home."[29]

In other words, the past for Polonsky is not treated as if it contained the origins of some future that is waiting to happen. Historical beginnings cannot be neglected, but it is dangerous to search for a usable past when driven by contemporary needs. History is an endless argument, and that is why *The World Above* ends up as a modern love story. Through much of the novel, Polonsky promotes a laissez-faire sexual philosophy with love unmoored from older ideas and representing an unknown quantity. One does in sex what one must do to meet the urgings of desire. "The World Above," that is, consciousness, is more or less at the mercy of "The World Below," the unconscious. But a series of rather shocking near-transgressions—first with the psychotic "Little Emily," then with Carl's brother's wife, Juley Meyer—raises questions about the absence of boundaries in Carl's surrender to lust and self-love. Carl's initial reaction to Juley, when married to his bother and pregnant, was both revulsion and desire. In the several years of her widowhood after World War II, he loses contact with her, and Juley drifts into a dubious relationship. She becomes the lover of Sam Halloran, the leader of the left wing in the UAW. Then, Val Curtin–like, Sam capitulates to the more conservative Cold War UAW establishment, presumably the Reuthers, while Juley stands fast, presumably with the Communists, against the new leadership.

When Carl and Juley finally reconnect in New York, they recognize each other as counterparts. This reconciliation brings him face-to-face with a tough, self-governing woman, and he sees the basis for a unified personal relationship that will endure the coming era. The bond of intimate love turns out to be a microcosm of the social world, one that enlarges critical understanding of the forms in which the autonomy and embeddedness of human consciousness move in a perpetual dance. This Communist literary modernist mode of inquiry was at the core Polonsky's best work, as it came to be for the finest writing of John Sanford and the Gildens. When first encountering Juley, Carl imagined that he had seen her—but he had not. Now he is free to boldly embrace the enigmatic.

ANALYTICAL REALISM

In the writings of Bert and Katya Gilden, the activist facet of the Jewish American Left would seem to be far more present than in *The World Above*, yet it is just as cloaked. Beginning in the late 1940s, the couple decided to become the joint authors of what they projected to be major novels. Katya, legally blind, was the writer in the technical sense, and Bert was a resource and guide for content. They paid special attention to fashioning publicity about themselves, a skill Bert had practiced professionally. This included the preparation of autobiographical materials for release, always repeated in reviews, articles, and reference books without independent verification, although Bert's 1956 testimony before HUAC contains contradictions to the story used for marketing.³⁰ Such well-crafted, plausible self-narratives effectively created public personae, but they systematically elided the genuine political emotions and ethnic experiences behind their work.

Bert D. Gilden is described in such publicity as having been born in Los Angeles but growing up in the industrial city of Bridgeport, Connecticut, among Hungarian and Swedish industrial workers. That he was from a Jewish socialist family with a father and grandfather active in the Workman's Circle is omitted, as well as his militant Communist views and activity for close to two decades. After working his way through Brown University, where he studied English and French literature, he was employed from 1936 to 1941 as a press agent for Warner Brothers. During World War II, probably on leave from the Communist Party, he was a lieutenant commanding a tank platoon in North Africa, Italy, and France, where he was wounded twice and awarded the Silver Star, the Bronze Star with Oak Leaf Cluster, and the Croix de Guerre with Vermillion Star. Returning home, he committed himself to a life of writing and political activism, moving to rural Georgia. He later claimed that he supported himself by organizing Veterans Farm Training courses offered under the G.I. Bill of Rights for both Black and white veterans who were farming in the area; but the details are murky, and it is likely that he was primarily involved in Communist Party activities. After he married Katya in 1947, she joined him in Georgia briefly, where together, as non-public Communist Party members using the coded language of Progressive politics, they organized interracial community action programs and worked on the stories that eventually became *Hurry Sundown*. In his 1956 HUAC testimony, Bert emphasized that he spent 1949–52 as a student in a writers' clinic at New York University, but the episode oddly disappears in the publicity prepared to promote the Gildens' two books.

In the press releases and interviews, Katya Gilden is always described as born in Bangor, Maine, growing up in a neighborhood of Irish and French Canadian railroad workers. She, too, never mentioned that her family was Jewish and had left-wing affiliations. An English literature major at Radcliffe College, she was the first woman published in the *Harvard Advocate*. After Radcliffe, she took jobs as a fashion copywriter and social worker. She lived in Harlem in the late 1930s and worked on a novel, but she later explained that her efforts to use the methods of Kafka, Hemingway, Proust, and Joyce were unsuccessful. During World War II, she moved back to Bangor, where she organized an interracial forum for the Negro USO (United Services Organization, which provided recreational activities for soldiers) and held a job as the information director of the Unitarian Service Committee.

In the public version of the Gildens' rise to fame, they returned to Bridge-

Katya and Bert Gilden, standing to the left of English professor I. J. Kapstein at a Brown University reception, were former Communists who wrote the successful *Hurry Sundown* (1964) under the name K. B. Gilden. (Courtesy of John Hay Library, Brown University Library)

port in 1949 and stayed there until 1964, when they moved to the suburb of Fairfield, Connecticut. They started publishing stories and writing TV and film scripts in the early Cold War, but the repressive political climate encouraged them to set their massive novel-in-progress far from home, in the post–World War II South. To support their three sons, Bert worked on the production line at several Bridgeport plants—General Electric, Remington, and Singer. Omitted from the story, and confirmed by his HUAC testimony, is that Bert ran for political office in Connecticut on the platform of the Progressive Party (the local name was People's Party) in 1950, along with Eslanda Robeson (married to Paul Robeson), and then he became its executive director in 1952. He probably participated in Communist Party efforts to unionize the local plants, and his dismissal from the Singer factory was a result of his unfriendly HUAC testimony. This labor movement experience became the setting for *Between the Hills and the Sea*. In 1964 the publication of *Hurry Sun-*

down was a triumph; translated into several languages, it was also made into a 1967 film directed by Otto Preminger.

This first novel's southern setting not only reflected the authors' postwar experiences but also allowed them to epitomize the forces they felt were shaping the future. The Gildens depict two former soldiers, one African American and one white, with adjoining farms that share a mutual right of way. In the face of a demand to sell their property from a new and powerful mechanized produce enterprise, the men must unite in order to effectively resist. Emanating from the dual protagonists is an interracial cast of characters representing a range of economic situations and thus a cross-section of a community in deep conflict. Yet the drama unfolds through the intimate lives and concrete personalities of intricate characters; this is not a thesis novel but one of process, where race and class are not abstractions but are met in the form of unpredictable people. Admiration for the Gildens' depiction of Black characters resulted in their presenting an address titled "The Novel and Its Social Relevance to the Negro Revolution," at the 1966 Fisk University Centennial Writers Conference on "The Image of the Negro in American Literature."

To the end of their lives, the couple was silent on their Communist Party membership, which likely began in the late 1930s and persisted until about 1958, after which they associated with a circle of former members. Among the few dribbles of details about their connection with the Communist Party that can be ascertained is that some difficulties with the organization began in Georgia, precipitated by a conflict with a statewide Communist Party leader.[31] In Connecticut in the early 1950s, Bert defended the Soviet Union against the charge of anti-Semitism; what survives of his views on the latter subject reflects the conventional outlook of apologists for the Stalinist state.[32] Perhaps he might have disclosed more about their political past, but at the age of fifty-six, on the eve of the publication of *Between the Hills and the Sea*, Bert suddenly died of a heart attack.

Katya revealed late in life that the writings of Georg Lukács, the Marxist critic, were a major influence on their literary work. Sometime in the late 1940s, they had read Lukács's "The Intellectual Physiognomy of Literary Characters" and taken extensive notes on it.[33] They immediately concluded that Lukács had unlocked for them a literary method that allowed the integration of the individual and social dimensions of experience. The Gildens claimed to sympathize with Lukács's notion of a socialist realism that promoted Tolstoy, Stendhal, and Thomas Mann as models; such a perspective enabled them to move beyond the versions modernism and naturalism that seemed inadequate literary strategies for expressing the reality that they had lived and seen. They called their transcendent method "analytical realism" and maintained that it was analogous to organic chemistry. They aspired to invent characters who represented more than themselves and to deeply explore these as individuals by placing them in an "essence situation" that encapsulated the issues of the time. An initial conflict would engage people with each other and their milieu and lead to an ever-mounting series of dilemmas in which the characters would be revealed and developed as they were tested by the historic events of the time.[34] In *Hurry Sundown* the Gildins intended to show what had happened to the postwar dream of peace and prosperity that was promised to returning veterans of World War II.[35] Underlying their literary theoretics, however, was a question well known to the Jewish American Left: how to live—for oneself alone or with concern for others?

The recognizable emotions of the Jewish Left are present in the background of the Gildens' second work of fiction. *Between the Hills and the Sea* is set in a northern industrial city in a purposeful contrast to the southern rural setting of *Hurry Sundown*. The novel was explicitly begun in 1964, as something of a message to a new generation of political rebels about the radical heritage. But the art is very much rooted in memories of the decade after World War II, enhanced by research (including personal interviews) into Left and labor activities. The narrative opens in March 1956, a time of conformity. The Gildens do their best to capture the crosscurrents of the emerging race, class, and environmental pressures that would explode in the 1960s. The novel's focus is on the life of Mish Lumin, who in the years following World War II was the young president of an 8,000-member union local. By 1956, his life has been reduced to that of a setup man in the switch department of a giant corporation, wonderfully named "United Vacuum." Mish is married to Priscilla Barth, the daughter of a local civil libertarian lawyer. She and a number of workers want him to return to leading the union, which he refuses to do. Priscilla then tries to compensate for his disillusionment with the union by cajoling Mish into the leadership of a tenants' movement in their housing project, one against the environmental menace of an adjacent dump. The arc of the novel follows Mish's being prompted into action at his plant by new developments, only to be defeated, and retreating into private life. In a compelling example of negative dialectics, the sense of the future has been amputated.[36]

Between the Hills and the Sea draws on elements from the personal activities of the authors in Bridgeport and undoubtedly from Bert Gilden's work experience in the large city; there may also be material extracted from the ethnic communities of Katya Gilden's childhood in Bangor. As in a Jane Austen novel, there is one character, Mish, whose consciousness is tacitly allowed a privileged standing and whose mental life is rendered more fully than others. A class-conscious worker, Mish is not a Communist Party member but willing to work with Communists. While he is increasingly skeptical of the Communist Party's worldview, his association with Party members is put into effect through his fervent friendship with Party leader Bob Ucchini, whose death occurs in the course of the novel. Bob, in turn, is depicted as existing in a rather impenetrable and almost mystical world of his own; there is more than a suggestion that Bob's moral certainty about Communism is a sublimation of his frustrated artistic drive to be a professional concert pianist.

An obvious discrepancy between the Gildens' biography and their fiction is that, although the Gildens were Jewish and there was a strong Jewish presence in the labor Left, neither Mish nor any other central character in the novel is Jewish. The leading actors are mostly Italians (the political antagonists Ucchini and Nick Coangelo), Russians (the Lumins), upper-middle-class WASPs (the Barths), or Catholics (Herb Cranston and Mari Ucchini). The one Jewish character may have been of significance for the authors' biographies but is a minor actor in the novel. Boris Kallen is known by both Mish's father and the Barths; Joe Barth had served as Kallen's lawyer when Kallen was once accused of being a subversive and threatened with deportation. Whether or not Kallen is a member of the Communist Party, he is depicted as a deluded man who nearly breaks up his marriage in battles about his preference for the Communist paper *Freiheit* over the socialist paper *Forward*. He raises funds for the mythical Jewish homeland of Birobidzhan set up by Stalin and is unperturbed by the 1956 Khrushchev Revelations.

The novel begins with a section humorously called "The Sensitive Plant," referring to the factory by way of Shelley's 1820 philosophical poem about the world of flux. The reason that Mish's "plant" (the factory) is sensitive is because the consciousness of the population of workers is sensitive; the employees are potentially passive or explosive or divided or playful or fearful, depending on the mix of personalities and events at any given juncture. Within the society depicted, certain characters in and out of the factory typify social and political trends: Grover Coffin, the rising new-style managerial class; Cranston, right-wing Catholic anti-Communism; Ucchini, proletarian idealism tied to the lie of the Soviet Union's socialism; Gene Bostic, Black pride and consciousness linked to self-preservation and advancement; Lucas Ford, homeless radicalism untethered to a community or class; and the Barths, a family, except for Priscilla, hesitant to live fully its commitments.

Yet many individual characters run a gamut of emotions, especially the political idealists who have various kinds of commerce with opportunism. Mish and Priscilla, for example, come close to engaging in adulterous relationships with characters who reflect the very components of their respective personalities that are forcing them apart. In the case of the politically uncooperative Mish, the flirtation occurs with the intransigent unionist Mari, whose Communist husband (at this point dead of a stroke or heart attack) always knew when it was time to fight and time to retreat; with the volatile Priscilla, it is with the déclassé, rootless Lucas. Mari herself uses her sexual allure with various men. She also ruthlessly calls on Bostic to pay his political debt to her late husband by supporting her union politics; Bostic had personally benefited from the Party's postwar campaign for super-seniority for African Americans.[37] As a result of their idealism, the Barths have eschewed the power and respectability that could easily have been theirs, although they still retain their safety-net control of a small business that Priscilla's brother Ted and Mish take over at the novel's end. This little factory, however, is not immune to the larger society; it is described as producing polluting waste and is about to institute Taylorist efficiency-methods in management. Only two main characters are depicted as less divided, and they are therefore less compelling: Coffin and Coangelo are on an inexorable path toward corruption. Little is revealed about their inner psychologies, although Coffin is associated with a lust for Mari and Coangelo with a lust for Priscilla.

The Gildens' novel intentionally evokes the nineteenth-century realism of Tolstoy that was championed by Lukács; there is a special effort to illustrate a panorama of class forces personified by typical characters of the 1946–56 era. Within that framework, it employs many of the tropes of naturalism with its portrayal of humans from a materialist, almost social Darwinistic, perspective: as animals with rumbling bowels, strong sex drives, surging emotions, and passions for food, sometimes stuck in a character's teeth. Likewise, the Gildens exploit at least a few techniques of modernism through the novel's structure of weaving the events of one week in 1956 with very full re-creations (more than flashbacks) of the past events that went into shaping the mid-1950s "moment." They make effective use of stream-of-consciousness passages with rapid shifts in perspective that are often unannounced. The overall architecture of the narrative demonstrates how characters are the sum of their pasts; the atmosphere links different episodes without requiring explicit causality.

Unlike *The World Above*, *Between the Hills and the Sea* addresses practical politics, but knotty ones. The historical setting of 1946 to 1956 disrupts the prevalent view of proletarian life as having dissolved after World War II into middle-class complacency; the Gildens want to show that workers are still workers. The legacy of the class struggle is very present as concurrently a formative element and a disappearing background; the 1930s is where the events of 1956 all began, captured in the earlier relationship of Bob Ucchini to the veteran union activist Frank Gavin, a son-father relationship that prefigures the postwar Mish-Bob relationship. The credit due the Communist Party in establishing CIO unions, and the essential justice of such unions, is a given in the novel. However, the expectations associated with the CIO erode when the labor movement becomes institutionalized and bureaucratized amid a changing society.

There are major social pressures on the CIO to accommodate, but that seems only possible by articulating a limited pro-union survival stance and jettisoning long-term socialist politics. This change is most convincingly represented by the mature, ex-Communist union veteran Gavin, who took all the risks during the 1930s and now serves as the union's éminence grise. Just as Scottsy (Jimmy Scott), the union's outstanding field organizer, was first discarded because of his homosexuality, Bob Ucchini next had to be jettisoned from membership because of his affiliation with the Communist Party. Of course, Bob and Mish face different situations. In 1956, Bob is what he is because the Communist Party gave him an identity, perspective, and faith; Mish is what he is because his stance as both a Leftist and an independent allowed him to play a crucial role in the 1946 strike. Mish now remains the conscience of the union to whom everyone runs for help when in trouble, especially women and African Americans.

This is the framework through which the Gildens present the reader with the truly thorny problems of working-class radicalism: the diminution of class consciousness in the workforce; the aging and growing family responsibilities of onetime militants; the disclosure of the sham of the Soviet Union in 1956; the bureaucratization of the union; and the introduction of clever co-management "Team Concepts" at the plant. All-pervasive in the narrative is the question of what happens to a marriage (Mish and Priscilla's) when the original vision that united the couple has disappeared. The Gildens never suggest a facile way out of this morass. Indeed, Mish's climactic, brutal ejection from the plant (he was betrayed to the bosses for an infraction by a second-rate informer, a woman to whom he and Mari had just given a lift to work) and his final stance en route to middle-class success are ironically pessimistic.

Still, the locus of the values in this novel remains uncompromisingly with the needs and struggles of working people, and capitalism itself is depicted as archetypal capitalism, not some new postindustrial system obviating the necessity of critical alternatives such as Marxism and socialism. The older versions of Communism have run their course, but Mish has resisted the ultimate sell-out of becoming Coffin's advisor. In a certain sense, he has emulated the protagonist of Ellison's *Invisible Man* by insisting on being his own man.

The Gildens, however, are not satisfied with that defiance alone; their point is that one can never find freedom in a socially created unfreedom. They recognize and wish to emphasize that one does *not* have a choice of being one's own person in the abstract, without context and consequences. Mish's hands will soon be dirty; even the small barrel company that he takes over at the novel's end is complicit in the system, although not on the scale of the plant from which Mish was discharged.

The theoretical statements of the Gildens could sound pontifical; in person they may have seemed doctrinaire politicos. But their fiction is replete with multilevel meanings and interlocking ironies. The question is posed to the reader: How can one be one's own man or woman by participating in a collective movement rather than an ally of the forces of exploitation through the illusion of rising above it? Their answer is characterized by the paradoxes and poignancies of Adorno's concepts of negative dialectics and commitment because they know the literary secret of expressing the political through the personal. If John Sanford was the John Dos Passos of the Jewish American twentieth-century experience in experimental style, the Gildens were its Jane Austen in social psychology; they followed both the minute presentation of daily life yet stood at ample distance to exhibit that same life objectively, and often comically. The Gildens paradoxically composed their novel with a knowledge that their generation had failed, yet they believed that when radicalism came again—and there were signs of a resurgence as they wrote— their failure would have nonetheless contributed encouragingly to the new impetus.

THE BOOK OF MEMORY

Anna Teller is a novel achingly attentive to the emotional pain in history of which memory is the censor. Set in Detroit between December 1956 and September 1957, Jo Sinclair's 600-page tome contemplates the unsettled anguish connecting a son to his mother. Fifty-four-year-old Emil Teller is a poet-turned-businessman, wary in the McCarthy era about his Communist past. At the outset of the narrative, he is speeding by train to New York to greet his refugee parent, Anna Teller, who will arrive shortly by plane from Europe. She is a seventy-four-year-old "freedom fighter" who took up arms in the 1956 Budapest uprising against Soviet tanks. Emil immigrated to the United States in 1923 in search of art and love while Anna chose to remain in Hungary to pursue her business options. Much of the novel reconstructs the world as filtered through their remembering minds. First there are ruminations pertaining to incidents of Emil's childhood near and in Budapest before and after World War I; then come episodes from their divergent routes through the 1930s, 1940s, and early 1950s. Together Emil and Anna personify the distinct experiences of secular Jewishness and Communism of two generations on two continents.

Jo Sinclair ponders the mid-twentieth-century dilemma of radical "Jews without Judaism" by means of a frank acknowledgment that the past is never past. Unlike the figures who populate *The World Above* and *Between the Hills and the Sea*, the major (and most of the minor) characters in *Anna Teller* are identified as Jews, although theology plays no part in their belief systems and physical characteristics are never mentioned. What is Jewish is a product of historical experience, the reworking of traditions passed on by families, and an identification with Jewishness largely created as a response to anti-Semitism.

Anna Teller is an imposing tour de force of narrative strategies that were residual and emergent in the postwar era. In Sinclair's unraveling of the Teller family's bi-continental and multigenerational history, an aura of the old social realism is at hand; it is useful to recall that the author, born Ruth Seid, chose the pseudonym "Sinclair" in honor of Upton Sinclair.[38] She draws appreciably upon the genre of the family saga novel in the sense of chronicling the lives and doings of interconnected relatives over several age groups. There is also the whiff of the historical novel in her effort to depict the customs and ways of thinking in precise times and cultures. Even more in evidence is the tradition of the classical psychological novel, with its accent on the life of the inner person animated by interior monologues and a questioning of one's motives in relation to circumstances.

In Emil Teller's progress after his 1923 arrival in the United States, one finds the commencement of what has been called the novel of "immigrant adjustment."[39] But this early-twentieth-century immigrant's (Emil's) adaptation to new opportunities for a prosperous future after World War II is monumentally disrupted in Sinclair's novel by the arrival of yet another immigrant— Emil's mother, Anna, who comes as a "stateless person" in December 1956. Anna embodies all that Emil's existence in the United States has enabled him to escape and evade, especially the horrors of the Holocaust and the lies of Stalinist postwar "liberation."

The consequences of the emotional upheaval precipitated by this confrontation between an old and a new immigrant also cuts across any real affiliation of *Anna Teller* with the arising 1950s genre of suburban literature.[40] Emil Teller and his family are certainly material beneficiaries of a Consumers' Republic, and even participants in white flight to Detroit's suburbs. But their psychological concerns are a sharp departure from contemporaneous novels that were out to craft private rebellions compatible with the emerging organization man in the gray flannel suit, or even ones in which the protagonist denies authentic middle-class identity. It is not merely Anna's arrival in the United States that unmoors the Teller family's evolving consciousness from characters in the growing body of literature associated with John Cheever, John Updike, and Richard Yates. There is also the presence of Emil's two curious non-Jewish stand-in children in *Anna Teller*, Abby Wilson and Mark Jackson, his recruits from his left-wing years on the WPA.

As a Communist writer on the WPA, Emil took Abby and Mark under his wing and gave them direction. He introduced them to music and literature as well as the life experiences of African Americans and the foreign-born. Abby and Mark are less representative of the working class than the "Common Man" or the "Little People" that the Left sought to empower during the Popular Front. Although Emil's pro-Communism has evaporated, he still feels responsible for these protégés. Emil and his wife, Liz, provide emotional support as well as financial assistance. They make gifts to Abby, and eventually, after a sojourn in New York where she fakes a marriage to give birth to David (Davey), she joins Mark as an employee in Emil's bookstore. Abby and Mark are regarded as Emil's "waifs" who became his acolytes; their ability to find lives of fulfillment is a test of his legacy, turning them into the equivalent of character references. Adrift without functioning families of their own, both look to the Tellers as a surrogate; they long for a commanding mother like Emil's legendary Anna.

The presence of Abby and Mark also constitutes an unsettling challenge to heteronormativity, which will be discussed in more detail below. There are multiple critiques of gender at work in this novel. At first, one encounters the story of Anna Teller herself, who wants to work and enjoy sex with the freedom of a man. Later, one views Emil, struggling to negotiate his own sense of masculinity amid warring desires for romantic adventure as a Marxist poet and a security to be found through marriage and recognition as head of a family. Emil is always aware that Anna stands above him in her strength, confidence, and certainty of beliefs. Finally, there come the stories of Mark and Abby, who enigmatically suggest the need for some new kind of understandings of gender and sexuality, although the particulars are unspoken or perhaps unknown.

Yet there are overlaps among these narratives. The love of Anna Teller's life turns out to be a woman, Margit Varga, a Jewish Hungarian friend, who plays a passive and subordinate, "wifely" role. Anna and Abby are frequently identified as like-minded spirits, with an affinity acknowledged on both sides. Mark and Abby, who have a peculiar sexual encounter, seem destined to create some unique kind of family. Since genital sexuality between individuals of the same sex is never directly addressed, an element of mystery is present as to how one might identify intimate relations between Anna and Margit or Mark and his older friend Sy, or in Abby and her revulsion at the male body. Moreover, for all its avant-garde thinking around gender, *Anna Teller* has an odd place in the second wave of feminism. It distinctly rejects the anti-psychology (although not necessarily anti-Freudian) perspective of works published just three years later, Mary McCarthy's *The Group*, Sylvia Plath's *The Bell Jar*, and Betty Friedan's *The Feminine Mystique*.[41] Even the topics of Jewishness and Communism are difficult to unravel from the persistent preoccupations of characters with oedipal feelings about one's mother and younger siblings.

The trouble with *Anna Teller* as a work of art is mostly in the prose, which is neither exquisitely crafted in the manner of Ann Petry nor a vehicle for energetic colloquial speech in the style of younger Jewish American writers such as Philip Roth. In some ways, *Anna Teller* is the ideal example of Dwight Macdonald's "midcult," half experimental novel and half soap opera.[42] There are moments when Sinclair's writing carries the risk of flirting with banality. Yet *Anna Teller* follows *The Narrows* by participating in the postwar shift toward new forms of realism.[43] Both works are significantly grounded in the representation of the characters' cognitive and emotional states, illustrated by the manner in which the memories of several protagonist-narrators revisit details of the past over which they brood and ponder.

The Narrows and *Anna Teller* are not novels where time ticks predictably and inevitably onward; it recurrently condenses, backtracks, or skips a beat. The authors are fully aware of the degree of entanglement between memory and imagination; how much of what we perceive exists outside ourselves, and how much is a product of our minds? Yet they share a relative certainty about the purported "objects" of the characters' memory; these are chiefly events in family history, although external reality impinges in baffling ways. Petry crowds an infinity of ambiguous passions into the smallest spaces, creating an "emotional cubism."[44] Sinclair presents proliferating strands of human tension, remaining closer to the aim of providing a far-reaching social panorama. Her teeming portrayals of consciousness reveal a story in flashbacks easier to assemble than Link Williams's history of traumas or Bill Hod's semimythical escapades.

Anna Teller, Sinclair's protagonist, is born Anna Horwitz in 1882 in a small village on the outskirts of Budapest with only ten Jewish families. At age nineteen, in 1901, she is married to the older Harry Teller, a silent Jewish man who owns land and a mill. Her sex life is a disappointment, but the couple has four children. Harry dies on the eve of World War I, and then the youngest boy,

Stephen, of sudden illness in 1917. Anna was at that time away from home, working at the mill in the company of her non-Jewish and adoring assistant, Janos. Subsequently, Anna moves her family to Budapest to pursue educational and financial opportunities.

Of the other children, Emil, the oldest (born 1902), becomes a revolutionary during the 1919 Communist uprising led by Béla Kun and then publishes a slim volume, *First Poems*. The book is dedicated to the memory of his brother, Stephen, and a poem titled "My Brother Dies" contains an alarming prophecy that Anna, upon receiving a copy, paraphrases in her mind: "If this boy, destined never to be a man, died for no reason . . . then may my sons die unconceived."[45] Emil then immigrates to the United States in 1923 in pursuit of a woman rejected as unsuitable by Anna. His brother Paul, two years younger and Anna's favorite, serves in the Hungarian military in the 1920s and by the 1930s finds a promising position in a department store. His sister, Louise, marries a successful factory owner, Andor, a non-Jew, and starts a family. Anna Teller's Budapest bakery becomes a sensation in the 1930s, and she befriends Margit Varga and her husband, Max, a dealer in diamonds. Although anti-Semitism is on the rise in Europe, Anna insists that in her country, "it is fantastic to think of Jews instead of Hungarians."[46]

In the United States, Emil lives the life of a young literary radical. He becomes a fellow traveler of the Communist Party in the 1920s and works as an editor of the Hungarian-language Communist paper published in Detroit. In 1932, Emil meets Liz Horvath, daughter of an educated Michigan Jewish family that owns dress shops. While Emil's friend Andy Kiraly (called "Andy K" because of difficulty in pronouncing his last name), a Party militant, goes off to fight the fascists in Spain, Emil finds a position as head of a WPA project. A charismatic poet and author of plays, Emil becomes a father figure to two young people who join the project, Abby and Mark. He initiates the former in the beauty of poetry and the latter to music.

With a growing family, Emil accepts financial backing of his in-laws to start the Pegasus bookstore in Detroit on the eve of World War II. Hiring Mark as an assistant, he originally features literary work in the shop, a replacement for his now-suppressed artistic aspirations. But the postwar growth in the auto industry and the advent of a new market in technical books induce Emil to change to a commercial direction. By the 1950s, Emil's family of four is enjoying the middle-class dream in a large suburban home with a maid. His sons are named Steven, for his dead brother Stephen, and Andrew, for Andy K. Emil, however, lives in dread of being exposed for his earlier political associations. He takes cold comfort in the fact that there is really only one person who could implicate him as a Communist sympathizer—Andy K. But Andy is dead; he committed suicide in political despair at the start of World War II.

Emil's guilt over Andy is compounded by a feeling of culpability for Paul. During the 1930s, Emil had been alarmed about the growing danger of fascism in Hungary, especially following his 1934 visit to Budapest. Yet he failed to take action in response to Anna's proposal that he find a woman in the United States who might marry his younger brother; this would have allowed Paul to emigrate. As Hungary moves to the Right in the 1930s, Louise is disowned by Andor, who emerges as a full-blown fascist, and the Tellers are ever more desperate. Toward the mid-1940s, Anna is in the company of Margit Varga, who now works at Anna's bakery and whose husband is taken prisoner in Vienna by the fascists. In 1944, Emil's sister Louise and her children are also apprehended by fascists while Anna and Margit are at work. Paul urges the two women to take shelter in the Swedish House, a rare place of sanctuary in Budapest. Paul then runs to retrieve Anna's jewelry from their home, although his main concern is to rescue the family copy of Emil's volume of poetry. He, too, is seized by the fascists, and Anna and Margit are left together to wait out the Nazi occupation of Hungary in the Swedish House.

Following Hungary's liberation by the Red Army in 1945, Anna continues to live with the seriously ill Margit. Taking loving care of her friend, Anna makes a comeback under the Communist regime by working in a hotel, although she develops other legal and illegal sidelines. She learns that Paul, Louise and her three children, and Max Varga were all exterminated at the Belsen concentration camp. Margit finally dies of illness in 1948, but Anna resists Emil's plea to come to the United States. She has found new meaning in her role as a leader of the working-class community, where she has long been known as "the General." Then, in 1956, Anna joins with the fifteen-year-old Laszlo Szabo, a boy from her neighborhood, to fight on the barricades in a revolt against the Soviet occupation. After loss of hope that the United States will come to their assistance, Laszlo is killed and Anna escapes across the Austrian border to the Traiskirchen refugee camp. Anna establishes that she has a son who is an American citizen and then boards a plane to the United States, which is the point at which *Anna Teller* begins.

A NOVEL OF EMOTIONS

There is, as in all of Sinclair's work, a strong basis for the narrative in events in Sinclair's own biography and the stories of her family and friends. Yet the particulars are murky. Like Petry, Sinclair was monumentally secretive about her personal history, not only in regard to intimate relations with other women but in details pertaining to her father and brothers as well as her radical political commitments in the 1930s and 1940s. Even though she left papers and a long autobiography, much of her existence was hidden away, just as her gender and ethnicity were camouflaged when she chose the pen name "Jo Sinclair." Yet enough documentation remains to assemble a scaffolding for the characters and events in *Anna Teller*.[47]

Emil Teller was modeled on Oscar Ban, Sinclair's mentor on the Cleveland WPA. Sinclair began working with Ban in 1936, depicting him as a union militant named "Molnar" in some of her unpublished writings of the Great Depression.[48] Sinclair was also close to Oscar's wife, Helen Ban, one of the three women to whom *The Changelings* (1955) is dedicated. Oscar was known for his research on foreign language newspapers in Cleveland, publishing on the subject in English in *New Outlook* in 1933 and *Common Ground* in 1941.[49] Later he became, like Emil, a successful businessman. Sinclair originally planned to dedicate *Anna Teller* to Oscar, but he was outraged when he viewed a draft that attributed to his prototype sexual infidelity and domination by his mother. Sinclair's bond with Ban was permanently damaged, causing considerable personal grief. The dedication was then shifted to Sinclair's editor, Edward C. Aswell.[50]

The character Anna, however, is unconnected to the Ban family. She is chiefly a blend of Sinclair's imposing grandmother on her father's side and her own mother, Ida Kravetsky Seid. The former managed with an iron will to move the entire Seid family from Russia to an agricultural commune in Argentina, and then back to Russia when she was dissatisfied with the difficulties in maintaining a kosher household. Sinclair's mother, Ida, underwent her own immigrant ordeal in the early twentieth century in New York and Cleveland, and several events from her life are redeployed to depict Anna's experiences in 1957. The design for the character of Anna Teller and her reactions to her forced immigration apparently arose from questions Ida raised in conversations with her daughter in the early 1950s. Ida wondered about the difficulty that an immigrant older than herself would have in trying to build a new life in the United States.[51] Moreover, the novel was an opportunity for Sinclair to explore unexplained feelings about her mother that paralleled Emil's toward Anna. Since childhood, Ida had been the cause of mysterious and confused pain for Sinclair. Her emotions were assuaged only in the 1940s and 1950s through the therapeutic interventions of Sinclair's older companion, the married Helen Buchman. By the time Sinclair wrote the novel, she was able to finally kiss her mother and stop abhorring her father.[52] One may conjecture that controversy about Sinclair's lesbianism played some part in this Seid family heartbreak, but she never candidly addressed it.

What is similarly unexplained in any directly autobiographical sources is how and why Sinclair came to write a novel with so many precise details about the Communist experience in the United States, and especially her inspired double focus: a left-winger in fear of Cold War repression comes face to face with a victim of European Stalinist authoritarianism. That Emil's Communist political past emanated from his generosity of the spirit, along with some degree of ego and opportunism, places him in a complicated relationship with the system and ideology of Communism that at first rescues and then nearly kills his mother. What is the explanation for the essential part played by this political duality in the novel?

The novel was most likely written as it was because a consciousness about the relationship of Jews and Communism was intrinsic to Sinclair's being, a knowledge shared by the closest friends and family members of her generation. The "fiction" was a substitute for what she could never tell in her autobiography, published eventually as *The Seasons: Death and Transfiguration* (1993). If she was going to communicate her deepest sentiments about the experience of Jewish American immigration and the situation of people who felt themselves outsiders and "displaced persons," the double face of Communism had to be a central part of the account. In fact, Sinclair had sketched out some of the characters of *Anna Teller* over some fifteen years beforehand, but lacked a means to make these portraits cohere. It was the eruption of the Hungarian uprising of 1956 that afforded her the opportunity to rework her sketches into a narrative of world-historic resonance. She seized the moment, and on 1 January 1957, she began to visualize a definite novel involving people from her personal past and started the outline of "A Breaking of Prison," the original title of *Anna Teller*.[53]

Anna Teller is a novel that melts the questionable borders between the "high culture" of elevated thoughts and one's ordinary life; at times, Sinclair goes further to simply dissolve the frontier between literature and life itself, as when people and experiences are depicted as poems.[54] There is a devotion to art as enhancing one's understanding and also a suspicion of its inadequacy in communicating truth. The "writers" in this novel, Emil and Abby, have written little in the past and are blocked in the present, despite efforts and aspirations. Yet they use literary forms and metaphors of the writing process to structure and describe the way they come to understand their lives and relationships.

Emil, a published poet when a young man in Hungary, in 1956 imagines himself as a budding novelist. But he never actually writes any fiction. When he returns later in *Anna Teller* to reread his youthful poems, he realizes he may never have been meant to be a serious poet. Abby, who published the poem "To the Wind" at the end of the 1930s and planned to write "We Were Born in Spain," often thinks of her life after Davey's birth as a long poem. Yet that life is a lie, inasmuch as she has covered up Davey's illegitimacy by fabricating the story of a husband who was killed in the Korean War.[55] There are several suggestive observations about life and literature attributed to the Communist Andy K. In the 1920s, when Emil was engrossed in writing love poems, Andy notes that he would produce less about sex in his art if he were getting more of it in life.[56] In the 1930s, facing the political crisis, Andy recommends that to attain "real literature," one should "shoot with one hand and write with the other."[57] As with all matters regarding Andy, who is a baffling and ambiguous presence in *Anna Teller* as is the Communist Bob Ucchini in *Between the Hills and the Sea*, the significance of this statement is indeterminate. Is Andy's main point that one is using *different* hands to write and shoot, or that both hands are attached to the *same* body and mind?[58]

Sinclair's modus operandi seems to resemble Petry's: all manner of narrative forms are necessary to grapple with complicated life circumstances, familial connections, and political realities. Even when characters forge their own mental tropes, they are adapted from literature and popular culture. In *Anna Teller*, there are citations of classical and original poems, re-creations of plays within the novel, simulated versions of psychotherapy, listings of newspaper headlines, depictions of movie-like scenes, dredged-up autobiographical and chronological reminiscences, and pages from diaries. Anna Teller herself relies on oral storytelling, of which she is a master. Mark sees the world through music. Emil episodically aspires to explain his emotions by outlining his own "immigrant" novel.[59]

An oddity is that *Anna Teller* is not a political novel even to the extent of *The World Above* and *Between the Hills and the Sea*, although I am implicitly making a case that the reclamation of emotion is an Adorno-like political move. Even the idealized hopes of Emil and Anna for a United Nations resolution in response to the Hungarian uprising fails to translate into anything like a political "line." The theme of political commitment is not addressed in any familiar form. For the major characters, this is a novel about political ambivalence, about the failure to commit, or an active decision not to commit. Political loyalties are never sustained, in many cases never even declared. The question of whether or not Anna had at any time been a Communist in Hungary remains puzzlingly unanswered.[60] Emil had been a fellow traveler of the Party but one noted for his unwillingness to join or go to Spain. Emil promises the reader of his imaginary novel that he will eventually clarify his relation to the Party but never does.[61] Andy K was a devout Communist but commits suicide at the beginning of World War II, when the Soviet Union entered its period of greatest popularity in the United States.

This act is apparently an expression of Andy's disillusionment but may be a symbol used by Sinclair to indicate the inability of the original ideals of Communism to address the new world political situation. After the 1930s, no character in the novel ever votes or even cares about political activity, although Emil has some residual Leftism inasmuch as he reads the *Nation* and is unenthusiastic about the Korean War. It is difficult to think of Anna's activities in terms of politics; she refuses to see the possibility of the Holocaust because the acknowledgment of growing anti-Semitism is against her interests as an enterprising businesswoman in Budapest. Her participation in the 1956 uprising is depicted as a spontaneous identification with the popular upsurge.

To some extent, *Anna Teller* is a cultural reflection of the adaptation of the Left to the framework of the Cold War, "the end of ideology." It is also a challenge to conformity and quiescence, a prefiguring of the 1960s slogan "The Personal Is the Political." The public sphere and private life seem to blend into each other in the same manner as the borders melt between high culture and ordinary life.[62] Evidence for Sinclair's own exact political thinking in the late 1950s is scarce. She was as selective in what she said and wrote to individuals in interviews and letters as about the contents of her autobiographical manuscript. The thoughts of Emil and Anna, the most political characters, suggest that both are indifferent to the professed international aims of either the United States or the Soviet Union; they may even hold the belief that, if the Soviets are mostly left alone and confined to their own space, some good may come of the Russian experiment. Clearly there is no sympathy in this novel for those who seek out and aim to stigmatize former (or even present) Communists in the United States.

In its own way, *Anna Teller* is a Jewish response to the anti-Communist confessionals of Whittaker Chambers, Louis Budenz, and others. The story Sinclair offers is not of betrayal and disloyalty but of human emotions, love, sex, loneliness, and desire, the felt experiences of the ordinary participants in the movement. The portrait of Anna Teller herself is also a corrective to *Time* magazine's frightening 20 September 1948 cover picture of Romanian Jewish Communist Ana Pauker, described as "the most powerful woman alive."[63] From another angle, Sinclair offers a very human (and feminist) response to the hyper-idealized "Hungarian Freedom Fighter" appearing on *Time*'s cover as the "Man of the Year" for 1956.⁶⁴ The novel is also, implicitly at least, an appropriate dismissal of Communist Herbert Aptheker's sickening apologetics for Soviet intervention in *The Truth about Hungary* (1957).

Like Petry, Sinclair's one-time attachment to Marxism migrated to a critical look at gender and heteronormativity. Neither could fully dramatize lesbians in the Cold War; coded language, desires, and relationships seem to mask the gay identity of characters, although sometimes stereotypes and allegedly negative aspects are uncomfortably featured. Most striking for *Anna Teller* are the frequent and various uses of the term "queer." Research indicates that the term emerged around 1500 from Scottish to mean strange, peculiar, and off-center; 1922 was the first time that "queer" was used in the United States to refer to homosexuals, and it became a noun only in 1935. In *Anna Teller*, "queer" is used well over thirty times, sometimes to modify feelings ("queer despair," "queer loneliness," "queer dread," "queer hurt") but also in more suggestive phrases ("in the queer mirror," "She always was queer," "the queer little girl," and "queer hesitancy in voice").⁶⁵

Many sexual issues are suggested in the novel without resolution. *Anna Teller* is partly the story of twenty-five years of marriage, 1932-57, between Emil and Liz. It also provides the "case histories" of Abby's and Mark's sexualities. Abby, who grew up with a father who violently demanded sexual intercourse several times a day from Abby's stepmother, a woman he despises, is at first quite happy to raise a child without the man being present. She casually uses a drunk soldier she meets for insemination and then invents a cover story about a quick marriage followed by the man's death in the Korean War. Only as Davey begins to grow does Abby mourn the absence of a father, but this is primarily in terms of Davey's needs. Mark, who thinks he hates his mother due to abandonment, is also inscrutable. Is Mark the portrait of a confused homosexual, or just a confused portrait of a homosexual? Both he and Abby manage to bring up the issue of homosexuality in their fictional biographies without actually addressing it. But Sinclair may aspire to present Abby and Mark as complicated persons whom one cannot label; by refusing to be more specific about same-sex desire, she may be declining to allow the characters to be reduced to mere symbols of sexual orientations that in the 1950s were depicted as manifestations of sexual infirmity.⁶⁶

At the core of *Anna Teller*'s artistic mission is the story of a man trying to write a novel of emotions, what Emil calls "the emotional study of a man"; what we receive is frequently described by him as just an outline.⁶⁷ Yet it is through Emil's effort that Sinclair reveals part of her own qualms in the production of *Anna Teller*. Emil's speculation about the ultimate impossibility of his being able to dramatize sex and emotion are Sinclair's own, along with his realization that it will be equally hopeless "to talk about Commie stuff."[68] Sinclair is also at one with Emil in wanting to write a book of memory. It must be a book with no ultimate chronology, containing "memories of two worlds," in which "all the [Teller] brothers stay alive" and where the dead and living are side by side regardless of year or war or job.[69] Like Emil, Sinclair is very much in mourning for the 1930s: "It was the whole era of the thirties he missed—as if he were an old man looking back with mournful nostalgia at the excitement of youth and vigor and love, the clamor of revolutionary thoughts and needs. Yes, and deeds: the WPA project had picked up a great piece of America, somehow. Fed it, housed it, but most of all freed its soul."[70] While Petry addresses the Cold War social stasis in a depressed African American community and Sinclair in an upwardly mobile Jewish American one, the novels put on display critical minds working at full stretch. Both women create novels seeking to acknowledge and thereby transcend the competing subjectivities to which even art contributes.

Chapter Eight

Off Modernity's Grid

THE STRANGE CAREER OF PEOPLE'S POETRY

On the bitterly cold morning of 8 February 1954, the year that the bipartisan Communist Control Act was passed by Congress, the thirty-three-year-old Marxist poet Aaron Kramer (1921–97) unfolded his New York City newspaper to lurid banner headlines about a sensational double murder. Maxwell Bodenheim (born Maxwell Bodenheimer, 1892–1954), the Jewish poet and novelist who had briefly joined the Communist Party at the outset of the 1930s and never repudiated his stance, had been shot in the heart with a .22 rifle bullet just a few blocks from where Kramer lived. Bodenheim's young third wife, Ruth Fagan, daughter of the socialist journalist Peter Fagan (once engaged to Helen Keller), had been knifed to death at his side. Their murderer, Harold Weinberg, soon caught and obviously deranged, argued in the defense at his trial: "I ought to get a medal. I killed two Communists."[1] The statement was made only nine months after the execution of Julius and Ethel Rosenberg.

Kramer had followed Bodenheim's career since first hearing him read at a socialist camp in 1930 or 1931. He considered Bodenheim a major literary influence, and Kramer was affected to his core by defiant lines from Bodenheim's famous "Pierrot Objects" (1920), as well as by the lesser-known "Upper Family" (1946) and "Sincerely Yours, Culture" (1946). By the 1940s, Bodenheim was for Kramer the youngest of a trio of senior poet-mentors associated with the Communist Left and living in New York City. The others were Shamus O'Sheel (born James Shields, 1886–1954), whose major books were published before World War I, and Alfred Kreymborg (1883–1966), whose final volume would be *No More War, and Other Poems* (1950).[2]

In 1944, Kramer achieved his first national recognition when his poems appeared along with Bodenheim's and Kreymborg's in the antifascist collection *Seven Poets in Search of an Answer*. The volume went through three

Aaron Kramer was a young Communist firebrand who after World War II wrote people's poetry such as *Roll the Forbidden Drums!* (1954). In the 1960s, he found a more supple voice and won a broader audience. (Courtesy of Aaron Kramer)

large printings in a short time and aimed to form a cultural bridge. On one bank was the people's poetry of the 1930s, sometimes called labor poetry or workers' poetry, openly revolutionary and characterizing all international wars as imperialist. On the other side was the emergent wartime progressive literature, also called people's poetry but aimed at carrying the antifascist vision to military victory and then to postwar peace and democracy undergirded by a sanguine view of the Soviet Union. The volume was introduced by O'Sheel, who explained that the question to be answered in the book was whether poets had the capacity to address "stern social and political issues." To him, this was the essence of "the great tradition" going back to Dante and Shakespeare, and O'Sheel had no doubt about how to translate the Great Tradition into the militarized literary practice of antifascism: "to stand less on the defensive, to attack more and on more fronts; to postpone the threnody and sound the clarion call; to learn to move men to anger and action, even at the sacrifice of analysis; and to find ways to co-operate as a phalanx where now each poet fights as a lone partisan."[3] The other four writers included in *Seven Poets* were all associated with the Communist movement going back to the Depression: Langston Hughes, Martha Millet (1919–2008), Norman Rosten (1913–95), and Joy Davidman (1915–60). At a public meeting to celebrate the book's publication, hosted by the Hotel Grosvenor on Fifth Avenue, the contributors read their verse, each presented by O'Sheel. Afterward, Kramer proudly introduced the wild-looking, and probably inebriated, Greenwich Village celebrity Bodenheim to his parents.[4]

Nine years later, on that grim winter day when the news of the double killing of Bodenheim and Fagan was announced, Kramer rushed to the home of Bodenheim's first wife, Minna, before reporting for work at his bookkeeping job. There he secured her enthusiastic agreement to read a eulogy at Bodenheim's memorial meeting, only to be devastated shortly afterward when his employer refused to let him take time off work to attend the commemorative event. Kramer then arranged for Kreymborg to read his tribute, which was published immediately afterward in the *National Guardian*. Kramer's remarks were as much about himself as his murdered comrade. He lauded Bodenheim's tenacity in maintaining his style and his point of view and bravely predicted a new day, twenty years hence, when Bodenheim's "simplicity" of expression would be remembered far more than the work of the then-popular poets of "cynicism and snobbishness."[5]

That same evening, O'Sheel sent Kramer a moving letter about the memorial event. O'Sheel concluded, in the recently recovered text of that letter: "Ah, me lad, Max and Alfred and I count on you to carry the fire forward now that he [Bodenheim] is gone and we are going."[6] Twenty years later, when he published his 1975 poem "Disappointed Ghosts," Kramer recalled O'Sheel's words a bit differently:

Max is dead;
I and Alfred soon will lose the game;
that leaves only you—lift high the flame!

In this poem, never reprinted, Kramer recalls that he wept and mouthed "a promise (which has not been kept)." He closes:

Deep in shadow now you crouch, all three, poised as if
  expecting light from me.
How am I to merit such command?
Lift high what flame?
Now ash is in my hand.[7]

The "ash" in Kramer's hand in 1975 was not a destroyed socialist vision but what remained of the political hallucination of late antifascism, a politics closely joined to the production of a people's poetry crafted by pro-Communists with techniques inspired by Heinrich Heine, Robert Burns, and Langston Hughes. The aesthetic goal was to declaim verse thriving in song and ballad forms that sought instant communication with working-class audiences.[8] This genre was defined in stark opposition to writing supposedly contaminated by T. S. Eliot and Ezra Pound, still denounced by Kramer as late as 1950 as the "hoot-owls of darkness and decay."[9] The workers' poetry tradition began as an effort to capture the ordinary lives of laborers and outcasts, but the people's poetry of late antifascism too often resulted in a political-literary Kabuki, stylized performances where the dramatization of progressive and reactionary arguments are as predestined as the ending. Within that confining framework, Kramer launched his career when still in public school and occasionally managed to attain bona fide artistry.

As a fiery young Communist militant in the postwar era, Kramer remained under the spell of dogmatic mentors such as O'Sheel who bombarded him with a constant stream of letters criticizing the Communist movement for alleged "negligence, blindness, and indifference toward earnest and serviceable anti-fascist poetry."[10] What O'Sheel said he meant by the latter was "not an art of decoration but an art of utterance, an art of saying things that the moral conscience demands shall be said." However, the target seemed to be occasional free verse or perhaps abstruse references, or maybe the complaint was about a perceived lack of regard for his own opinions or the work of his young protégé. The sixty-eight-year-old author of the famous lines "They Went Forth to Battle, but They Always Fell" (1917) joined Kramer in the promotion of a "turn to rhyme": "only rhymed verse in metrical rhythm can reach the minds and emotions of masses of people, and can take hold and be remembered and repeated." O'Sheel was not in principle against blank verse and vers libre, although he despised "similes, metaphors, and hyperboles inclined to the odd, far-fetched, cryptic." His stance was that these modern approaches had been overworked; the new strategy he recommended for Kramer was to use "freer rhythms" and "shaken-out rhythms, rather than the old standard strictly measured and standard rhythms." O'Sheel would go line-by-line over Kramer's writings, pointing out instances where the syllables seemed too crowded and figures of speech were too puzzling.[11]

Although Kramer had other Left literary friends, such as Norman Rosten (1913-95), who urged him to break with the stifling conventions of the proletarian poetry of the 1930s, it was the stern guidance of O'Sheel and Kreymborg (by the 1940s, Bodenheim was nearly a derelict) that inspired him during the nastiest years of the Red Scare.[12] Like a literary warrior with a take-no-prisoners approach, Kramer wanted to strike poetic blows at McCarthyism. A volume of poems advocating resistance with a formidable title, *Roll the Forbidden Drums!* (1954), was in press, at the liberal William-Frederick publishing house, on the day that Maxwell Bodenheim was murdered. Suddenly, apprehensive of the risk involved in such a publication, the owner of William-Frederick pulled out and offered to secretly assist by making the book's plates available to another publisher, only increasing Kramer's feeling of harassment. Angus Cameron (1908-2002), the recently blacklisted former vice president of Little Brown and Company, seized the opportunity with his partner, the journalist Albert E. Kahn, to issue the volume under the imprint of their new Cameron and Kahn Associates.

Roll the Forbidden Drums! was one of four volumes of poetry written by Kramer during the high Cold War. His books were aimed expressly and insolently at keeping alive the spirit of confrontation, as well as to affirm a tradition of a people's art. The other volumes were *The Golden Trumpet* (1949), *Thru Every Window* (1950), and *Denmark Vesey and Other Poems* (1952). Kramer's intended audience of workers was, of course, comprised of the dwindling Communist-led Left, but it was a following that could still fill auditoriums of hundreds of seats. Kramer's most sustained single work of the era—the long "Demark Vesey," in which the slave rebel is invoked as a model for the 1950s—was written to be performed before large audiences in Los Angeles.[13]

During the early 1930s, a tradition of worker ballads and romantic poetry was one-sidedly favored by the *Daily Worker* and had more or less received an official imprimatur as far back as the publication of *Poems for Workers* in 1927. Yet this legacy was cautiously sidestepped by a new generation of Communist poets such as those who published in *Dynamo* in 1934-36—Sol Funaroff, Herman Spector (1905-59), Edwin Rolfe (1909-54), Kenneth Fearing, Horace Gregory, Muriel Rukeyser, Alfred Hayes, and Ben Maddow (1909-92).[14] While sharing a common ground in the Left's adulation of Walt Whitman, this circle of writers more accurately embodied a proletarian avant-garde tendency of poets who aspired to quietly adapt the modernist forms of Eliot, Pound, and Yeats for revolutionary ends.[15] On occasion, select portions of their writing were included in Party venues, but the larger corpus was kept apart, a practice that would continue in the postwar era. To all intents and purposes, the Communists' Third Period had effectively energized both workers' poetry and an avant-garde proletarianism, but the political priorities of the Communist Party's turn to the Popular Front in 1935 pushed the Left-modernist strain into the background.

From the advent of the Hitler-Stalin Pact and even into World War II, the incidence of published poetry of any type in the *New Masses* declined and the austere verse of Alexander Bergman was held up as a model.[16] Even so, the drive toward some form of modernist difficulty retained a behind-the-scenes presence in the two circles of fledgling writers that Kramer entered in the late 1930s. At the age of fifteen, Kramer joined the Communist Party's Young Labor Poets, led by Eli Siegel (1902–78), a genial Village bohemian assigned to this work by the Communist Party. At sixteen Kramer entered Brooklyn College, where he joined the staff of the literary magazine, the *Observer*, where youthful Communists were a real force. Among the Young Labor Poets, Kramer felt disparaged by aspiring writers like Raphael Hayes (1915–2010), the handsome younger brother of Alfred Hayes, who reportedly mocked Kramer as a mere balladeer.[17] While not deflected from his stance as a people's poet, Kramer's behavior in at least two instances demonstrated a troubling insecurity. When his first book of poetry, *The Alarm Clock* (1938), led to a community celebration of 300 of his neighbors in Bensonhurst, Kramer stood on the platform but refused to read a single poem because he was overwhelmed by doubts about the quality of his work. Then, on the eve of his graduation from Brooklyn College, Kramer capitulated to pressure from his pro-modernist literary friends and wrote an Audenesque "Valedictory Ode, 1941."[18] As expected, his poem was warmly greeted by his *Observer* colleagues, but Kramer would guiltily refuse to include it in his later volumes.[19]

After World War II, Kramer was disturbed by reports of disappearances and executions in the Soviet Union but held back from reaching any larger conclusion about the Soviet state. A fear of the slippery slope of renegacy was lodged in his brain; a critic of Stalin was judged to be a person en route to becoming an "anti-Sovieteer" and tool of reaction. Kramer several times withdrew from Communist Party commitments in the 1940s for personal reasons, yet various events and incidents would push him back into frenetic activism. One such moment followed the 1947 death of his father; the loss not only increased his fidelity to the Communist Party but inflected his poetry with renewed fervent simplicity. Finally, in 1952–53, the contradictions of Communism seemed too great. Provoked by the excesses of the internal Party campaign against "white chauvinism," Kramer quietly dropped his membership in the Party when he moved with his family to the East Village. At news of the 1956 Khrushchev Revelations, he found himself less surprised than confirmed in what he already knew. Kramer mailed off a sonnet called "Threnody" to the *New York Times*.

The *Times* published "Threnody" on its editorial page, as was normal then; although comrades immediately knew the subtext, Kramer believed that the editors did not grasp the point of reference as a loss of faith in the Soviet utopia.[20] Later incorporated into a sonnet sequence in *Rumshinsky's Hat* (1964), a series that might be read as a lamentation for the Third International, "Threnody" concludes: "the dream by which I lived is dead ... / And I, that bellowed so, must learn to be silent—except for this one threnody."[21] Abandoning his Communist poetic persona, Kramer constructed over the next four decades an alternative presence as an independent revolutionary, a popular figure on the New York Jewish Left cultural scene, and the most consistently published white writer in the left-wing African American journal *Freedomways*. He was a major anthologist of left-wing poets in English and Yiddish and a public and unabashed opponent of U.S. policy in Vietnam and of every instance of imperialist aggression by the West.[22] He never recanted rhyme, music, and simplicity but found his own way of using modes of expression appropriate to many-layered emotions and meditations too intricate for instant communication to a working-class audience, real or hypothetical. For many poets, the finest verse is written mainly early in their careers; this was not true of Kramer, who over the years acquired a far more supple voice.

IMAGINARY FRIENDS

With the important exception of the *Daily Worker*, the cultural organs of the Communist Party in the 1940s and 1950s were not as hospitable to Kramer's work as one might expect in light of his complete identification with the Party's politics as well as with the tradition of workers' poetry. Kramer was hypersensitive to possible slights, but he was ignored if not outright disrespected by the fugitive but nonetheless influential Left-modernist writers and editors who had a presence on the boards of *California Quarterly* (1951–56) and the poetry journal *Coastlines* (1955–64) on the West Coast and gained influence at *Masses & Mainstream* on the East Coast in 1956. Kramer had some justification in seeing himself as beleaguered in comparison to Thomas McGrath, which seems contrary to an influential E. P. Thompson essay, "Homage to Thomas McGrath,"[23] asserting the opposite. On balance, McGrath and

Kramer received somewhat equal treatment. The Communist Party publishing house published two books by McGrath, one of poetry and one of fiction, which is the same number as published by Kramer. The *Daily Worker* and less prestigious Party publications tilted toward Kramer, but neither poet was particularly championed by *Masses & Mainstream* before 1956. And in Communist Party venues, McGrath's early books by non-Party publishers were as consistently reviewed as were Kramer's, neither uncritically. When Samuel Sillen and Howard Fast dropped out of the Communist Party over the Khrushchev Revelations in 1956 and V. J. Jerome was imprisoned under the Smith Act, McGrath's ally Charles Humboldt took over as perhaps the most vital cultural critic in the Communist Party through his workaholic devotion to the editing of *Masses & Mainstream*, renamed *Mainstream* in 1956.

McGrath then began appearing as a regular in its pages, as both a poetry contributor and reviewer, by far eclipsing Kramer. Moreover, McGrath was listed as an advisory editor, an honor never accorded Kramer. Kramer, who remained publically silent regarding his misgivings about the Soviet Union until the 1960s, was found more acceptable for publication in Party-supported albeit technically independent journals such as *Freedomways* and *Jewish Currents*. In 1955, McGrath took a swipe at Kramer that caused considerable pain. In his introduction to the posthumous collection of Communist poet Edwin Rolfe's, *Permit Me Refuge*, McGrath holds up Rolfe as a "serious poet" in contradistinction to those who try to "create a whole corpus of work out of little moral or mock-moral allegories concerning birds and animals."[24] This was an unmistakable dismissal of the core of Kramer's anti-McCarthy resistance poems that did, indeed, allegorically employ forms and structures from popular, romantic, and children's myths.

Although their personal relations were always cordial, both men saw themselves embattled in different ways; one suspects that this was a commonplace experience in such a movement with limited resources and the persistence of political criteria for art. The force field of the postwar Communist cultural movement was riven by contested impulses, and the war behind the scenes between Kramer and McGrath was characteristic. Kramer had the backing of the Communist Party hierarchy and pro-Communist Jewish cultural institutions, while McGrath had extra support from the more sophisticated elements of the literary Left. This meant that Kramer had a real audience of working people, while McGrath, Charles Humboldt, and others were partisans of labor but had a more hypothetical working-class audience. To a poet, however, the confirmation of other writers and cultural figures trumps all. The clash between the two was less over politics than literary strategy. Kramer

Thomas McGrath, an unflagging Communist in his political views, was blacklisted from teaching in 1954 but wrote groundbreaking verse and inspired a younger generation of poets in Southern California. In the photograph on the right, he is shown with Alice Greenfield McGrath, a Communist activist in Los Angeles who became his second wife. (Courtesy of Elwyn B. Robinson Department of Special Collections, Chester Fritz Library, University of North Dakota)

had an antifascist literary discipline, but it took decades for him to forge an independent poetic vision. In this respect, McGrath triumphed early and has only increased in standing.

Born in Ranson County, North Dakota, the son of second-generation poor farmers of Irish ancestry, McGrath was the oldest of six children. His mother, Catherine, was a devout, churchgoing Catholic. Like the Kramers, there was radicalism in the family history; McGrath's father, James, who loved to recite poems and tell stories, was shaped by the culture and outlook of the IWW. A decisively painful event occurred in McGrath's childhood during the course of a strike when a charismatic union organizer was badly beaten by an uncle, the brother of McGrath's mother. The other workers stood by, and the strike was lost. McGrath's major work, *Letter to an Imaginary Friend* (1962–85), memorializes and seeks to redeem this worker, called "Cal," along with others who played crucial roles in creating McGrath's political and literary vision. His cast of characters includes militant workers, revolutionary comrades, and a few poets and family members.

The concept of an "imaginary friend," which came to McGrath in the postwar era of repression and blacklisting, introduced an alternative approach to the dilemma that vexed Aaron Kramer in the same years: the problem of audience. McGrath rotated among several claims about his intended addressees; he variously affirmed that they consisted of educated workers, comprised an unknown and uncertain quantity, or made up an entity that lay in the future. This complex vision of his readership allowed McGrath a marvelous range of techniques and materials. On the other hand, for McGrath the "imaginary friend" was an indubitably masculine one, and his writing is full of the language of the male proletarian experience, male sexual and domestic preoccupations, and a male rhetoric of military-like class struggle. McGrath's "imaginary friend" was clearly a buddy, a comrade in the struggle, an alter-ego serving as a synecdoche of the revolutionary forces that had fought and failed yet needed to rise again.[25]

McGrath's early literary and political formation took place in isolation from the urban and East Coast centers of the Left; his evolution toward modernism came simultaneously with his initial publications. As a child, in imitation of his father, he took to reading poetry in whatever collections he found available. These were mostly romantic and Elizabethan classics. He also was drawn to the idea of becoming a playwright as a means of expressing the oral culture of the region. Politically, the young McGrath thought of himself only as a "rebel," which produced an erroneous identification with Franco (who led the "rebels" against the Republic) when he read the first press reports about the Spanish Civil War. Shortly afterward, he was drawn to Marx while he also stumbled across modern poets such as E. A. Robinson and Hart Crane.

After graduating from high school in the nearby town of Shelton, McGrath worked at odd jobs to raise money so that he might attend a state university. In 1935, he matriculated at the University of North Dakota and quickly joined the local branch of the Communist Party. This was the moment of the advent of the Popular Front, and as a new Party member, McGrath found himself somewhat preferring the older policies to what seemed to him a growing liberal ethos. Yet he admired the Third Period's emphasis on political discipline, so he subordinated himself to the new orientation despite a discomfort that he would feel ever afterward. An immediate expression of his fierce commitment to the movement was a determination to volunteer for combat in Spain. McGrath claimed that he was ready to embark just as the decision was made for the International Brigades to pull out of the war.[26]

During four years at North Dakota, McGrath read widely in modernism, especially fiction by Joyce and Proust. In the late 1930s, he began sending submissions of poetry to the *New Masses*. To his dismay, he received back letters from assistant editor Norman Rosten apologetically explaining that McGrath's offerings were too difficult and even too demoralizing to be published.[27] By the time of his college graduation in 1939, the precocious McGrath had received a Rhodes scholarship for study abroad and was also besieged with bids to do graduate work at Harvard University and other institutions around the United States. Due to the signs that the United States would be drawn into a world war, McGrath made an arrangement to defer the Rhodes scholarship. He set off for Louisiana State University, where he completed coursework for an M.A. in 1939–40.

Baton Rouge was the setting for three crucial events in his life. First, McGrath became a student of Cleanth Brooks (1906–94), who had just published the text *Understanding Poetry* (1939) and the scholarly book *Modern Poetry and the Tradition* (1939). Both works expostulated the principles of tension, paradox, and ambiguity that would become the foundation for the New Criticism. Brooks took a liking to McGrath and dragooned him into taking all his classes, in addition to passing hours in private conversation in a local tavern. While McGrath was antipathetic to Brooks's conservative politics, rooted in Southern Agrarianism, he respected his gentle nature and responsiveness to modern poetry. The second influential moment of McGrath's Louisiana years was his decision to deepen his commitment to Communist politics; in Baton Rouge, he was active in political work both on the waterfront and in African American districts. The third event was the cementing of a lifelong friendship with Alan Swallow (1915–66), a poet and publisher who would bring out most of McGrath's important volumes.[28]

From 1940 to 1941, McGrath, newly married, tried teaching at Colby College, but he was bitten by a political bug too strong to allow him to rest easy in a small college environment. Teaching seemed dull and unsatisfying in comparison to the pull of New York City, so he moved to Manhattan at the end of the academic year. From that time until he began military service in 1942, McGrath immersed himself in militant labor activities rooting him all the more in the traditions of the Communist Left. His memories of these years would sustain him through the postwar decade, when he underwent an ordeal of political persecution that would banish him from academic and mainstream poetry circles until the 1960s. Yet the rebound would be a triumphant breakthrough in Marxist poetry of the United States.

McGrath's earliest volumes of poetry indexed his radicalism, but he had no connection to the cultural organizations and institutions that were guided by Party members. By inclination, his writing was closer to the Marxist-modernists of the *Partisan Review*, even though he regarded the editors as politically reactionary. Complicating the matter was McGrath's antipathy to Walt Whitman. He saw Whitman as an outright danger to the Left for both his loose style and non-revolutionary politics. McGrath was similarly at arm's length from William Carlos Williams; he rejected what he saw as Williams's fetishization of the object (for example, in his 1923 "The Red Wheelbarrow").[29] Added to these heresies was McGrath's own positive early response to surrealism and his partisanship for Bertolt Brecht's pro-modernist views in his debates with Georg Lukács.

For a committed Communist, a startling number of McGrath's poems from his early period, those included in *First Manifesto* and "The Dialectics of Love" (in *Three Young Poets: Thomas McGrath, William Peterson, James Franklin Lewis*, 1942), describe an isolated consciousness in an existential hell. In "Up the Dark Valley," the narrator finds no companionship or consolation in nature, only decay and echoes of his own voice. In "A Way You'll Never Be," he whistles in the dark against a dread of isolation. "Gotterdammerung" illustrates paralysis in the face of impending calamity. Themes of socialist solidarity and community are hard to find. "Get Out of Town," an early poem on the temptations of political betrayal, is marvelously crafted in its fusing of new imagery with rhythmic half-rhyming quatrains. Intimations of the threat of death are time after time associated with cold temperatures, and the case made by the protagonist for flight from "the cops snoring in the frost-hung parlor" seems airtight until the last two lines reveal that personal escape would leave "the boys" (presumably radical workers to whom the protagonist has promised aid) isolated and trapped.[30]

McGrath's literary and political yearning jelled in a central way during the two periods he spent in New York City collaborating with waterfront Communists.[31] In these sojourns, 1941–42 and 1945–47, McGrath was exposed to a vibrant working-class culture that was tough, ethnic (mostly Irish), and witty, apparently generated by autodidacts in or close to the Communists organizing the waterfront. When McGrath arrived in Chelsea in 1941, he quickly fell under the spell of a man named Arthur Blair who called himself Mac McClain but was known simply as "Mac." Mac led caucuses of dissident longshoremen, checkers, and teamsters in the union locals and on the docks. Among Mac's closest associates, whom he loved to debate on issues of politics and ethics, was a former Marxist turned gangster, Ky Costello. Costello worked alternately as a gun-packing goon for shipowners and a defense guard for the unions—whoever would pay the higher price.

In the late 1940s, Costello was killed by an infamous waterfront thug, John M. "Cockeye" Dunne, who in 1949 was electrocuted for the murder of at least thirty men.[32] Dunne was a terror in the community but tolerated by the police and clergy. He was opposed mainly by Mac and his circle of working-class radicals. These militants published a four-page broadsheet called the *Shamrock* under the editorship of Ray Condon. This was McGrath's milieu, and he registered its impact in two book dedications. His 1949 collection *Longshot O'Leary's Garland of Practical Poesie* was dedicated to *Shamrock* editors "Mac, Ray and Jody," and his 1988 novel *This Coffin Has No Handles* was to "the great Mac Blair." Mac also appears as a character throughout *Letter to an Imaginary Friend, Part I*.

The amazing Mac reportedly had a background as an agricultural organizer in the Salinas Valley of California and as a strike leader in Camaguay, Cuba, and he was one of the militant seamen who in 1935 tore the Nazi flag from the mast of the German ship *Bremen* when it was docked in New York Harbor.[33] Others in the group also boasted proletarian credentials and legendary courage. Harold Gates, one contributor to the *Shamrock*, was an open Party member and employed McGrath on the rank-and-file newspaper for his local. Their union activities were targeted by local gangs who wanted to "clean up" the unions in regard to the Communists, who posed a threat to their shakedown operations. Associates of the *Shamrock* were beaten and murdered, while the police appeared more sympathetic to the gangsters than to the union activists.

At the same time, McGrath carried out political work by aiding the

Communist-led International Labor Defense in doing research for the Philadelphia deportation case of Communist leader Samuel Adams Darcy (born Samuel Dardeck, 1905-2005). Later, McGrath was assigned by the Party to obtain a job at the Federal Drydock Company in Kearney, New Jersey, assisting in the organizing of shipyard workers. In 1942, McGrath entered the army, serving three years in the Aleutian Islands, where he obtained the rank of sergeant. Inasmuch as most of the other writers for the *Shamrock* joined the military around the same time, the *Shamrock* folded. Immediately after the war, there was a brief effort to revive the paper. McGrath returned to Chelsea and began to work again with Harold Gates, but one day Gates simply vanished. McGrath joined forces with Mac Blair, Maggie Blair (Mac's wife), Ray Condon, and other activists from the National Maritime Union to search every building and back alleyway, but it was to no avail.

That same year, 1947, McGrath had his chance to make use of his Rhodes scholarship with an offer to study at New College in Oxford. Once in residence, he prepared a proposal for a thesis on the prominent Communist critic Christopher Caudwell (1907-37), whose blend of Marx and Freud was a foremost influence on McGrath's creative thinking. When this idea was rejected, he relocated to southern France, where he wrote the two works reflective of his waterfront experiences, *Longshot O'Leary's Garland of Practical Poesie* and "All But the Last" (published three decades later as *This Coffin Has No Handles*). The first contains McGrath's cultural declaration of independence, "Ars Poetica; Or: Who Lives in the Ivory Tower"; a memorable satire, "Poor John Luck and the Middle Class Struggle"; and an elegy for his brother who was killed in the war, "Blues for Jimmy." *This Coffin Has No Handles*, a work of proletarian pulp, is a perfect prose counterpart to his poetry, something of a cross between James Joyce and noir fiction. Written in the form of a log, the novel vivifies New York in hard-boiled style with descriptions that can resonate as powerfully as his most compelling verse. The cast of characters includes Joe Hunter, a McGrath stand-in who has just been released from wartime service in the army; Barney Last, leader of the Communist waterfront workers and an honorable veteran of the Spanish Civil War; Alton Husk, an anti-Communist authority from a wealthy family; Kay, Joe Hunter's lover, who tempts him to abandon Communist commitment to indulge in the fantasy of an escape to a small town in Colorado; Crip, a club-footed professional killer; Landers, a vicious Trotskyist; and Jim Keyes, a union activist who mysteriously disappears and then is found murdered in the river.

Returning to the United States, McGrath saw the thirty-two page *Longshot O'Leary* come out in the same International Publishers Poets' Series as books by Milton Blau (1921-2009) and Aaron Kramer.[34] The volume contained a mixture of verse that he knew met the approval of his comrades due to its tactical relevance to current policy, along with a few that he thought to be provocative for the long-term raising of consciousness. Encouraged by this small success, he circulated the manuscript of his waterfront novel to both mainstream and left-wing publishing houses. It met with so many negative responses that he squirreled it away for the next thirty years. In the interim, he discovered that he could make some money by writing for pulp magazines, especially Westerns, and developed pseudonyms that he kept hidden and still remain unknown. This activity eventually led to a crisis in his poetry; he found that he could not do both genres of writing simultaneously, so he abandoned the pulp.

MEMORIES OF THE FUTURE

By 1946, McGrath began to publish poetry reviews in *New Masses*, and when his book from International Publishers appeared, he found himself more accepted in the Communist Party network. He quickly took sides in the aesthetic split over difficult poetry forms, creating tensions when he criticized the Communist poet Vincent Ferrini (1913–2007) for his short-term vision. Such opinions led to his close rapport with Charles Humboldt.[35] Then McGrath's personal circumstances transformed after he moved to California at the start of the 1950s. His marriage to his first wife, Marian, disintegrated during the war, and he was soon in the company of Alice Greenfield (1917–2009), a local Communist well known for her activities in the 1942 Sleepy Lagoon Case.[36] In addition, there was an unanticipated situation in regard to cultural work. The Los Angeles Party was the home of a strong cultural section led by John Howard Lawson, a brilliant, courageous, and single-minded playwright and screenwriter who held aesthetic views that McGrath regarded as socialist realist dogmatism. The older and authoritative Lawson easily prevailed in any discussion, which gave McGrath the feeling there was no role for him as a poet in the Party. Increasingly he drifted into individualist activities.

McGrath initially struck it lucky and without much effort landed a teaching post at Los Angeles City College in 1951. But within three years, he was called before HUAC and dismissed from his job because of his non-cooperative stance. Student protests could not reverse the decision, so he began a sequence of low-paying jobs. This included carving wood animals, teaching at a private secondary school, and episodic television and film work. Since McGrath excelled at inspiring young writers, he decided to launch a school for poetry writing that he called the Sequoia School. It lasted only from 1954 to 1955 but left a big imprint on local culture. Los Angeles painters were attracted along with writers. McGrath, at this point immersed in the poetry of Ezra Pound and the jazz of Sidney Bechet, had a reputation as a fabulous reader of others' verse with an impeccable eye.

McGrath also established friendships with other Los Angeles Communist poets, especially Don Gordon (1902–89) and Edwin Rolfe, both of whom would occasionally take over his classes at the school. Gordon especially shared McGrath's attraction to Freud, although he strangely disparaged McGrath's long poems in favor of the short ones.[37] In the first half of the 1950s, McGrath assisted Philip Stevenson in editing the publication *California Quarterly*; his wife, Janet Stevenson (1913–2009), was another blacklisted teacher who had collaborated in the Sequoia School. Next McGrath moved on to become the behind-the-scenes inspiring figure behind the journal *Coastlines*. At the end of the 1950s, he published two children's books, *About Clouds* (1959) and *The Beautiful Things* (1959).

When McGrath first arrived in California, Alice Greenfield noticed him at a political fund-raiser. He was a very handsome man with light brown hair, blue eyes, and attractive Irish features, including a McGrath family trait—a tendency for one's eyes to go down at the corner. Greenfield also imagined that he was a strong man who would enjoy long strolls, although it would turn out that he was an entirely sedentary person who chain-smoked and had contempt for athletics and exercise. He also had dark moods and a romantic fixation on the old days (the 1930s and 1940s) that would grow more pronounced. Greenfield was already married but became convinced that she was experiencing instantaneous love. It took over a year for her to decide to leave her husband, and even then she hesitated before marrying McGrath.[38] The initial months after the wedding were happy. They made a strikingly attractive couple, arriving in black leather on Tom's motorcycle for late night parties. McGrath adored jazz music and loved witty, intense conversation, above all with poets and painters. But he was also a heavy drinker, which would become a factor in their eventual divorce.[39]

Tom was politically content with Communist ideology and very pro-Soviet, but the climate in the Party became increasingly uncomfortable due to the hostility he felt from Lawson.[40] He probably would have quit if he had seen a possible alternative. Between the fall of 1950 and May 1956, nothing at all of McGrath's appeared in *Masses & Mainstream*, although he submitted frequently.[41] A particularly galling incident occurred at the time McGrath was fired from his teaching job. His students issued a volume of his poems to express their support, and Charles Humboldt, by now known to be McGrath's literary champion, wrote a review for *Masses & Mainstream*. The editorial board, however, led by A. B. Magil, rejected the review on the grounds that it was uncritical.[42] Magil spoke on behalf of Samuel Sillen and Herbert Aptheker, regarded by the Communist Party as leading people in the cultural field. The complaints of the editors about the poetry submissions of Humboldt himself were characteristic of the mentality of late antifascism, and Humboldt's writing was identified with that of McGrath's. In rejecting Humboldt's poem "To Certain Men of Learning," about the cowardice of academics in the face of McCarthyism, the editors found the "form" to be unsuitable, especially in the 1950s, "when the imperialist bourgeoisie is cultivating and utilizing decadence, formalism, abstraction.... We have to beware of permitting formalist and abstractionist infiltration." The editors pontificated that "there is a conflict between form and content and it reaches the point where form invades content, disorients it, takes it captive."

The poem was rejected as marred by obscure lines and a stanza "especially laden with elliptical, over-symbolic language," so that "the whole spirit of the writing ... is wrong, the isolation and aloofness it expresses, however much you intended it to be otherwise." Returning to the submission under dispute, Magil put forward a bizarre argument: "If Yvor Winters wrote 'To Certain Men of Learning' and sent it to *Masses & Mainstream*, it would mean progress for him and under those circumstances we might consider publishing it." The board's summary point expressed the longtime Achilles' heel of the kind of Communist criticism prevalent in its cultural wing: "For whom are we writing? To me [Magil] it seems that this is the central question. If poetry does not communicate, if its form is such that its content or intended content is incapable of influencing people and becomes a kind of private speech understood by a small coterie of the initiate, it loses its character as a weapon in our struggle. Form inbred to formalism is alien to everything we stand for—and not merely alien, but inimical."[43]

After 1956, the state of affairs at *Masses & Mainstream* altered considerably. Humboldt was left in charge of the publication and for the next four years made a large effort to put into practice a procedure that did not prioritize one style of poetry over others. McGrath appeared regularly as both a poetry contributor and book reviewer, and the publishing house associated with the magazine issued McGrath's *The Gates of Ivory, the Gates of Horn* (1957), with an introduction by Humboldt. This was science fiction thriller-like satire of a McCarthyite Consumers' Republic featuring an Investigator in a mechanized and soulless California of the future.

McGrath's own poetry continued to flow unabated throughout the 1950s, with *Figures from a Double World* appearing in 1955. That was the year he began writing *Letter to an Imaginary Friend*, with volume 1 coming into print in 1962, followed by volume 2 in 1970 and volumes 3 and 4 in 1985. By 1960,

McGrath's marriage to Alice was over, and he moved to New York City to take a teaching position at C. W. Post College. Now in a third marriage, with Eugenia (Genia) Johnson, McGrath that year launched a radical poetry journal called *Crazy Horse*, still in existence and a leading magazine. Although the first issue states that "*Crazy Horse* is an irregular publication, edited by a dead Sioux chief who is presently reincarnated by a group of Western poets," every single poet featured had a connection to the Communist movement in the United States (Thomas McGrath, Bert Meyers, Naomi Replansky, Charles Humboldt, Alvaro Cardona-Hine), England (Edgell Rickword, Jack Beeching), or Latin America (César Vallejo).

In 1962, McGrath took up a position at North Dakota State University at Fargo and then taught at Moorehead State University in Minnesota from 1969 until his retirement in 1983. Throughout these years, McGrath remained politically associated with the milieu of the Communist Party but very much a maverick in regard to political activity, occasionally identifying with groups such as the Far Left extraparliamentary Lotta Continua in Italy and the Maoist Progressive Labor Party in the United States. His own account of his membership has him joining the Communist Party in 1935, resigning according to official policy during his period of World War II military service, not having membership in the technical sense when he was called to testify before HUAC, yet holding some form of informal Party status in subsequent decades. This actually became firmer in the years before his death when he began to admire Gus Hall (born Arvo Kustaa Halberg, 1910–2000), one of the most Stalinist leaders in the history of the movement.[44]

By an order of magnitude, McGrath stands with writers such as George Oppen (1908–84) as among the finest postwar poets, Communist or otherwise. His *Letter to an Imaginary Friend*, first appearing in magazine selections in 1957, and then completed in four volumes by 1985, remains the core of his heritage. This is a nonlinear memoir in verse, simultaneously comprising memories of the future or perhaps a history for an unborn generation. A long poem organized around the autobiographical episodes, it alternates between passages of brilliant lucidity and those of impenetrably obscure personal references, some of which he later explained in interviews. The early sections go over his childhood; further on, many of the most commanding episodes relate to his adventures on the New York waterfront; and some of the concluding materials are set in Lisbon, Portugal, during the revolution against the Salazar dictatorship.[45]

Letter to an Imaginary Friend establishes McGrath as a master of the expansive poem, putting on display his baroque verbal qualities. He presents a cul-

Gene Frumkin and Alvaro Cardona-Hine were young Los Angeles poets inspired by Thomas McGrath during the Cold War. Their work appeared in the Communist publication *Mainstream* as well as the poetry journal *Coastlines*. (Courtesy of Gene Frumkin)

tural and linguistic amalgamation with proliferating allusions and metaphysical murkiness. He draws on numerous rhetorical elements—song, citation, conversation, prose, meter, rhyming, fragmentation, ellipse, and unusual diction. He also reveals himself a talented ranter offering a beguiling mix of the profane and the sacred. McGrath's cantos exist partly to defy paraphrase, yet the reader must speculate and grope for meanings because nothing feels wholly random or impressionistic. His rejoinder to the postwar memory loss suffered by the radical workers' movement puts on display numerous unmatched phrases:

Still, in the streets, sometimes, I see them moving—
Sleepwalkers in nightmare, drifting the battlefields of a war
They don't even know what is happening—
                                O blessed at the end of a
                                nightstick....
Machined to fit the print in a rack'n'gawk jukebox.... shot full of holes
    by the bounty hunters of Mad Avenue, brains drawn off
By the oak-borers of Ivy League schools' mistletoe masters.
Everything's been Los Angelized...
Alone, now, in the street....

He expresses revolutionary desire free of the familiar cant of late antifascism, and with just the right measure of wit:

What sign, what blazed tree, what burning lightning of the radical Word
Shall write their names on the wall break down that mind-framed dark?
Northern lights in winter; in summer the eccentric stairs
The firefly climbs...
But where is the steering star
Where is
The Plow? The Wheel?
Made this song in a bad time...
No revolutionary song now, no revolutionary
Party
sell out
false consciousness
yet I will
Sing
For these poor
For the victory still to come
RSVP[46]

"RSVP," we learn from an interview with McGrath years after the poem was written, was a private name he proposed for a socialist regroupment during the Cold War—Ramshackle Socialist Victory Party. It works flawlessly if only intended as a call for a response to his visionary song.[47]

McGrath's version of political Marxism was retrograde compared to Kramer's; like John Sanford, he lived in a world of his own private Stalinism. But also like Sanford, McGrath early on took a literary leap of a rare commitment to fierce experimentation that he shared with disciples in Los Angeles and elsewhere. It was Communist literary modernism, whatever his formal doctrinal allegiances. In the looping, cyclical, autobiographical narrative of *Letter to an Imaginary Friend*, saturated by an incantatory, noir-like voice-over, his imagination was never really in sync with the genre of people's poetry, even if he was writing an epitaph for the destruction of older ideals of working-class community. McGrath's literary statements are wild, raucous, and assaultive, an accumulation of alertly observed detail. He is erudite but impetuous, raised on classics but avant-garde in disposition, a reflective poet who is nonetheless resolved to imbibe the factual world in its dregs, sometimes regurgitating toxically cacophonous lines. McGrath had the genius to cultivate his singularity as a visionary Marxist poet, leaving a verbal imprint on his oeuvre like a darkening red watermark.

SOCIALIST SURREALISM

Paradoxically, the Communist poet who became most influential in the 1960s as an open Party member with no apologies was the one who had been among the most profoundly shaken by the revelations of the Twentieth Congress. Recovering from the crisis, he made a dramatic turn toward the emerging culture of the New Left and combined perhaps the least sectarian literary tastes of any of the poets in the Communist movement with the most naive optimism about the possibilities—indeed, the realities—of Soviet and Eastern Bloc reform during the post-Khrushchev era. This was the irrepressible Walter Lowenfels (1897–1976), who became the cultural face of the Communist Party for the new generation.

And what a remarkable success he was! To describe him only as a writer is less than half the story. Lowenfels's literary qualifications were those of legend, but the mad energy of the man was staggering; he got up at four or five o'clock in the morning every day and worked ten hours straight. A prize-winning poet and original among originals in the Parisian expatriate years of the late 1920s and early 1930s, he returned to the United States in mid-Depression to devote his literary skills to the Pennsylvania edition of the *Daily Worker*. After a brief and never explained Party assignment in Mexico, he was arrested under the Smith Act in July 1953.[48] As part of the "Philadelphia Nine," Lowenfels was charged with sedition and conspiracy to overthrow the U.S. government. Although he was found guilty, the case was overturned in 1957. In 1954, Walter was arrested yet again, this time for distributing "subversive" materials, and he was locked up for treason in the Holmsburg County Prison in Philadelphia. Due to lack of evidence, this second conviction was overturned, too. In the midst of these arrests, Lowenfels's wife, Lillian, who supported the family by teaching Romance languages in the public schools, was fired when she pleaded the Fifth Amendment instead of signing a loyalty oath. The stress no doubt assisted in producing the debilitating stroke that Lillian suffered in 1958, leaving her half-paralyzed for the twenty remaining years of her life.

It was during the first long courtroom proceedings that Walter Lowenfels found himself keeping busy by writing sonnets and translating works of other poets, after which he decided to relaunch his literary career. In 1954, he issued *The Prisoners: Poems for Amnesty*, which is of little value beyond underscoring the absurdity of the indictment along with the literary embarrassments of late antifascism. In "Sonnet for Ben Davis," an African American Party leader, Lowenfels writes:

> I one Jew tell you it will not be!
> Not more undone, unraveled human grain,
> gas chamber scarred with unhuman pain,
> no, not more! (But why is Ben not free?)

Toward the end of the volume, he cites Chinese Communist leader Mao Zedong, a brutal tyrant, on behalf of his own conviction that "every poem tends to be a love poem."[49] But these awful writings turned out to be misleading.

Lowenfels had commenced as a poet over three decades earlier, in what was yet another illustration of the severe anxiety disorder in literature produced by the impact of World War I. In the avant-garde writings of the Lost Generation, a godless world was besieged by death on all sides; salvation, or at least the closest thing to immortality, was available only through an artistic creation unburdened by social action. Lowenfels, who precipitously rejected his entire family as crass and business-oriented, became a quintessential exponent of such a wasteland mood starting with *Episodes & Epistles* (1925) and appearances in *transition* and *This Quarter*. His manifesto with Michael Fraenkel (1896–1957), called *Anonymous: The Need for Anonymity* (1930), was immediately joined by Lowenfels's own anonymous musical play *USA with Music: An Operatic Tragedy* (1930).

The early Depression revealed a new literary forte for Lowenfels. He published three long poems, each celebrating dead writers: *Apollinaire: An Elegy* (1930), *Elegy in the Manner of a Requiem in Memory of D. H. Lawrence* (1932), and *The Suicide* (1934), which was about Hart Crane. In that same period, Lowenfels was drawn to the Communist movement in France in 1932, and even more to the U.S. Party when returning from abroad in 1934. His literary strategy was now in an uncertain relation to his politics. At first he tried to apply some of his experimental techniques to poems about the Spanish Civil War and the CIO organizing drive. This resulted in *Steel 1937*, a fizzle in left-

Off Modernity's Grid 273

Walter Lowenfels spent the late 1920s and early 1930s in Paris as an avant-garde poet and publisher. (Courtesy of Judy Jacobs)

wing and all other circles. The chapbook turned out to be the prelude to a dry spell in verse for about fifteen years.⁵⁰

Only shortly after his 1954 collection, Lowenfels managed to pick up the thread of his earlier work and was reformulating his poetic mission through his fresh reading of Walt Whitman. The gist of his newly announced sensibility was that the death and suicide themes that obsessed him in his expatriate period were to be understood as the result of the reifications of capitalism and imperialism; life would be forged through creative action in harmony with the engagements for social redemption.[51] As time went on, Lowenfels found inspiration far beyond the orthodoxies of the Soviet Union and the Communist parties, and least of all in the limitations of workers' poetry or people's poetry. For him, Stalinism was never refuted, just sidestepped. A master of changing the subject and finessing stale tenets from the Left, Lowenfels, by example and through his devotion to anthologies, built a welcoming bridge back to poets who had drifted away from official Communism or whose roots were in the 1960s radicalization.

Responsive to jazz and African American culture, Lowenfels in the early 1960s launched a major attack against the "White Poetry Syndicate" and "The (Lily-White) Oxford Book of American Verse" that drew national attention to the Eurocentrism of U.S. literary culture.[52] He developed friendships with Black writers Clarence Major, Calvin Hernton, Ishmael Reed, and other younger African American literary voices. He became a buddy of Kenneth Rexroth in the San Francisco Bay Area, hit it off with Allen Ginsberg and the Beats, and single-handedly created the genre of multicultural, multigenerational left-wing literary anthologies thematically centered on the Third World, the war in Vietnam, the radical protest tradition in the United States, and the 1973 coup in Chile.

Political and personal mysteries undergird this trajectory. At the time of the Khrushchev Revelations, Lowenfels drafted a letter to the *Daily Worker*, which, unfortunately, was never sent. It is a document worth quoting at length:

> It isn't only that our singing tomorrows were having their jaws busted in confession chambers but that we became people who couldn't hear them even when their brains were being beaten into pulp with bullets. It's not the dead who wake us at night, though we think we hear their voices from the execution walls, it's ourselves. I think of the mine disasters I have covered as a [*Daily Worker*] reporter—the crowd—women and children huddling on the slag-bitten hillside, waiting in the December rain, as I saw them at Pine Creek, Kentucky—waiting for the bodies of lovers, husbands, fathers to be brought out. . . . That inhuman shriek from a woman when the first men came up out of the dark mouth of the mine, even before she saw the canvas-covered car, as if she knew beforehand what the shroud covered. . . . That was ones and twos—or hundreds like Centralia—not thousands, tens of thousands. . . . For us, the living, in the USA—it is not the dead who need rehabilitation—it is we, the selves, we have to wake up with in the morn-

By the 1970s, Walter Lowenfels was a successful literary anthologist and the public face of the Communist Party in poetry circles. (Courtesy of Judy Jacobs)

ing. . . . We are saying good-bye to our childhood. It is not easy at my age, 59, to grow up. What lies beyond the horizon for us all, I believe, is the real contour of human beings—not their make believe, but what they really are. A new dimension in human character that we had missed has been supplied. It gives all things a new angle, a new depth, a new height.[53]

By the 1960s, Lowenfels had somehow compartmentalized these political quarrels with the orthodox wing of the Communist Party. He always aligned himself with the political leadership associated with William Z. Foster by focusing mainly on the battle for good poetry. Lowenfels even wanted poetry to be integrated into Communist Party life to the point of having verse read at national conventions. When the Communist Party's *Mainstream* finally failed in 1963, as financially unviable, Lowenfels fought against its dissolution. When *American Dialog*, published by the Party from 1963 to 1973, seemed to be growing thinner on literature and narrower, Lowenfels battled hard to keep it cultural. He hoped to guide the contents while longtime colleague Joseph North managed the financial angle. In the end, North was pulled out against

Lowenfels's wishes. Disappointed with the way the magazine was going, he angrily dissociated himself.

The Communist Party, to which Lowenfels was unshakably loyal, did publish some of his odder books, such as *The Revolution Is to Be Human* (1964), in which he declared, "In the movement, we are all poets," and, "We are long past the age of socialist realism. What we are working toward is socialist surrealism."[54] What Lowenfels actually meant by "socialist surrealism" was never made precise. The phrase may have been a brilliant maneuver around theoretical issues that he was incapable of addressing, but it served him well as a talisman for his second life as a poet. Refusing to accept the idea that the Communist Party's emphasis on people's poetry had derailed his own development, Lowenfels's autobiographical narrative became that his poetic inspiration evolved directly into his political activities in the late 1930s and 1940s. He said he had given his best writing to the *Daily Worker*, but this journalism has never been reprinted, and there seems to be little interest in it.

The Lowenfels personality was as extraordinary as his political balancing acts. He was the reincarnation of a successful businessman in the heyday of the 1920s: entrepreneurial, evidencing no fear, and demonstrating a concentration so intense that he was never sidetracked. He also exhibited utter ruthlessness in terms of goals, breaking completely with individuals over political matters or losing interest when they were no longer serviceable. He spoke loudly in a voice that was not strong but at top volume and brandished a New York accent so thick that it seemed like a speech impediment. Nothing could faze Walter Lowenfels; resilience was so strong that he barreled his way through all of life like a Buster Keaton with a smile on his face. But Walter did require all the attention; he had to be flamboyantly at the front of the stage. When he was forced to get involved in day-to-day affairs, he showed himself to be a clumsy luftmensch. This may have been a spur to his reengagement with poetry. During his Pennsylvania political trials, Lowenfels complained about being pushed into the background; everyone had a role but himself. Then he chose to create a major part by writing sonnets and communicating with writers around the world.

Despite his aristocratic background, Lowenfels was never known to be condescending. A special interest in African Americans may have been instigated by his friendship with the British antiracist heiress Nancy Cunard (1896–1965), married to a Black man. During his Parisian expatriate years, he had been fascinated with jazz and Africa. In Philadelphia or New York City, Lowenfels could walk into a bar in a poor community and be immediately surrounded by Black people in conversation with him. He was at home with jazz musicians and great friends with Black Communists such as Ben Davis

Sarah Wright with Lucy Smith at the time that both were poets close to Walter Lowenfels and the Communist movement. In 1969 Wright published *This Child's Gonna Live*, a classic of Black women's fiction. (Courtesy of Joe Kaye)

and Edward and Augusta Strong. In Philadelphia, he mentioned and published in the *Daily Worker* two Black women writers close to the Communist Party, Sarah Wright (1928–2009) and Lucy Smith (dates unknown). In 1969, Wright published the acclaimed novel *This Child's Gonna Live*.[55]

When considering the oddities of Lowenfels's evolution and personality, the circumstances of his unusual childhood may be critical. Lowenfels's voluminous archives are filled with his efforts to answer complicated questions about "the Marxist view of death" and the meaning of a life of a committed artist. There are no reflections, however, on his family or background, only anecdotes in connection with his father wanting him to carry on the family "Hotel Butter Bar" business. (All his life, Walter would taste the butter in restaurants in a professional manner.) He never mentioned that his mother, a woman who was from a wealthy German Jewish background, was mentally ill and was often out of the picture. Another peculiarity concerns a sister who died shortly before Lowenfels's birth; his parents, desperate for a replacement, started dressing Walter as if he were female. Photos of Walter at age two show him very feminine-looking with huge brown curls. When he had his own daughters, he entertained them with stories that began, "When I was a little girl..."[56] As a result of this bizarre homelife, Walter rebelled early, managing to be expelled from numerous elite New York City high schools and never attending college.

Lowenfels's life-long relation to the Apotheker sisters is another riddle. The Communist Party would become Lowenfels's real family, but part of the romance started in the 1920s when he first met Nan and Lillian. They were brilliant young women who came from a Far Left background. Their father was a Yiddish contributor to the Communist press, a humorist using the pen name Hinke Dinke Schlemazel ("limping ne'er-do-well" in English). He died when they were young, and little information is available about him. Walter encountered the sisters in the 1920s, after he had returned from his World War I military service, during which time he had not actually left the United States. He was then working somewhat unhappily in the family business, although he is credited with devising the new wax paper wrapping for butter and date-stamping techniques to keep butter fresh. First Walter began to date the older Nan, an aspiring Greenwich Village poet who had already published in the *Masses* and *Seven Arts*. Nan was a committed left-winger, friends with Scott Nearing and Marc Blitzstein, and skilled as a translator and editor. From the 1930s until her death, she worked on Communist Party cultural projects and in organizations of Progressives, frequently collaborating with her brother-in-law.

As soon as Walter met the younger sister, his love interest switched. Lillian was short, five feet two inches tall, with reddish hair and freckles; eventually she became a chain smoker with weight problems. Like Nan, Lillian was intellectually brilliant; she had completed a master's thesis on Walt Whitman at the University of Pennsylvania, which is how Walter became involved in the topic of Whitman. The events leading to the marriage itself remain bewildering, as would the dynamics of the relationship in later years. Apparently Lillian had raised the funding for Walter's first book of poems in New York, but then the couple broke up. Walter quit the butter business and moved to Paris with a financial subsidy from his father, having made the agreement (never honored) that Walter would seek psychoanalysis with Freud in Vienna to address his irresponsible behavior toward the Lowenfels family. Soon Lillian arrived in Paris, pregnant with their first daughter, Micah. The couple reunited and a wedding ensued.

Lillian had greater organizational skills than Walter but lacked his personality. She became and always remained Walter's chief ally as he endlessly tapped her energy and intelligence. She was certainly frustrated with his irresponsibility in daily living, but she made it possible for him to focus on his poetry. Walter additionally had the capacity to display a terrible temper, at such moments becoming a different character from the accepting and patient persona that appears in his writing. But Lillian was a powerhouse, and even after her stroke, she read and criticized all of Walter's material. The stroke, however, meant that she no longer brought in an income.

Fortunately, Walter's father had arranged for him to receive annuities from successful stocks in GM and shares in buildings; due to the postwar boom, this money increased noticeably in the 1950s, just when it was needed. Walter's father was bitter that his son had forsaken the family business and held the mistaken opinion that the ambitious Walter was decadent and lazy. Walter in turn hated his father even to the point of being unmoved by his death. But the senior Lowenfels had gone ahead and made arrangements for Walter's own good. In particular, the father made certain that Walter received dividends but could not personally gain control of the stocks, ensuring that they would eventually go to his daughters. Otherwise, Walter would have most certainly tapped immediately into as much money as was available and turned over the rest upon his death to the Communist Party. To solve the problem of taking care of Walter's need for a typist after Lillian's stroke, Nan came back on the scene. She was divorced in 1954 from the inventor Lawrence Braymer and took up a number of Lillian's former duties. In the last decades, Nan Braymer was a part of the household and fully involved in many of Walter's projects.

The Lowenfels marriage remained stable but in an idiosyncratic way. Lillian had sexual relations with other men, and Walter was apparently incapable of jealousy. He remained personally devoted, although his own fidelity is uncertain. At one point, Lillian wrote some short stories suggesting emotional pain and a desire to leave the marriage, yet she continued to wait on him and almost single-handedly raised their children. However, after Lillian's disabling stroke, Walter repaid her sacrifices with absolute dedication. He took her along wherever he went, whatever the inconvenience. On one occasion, Walter was invited to the Lower East Side residence of poet Paul Blackburn (1926–71), which was on the fifth story of an apartment building. He easily collected from the street a group of young people who cradled Lillian in their arms and brought her up to the apartment.[57]

With irrepressible activism, Walter began writing for the Pennsylvania edition of the *Daily Worker* in 1938, later rising to the position of editor, which he held until 1953. As a Communist journalist, his work focused on the lives of working people, especially African Americans.[58] He was active in various causes, including the campaigns to free the Scottsboro Boys and Willie McGee, an African American veteran accused of rape in Laurel, Mississippi. (McGee was executed in 1951.) He supported striking coal miners and campaigned to draft Franklin Roosevelt for a fourth presidential term. During this time, he worked only half-time for the paper, supplementing his income by selling intercommunication devices door-to-door. The Lowenfels family's primary means of support, however, was Lillian's teaching salary. The situation in the household was further complicated by the presence of folksinger Lee Hays throughout much of the 1940s, when a short stay-over turned into a long visit that ended badly.[59]

Lowenfels was six feet one-and-one-half inches tall and handsome. He kept generally trim and had big hands that were all over the place. His hair was originally black, but he began balding early, ending up with lots in back and nothing up front. A mustache was there for most of his adult life. Suddenly he shaved it in the early 1970s to reveal a countenance that was very smooth and with no wrinkles. Lowenfels was also noteworthy for bizarre sleeping habits, never lying down for more than two or three hours and getting his rest by a sequence of naps. He could easily conk out on a sofa with noisy kids all around, then wake up after thirty minutes and be fully alert. Lowenfels's high energy level and robust sense of life were magnets; scores of people ended up gathering in his house. Never in a depression, Walter was barely fazed by a heart attack in his early fifties, giving up in an instant his addiction to cigarettes. He seemed to ignore the aging process.

Only a week after Lillian died in 1975, Walter learned that he had a fatal tumor. Faced with his own death, he responded in a remarkable way, never mourning his situation. He simply made his treatments into a big joke, taking a sign from the radioactive part of the hospital and putting it in his living room: "Caution: Do Not Enter." He also kidded about the tumor itself, as if it were a person. When he had a tracheotomy, his grandchildren came to visit him at the hospital and were terrified when they saw the tube coming out of his throat. Then Walter started making fun of the apparatus as "the latest style," and the kids burst into laughter. This was a natural response of Walter's, not a conscious strategy. There seemed to be no guile in political or personal identity. After 1954, Lowenfels formulated an idea about being an open and proud Communist, presenting himself as an example of a fulfilled Marxist literary life; the idea inspired him to the end.

When asked the $64,000 question, "Are you now or have you ever been?," Walter would quip: "What! Me, a Communist? Why, I've never done a decent thing in all my life."[60] Such a demeanor caused some, like the art critic Harold Rosenberg, to comment, "Oh, Walter—he belongs to a Party all his own!"[61] But Lowenfels, who felt that U.S. Communist writers should drop their inferiority complex as cultural pariahs and behave as if they belonged in the company of universally admired Communist artists such as Neruda, Picasso,

Brecht, Siqueros, and O'Casey, had the drive and vision to enter the mainstream. He was most successful for his anthology *Where Is Vietnam?* (1967, co-edited with Nan Braymer) and two books on Walt Whitman, *Walt Whitman's Civil War* (1961) and *The Tenderest Lover: The Erotic Poetry of Walt Whitman* (1970). Lowenfels's poetry lacks the power and profundity of McGrath's, offering instead an unreal reality in his late verse, a sensibility that gives way to perceptions that might be called a realistic surreality. At his worst, he seems a lamebrain socialist clone of Lawrence Ferlinghetti, with lines like the following ones from his twenty-page-long "The Poem That Can't Be Stopped":

> The last argument of nothingness conquered....
> And quick as a spark
> Liberty is conquered
> Liberty is a leaf growing on May Day
> The five-star extra
> The flame inside the cloud
> The fire in the bird's throat
> The light in the caves
> And everywhere men
> Taking over everything
> Including the walls[62]

Some of Lowenfels's best lines are found in the charming monologues of his prose poems in *To an Imaginary Daughter* (1964) and in the letters of *The Autobiography of My Poems* (1968). There are assuredly lyrical heights scattered throughout his verse of five decades, but what one specifically remembers is Lowenfels's relentless cheerfulness and his gift of a phrase that lingers in a reader's head. Some of these are in titles—"Shoes That Walked for Willie McGee," "Every Poem Is a Love Poem," "My Spectrum Analysis," and "Loving You in the Fallout." An outsized literary personality who could be enthralling and infuriating, he loved to tell anecdotes about his favorite literary character—Walter Lowenfels.

AUDEN IN BROOKLYN

Aaron Kramer, Thomas McGrath, and Walter Lowenfels provide the more conspicuous routes for tracing the postwar Communist presence in poetry. Their prominence in books published by the Communist Party is itself a tidy assist to establishing the homologous political origins. The larger picture of the postwar Left in poetry is thornier to grasp. The literary movement around the Party certainly bequeathed anthologies of verse on political themes by which one might take the pulse of left-wing poetry at different stages after the Great Depression, but few of them show the patient doing very well. Only rare book collectors or academic specialists on the literary Left might own copies of *War Poems of the United Nations* (1943), *Seven Poets in Search of an Answer*, *The Rosenbergs: Poems of the United States* (1957), *The Writing on the Wall* (1969), and *On Freedom's Side* (1972). They contain absorbing documents and poems that inspire respect but mainly point to an unfinished movement. Apart from such publications, there were several poets of real stature politically attracted to Communism but privately drawn to the otherness and occasionally the impenetrability of modernism. George Oppen, Carl Rakosi, and Muriel Rukeyser are the most obvious, although the first two were mute for much of the 1940s and 1950s.

Nevertheless, in the work of little-known Communist and former Communist poets during the postwar period, there is also writing that is far from the prisoner or creature of officialdom. One must turn to more politically neutral chapbooks and small press editions, a number of them privately published, to make out that there was power, brilliance, and sometimes a high order of imagination among a significant number of poets whose affiliations are less well-defined. This is verse that has attracted flickering rather than sustained attention. But any study of postwar U.S. verse that aspires to historical density is mistaken if it dismisses vast amounts of poetry simply because a poet's reputation is not "as great as" Robert Lowell's or that of similar postwar icons; this would produce an interpretive vacuum. Far better to err by generosity toward the many neglected than by circling wagons around the iconic few.

One group of minor figures, a number of whom also illustrate the homosexual presence discussed in chapter 4, emerged from the Communist movement at Brooklyn College in the Depression. W. H. Auden (1907–73), a writer who was openly pro-Communist for much of the 1930s, served as muse for several of them. Like Auden, several of the Brooklyn poets were gay, including Robert Friend (1913–98), Harold Norse (born Harold Rosen, 1916–2009), and, of course, Chester Kallman (1921–75), Auden's lover from 1939 to 1941. The students were also close to three gay Communist faculty members who taught English literature and served as their advisors: Murray Young (1907–69), David McKelvy White (1901–45), and Bernard Grebanier (1903–77).

There is a convoluted political, personal, and literary history entangled in this Brooklyn College milieu. All originated as Communists, but the fate of the faculty members is a reminder of how inhospitable academe was for the Left in those years. One of these professors, Bernard Grebanier, earlier named

David McElvey White with Kate Lenthrer. White was an inspiring teacher of English literature at Brooklyn College who joined the Communist Party and served in the George Washington Battalion of the Abraham Lincoln Brigade as a machine gunner in Spain. His 1945 suicide remains a mystery. (Courtesy of Abraham Lincoln Brigade Archives, New York University)

to an investigating committee Young and White as having been Communist Party members; this was during the 1941 Rapp-Court investigation of subversive activities in the New York public school system.[63] White had already resigned from the faculty to join the George Washington Battalion in Spain, and by the time of the hearings engaged in full-time Communist Party work. A second witness could not be induced to identify Young, so his (unconvincing) denial of Communist Party membership stood, and he was allowed to keep his job.

Four years later, White committed suicide, although there remains disagreement as to whether the reasons were personal or political, and some sources have inaccurately attributed his death to illness and accident.[64] In the fall of 1952, Young, who was handsome, Irish, and candid about his sexuality, was again called to testify, this time before the Senate Internal Security Committee. Once more he refused to answer questions about his Communist affiliations. But now a second person corroborated Bernard Grebanier's claim, so Young was dropped from the Brooklyn College faculty in March 1953 after twenty years of service. He then went to work as the managing editor and book review editor for the pro-Communist *New World Review*, which had changed its name from *Soviet Russia Today* in 1951, until he retired in the spring of 1969.[65] Nearly fifteen years after his death, Young's estate received $20,000 as restitution for his dismissal, a determination by Brooklyn College that was declared unconstitutional.[66]

The Communist faculty's protégés who worked on the *Observer* at Brooklyn College followed an intriguing array of life trajectories as well. The most curious is that of a minor poet, Sheldon Kranz (1919–80), who became a disciple of the former Communist Eli Siegel, the leader of the Young Labor Poets, which was an assignment given by the Communist Party to the somewhat older man.[67] In the early 1940s, Siegel moved from the social realism of people's poetry to his own philosophy, which he called "Aesthetic Realism," and in the process founded a cult promoting the bizarre cause of switching homosexuals to heterosexuals.[68] The conversions of the new group frequently came in the form of arranging marriages among Siegel's followers. In the late 1950s, Kranz himself became a poster boy for Siegel's purported success with such switches in sexual orientation, and remained his loyal follower through the 1960s and 1970s while Aesthetic Realism achieved some notoriety in the New York press. When Siegel committed suicide at the home of one of his disciples in 1978, the Aesthetic Realists disputed the fact, bizarrely insisting that Siegel "died of a broken heart" after fifty years of unjust neglect by the literary establishment.[69] Kranz passed away two years later; his widow, Anne Fielding, maintains a website devoted to his writing and Aesthetic Realism.[70]

The three more accomplished gay poets were to some extent in the Auden tradition. Friend, Norse, and Kallman exhibited moments of exhilarating versatility, although none possessed Auden's intellectual scope and ambition. Their reputations were appreciable, at least among other poets, and their writings represented literary gayness in a range of approaches that went from the openly sexual to delicately sensual to a disembodied ideal. In such verse, the lover or object of lust can be portrayed through nonspecific gender identification, or as a deep friendship without physical passion.[71] Obscurity of various sorts, including elaborate syntax and layers of meaning, an attribute of modernism, also served as a useful device for these postwar gay writers. Ambiguity allowed a writer to address a heterosexual public and a homosexual private audience simultaneously. The difference between public and private representations of eros is conspicuous when comparing the two love poems written by Auden to Kallman. The first, composed in May 1939 and eventually published as part of "The Prophets," situates a same-sex attraction in the conventions of romantic love without explicit reference to gender. The second, composed in January 1941 and unknown to the public until 1984 when it was published as "To Chester Kallman, b. Jan. 27, 1921," refers to the "amorous antics in the bed" of two "introverts."[72]

Robert Friend, who is today included in gay poetry anthologies albeit without his political biography, was a characteristic product of Depression-era Brownsville in Brooklyn—poor, Jewish, and radical. After his father abandoned the family, he threw himself into a search for culture and thrived on political debate. In high school, he organized a poetry group called the "Houynyms," after the enlightened horses created by Jonathan Swift; the group met in his mother's kitchen. As a student at Brooklyn College from 1930 to 1934, Friend took part in political protest rallies and immediately gravitated toward the Communists. He joined the Communist Party only after graduation, remaining a member for the next four or five years and then a sympathizer "for many years."[73]

This commitment was most ardent when Friend, a young man with dark curly hair and owlish glasses, was in Puerto Rico. In 1937–38, Friend taught English, returning again in 1938–40 to edit an English-language page of a pro-Communist Puerto Rican newspaper. Friend was investigated by the FBI on several occasions, especially in Panama, where he taught at the Inter-American University during World War II. In 1947, Friend left the United States to live in Europe and eventually Israel after 1950. He felt at home there, no longer in exile, and Zionism gradually replaced Communism as his ideological perspective.[74]

Friend's radical political convictions are most explicit in his first book, *Shadow of the Sun* (1941). A poem called "History" marks the moment when Mussolini's troops completed the conquest of Ethiopia, and a second verse with the same title tells how Friend's artistry emerged from conditions of poverty and abandonment.[75] Candidly gay writings for a public audience were a long time coming. A later poem, "Ars Poetica," recalls a transformative time when Friend, depicting himself as previously repressed, embraces his sexuality during his Puerto Rican sojourn. In the verse, he is self-created initially as a fervid sonneteer with a description borrowed from a remark of his Brooklyn College classmate Irwin Shaw (1913–84) that he was a young poet "thin enough for any wind to blow him back as far as Tennyson." In the lobby of a San Juan hotel, the narrator of "Ars Poetica" encounters a Dr. Williams, presumably the free verse poet William Carlos Williams, who was a pediatrician partly of Puerto Rican ancestry. In the poem, Dr. Williams proceeds to "diagnose... the case" by way of directing the young poet to the sight of bathers (unidentified by sex) playing on the beach and in the waves.[76] A careful reading of the following verses indicates that conventional literary forms, sexual repression, and Communist orthodoxy are interlinked as expressing a prior way of life that has been dispelled during Friend's first exile from his homeland.

Friend's work was the product of endless rewritings and frequently exhibits a sure sense of narrative pungency and immediacy. In "Ars Poetica," the shatterings of poetic, sexual, and even Leftist political conventions are conceived as being of one piece, which reinforces a comment that Friend made in a personal letter late in life. He stated that his work was "homosexual poetry, which may by its very nature be considered protest poetry."[77] Such an imbrication of protest against homophobia and class oppression is evident in some of the work of pro-Communist writers. Yet representations of gayness are not always affirmative; Friend elsewhere depicts sexuality as a form of predatory cruelty and his own sexuality as a function of his "lower self" or, as late as 1965, as marking the homosexual as a hunchback or cripple.[78] On the other hand, his indignation about heterosexual prejudice is obvious in his indictment of the "ignorant rage" of homophobes in his poem "At the Tomb of Oscar Wilde" (1975). More typical of Friend's embracing poetic eye is the suffusion of such views in his pithy and elegantly witty poems "The Irrational Source" and "The Teacher and the Indian."[79]

In "Ars Poetica," what is prominent in light of Friend's biographical and historical context is his description of the young poet having earlier taken on the sonnet form as a "cause." When Friend embraces Dr. Williams's apparition of the frolicking bathers as a surrogate vision of a workers' utopia, a triumvirate of literary, sexual, and political liberation is established. Knowledge of gender, politics, and poetic form as they relate to Friend's poetry additionally augments the meaning of his shift from Tennyson to William Carlos Williams. To be sure, Tennyson wrote in classical forms prized as accessible by proletarian and people's poets in the 1930s, but the Victorian iconic poet was no social rebel. However, his "In Memoriam" (1849) may fall into a convention of gay writing as it blurs the boundary of Tennyson's love for Arthur Henry Hallam as being both platonic and actively erotic. At the same time, the mood of this and other of Tennyson poems tends toward a moralizing and self-indulgent melancholy that fed Friend's propensity toward repression. In contrast, William Carlos Williams, though he was episodically attracted to the Communist literary movement in the Depression, was an independent radical who prized inventive literary forms that were centered on the everyday life of common people. Noted for his brief imagistic and sometimes sexist portraits of women, Williams wrote poems that were often erotically charged; unlike T. S. Eliot, Williams held that sexual relations could reorient people toward a natural healing process and away from the harmful aspects of twentieth-century culture.

These gay poets emerged from the Communist Left but lacked a manifesto of their own, rendering it difficult to grasp their relationship to the rhymed simplicity of workers' poetry and people's poetry embraced during late antifascism. Were they writing in conscious rebellion or simply going their own ways? Their relative anonymity in literary history poses a problem of evaluation for literary methodology, thereby vexing a book such as this one. Left poets from the Communist tradition produced an enormous body of writing even though they have fallen off the radar screen of what is considered a successful poetry career during the late twentieth century.[80] Yet writers are often remembered for a small body of excellent material, and it is rare for any poet to consistently write genuinely powerful poems. For Left poets in particular, one has even fewer guideposts for assessing the achievement of the postwar years.[81]

Most likely, the strategy of a proletarian avant-garde—my term for the social realist sensibility among 1930s poets who engaged modernist techniques—triumphed over people's poetry not in any formula but in its epistemological posture. The stance of such writers going back to the journal *Dynamo* in the early 1930s was against the imposition of meaning upon the reader; they held that meaning should be achieved through a collaboration necessary to further one's personal understanding. However, this attitude is far from operative to the same degree in all instances. A pronounced resistance to instantaneous understanding is obviously a feature of the poetry of one-time Communists George Oppen, Muriel Rukeyser, Louis Zukofsky (1904–78), and Carl Rakosi. If this defiance was intended as their objective, it was well achieved.

On the other hand, a Left poet would also be one who steered clear of any fallacy of aesthetic reduction to language. An active or even residual socialist commitment usually contradicted any rival temptation to allow references to history, ethics, and especially a yearning for utopia to disappear into an independent verbal structure. One doubts that even poets like Oppen, grounded in the school of objectivism, saw their poems merely as inert raw material to be given meaning solely by the one-sided proclivities of the reader. Instead, genuine achievement is found in many forms; colloquial directness and graceful elegance are among the more common strategies. Some who passed themselves off as people's poets in one context were in others more accurately part of a proletarian avant-garde. A figure such as Langston Hughes might be read either way. Others, such as David Ignatow (1914–97), had a onetime Communist association but kept the details so well hidden that he and his work are almost never discussed in the appropriate context.[82] A handful of brief examples must serve as a synecdoche for a cultural undercurrent so disrupted by Cold War memory loss that it cannot be convincingly named.

In a minor California poet such as Don Gordon, one finds the sweet surprises of his 1958 collection *Displaced Persons*. On "Sunday Afternoon," "Time floats in the living room / as innocent . . . as soft . . . as smoke."[83] Gordon was a gentle lyricist whose works were touched by a reticent melancholy. Such sentiments are displayed in his passing reference to the death of his comrade Edwin Rolfe: ". . . the poet, his sun blackened in Spain / Who lived among us by reflection for a time."[84] Gordon could write verse with personal emotions that are vigorous and polished, and he could address political issues in a style revealing tremendous self-assurance and a lack of histrionics, as in his own rendition of the mood of late antifascism:

> Barbed wire is the exposed nerve between the war and the peace;
> The mice hearing them tapping on the dry monotone of the cage.
> The brain in its double grave emits the obscene word: *tomorrow*.[85]

This is the political anger of a reserved and self-effacing man, whose courtly verse seems to have sprung miraculously from his very ordinary life.[86]

Olga Cabral (1909–97), of Portuguese ancestry, created poems that luminously portray the intricacies of the human mind in her memories of her departed husband, Yiddish Communist writer Aaron Kurtz (1891–1964). This capacity coexisted with political sentiments unchanged since the 1930s. Of the table where Kurtz worked on his poems:

> There are acres of dull desks
> that never were airborne:
> your table floats in time
> around the sun, in its own parabola
> set with moons for dishes.[87]

She begins a seven-part "Kaddish" for Kurtz:

> Nightly I write you letters
> but morning is always cancelled by a gray envelope
> stamped ADDRESS UNKNOWN.

A phantom Kurtz hugs her in a dream:

Don Gordon, a script reader for Hollywood studios who was blacklisted after 1951. Gordon was one of many accomplished modern poets associated with the Communist movement. (Courtesy of Eva Russo)

> your bones
> had the same span, your heart
> beat on its ribcage—
> only your face was turned away
> and that seemed strange.⁸⁸

Ben Maddow (1909–92), from New Jersey, was a poet from first to last but contributed prolifically in Hollywood film scripts (for big studios as well as for independent companies), studies of photography, short fiction, drama, and more. In the lyrically hard-boiled prose of his neglected noir novel, *44 Gravel Street* (1952), he exhibits a nervous melancholia. The narrator withdraws so deeply into his fictive environment in self-protection that he reveals nothing about his identity or beliefs, producing a strangely dreamlike reality recalling Dostoyevsky and Gorky. In contrast, Maddow's collected poems, *A False Autobiography, Poems: 1940–1990* (1991), are saturated with self-lacerating if imprecise revelations, sometimes about his sex life. Of his Communist years, he writes:

> I lunged at thirty to the rhetorical left,
> Marx was my failed father, Lenin my clever
> Cousin, leading the phalanx of the bereft
> Under blind flags toward a counterfeit star.
> And in those lurid decades, illusory or real
> And generally both, a sequence of women
> Loaned me, in the perfumed rains of April,
> The luxury of their infidel passion.⁸⁹

These are a small number of illustrations of the poets of the post–World War II Left who were fugitives from the prevailing mainstream as well as Communist literary culture. Gordon and others published in the 1940s and 1950s mostly on the margins of those publications and anthologies that carried Party endorsement. What they frequently put on display seems now like a remixing of radical politics in consonance with "The New American Poetry" (the term for what was thought to be a third generation of U.S. modernists), but the roots of Gordon and others are in social realist traditions that encountered new contingencies.

In contrast, to revisit, via old Communist newspapers and journals, the Left poetry associated directly with the workers' poetry or people's poetry tradition is mostly to drop in on a vanished moment that was decidedly off modernity's grid. Like Banquo's ghost, the memory of these earnest but stilted expressions of righteousness still hovers over the promise of a Communist literary modernity of McGrath and others who are simply not seen for what they were. The pressure of late antifascism aimed to instrumentalize verse, subsuming the intricate relations of politics and art to the limited language of indignation and vitriol. Genuine talent and priceless dreams were sometimes surrendered to unworthy rhetorical notions of politics, history, and cultural commitment. Some of this dull verse might have been enlivened by the promotion of poetic empathy beyond one's own ideological blinders, which is the natural tendency of forceful literature. But too many skillful poets based their art on political certitudes that missed the point that art must be risky and dangerously imaginative. What one should seek in radical poetry is not the moral certainty that consoles but discernment advancing toward difficult veracities.

Conclusion

The Sense of an Ending

THE AFTERLIFE OF LITERARY COMMUNISM

It would be simpler if the end of the Communist literary tradition happened quickly, if the demise of the authority of the Soviet Union and the Communist Party over culture suddenly gave rise to liberating impulses producing a massive prison break, a cultural Prague Spring. Yet the afterlife of Literary Communism began much earlier than 1956 and goes on and on; one still does not have the sense of an ending. The 1930s set the stage for intersections of social realism and the avant-garde, while the postwar years produced the new contingency and then Communist literary modernism. The calamity of 1956 was as much a corroboration as an eye-opener, and its cultural ramifications were repeated in miniature in 1960–61 for the small circle of cultural workers still close to the Party. For any remaining political adherents among writers, the last straws were in 1968 and 1989. But the political fortunes of the Soviet Union and similar systems had a lessening significance for writers in the United States long before then; the cultural workers were moved by something that went deeper than Stalinism.

Most attempts to revisit Left literature in the years after the high Cold War have tended to wax nostalgic chiefly about the 1930s achievement; there was a comparatively superficial treatment of the evolution of the Communist cultural presence in the 1940s, and even scholars sympathetic to Marxism saw the 1950s as mainly "The Time of the Toad," focusing on aspects of blacklisting and persecution.[1] The rise of the 1960s New Left escalated historical and biographical interest in radical intellectuals, but these, once again, were associated mainly with the Great Depression. The method of recoupment was to view cultural workers through presentist glasses: Tillie Olsen and Meridel Le Sueur as feminist icons, Richard Wright and Langston Hughes as precursors of the Black Arts movement, and the Popular Front as the champion of multiculturalism and the political resistance found in popular and even mass culture. The decline of the New Left social movements in the 1970s spawned a spectacular increase in Marxist cultural theory, but the outstanding new scholars (none more brilliant than Fredric Jameson) had only a minor interest in the U.S. Communist legacy, and almost none addressed the literary criticism produced by the immediate postwar Left.

This treatment of the 1940s–1950s Communist presence was poor preparation for what occurred next. In literary history, as in personal life, the repressed tends to return. Even as the Communist movement died, an outpouring of novels, poems, plays, films, and autobiographies emerged in the second half of the twentieth century with reference to the postwar Communist past; they have provided a continual flow within the larger culture to this day that is likely to persist. This body of writing began as the slender but powerful and expanding trend that expressed many of the virtues pioneered in the 1930s and revitalized through the new contingency and Communist literary modernism.

At first there was a sequence of unusual works of literature starting in the late 1950s by onetime members of the Communist Party: Warren Miller's *The Cool World* (1959), Lorraine Hansberry's *A Raisin in the Sun* (1959), Clancy Sigal's *Going Away* (1961), Tillie Olsen's *Tell Me a Riddle* (1961), John Oliver Killens's *And Then We Heard the Thunder* (1962), Jose Yglesias's *A Wake in Ybor City* (1963), Margaret Walker's *Jubilee* (1966), Lillian Hellman's *An Unfinished Woman* (1969), and Helen Yglesias's *How She Died* (1973), along with the works of Bert and Katya Gilden and John Sanford. A somewhat younger generation, personally familiar with Communists, would diversely carry on this tradition through novels such as Leo Litwack's *Waiting for the News* (1969), Lawrence Bush's *Bessie* (1983), Meredith Tax's *Union Square* (1988), Brian Morton's *The Dylanist* (1991), and Paul Levitt's *Dark Matters* (2004).

Then the quality of the tradition escalated with the publication of several books coming from other nations but widely discussed in the United States, such as the very early novels of the still-Leninist Aleksandr Solzhenitsyn and *The Joke* (1964) by Milan Kundera, followed by other Kundera books. Doris Lessing's *The Golden Notebook* drew upon the 1956 political crisis over "de-Stalinization" of the British Communist Party as the setting for the emotional finale of the female protagonist's love affair with an expatriate U.S. radical, modeled on former Communist Clarence ("Clancy") Sigal (b. 1926). Nadine Gordimer's *Burger's Daughter* (1979) investigated the generational conflict between a recently deceased South African Communist and his New Left daughter, who was concurrently negotiating a love affair. Mario Vargas Llossa's *The Real Life of Alejandro Mayta* (1985) portrayed the search for the ultimately indeterminate truth about the life of a legendary (and possibly gay)

Trotskyist revolutionary who led an insurrection in the Peruvian Andes in the late 1950s. Margaret Atwood's *The Blind Assassin* (2000) revealed the extramarital affair of the narrator with a Canadian Communist science-fiction-writer-turned-strike-leader and then volunteer in the Spanish Civil War.

African American writers broke new ground in Communist literary modernism in the United States in the 1940s and 1950s and were followed by others such as John A. Williams, especially in *The Man Who Cried I Am* (1967). But many of the most complex and sophisticated narratives of the afterlife of Literary Communism were by and about Jewish Americans: E. L. Doctorow's *The Book of Daniel* (1971), Chaim Potok's *Davita's Harp* (1985), and Philip Roth's *I Married a Communist* (1988) top the list. What invigorates the quality of these three novels is the perspective of belatedness (seeing how it all came out) combined with a healthy emotional distance. Each provides a captivating excursion into the inner living of their subjects and the social worlds they transited; the writers depict with care and sympathy how the vision of the 1930s, even after World War II, gave meaning to lives as various religions had once done. By tracing the particular interests of each individual character with such freedom and subtlety, the nature of the pulsing, multifarious, collective Communist presence becomes more accurately studied. Insisting on complexity is the best challenge to deceitful simplifications, Left and Right.

American Night, however, is grounded in a collective biography of a cross-section of pro-Communist writers of an earlier time; its focus is closer to the moment when lives and writings were vexed by the crossroads where the idealism of the radical movement in the United States entered into lethal encounters with world events. Imaginative writings rooted in the pre-1960s (even if published a bit later), although certainly varying in quality and effectiveness, are artistically crafted narratives and explorations of social and emotional history. The most compelling bring into interaction the clashing perspectives of individuals who are viewed as flawed, admirable, talented, or merely human in recognizable ways.

Responsive readers of novels such as *The Narrows* and the long poem *Letter to an Imaginary Friend* discover on each successive reading that one's understanding of the world has been heightened and general knowledge of life and grasp of the overdetermination of historical moments have been enhanced. Even when presented in social realist style, as in *The Great Midland*, the writings of the Left are not simply reprisals of documented facts, nor are they vessels of "political theory." The most forceful works cast emotions and experience with precision and economy and sketch mental images permitting readers to imagine themselves at events and to undergo the passions of the protagonists. If one wishes to go beyond the blinders of official political line and to pay more attention to recovering intention and significance, imaginative literature and biography are above all critical in regard to the Communist cultural movement.

American Night began in a moment of peripeteia, the postwar reversal of fortune, but the afterlife of Literary Communism defies any notion of a predestined end, even a final unexpected turnaround. Frank Kermode claimed that peripeteia is present in all fiction but by the mid-twentieth century it became elevated to an ending in which one's expectations are falsified; this is due to a failure to reach discovery or recognition even by an unexpected route.[2] In the new contingency and Communist literary modernism, the reader is not actually denied an ending per se, but what we get is one that defies the very Communist cultural tradition from which the literature emerged, a trajectory that had been animated by positivist rationalism. The particular texts emphasized in *American Night*, as well as the literary history that they generate, are not congruent with the Communists' proclivity toward the Cult of Reason in which this cultural movement was nurtured.

Readers familiar with Frankfurt School writings will already guess, as the preface to *American Night* advised, that the phenomenon in fiction and poetry that I have described might be regarded as a correlative in imaginative literature to Theodor Adorno's searching critique of modernity by way of "negative dialectics."[3] This term, although used later, was formulated for analyzing the cultural and political terrain after World War II, when Adorno become increasingly uncertain of the possibility of the socialist transformation that he regarded as the synthesis or third stage in Hegelian dialectics. The writers featured in *American Night* are, from an Adornoesque angle, aspiring to introduce, through fiction and poetry, an element of critical rationality into the postwar literary imagination. The hope is that a transformation in consciousness might be effectuated.

This trend toward expanding perception parallels Adorno's judgment that capitalism had become more entrenched through its attack on critical consciousness in mass society, an analytical awareness required for any revolutionary transformation to emerge from conditions of oppression. Despite the aura of darkness and gloom, neither the writers featured in this book nor Adorno are engaged in offering metanarratives of universal decline. The work of these texts is to expose the ideological and destructive tendencies within positivist rationality and instrumentalized reason, no matter what the source. That's why it is a mistake to attribute even to a cynical Kenneth Fearing an entirely pessimistic view in which all intellectual reflections are rendered hopeless. *The Big Clock* and its successors have the goal of illuminating human experience in capitalist society as a process that contrasts with reified forms of consciousness; in particular, ones associated with the positivist rationality of conventional philosophy and social theory, and Marxism dogmatically ensnared in moral certainty and a cult of reason.

Following Adorno, most of the writers began to register after World War II the significant changes occurring in the structure of capitalism, ones that required a rethinking of predictions made in the name of Marxist reason. The socialist struggles of the past had not gone away; they were the matrix of the Cold War cultural present. Even those writers profoundly alienated by the Stalin regime were, like the Frankfurt Marxists, unwilling to forgive the West its legacy of empire, racism, and class brutality. They remained Marxist materialists in their view of art as embedded in society; novels and poems expressed the unavoidable conflicts and tensions of the larger historical process from which such writings arose and to which they belong. But affected as they were by the phenomenological turn and new contingency, Fearing, Ann Petry, Thomas McGrath, and the others do not lecture the reader on permutations of Hegelianism; they demonstrate through the experiences that they depict in imaginative literature that thinking in contradictions is forced on those living in a society driven by the fundamental antagonism of commodity production.

The "political" aim of their art is to induce the reader to move beyond mere contradictory judgments, revealing that the criteria and categories of inherited truth by which one operates are clearly inadequate. Like Adorno, these writers recognize that postwar capitalism is something different from the military vision of class war; it is not just one class working against others. There has developed an intensified commodification of desire brought on by a Consumers' Republic. Individuals have become increasingly transformed into "things" obeying the inexorable laws of the marketplace. The answer to the Leninist "What is to be done?" does not translate into the old parties and programs. There is little to suggest in these writings—even the intransigent McGrath's—that a revolutionary working class is simply destined to overcome such reification, or that transitory praxis can make a palpable difference now that postwar socialism has missed its moment of realization. History is a long debate; sometimes it is better to be defiant than programmatically "correct."

THE INDETERMINACY OF ART

My search in *American Night* for a Communist presence in literature, semi-modernist or not, has proved to be particularly demanding during the postwar era when writers thwarted certain generic expectations handed down by the 1930s to sometimes use literary strategies that hamper an invasive gaze. Inasmuch as my predilection is to prize texts of imaginative literature for their artistic capacity as truth-tellers affected by, yet transcending, any formal partisan affiliation of their authors, I began as dubious that postwar works by writers profoundly shaped by the Communist movement might achieve this standard. Could a moral complexity worthy of the name exist in literature produced by those variously associated with Communism in the more constricted era of late antifascism? The discernment of a considerable presence of Communist literary modernism came when I began to set apart several imaginative texts as paradoxical memory screens. Due to the anti-Communist culture war of the 1940s and 1950s, significant political energies and identifications were displaced by Left writers onto closely associated but ostensibly less significant details, with mnemic symbols reenacting social trauma. To express what cannot candidly be made public, imaginative literature, even and perhaps especially when reverting to the most popular forms, makes use of camouflaged and inventive artistic formulations of political circumstances and emotions.

Those postwar writers who were unrepentant about a past or still lingering Communist allegiance nevertheless were obligated to retreat into aliases of nomenclature about ideology (calling themselves Progressives, liberals, antifascists, New Dealers) and fudged personal histories in autobiographical statements. This evasiveness allowed too many scholars, especially authors of overviews of literary history, to fluctuate between near-silence about writers' political biographies and oversimplifications regarding the Communist tradition.[4] The result has been the consolidation in traditional scholarship over the past five decades of a retrospective Cold War collective literary identity that is fundamentally disfigured by the absent presence of a tradition that dared not speak its name.

Among the missing elemental points in most constructions of this era is an awareness that U.S. Communism, relegated to "outside" status by the state, business, and the Right, naturally attracted other "outsiders" — especially Jews and African Americans but also homosexuals, "race traitors," bohemian artists, and various other diverse minorities and idealists.[5] The presence of Jews and other outsiders in the Communist Party was an effect, not a cause; the Party offered outsiders a vision and an opportunity. This multilayered "outsideredness" of the Communist movement further complicates the elusiveness of Communist identity, a fostered secretiveness by instinct and design that facilitated a writer's self-preservation in the face of political hounding. This blurriness about the Communist presence in existing literary history of the postwar years is why I have tried to craft a book that, among other priorities, expands an appreciation of these many outsider constituents within the Left.

Communist literary modernism often showcases its critique of positivist rationality through multiple perspectives. The target is not just a Consumers' Republic but also the very Communist social movement to which the writers' emotions were still loyal. Ann Petry, of course, proposes an "enlightenment of the Enlightenment" in regard to the all-consuming industrial engines of the Treadway munitions company that invisibly shaped the lives of the people of Monmouth.[6] Moreover, Petry recalls no one more pointedly than Adorno in her use of Cesar the Writing Man's biblical quotations throughout *The Narrows*. Their strategic insertions suggest that the myths of older religious philosophies may actually provide a superior enlightenment; the official mode of rationality of postwar industrial society is at odds with the critical rationality that can motivate new judgments, potentially leading to a revision of society.

The focus of Richard Wright, in contrast, is almost exclusively on the Communist movement, which presents its own version of the Enlightenment that encourages the growth of an egotism among an elite of "superior" individuals to whom the hopes of the future are to be entrusted. The sequence of events in *The Outsider* takes shape in the dynamic flux of characters who are locked in this same story but have radically different positions within the narrative. Works of fiction by the Gildens, Abraham Polonsky, Jo Sinclair, and John Sanford burrow deeply into related territory, but only the last exhibits comparable rage. The others construct variously muted simulacrums of anger at Communist deceptions and rigidity and are more persuasive on that particular matter for their restraint.

The afterlife of Literary Communism continues to be bolstered by the fresh unearthing of previously unknown writings—outsider texts in more ways than the ones already considered. One major unfinished novel of Communist literary modernism, unheard of until decades after the death of its author, travels to the heart of the selfhood of the revolutionary artist himself. Carlos Bulosan (1911?–56), born in the rural Philippines and coming to the West Coast of the United States as a migrant laborer in 1930, never ceased reinventing himself as an activist, poet, short story writer, journalist, and autobiographer. In *The Cry and the Dedication*, drafted between 1949 and 1955, Bulosan delivers a surprising and unorthodox work of artistic truth and grueling intensity.[7]

It is a work close to poetry of the unconscious, significantly a novel of psychosexual revelation, and even raises contemporary questions about the place of narrative in the architecture of historical knowledge. Above all, *The Cry and the Dedication* addresses the "moral certainty" of the Communist

Carlos Bulosan was born in the Philippines and became active in literary and labor circles around the Communist movement on the West Coast in the 1930s. During the early Cold War, he worked on a book about the emotional and moral life of revolutionaries that was published posthumously as *The Cry and the Dedication* (1995). (Courtesy of Special Collections, University of Washington Libraries, neg. no. UW 513)

Left. Bulosan depicts the revolutionary Huk fighters in the postwar Philippines as pieces in a political puzzle. They are men and women motivated by political aims that are altruistic and humanitarian, inspired by pity and compassion for human suffering. But under the conditions of guerrilla war, such ends can be achieved only by suppressing the spontaneous outflow of the very same feelings. Bulosan's Huks thus rely on "reason" as a version of utilitarian calculation poised to master all the contradictions. This depiction, revealing and groundbreaking, was not a refusal to take sides but the mark of indeterminacy in an art that had become, postwar, more emotional than cerebral in force.

A painful personal reassessment on the author's part during the 1950s may to some extent explain why *The Cry and the Dedication* is written less in the mode of social realism Bulosan used in the 1940s. Although some of his letters of the 1950s express a mechanical "cult of reason" view of world politics and even illusions about the Soviet Union, in a 1955 letter to a friend identified only as "Ray," Bulosan confesses that the last ten years (1945–55) had been "a decade of silence and heartbreak and re-evaluation of my life and career."[8] Others among Bulosan's letters suggest that he underwent some type of reexamination of his sexuality. Living in Seattle in the 1950s, Bulosan greatly admired the early homoerotic stories of Truman Capote and transformed passages from Capote's work into his poetry, insisting that they had private meaning.[9] What exactly was the affliction that plagued Bulosan? The fine points of his personal and political thinking may never be known. Concealment had been a feature of his literary life since the early 1930s, a strategy of erasing traces. There are documented episodes of alcoholism and plagiarism and plenty of sexual inscrutability, but perhaps there is no simple secret. The dates, however, of his postwar crisis coincide with the writing of *The Cry and the Dedication*.

Bulosan's new thoughts occurred against the background of his sometime stormy relation to the Communist movement. In its outward form, Bulosan's political career during the 1950s remained mostly consistent with his 1930s commitments, albeit his radical friends acknowledged that he was no longer active. Bulosan, possibly a member of the Communist Party briefly in the 1930s or at the start of World War II, had severely criticized the pre-1935 sectarianism of Communist practice in his fictionalized autobiography, *America Is in the Heart* (1946); at the same time he declared that his genuine sympathy to Communism came with the Popular Front. Toward the end of the war, he expressed a controversial attraction to the puppet government associated with Manuel Roxas; this brought bitter denunciations in West Coast Communist circles and the claim that he had underworld ties.[10] Bulosan reversed course, but he appeared in Communist publications very rarely after 1946, retaining close relations mainly on a personal basis with pro-Communists in the Cannery Workers Union and the Committee for the Protection of the Foreign Born in Seattle during the last few years of his life.[11] But his companion of that time, a well-known Party activist named Josephine Patrick, reported to him that the organization was putting pressure on her to end the affair. Less than two years after Bulosan wrote the letter to Ray, Patrick broke with the Communist Party to become a Trotskyist, a leading figure in the Seattle branch of the Socialist Workers Party.[12] This adds even more mystery to Bulosan's final political thinking.

The Cry and the Dedication is not a literal representation of personal, family, or community experience and could not be based on any physical participation of Bulosan's in the guerrilla war in the Philippines. The novel's texture is akin to Bulosan's most striking poem of the early 1950s, "Theseus." What emerges from these two weird and wonderful texts suggests the articulation of a sexual and political impasse that Bulosan, perhaps to his own surprise and artistic frustration, was driven to put on paper but never published. Underlying these parallel writings is the disguised demand of the narrative to challenge moral certainty; Bulosan even seems to be toying with the idea that reason has proved so treacherous that faith may be required.

The poem "Theseus" conforms to an established tradition; the Minotaur is unreason and Theseus reason, with Ariadne's thread serving as reason's instrument. Yet in Bulosan's version, reason kills unreason only to find that the two are brothers and Theseus's heroism a sham. This revision implies an uncertainty on Bulosan's part about the Enlightenment heritage of Marxism as the tool of liberation. The heroic warrior Theseus, playing to the crowd and worshiped by "a boatload of virgins" for his decapitating of the Minotaur, had not actually killed a "many-headed monster," but only a simulacrum of his own brother.[13] Theseus is thus transformed from the prototype of the artist or revolutionary of the Enlightenment, one who chooses to live a symbolic, inspiring life, into a self-deceiving and tormented murderer. Bulosan's *The Cry and the Dedication* has a near-identical climax when the leading revolutionary protagonist and Bulosan persona, Dante, is murdered by his brother.

The novel is further haunted by a sexual strangeness suggesting a defiance of conventional notions of revolutionary manhood prevalent on the Left. Both of the central male figures, Dante and Felix, have their genitals mysteriously damaged. One central thread of the plot involves Mameng, a facially disfigured female guerrilla in men's clothes, whose sexual services are offered to achieve political objectives. As the Huks trek through the forest, the novel's narrative voice refers to "the well of loneliness" and "the phallic truth."[14] When two of the guerrillas, Hassim and Dabu, have a private moment, Bulosan says that "their silence spoke louder than words, meant more than words, for it was the tranquil silence of conspirators against a world they did not make."[15] This is a paraphrase of the gay Victorian poet A. E. Housman's words "I, a stranger and afraid, / In a world I never made."[16] It is unlikely that a book full of this mystical, heterogeneous blend of sexual and political material could have been published in the 1950s by a writer now so isolated from the publishing world. If so, it would have been greeted with hostility by his Filipino and Communist comrades still limited by puritanical and political orthodoxies.

Bulosan does not provide an ending to *The Cry and the Dedication*, only shapes fleeing in different directions. Whether something more was intended is unclear; the reader is left in a darkness of exploding contradictions. But it seems fitting that brothers end up murdering brothers, and allies arrive who have no political identity or history. Bulosan's core group of Huk guerrillas are technically victorious in their immediate killing but end up lost in the night, trapped in their own thread of rationalistic reasoning that amounts to an "end justifies the means" form of brutality. The sexual rethinking is also present in a manner that recalls the variety of bisexual writing where loneliness takes on an allegorical intensity marked by sexual confusion and alienation. *The Cry and the Dedication* is filled with destructive triangles, three-way relationships, sexual ambivalence, and the inability to fit into prescribed social structures.

In the end, *The Cry and the Dedication* goes nowhere marvelously. Although it is not exactly a work of self-psychoanalysis, on some level Bulosan's method operates through a free association guided by what his instincts are telling him. Bulosan was an author who saw art in transcendent forms. His novel is yet another example of postwar Left fiction offering a vehicle for expressing what cannot be made public, the artistic formulation of circumstances and emotions its author may not wish to directly disclose. In Bulosan's case, the result is a weirdly breathtaking Communist literary modernism, perhaps more in the conception than in the uneven writing. Bulosan could be a master of literary tropes as he very consciously sought out images that deepened his themes and offered analogues of the way his mind operates, the workings of a consciousness. Irrationalism in the novel is killed along with rationalism, suggesting that the reductive nineteenth-century naturalism evident in his earlier *America Is in the Heart* may be under assault. The abstract logic by which the Popular Front against fascism would produce concrete democracy for the exploited and oppressed, bound up in the mystique of the Soviet Union, is unmentioned and conceivably no longer compelling. In his narrative refusal of a simple vanguard literary style, Bulosan aspires to make a radically new kind of art and tentatively moves toward an early version of magical realism or at least irrealism.[17]

To explore the labyrinth of postwar Communism, negative dialectics is the most promising guide. Communist literary modernism is not a development within modernism, a "late modernism," but an evolution of the social realism already in commerce with a modernism that emerges into a third tradition through a strategy of psychological intensities.[18] One observes this explicitly in the step-by-step movement of writers such as Paul Bowles, Kenneth Fearing, and Richard Wright, from a 1930s self-identification with Communism to a late-1940s affinity with the angst of the Parisian Sisypheans. For the Communist literary modernists of the 1950s, historical explanation and narrative understanding are given each in the other. Petry, Sinclair, the Gildens, and Sanford "feel" history as the human experience of time is rescued from linear chronology.

Yet this is distinct from the modernism of formalism; the originality of forms in the fiction and poetry of Communist literary modernism is owing to its "contentism," its emphasis on experience and perception. In the novels of Polonsky, the Gildens, Sinclair, Sanford, and Bulosan, narratives develop in the liminal space between devotion and disillusion to arrive at a point of delicate equilibrium. Much is happening in the felt texture; the unquiet dead stir about in the unstable substrata of memory, and the political landmarks of the Communist past are animated by maintaining an uncanny elusiveness. What we repeatedly learn from Communist literary modernism is that the psychic mechanisms that function for us in political crises are hardly disconnected from those that regulate our behavior in private situations. McGrath's *Letter to an Imaginary Friend* provides an alternative to that prevailing trend within modernism where the poet's interior is placed in opposition to the world. McGrath encompasses the world alternatively in the disjointed flow of consciousness; his poetry produces a pattern of unobtrusive echoes that is largely responsible for its lyrical and emotional force.

Modernism as a cultural movement comes within the Western industrial period of the modern and modernity, which contains the development of Marxism, psychoanalysis, and existentialism. Writers drawn to its mood often reject traditional forms, topics, and narratives in favor of individualized experimentations. But the individuality of Communist literary modernism is not cut from the same cloth as the 1950s celebrations of nonconformity that claim to go beyond ideology. Petry, Wright, McGrath, Bulosan, and the others have a mutual investment in history—especially in the Marxist understanding of racism and colonialism—that justifies an off-the-record link between texts. Their writings realize historical moments in a culturally specific way while reaching toward a perspective that transcends short-term considerations. Similar to Ralph Ellison's *Invisible Man*, these texts are out of the reach of either straightforward referentialism or abstract universalism. Yet, in contrast to Ellison, their artistic equal at the very least, they refuse to join the postwar American celebration, seen as a mask for the reification of commodity culture and world economic expansionism.[19]

THE PRESENCE OF AN ABSENCE

The original master plot of the imagined literary lives of former Communists such as Bulosan was inspired by a commitment that involved a growing sacrifice and self-discipline on behalf of a bright and shining cause. The pattern of their literary second acts, emerging from late antifascism, was often a healthy conduit toward diverse renovations and renewals, few more extraordinary than *The Cry and the Dedication*. In several respects, the evidence of this literary record grew more robust as the political climate relaxed; an increasing number of volumes of fiction and poetry would be reprinted and the canon revised. But memory loss and enforced forgetting of the personal truth of what happened to many of the writers in the postwar years obscured a discernment of the new contingency and Communist literary modernism. The effect was frequently research conducted backward through contemporary definitions, an attempt to create a heroic past of resistance to victimization. Too often omitted was a perception of the kind of pain indicated in Bulosan's 1955 letter to Ray and in the subtext of *The Cry and the Dedication* and "Theseus."

Such pain, combined with self-hate and self-disgust, can be found in anguished letters sent out by one-time Party intellectual Richard Bransten during the early 1950s. Bransten, from a wealthy California family, was originally an aspiring novelist radicalized by the 1934 West Coast Longshoremen's Strike. After publishing a few short stories, he started writing on labor and economics for the *New Masses* in the mid-1930s as Bruce Minton. Several books appeared in collaboration with John Stuart (a pseudonym for Jacob Winogur, dates unknown). In 1946, he and his second wife, novelist Ruth McKenney (1911–72), were expelled from the Communist Party after expressing a fit of hyper-orthodoxy. As reported in his letters, Bransten was immediately denounced by his friends and collaborators as a liar, thief, betrayer, and FBI agent.[20]

Working in the publishing industry at the start of the Cold War, Bransten moved to Western Europe for some jobs, then went back to the United States for a spell with the publishing house Rinehart and Company, and then returned to London to try writing again. In his isolation and misery, Bransten came to realize that he had done very much the same thing to others over the years as had been done to him. He rebuked himself endlessly over the way in which he had blindly and foolishly abandoned his conscience and humanity in a worship of Stalin, Browder, and the Communist Party hierarchy. For personal reasons, he was estranged from the son of his first marriage, to Louise Rosenberg Bransten. Louise herself, remarried to the brilliantly eccentric Communist functionary Lionel Berman (1906–68), was still a Party loyalist and under suspicion by the federal government for espionage. There were rumors that Richard Bransten had retaliated against his comrades by informing, which was hard to prove or disprove. He had now painted himself into a corner, financially, intellectually, and emotionally. After such knowledge, what forgiveness? In 1955, Bransten committed suicide.[21]

There was also the pain of paralyzing and indescribable disillusionment that haunted the once-flourishing Communist literary agent Maxim Lieber (1887–1993), a close collaborator of Whittaker Chambers's, who fled to Mexico in 1951. Lieber had launched a sensational career as a publisher in the 1920s, then started his own "Maxim Lieber Literary Agency" in 1930, attracting scores of clients who became major writers. All but a few of these were close to the Communist movement, which allowed for a unique intimacy as Lieber was able to promote his own Communist convictions along with their careers. Named by Chambers as a coworker who could confirm charges against Alger Hiss, Lieber was called to testify before a grand jury in New York in 1948 and then before an executive session of HUAC in 1950. He pleaded the Fifth Amendment on all occasions, spiriting his wife and two children out of the country at the first opportunity, an event recounted in Anthony J. Sacco's novel *Little Sister Lost* (2004). Following several years in Cuernavaca and Mexico City as a stateless person, Lieber moved to Warsaw, where he worked in publishing, and then was joined by his family. But disenchantment, especially with Poland's anti-Semitism, quickly set in. Lieber was a single-minded man; without conviction, he was politically useless and quickly devolved to a minor proofreader.

In the mid-1960s, Lieber attempted to relocate to the United Kingdom but was expelled by the British Home Office. Fortunately, his U.S. citizenship was restored in 1964, as his Communist associations were over, and in 1968 he found an obscure job as a proofreader for a printing company in Hartford, Connecticut. He never raised the issue of Chambers and Hiss on his own; when others brought it up, he instantly expressed hatred for Chambers but did not forthrightly defend Hiss or deny his own involvements.[22] For the next twenty-five years, he nursed his wounds in near-silence, occasionally trying to reestablish relations with old friends and clients such as novelists Erskine Caldwell and Albert Halper, only to be rebuffed.[23]

Sometimes the pain was communicated by indirection, as in Ben Maddow's moving depiction of photojournalist W. Eugene Smith (1918–78) as "The Wounded Angel" in his study of Smith's photographs.[24] Smith had assumed presidency of the Film and Photo League at the time it was accused of being a subversive organization. Maddow circumvents such political history but provides a beautifully crafted sentence-after-sentence etching of the agonized emotional life of this fellow artist throughout the postwar years. Behind his words is in all probability the untold tale of Maddow's own decades of moral certainty as a Communist, followed by a dispiriting period of resistance to HUAC. In the late 1950s, Maddow reached a compromise with the Hollywood studio blacklisters that he struggled to keep in the veiled background of consciousness.[25] His heartbreaking tribute to the founder of the photo-essay bears out the insight that the eulogy is the most revealing form of autobiography.

The pain was on occasion unspoken but reported by others. Samuel Ornitz was a screenwriter and novelist who was convicted as one of the Hollywood Ten and served a year in prison, ending his career. Once a humorless Party pontificator who spoke in beautifully composed and well-rounded sentences that tended to go on and on, Ornitz was one of those who acted as if he had received the Communist "word." He had been a good-looking ladies' man but in the postwar years become jowly with a disfiguring benign tumor on his neck. In prison, Ornitz had passed the time listening to stories of murderers, which did not help his disposition when he began to learn the truth about Soviet despotism in the early 1950s. He claimed to be writing a sequel to *Bride of the Sabbath*, but this was just an excuse to hide himself away as he mulled over the news about the Katyn Massacre and the Soviet suppression of the Hungarian revolt. He never could write a word on politics after the early 1950s, but agonized to a few friends over his personal responsibility for the "Great Crimes" of Stalinism. In 1957, still widowed to the shame of his corrupted fantasy, his life was taken by cancer at the Hollywood Motion Picture Home.[26]

Not everyone was so grim about the situation regarding the postwar Soviet Union. Medieval scholar Margaret Schlauch, a political refugee from New York University after 1951, lived in Warsaw and seemed happy with her new life. Although she never really learned Polish, she became head of the English department at the University of Warsaw, socializing regularly with her sister and brother-in-law, also in exile. It is possible that Schlauch muted criticisms out of fear, but she gave friends in the United States the impression that she had everything she needed and was quite content. She was also unabated in the production of rigorous scholarship in medieval studies, comparative literature, and linguistics; students and international colleagues produced an admiring festschrift in 1966.[27] Twice in the 1960s she visited the United States to teach temporarily at the University of Connecticut in Storrs. She remained close to Lieber, whom she had known in Warsaw and saw again in Connecticut, by all accounts able to separate the personal from the political. Even when martial law was declared in Poland, she talked favorably about developments in the Soviet Union and Eastern Europe, never considering a permanent return.[28]

One psychological defense against the pain of the past was to turn the bad experiences into a rueful joke. Earl Conrad (born Earl Cohen, 1912–66) was an activist in the John Reed Club and a member of the Communist Party in the 1930s. In the 1940s he worked out of the New York office of the Black newspaper the *Chicago Defender*, shifting his status to that of a fellow traveler. Conrad came to national attention as an antiracist with his 1943 book on *Harriet Tubman*, and continued his success with *Jim Crow America* (1947) and *Scottsboro Boy* (1950). When his popular novel called *Rock Bottom* appeared in 1952, Conrad found himself caught up in the Party's internal campaign against "white chauvinism." He had imagined that his brutal depiction of the life of an African American woman in Mississippi and Harlem was consistent with the Party view that Black Americans had been subject to a genocidal assault. Suddenly he was the target of his own comrades who denounced him as a racist for treating Black characters with insufficient humanity. When later asked about his Communist years, Conrad simply reformulated the famous lines of Lincoln Steffens: "I have seen the future and it worked me over."[29]

Generally, there was public silence on the matter of the Soviet Union in this milieu. Several prominent Communist Party writers either denied outright their former membership or wrote letters and memoirs that were misleading: Milton Howard (born Milton Halpern, 1909–2000), Ben Field (born Moe Bragin, 1901–86), Edwin Seaver, and Eve Merriam (born Eva Moscowitz, 1916–92).[30] Several of the writers for the *Daily Worker* and *New Masses* worked in fields unconnected with politics and did well. A. B. Magil was one of a dozen former Communists who found jobs in medical journalism, especially *Medical Tribune* and *MD* magazine. The first openings came in the 1950s through the William Douglas McAdams agency, specialists in medical advertising. The agency was bought up by the Sackler Brothers, all three of whom had briefly passed through the Communist Party. Arthur Sackler (1913–87), a prominent medical researcher and later a major philanthropist, became chairman of the board. Sackler had got his start in publishing as a

Earl Conrad was the author of popular books about racism such as *Scottsboro Boy* (1950). He was first a member and then a supporter of the Communist Party until he was denounced by his own comrades for his novel *Rock Bottom* (1952). (Courtesy of Alysse Conrad)

Conclusion   309

Milton Meltzer was a Communist contributor to the *New Masses* and *Daily Worker* before World War II. During the Cold War, he emerged as a popular liberal historian and biographer for young adults. (Courtesy of Milton Meltzer)

student activist who single-handedly put out a crude strike bulletin; decades later, at its peak, the flourishing *Medical Tribune* appeared throughout the United States three times a week.[31]

A few writers found prominence and managed to mostly sidestep stigmatization for their Communist past. Milton Meltzer (1915–2009), who had been a member of the Party and on the *New Masses* staff prior to World War II and stayed sympathetic during the 1940s, expressed Left-liberal politics through prize-winning books on African Americans and American history.[32] Ira Wallach (1913–95), who in the postwar years wrote the *Daily Worker* humor column as "Ted Tinsley," specialized in satires and comedies in theater, fiction, and screenplays. Among his many works were *Hopalong Freud*

Ira Wallach wrote a humor column in the *Daily Worker* during the Cold War as "Ted Tinsley" while also publishing satirical essays, plays, novels, and films that were popular in the 1950s and 1960s. (Courtesy of Ira Wallach)

and Other Literary Characters (1951), *Muscle Beach* (1959), and *The Absence of a Cello* (1960).

Neither man regretted his past. In his late seventies Wallach published an essay on aging, "Strolling to the Finish Line," in which he said with equanimity about his Party experiences over several decades, "I think my mistake was to confuse the criminal distortion of Marxism with Marxism itself. . . . My allegiance to the Communist Party was an allegiance to what I thought it was and not to what it actually was."[33] Similar sentiments appear in late-life autobiographies of one-time Communist women writers such as *Fireweed: A Political Autobiography* (2003) by Gerda Lerner (b. 1920), *A Fine Old Conflict* (1977) by Jessica Mitford (1917–96, a U.S. citizen after 1944), and *Close to My Heart* (2005) by Dorothy Sterling (1913–2008).

A handful of ex-Communist writers evolved to the Far Right, such as Whitaker Chambers, Grace Lumpkin, and E. Merrill Root (1895–1973). Several are noted for a switch in allegiance from the Soviet Union to fervent identifications with Israel, as evidenced by the novels of Michael Blankfort

(1907–82) and Meyer Levin (1905–81). Ralph Ellison was alone among African Americans as a one-time Communist writer who became a Cold War liberal. He seemed indifferent to the civil rights movement and supported the War in Vietnam. Robert Hayden (born Asa Bundy Sheffey, 1913–80) left politics for religion, joining the Bahá'í faith in 1943 but still writing astonishing poems to the end of his life.

Other veterans simply dropped from sight in the world of writing, going in diverse political directions without leaving a literary summing up. W. L. River was expelled from the Communist Party for alcoholism in the early 1950s. He resisted attempts by the FBI to have him inform on former comrades and survived by operating a laundry. Eventually River made a comeback as an important Democratic Party official in Southern California, and a park was named in his honor. John Michel, perhaps the most talented of the science fiction writers who were known as the Futurians, was also expelled from the Communist Party a few years earlier, in 1949, for alleged cowardice on a picket line. Usually as "Hugh Raymond," Michel appeared in numerous fantasy magazines into the 1950s, even as he struggled with alcoholism and a depression requiring frequent shock therapy. After a minor success as a pornographer, he was found drowned in a foot of water on New Year's Day in 1969 on the Connecticut ranch where he worked as a caretaker.[34]

Novelist and scenarist A. I. Bezzerides (1908–2007) evaded the blacklist but spent his last thirty years unsuccessfully trying to write a great novel that his friend William Faulkner had seen in him. Janet Stevenson was fired in 1952 from her position as a lecturer in the Theater Department at the University of Southern California after refusing to cooperate with an investigating committee. She wrote widely on civil rights and the women's movement. In 1986, when she was in her mid-seventies, she was elected mayor of the small town of Hammond, Oregon. Proletarian novelist Edward Newhouse, once a *Daily Worker* sports columnist and *New Masses* regular, pursued a career at the *New Yorker* in the 1940s. In 1949, he published a satire of his experiences at the Communist-influenced Modern Age publishing house, *The Hollow of the Wave*, after which he spent the rest of his long life living on the proceeds of his successful stock market ventures and enjoying his wife's musical profession.[35]

Philip Stevenson remained loyal to the Communist movement, publishing four novels without much success as "Lars Lawrence." He died of a heart attack in 1965 during his first trip to the Soviet Union. This was before he could complete the last two volumes of his six-novel epic about New Mexican labor battles in the Great Depression. In 1953 Stefan Heym, who had been known as a Communist novelist in the United States, relocated to East Ger-

Edward Newhouse, a proletarian novelist popular for short stories in the *New Masses* as well as the *New Yorker*, looked back on his Communist experiences with mockery in *The Hollow of the Wave* (1949). (Courtesy of Alison Dinsmore)

many, where he became an even better-known dissident. In the twenty-first century, Phillip Bonosky remained nominally a member of the Communist Party but was convinced that it had reverted to Browderism in the years after the collapse of the Soviet Union.

The 1960s brought new political challenges to those who departed the movement yet wished to remain active. African American writers of Communist backgrounds who shed their official affiliations but pursued antiracist objectives with a class perspective included John Oliver Killens, Julian Mayfield, Shirley Graham, Rosa Guy, Alice Childress, Audre Lorde, and Sarah Wright. Between 1981 and 1985, most of these men and women appeared in the pages of *Freedomways*, an impressive journal founded by African American pro-Communists, and with Communist Party assistance. Contributors of greater political breadth also published there. Although the journal originated out of a special interest in the southern civil rights movement, much in the spirit of the Southern Negro Youth Congress (1937–49), its pages included coverage of antiracist developments in the North as well as international movements against colonialism.

The Jewish American Warren Miller and the Latino (Cuban American and Spanish American) Jose Yglesias (1919–95), close friends, strongly identified with the Cuban Revolution. They supplemented their numerous novels with the nonfiction works *Ninety Miles from Home* (1961) by Miller and *In the Fist of the Revolution* (1968) by Yglesias. Pietro Di Donato (1911–92) never regained the success of his best-selling *Christ in Concrete* (1939) in his Communist Party years (he had joined in 1927). He became a conscientious objector during World War II and then surfaced as a sympathizer of the Italian terrorist Red Brigades in the 1970s. Truman Nelson (1911–87), an astonishing throwback in temperament to nineteenth-century New England abolitionism, stayed loyal to his Communist commitment as a union activist in the 1930s and 1940s. In the 1950s, as he launched a career as a novelist with *The Sin of the Prophet* (1952) and *The Passion by the Brook* (1953), he felt deserted by the Party's semi-underground existence. He then concluded that it was "revisionist" and became a prophetic revolutionary novelist allied with the Black Power movement in the 1960s.[36]

Commitment to peace and advocacy of civil rights were the prevailing forms in which Left activism continued, but the beckoning of utopia took nonpolitical shapes as well. *Exiles from a Future Time*, the first volume of this trilogy, begins with a portrait of Guy Endore, the Hollywood screenwriter famous for *The Werewolf of Paris* (1933). An improbable rabble-rouser, he looked like the introvert genius that he was, wispy and sensitive as a violin string. Although he was called "Blondie" in college, by the 1950s his dark blond hair was tinged with gray. Yet he remained a gentle, slim, wiry man, and at sixty he otherwise looked forty. In the postwar years, his political story was parallel to that of his friend Samuel Ornitz, with whom he met in Los Angeles for long walks and political discussion nearly every day.

Endore later claimed that toward the end of the 1940s he broke away from the Communist Party, but he probably remained part of the organization into the 1950s. He found himself repeatedly named in public hearings as a member of the Hollywood branch. The first time, in 1947, resulted in his name being withdrawn from those identified at the request of studio magnate Jack Warner. But the second time, when he was named in 1951 by former Communist screenwriters Martin Berkeley (1904–79) and Roy Huggins (1914–2002), it stuck and he was blacklisted. Then Whittaker Chambers, a Columbia College classmate who was instrumental in convincing Endore that to be moral he must give the whole of his life to the Communist movement, published *Witness*. Endore went into a rage, offering to collaborate on a rebuttal and declaring that Chambers had to be destroyed. But part of his brain raised the question as to whether he himself was really any better than Chambers as a human being.[37]

Gradually Endore began to accept that he had been completely misguided about the Soviet Union, and he wanted off the blacklist. In 1956, he wrote a letter to California State Senator Hugh Burns, of the local affiliate of the House Committee on Un-American Activities, offering to make a statement, but there was no response. He then tried crafting different kinds of letters, always trying to minimize his Party involvement in ways that demonstrate the camouflage techniques used by so many of his contemporaries. His various versions show him switching the date of his attraction to Communism from the early 1930s (Third Period) to the late 1930s (Popular Front) and changing his affiliation from member to participant only in a Party-sponsored study group. Finally, in 1958, he gave testimony in a closed session of the committee in Washington, D.C., and signed an affidavit. But he revealed little, and not much changed in his employment status.[38]

Except for an unpublishable autobiography, "Tell Me! Tell Me!," Endore wrote fiction for markets and money, although his themes and subjects drew directly on his own emotional itinerary. In a notation for himself, he reflected that all of his novels indirectly dramatize episodes in his life and career, feelings about himself and the world. Now he made the most of it, expressing his divided sense of self in *King of Paris* (1956), a book-of-the-month-club pick about the ambivalent emotions between Dumas *père* and Dumas *fils*, and then in *Voltaire! Voltaire!* (1961), focusing on Voltaire's fanaticism in his jealous coexistence with Jean-Jacques Rousseau. While writing *Satan's Saint*

(1965), his book on the Marquis de Sade, he privately meditated on his experiences with Stalinism, twisting Wordsworth's reflections on the French Revolution to quip that "it was hell that yawned instead of heaven."[39] On his desk when he died were notes for a fictionalized biography of Balzac. Endore's books, however, are unlikely to play the part of disclosing the personal truth of the Communist experience in the manner of Sanford's or Sinclair's works; his autobiographical subtext is far too hidden.

Endore had always regarded himself as a mystic, and he also took excursions into linguistics and psychoanalysis to populate his imaginative world. Religious feelings were part of what drew him to the drug rehabilitation center Synanon in the early 1960s. Endore was fascinated by its communal living and the stories that were being told. He recruited more former Communists to the cause, and he and blacklisted screenwriter Bobby Lees (Robert Lees, 1912–2004) supported their own children who wanted to live on the premises. Endore grew close to the Synanon cult founder Charles Dederich (1913–97), became the organization's chief pamphleteer and publicist, and authored yet another best-selling book, *Synanon* (1968). Perhaps it was fortunate that Endore died before this dream, too, collapsed in shocking reports about Synanon's criminal activities and an attempted murder.

As usual, when literary history is deliberated, the stakes are not just the past but also the present and future. Daniel Aaron's *Writers on the Left: Episodes in the History of U.S. Literary Communism* (1961) was followed by decades of scholarship in which the 1930s served as a political football. Originally those leaning toward the Left (especially literary scholars) dominated the game, deeming what happened in the 1930s a manifestation of collectivist hope; later, those leaning toward the Right (especially political scientists and former radical historians) took the field, presenting Marxist culture as a catastrophic detour that led toward perilous utopian fantasies. Since the new millennium, however, with many new shifts in political culture, the 1930s have become virtually synonymous with the New Deal, driven primarily by an early-twenty-first-century fixation on whether the elected government aims to dismantle or reinstate FDR's policies and practices.

For the literary Left, as demonstrated in Aaron's book, the New Deal as pragmatic policy was never the main show. The New Deal was more accurately a symbol or perhaps an index of a larger, more complicated, and more central episode. The real game on the cultural front was the gathering storm of the social movements that were animated by a distinct and inspiring vision on the upswing in the 1930s. And the core perspective of that vision began to ascend even before the term "New Deal" was coined. As one looks back after seventy years, the Great Question is still there: Was the era of the New Deal and the unique vision of the 1930s merely an aberration occasioned by economic decline and the rise of European fascism? Or was it the beginning of a project that remains unfinished?

This has been a difficult book to write. How does one compose a cultural history that covers so much diversity in ethnicity, geography, sexual mores, and psychological temperament? How does one characterize a political movement whose mind-set and structure are spurred by the traumatic particulars of national and international events, yet discussed by the movement's leaders and cadre through means of classic texts from other languages (especially German and Russian) and emotionally driven by allusions to a country 5,000 miles away (and no longer in existence)? Was the Communist-led literary movement even a coherent project, or was it just a historical conglomeration? How great is the risk of trying to smuggle a sense of shape into recalcitrant history?

Communist literary modernism plays a dual role in *American Night*. The expression suggests both the mark of aesthetic quality and the interpretative system used to explore the figurative formations (tropes, metaphors, synecdoche, metonymy) in imaginative texts. This term for the new contingency and postwar phenomenological turn indexes the artistic possibility available when the writer uses the full range of the literary imagination to bring the moral certainties of late antifascism and the enforced forgetting of a Consumers' Republic under a relentless questioning; the aim is not to present absolute contrasts and definitive choices but to grasp this mental process.

History is the puzzle and the resolution. The writings examined in *American Night* reverberate incessantly with a particular clandestine narrative that must be unshackled, what Paul Ricoeur calls "the enigma of the presence of absence."[40] Only in grasping how literature's structures of figuration are tied to the shared but hidden presence of Literary Communism can one appreciate the mysterious patterns in writing, ones produced by an author's personal life. Shuttling between the individual author and the larger group under examination, *American Night* has aspired to meet head-on the postwar moment's special reference to the crumbling vision of the 1930s. This informs cultural production after 1946 as nothing less than the specter of a lack, the literary counterpart of negative dialectics that is registered above all in the inner life of the novel.

The mission for future scholarship is to reverse enforced forgetting. My own strategy has not been to simply make room in our memory for something additional but to restore complexity to our sense of the past. I have spent much of my time writing about books that I feel are wrestling true discourse away from the vertiginous falsifications consolidated in the postwar decades. The Communist presence in postwar U.S. literature and culture is hardly the be-all and end-all of literary history, but it surely is much more than the long footnote that it became in general literary histories of the era. Demonizers and subterfugers play parallel games of manipulating political identities that impoverish cultural understanding. At the same time, the enforced forgetting of the extensiveness and intricacy of left-wing literature that emerged from a climate of fear cannot be entirely blamed on state repression.

Late antifascism, we now see, was for pro-Communists and Progressives a moral certainty, one that contradicted Marxism by transforming what it called "Marxism-Leninism" from an experimental method into a metaphysic. Moreover, Marxism was supposed to be superior to liberalism by being rooted in an ethics exceeding the agenda of any nation-state. The crowning irony is that Soviet Marxism, far from liberating people, was the ideology by which people were oppressed. As a consequence, the rhetoric of late antifascism itself became infected by the marks of that awful national time in the United States known as McCarthyism, a decade of fanaticism, paranoia, corrupted demands for "unity," and the demonization of difference. The Progressive culture of late antifascism was intrinsically the product of a literary movement that allowed too much to grow dim behind clichés and ungenerous perceptions.

Yet the good accomplished by those under the spell of moral certainty, in literature and in practical life, is not nullified by knowing more about the consequences, even if full disclosure can be dispiriting. The paradox of Marxist wisdom is that it becomes folly when it does not know its own limits. The real stories embedded in the novels and poems of the Left occur outside the familiar realm of echoes, allusions, and putative references that we have inherited as a means to interpret and evaluate. Given this complicated background, it is understandable that the antidote to late antifascism, Communist literary modernism, should agonize over the objectivity of perception. Ann Petry and others understood all too well that a person sees what he or she believes to be true, but that this may not be the *whole* truth.

What is to be concluded, then, about the years treated in *American Night*? Postwar, the still forceful confederation of writings animated by the vision of the 1930s raced like a giant asteroid, one out of the science fiction imagination, into the toxic atmosphere of an unfamiliar planet. Encountering the inhospitable environment of the Truman era, the once commanding edifice of 1930s radical culture was after 1946 pounded externally by persecution from business and government while undermined internally through a corrosive loss of political trust in its Soviet beacon. During the 1950s, because of the power of anti-Communist ideology as an instrument of reactionary demagogues, the more the Communists were defanged, the more they were trampled. Accordingly, the 1930s socialist dream in the form of novels, poems, and plays fragmented in tandem with the disintegration of the organized Left, breaking off into meteoroid-like shards of sundry shapes and sizes. Some blazed a moment, like shooting stars; others vanished into the blackness; and still others await discovery in some yet undisclosed location on the cultural landscape.

A Note on Methodology

This book was written with the conviction that postwar U.S. literature, while the focus of several acute studies, remains an era in search of a critic. The method of *American Night* follows an observation of Walter Benjamin's: "To write history is to give the dates a physiognomy."[1] Aiming to craft a "humanscape" of several generations of Left writers, I have also tried to respond to an intellectual challenge posed by Theodor Adorno: "Even the biographical individual is a social category. It can only be defined in a living context together with others; it is this context that shapes its social character and only in this context does an individual acquire meaning within given social conditions."[2] The Marxist poet Thomas McGrath, from whose long poem *Letter to an Imaginary Friend* this book derives its title, put it this way: "All of us live twice at the same time—once uniquely and once representatively. I am interested in those moments when my unique personal life intersects with something bigger."[3]

In fiction even more than in poetry, the street runs both ways. One cannot help but look for clues to illuminate the lives that dreamed the sometimes fantastic narratives of Kenneth Fearing, Alexander Saxton, Richard Wright, Ann Petry, Abraham Polonsky, Jo Sinclair, Carlos Bulosan, and others. Theory remains indispensable in grasping the workings of artistic form, yet there is a power in the most affecting components of the literary legacy of the Left that begs to be considered against a flesh-and-bone dimension of human existence and historical chronology. Moreover, events of the postwar era make up a trauma that ought to be returned to critical discussion; a critic must sometimes employ a variety of talk therapy, one exploring the writer's emotional architecture. A particular effort has been devoted to tracing the networks of association—friends, lovers, comrades—that ran through the pro-Communist literary milieu. Details about intimate affairs (alcoholism, infidelity) are incorporated not to censure or scandalize but to gain insight into the actual culture of the day. A particular point about private life as a matrix of the literary imagination must be made even as one is mindful of a major pitfall of biography—the reduction of an author's ideas to his or her idiosyncratic psychology, an outgrowth of some peculiar aspect of the writer's personal development.

There were hundreds of cultural workers who lived and worked in this complex postwar era. Some dwelled in the literary past, and others wrote in an experimental and explorational spirit that nonetheless linked back to a preceding tradition forged in the Depression by pro-Communists in dialogue with modernism, such as John Dos Passos, Henry Roth, Muriel Rukeyser, Nathanael West, and the *Dynamo* poets. Given that *American Night* aspires to rethink from innovative slants the obfuscations of 1940s–1950s converso culture, there has been little room to simultaneously reiterate some of the customary iconic figures and episodes of the Cold War cultural Left. Nor could the book touch on every sphere of cultural practice or dispute. Students of the era should already be familiar with, or can readily access information about, emblematical events that include the 1946 testimony of the Hollywood Ten, Norman Mailer breaking ranks with the pro-Communist Left at the 1949 Waldorf World Peace Conference, Dashiell Hammett and Lillian Hellman defying the House Committee on Un-American Activities in the late 1940s and early 1950s, Langston Hughes's 1953 arrangement with the same committee to cooperate but not to inform on any individuals, the controversy over the 1954 film *The Salt of the Earth*, and Arthur Miller's refusal to name names in 1956 and 1957.[4]

American Night is designed to offer a map to help us see, locate, and analyze a much larger number of radical writers than these celebrity ones. A glance at the list of photo illustrations for *American Night* will provide quick orientation to the breadth of the study, consistent with the first two volumes. There is a special exertion to understand cultural workers who make up a substratum or even a rank and file, without denying that there were well-known Left authors or superior artistic achievements. Among postwar writings of the Left selected for close readings, I say less about those already in the limelight— *The Naked and the Dead* (1948), *The Crucible* (1953), *The Dollmaker* (1954), *A Raisin in the Sun* (1959)—than about those works that are neglected or (in my view) misread. Only a small number of these lesser-known volumes are offered as artistic equals of Mailer and others for a broad readership—*The Narrows*, *Letter to an Imaginary Friend*, and *Scenes from the Life of an American Jew*. Many more are likelier candidates to be the favorites of specialized audiences—*The Big Clock*, *The Outsider*, and *The Cry and the Dedication*.

American Night uses the same structural pattern as the earlier two volumes, alternating between sections devoted to individuals, discrete traditions, and more collective considerations to express involvedness and fine distinctions. There is a chronological center, 1946 to 1956, yet excursions back to the 1930s and forward even past the 1960s are frequently required to comprehend the trajectory of lives, careers, and cultural issues. The creation of several less linear stories, as in the evolution of gay writing (chapter 4), leaves greater freedom for the unpredicted and the perplexing. Still, intellectual investigation invariably fluctuates on many levels between manifestations of abstraction and distinctiveness, and my choices are not immune from criticism apropos flaws in choices, overly intricate speculation, and limits regarding how far to pursue hypotheses.

A concern for complexity and nuance, however, does not moderate the book's passionate sympathy with the Marxist partisans of social justice. This perspective is precisely what accounts for the constant critique of the Stalinist experience in *American Night*. Communists emerged from an indigenous radical movement, but their passage through Stalinism left a non-biodegradable stain on the Left tradition. It is a reminder of the calamity that results from the subordination of one's socialist commitment to an idealized regime professing political values one endorses, blotting out one facet to embellish another. Marxist commitment should be consistently aimed at the primacy of abolishing exploitation and political persecution. Pro-Sovietism and its offshoots have been as damaging to the Left as comparable ingenuousness about the inconsistencies of Western democracies has been for well-intentioned liberals and conservatives.[5]

The pertinent autobiographical subtext here is that I came to social consciousness during the civil rights era in an ambience of radicalization utterly different from the one discussed in this trilogy, that of the post-1950s, when the writers and activists who shaped my own worldview were attempting to redefine internationalism on the basis of emerging social movements in opposition to racism, against colonialism, and in defiance of imposed conformity. Like other student "sixty-eighters," I witnessed the lies about Vietnam and the hypocrisy of racial codes and the free market in the United States, alongside the cruelty of one-party systems in the Soviet Union, Eastern Europe, and China. The juxtaposition made me acutely aware of the moral perils of misplaced trust in any state regime, and the matter became further clarified in the 1970s as I read the pages of *New Left Review*. Thus it is no surprise that the literary works by politically committed writers that have fascinated me throughout a thirty-five-year career have been those that have helped illuminate my comprehension of the reservations I experienced then and subsequently, ones that signal a longing to recapture the critical imagination in socialist literature. Research for this volume led me to find such moments in unexpected places, including among writers who did not openly embrace the politics with which I identify.

This is not a book about aesthetic monuments, and there is no assertion of consistently high literary merit in my particular selections. Most of the writers I discuss had a talent and competence equal to many other authors who sustained a popular following in diverse genres; several are occasionally esteemed by the academy. Others may be recalcitrant to all but the most tenacious readers. Literary scholars traditionally dispute each other's claims about exceptional success, and alternative valuations are expected. The comprehensive achievement of the literary Left after the mid-1940s is indicated by the many more names cited in passing as well as in the endnotes. The centrality of Left culture is a fact of the early Cold War but tougher to sort out than during the Great Depression, when a coherent movement gathered steam around models undergirded by a vision of triumph. The postwar collapse of confidence in portions of this worldview launched its onetime partisans on a sometimes feverish voyage through unfamiliar terrain. As the Cold War persecution began, the Marxist project, like Franz Kafka's *Deus absconditus*, gave the impression of retreating into a protective darkness, which is part of the reason why I titled this book *American Night*.[6]

To conduct a postmortem on an acute fifteen-year subdivision in what Eric Hobsbawm called "The Short Twentieth Century, 1914–1991,"[7] puts one in uncomfortable positions. Here I will present just three examples of the likely insoluble questions with which I wrestled. The most excruciating is that of placing under examination the allegedly idealistic motives of writers, even though motivations are by no means straightforward to sort out and often hopeless to judge. U.S. Communism, a small oppositional movement, was in several respects the obverse of its tyrannical Soviet inspirer by doing more good than harm. This is the understandable perception of political activists who prize racial justice and trade union rights; literary scholars can add that the movement gave voice and vision to generations of writers and artists early in their careers. Yet there were still victims in its wake.

A narrative of this period that flattens complexity, reducing tragedy to a melodrama that demonizes either the Left or Right, satisfies only constituencies of the already convinced or naive. The Communist writers depicted in *American Night* are certainly not the soulless hacks that populate the vast industry of anti-Communist studies, but to restore their humanity means to avoid the see-no-evil cheerleading of the Popular Front that sometimes characterizes the quest for ancestors to comfortably validate present needs. I anticipate making no one happy in this irresolvable endeavor to locate a modicum of balance but felt it would evade the tough questions if I did not at least take a stab at illumination.

The second of the insolubles is the riddle of how pro-Communism should be defined. Is there a specific list of political positions mandatory to the characterization of a writer as a Communist? How deep a belief in the Soviet Union as the working future of humanity is required? Did the political tag "Progressive," increasingly popular in the 1940s and 1950s, refer to an independent category of radicals, or was it mostly meant to cloak a pro-Soviet faith with a euphemism? Trying to pin this down—who is a Communist and who is a Progressive—can be like putting one's thumb on a blob of mercury. For me, the answers that work best come on an individual basis. Genuine political blends, plainly evident in a career such as that of Congressman Vito Marcantonio's (1902–54), may be found among cultural figures, but the particulars of ideological commitment are far from interchangeable.[8] This need to make distinctions in each instance sometimes results in a surfeit of facts about the political activities and associations that inform my conclusions about a writer's specific interrelations with Communism. However, as an admitted "detail junkie," I have endeavored to develop strategies to avoid data overload in the narrative, including using some long, old-style endnotes for additional material about lives, plots, and scholarly sources. Nevertheless, as the introduction to this volume makes clear, despite the latest archival findings, post–World War II Communist literary affiliation, as remembered (and misremembered) by those seeking to mask, demonize, minimize, sensationalize, or just forget, will always remain something of a Rubik's Cube. In some cases, the solution may be lodged in a subterranean stratum of the particular writer's brain that an interpreter can never fully excavate.

The third and final matter in dispute concerns the Cold War as a time when recognized writers came under uniquely personal strains with reference to their ability to earn a living. To refuse to "name names" to an investigating committee became an institutionalized means of effectively firing oneself from any job outside the small political apparatus of the Left, a problematic martyrdom for those who were growing dubious of Communism as the ally of justice. Was Hollywood screenwriter Dalton Trumbo accurate in his claim before the Writers Guild in 1970 that there were in the bitter brawl about blacklisting "only victims," ultimately "good and bad on both sides"?[9] If so, should the borders of a tradition of literary radicalism be expanded to embrace "informers" who otherwise remained on the Left—including a defiant Budd Schulberg and a shamefaced Ben Maddow? The short answer to this last question is yes, even if the center of the tradition remains the "unfriendly" witnesses. But responses to further inquiries about the eventual significance of apostasy will require additional debate that exceeds the boundaries of *American Night*. As James Thurber quipped, "It is better to ask some of the questions than to know all of the answers."[10] The texts and careers that I have chosen for analysis will not satisfy every reader's personal predilections but are ones that I hope will help the reader navigate through so much of the ostensible "indecipherability" of the postwar literary Left.

I wrote this book for the specific reasons mentioned above but also because I wish to participate in the conversation about the "ways and means" of U.S. literature. A scholar must be alert to techniques of reevaluating and regrouping writers. Only with the forthright inclusion of former and ongoing pro-Communists of the era, who were abundant and often central, can one come to fully realize one's literary heritage. The result will not be one narrowly Left-leaning but surely will be one that contests all previous critical efforts to contain what really happened in U.S. literature in the postwar years. In particular, a frank acknowledgment of the breadth of U.S. literary radicalism during the Cold War will flesh out the transnational arc that previous scholars have traced from proletarian literature to magical realism.[11]

Notes

PREFACE

1. Terms such as "memory crisis," "memory loss," and "enforced forgetting" are adapted from the study of cultural memory. For a sustained overview and influential interpretation of these concepts, see Anne Whitehead's *Memory* (London: Routledge, 2008) and Richard Terdiman's *Present Past: Modernity and the Memory Crisis* (Ithaca, N.Y.: Cornell University Press, 1993). Of course, a central place in any consideration of memory must go to Paul Ricoeur, *History, Memory, Forgetting*, trans. Kathleen Blamey and David Pellauer (Chicago: University of Chicago Press, 2004).

2. My general view of the aims of twentieth-century socialism follows the argument of Geoff Eley in *Forging Democracy: The History of the Left in Europe, 1850–2000* (New York: Oxford, 2002), in the sense that its ideal was of "making democracy social" (13).

3. For a compelling analysis of the impact of the Khrushchev Revelations on the Communist Party, see Maurice Isserman, "The Collapse of the Communist Party," *If I Had a Hammer: The Death of the Old Left and the Birth of the New Left* (New York: Basic Books, 1987), 1–34.

4. Robin D. G. Kelley, *Hammer and Hoe: Alabama Communists during the Great Depression* (Chapel Hill: University of North Carolina Press, 1990), 229.

5. The expression "A Consumers' Republic" is from Lizabeth Cohen, *A Consumers' Republic: The Politics of Mass Consumption in Postwar America* (New York: Random House, 2003). Cohen's book is about neither imaginative literature nor the Left, but her investigation is important to accentuate that the postwar crisis came to a head within a context of greatly intensified consumerism.

6. The term "Cultural Cold War" usually refers specifically to the collaboration between the CIA and Cold War liberals to combat fellow travelers and European "neutralists." The literature about this is endless, and I have addressed some of the issues in *The New York Intellectuals: The Rise and Decline of the Anti-Stalinist Left from the 1930s to the 1980s* (Chapel Hill: University of North Carolina Press, 1987).

7. In a recent book, *Turncoats, Traitors, and Fellow Travelers: Culture and Politics of*

the Early Cold War (Jackson: University Press of Mississippi, 2008), Arthur Redding proposes the expression "fugitive culture" to address analogous artistic concerns. He characterizes fugitive culture as follows: "in part complicit but largely and in complex ways resistant, emerg[ing] as various 'popular front' writers and activists fled into exile, went underground, or grudgingly accommodated themselves to the new order" (4). To capture another facet of multilayered literary representation, Lillian Hellman makes thought-provoking use of the artistic term "pentimento," the alteration of a painting, in her 1973 autobiography, *Pentimento: A Book of Portraits* (Boston: Little, Brown, 1973). I prefer the phrase "converso culture" as more accurately conveying the ambiguities of the enforced forgetting and memory crisis central to *American Night*, but no term will be entirely satisfactory.

8. Michael Denning, *Culture in the Age of Three Worlds* (London: Verso, 2004).

9. See, for example, Jack B. Tenney, *Red Fascism: Boring from Within by the Subversive Forces of Communism* (Los Angeles: Federal Printing, 1947). Many of the writers discussed in *American Night* are cited in this volume.

INTRODUCTION

1. Howard Fast, "An Epitaph for Sidney," *Departure and Other Stories* (Boston: Little Brown and Company, 1949), 76.

2. Morris U. Schappes, "Commentary on 'An Epitaph for Sidney,'" *Jewish Life*, February 1949, 25–27. Schappes is critical of the story mainly because of its thin treatment of Jewish identity; Sidney sees himself as Jewish only in relation to anti-Semitism. Schappes's reader's report for the magazine urged that the story not be published and pointed to the undistinguished prose style and absence of Sidney's distinctive personal traits as well. See *Jewish Life* Manuscript Report for "An Epitaph for Sidney," box 25, folder 19, Papers of Morris U. Schappes, Tamiment Library, New York University.

3. Fast, "An Epitaph for Sidney," 60.

4. Ibid., 61. Current estimates for deaths occurring in World War II are now double this number.

5. Ibid., 62.

6. Ibid., 59.

7. Ibid., 71.

8. Ibid., 57.

9. Ibid., 70.

10. Ibid.

11. Ibid., 73.

12. Ibid., 74.

13. In 1932, William Z. Foster, in the post of Party chairman, published the book *Toward Soviet America* (New York: International Publishers, 1932), the title of which invokes the Communist aspiration of the time. In April 1935, the Communist-led League of American Writers was formed to counteract the sectarianism of the Party-

led John Reed Club by uniting convinced Communist writers with those who saw themselves as middle class and unwilling to submit to the discipline of formal Party membership; the prevalent term at that moment was "revolutionary writer." Waldo Frank (1889–1967), the league's chairman, wrote the following in his published address, "Values of the Revolutionary Writer": "My premise and the premise of the majority of writers here assembled is that Communism must come, and must be fought for." See Henry Hart, ed., *American Writers' Congress* (New York: International, 1935), 71.

14. The titles of Party national secretary Earl Browder's publications in those years reflect the political sea-change from the days of Foster: *Lincoln and the Communists* (New York: Workers Library, 1936), *Democracy or Fascism* (New York: Workers Library, 1936), *Unity for Peace and Democracy* (New York: Workers Library,1939), *The Heritage of Jefferson* (New York: New York Workers School, 1943), *Communists and National Unity* (New York: Workers Library, 1944), *The Future of the Anglo-American-Soviet Coalition* (New York: Workers Library, 1944), and *The Road Ahead to Victory and Lasting Peace* (New York: Workers Library, 1944).

15. There is no authoritatively consistent use of the terminology; perhaps the fullest application of the Progressive and Great Tradition perspective can be found in the books of Annette T. Rubinstein, *The Great Tradition: From Shakespeare to Shaw*, 2 vols. (New York: Monthly Review, 1953), and *American Literature: Root and Flower: Significant Poets, Novelists and Dramatists, 1775–1955* (Beijing: China Foreign Teaching and Research Press, 1988).

16. The role of liberals in the Popular Front is discussed in many books, but one that provides unusual documentation and details is Judy Kutulas, *The Long War: The Intellectual People's Front and Anti-Stalinism* (Durham, N.C.: Duke University Press, 1995).

17. A review of the history of this term appears in Paul Buhle's entry under "Progressive" in *Encyclopedia of the American Left*, ed. Mari Jo Buhle, Paul Buhle, and Dan Georgakas, 2nd ed. (New York: Oxford University Press, 1998), 632–35.

18. The January 1948 issue of the *New International*, journal of the Trotskyist Workers Party led by Max Shachtman, devoted several articles to the phenomenon of "Stalinized Liberals" and the "Neo-Stalinist Type" in the postwar era. Some of the independents so designated held that the Stalinist system was all right for others; some saw the tough reality of the Soviet Union and liked it; some were not attracted to life under the regime but thought that much could be learned from the experience and that the Soviet Union might be moving in the same direction as the United States. Part of the *New International*'s argument was also that, prior to World War II, the fellow travelers were significantly influenced by socialist idealism; afterward, the "Stalinist liberal" was more likely to be in pursuit of capitalist aims without capitalist methods, or Stalinist aims with capitalist methods.

19. Daniel S. Gillmor, ed., *Speaking of Peace* (New York: National Council of the Arts, Sciences and Professions, 1949), 144–47.

20. See editorial, "Memo for Progressives," *Masses & Mainstream* 1, no. 10 (December 1948): 3-5.

21. Boyer believed that he had the right to declare his politics forthrightly and refused to cooperate in HUAC investigations. See his obituary in the *New York Times*, 9 August 1973, online at New York Times Archive. Once blacklisted, he wrote influential books on labor and abolitionist John Brown. Sandy Boyer, phone interview with the author, 12 September 1990.

22. See Peter Dreier, "The Fifty Most Influential Progressives in the Twentieth Century," in the 16 September 2010 issue of the *Nation* and online at http://www.thenation.com/article/154816/fifty-most-influential-progressives-intro.

23. Fast, "An Epitaph for Sidney," 74.

24. The subject is not mentioned beyond Sidney's having once joined the Young Communist League; if a Party member at the time of World War II, he would have taken a leave of absence in order to serve in the military.

25. See Geoff Eley in *Forging Democracy: The History of the Left in Europe, 1850-2000* (New York: Oxford University Press, 2002).

26. Paul Buhle provides a history of antifascism in his entry under this topic in *Encyclopedia of the American Left*, ed. Buhle, Buhle, and Georgakas, 54-56.

27. Ibid., 55.

28. Ibid.

29. One of the major anticolonial efforts that the Communist Party helped to keep alive was the Council on African Affairs. See the study by Penny Von Eschen, *Race against Empire: Black Americans and Anti-Colonialism, 1937-1957* (Ithaca, N.Y.: Cornell University Press, 1997).

30. Ibid., 55.

31. Jonathan Haidt, "The Emotional Dog and Its Rational Tail: A Social Intuitionist Approach to Moral Judgment," *Psychological Review* 108, no. 4 (2008): 814-34.

32. Ibid., 814.

33. As Larry Ceplair observes in *Under the Shadow of War: Fascism, Anti-Fascism, and Marxists, 1918-1939* (New York: Columbia University Press, 1987), 204: "Stalin was not cunningly biding his time or secretly preparing to open a second front against Germany. He was prepared to maintain a working relationship with Hitler, watch the defeat of the democracies, and adhere to the Tripartite Pact (with Germany, Italy, and Japan) if the necessary guarantees could be arranged. As late as April 1941, with Operation Barbarossa pending against it, the Russians continued to observe their commercial arrangements with Germany and deliver considerable amounts of raw material to it."

34. Historian Leo Ribuffo has discussed this episode in his chapter "Brown Scare" in his 1985 book *The Old Christian Right* (Philadelphia: Temple University Press, 1983).

35. Earl Browder, "Hitler's Uprisings in America," *New Masses*, 14 September 1943, 3-5.

36. See Alan M. Wald, *Trinity of Passion: The Literary Left and the Antifascist Crusade* (Chapel Hill: University of North Carolina Press, 2007), 108-45.

37. Stuart Hall, "Life and Times of the First New Left," *New Left Review* 61 (January–February 2010): 177.

38. Howard Fast, *Intellectuals and the Fight for Peace* (New York: Masses and Mainstream, 1949), 3, 5.

39. The Editors, "Preface for Today," *Masses & Mainstream* 1, no. 1 (March 1948): 3–4.

40. Ibid.

41. The centrality of the belief in imminent war and fascism to the Communist Party's behavior is emphasized in the chapter "Expectations of War and Fascism" in David A. Shannon, *The Decline of American Communism: A History of the Communist Party of the United States since 1945* (New York: Harcourt, Brace and Company, 1959), 191–95.

42. See Dorothy Healey and Maurice Isserman, *Dorothy Healey Remembers: A Life in the Communist Party* (New York: Oxford University Press, 1990), 125–32. She begins: "The great irony of the McCarthy period is that we did almost as much damage to ourselves, in the name of purifying our ranks, as Joe McCarthy and J. Edgar Hoover and all the other witch-hunters combined were able to do."

43. Ibid., 137–38.

44. The literature on the case is enormous. For two of the most noted works, see Ronald Radosh and Joyce Milton, *The Rosenberg File: A Search for the Truth*, 2nd ed. (New Haven: Yale University Press, 1997), and Walter Schneir and Miriam Schneir, *Final Verdict: What Really Happened in the Rosenberg Case* (New York: Melville House, 2010).

45. A dozen novels have re-created aspects of the Rosenberg case, but the most compelling remains E. L. Doctorow, *The Book of Daniel* (New York: Random House, 1971).

46. See Wald, *Trinity of Passion*, 221–28.

CHAPTER ONE

1. Kenneth Fearing, "Man versus Man," *New York Times*, March 26, 1944, 5, 15.

2. Donald A. Klopfer to Kenneth Fearing, 18 December 1939, Random House Records, Rare Book and Manuscript Library, Columbia University, New York; James Atlas, *Saul Bellow: A Biography* (New York: Random House, 2000), 131; Bennett Cerf to Kenneth Fearing, 7 July 1942, Random House Records. For original title, see DSK to Kenneth Fearing, 19 January 1942, Random House Records. A memo from Emanuele E. Harper in the Random House records gives sales figures of 1,250 for *Clark Gifford's Body* through 31 July 1942.

3. Kenneth Fearing, "The Judas Picture," *American Magazine* 142, no. 4 (October 1946): 157–80. The cover says "Complete American Mystery Novel," so this may actually be an early version of *The Big Clock* despite its publication seven months later.

4. In 1980, a second film version, set in CIA headquarters, was made as *No Way Out*, and a new paperback edition of *The Big Clock* was issued under that title as well.

5. Horace Gregory, *The House on Jefferson Street: A Cycle of Memories* (New York: Holt, Rinehart and Winston, 1972), 121.

6. Statement published in Stanley J. Kunitz and Howard Haycraft, *Twentieth Century Authors: A Biographical Dictionary of Modern Literature* (New York: H. H. Wilson, 1942), 444–45.

7. The introduction also appeared as a review, "Kenneth Fearing: Poet for Workers," in *New Masses*, 21 May 1935, 24–25.

8. Early evidence of Fearing's fascination with Wells can be found in "A Voice from the Past," in his film review column, "The Screen," in *New Masses*, 5 May 1936, 27.

9. For a listing of scholarship about Fearing, see Alan M. Wald, *Exiles from a Future Time: The Forging of the Mid-Twentieth-Century Literary Left* (Chapel Hill: University of North Carolina Press, 2002), 334n1. The most extensive recent essay about Fearing's poetry is Nathaniel Mills, "The Dialectic of Electricity," *Journal of Modern Literature* 30, no. 2 (Winter 2007): 17–41.

10. See "Dirge," *New Masses*, 18 September 1934, 14.

11. This is the title of a celebrated symposium in *Partisan Review* that ran for four issues in 1952.

12. Bennie Graves, "Literature Forms Social Myths, Says Fearing," *Indiana Daily Student*, 29 July 1948, 4.

13. See the stimulating if to some extent controversial argument of Lizabeth Cohen, *A Consumers' Republic: The Politics of Mass Consumption in Postwar America* (New York: Random House, 2003).

14. Kenneth Fearing, "Reading, Writing, and the Rackets," *New and Selected Poems* (Bloomington: University of Indiana Press, 1956), xv.

15. Fearing, "Man Versus Man," 15.

16. Lung cancer, however, was the immediate cause of his death. See Patricia Santora, "The Poetry and Prose of Kenneth Flexner Fearing" (diss., University of Maryland, 1982), 48.

17. See the correspondence file on Fearing of the *New Yorker* magazine for copies of numerous such letters of rejection.

18. Kenneth Fearing to Bennett Cerf, June 1940, Random House Records.

19. Kenneth Fearing, *Stranger at Coney Island* (New York: Harcourt, Brace, 1948), 3–4.

20. Kenneth Fearing, "Goofy but Tragic," *New Masses*, June 1928, 2. One of several places that the identification of Fearing as the main character is mentioned is in the review of *The Hospital* in *Time*, 4 September 1939, 52.

21. Margery Latimer, *This Is My Body* (New York: Jonathan Cape, 1930), 165.

22. Ibid., 166.

23. Ibid.

24. Ibid., 315.

25. Gregory, *House on Jefferson Street*, 120.

26. Kenneth Fearing, "Champagne and Bitters," *Ed McBain's Mystery Book* 2 (1960):

71–81. Although based on an actual case of murder and suicide, Fearing narrates the events in a way that echoes troubling issues in his own life involving parents and friendships.

27. Gerald L. Belcher and Margaret L. Belcher, *Collecting Souls, Gathering Dust* (New York: Paragon, 1991), 158.

28. Mary Beth Hinton, ed., *The Diaries of Marya Zaturenska* (Syracuse, N.Y.: Syracuse University Press, 2002), 135.

29. Gertrude Hayes, interview with the author, New York City, 8 October 1989.

30. Nathan Adler, interview with the author, Mill Valley, Calif., 12 September 1989. Adler believed that Fearing probably participated in May Day parades and felt that young Communist poets like himself took Fearing seriously as a revolutionary. The main difference was Fearing's middle-class background and his conflicted sense of Jewish identity.

31. Margery Latimer urged him to join the supporters of the Passaic Strike, but he couldn't be bothered. See Robert Ryley, "Fearing's Politics," draft chapter of biography of Kenneth Fearing, in possession of the author.

32. *New York Times*, 3 November 1935 (online at *New York Times* Article Archive).

33. Horace Gregory and Marya Zaturenska, *A History of America Poetry, 1900–1940* (New York: Harcourt Brace and Company, 1946), 467.

34. Jerre Mangione, *The Dream and the Deal: The Federal Writers Project, 1935–43* (Boston: Little, Brown, 1972), 177.

35. It was released on 14 August 1939 and appeared in *Soviet Russia Today* 8, no. 5 (September 1939): 24–25, 28. The first pro-Soviet statement on which Fearing's name appears was issued by the John Reed Club and reported in "Group Here Scores Anti-Soviet Drive" and also in the *New York Times*, 16 March 1930 (online at *New York Times* Article Archive).

36. Anita Tilkin, "The Poetry of Irony," *Daily Worker*, 20 December 1938, 7. For sophisticated assessments by two veterans of the Communist cultural movement, see Kenneth Burke, "Two Kinds of Against," *New Republic*, 26 June 1935, 198–99; and F. W. Dupee, "Sinister Banalities," *New Republic*, 28 October 1940, 597. In the mid-1930s, Burke explained that Fearing had a Communist set of values for his frame of reference. Five years later, Dupee insightfully noted that Fearing had come through the Communist movement but that his poetry had remained intact because he ignored propaganda while absorbing its negations. He also characterized Fearing's Communist phase as the last phase of post–World War I rebellion.

37. Carl Rakosi to Robert Ryley, 19 July 1984, Memorial Library, University of Wisconsin.

38. Sol Funaroff to Nathan Adler, May 5, 1937, in possession of the author.

39. "Kenneth Fearing (1902–)," in Kunitz and Haycraft, *Twentieth Century Authors*, 444.

40. Most adamant that Fearing was "a-political" was Carl Rakosi: "Nobody else seems to think this, but I knew him, he was my roommate. I was so sure that he was

a-political because he used to make fun of me for being political. 'Cause I was always political." See Steve Dickison, "An On-Line Interview with Carl Rakosi" (1999), at http://www.english.illinois.edu/Maps/poets/m_r/rakosi/online_interview.htm.

41. William Phillips, *A Partisan View: Five Decades in the Politics of Literature* (New York: Stein and Day, 1983), 56.

42. Ibid.

43. "The Situation in American Writing," *Partisan Review* 6 (1939): 33–35; "U.S. Writers in War," *Poetry* 56 (1940): 318–23. Fearing wrote in *Partisan Review* that the coming war could take only two forms: either civil war would break out in France, and the American public should support the antifascist resistance in the same manner as the Spanish Republic had been supported, or there would be a repeat of World War I, in which case the United States should give aid to any enemy of the Axis but denounce the governments of France and England for their policies and practices. A year later he reaffirmed his revolutionary antiwar views in *Poetry*, stating that the "old answers are not wrong" but had been made in "innocence." Now that international war was a reality, one could find any explanation for it only in the "social rivalries and contradictions" that had created many wars growing from "conflagrations that are in the structure of twentieth century society" and that need to be "brought under control."

44. Bennett Cerf to Kenneth Fearing, 5 August 1942, Random House Records.

45. T. C. Wilson, "The Real Thing," *Poetry* 54, no. 1 (April 1939): 26–27.

46. A. B. Magil, interview with the author, New York City, August 1990.

47. The most successful novel by River was *The Torguts* (New York: Frederick A. Stokes, 1939). Two of the most important Hollywood films that he scripted are *The Adventures of Martin Eden* (1942) and *City without Men* (1943).

48. Among Fearing's lesser-known connections were music and dance. For example, Fearing wrote a poem called "Nevertheless, Come Back" that was put to a musical setting by Lionel Nowak, a composer who taught at Bennington College, and it was read in a public performance by Lee Sherman. See *New York Times*, 4 January 1943 (online at *New York Times* Article Archive). The poem is one of several omitted from all collections of Fearing's work, including Robert M. Ryley, ed., *Kenneth Fearing: Complete Poems* (Orono, Maine: National Poetry Foundation, 1994). Fearing also had an interest in urban photography and tried to connect Robin Carson with editor Bennett Cerf. Fearing to Bennett Cerf, July 1940, Random House Records.

49. Herald may have already joined the Communist Party before arriving in Madison. Rakosi was previously influenced by his father's socialist views. Gregory shared some of Fearing's divided consciousness and became an intellectual devotee of the Communist Party but without much organizational activity. Rakosi, Herald, Fearing, and Margery Latimer were all publishing in the *New Masses* in 1926. Herald appeared as a minor figure in the Hiss-Chambers case, coming forward to accuse Chambers of making a homosexual advance toward him. He was the father of the popular folksinger John Herald (1939–2005).

50. Carl Rakosi, interview with the author, San Francisco, 1 July 2003.

51. Ryley, "Fearing's Politics."

52. This may be the source for an article by John Chamberlain in "Books of the Times," *New York Times*, 27 May 1935 (online at *New York Times* Article Archive), stating Communist literary representative Maxim Lieber's view that Fearing had been a first-rate student in economics at Wisconsin: "His poems are what [Marxist economist] Scott Nearing would write if he were a poet, not an economist."

53. Anita Tiktin, "The Poet of Irony," *Daily Worker*, 20 December 1938, 7. The incident is described in Wald, *Exiles from a Future Time*, 10.

54. Ryley, "Fearing's Politics."

55. See James Weschler, *Edward Landon*, exhibition brochure for Mary Ryan Gallery, 24 West 5th Street, New York, 15 June–15 July 1994. The marriage was in 1948. Rachel Fearing's sister, Doris Meltzer, was also an artist and knew Landon.

56. Elizabeth Seaton, "Nan Lurie," *Paths to the Press: Printmaking and American Women Artists, 1910–1960*, brochure for Mariana Kistler Beach Museum of Art, Kent State University, Kent, Ohio. See letters of reference for Nan Lurie in the Yadoo Papers, New York Public Library. Lurie came from a Russian Jewish family and was briefly married to a writer named Byron Bishop around 1940.

57. Joseph Freeman to Horace Gregory, 29 June 1961, Horace Gregory Papers, Syracuse University, Syracuse, N.Y.

58. The cover featuring Fearing and a selection of poems appeared in *Mainstream* 14, no. 8 (August 1961): 26–34. Fearing's explanation of his refusal to allow *Masses & Mainstream* to reprint his essay is discussed in Ryley, "Fearing's Politics."

59. Ryley, "Fearing's Politics."

60. "The poet Kenneth Fearing... was one of the Project's most popular staff members and had friends in all camps. The same was true of Richard Wright, whose Communist party affiliation was well known." Mangione, *The Dream and the Deal*, 177.

61. In a letter of 5 May 1937 from Sol Funaroff to Nathan Adler, Funaroff reports that he witnessed Hayes at Fearing's apartment carping about the Communist Party's stand on Spain and the Moscow Trials. Letter in possession of the author.

62. This new title was suddenly proposed in June 1938 for the collection, already assembled. The switch suggests ambivalent feelings about the certainty of his views, or at least Communism's pretense to scientific authority. See Kenneth Fearing to Bennett Cerf, 6 June 1938, Random House Records.

63. Nelson Algren, "Fearing's Verse Catches Tempo of Modern Times," *Daily Worker*, 6 April 1939, 7.

64. At the same time, he made a point of noting that some of the questions addressed to him might be aimed at intensifying factional differences within the Left; if so, his answers were not intended to assist that aim.

65. "Pact" was originally published in the *New Yorker*, 23 September 1939, 25. The Hitler-Stalin Pact was signed in August.

66. Meridel Le Sueur reported this to Robert Ryley, who discussed it with me in a phone conversation on 12 August 1990. Ryley refers to it in his edition of *Kenneth Fearing: Complete Poems*, liv.

67. Bergman was a protégé of the up-and-coming Communist poet Joy Davidman (1915–1960) and, oddly, a patient of Fearing's first wife. Although Rachel maintained that Fearing and Bergman were unacquainted, Bergman's correspondence with Raphael Hayes suggests otherwise. Letters in possession of the author.

68. Alexander Bergman, "Fearing's Poems," *New Masses*, 19 November 1940, 25–26.

69. Fearing, "Reading, Writing, and the Rackets," ix–xxiv.

70. Sally Alford, "Chaos in Ivory," *New Masses*, 4 August 1942, 25–26.

71. See Fearing, "U.S. Writers in War," 318–23; and Ryley, *Kenneth Fearing: Complete Poems*, xxvi.

72. Fearing, "Seven Questions," *Partisan Review* 6, no. 4 (Summer 1939): 39.

73. See "Agent No. 174 Resigns" as the clearest expression of his search. It was originally published under the title "Operative 174 Resigns," *New Yorker*, 26 August 1939, 19.

74. Fearing to Lambert Davis, Harcourt, Brace Publishers, 1946, Harcourt Brace Papers, Butler Library, Columbia University.

75. Much new information about the relationship between the two men appears in Alan Brinkley, *The Publisher: Henry Luce and His American Century* (New York: Random House, 2010). It is likely that Fearing picked up information about the history of the corporation during the time of his employment there and reworked this variously into his literary portraits.

76. Isaiah Wilner, *The Man Time Forgot: A Tale of Genius, Betrayal, and the Creation of "Time" Magazine* (New York: HarperCollins, 2006).

77. Janoth also brings to mind "mammoth" (of gigantic size and importance), and Delos suggests "Lesbos" (the Greek island that was the home of the poet Sappho, who wrote of love between women).

78. Fearing, *The Big Clock* (New York: New York Review of Books Classics, 2006), 66.

79. See extensive references to the case in Charles Kaiser, *The Gay Metropolis: The Landmark History of Gay Life in America* (Boston: Houghton Mifflin, 2007).

80. Fearing, *The Big Clock*, 40.

81. Ibid., 90.

82. See the following reviews: Lee E. Cannon, "Tick, but No Tock," *Christian Century*, 1 January 1947, 17; Charles Poore, "Books of the *Times*," *New York Times*, 21 September 1946 (online at *New York Times* Article Archive); C. V. Terry, "High-Powered Whodunit in Reverse," *New York Times*, 22 September 1946 (online at *New York Times* Article Archive).

83. Gil, the tavern owner, brings out various objects that he has collected, mostly pieces of junk such as a used football helmet, a stuffed bird, a bowl of foreign coins, or an old toy. He combines these with an ad hoc explanation to accommodate his customers' requests to see items that could not plausibly be on hand—such as a locomotive or a crystal ball. (A steamroller is the item ominously requested by Pauline, who is about to be crushed by the formidable publishing magnate, Janoth.) Gil's objects are not commodities but the raw material of civilization that can be worked up by

the imagination to fulfill needs. Mostly the customers are satisfied and shell out for a drink.

84. Fearing, *The Big Clock*, 114. A literary journal called the *Creative Quarterly* is carried about by one of Janoth's reporters, Edward Orlin. Orlin takes the magazine to Gil's Tavern, where he reads about the postwar Henry James revival, missing out on obtaining the vital information about Stroud that he has been sent to acquire. The name of the journal likely refers to the *Partisan Review* and the overweight reader to Edmund Wilson. Parts of the first or last names of other writers employed by Janoth hint at contemporaries such as Philip Rahv, Lionel and Diana Trilling, Eleanor Clark, and Mary McCarthy. The one writer favored by Stroud, Emory Mafferson, brings to mind F. O. Matthiessen, a Harvard professor and Communist fellow traveler of the time.

85. These invariably possess implications for the larger scheme of the novel, or else unconsciously reveal Stroud's personal fears, such as the danger of self-absorption.

86. In this respect, she closely resembles the Alice Neel who is dubbed the "quintessential bohemian" by Phoebe Hoban in *Alice Neel: The Art of Not Sitting Pretty* (New York: St. Martin's, 2010), 1.

87. Ibid., 3.

88. This reinforces the links in the novel between Patterson and Delos, already suggested by Patterson's ability to instantly perceive Delos as a lesbian. What may be pertinent to the identification of the two women as perhaps deriving from a single prototype is that Patterson's model, Alice Neel, did not physically resemble Patterson in the 1930s but was closer to the blond and attractive Delos. Moreover, Neel was assaulted and nearly killed by her jealous lover, Kenneth Doolittle, in an incident in which most of her paintings were destroyed. As "free women," Delos and Patterson are sisters living with similar risks.

89. This is not to suggest that Bellow became apolitical. A combination of a morality derived from personal life and withdrawal from public activism may have formed the dimensions of a political position, and Bellow became increasingly conservative after the 1950s. Among the many writings on Jewish American authors in the 1940s and 1950s, I especially commend the treatment of Bellow in Morris Dickstein's *Leopards in the Temple: The Transformation of American Fiction* (Cambridge: Harvard University Press, 2002), 62–66; and Mark Shechner's "Jewish Writers" in Daniel Hoffman, *Harvard Guide to Contemporary American Writing* (Cambridge: Belknap Press of Harvard University Press, 1979), 220–25.

CHAPTER TWO

1. Josephine M. Guy, ed., *The Complete Works of Oscar Wilde: Volume IV* (New York: Oxford University Press, 2007), 90.

2. The definitions for these and other critical terms have been provided in the preface and introduction. The most sophisticated survey of cultural policy in the U.S. Communist movement from the 1920s through the 1950s is Andrew Hemingway,

Artists on the Left: American Artists and the Communist Movement, 1926-1956 (New Haven: Yale University Press, 2002). The outstanding book on socialist realism and the novel in the Soviet Union is Katerina Clark, *The Soviet Novel: History as Ritual*, 3rd ed. (Chicago: University of Chicago Press, 2000).

3. The most thorough study of the proletarian novel is Barbara Foley, *Radical Representations: Politics and Form in U.S. Proletarian Fiction, 1929-1941* (Durham, N.C.: Duke University Press, 1993). Foley's personal view is that the Communist-led movement ceased its championing of proletarian literature by the end of 1936 and that the early 1930s proletarian literary movement was doomed not by sectarianism but by its failure to break "with an aesthetic theory that was essentially bourgeois" (128).

4. The most influential polemic is probably Philip Rahv, "Proletarian Literature: A Political Autopsy," *Southern Review* 4, no. 3 (Winter 1939): 610-28.

5. Howard Fast provides numerous examples in *Literature and Reality* (New York: International Publishers, 1950), where he claims that Franz Kafka serves the ruling class in his "equation of man and cockroach" (11) and George Orwell "equated mankind with the inhabitants of a pigsty" (96).

6. Ibid., 62.

7. A characteristic late-1930s discussion of the issue of the continuance of proletarianism was published as "In Defense of a Term," *New Masses* (Literary Section), 12 July 1938, 145-47. This consists of a letter from Walter Lowenfels, then a recent Party recruit, and a reply by Joshua Kunitz, then an authoritative Party spokesman at the time on cultural matters, although no longer technically a Party member. With the post-Popular Front legitimization of the term "People's Literature," Lowenfels proposes to set aside "Proletarian Literature" entirely on the grounds that there is so little poetry (his frame of reference) that has a working-class audience. Kunitz insists that "Proletarian Literature" describes a real phenomenon, alongside people's literature, and that the use of the term will help to increase its presence. By the late 1940s, the prevailing view in Party criticism was that 1930s proletarianism was sectarian only in efforts to restrict its subject matter to the proletariat; what was still valid was for "the proletarian world outlook [to] claim the whole of the world and all of experience as its literary material." See Fast, *Literature and Reality*, 63.

8. Joseph Davis, "*The Grapes of Wrath* Is a Great Proletarian Novel," *Daily Worker*, 4 April 1939, 9.

9. Granville Hicks, "Steinbeck's Powerful New Novel," *New Masses*, 2 May 1939, 22-24.

10. Samuel Sillen, "Sammy Glick and Johnny Dobrejack," *New Masses*, 29 April 1941, 22-24.

11. All reviews by Glenn of Schulberg's books have been reprinted, along with Schulberg's 23 May 1951 testimony before the House Committee on Un-American Activities, in Nicholas Beck, *Budd Schulberg: A Bio-Bibliography* (Lanham, Md.: Scarecrow Press, 2001).

12. Nancy Lynn Schwartz, *The Hollywood Writers' Wars* (New York: Knopf, 1982), 168.

13. Budd Schulberg, "Collision with the Party Line," *Saturday Review of Literature*, 30 August 1952, 6-8, 31-37.

14. "How I Feel about the War," *New Masses*, 29 July 1941, 16-17.

15. See W. L. River, "Conniving and Copulating Ghosts," *Clipper* (June 1941): 20-22; and Edwin Seaver, "Books," *Direction* 4, no. 4 (April-May 1941): 26.

16. To read different treatments from mine of the Schulberg episode, see Kenneth Lloyd Billingsley, *Hollywood Party: How Communism Seduced the American Film Industry in the 1930s and 1940s* (Rocklin, Calif.: Forum, 1998); and Ronald Radosh and Alis Radosh, *Red Star over Hollywood: The Film Colony's Long Romance with the Left* (San Francisco: Encounter, 2005). The only scholar to notice that the *New Masses* review was positive is Saverio Giovacchini, *Hollywood Modernism: Film and Politics in the Age of the New Deal* (Philadelphia: Temple University Press, 2001), 119. Gerald Horne, who does not mention the Glenn reviews, notes that Schulberg was a supporter of the Hollywood Ten in *The Final Victim of the Blacklist: John Howard Lawson, Dean of the Hollywood Ten* (Berkeley: University of California Press, 2006), 206. In accordance with the deepening sectarianism of the Communist Party, Howard Fast signaled out Schulberg for renewed attack even before Schulberg's testimony, in *Literature and Reality*, 56.

17. Fast, *Literature and Reality*, 40.

18. According to Franklin Folsom, executive secretary of the League of American Writers, Gold had addressed the First American Writers Congress, prior to the Popular Front, but "had not found the right voice with which to speak prominently at the Second and Third Congresses," because of their intimate connection with the Popular Front. See Folsom, *Days of Anger, Days of Hope: A Memoir of the League of American Writers, 1937-1942* (Niwot: University Press of Colorado, 1994), 208.

19. The announcement of Gold's lecture appeared in *New Masses*, 3 June 1941, 32, and his talk was published in Michael Folsom, ed., *Mike Gold: A Literary Anthology* (New York: International Publishers, 1972), 243-54, under the title "The Second American Renaissance." Irving Howe and Lewis Coser's *The American Communist Party: A Critical History* (New York: Praeger, 1962) provides an accurate if unforgiving review of the shifts of Communist Party policy after 1939 but omits a consideration of its cultural policy.

20. Samuel Sillen, "The Intellectual under Fire," *New Masses*, 24 June 1941, 8-11.

21. Samuel Sillen, "Too Quiet on the Western Front," *New Masses*, 8 September 1942, 42.

22. See Alvah Bessie, "Telegram from Heaven," *New Masses*, 20 September 1942, 26, and "Drama Review," *New Masses*, 15 December 1942, 30-31. A few weeks after his first piece on Manoff, Bessie argued that his novel should be turned into a film. See *New Masses*, 27 October 1942, 21. For a discussion of James and *Famous All Over Town* (1983), see Marcial González, *Chicano Novels and the Politics of Form: Race, Class, and Reification* (Ann Arbor, Mich.: University of Michigan Press, 2009). Under a pseudonym, the seventy-two-year-old Yale-educated James published what was regarded as an important working-class Chicano novel.

23. Samuel Sillen, "Trends in War Writing," *New Masses*, 8 December 1942, 23–25.

24. See the extraordinary pamphlet by Earl Browder, *Teheran and America* (New York: Workers Library, 1944).

25. Samuel Sillen, "The Challenge of Change," *New Masses*, 16 May 1944, 3–5.

26. "The Man Who Made Good in America" was featured in *Mainstream* 1 (1947).

27. Budd Schulberg to Arthur Mizener, 20 October 1951, Schulberg Papers, Mudd Manuscript Library, Princeton University, Princeton, N.J.

28. Gertrude Stein, *The Making of Americans: Being a History of a Family's Progress* (New York: Albert and Charles Boni, 1926), 3.

29. Highsmith was a member of the Young Communist League at Barnard College from 1939 to 1941.

30. Samuel Sillen to Janet Feder, 7 July 1935, Janet Sillen Papers (current location unknown).

31. Ibid., 3 November 1935.

32. See the discussion of this episode in Alan M. Wald, *Trinity of Passion: The Literary Left and the Antifascist Crusade* (Chapel Hill: University of North Carolina Press, 2007), 210–35.

33. See Stanley Edgar Hyman, *The Armed Vision: A Study in the Methods of Modern Literary Criticism* (New York: Knopf, 1948), 193.

34. Samuel Sillen, "A Guide for Understanding and Struggle on the Cultural Front," *Political Affairs* 17, no. 3 (March 1948): 283–88.

35. Many of the biographical details of Sillen's life are from a letter from Dr. Estelle Fuchs (Sillen's sister) to the author, 29 October 1989; Janet Sillen (his widow), interview with the author, San Diego, March 1990; and private papers of Sillen's in possession of Janet Sillen.

36. Several letters from Virginia Woolf to Samuel Sillen are in the Janet Sillen Papers.

37. Samuel Sillen to Janet Feder, 24 September 1935, Janet Sillen Papers.

38. Janet Sillen interview.

39. This was probably a visit in connection with a tour to promote her book *I Change Worlds* (1935). See Tracy B. Strong and Helene Keyssar, *Right in Her Soul: The Life of Anna Louise Strong* (New York: Random House, 1983), 162.

40. Samuel Sillen to Janet Feder, 14 July 1935, Janet Sillen Papers.

41. Ibid., 8 October 1935.

42. Samuel Sillen, "A Proletarian Novel," *Point: An Independent Literary Quarterly* 1, no. 1 (1934): 54–56.

43. Samuel Sillen to Janet Feder, 13 July 1935, Janet Sillen Papers.

44. Ibid., between August and November 1935.

45. Ibid., 16 August 1935.

46. Ibid., 22 October 1935.

47. Ibid., 16 October 1935.

48. Ibid., 25 October 1935.

49. F. W. Dupee, interview with the author, Carmel, Calif., August 1973.

50. See Walter Ralston, "California Battleground," *New Masses*, 18 February 1936, 22–33; and Mary McCarthy, "Minority Report," *Nation*, 11 March 1936, 326–27.

51. Philip Rahv, "Insidious Innocence," *New Masses*, 16 March 1937, 22–24, and "Readers' Forum," *New Masses*, 23 March 1937, 19.

52. Samuel Sillen to Janet Feder, 24 September 1935, Janet Sillen Papers.

53. Ibid., undated.

54. See Samuel Sillen, "Alexei Tolstoi, Soviet Humanist Fought the Enemies of Culture," *Worker*, 4 March 1945, 14.

55. Samuel Sillen to Granville Hicks, 10 June 1938, Granville Hicks Papers, Special Collections, Syracuse University, Syracuse, N.Y.

56. Ibid.

57. Ibid., 7 February 1939.

58. Ibid., 29 June 1939.

59. Ibid., 10 June 1938.

60. Samuel Sillen, "The People, Yes," *New Masses*, 6 June 1939, 6.

61. Janet Sillen interview.

62. Samuel Sillen, "Thumbs Up on 'The Moon is Down,'" *New Masses*, 14 April 1942, 42.

63. Trilling's essay was "Sermon on a Text from Whitman," *Nation*, 24 February 1945, 15–20.

64. See anecdotes about Jerome in Alan M. Wald, *Exiles from a Future Time: The Forging of the Mid-Twentieth-Century Literary Left* (Chapel Hill: University of North Carolina Press, 2002), 169–71.

65. Czeslaw Milosz, *The Captive Mind* (New York: Knopf, 1953), 191.

66. See Joseph North's uplifting description of the "objective factors" guaranteeing the future of the new Communist publication in "And Fighting All the Way . . . *New Masses*' Journey through a Generation," *New Masses*, 13 January 1948, 3–7.

67. See the assessment of Jerome in Wald, *Exiles from a Future Time*, 163–78.

68. This is cited in Aileen Kraditor's insightful *Jimmy Higgins: The Mental World of the Rank and File American Communist, 1930-58* (Westport, Conn.: Greenwood Press, 1988), 4.

69. Samuel Sillen, "Victory in Europe," *Daily Worker*, 17 January 1945. From Sillen's personal clipping file, in possession of Janet Sillen.

70. Sillen, *Daily Worker*, "Progress of the War," 12 January 1945. From Sillen's personal clipping file, in possession of Janet Sillen.

71. Sillen instantly withdrew from activity but nominally held onto his membership until the Smith Act victim Eugene Dennis completed the terms of his conditional release from prison. Janet Sillen interview.

72. Samuel Sillen, preface to 100th anniversary *Leaves of Grass* edition of *Walt Whitman: Poet of American Democracy* (1944; New York: International Publishers, 1955), 9.

73. Samuel Sillen, *William Cullen Bryant: Selections from His Poetry and Prose* (New York: International Publishers, 1945), 28.

74. Annette T. Rubinstein, "Charles Humboldt, 1910-1964," box 9, file 292, Humboldt Papers, Sterling Memorial Library, Yale University, New Haven, Conn.

75. See *Poetry* 33, no. 4 (January 1929): 227-29, and 37, no. 1 (October 1930): 50-53.

76. For much biographical information, I am indebted to a letter from Mimi Schwartz, 28 May 1992.

77. Rubinstein, "Charles Humboldt, 1910-1964," Humboldt Papers.

78. "Romans," *Poetry* 36, no. 3 (May 1930): 59-65.

79. McGrath quoted by Rubinstein in "Charles Humboldt, 1910-1964," Humboldt Papers.

80. See, for example, Charles Harrison, *Art in Theory, 1900-2000: An Anthology of Changing Ideas* (Oxford: Blackwell, 2002). See the discussion of Humboldt's role on *Art Front* in Gerald M. Monrie, "*Art Front*," *Archives of American Art Journal* 13, no. 3 (1973): 13-19.

81. For the vivid recollections of Humboldt by Harold Rosenberg, see oral history interview with Harold Rosenberg, 17 December 1970-28 January 1973, Oral Histories, Archives of American Art, Smithsonian Institution, Washington, D.C.

82. See Clarence Weinstock, "Three-Penny Opera," *New Masses*, 29 November 1938, 31.

83. The document is undated but refers to activities in the late 1950s. See Humboldt Papers.

84. Mimi Schwartz to author, 28 May 1992.

85. See Charles Humboldt, "The Novel of Action," *Mainstream* 1, no. 4 (Fall 1947): 389-407.

86. Charles Humboldt, "The Lost Cause of Robert Penn Warren," *Masses & Mainstream* 1, no. 5 (July 1948): 8-20.

87. Charles Humboldt, "Communists in Novels," *Masses & Mainstream* 2, no. 6 (June 1949): 13-21, and 2, no. 7 (July 1949): 44-65.

88. Annette T. Rubinstein to author, 13 January 2003.

89. Charles Humboldt to Tom McGrath, 6 January 1959, Humboldt Papers.

90. Column by Michael Gold, *Worker*, 16 August 1959, 8.

91. John Condell, "Hands Off the Imagination," *Mainstream* 12, no. 12 (October 1959): 48-51.

92. Ibid.

93. Mike Newberry, "The Mainstream of What?" *Worker*, 8 November 1959, 10. As Stan Steiner, he would later publish numerous multicultural histories, but his Communist literary connections go back to the 1940s when as an activist in the American Youth for Democracy he launched a short-lived project called the New Writing Foundation.

94. Exchange between Annette Rubinstein and Mike Newberry, "The Arts," *Worker*, 3 January 1960, 10.

95. Ibid.

96. *Mainstream*, November 1960, 47.

97. The phrase appears in "A Sort of Song" (1944), among other places.
98. A carbon of this letter, dated 4 May 1956, was given to me by Annette Rubinstein.
99. Charles Humboldt, "The Salt of Freedom," *Mainstream* 9, no. 9 (October 1956): 21.
100. I am grateful to *Guardian* writer Michael Munk for a 3 March 2008 email with recollections of the last days of Humboldt.
101. Charles Humboldt, "The Art of Ingmar Bergman," *Massachusetts Review* 4, no. 2 (Winter 1963): 352.
102. Charles Humboldt, "The Voice Persisted until Death," *Trace* 46 (Summer 1962): 217–22.
103. Charles Humboldt, "The Fifth Season," *Mainstream* 10, no. 6 (June 1957): 32–33. The original manuscript in the Humboldt Papers indicates that the dedication was "To Mimi."
104. The only time that the gentle George Oppen seems to rise to anger in his 436-page collection of correspondence is in reply to a criticism of him made by Humboldt; see Rachel Blau DuPlessis, ed., *The Selected Letters of George Oppen* (Durham, N.C.: Duke University Press, 1990), 59.
105. Two occasions when he did so was in "To the Mad Hatters," *New Masses*, 11 March 1947, 13–17, and "Nest of Vipers," *New Masses*, 29 April 1947, 24–26.
106. Qtd. in Rubinstein, "Charles Humboldt, 1910–1964."
107. See Charles Humboldt, "The Atkinson Formula," *New Masses*, 22 October 1946, 11–12.
108. Humboldt, "The Voice Persisted until Death," 217–22.

CHAPTER THREE

1. "The Long Retreat" is the title of the concluding chapter of Walter Rideout's *The Radical Novel in the United States, 1900–1954: Some Interrelations of Literature and Society* (Cambridge, Mass.: Harvard University Press, 1956).
2. See Harvey Klehr and John Earl Haynes, *The American Communist Movement: Storming Heaven Itself* (New York: Twayne, 1992), 100–101.
3. The Cultural Division was temporarily disbanded in the early 1950s, then reconstituted in 1954–55. The work was supervised by a sub-body of the Party's Central Committee known as the Cultural Commission and led by V. J. Jerome. This information was provided in emails of 7 and 14 December 1999 from Irwin Silber, who was active in both the writers and music sections.
4. An accurate history of the National Council of the Arts, Sciences and Professions is contained in Andrew Hemingway, *Artists on the Left: American Artists and the Communist Movement, 1926–1956* (New Haven: Yale University Press, 2002), 195–98.
5. The premier study of People's Songs is Robbie Lieberman, *My Song Is My Weapon* (Urbana: University of Illinois Press, 1995).

6. Cohen joined the National Committee for the Defense of Political Prisoners delegation that investigated the condition of miners in Kentucky in November 1931; endorsed the Communist Party presidential campaign in 1932; and was a founding member of the League of American Writers in 1935. He remained active in the league to the end of the Hitler-Stalin Pact, during which time he served on its national council, taught at its New York School, and signed the call for its Third Congress. Cohen's name is conspicuously absent from the Fourth Congress call in 1942, by which time the league was supporting the Allied intervention. FBI records of the League of American Writers designated him as still active in the Hollywood chapter in 1942.

7. Kenneth Fearing, "Other Recent Spring Novels," *New York Times Book Review*, 13 May 1945, 21.

8. Hy Hurwitz, "The Returned G.I.," *Boston Globe*, 23 May 1945, 13.

9. This is a traditional topic in studies of 1930s literary radicalism. See Sylvia Jenkins Cook, "The Gastonia Strike and Proletarian Possibilities," *From Tobacco Road to Route 66: The Poor White in Southern Fiction* (Chapel Hill: University of North Carolina Press, 1976).

10. For further information on Brown and Bonosky, see Alan M. Wald, "Lloyd Brown and the African American Literary Left," foreword to *Iron City*, by Lloyd Brown, Northeastern Library of Black Literature Reprint (Boston: Northeastern University Press, 1994), vii–xxxvii; and Wald, "The Wager of Benedict Bulmanis," introduction to *Burning Valley*, by Philip Bonosky (Urbana: University of Illinois Press, 1997), vii–xxxv. For Alfred Hayes, see Wald, *Exiles from a Future Time*, 214–27.

11. A fuller study of Maund can be found in Alan M. Wald, "A Southern Rebel in Cold War America," introduction to *The Big Boxcar*, by Alfred Maund (Urbana: University of Illinois Press, 1998), vii–xxx.

12. For an examination of Le Sueur's career, see Wald, *Exiles from a Future Time*, 95–102.

13. Quoted in John Gassner and Sidney Thomas, eds., *The Nature of Art* (New York: Crown, 1964), 153.

14. See Barbara Foley, *Radical Representations: Politics and Form in U.S. Proletarian Fiction, 1929–1941* (Durham, N.C.: Duke University Press, 1993).

15. More details about Stevenson's career can be found in Alan M. Wald, "Stevenson, Philip Edward (1896–1965)," in *Encyclopedia of Literature and Politics*, ed. M. Keith Booker (Westport, Conn.: Greenwood, 2005), 697–99.

16. More on the personal and political life of Neugass can be found in Alan M. Wald, "Hero — International Brigade," review of *War Is Beautiful: An American Ambulance Driver in the Spanish Civil War*, by James Neugass, *Against the Current* 17 (November–December 2009): 17–20.

17. Giles's career is discussed in Alan M. Wald, "Marxist Literary Resistance to the Cold War," in *Cold War Literature: Writing the Global Conflict*, ed. Andrew Hammond (New York: Routledge, 2006), 100–113.

18. In the "Special War Issue," *New Masses*, 1 July 1941, 16–17.

19. See Alexander Saxton, preface to *The Great Midland* (Urbana: University of Illinois Press, 1987).
20. Saxton, *The Great Midland*, 192-95.
21. See Harold Bloom, *The Anxiety of Influence: A Theory of Poetry* (New York: Oxford University Press, 1997).
22. For the belated recognition of Stephanie's centrality, see the crucial analysis by Constance Coiner, "The Old Left and Cross-Gendered Writing," along with Alexander Saxton's introduction and "To Constance Coiner" in *The Great Midland*, xi-xxx.
23. See Howard Fast, "Railroad Men," *Masses & Mainstream* 1, no. 9 (November 1948): 81-84.
24. Saxton, introduction to *The Great Midland*, xxv.
25. Kenneth Fearing, *New and Selected Poems* (Bloomington: University of Indiana Press, 1956), xv.
26. Josephine Herbst, "The Ruins of Memory," *Nation*, 14 April 1956, 302-4.
27. See the substantial discussion in Elinor Langer, *Josephine Herbst: The Story She Could Never Tell* (Boston: Little Brown, 1984), 245-58.
28. To clarify these "histrionics," Light reveals that he was recently dismissed from a government job: "His 'enemies' had belatedly discovered that he had been too assiduous, several years before, in behalf of the defeated cause of Republican Spain. Then, he confessed, he had signed some petitions showing concern for the underdogs. Finally, he had ventured to protest that all Germans might not be evil. That gave a little ammunition to everyone." Josephine Herbst, *Somewhere the Tempest Fell* (New York: Charles Scribner's Sons, 1947), 232.
29. Ibid., 272-74.
30. Johns had linked up with Adam Snow in 1935 in Europe, at the advent of the Popular Front. Both had, like Harry and Bart, Left sympathies, although the details of them are never provided. For undisclosed reasons, Johns now feels "slugged by history" and doubts that he any longer believes in progress. He frequently observes that he is politically and personally lost, but one thing that he claims to understand is the suicide of the German poet Ernest Toller (1893-1939): "I understand it too damn well. . . . [He] died in despair that one plan after another for the redemption of the world had failed." Johns himself mourns "for the shambles that had overtaken the promise." By promise, does John mean the pacifist one of ending international wars, the liberal one of the triumph of reason, or the Soviet one of a new world? The postmortem goes no further. Herbst, *Somewhere the Tempest Fell*, 130-31.
31. It is disclosed early in the novel's narrative that, while living in Italy in the late 1930s, Adam collaborated with members of an anti-Mussolini underground. There he was so traumatized by the transformation of a comrade, Portalini, into a traitor that he subsequently imagined that the same route was being followed by another associate, Pietro. Upon encountering Pietro on the street, Adam ironically had given him the antifascist salute, and he later learns, from the mysterious Zabo, that this had triggered Pietro's arrest and execution. Realizing that he is now judged an informer

by virtue of his inadvertent gesture, Adam longs to return to Italy following the impending defeat of Mussolini and make contact with his old comrades to ensure that a new order will truly come to pass.

32. Isidor Schneider, "The Fetish of Simplicity," *Nation*, 18 February 1931, 184–86.

33. By 1987, the subject came to national attention with the publication of Charlotte Nekola and Paula Rabinowitz, eds., *Writing Red: An Anthology of American Women Writers, 1930–1940* (New York: Feminist Press, 1987).

34. See the 1,000-page-long volume by Cathy N. Davidson and Linda Wagner-Martin, *The Oxford Companion to Women's Writing in the United States* (New York: Oxford University Press, 1995). A perspective on the novel by women in the 1940s and early 1950s is difficult to locate in Emory Elliot, ed., *The Columbia History of the American Novel: New Views* (New York: Columbia University Press, 1991), and nothing has appeared since then to correct the situation. One recent exception to this record: Gordon Hutner's study of the middle class and fiction over four decades, *What America Read: Taste, Class, and the Novel, 1920–1960* (Chapel Hill: University of North Carolina Press, 2009), has a chapter surveying the 1940s and a few pages on "Invisible Women." His concern is fiction addressed to the postwar reinvention of women by authors of both sexes, and he concludes that "in part, American women writers would be slighted in the years that followed for not being veterans of the recent war" (268). Among the few sources for literary recovery is Diana Trilling's anthology of her book reviews from the *Nation*, *Reviewing the Forties* (New York: Harcourt, 1978). While Trilling provides no synthesis, there are at least brief, often insightful, commentaries on novels by Eleanor Clark, Elizabeth Hardwick, Ruth McKenney, Carson McCullers, Edita Morris, Dawn Powell, Elinor Rice, Caroline Slade, Betty Smith, and Eudora Welty—almost all women with left-wing backgrounds. A closer look at the literary substructure of the era, beneath the exterior of the few works widely acclaimed at the time or later (usually by Eudora Welty and Carson McCullers), provides evidence of the expansion of women writers into new genres, including those associated with pulp fiction and mystery. In the last years of the decade, there are also landmarks of African American women's fiction by two authors with left-wing backgrounds, Ann Petry's *The Street* (New York: World Publishing Co., 1946) and Dorothy West's *The Living Is Easy* (New York: Random House, 1948). Postwar conservative fiction by women made a strong debut as well: not only Ayn Rand's *The Fountainhead* (Indianapolis: Bobbs-Merrill, 1943) but also a novel-a-year from future John Birch Society spokeswoman Taylor Caldwell and two from Southern Agrarian Caroline Gordon.

35. Reports are quoted and summarized in a 27 September 1939 letter to Johnson from Simon and Schuster, Inc., signed by Maria Leiper, Johnson Collection, Washington University Library, St. Louis, Mo.

36. See the discussion in Kathy Cantley Ackerman, *The Heart of Revolution: The Radical Life and Novels of Olive Dargan* (Knoxville: University of Tennessee Press, 2004), 34–40. Ackerman assumes that Dargan must have become disillusioned with the Communist Party at the time of the 1939 Hitler-Stalin Pact, but there is no clear documentation regarding the matter.

37. See Dee Garrison, *Mary Heaton Vorse: The Life of an American Insurgent* (Philadelphia: Temple University Press, 1989).

38. A formulaic Dell Mystery called *The Visitor* appeared in 1944, but short fiction submitted under the joint pseudonym "George Newton, Jr." was universally rejected. See Abe Ravitz, *Leane Zugsmith: Thunder on the Left* (New York: International, 1992), 108. Abe Ravitz, interview with the author, Redondo Beach, Calif., July 1990.

39. Myra Page, interview with the author, New York, September 1990.

40. For Page's version of her life, see Christina Looper Baker, *In a Generous Spirit: A First-Person Biography of Myra Page* (Urbana: University of Illinois Press, 1996). See my discussion of the novel in Alan M. Wald, *Writing from the Left* (London: Verso, 1994), 92–94.

41. This is one of the revelations of her autobiography, *The Secrets of Grown-Ups* (New York: McGraw-Hill, 1979).

42. Nevertheless, Caspary's numerous later novels are fun to read and contain informative portraits of independent women. In particular, *Bedelia* (New York: Blakiston, 1945) is an insightful study of gender roles in a marriage that occurs on the eve of World War I.

43. See the discussion of Caspary's political career and her role as a Jewish American author of *The White Girl* (New York: J. H. Sears, 1929) in Alan M. Wald, *Trinity of Passion: The Literary Left and the Antifascist Crusade* (Chapel Hill: University of North Carolina Press, 2007), 192–93. Caspary has been the subject of several well-researched and insightful essays by A. B. Emrys. One is "Laura, Vera, and Wilkie: The Sensation Roots of a *Noir* Novel" in *Clues* 23, no. 3 (Spring 2005): 5–13. The other appears as the afterword to the 2005 Feminist Press edition of *Laura* in its Femme Fatales: Women Write Pulp series.

44. This description of the process is reported in Caspary, *The Secrets of Grown-Ups*, 188–96.

45. Vera Caspary, *Laura* (New York: Feminist Press, 2005), 167.

46. In light of the references to Lydecker's dependence on a cane (used as a weapon) and McPherson's receiving a wound in the leg requiring a steel implant, the fact that Woollcott's close friend Duranty had only one leg (the result of an accident) may have some significance.

47. Caspary, *Laura*, 168.

48. The relations between Laura and Diane suggest a parallel in their efforts to negotiate sexual and social power. Both are exploited by Shelby Carpenter, who is drawn by Diane's superior physical beauty and Laura's status in the advertising profession. The women are linked through Laura's ad campaign called "Lady Lilith," for which Diane serves as photographic model. *Lady Lilith* was the well-known painting by D. G. Rossetti depicting a female as both an excessively sexualized object and empowered woman. That Laura's mistaken attraction to Carpenter grew out of misplaced female desire is suggested by the perverse eroticism of Diane's being murdered while naked (she had quickly donned Laura's mules and robe to answer Lydecker's knock at the door).

CHAPTER FOUR

1. The query had a disturbing resemblance to the ultimatum of federal and state investigating committees at the time: "Tell us whether you have ever been or are now a member of the Communist Party?" This version of the question appears in David Holmes, *Stalking the Academic Communist: Intellectual Freedom and the Firing of Alex Novikoff* (Hanover, N.H.: University Press of New England, 1989), 68.

2. Junius Irving Scales and Richard Nickson, *Cause at Heart: A Former Communist Remembers* (Athens: University of Georgia Press, 1987), 223–24; and the author's interview with Scales, New York City, May 1993. For information on the approach to this issue in the Edenville section of Los Angeles, see Daniel Hurewitz, *Bohemian Los Angeles and the Making of Modern Politics* (Berkeley: University of California Press, 2007), 236. Jim Kepner, an early gay rights activist and columnist for the daily *People's World* in 1949, claimed that he was expelled from the Communist Party for homosexuality. See David W. Dunlap, "Jim Kepner, in 70s, Is Dead; Historian of Gay Rights Effort," *New York Times*, 30 November, 1997, C26. Yet he continued to write for the paper. See the unpublished essay by Aaron Lecklider, "'Fight Hardens in My Fists': Gay Male Sexuality and the American Left from the Popular Front to the McCarthy Years," for more details as well as excellent commentary on the relationship of early gay rights organizations to the Communist Party experience and the impact of McCarthyism.

3. See Peter Drucker, "The New Sexual Radicalism," *Against the Current* 146 (May–June 2010): 23–28. For an overview of the Left and homosexuality, see Gert Hekma, Harry Oosterhaus, and James Huxley, eds., *Gay Men and the Sexual History of the Political Left* (New York: Hayworth Press, 1995); and Sherry Wolf, *Sexuality and Socialism: History, Politics and Theory of LGTB Liberation* (Chicago: Haymarket, 2009). For a unique perspective, see Christopher Phelps, "A Neglected Document on Socialism and Sex," *Journal of the History of Sexuality* 16 (January 2007): 1–13.

4. The authoritative study of this development is George Chauncey, *Gay New York: Gender, Urban Culture, and the Making of the Gay Male World, 1840–1940* (New York: Basic Books, 1994). A recent theoretical work on Marxism and queer theory with case studies from American culture is Kevin Floyd, *The Reification of Desire: Toward a Queer Marxism* (Minneapolis: University of Minnesota Press, 2009).

5. See Stuart Timmons, *The Trouble with Harry Hay: Founder of the Modern Gay Movement* (Boston: Alyson Publications, 1990), 69. Hay sometimes wrote as Eann McDonald.

6. The story is told in John Sanford, *A Very Good Land to Fall With* (Santa Rosa, Calif.: Black Sparrow Press, 1987), 284–86. A sense of guilt about the treatment of homosexuals in the Communist-led movement is also reflected in the 1971 novel *Between the Hills and the Sea* (New York: Doubleday, 1971), by former Communist Party members Bert and Kayta Gilden (writing as K. B. Gilden). The memory of the removal of a gay union organizer, Scottsy, during a strike, because he is allegedly a security

risk, comes to haunt the pro-Communist activists in later years as their movement crumbles under the simultaneous blows of repression and disillusionment.

7. Timmons, *The Trouble with Harry Hay*, 109. See the excellent biography by Eric A. Gordon, *Mark the Music: The Life and Work of Marc Blitzstein* (New York: St. Martin's Press, 1989).

8. Irwin Silber, email to the author, 7 December 1999. Hays's biographer, on the other hand, maintains that his non-membership was due to Hays's anti-authoritarian personality. See Doris Willens, *Lonesome Traveler: The Life of Lee Hays* (New York: W. W. Norton, 1988), 233.

9. Arthur Laurents, *Original Story By: A Memoir of Broadway and Hollywood* (New York: Knopf, 2000), 36.

10. For further details, see Martin Duberman, *The Worlds of Lincoln Kirstein* (New York: Knopf, 2007); Barry Seldes, *Leonard Bernstein: The Political Life of an American Musician* (Berkeley: University of California Press, 2009); Howard Pollack, *Aaron Copland: The Life and Work of an Uncommon Man* (Urbana: University of Illinois Press, 2000); and Deborah Jowitt, *Jerome Robbins: His Life, His Theater, His Dance* (New York: Simon and Schuster, 2005).

11. See Arthur D. Kahn, *The Education of a 20th Century Political Animal: Book 2: Resisting Truman's Loyalty Oaths and McCarthy-ite Hysteria, 1946-1959* (Bloomington, Ind.: Author House, 2009), 104.

12. See the discussion of Wilson in relation to the *New Masses* in Alan M. Wald, *Exiles from a Future Time: The Forging of the Mid-Twentieth-Century Literary Left* (Chapel Hill: University of North Carolina Press, 2002), 126-27. Also, see the T. C. Wilson Papers at the Beinecke Rare Book and Manuscript Library, Yale University, with their descriptions of his attraction to male soldiers and sailors, and the references to Wilson in Mary Beth Hinton, ed., *The Diaries of Marya Zaturenska, 1938-1944* (Syracuse, N.Y.: Syracuse University Press, 2002). These sources suggest that Wilson had a period of sympathy for Trotskyism in 1939, but then returned to Communism for a while in the early 1940s. They also indicate that Horace Gregory and Marya Zaturenska were fully aware of Wilson's homosexuality and that Gregory served as his advisor and confidant.

13. Except for Paul Peters, the political, marital, and sexual information about all the others now appears in scholarly books. Peters was at first married to the artist Katherine Larkin (sister of Margaret Larkin and sister-in-law of Albert Maltz) and later lived with his partner Ivan von Auw, a well-known literary agent. During the Cold War, they moved to the Caribbean. Von Auw died in Puerto Rico, and Peters was subsequently reported to be in London and Portugal. See Tom Nolan, *Three Chords for Beauty's Sake: The Life of Artie Shaw* (New York: W. W. Norton, 2010), 186; and Douglas Gilbert, "Sugar Coatings Have No Place in His Writings," *New York World Telegram*, 19 May 1934, 14. Willard Maas was a poet and filmmaker. See references to Maas in Alan Filreis, *Modernism from Left to Right: Wallace Stevens, the Thirties, and Literary Radicalism* (Cambridge: Cambridge University Press, 1994) and *Counter-*

Revolution of the Word: The Conservative Attack on Modern Poetry, 1945–1960 (Chapel Hill: University of North Carolina Press, 2008); and Alan Filreis, email to the author, 23 April 1994.

14. Alex Williams, "Notoriety in a Tight Embrace," *New York Times*, 10 June 2010, E9.

15. In *Memoirs of a Bastard Angel* (New York: William Morrow and Company, 1988), 77, Harold Norse claims that he coined the term in 1939 and included it in a letter to W. H. Auden, who subsequently used it in the *Partisan Review* two years later. Norse states that his intention was to identify a "global sexual community." However, there is no evidence that Auden used the phrase until many years later, in his book review of George Woodcock's *The Paradox of Oscar Wilde*, "A Playboy of the Western World: St. Oscar, the Homintern Martyr," *Partisan Review* 17 (1950): 390–94. For further consideration of the term, see the unpublished essay by Aaron Lecklider, "Picturing the Herrin Massacre: Paul Cadmus's 'Unspeakably Bad and Gory' Study of Radical Politics and Queer Desire." For a first-rate consideration of the anxiety caused by this somewhat closeted gay presence, see Michael S. Sherry, *Gay Artists in Modern American Culture: An Imagined Conspiracy* (Chapel Hill: University of North Carolina Press, 2007).

16. Some of these individuals, such as Elizabeth Gurley Flynn (1890–1964) and Grace Hutchins (1902–68), lived with other women in what has come to be known as a "Boston marriage."

17. On the career of Martha Dodd, see Kathlene McDonald, "Postwar Left Feminism and Anti-Fascist Resistance in the Cultural Work of Martha Dodd," in *Invisible Suburbs: Recovering Protest Fiction in the 1950s*, ed. Josh Lukin (Jackson: University Press of Mississippi, 2008), 41–61.

18. Eleanor Flexner was the author of *American Playwrights: 1918–1938* (New York: Simon and Schuster, 1938) and *Century of Struggle: The Women's Rights Movement* (Cambridge, Mass.: Harvard University Press, 1959). She did not reveal that she had held Communist Party membership (she joined in 1934) until 1981. For Highsmith's politics, see n. 29 on p. 338.

19. These are available in the Herbst Collection, Yale University Library, New Haven, Conn.

20. For details of Pitts's intimate life, I am grateful to Debra White for the information she obtained through research undertaken for a graduate research essay at Emory University in 1997, "My Life Had Stood: A Loaded Gun—The Dissent of Rebecca Pitts, Indianapolis Poet and Philosopher."

21. Rebecca E. Pitts, "The American Scene and American Character Types in the Representative Work of Henry James" (M.A. thesis, University of Chicago, 1930).

22. Two of Pitts's most important writings are "Women and Communism," *New Masses*, 19 February 1935, 14–18, and "Women and the *New Masses*," *New Masses*, 1 December 1936, 15–18.

23. White, "My Life Had Stood."

24. Wright mentioned the importance of Pitts's early 1930s writing in a manu-

script probably from the late 1940s, "Writing from the Left," unpublished typescript, 3, Richard Wright Archives, Yale University Library, New Haven, Conn. The "Woman Question" inspired Wright in drafting a novel in 1939 called "Little Sister," the unpublished manuscript of which is in the Richard Wright Archives.

25. Pitts is referred to many times throughout George T. Blakey's *Creating a Hoosier Self-Portrait: The Federal Writers Project in Indiana* (Bloomington: Indiana University Press, 2005).

26. Micki McGee, *Yadoo: Making American Culture* (New York: Columbia University Press, 2008), 7.

27. White, "My Life Had Stood."

28. Rebecca Pitts, "Something to Believe In," *New Masses*, 13 March 1934, 14; "Prayer and the Incarnation," *Hibbert Journal* 51–52 (April 1953): 242–46; "Are We 'Our Own Worst Enemies'?" *Womankind*, cited in Allegra Stewart's foreword to *Brief Authority: Fragments of One Woman's Testament*, by Rebecca E. Pitts (New York: Vantage, 1986).

29. The Dickinson poem is called "My Life Had Stood—a Loaded Gun."

30. Pitts, *Brief Authority*, 1.

31. Pitts, "World Sacrifice," *Brief Authority*, 61.

32. Pitts, *Brief Authority*, 10, 36.

33. Ibid., 62.

34. White, "My Life Had Stood."

35. Parker Tyler, "Politics and Art," *New International* 4, no. 5 (May 1938): 158–59, and "Magic and Machine," *New International* 4, no. 10 (October 1938): 316.

36. See the discussion of *The Young and Evil* (Paris: Obelisk Press, 1933) and *Butterfly Man* (New York: Macauley, 1934) in the context of similar writings of the era in Roger Austen, *Playing the Game: The Homosexual Novel in America* (Indianapolis: Bobbs-Merrill, 1977). For biographical information on Levenson, see Richard L. Levenson to the author, 25 August 1998. In Al Richmond's autobiography, *A Long View from the Left: Memoirs of an American Revolutionary* (New York: Houghton Mifflin, 1975), 259–60, there is a description of a prolific *Daily Worker* staff member named Lew Levinson [sic], "a mild-mannered man and no political heavy," who used pen names such as "Benjamin Cardozo" and "Annette Castle" in pieces aimed at striking "a popular chord." Richmond believed that his colleague also wrote prolifically for pulp serials.

37. Lew Levenson, "California Casualty List," *Nation*, 29 August 1934, 245.

38. Lester Rodney to the author, 6 August 1991. Rodney recalls that Levenson ran the *Daily Worker*'s arts and culture section and included more regular play and film reviews. Not only did he impress his coworkers with a knowledge of theater, art, dance, and music, but he also instituted a weekly sports section. He often used the names "Charles Dexter" and "Scorer" for his own writings and won membership for the paper in the hitherto sacrosanct Baseball Writers Association, which gave him entry to press boxes. Levenson was about five feet ten inches tall and seemed to have one bad eye—he wore a smoked lens over it—and had a reputation as a womanizer. An episode in which he startled a young female volunteer at the paper by pursuing

her around his desk was one of a number of incidents that kept Levenson from being taken sufficiently seriously as a Communist and placed on the *Daily Worker* editorial board.

39. The *New York Times* covered the accusations against WPA writers in a number of front-page articles: "Somervell Drops 300 of His Staff," 22 August 1936, 1; "Alsberg Denies He Is a Red," 2 November 1936, 1; "Anti-Red Writers Barred from WPA, Witness Declares," 16 September 1938, 1, 16; "House Group Told of Red Domination over WPA Writers," 2 May 1939, 1, 6.

40. Letter from Richard L. Levenson to the author, 25 August 1998.

41. The poems were "There Was a Man," *New Masses*, 1 June 1929, 12, and "Puget Sound: A Contrast," *New Masses*, December 1929, 12.

42. The full story of Brinig is well told in fictionalized form in Earl Ganz, *The Taos Truth Game: A Novel* (Albuquerque: University of New Mexico Press, 2006).

43. Baldwin alone moved into Left activism during the civil rights movement and even wrote for *Freedomways*, which had ties to the Communist Party.

44. Most information about Bowles and Communism comes from his own writings and is summarized in Christopher Sawyer-Laucanno, *An Invisible Spectator: A Biography of Paul Bowles* (New York: Weidenfeld and Nicholson, 1989), 162, 205–6, and 218. He started reading the *New Masses* faithfully as an adolescent, but his positive feelings about Communism did not manifest themselves in terms of investigation into the Party itself until 1935.

45. Two provocative studies of the relationship of Paul Bowles's fiction to Communism during the Cold War are Brian Edwards, "Sheltering Screens: Paul Bowles and Foreign Relations," *American Literary History* 17, no. 2 (Summer 2005): 307–34; and Arthur Redding, *Turncoats, Traitors, and Fellow Travelers: Culture and Politics of the Early Cold War* (Jackson: University Press of Mississippi, 2008), 110–32.

46. An intensification of anti-homosexual prejudice combined with government persecution occurred simultaneously with the Red Scare. See David K. Johnson, *The Lavender Scare: The Cold War Persecution of Gays and Lesbians in Federal Government* (Chicago: University of Chicago Press, 2004). The Left, however, did not defend homosexuals and anti-McCarthy forces were implicated in homophobic smear tactics; see Andrea Friedman, "The Smearing of Joe McCarthy: The Lavender Scare, Gossip, and Cold War Politics," *American Quarterly* 57, no. 4 (December 2005): 1105–29. For more information and perspectives on this phenomenon, see Louise Robbins, "The Library of Congress and Federal Loyalty Programs, 1947–1956: No 'Communists or Cocksuckers,'" *Library Quarterly* 64, no. 4 (October 1994): 365–85; Barbara Epstein, "Anti-Communism, Homophobia, and the Construction of Masculinity in the Postwar U.S.," *Critical Sociology* 20, no. 3 (1994): 21–44; and Lise E. Davis, "The FBI's Lesbian, Eleanor Roosevelt, and Other Tales from the Red Scare," *Rethinking Marxism* 21, no. 4 (October 2009): 621–33.

47. See Scott Donaldson, *John Cheever: A Biography* (New York: Random House, 1998), 78.

48. In an autobiographical statement submitted to *Story*, McCullers states that in

the winter of 1935, she did her part in promulgating Communism and quotes Marx. This was never published in the magazine. In the late 1930s and early 1940s, many of McCullers's most intimate friends had backgrounds in the Communist cultural movement, such as Edward Newhouse and Louis Untermeyer. See "Carson Smith, Author of *Wunderkind*," December 1936, *Story* Magazine Archives, Princeton, N.J.; and Virginia Spencer Carr, *The Lonely Hunter: A Biography of Carson McCullers* (New York: Doubleday, 1975). For the full story of 7 Middagh Street, see Sherrill Tippins, *February House* (New York: Houghton Mifflin, 2003).

49. Gleason, who came from a Protestant family in Boston, also published Popular Front magazines such as *Friday* and *Salute* and was not shy about declaring his own pro-Communist views before the Cold War. In 1947, Gleason was interrogated, fined $500, and given a three-month suspended prison sentence by HUAC for refusing to provide information about the Anti-Fascist Refugee Committee. By the 1950s, as president of the Association of Comics Magazine Publishers, he was targeted by the "Anti-Comics Crusade," in which Fredric Wertham (1895–1981), who had had his own associations with the Communist movement, was central. Gleason's publishing career ended in 1955, and, while remaining a radical, he afterward went into real estate and then ran a small business on Cape Cod selling patriotic home ornaments featuring the American eagle. David Hajdu, *The Ten-Cent Plague: The Great Comic Book Scare and How It Changed America* (New York: Farrar, Straus and Giroux, 2008). Other information comes from Brett Dakin, telephone interview with the author, 30 June 2010, and Dakin's short manuscript "Lev Gleason: The Family Speaks." Dakin is a relative of Gleason's and is preparing a biography of him.

50. See Barry Werth, *The Scarlet Professor* (New York: Doubleday, 2001), 100–101. Werth mentions that around the same time, Capote had a brief relationship with Howard Doughty, a Smith College colleague, who had also been pro-Communist in the 1930s. Arvin seems to have followed the political path of Granville Hicks to anticommunist liberalism after the Hitler-Stalin Pact, but not as publicly or vociferously.

51. His presence in the organizations is noted in Hazel Rowley, *Richard Wright: The Life and Times* (New York: Henry Holt, 2001), 109; Jerre Mangione, *The Dream and the Deal: The Federal Writers Project, 1935–43* (Boston: Little, Brown, 1972), 127–28; and Franklin Folsom, *Days of Anger, Days of Hope: A Memoir of the League of American Writers, 1937–1942* (Niwot: University Press of Colorado, 1994), 284.

52. Mangione, *The Dream and the Deal*, 127.

53. Edwin Berry Burgum, "Two Realistic Novels," *New York Teacher*, March 1937, 24–25; and Mark Seinfelt, *Final Drafts: Suicides of World-Famous Authors* (New York: Prometheus Books, 1999), 384.

54. James Levin, *The Gay Novel in America* (New York: Garland, 1991), 73.

55. James Baldwin, "Without Grimly Gaiety," *New Leader* 30 (September 1947): 12.

56. Anthony Slide, *Lost Gay Novels: A Reference Guide to Fifty Works from the First Half of the Twentieth Century* (New York: Harrington Park Press, 2003), 82. Wilhelm Stekel, a dissenting disciple of Freud, committed suicide in London.

57. James Baldwin, "Nursery Rhyme," *New Masses*, 21 May 1946, 10.

58. Miller contributed theater reviews to the *New Masses* as "Matt Wayne."

59. Smith was active on the Left in the Minneapolis area and was a friend of Meridel Le Sueur's. He published eight books of poetry and one of short reviews and left an unpublished manuscript. One substantial study of his poetry, with only vague references to a Leftist idealism, is James Naiden, "Motions of Grace: The Poetry of Ray Smith," *North Stone Review* 12 (1995): 111–50.

60. Geraldine Murphy wrote about the early politics of James Baldwin in "Subversive Anti-Stalinism: Race and Sexuality in the Early Essays of James Baldwin," *ELH* 63, no. 4 (Winter 1996): 1021–46, but her work omits the first half of the 1940s.

61. See Michel Fabre, *Black American Writers in France, 1840–1980* (Urbana: University of Illinois Press, 1991), 203; and F. Folsom, *Days of Anger, Days of Hope*, 77.

62. Lesley Conger, "Jimmy on East 15th Street," *African American Review* 29, no. 4 (1995): 557–66. Conger was a member of the Young People's Socialist League. Saville Sax was one of the two people with whom a "commune" in the form of a common living arrangement was fantasized by Conger and Baldwin in 1945; other associations between Baldwin and Sax are also described. According to the *New York Times*, Sax had recruited his Harvard roommate Theodore Hall to engage in espionage, and in 1944 Sax approached a Soviet trading company in New York to supply critical information about the atomic bomb project obtained from Hall. See Alan Cowell, "Theodore Hall, Prodigy and Atomic Spy, Dies at 74," *New York Times*, 10 November 1999, 24. That the poem "Nursery Rhyme" was written by Baldwin is confirmed by the author's name under which it was published and its style, recalling the early poetic influence of Countee Cullen and Langston Hughes. Moreover, the writer Lesley Conger shared an apartment with Baldwin in 1945; she has in her possession a carbon copy of "Nursery Rhyme" that was given to her by Baldwin together with several of his rejection slips dated that year.

63. See Stan Weir, "Meetings with James Baldwin," *Against the Current* 18 (January–February 1989): 35–41. Weir gives the impression that Baldwin understood the ins and outs of the Trotskyist movement. Baldwin's main objection to the Workers Party concerned its attitude toward homosexuality; homosexuals were not expelled from membership if discovered, but the subject was simply not discussed. In *James Baldwin: A Biography* (New York: Knopf, 1984), David Leeming states that Baldwin was briefly a member of the Young People's Socialist League and a "Trotskyite" but does not provide details or clear sources (46). His bibliography begins only in 1947. Regarding the *New Leader*, see the unusual reviews by Parker Tyler and Baldwin in the issue of 20 September 1947, 12.

64. I've tried reading the poem from the opposite direction, interpreting the "sunless dawn" as a stand-in for the persistence of a fruitless existence, but such a reading contradicts not only its prophetic voice but its consistent theme that one's hopelessness will end at dawn.

65. James Campbell, *Talking at the Gates: A Life of James Baldwin* (New York: Viking, 1991), 21.

66. Baldwin, "Nursery Rhyme."

67. For Arvin, see the book-length study by Barry Werth, *The Scarlet Professor* (New York: Doubleday, 2001). For Matthiessen, see Douglas Shand-Tucci, *The Crimson Letter: Harvard, Homosexuality, and the Shaping of American Culture* (New York: St. Martin's, 2003), 149-55.

68. Dana's role as a controversial figure is the centerpiece of Shand-Tucci's *The Crimson Letter*, especially the chapter titled "Pal Hal," 129-37.

69. Dana was a source of many sensational headlines in the *New York Times*. Articles that mentioned him can be found in its online archive: "Columbia Ousts Two Professors," 2 October 1917; "Longfellow's Son Cuts Off Nephews," 4 October 1922; "Prof. Dana Barred from Britain Again," 27 August 1932; "H. W. L. Dana Is Arrested," 5 April 1935; "Longfellow Kin on Trial," 22 May 1935; and "Professor Dana Acquitted," 30 May 1935.

70. For Dana's family background information, see Rosamond Wild Dana, "Privileged Radicals: The Rebellious Times of Six Dana Siblings in Cambridge and New York in the Early Twentieth Century" (M.A. thesis, City University of New York, 1991). An extraordinary resource is the collection of family materials held at the Longfellow National Historic Site in Cambridge, Massachusetts, which are summarized in the "Finding Aid for Henry Wadsworth Longfellow Dana Papers," Revised, Summer 2007.

71. Zechariah Chafe Jr., *The Fiftieth Anniversary Report of the Harvard Class of 1903* (Cambridge, Mass.: Harvard University Press, 1950), 198.

72. Charles Beard, "A Statement," *New Republic*, 29 December 1917, 249-50.

73. Richard S. Kennedy, *Dreams in the Mirror: A Biography of E. E. Cummings* (1980; New York: Liveright, 1994), 310.

74. "Longfellow's Son Cuts Off Nephews."

75. Dana to Roger Baldwin, 23 November 1925, Longfellow National Historic Site.

76. Shand-Tucci, *The Crimson Letter*, 129-37, 149.

77. Blake Baily, *Cheever: A Life* (New York: Knopf, 2009), 53-54.

78. J. Louis Engdahl to Dana, 5 December 1921, Longfellow National Historic Site.

79. Bert Miller to Dana, 1 June 1926, Longfellow National Historic Site.

80. See letters and clippings from James P. Cannon, Longfellow National Historic Site.

81. Unsigned letter, 9 September 1933, Longfellow National Historic Site.

82. He contributed several pieces to *New Theater* in 1935 — "Meyerhold's New Theater," January 1935, 10-12, and "A Letter from H. W. L. Dana," November 1935, 7-8 — and he wrote the poem "Moscow" for the tenth anniversary issue of *Soviet Russia Today* in May 1942.

83. See 1933 leaflet for the West meeting as part of a series of meetings for recent visitors to the USSR, Longfellow National Historic Site. Dana was designated as chair of the meeting.

84. "H. W. L. Dana Is Arrested."

85. Granville Hicks to Dana, 29 April 1935, Longfellow National Historic Site.

86. Lamont to Dana, 7 May 1935, Longfellow National Historic Site; permission granted to quote.

87. Apparently Dana offered to take Hicks with him to the Soviet Union, but Hicks declined and Dana located the material himself. Hicks to Dana, 14 January 1936, Longfellow National Historic Site.

88. Leonard Bernstein to Dana, 17 April 1941, Longfellow National Historic Site.

89. Joseph North to Dana, 31 August 1941, Longfellow National Historic Site.

90. Medical report, 31 May 1946, Longfellow National Historic Site.

91. Townsend Ludington, ed., *The Fourteenth Chronicle: Letters and Diaries of John Dos Passos* (Boston: Gambit, 1973), 314.

92. Information on Rollins is based on the following sources: Jerre Mangione, *An Ethnic at Large: A Memoir of America in the Thirties and Forties* (New York: Putnam, 1978), and *The Dream and the Deal*; Mangione to the author, 30 November 1988 and 5 November 1991; Mangione to Hansell Baugh, undated, Mangione Archive, University of Rochester Archives, Rochester, New York; Stephen Underhill, National Archives, College Park, Maryland (regarding FBI and HUAC records on Rollins), email to the author, 18 October 2007.

93. Two of the stories are "A Song of India," *Black Mask* 6, no. 9 (August 1933): 64–77, and "K. O. Comes Clear," *Black Mask* 15, no. 12 (February 1933): 61–78.

94. Claude J. Summers, *Gay Fictions* (New York: Continuum, 1990), 21.

95. Richard Wright, "Adventure and Love in Loyalist Spain: Review of *The Wall of Men* by William Rollins, Jr.," *New Masses*, 8 March 1938, 25–26.

96. William Rollins Jr., "The Collective Novel," *Partisan Review* 4 (September–October 1934): 59–61.

97. "What Is a Proletarian Writer?" *New Masses*, 7 January 1935, 22–23; and William Rollins Jr., "Strike!" in *Proletarian Literature in the United States*, ed. Granville Hicks et al. (New York: International Publishers, 1935), 123–33.

98. See *Daily Worker*, 23 September 1940, 7.

99. William Rollins Jr., "I Wish It Was More," *Soviet Russia Today*, November 1941, 28–29, is an article favorable to establishing a committee for Russian War Relief in New York. "Lyosha: A Short Story Based on Actual Events," with illustrations by Fred Ellis (1885–1965), appeared in *Soviet Russia Today*, January 1943, 31–32. This is a war story set in the Ukraine, featuring a fourteen-year-old boy who joins the fighting against the Nazis, "his boyhood, left forever behind him, a harsh, purposeful future ahead."

100. Mangione, *An Ethnic at Large*, 76.

101. Ibid.

102. Ibid., 122–23.

103. Jerre Mangione to the author, 5 November 1991.

104. Ibid.

105. Horace Gregory, *New York Herald Tribune Books*, 11 March 1934, 7; Robert

Cantwell, *New Outlook*, March 1934, 56; John Dos Passos, *New Republic*, 4 April 1934, 220; Louis Kronenberger, *New York Times*, 18 March 1934, 6.

106. John A. Salmond, *Gastonia 1929: The Story of the Loray Mill Strike* (Chapel Hill: University of North Carolina Press, 1995), 170. Rollins may not have known about Beal's sexual orientation. His literary portrait is consistent with others such as the one by Mary Heaton Vorse in *Strike!* (New York: Liveright, 1930), which depicts Beal as being sexually aloof from the young women who flock after him.

107. Drouet's part may also be noteworthy as an unanticipated role-reversal inasmuch as the French Canadians in the region were not known as particularly sympathetic to striking workers.

108. One source of this anecdote about Tiomkin's query is Myers's oral history housed at Columbia University, June 1959, 43. Myers responded in the negative, but when Tiomkin persisted in pursuing his question, Myers elaborated that he had no feelings about it one way or the other.

109. Norma Barzman to the author, 17 October 1995.

110. Norma Barzman believes that an enduring source of financial support was Edelaine Gorney, first married to Jay Gorney and then to E. Y. "Yip" Harburg. Norma Barzman, interview with author, Hollywood, Calif., 19 December 1995.

111. Norma Barzman told the story first in an unpublished novel, "The Violins of Cremona," which she was kind enough to show me in manuscript form in 1995. It was reworked into *End of Romance: A Memoir of Love, Sex and the Mystery of the Violin* (New York: Nation Books, 2006). The events are set in 1973, when Norma is fifty-three and Myers nearly eighty. At the time, she was living in southern France and she and Myers traveled to Italy to investigate the career of a brilliant violin-maker for the purpose of providing Myers with plot material for a new novel. During the trip, Norma is drawn erotically to a young American and begins to have flashbacks of Myers fondling her as a preteen, followed by memories of sexual encounters with him between 1932 and 1942 that she instigated. Much of the biographical information about Myers is drawn from Norma Barzman's 2006 memoir; my interview with Norma and Ben Barzman in Hollywood, 12 May 1988; the Columbia University Oral History Project interview with Henry Myers, June 1959; and my interview with Norma Barzman, 19 December 1995. Norma Barzman also published a highly informative memoir, *The Red and the Blacklist* (New York: Nation Books, 2004).

112. Norman Barzman's observation seems plausible in light of his frequent association with Offner and Collier in gay cinematic culture in Hollywood and his association with George Cukor and Christopher Isherwood.

113. His only other novel with a dedication is *O King, Live Forever* (New York: Crown, 1953), "To E. and Y. with love," presumably Edelaine and Yip Harburg.

114. Barzman, *End of Romance*, 146.

CHAPTER FIVE

1. The basic facts about Wright's and Ellison's involvement in Communism can be found in Alan M. Wald, *Exiles from a Future Time: The Forging of the Mid-Twentieth-Century Literary Left* (Chapel Hill: University of North Carolina Press, 2002), 90–93 and 286–89; those about Himes's involvement can be found in Alan M. Wald, *Trinity of Passion: The Literary Left and the Antifascist Crusade* (Chapel Hill: University of North Carolina Press, 2007), 66–73. A discussion of both *Invisible Man* and Himes's fiction can be found in Wald, *Trinity of Passion*, 57–61 and 66–73.

2. Barbara Foley, *Wrestling with the Left: The Making of Ralph Ellison's "Invisible Man"* (Durham, N.C.: Duke University Press, 2010), 6.

3. See correspondence between Ellison and Wright, April 1940, Library of Congress. In particular, note Ellison's letter of 26 May 1940 where he expresses hope for Hitler's invasion of England. Of course, Wright and Ellison were for the destruction of Nazi Germany as well.

4. Wright's personal papers, housed at the Beinecke Library, Yale University, contain many pages of notes about changes in Communist Party policy after it began to support the war. Among his claims are that the Communist Party pulled back on its assistance to various types of legal cases against discrimination and segregation and was in actuality sabotaging the militancy of Blacks who wanted to fight for justice during the war. Wright refers to "Stalinism," but he does not theorize the concept. Wright places the blame for the new Communist Party situation on Black Communist leaders as much if not more than on whites and increasingly traces the cause of its wartime policies back to the Popular Front. His attitude toward the Party evolves further after 1944; however, his view in a memo from 2 January 1945 is clearly that the problem is not Communism itself but the leaders who run the Communist Party. He claims that, as a Communist journalist, he had lied consciously and deliberately, but now he wants to be honest. In 1944, he felt satisfied with the idea of publishing an exposé of his experiences (called "I Tried to Be a Communist") and did not plan to write any further either for or against the Party; anti-Communism, he believed, was as much a form of psychological slavery as pro-Communism. By 1949, however, Wright returned to the subject in a more conceptual manner based on his new conclusion that his own writing must be grounded in concepts entirely opposed to the Communist Party's doctrine. This paved the way for *The Outsider*.

5. The politics and fiction of John Oliver Killens are discussed at length in Wald, *Trinity of Passion*, 46–55. See the excellent recent biography by Keith Gilyard, *John Oliver Killens: A Life of Black Literary Activism* (Athens: University of Georgia Press, 2010).

6. James's review was published under the name J. R. Johnson in the May 1940 issue of *New International*; it was republished in Scott McLemee and Paul Le Blanc, *C. L. R. James and Revolutionary Marxism: Selected Writings of C. L. R. James, 1939–1949* (Atlantic Highlands, N.J.: Humanities Press, 1994), 88–91.

7. His famous statement on nationalism and literature appears in "Blueprint for Negro Writing," *New Challenge* 2, no. 2 (Fall 1937): 53–65.

8. The most detailed statement of Wright's fascination is contained in his unpublished manuscript of the early 1940s, "Memories of My Grandmother," held by the Beinecke Rare Book and Manuscript Library at Yale University.

9. Wald, *Exiles from a Future Time*, 90–93.

10. David Rousset was a leader of the French Trotskyist movement from 1935 to 1943 and active in the Resistance until he was arrested by the Gestapo in 1943, tortured, and sent to the Buchenwald concentration camp. In 1947, Rousset published *L'Univers concentrationnaire* (translated as *The Other Kingdom* [New York: Reynal and Hitchcock, 1947]), an award-winning book about the concentration camps. In the late 1940s and 1950s, he was active in a variety of left-wing political causes, including exposés of forced labor camps in the Soviet Union.

11. The details of Wright's activities in Paris can be found in Michel Fabre, *The Unfinished Quest of Richard Wright*, 2nd ed. (Urbana: University of Illinois Press, 1993), 326–31. A fuller assessment of the RDR, including its relations with Trotskyist intellectuals and organizations, can be found in the fascinating study by Ian H. Birchall, *Sartre against Stalinism* (New York: Berghahn Books, 2004), 93–107.

12. Beginning in the late 1970s, Wright's fiction became an object of criticism by Black feminists. See Sherley Anne Williams, "Papa Dick and Sister Woman: Reflections on Women in the Fiction of Richard Wright," in *American Novelists Revisited: Essays in Feminist Criticism*, ed. Fritz Fleischmann (Boston: G. K. Hall, 1982), 394–415.

13. This claim is discussed in many places; one of the first and most effective challenges is Nina Kressner Cobb, "Richard Wright: Exile and Existentialism," *Phylon* 40, no. 4 (1979), available at http://www.jstor.org/pss/274533.

14. This claim is stated forthrightly in Michel Fabre, "Richard Wright and the French Existentialists," *MELUS* 5, no. 2 (Summer 1978), available at http://www.jstor.org/pss/467459.

15. The relationship between Wright and the work of Simone de Beauvoir has been cited but insufficiently developed. This association is currently being pursued in a doctoral dissertation by graduate student Konstantina Karageorgos at the University of Michigan, who has presented some of her findings in a paper on *The Outsider* called "Richard Wright's Search for a Method."

16. See, for example, Hazel Rowley, *Richard Wright: The Life and Times* (New York: Henry Holt, 2001), 474. Documentation of Wright's collaboration with U.S. authorities had appeared earlier in James Campbell's *Exiled in Paris: Richard Wright, James Baldwin, Samuel Beckett, and Others on the Left Bank* (New York: Scribner, 1995).

17. In 1983, Cedric Robinson raised several facets of this aspect of Wright's cosmopolitanism when he featured him in the climactic chapter of *Black Marxism: The Making of the Black Radical Tradition* (Chapel Hill: University of North Carolina Press, 2000). Ten years later, Paul Gilroy wrote one of the most powerful reconsiderations of Wright in a chapter of *The Black Atlantic: Modernity and Double Conscious-*

ness (Cambridge, Mass.: Harvard University Press, 1993). Scholarship about Richard Wright has gone in many other directions as well. For his relation to the visual arts and mass culture, see Paula Rabinowitz, *Black & White & Noir: America's Pulp Modernism* (New York: Columbia University Press, 2002); Joseph Entin, *Sensational Modernism: Experimental Fiction and Photography in 1930s America* (Chapel Hill: University of North Carolina Press, 2007); and Sara Blair, *Harlem Crossroads: Black Writers and Photography in the Twentieth Century* (Princeton: Princeton University Press, 2007). For the treatment of gay themes in Wright, see Gary Richards, *Lovers and Beloveds: Sexual Otherness in Southern Fiction, 1936–1961* (Baton Rouge: Louisiana State University Press, 2007). For a theoretical approach to Wright engaging concepts from Marx, Heidegger, and Hegel, see Abdul R. JanMohamed, *The Death-Bound Subject: Richard Wright's Archaeology of Death* (Durham, N.C.: Duke University Press, 2005). Recently, two specialists in Wright's Paris years provide contrasting assessments: Hazel Rowley, "The Exile Years?" *Book Forum* (December–January 2006), at http://www.hazelrowley.com/exileyears.html; and James Campbell, "Richard Wright: Black First," *Times Literary Supplement*, 11 June 2008, at http://entertainment.timesonline.co.uk/tol/arts_and_entertainment/the_tls/article4112123.ece.

18. Cornel West, introduction to *Black Power: Three Books from Exile*, by Richard Wright (New York: HarperCollins, 2008), xiii.

19. Richard Wright, *American Hunger* (New York: Harper and Row, 1997), 27–28.

20. In Wald, *Exiles from a Future Time*, Walker's relationship with Wright is discussed on p. 273 and the relationship between West and Minus on p. 275. Walker's private correspondence in the Richard Wright Papers, Yale University Library, New Haven, Conn., refers to much gossip, including about Theodore Ward. In his excellent chapter "Richard Wright and Compulsory Black Male Heterosexuality" in *Lovers and Beloveds*, 62–93, Gary Richards presents the evidence for speculation that Leon Wright was gay and emphasizes some of Margaret Walker's observations about Richard Wright's own sexuality.

21. See the dissertation by Joachim Gerhard Ludovicus Riesthuis, "Blacks and Exiles: African American and German Exiled Authors, 1933–1952" (University of Chicago, 2004).

22. Rowley, *Richard Wright*, 407–8.

23. See the discussion of this aspect of Wright's work in Rabinowitz, *Black & White & Noir*, 83.

24. Gil Blount's name also recalls Carson McCullers's deluded revolutionary, Jake Blount, in *The Heart Is a Lonely Hunter*; Wright had reviewed her novel for the *New Republic* and later came to be friends with McCullers and her husband, Reeve McCullers. See Richard Wright, "Inner Landscape," *New Republic*, 4 August 1940, 195.

25. For a Communist view in the postwar era, see William Thor Burger, "'New Realism' or Old Hat?" *New Masses*, 23 April 1946, 25–29.

26. See the discussion of Amter's public criticism of Ruth McKenney in Wald, *Trinity of Passion*, 174.

27. The most reliable details about Poplar can be found in Rowley, *Richard Wright*,

especially following 232. I am indebted to Konstantina Karageorgos for research assistance on Ellen Poplar.

28. After the couple moved to Paris, Simone de Beauvoir reported that she was surprised that the Wright relationship was conventional with Ellen accepting of the double standard. Following the separation of the Wrights, Ellen had a love affair with Nelson Algren and moved to London with the Wright children in 1959. Rowley, *Richard Wright*, 518. The affair is possibly the basis for the episode in John A. Williams's novel *The Man Who Cried I Am* (Boston: Little, Brown, 1967), where the wife of the Wright-like character, Harry Ames, has an affair with one of his literary friends, Max Reddick; however, Reddick is Black and has personality traits suggestive of Chester Himes.

29. She is the mother of Peter Gourfain, later distinguished for his sculptures, carvings, and prints.

30. One of her pieces, intended for *Weird Tales*, edited in Chicago by the politically sympathetic J. C. Henneberger, was unsuccessfully channeled by Ed Gourfain to the *New Masses*.

31. This appeared in 1956 under the auspices of the Seven Arts Workshop.

32. Joyce Gourfain to Wright, 17 August 1939, Wright Papers. Joyce also confided to Wright that she was distressed because her children limited her ability to write. Joyce Gourfain to Wright, undated letter, early 1940s, Wright Papers. I am grateful to Sarah Ehlers for her research on Gourfain and related matters in the Wright Papers.

33. See Robert Minor, "To Tell the Truth," *Daily Worker*, 15 August 1944, 6.

34. Some biographers spell her last name "Meadman," although in this respect I am following Hazel Rowley's research. References in the press are always to "Dhimah," her stage name. Rowley says that Dhimah's parents, Aaron and Eudice Meidman, were from Odessa and had left Russia in 1905 and that she had two brothers, Samuel and Harry.

35. Under the name "Dhimah," she published "Dance for Moscow" in *New Theater*, October 1935, 25. See the article about her by Chen-I-Wan, "American Dancers in Moscow," *New Theater*, August 1935, 21. I am indebted to Konstantina Karageorgos for research assistance on Dhimah Meidman.

36. Rowley, *Richard Wright*, 205–6.

37. See ibid., 552. Several of her paintings called "Abstract" can be viewed at http://www.aspireauctions.com/auction13/2230.html.

38. She also received some notice for her story "The Love Affair," originally published in the *Kenyon Review* and reprinted in Martha Foley, ed., *The Best American Short Stories of 1946* (New York: Houghton Mifflin, 1946). I am indebted to Konstantina Karageorgos for research assistance on Henrietta Weigel.

39. See Henrietta Weigel, "Personal Impressions," in *Richard Wright: Impressions and Perspectives*, ed. David Ray and Robert Farnsworth (Ann Arbor: University of Michigan Press, 1973), 71–75.

40. Replansky's communications with Wright are preserved in his papers. In the mid-1940s, frequently from California, she sent Wright poems, reported on her meet-

ings with Bertolt Brecht, and described her stay with Natalie Moffat (a lover of Simone de Beauvoir's, then married to the director George Stevens). See letters of Replansky to Wright of 8 September 1945, 18 June 1946, 7 September 1946, and 31 January 1947, Beinecke Library.

41. See Rowley, *Richard Wright*, 355–56 and 408.

42. Less is known about Wright's affairs with women in Europe—Madelyn Jackson, Vivian Werner, and Celia Hornung—which probably occurred after most of the novel was written.

43. In *The Outsider*, the Communist activist Bob Hunter, like C. L. R. James, is from Trinidad and is eventually imprisoned by immigration authorities on Ellis Island, as later happened to James (1953). In a private conversation in Paris in July 1993, Wright biographer Michel Fabre, usually a reliable source, told me that Wright and Webb had been lovers during the late 1940s, meeting under the pretense of his teaching her how to drive. If so, this was not acknowledged by Webb in her autobiography, *Not Without Love: Memoirs* (Hanover, N.H.: University Press of New England, 2003), and remains unconfirmed.

44. These observations and those on the following pages are all summarized from Wright's draft perspectives for "American Pages," although it is not possible to include all of his ideas. One can view the full document in the Wright Papers.

45. Hank Johnson's father had been a member of the IWW. Hank had come from Texas to New York to attend City College from 1930 to 1934, during which time he worked for the International Workers Order (1932–34). Johnson then joined the CIO Steel Workers Organizing Committee in 1936 and became one of the most important organizers of the meatpacking unionization drive in Chicago in 1937. One of the founders of the Communist-led National Negro Congress, he was believed to be a Communist but never publically identified himself with the Communist Party. References to Hank Johnson can be found in Wright's diary for 1945, box 117, folder 1860, Wright Papers.

46. Arthell Shelton and Hank Johnson were featured prominently and favorably in a *Chicago Defender* article replete with photographs, "What Goes On in Packingtown?," by the pro-Communist Harold Preece, 23 September 1939, 13.

47. Wright's diary for 1945, Wright Papers.

48. Roger Horowitz, email to author, 15 July 2008. The only way that Shelton could conceivably have been linked to the Communist movement in the 1940s concerns an incident in the August prior to the murder. At that time, Shelton, the bodyguard for AFL officer Norman Zuckowsky, assaulted a police officer. A Judge Quilici managed to get the charges against Shelton dismissed and apparently participated in a cover-up. Perhaps Quilici, a former president of the National Lawyers Guild, an organization then significantly influenced by Communists, might once have been a fellow traveler.

49. Edward Bland Jr., emails to the author, 10, 17, 19 April 2010.

50. Richard Wright, "Not My People's War," *New Masses*, 17 June 1941, 8–9.

51. This led to a congressional inquiry into the comic book industry and creation of the Comics Code. Wertham was influenced by Freud, but his main emphasis was

on the environment and social background as having major effects on psychological development. Among Wertham's many connections to the Left was that he helped the imprisoned Ethel Rosenberg and served as an advisor in the adoption of the Rosenberg sons.

52. Isidor Schneider, "One Apart," *New Masses*, 23 April 1945, 23–24. Diana Trilling comments on the affair in *The Beginning of the Journey* (New York: Houghton Mifflin, 1995), 215.

53. Gil Blount's real name is said to be Bernstein in *The Outsider* (New York: Perennial, 1993), 329. Ben Burns published a revealing autobiography in which he discusses his version of his conflict with Wright, *Nitty Gritty: A White Editor in Black Journalism* (Jackson: University Press of Mississippi, 2007).

54. Samuel Sillen, "Richard Wright in Retreat," *Daily Worker*, 29 August 1944, 25–26.

55. This debate is discussed at length in Wald, *Trinity of Passion*, 222–27.

56. Hunter's personal situation also has some resemblance to that of C. L. R. James's, as he is under threat of deportation to the Caribbean. One leading African American Communist who attacked Wright in print was James W. Ford, "A Disservice to the Negro People," *Daily Worker*, 5 September 1944, 6. Ford insists that Wright had been well treated by the Communist Party, which had never tried to hold him back in his career.

57. See the articles "Anna Damon Dies after Long Illness," *Daily Worker*, 14 May 1944, 5, and "Communist Party Mourns Death of Anna Damon, ILD Leader," *Daily Worker*, 20 May 1944, 9. The suicide is mentioned in Bella Dodd's *School of Darkness* (New York: P. J. Kennedy, 1954), 172. The Communist press reported only that Damon died after a protracted illness, in the throes of excruciating pain, while preparing to attend the Communist Party national convention as a delegate. Damon's funeral may have been dramatized in the novel as the basis for Gil Blount's. "Many at Rites for Damon," *Daily Worker*, 21 May 1944, 12, reports that over 100 people attended an interracial farewell tribute at the Plaza Funeral Home.

58. "Mysterious Death in Communist Row," *Chicago Defender*, 5 July 1930, 11, reports that Alfred Levy died in a Harlem hospital of a skull fracture. The detectives were told that he had been hit by brick thrown from a building after police dispersed a Communist rally, but another version was that he fell in Communist Party headquarters after police had come because of trouble between the Communist Party and followers of Marcus Garvey. For more conflicting versions of the story, see also "Two Died in Harlem Reds Street Riot," *Chicago Defender*, 5 July 1930, 4, and "8,000 Attend Red Funeral in New York," *Chicago Defender*, 5 July 1930, 2.

59. Fabre, *Unfinished Quest of Richard Wright*, 275.

60. Franklin Folsom, *Days of Anger, Days of Hope: A Memoir of the League of American Writers, 1937–1942* (Niwot: University Press of Colorado, 1994), 255.

61. Wright, *The Outsider*, 359.

62. Michel Fabre, *Richard Wright: Books and Writers* (Jackson: University of Mississippi Press, 1990), 72.

CHAPTER SIX

1. "Hypersleep," a term of science fiction theory, denotes a complete cessation of activities that may readily restart, whereas "suspended animation" is a reduction of life and social processes with an unknown future.

2. James argues: "Melville took great pains to show that revolt was no answer to the questions he asked. . . . [Steelkit's] revolt is in the end successful. But what happens? . . . Everything goes back to just what it was before. That is exactly what would have happened if there had been a revolt on the *Pequod*. We would have been left in the end exactly where we had been at the beginning." See C. L. R. James, *Mariners, Renegades, and Castaways: The Story of Herman Melville and the World We Live In* (1953; Hanover, N.H.: University Press of New England, 2001), 53–54. Of course, James saw the political situation a hundred years later rather differently.

3. Ann Petry, *The Narrows* (New York: Dafina, 2008), 67. Actually, this origin for his name is an assumption of Link's; as an orphan, he never knew his biological mother.

4. Herman Melville's "Bartleby the Scrivener" (1853) features a demoralized clerk who is reported to have held a previous position in a dead letter office in Washington, D.C. Inasmuch as Petry read poetry throughout the 1940s, it is possible that she encountered William Meredith's *Love Letter from an Impossible Land* (New Haven: Yale University Press, 1944), containing poems written while Meredith was stationed in Hawaii. The title poem, p. 38, has lines that resonate with Link in *The Narrows*, such as the reference to "exile islands of the mind" and "the fog is real."

5. Elisabeth Petry cites a diary entry of her mother's where this identification of Link with her husband and Offord is made; see *At Home Inside: A Daughter's Tribute to Ann Petry* (Jackson: University Press of Mississippi, 2009), 84. George Petry is identified as a left-wing writer on the Federal Writers Project by Jerre Mangione, *The Dream and the Deal: The Federal Writers Project, 1935–43* (Boston: Little, Brown, 1972), 248, and Paula Rabinowitz notes references in Petry's diary to her husband's work on the *People's Voice* in "Pulping Ann Petry," in *Revising the Blueprint: Ann Petry and the Literary Left*, ed. Alex Lubin (Jackson: University Press of Mississippi, 2007), 153. Both pieces of information are also given in a 6 January 2005 email from Elisabeth Petry to the author. Carl Offord's politics are discussed in Alan M. Wald, *Trinity of Passion: The Literary Left and the Antifascist Crusade* (Chapel Hill: University of North Carolina Press, 2007), 137–40.

6. Link thinks Camilo has "legs like Dietrich" and that she "had a pink and white figure straight out of one of those Fifth Avenue store windows." A. Petry, *The Narrows*, 85 and 316.

7. Ibid., 309, 96, 282, 261, 146, and 127.

8. Ibid., 95.

9. Ibid., 73, 90. Link's male chauvinism toward Camilo is a persistent theme. He insists on being the driver when they are together and resents her paying any bills.

10. Edmund Wilson's story, too, invokes ideas of commodity fetishism, which is also the Marxist concept about which Wilson famously wrote in his chapter "Karl

Marx: Poet of Commodities and Dictator of the Proletariat," in *To the Finland Station: A Study in the Writing and Acting of History* (1940; New York: Anchor Books, 1953). Wilson states that "Marx presents us with a picture of the world in which the commodities appear to command human beings." Camilo operates on Link like the objects described by Wilson that take on "the fetishistic character which is to make them appear ends in themselves, possessed of a value of their own, then acquiring a potency of their own, which seem to substitute itself for human potency" (A. Petry, *The Narrows*, 291–92). From another angle, Bill V. Mullen fruitfully discusses commodity fetishism in Petry's *The Street* in "Object Lessons: Fetishization and Class Consciousness in Ann Petry's *The Street*," in *Revising the Blueprint*, ed. Lubin, 35–48.

11. See Simon Karlinsky, *Dear Bunny, Dear Volodya: The Nabokov-Wilson Letters, 1940–71* (Berkeley: University of California Press, 2001).

12. A. Petry, *The Narrows*, 5. Other names for this community are "Eye of the Needle," "the Bottom," "Darktown," and "Niggertown." A "narrows" is a small body of water, often the thinnest part of a strait, connecting two larger bodies. In Petry's novel, the River Wye is next to the community but is always called "the river," so the term "narrows" must refer to land. Otherwise, the expression "the Narrows" usually means the strait in New York City separating the boroughs of Staten Island and Brooklyn.

13. A 15 June 2006 email to the author from Elisabeth Petry states that Monmouth is not Old Saybrook, which was more accurately depicted as the town of Lennox in Petry's novel *Country Place* (New York: Houghton Mifflin, 1947). Monmouth is supposed to be a city, whereas Old Saybrook had only 1,500 residents into the 1950s. Moreover, there were but four Black families in Old Saybrook, certainly not an entire African American district. Monmouth appropriates some features from Hartford (which had a Franklin Avenue and was known for gun manufacturing) and New London (which was a port full of sailors). Both had small but longtime African American populations. Hartford's population peaked in 1950 at 177,397. In 1968, following the assassination of Dr. Martin Luther King Jr., Hartford's predominantly African American North End erupted in riots. The state's capital was in the city's southeast side. Hartford is on the Connecticut River, called the Wye River in the novel, which is the boundary between Hartford and East Hartford. Historically, Hartford was a center of abolitionism—the home of Harriet Beecher Stowe. The daily newspaper was the *Hartford Courant*.

14. "In fact, she had been working on the sketches for characters that would populate *The Narrows* since 1944. Her notebooks are full of descriptions of Abbie Crunch and Mamie Prowther as well as variations on the many plot twists—including rape, murder, pedophilia, bribery, gambling, and so forth, piling on details over the public outrage Paul Robeson's son's interracial marriage generated in photographs and reports in local newspapers and radio broadcasts." See Rabinowitz, "Pulping Ann Petry," 56. Petry's notebooks are available at the Howard Gottlieb Research Center at Boston University.

15. E. Petry, *At Home Inside*, 5.

16. Ibid., 23.

17. Ibid., 139, 34, 132.

18. They were remarried in 1938 to please Ann Petry's parents, which is the marriage date given in all available scholarship on Petry. The documentation of the 1936 marriage is presented in E. Petry, *At Home Inside*, 43–44.

19. Ibid., 45; a reproduction of the article is on the second page of the insert following p. 96.

20. Ibid., 27.

21. Ibid., 156.

22. Ibid., 85.

23. Ibid., 77.

24. Ibid., 84, 85, 151, 155.

25. This is the recollection of Petry's daughter, who is certain that "Mother saw Weegee's photographs." Elisabeth Petry, email to the author, 15 June 2006.

26. See Wald, *Trinity of Passion*, 108–18, for a history of Petry's association with *People's Voice*.

27. A. Petry, *The Narrows*, 50. These are the thoughts of Peter Bullock about Jubine: "With a few added touches, it would be a clown's face; the potential was there, the mouth a little too large, the nose too prominent, the eyes bulged, the ears stood out, too big. Clown's face." This description resembles any number of self-portraits of Weegee, especially his 1944 *Self-Portrait with Speed Graphic Camera*.

28. A. Petry, *The Narrows*, 48.

29. Ibid., 362–63.

30. Dan Wakefield, "C. Wright Mills: Before His Time," *Nation*, 18 March 2009, available at http://www.thenation.com/article/c-wright-mills-his-time.

31. A. Petry, *The Narrows*, 15 and 47.

32. The Photo League was descended from the Film and Photo League, originally the Workers Film and Photo League in its pre–Popular Front days. The Photo League sponsored an influential show of Weegee's work in 1941.

33. Petry had followed the 1946 Communist Party debate about this matter, siding with Albert Maltz. See Wald, *Trinity of Passion*, 118–19.

34. A. Petry, *The Narrows*, 45.

35. Hannah Arendt, *Men in Dark Times* (New York: Harcourt Brace, 1968), 97.

36. A. Petry, *The Narrows*, 329.

37. The Krupp Trial was the tenth of the twelve war crimes trials following World War II. The directors of the financial empire known as the Krupp Group were accused of enabling the Nazi preparation for an aggressive war. The trial was held from December 1947 to July 1948, after which prison sentences were given out. But the Krupp family would have been in the news well into the 1950s when the defendants were released from prison and gained control of the firm once more. The most famous of Krupp's guns was "Big Bertha," the World War I howitzer gun named after Bertha Krupp, heiress to the Krupp industrial empire. Petry also mentions the British engineering firm of Vickers, which was founded in Sheffield (the last name of Camilo and her husband) and expanded into artillery manufacture.

38. Abbie slowly comes to realize that the Hangman was named for its resemblance to trees used for lynching. See A. Petry, *The Narrows*, 5.

39. One exception might be the working-class couple of Miss Doris, Frances's housekeeper, and her husband, called Sugar. But few details are given about the marriage, and it is Doris's personal strength and convictions that are most memorable. Some important observations about the role of Doris are present in Rachel Peterson, "Invisible Hands at Work: Domestic Service and Meritocracy in Ann Petry's Novels," in *Revising the Blueprint*, ed. Lubin, 72–96.

40. There is no suggestion of genital sexuality, but marriage-like references are numerous: Abbie and Frances are said to be Link's two mothers, Frank is Abbie's husband, Frances has a man's mind, and Frances asks Abbie to come live with her so that Frances can take care of her.

41. Their personal relationship is discussed in Judith Schwartz, *Radical Feminists of Heterodoxy: Greenwich Village 1912–1940* (Norwich, Vt.: New Victoria Press, 1986), 36–39.

42. Butler Library at Columbia University holds papers of Mabel Louise Robinson. I am indebted to Konstantina Karageorgos and Emma Garrett for research assistance on Robinson and Hull.

43. The letter is incomplete and marked only "151." I wish to express my appreciation to Emma Garrett for locating this item.

44. E. Petry, *At Home Inside*, 74.

45. Ibid., 130.

46. See A. Petry, *The Narrows*, 246. On 236 and 237, she repeats the following thought: "Accident? Coincidence? It all depended on what happened in the past. We carry it around with us."

47. Ibid., 229.

48. The Soviet Union is referred to on several occasions but without illusions. Weak Knees declares that it is an oppressive society but not based on race. He specifically observes that Paul Robeson might be shot in the Soviet Union for proposing social change, but no one would care if his son married a white woman. See ibid., 266.

49. Prowther refers to the Treadway chauffeur as "Al the Nazi," but the two soon become fast friends. See ibid., 162. When Camilo calls Link's psychiatrist friend Wormsley a "fascist" because he desires to be a "kingmaker," Link dismisses this quality as a human trait. Ibid., 147.

50. Ibid., 86.

51. Ibid., 73.

52. Ibid., 69. She is recalled again, by Abbie, on p. 226.

53. Ibid., 71, 79, 94, 148, 257, 319.

54. Ibid., 9.

55. Ibid., 20.

56. Ibid., 28.

57. Ibid., 51.

58. A sermon on Cain and Abel by Reverend Longworth is in progress in *The Nar-*

rows when Prowther fingers Link. See ibid., 384–85. The association with Chambers is likely from a perception that Chambers was jealous of Hiss and was seeking to ingratiate himself with those in power. The case is briefly cited in ibid., 362, but more extensively in Petry's notebooks for the novel.

59. E. Petry, *At Home Inside*, 95, 13, 40.

60. This remark appeared in an April 1929 issue of *Harper's* magazine and is reprinted in Robert Deming, ed., *James Joyce, 1928–1941* (New York: Psychology Press, 1997), 417.

61. Robinson and Hull were authorities of their time in the use of modern literature as an instructional guide. Some of their ideas can be found in the volume they co-edited with Roger Sherman and Paul Kavanagh, *The Art of Writing Prose* (New York: R. R. Smith, 1930). Faulkner is also mentioned, for his skill at creating tension.

62. "On an Author," *New York Herald Tribune Weekly Book Review*, 8 August 1953, 3.

63. McTell's lyric is: "Describe your woman, and I'll tell you what road she's on." I am grateful to the assistance of Bruce Conforth for tracking down this information.

64. A. Petry, *The Narrows*, 234.

65. Ann Petry, "Playwright's Letter Stirs Dissent," *New York Times*, 4 September 1949, 46.

66. Frances's blouse is "cut almost like a man's shirt"; she is said "to have a man's mind"; and Link remarks, "She was here so often that I used to think she was my father and you were my mother." See A. Petry, *The Narrows*, 233, 234, 14. In an email of 10 May 2011, Elisabeth Petry points out that Frances Jackson, originally called Naomi Jackson, also bears a resemblance to a close friend of Ann Petry's named Charlotte Crawford, who attended Wellesley. Abbie, as well, bears a resemblance to Petry's own mother, Bertha James Lane, who was of a conservative temperament and intimidated by her husband's more outgoing family.

67. A. Petry, *The Narrows*, 246.

68. Only Helen Hull was technically a member; Louise Robinson attended activities.

69. The most compelling treatment of *The Narrows* as a political novel is Farah Jasmine Griffin, "Hunting Communists and Negroes in Ann Petry's *The Narrows*," in *Revising the Blueprint*, ed. Lubin, 137–49.

70. Why does China observe the beating of Link by Bill? Is it due to concern as his mother, or due to a victim's finding pleasure in the victimization of another? Is there some connection between her name, China, and Bill's launching his criminal career as the murderous smuggler of Chinese laborers into the United States? As in the case of Bill's possible parentage of J. C., suggested by their physical resemblance and the circumstances of J. C.'s birth, the narrative is strewn with signs that offer incomplete or even multiple explanations.

71. A. Petry, *The Narrows*, 118.

72. Ibid., 119.

73. He always thinks of her as "Miss pause Dwight" and mocks her speech habit.

Ibid., 135. She later returns to express racist ideas at the climax of the novel. Ibid., 374.

74. The use of the name Valkill seems to be another of the homophobic associations in the book; Val-kill was the Hyde Park, New York, retreat for Eleanor Roosevelt where she planned some of her progressive activities and conducted intimate relations with other women, especially Lorena Hickock. Today it is listed as a Gay and Lesbian Historic Site; see http://queerestplaces.wordpress.com/2009/01/16/er-at-val-kill/.

75. This is one of many interconnected references in the novel to the operations of race and ethnic hatred. On p. 235 of *The Narrows*, Frances explains how she overcame her unbearable reaction to hearing the epithet applied to herself.

76. A. Petry, *The Narrows*, 62.

77. Ibid., 124. On p. 125, Link recognizes that "it was a song about death" but also feels that sex is implicated. On p. 127, as he waits for Camilo on the dock at four o'clock, he thinks again "of Mamie singing Same Train."

78. Ibid., 155, repeated on 258, 259, 271, 275.

79. In *Laura*, the wealthy aunt of the protagonist is Mrs. Treadwell, echoed by the name of the wealthy Mrs. Treadway in *The Narrows*.

80. The novel explains that J. C.'s birth came three years after the birth of the twins, Kelley and Shapiro, during which time Mamie had commenced to receive gifts of dresses from Bill Hod, obviously her lover. Mamie refers to J. C. looking at her "just like Bill." See A. Petry, *The Narrows*, 296.

81. The episode of J. C. breaking through the Major's hat, an odd image of the destruction of a symbol of her memory fixation and a rebirth, seems to symbolize what is psychologically at work following the funeral for Link. See ibid., 416.

82. Ibid., 414, 415.

83. J. C. was given initials at birth so that he could fill them in later. In addition to the possibility of a reference to Jesus Christ, another is Jonathan Copper, the son of the lecherous Old Copper, who infected Malcolm Prowther with a lust that led to humiliation and betrayal.

84. See A. Petry, *The Narrows*, 77, when Link compares the experience to "the power and the glory" from the Lord's Prayer, and p. 78, where he says that he felt he could "conquer the world." The same expression is used on p. 98 when he acknowledges that he loves Camilo.

85. The artist was Clark Hulings. Paula Rabinowitz reproduced the cover in her essay "Pulping Ann Petry," 69.

86. Camilo first uses the epithet in A. Petry, *The Narrows*, 257, and it is repeated in Link's memory on 259, 260, 264, 271, 275, 314, 330, and 430.

87. In *The Narrows*, 258–59, Link's memory of the beating he received from Hod, which inspired his effort to shoot him, is tied to his desire for violent revenge on Camilo's body.

88. E. Petry, *At Home Inside*, 82–83.

89. One of the more recent books on the case is David E. Stannard, *Honor Killing: How the Infamous "Massie Affair" Transformed Hawaii* (New York: Penguin, 2006).

90. After Thalia Massie's daughter had made a scene at a nightclub and left for home, she claimed that she had been raped by Hawaiian men (called "niggers" by the U.S. whites). She eventually produced the license plate of a car, and an arrest was made of a group of five men, including the prizefighter. But gossip circulated that Thalia had been involved with several men, including one Hawaiian and one white. Her angry mother then came to Hawaii and began to defend her daughter by attacking the defendants. The story was at first kept out of mainland U.S. press for fear that it might harm the tourist industry.

91. The Massie story eventually hit the mainland press and took on a racist character against Hawaiians, claiming that this was an honor killing. The four whites were convicted of manslaughter and then left the island after a sentence of one hour served in the territorial governor's office.

92. See Ann Petry, "Harlem Women Wax Indignant over Latest 'Crime' Campaign," *People's Voice*, 15 August 1942, 3; *The Narrows*, 374–78.

93. I am grateful to the brilliant "Introduction: Lighting the Circle" in Clive Bush's *The Century's Midnight: Dissenting European and American Writers in the Era of the Second World War* (Oxford: Peter Lang, 2010), 1–20, for a perspective on several of these issues.

94. Paule Marshall, *Triangular Road: A Memoir* (New York: Basic Civitas Books, 2009), 7.

95. Harold Cruse, in *The Crisis of the Negro Intellectual: A Historical Analysis of the Failure of Black Leadership* (New York: William Morrow, 1967), provided the most candid information about the substantial background of figures associated with the Harlem Writers Club and then Guild in the Communist Left, although the book is marred by Cruse's self-serving attacks on personal rivals. Marshall is depicted as both a part of the Killens group and somewhat different, due to her age and Caribbean family background.

96. Paule Marshall, "Brooklyn," in *Reena and Other Stories* (New York: Feminist Press, 1983), 27–48.

97. In a personal interview with the author in Paris, June 1993, Paule Marshall confirmed that the model of Berman was Slochower.

98. Leslie Fiedler, *Love and Death in the American Novel* (New York: Stein and Day, 1960), 12. For a superb analysis of this book, see Robyn Wiegman, "Fiedler and Sons," in *Race and the Subject of Masculinities*, ed. Harry Stecopoulos and Michael Uebel (Durham, N.C.: Duke University Press, 1997), 47–68. Wiegman is among those who most effectively interrelate the provisional and performative aspects of ethnic and gender identities, notwithstanding the immense shaping powers of inherited and ongoing racism and heterosexism. A few of the books in the field of Black queer studies especially helpful in addressing Black gay writers are Maurice O. Wallace, *Constructing the Black Masculine: Identity and Ideality in African American Men's Literature and*

Culture, 1775–1995 (Durham, N.C.: Duke University Press, 2002); Roderick A. Ferguson, *Aberrations in Black: Toward a Queer of Color Critique* (Minneapolis: University of Minnesota Press, 2004); Siobhan B. Somerville, *Queering the Color Line: Race and the Invention of Homosexuality in American Culture* (Durham, N.C.: Duke University Press, 2000); Marcellous Blount and George P. Cunningham, eds., *Representing Black Men* (New York: Routledge, 1996); E. Patrick Johnson and Mae G. Henderson, *Black Queer Studies: A Critical Anthology* (Durham, N.C.: Duke University Press, 2005); and Marlon B. Ross, *Manning the Race: Reforming Black Men in the Jim Crow Era* (New York: New York University Press, 2004).

99. Theodore Pierce, interview with the author, Madison, Wisc., September 1993.

100. Ibid.

101. Zev Braun, phone interview with the author, August 2001.

102. See Jerome Klinkowitz, ed., *The Diaries of Willard Motley* (Ames: Iowa State University Press, 1979), 100–101.

103. Zev Braun interview.

104. In 1976, Andrews published *The Darkness Is Light Enough* (Philadelphia: Fellowship Press, 1976), with artwork by her companion, Ruby Morris. The FBI took note of Andrews's sexual orientation, also known to Motley's friends. Her recommendations about *Knock on Any Door* can be found in her correspondence with Motley in the Motley Collection, Northern Illinois University Library, DeKalb.

105. A compelling case for Motley as a social realist novelist appears in Stacey I. Morgan, *Rethinking Social Realism: African-American Art and Literature, 1930–53* (Athens: University of Georgia Press, 2004), especially 254–75. Morgan provides a rare appreciative discussion of the political themes of *We Fished All Night* (New York: Appleton-Century-Crofts, 1951). However, my own research comes to very different conclusions as to when Motley discovered the circumstances of his birth and the pivotal role of this revelation as well as homosexuality in his life and work.

106. Theodore Pierce, interview with the author, Madison, Wisc., September 1993.

107. "Notes for 'Ho' Book," Motley Papers, Special Collections, University of Wisconsin, Madison. See Motley to literary agent Liza McKee, 31 October 1961, available in Special Collections, University of Wisconsin.

108. FBI file for Willard Motley, #100-21911. I am grateful to Joe Allen for sharing this with me.

109. This was affirmed in all the biographical interviews conducted for this book, especially those with Frederica Westbrook, Archibald Motley III, Zev Braun, and Ted Pierce.

110. The scholar Robert Flemming established the accurate date of birth; I was shown the birth certificate in the home of Frederica Motley Westbrook in Chicago in 1993.

111. Walter Roth, phone interview with the author, 3 June 1993.

112. Willard Motley, "Negro Art in Chicago," *Opportunity*, January 1940, 19–22, 28–31.

113. Zev Braun interview. See also Motley's "The Education of a Writer," *New Idea: Magazine of Student Thought and Writing*, Winter 1960, 11–28.

114. Willard Motley to Ted Purdy, 21 March 1947, available in Motley Papers, Special Collections, University of Wisconsin.

115. Willard Motley, *Let No Man Write My Epitaph* (New York: Random House, 1958), 224.

116. See Klinkowitz, *Diaries of Willard Motley*, 64.

117. Willard Motley to Frederica Westbrook, 14 April 1960, Motley Collection.

118. See "Lonely Crusade," *Chicago Daily Sun-Times*, 2 October 1947, 33; and "Stand Up and Be Counted," *Time*, 7 June 1963, 11.

119. See Klinkowitz, *Diaries of Willard Motley*, 86.

120. See ibid., especially 22, 32, 52, 72, 86, 100, 101, 119.

121. Willard Motley, *We Fished All Night*, 251.

122. Klinkowitz, *Diaries of Willard Motley*, 56.

123. Diana Anhalt, *A Gathering of Fugitives: American Political Expatriates in Mexico, 1948–1965* (Santa Maria, Calif.: Archer Books, 2001), 112.

124. Motley, *Let No Man Write My Epitaph*, 274.

125. FBI file for Willard Motley, #100–21911.

126. Both novelists have been the subject of informative book-length biographies: Douglas Wixson, *Worker-Writer in America: Jack Conroy and the Tradition of Midwestern Literary Radicalism, 1898–1990* (Urbana: University of Illinois Press, 1994), and Bettina Drew, *Nelson Algren: A Life on the Wild Side* (New York: Putnam, 1989).

127. Motley, *We Fished All Night*, dedication.

128. See the correspondence to Motley from Dorothy Andrews and from Motley to Alexander Saxton, Motley Papers.

129. Motley, *We Fished All Night*, 239.

130. FBI file for Willard Motley, #100–21911.

131. Alexander Saxton, interview with the author, Los Angeles, September 1992.

132. The FBI identified Motley as a "Trotskyist"; see FBI file for Willard Motley, #100–21911. For the full story of the Hickman case, see Joe Allen, *People Wasn't Made to Burn* (Chicago: Haymarket, 2011).

133. See James Kutcher, *The Case of the Legless Veteran*, rev. ed. (New York: Pathfinder Press, 1973).

134. Zev Braun interview.

135. Walter Roth interview and Theodore Pierce interview.

136. Alexander Saxton interview and Zev Braun interview.

137. Obituary, *New York Times*, 5 March 1965.

138. Zev Braun interview.

139. A superb study of these two works is featured in Rebecca M. Schreiber, *Cold War Exiles in Mexico: U.S. Dissidents and the Culture of Critical Resistance* (Minneapolis: University of Minnesota Press, 2008), 137–70.

140. Motley, *Let Noon Be Fair*, Department of Special Collections, UCLA, 414.

141. Ibid., 415.

CHAPTER SEVEN

1. Ruth Wisse presents a version of 1940s–1950s "Jewish American Renaissance" in Michael Kramer and Hannah Wirth-Nesher, *The Cambridge Companion to Jewish American Literature* (Cambridge: Cambridge University Press, 2003), 190–211.

2. For Uris, whose father was a leading figure in the Jewish Communist movement, see Ira B. Nadel, *Leon Uris: Life of a Best Seller* (Austin: University of Texas Press, 2010). For Miller, the most candid information is now available in Christopher Bigsby, *Arthur Miller* (Cambridge: Harvard University Press, 2009), especially 88–90. Still missing are details about the political convictions of Miller's older brother and perhaps other family members.

3. The most useful discussion of Walter Benjamin in this regard is Wendy Brown, "Resisting Left Melancholia," in *Loss: The Politics of Mourning*, ed. David L. Eng and David Kazanjian (Berkeley: University of California Press, 2003), 458–56.

4. "Deconversion" refers to the rejection of a belief system. The word "disavowal" (*Verleugnung*), frequently translated as "denial," means the mental act of refusing the truth of a perception because of its latent traumatic associations.

5. A first-rate discussion of this genre can be found in David Seed, "The Ex-Communist Memoirs of Howard Fast," *Prospects* 24 (1999): 605–24.

6. See Hannah Arendt, "The Ex-Communists," *Commonweal* 57 (20 March 1953): 595–99; and Isaac Deutscher, "The Ex-Communist's Conscience," *Russia in Transition* (New York: Grove Press, 1960), 223–36.

7. For background, see Alan M. Wald, "The Conversion of the Jews," *Trinity of Passion: The Literary Left and the Antifascist Crusade* (Chapel Hill: University of North Carolina Press, 2007), 176–209.

8. See the discussion and application of Itche Goldberg's ideas in this respect in Paul Buhle, *From the Lower East Side to Hollywood: Jews in American Popular Culture* (London: Verso, 2004), especially "Reflexive Jews," 215–70.

9. See Werner Sollors, *Beyond Ethnicity: Consent and Descent in American Culture* (New York: Oxford University Press, 1987).

10. Eugene Goodheart, *Confessions of a Secular Jew: A Memoir* (New Brunswick, N.J.: Transaction Books, 2005), xv. Goodheart recalled that at Camp Kinderland, the largely Jewish children's resort of the pro-Communist International Workers Order, there was a special emphasis on identification with Native American Indians. The bond was promoted by an elderly Jewish counselor who wrote a Yiddish book about Native Americans and occasionally wore his hair in braids: "Every Sunday we marched to breakfast and saluted the flag with a defiant Indian salute. We were the Jewish Indians of Camp Kinderland, multicultural before the word ever existed." See pp. 29–30.

11. For an expression of the aim of writing about Communist characters, see the undated letter (probably 1947) from Katya Gilden to "Darling" (presumably Bert Gilden), Gilden Papers, John Hay Library, Brown University, Providence, R.I.

12. Among the many limitations of *American Night* is that restrictions of space, and

of the expertise of the author, do not allow for treatment of Yiddish-language publications. However, much of the creative work of the Yiddish American literary Left tends to be in poetry, and the subject has been gaining increasing attention; see, for example, the important volume by Amelia Glaser and David Weintraub, *Proletpen: America's Rebel Yiddish Poets* (Madison: University of Wisconsin Press, 2007).

13. For this and many other insights about international Communist autobiography and fiction, I am indebted to Gina Herrmann's dazzling *Written in Red: The Communist Memoir in Spain* (Urbana: University of Illinois Press, 2010).

14. For a history of *Jewish Life* and its successors, see Wald, *Trinity of Passion*, 205–9. Some aspects of the role of the pro-Soviet Jewish Left in equating anti-Stalinism with pro-fascism is discussed in Hasia R. Diner, *We Remember with Reverence and Love: American Jews and the Myth of Silence after the Holocaust, 1945–1962* (New York: New York University Press, 2009), 287–93.

15. The significance of the March 1948 *Jewish Life* essay "Concerning Jews Who Write" is discussed in Wald, "Arthur Miller's Missing Chapter," *Trinity of Passion*, especially 232–33.

16. Alman was the author of *The Hourglass* (New York: Simon and Schuster, 1947), *The Well of Compassion* (New York: Simon and Schuster, 1948), *World Full of Strangers* (New York: Doubleday, 1949), and *Generations* (Chicago: H. Regnery, 1971).

17. David Alman, "Samuel Ornitz's New Novel," *Jewish Life*, January 1952, 30–31.

18. Guy Endore to *Jewish Currents*, Endore Papers, Department of Special Collections, UCLA.

19. See John Sanford to Lloyd Brown, Sanford Papers, Howard Gottlieb Research Center, Boston University, and Sanford interview with author, 30 July 1989.

20. Sanford wrote several letters to Melitta Amster in 1991 that show a dogmatic loyalty to the Soviet Union as well as to the Israeli State. See the Sanford Papers in the Howard Gottlieb Research Center, 22 August and 9 September 1991.

21. Fortunately, the full story of Polonsky has been competently told in Paul Buhle and Dave Wagner, *A Very Dangerous Citizen: Abraham Lincoln Polonsky and the Hollywood Left* (Berkeley: University of California Press, 2002).

22. Abraham Polonsky, *The World Above* (Urbana: University of Illinois Press, 1999), 310.

23. The name suggests scriptwriter Val Lewton (1904–51), whose career overlapped with Polonsky's.

24. Polonsky, *The World Above*, 249.

25. Ibid., 502.

26. Abraham Polonsky, phone interview with the author, 1 August 1997.

27. The Communist press seems to have been uninterested in and even hostile to Polonsky's work. See Robert Friedman, "Abraham Polonsky's *The World Above*," *Daily Worker*, 13 April 1951, 11. Friedman oversimplifies Polonsky's argument, so that it seems unoriginal, and criticizes the novel for its incoherence and use of psychological jargon. Polonsky's book is one of a group of Marxist novels by one-time Communists

addressing psychology, most famously Millen Brand's *The Outward Room* (New York: Simon and Schuster, 1937) and William Gibson's *The Cobweb* (New York: Knopf, 1954).

28. The outstanding scholar on U.S. Marxism and psychiatry is Benjamin Harris. See his entry on "Psychology" in *Encyclopedia of the American Left*, ed. Mari Jo Buhle, Paul Buhle, and Dan Georgakas, 2nd ed. (New York: Oxford University Press, 1998), 610–12.

29. Ibid., 368.

30. This includes information sent to East Germany, very detailed in respect to everything except personal politics and ethnicity, about which there is total silence. See the long letter from Katya Gilden to Otto Brandstadter, 8 August 1973, Gilden Papers. The same information is given in numerous reviews of the Gildens' books and articles about their lives, including some by fellow Leftists who surely knew some of the facts. See Helen Yglesias, "Chronicle of the Class Wars," *Women's Review of Books* 7, nos. 10–11 (July 1990): 46. In some respects, Bert Gilden's testimony before the House Committee on Un-American Activities in 1956 provides an index for the political and ethnic omissions in the Gildens' subsequent autobiographical statements. There are important differences: in his HUAC testimony Bert Gilden insists that he had no job and did not engage in political activity while in Georgia, and that his work experiences in Bridgeport were minimal and involved no union activity. This testimony is on-line at http://www.archive.org/stream/investigationofc256unit/investigationofc256unit_djvu.txt

31. David Gilden, phone interview with the author, 18 May 1992. See also letters from Jairus M. Gilden to Wald, 1 April 1992 and 1 June 1992.

32. See letter from Bert Gilden to Sam Gruber, 12 January 1953, John Hay Library.

33. The Gildens sometimes use variants of this title but are probably referring to the version that appeared in *International Literature* 8 (August 1936): 55–83.

34. These ideas are expressed in many places including their manuscript "Notes on the Mode of Analytical Realism," Gilden Papers.

35. A critical essay especially insightful on gender and Lukács is Tim Libretti, "Between False Promises: K. B. Gilden's *Between the Hills and the Sea* and the Rethinking of Working-Class Culture, Consciousness, and Activism," *Women's Studies Quarterly*, nos. 1–2 (1998): 159–79. See also the informative interview of Katya Gilden with Paul Buhle, 21 November 1976, Oral History of the American Left, Tamiment Library, New York University.

36. Before Bert Gilden's death, the couple had planned to write a second volume about Mish's subsequent adventures, but the outline for it seems like an uninspired analogue to the later volumes of John Updike's *Rabbit* series. See the Gilden Papers.

37. The policy was subsequently used by union rivals to discredit Bob as a Party fanatic but had nonetheless resulted in Bostic's promotion.

38. See the personal and political biography of Jo Sinclair in Wald, *Trinity of Passion*, 250–59.

39. See the discussion of this literary trend in Tim Prchal, "New Americans and

the Immigrant Novel," in *The Cambridge History of the American Novel*, ed. Leonard Cassuto et al. (New York: Cambridge University Press, 2011), 426–36.

40. See Catherine Jurca, "The American Novel and the Rise of the Suburbs," in *The Cambridge History of the American Novel*, ed. Cassuto et al., 879–92.

41. See Maria Farland, "Literary Feminisms," in *The Cambridge History of the American Novel*, ed. Cassuto et al., 925–40.

42. Dwight Macdonald's much reprinted essay "Masscult and Midcult," which argues that the latter acts as if it esteems the values of high culture while diluting and vulgarizing them, was first collected in his volume *Against the American Grain* (New York: Random House, 1962).

43. I am grateful to the brilliant essay by Andrew Hoberek, "The Jewish Great American Novel," for a number of observations about this shift. See *The Cambridge History of the American Novel*, ed. Cassuto et al., 893–908.

44. "Emotional cubism" is an expression coined by James Wood and used by Hoberek, ibid., 896.

45. Sinclair, *Anna Teller* (New York: Feminist Press, 1992), 29.

46. Ibid., 41.

47. The outstanding source for biographical information on Jo Sinclair remains Elisabeth Sandberg, "Jo Sinclair: Toward a Critical Biography" (diss., University of Massachusetts, 1985).

48. See Wald, *Trinity of Passion*, 252.

49. See Oscar Ban, "Death Comes to the Foreign Press," *New Outlook* 162 (July 1933): 44–48, and "Cleveland's Foreign Language Newspaper Digest," *Common Ground* 1, no. 4 (Summer 1941): 120–24.

50. Sinclair had previously dedicated *The Changelings* to Oscar Ban's wife, Helen Ban. See Sandberg, "Jo Sinclair," 179.

51. See ibid., 153.

52. Ibid., 1–49.

53. Ibid., 214. The personal stories in the novel are partly Sinclair's own. There is an aspect of her in Mark Jackson's love of music as there is in Abby's relation to Emil and his wife, although Sinclair was far more political, advanced in her writing, and certain of her sexual identity than Mark at the time she worked under Oscar Ban on the WPA. The mentor relationship of Emil to Abby also incorporates some of Helen Buchman's role in relation to Sinclair as guide and teacher. Sinclair first met Buchman when Buchman was founder of Cleveland's left-wing Contemporary Theater in 1938, preparing a local production of *One-Third of a Nation*, the Living Newspaper performance of the WPA. Later, the Buchman family had a garden next to their suburban Ohio home that is re-created in the novel. Sinclair was acutely aware that, during the McCarthy years, Buchman, like Emil, lived in fear that she would be tainted by one-time Communist associations. Most notably, Buchman's sister-in-law and husband, Helen and Philip Sharnoff, had visited the Soviet Union several times and were known in Cleveland as Communists. Helen was a left-wing poet and Sharnoff a teacher at the Communist Party school. Alex Buchman to the author, 12 June 1997; Philip Sharnoff

to the author, 24 January 1998. As a result of this geographical relocation, the Detroit environment, including nearby University of Michigan, has a thinness of detail as compared to the block-by-block descriptions of Cleveland found in *The Changelings*. To protect identities, Sinclair moved the setting of *Anna Teller* from Cleveland to Detroit, changed the successful business venture of Oscar Ban into Emil's Pegasus bookstore, and made the ages of Emil's children different from those of Ban's.

54. See Sinclair, *Anna Teller*, 95 (referring to Abby's vision of Emil in an adulterous relation with his co-worker Grace), 106 (referring to Abby's living a poem as a mother), 141 (referring to Abby's son, Davey, as a poem), and 187 (Liz suggesting that Emil call his son "your little poem").

55. The highly complex role of poetry in this novel is explored in a graduate seminar essay by Sarah Ehlers, "Soul/Poem/Self: Uses for Poetry in Jo Sinclair's 'Anna Teller,'" 16 April 2008, University of Michigan.

56. Sinclair, *Anna Teller*, 161.

57. Ibid., 180.

58. There is a continuous flow of portentous literary references throughout *Anna Teller*: Eugene O'Neill, Rainer Marie Rilke, Henrik Ibsen, Matthew Arnold, John Keats. Without difficulty, most can be used to develop interpretive arguments. From *Peer Gynt* there are a dozen mentions of the "Solveig Song," cited to suggest that Emil is prisoner to the bourgeois ideal of a subservient wife in his love of Liz. But *Peer Gynt* is also the story of the search for an inner consistency of identity over a long and varied career marked by outward transformations—very much Emil's quest in *Anna Teller*. Matthew Arnold's "Dover Beach" is drawn on to bring to mind how the sea of faith in Marxism (embodied in the characters' reverent attitude toward the Spanish Civil War) is fading. The quote from John Donne, appearing as a frontispiece, links phrases that appear in the Communist hymn "The Internationale" with Freudian notions of the social necessity of repression. And such allusions are intertwined with numerous other patterns—the parallel suicides of Mark's mentor Sy and the Communist Andy K; the fate of the four copies of the book of poems that Emil has distributed; the strangely shared view of Andy K and Anna that the United States must earn feelings of gratitude from potential citizens such as themselves; the suggestion of analogies between "displaced persons" as legal and psychological conditions; the pattern of troubled interactions between money and art; and the peculiar climax in the novel in which psychological fears become transformed into biological ones (the spread of typhoid). For a compelling interpretation of this last point, see the graduate seminar essay by Logan Scherer, "Red Fever: Jo Sinclair's *Anna Teller* and the Foreign Germs of Communism," 22 April 2011, University of Michigan.

59. Subjective narratives, not orderly sequences or cause and effect, are the mode of development in *Anna Teller*. The novel begins by moving among the subjectivities of five characters on a single day in 1956 as they contemplate Anna's arrival. As a literary technique, this serves to get a quantity of information across at the outset. Anna Teller is in the plane, escaping from Hungary to the United States, trying to reconstruct her life. Her grandson Steve is in Detroit, thinking about his father, Emil.

Emil has started to act like a "sissy" following news of the events in Hungary, a nighttime father with "queer" emotions. Sinclair, *Anna Teller*, 69, 272. Abby, also in Detroit, is reconstructing an imaginary dialogue with her ambiguously named psychiatrist, Dr. Loren. (Loren, like Jo, can be either a male or a female name.) Mark is ruminating about his sexuality and his relation to the godlike Emil. And Emil is meditating on how to organize a "novel of emotions." The insertion of Anna into this larger group establishes that, despite its title, *Anna Teller* is not the story of just one woman. In a 22 December 1959 letter to one of her editors, available in the Howard Gottlieb Research Center at Boston University, Seid explains that her preferred title is "A Breaking of Prison" (from the Donne quotation in the front of the book). She insists: "This is not a one-character novel. It cannot be, no matter how strongly Anna comes through. The very importance of these younger, and very-lost, very imprisoned people about her is diminished too much. The book is a picture of people chained by themselves (and, of course, by their past—which they have never understood). . . . I consider Abby almost as important as Anna."

60. See Sinclair, *Anna Teller*, 139–43.

61. Ibid., 162.

62. This is demonstrated in the use of the concept of "war." In addition to the Spanish Civil War, World War II, and the Korean War, Sinclair writes of personal experiences as "wars." Steve has his "private, screwy war" with his father; Anna, who throughout the novel is equated with Europe itself ("with its dirt. Wars. Its death"), has her personal wars with various characters; and Emil imagines his book covering all "the wars in a man's life." Ibid., 80, 589, 70, 151. Psychological and private wars seem to be treated as microcosms of concurrent as well as of historical political conflicts. At one point, thinking about the McCarthyite witch hunt, Emil says that he has a "senate committee sitting in his head." Ibid., 213. At another, thinking of the work he will accomplish with his novel, he declares that he will "write the Nazi into eternal oblivion, the Russian to a standstill and defeat." Ibid., 387. If there is a central political idea in *Anna Teller*, it comes from the original title, "A Breaking of Prison." But to break chains, one must first notice them, which for Anna and others is a slow and hard process.

63. See http://www.time.com/time/covers/0,16641,19480920,00.html.

64. This striking picture is available at http://en.wikipedia.org/wiki/Hungarian_Revolution_of_1956.

65. Sinclair, *Anna Teller*, 223, 400, 9, 463, 578, 73, 530, 303. The novels by Sinclair and Petry are closer to the concerns of queer theory than gay and lesbian studies in the sense that the authors are not simply concerned with homosexual behavior, and whether it is seen as natural or unnatural, but point toward a consideration of all sexual identities that do not fit into the ways that gender and sexual activity were fixed and labeled at the time.

66. It is the genius of the novel that it is impossible to estimate just how admirable the character Anna Teller actually is. To some, she is a superwoman fantasy that the characters need as a substitute for religious faith or the absence of role models in

their lives. A great deal rides on her emigration from Hungary to the United States for Steve (her grandson), Emil, Abby, and Mark. Yet there are signs that she bears some responsibility for the death of Stephen (her son), a failure to acknowledge the danger of fascism, and a failure to leave Hungary under Communism. She seems to care little for her daughter other than market value in securing a rich husband, and she is a know-it-all in regard to her sons' selection of potential mates. The motivation for her part in the Hungarian fighting is not explained.

67. Sinclair, *Anna Teller*, 218, 225.
68. Ibid., 167, 157.
69. Ibid., 226, 157.
70. Ibid., 205.

CHAPTER EIGHT

1. Jack B. Moore, *Maxwell Bodenheim* (New York: Twayne, 1970), 172–73. In 1940, Bodenheim was dismissed from the WPA on charges that he had falsely signed an affidavit denying that he was a Communist Party member. See "Bodenheim Dropped in WPA Red Inquiry," *New York Times*, 2 August 1940 (see online at *New York Times* Article Archive). The same paper played up the sensational aspect of the murder under the headline "Maxwell Bodenheim, Wife Slain in the Poet's Dingy Bowery Room," *New York Times*, 8 February 1954 (see *New York Times* On-line Index). Sources disagree as to whether Fagan was a third or fourth wife and as to the spelling of her name (sometimes "Fagin").

2. O'Sheel, an Irish nationalist who never visited Ireland, was also a public Communist who held some differences with Soviet foreign policy. Kreymborg limited his Communist associations to literary matters. Neither seems to have held Party membership, although O'Sheel claimed to be in personal contact with Party leaders. See http://library.syr.edu/digital/guides/o/osheel_s.htm.

3. Shamus O'Sheel, "Introductory Note," in *Seven Poets in Search of an Answer*, ed. Thomas Yoseloff (New York: Bernard Ackerman, 1944), 8–9.

4. Aaron Kramer, phone interview with the author, September 1990.

5. Aaron Kramer, "A Tribute to Maxwell Bodenheim," *National Guardian*, 22 February 1954, 7.

6. The quotation and further details on the episode can be found online at http://www.gvsu.edu/english/cummings/issue3/Kramer3.htm.

7. Aaron Kramer, "Disappointed Ghosts (For Shaemas O'Sheel)," *Xanadu* 1, no. 2 (Winter 1975): 49. On my copy of the poem, Kramer notes that it was written several years earlier.

8. See Alan M. Wald, "American Jeremiad," *Exiles from a Future Time: The Forging of the Mid-Twentieth-Century Literary Left* (Chapel Hill: University of North Carolina Press, 2002), 9–38.

9. Aaron Kramer, "A May Day Poem for T. S. Eliot and Ezra Pound," *Thru Every Window* (New York: William-Frederick Press, 1950), 5.

10. O'Sheel to Kramer, 27 February 1945, Kramer Papers, Labadie Collection, University of Michigan, Ann Arbor.

11. O'Sheel to Kramer, 24 April 1945, ibid.

12. See Rosten to Kramer, 20 March 1946, ibid. Rosten wanted Kramer to develop as a lyric poet. Despite their pro-Communist views, both Kramer and Rosten were sometimes under attack by more sectarian critics in the Communist press, especially Mike Hecht in Chicago.

13. For a fuller discussion of this work and the circumstances of production, see Alan M. Wald, "Cultural Cross-Dressing: Radical Writers Represent African-Americans and Latinos in the McCarthy Era," *Writing from the Left: New Essays on Radical Culture and Politics* (London: Verso, 1994), 152–61.

14. See the discussion of this background in Wald, *Exiles from a Future Time*, 193–263, 299–326.

15. Ibid., "The Antinomies of a Proletarian Avant-garde," 299–326. The whole issue of the relation between politics and poetic form has received considerable attention, but among the most subtle and provocative treatments is Laurence Goldstein's "Politics by Parable: Denise Levertov and the Gulf War," *Triquarterly* 135 (April 2010): 105–21.

16. Bergman's work was collected by the Communist Party as *They Look Like Men* (New York: B. Ackerman, 1944). The volume was edited by Joy Davidman, whose husband, William Lindsay Gresham, wrote a novel about the death of Bergman from tuberculosis, *Limbo Tower* (New York: Rinehart, 1949).

17. Today, Raphael Hayes is best remembered for writing the Three Stooges comedy *Have Rocket Will Travel* (1959), but there were other young Communists, more serious poets on the leading staff of the Brooklyn College *Observer*, who looked down on Kramer for the same reasons as did Hayes. These included Harold Albaum (later Harold Norse) and Chester Kallman.

18. Aaron Kramer, "Valedictory Ode," *New Observer* (Brooklyn College) 15, no. 2 (April 1941): 18.

19. It does not even appear in his posthumous magnum opus, *Wicked Times: Selected Poems*, ed. Cary Nelson and Donald Gilzinger (Urbana: University of Illinois Press, 2004).

20. Aaron Kramer, "Threnody," *New York Times*, 21 July 1956, 14.

21. "Threnody" was first published in the *New York Times* on 12 July 1956 and is printed in *Wicked Times*, 309.

22. In 1961, Kramer became a professor of English literature at Dowling College, in Oakdale, New York, and was a founding editor of *West Hills Review: A Whitman Journal*. After receiving a Ph.D. in English from New York University in 1966, he crafted such scholarly works as *The Prophetic Tradition in American Poetry* (Madison, N.J.: Fairleigh Dickinson University Press, 1968), *Melville's Poetry: Toward the Enlarged Heart* (Madison, N.J.: Fairleigh Dickinson University Press, 1972), and *Neglected Aspects of American Poetry* (New York: Dowling College Press, 1997). Also a noted trans-

lator, Kramer contributed to *Rilke: Visions of Christ* (Boulder: University of Colorado Press, 1967); *A Century of Yiddish Poetry* (New York: Cornwall Books, 1989), which includes his 370 translations of 135 poets; *All My Yesterdays Were Steps* (New York: Dora Teitelbaum Foundation, 1995), the selected poems of Dora Teitelboim; and *The Last Lullaby: Poems of the Holocaust* (Syracuse, N.Y.: Syracuse University Press, 1998). His 1975 translation of Viktor Ullmann and Peter Kien's opera, *The Emperor of Atlantis* (premiere in 1977), which they had created in the Terezin concentration camp, was performed worldwide. The forms of Kramer's poetry evolved in a dozen more volumes of his own verse.

23. The long essay has been reprinted several times and cited as a source regarding U.S. poetry and Communism in the Cold War. See E. P. Thompson, "Homage to Thomas McGrath," in *The Revolutionary Poet in the United States: The Poetry of Thomas McGrath*, ed. Frederick C. Stern (Columbia: University of Missouri Press, 1988), 104–49.

24. Thomas McGrath, introduction to *Permit Me Refuge*, by Edwin Rolfe (Los Angeles: California Quarterly, 1955), 3.

25. Women were welcome in McGrath's world, as lovers and companions, and celebrated if, like Communists Mother Bloor and Elizabeth Gurley Flynn, they took on features of the masculinized revolutionary persona. Native American culture also played an increasingly prominent role in McGrath's vision. This was partly due to the view he assimilated from British Marxist Christopher Caudwell that poetry was a form of functional magic. Moreover, as the postwar political wasteland continued, the outcast revolutionary McGrath identified with the lonely struggle of indigenous peoples against an invasion of a mass culture foreign to the values of its own traditions.

26. These and some other details about McGrath's political history can be found at http://www.english.illinois.edu/maps/poets/m_r/mcgrath/radicalism.htm. For additional sources, see also my interviews with Thomas McGrath in Ann Arbor, Michigan, on 23 December 1983; Alice Greenfield in Los Angeles, California, on 6 February 1994; Richard Nickson in New York City on 3 March 1991; and Gene Frumkin in Albuquerque, New Mexico, on 6 April 1998.

27. See http://www.english.illinois.edu/maps/poets/m_r/mcgrath/tactical.htm.

28. *First Manifesto* (Baton Rouge, La.: Swallow Press, 1940), *To Walk a Crooked Mile* (New York: Swallow Press, 1947), *Fugitives From a Double World* (Denver, Colo.: Swallow Press, 1955), *Letter to an Imaginary Friend, Part I* (Chicago: Swallow Press, 1962), *New and Selected Poems* (Chicago: Swallow Press, 1964), *Letter to an Imaginary Friend, Parts I and II* (Chicago: Swallow Press, 1970), and *The Movie at the End of the World* (Chicago: Swallow Press, 1973). Swallow also edited an early collection in which McGrath appeared, *Three Young Poets: Thomas McGrath, William Peterson, James Franklin Lewis* (Prairie City, Ill.: James Decker Press, 1942). The title *Figures From a Double World* was a misprint; it should have been *Figures of a Double World*.

29. See http://www.thephora.net/forum/archive/index.php/t-22736.html.

30. These poems are reprinted in *Thomas McGrath, Selected Poems: 1938-88*, ed. Sam Hamil (Port Townsend, Wash.: Copper Canyon Press, 1988), but the precise publication histories are not available.

31. The best source is Joe Doyle, "Longshot O'Leary: Thomas McGrath's Years on the New York Waterfront," *North Dakota Quarterly* 50, no. 4 (Fall 1982): 32-40.

32. See http://www.english.illinois.edu/maps/poets/m_r/mcgrath/radicalism.htm.

33. See Bill Bailey, "Ripping the Swastika Off the *Bremen*," *The Kid From Hoboken: An Autobiography* (San Francisco: Circus Lithograph Press, 1993), 257-67.

34. Blau departed the Communist movement in 1956 and under the name Eric Blau became famous as the author of the off-Broadway show produced in 1968, *Jacques Brel Is Alive and Well and Living in Paris*.

35. Thomas McGrath, "Form and Content," *New Masses*, 16 July 1946, 20-22. McGrath was rebutted by Alexander Manderal, "Mr. McGrath—For and at the People," *Great Concord Tide*, February-March 1947, 13-16, 33-34. For an excellent biographical and critical study of Ferrini, see Kenneth Warren and Fred Whitehead, eds., *The Whole Song: Selected Poems of Vincent Ferrini* (Urbana: University Illinois Press, 2002), xi-xxv.

36. She is the model for "Alice" in the 1995 film *Zoot Suit*.

37. Richard Nickson, interview with the author, New York City, 3 March 1991.

38. "The Education of Alice McGrath," Oral History Collection, UCLA, 130; Alice McGrath, interview with the author, Los Angeles, 6 February 1994.

39. Alice McGrath's recollection is that Tom mostly had little episodes of alcoholic behavior, but the incidents increased until they became one big event. The usual pattern was for Tom to gain access to hard liquor, then do something mean and self-destructive. Next came a period of remorse, which could be just as bad, followed by an antagonistic denial that he had done anything that should upset anyone. Alice McGrath, interview with the author.

40. Politically, the Party assigned McGrath to one of the Hollywood branches, but he did little other than focus on the craft of poetry. Although Alice and Tom followed the Communist press, Alice saw little evidence that he studied much Marxism. Occasionally, McGrath would read his poetry in public, but his manner struck some of his listeners as unexciting due to his belief that one should always read in a monotone so as not to distract from the content of the poem.

41. This was claimed in a letter from Charles Humboldt to Olga Cabral, 18 March 1957, Humboldt Papers.

42. This is discussed in a letter from Humboldt to Magil, 25 April 1954, Humboldt Papers. Humboldt accused Magil of never having read the poems. For biographical information about Magil, see Wald, *Exiles from a Future Time*, 179-80.

43. A. B. Magil to Charles Humboldt, 4 April 1953, Humboldt Papers.

44. Alice McGrath interview.

45. Perhaps the most compelling reading of *Letter to an Imaginary Friend* to date is by John Lowney, "A Metaphoric Palimpsest: The Underground Memory of Thomas McGrath's *Letter to an Imaginary Friend*," *History, Memory, and the Literary Left:*

Modern American Poetry, 1935–1968 (Iowa City: University of Iowa Press, 2006), 161–91.

46. Thomas McGrath, *Letter to an Imaginary Friend* (Port Townsend, Wash.: Copper Canyon Press, 1997), 162–63.

47. Quoted in Stern, *Revolutionary Poet in the United States*, 120.

48. Details on the Mexican sojourn are vague, but it is likely he was asked to go by the Communist leadership in connection with efforts to evade an expected outlawing of the Party.

49. Walter Lowenfels, *The Prisoners: Poems for Amnesty* (Philadelphia: Whittier Press, 1954), 9, 22.

50. One of the best commentaries on Lowenfels's work is Roger Asselineau, "A Neglected Transcendentalist Poet of the Twentieth Century," in *Proceedings of a Symposium on American Literature*, ed. Marta Sienicka (Poznan, Poland: Uniwersytet im. Adama Mickiewicz w Poznaniu, 1979), 31–42.

51. Joel Lewis handles this transition effectively in his introduction to Walter Lowenfels's *Reality Prime: Selected Poems* (Jersey City, N.J.: Talisman, 1998), 3–14.

52. Walter Lowenfels, "The White Poetry Syndicate," *Arts in Society* 8 (January 1971): 413.

53. Lowenfels included this text twelve years later in *My Many Lives: The Autobiography of Walter Lowenfels, Volume II, The Poetry of My Politics* (Homestead, Fla.: Olivant Press, 1968), 25–27.

54. Robert Grover, ed., *The Portable Walter: From the Prose and Poetry of Walter Lowenfels* (New York: International, 1968), 118.

55. Sarah Wright, interview with the author, New York City, 27 February 2002.

56. Judy (Dew) Lowenfels, interview with the author, New York City, 6 April 1990.

57. Judy Lowenfels, interview with the author, New York, 6 April 1990.

58. He was also involved in a controversy about sexism. On Christmas Day, 1949, Lowenfels published an article in the *Worker* entitled "Santa Claus or Comrade X?" in which he mused about the "difficulties" of living with five women (his wife and four daughters) who spent their time washing, sewing, and worrying about their clothes. The article was fiercely criticized by women who read the paper. Lowenfels's attempts to redeem himself in subsequent articles served only to anger his critics further, and the incident damaged his standing within the Party and the larger movement. This incident is treated as an example of efforts to confront male supremacy within progressive movements in historian Kate Weingard's *Red Feminism* (Baltimore: Johns Hopkins University Press, 2001).

59. The reasons are not clear why; there might have been disagreements over money and later over politics. Hays would dispute Lowenfels's collaboration in writing the song "Wasn't That a Time." See references to members of the Lowenfels family in Doris Willens, *Lonesome Traveler: The Life of Lee Hays* (New York: Norton, 1988).

60. Grover, *The Portable Walter*, 53.

61. Ibid., 53.

62. Walter Lowenfels, *Some Deaths* (New York: Nantahala Foundation, 1964), 89.

63. See the discussion of Grebanier in Wald, *Exiles from a Future Time*, 164–65.

64. As of spring 2010, the Taminent Library's Guide to the White Papers maintains that he died "from a heart attack at the age of 44." The scholar Matt Young believes that White committed suicide while facing imminent expulsion from the Communist Party as being both gay and a Browderite; see http://www.albavolunteer.org/2010/06/david-mckelvy-white-1901-1945. Junius Scales, close to White, maintains (with Richard Nickson) in *Cause at Heart: A Former Communist Remembers* (Athens: University of Georgia Press, 1987), 150, that White was associated with Browder and that the suicide may have been connected to Browder's fall in the Communist Party. Strangely, Harold Norse, in *Memoirs of a Bastard Angel* (New York: Morrow, 1989), 142, claims that White (referred to by the name David Blake) was killed in a private airplane accident while performing stunts that he learned in Spain. Others believed he died in Spain.

65. See "Murray Young, 1907–1969," *New World Review* 38 (1970): 221; and an email to the author from David Laibman, 19 May 2010. Laibman remembers Young as second in command to Jessica Smith under the title of managing editor. In the early 1950s, the *New World Review* was broadening its scope to include Eastern Europe and China. Laibman recalls that Young did not really seem to be a Marxist but was more of a Left anarchist. He was Catholic, a poet, and obviously gay, an issue that the Communist Party members did not discuss openly. Young's political relationship with the Communists became increasingly uneasy in the early 1960s because, while sympathetic to the Soviet Union, Young needed constant confirmation of his convictions on the basis of observable realities—especially in cultural achievements and education. By the late 1960s, he was frequently complaining about the harmful effects of bureaucracy and privilege in the Soviet bloc; he was tolerated on the magazine primarily because of his personal connection with the editor, Jessica Smith.

66. *New York Times*, 29 April 1982, 110. The teachers ousted in the 1950s were given restitution by New York City inasmuch as the laws under which the teachers were dismissed had been deemed unconstitutional in 1967–68.

67. Aaron Kramer, interview with the author, 6 June 1994. For further information on Krantz, see http://www.sheldonkranz.com/Aesthetic-Realism-Class-Report-3-8-48.html. Krantz was an early student of Aesthetic Realism with Siegel and became a consultant who taught Aesthetic Realism. In 1957, he married Anne Fielding and later described how he had been a homosexual who had permanently changed the way he saw women.

68. For sources alleging cult behavior and detailing Siegel's homosexual conversion campaign, consult http://en.wikipedia.org/wiki/Aesthetic_Realism.

69. See Michael Bluejay, "Aesthetic Realistic Founder Eli Siegel Killed Himself," at http://michaelbluejay.com/x/suicide.html.

70. See http://www.sheldonkranz.com/.

71. For additional perspectives on the evolution of postwar gay poetry, see Walter Holland, "The Calamus Root: A Study of Gay American Poetry since World War II," in *Gay and Lesbian Literature since World War II: History and Memory*, ed. Sonya L.

Jones (New York: Routledge, 1998), 5-25, and many other fascinating essays in that work.

72. See Dorothy J. Farnan, *Auden in Love: The Intimate Story of a Lifelong Love Affair* (New York: Simon and Schuster, 1984), 20, 26.

73. Robert Friend to the author, 26 April 1992.

74. Ibid. The poet Edward Field (b. 1924) is certain that Friend had learned that his passport was to be confiscated and he immigrated to Israel just "one step ahead of the American authorities." Edward Field, "Editor's Preface," in *Dancing with a Tiger: Poems 1941-1998*, by Robert Friend (New York: Spuyten Duyvil, 2003), 22.

75. The poems are reprinted in Friend, *Dancing with a Tiger*, 29, 31.

76. Friend, *Dancing with a Tiger*, 40. The source from Shaw is provided as a footnote.

77. Robert Friend to the author, 26 April 1992.

78. See Robert Friend, "The Hunchback," *Dancing with a Tiger*, 35, and discussion of Edward Field, "Robert Friend: A Life in Poetry," *The Gay and Lesbian Review Worldwide* (May 2003): 22-23.

79. Friend, *Dancing with a Tiger*, 131, 68, 84.

80. The list of names of capable postwar poets from Communist backgrounds goes on and on: John Beecher (1904-80), Millen Brand (1906-80), Ray Durem (1915-63), Estelle Gershgoren (b. 1940), Robert Hayden, David Ignatow, George Hitchcock, Norman Rosten, Alvaro Cardona-Hine, Gene Frumkin, Naomi Replansky, Vincent Ferrini, Lawrence Fixel (1917-2003), Leslie Woolf Hedley (dates unknown), Lance Jeffers (1915-85), Ettore Rella (1907?-88), William Pillin (1910-85), and Audre Lorde. Perhaps writers such as Dudley Randall (1914-2000) and even John Berryman (1914-72) might be added if more were known about their youthful commitments. There are dozens of still lesser-known authors of collections of poetry rooted in the Left— George Abbe (1891-1989), Martha Millet, Neil Wesson (1906-74), Art Berger (dates unknown), Richard Davidson (1930-93), Irene Paull, Sid Gershgoren (b. 1937), and Lucy Smith (dates unknown).

81. There are many excellent books on poetry in the Cold War but only two or three that address writers from the Communist movement, and these tend to be the few well-known figures. One major exception is Alan Filreis, *Counter-revolution of the Word: The Conservative Attack on Modern Poetry, 1945-1960* (Chapel Hill: University of North Carolina Press, 2008). Also see the excellent work of James Smethurst, *The Black Arts Movement: Literary Nationalism in the 1960s and 1970s* (Chapel Hill: University of North Carolina Press, 2005) for information about the importance of the 1950s to Left poets of color.

A list of titles of some of the other works I have found useful to understanding the poetry of the postwar era includes Charles Altieri, *The Art of Twentieth-Century American Poetry: Modernism and After* (Oxford: Blackwell, 2006); Edward Brunner, *Cold War Poetry* (Urbana: University of Illinois Press, 2001); Maria Damon, *Dark End of the Street: Margins in American Poetry* (Minneapolis: University of Minnesota Press, 1993); Michael Davidson, *Guys Like Us: Citing Masculinity in Cold War Poetics*

(Chicago: University of Chicago Press, 2004); Andrew Epstein, *Beautiful Enemies: Friendship and Postwar American Poetry* (New York: Oxford University Press, 2006); Walter Kalaidjian, *The Edge of Modernism: American Poetry and the Traumatic Past* (Baltimore: Johns Hopkins University Press, 2006); David Lehman, *The Last Avant-Garde: The Making of the New York School of Poets* (New York: Anchor Books, 1998); James Longenbach, *Modern Poetry after Modernism* (New York: Oxford University Press, 1997); Cary Nelson, *Revolutionary Memory: Recovering the Poetry of the American Left* (Madison: University of Wisconsin Press, 2001); Camille Roman, *Elizabeth Bishop's World War II–Cold War View* (New York: Palgrave Macmillan, 2001); and William Watkin, *In the Process of Poetry: The New York School and the Avant-Garde* (Lewisburg, Pa.: Bucknell University Press, 2001).

82. At the 1992 National Poetry Conference in Orono, Maine, Ignatow told me that he had briefly been a member of the Communist Party in the 1930s.

83. Fred Whitehead, ed., *Don Gordon: Collected Poems* (Urbana: University of Illinois Press, 2004), 71.

84. Ibid., 89.

85. Ibid., 71.

86. He worked in the Hollywood Studios rising to assistant head of the story department of MGM in 1951. Then he was called before the House Committee on Un-American Activities. Refusing to testify, Gordon lived in obscurity as a blacklisted Communist, supporting himself mainly by working in day care centers, halfway houses, and hospitals.

87. Olga Cabral, "The Table," *Tape Found in a Bottle* (Homestead, Fla.: Olivant Press, 1971), 31.

88. Olga Cabral, "Kaddish," *The Evaporated Man* (privately published, 1968), n.p.

89. Ben Maddow, *A False Autobiography, Poems: 1940–1990* (Carmel, Calif.: Other Shores Press, 1991), 12.

CONCLUSION

1. The title of a 1950 pamphlet on blacklisting by Dalton Trumbo.

2. Frank Kermode, *The Sense of an Ending: Studies in the Theory of Fiction* (New York: Oxford University Press, 1967).

3. See Theodor W. Adorno, *Negative Dialectics*, trans. E. B. Ashton (London: Routledge, 1990).

4. To get a sense of the skimpiness of the treatment of the Communist presence in post–World War II literary history, one has only to examine the most comprehensive treatments of the period: Emory Elliot, ed., *The Columbia History of the American Novel: New Views* (New York: Columbia, 1991); Emory Elliot, ed., *Columbia Literary History of the United States* (New York: Columbia, 1988); Daniel Hoffman, ed., *Harvard Guide to Contemporary American Writing* (Cambridge: Harvard University Press, 1983); and Fredrick R. Karl, *American Fiction, 1940–1980* (New York: Harper and Row, 1983).

5. The term "race traitor" was originally an epithet employed by racialists against those supposedly working against the interests of their own privileged ethnic group, but the term currently refers to the laudatory stance of antiracists and internationalists.

6. The phrase is associated with the work of the Frankfurt School; see http://jaysanalysis.com/2011/06/03/horkheimer-adorno-habermas-and-the-dialectic-of-enlightenment/.

7. The manuscript was originally published in 1977 with the misleading title *The Power of the People* and then was issued in a definitive edition by E. San Juan Jr. in 1995.

8. The passage is quoted in Augusto Fauni Espiritu's wonderfully researched *Five Faces of Exile: The National and Filipino American Intellectuals* (Stanford, Calif.: Stanford University Press, 2005), 54. The full text is available in the Bulosan Papers in Special Collections, University of Washington, Seattle, Wash. A 17 January 1955 letter in Special Collections addressed to "Florentino," is filled with conventional Communist Party rhetoric about science versus superstition.

9. See the letter identified as "Saturday night" in the Bulosan Papers. This appears to be part of a sequence of communications to Josephine Patrick starting in 1953.

10. Letter to *New Masses*, Isidor Schneider Papers, Rare Book and Manuscript Library, Columbia University, New York.

11. The *People's World* ran a positive obituary for him by his friend Chris Mensalvas. Chris Mensalvas, "Reporting for Carlos Bulosan," *Daily People's World*, 28 December 1956.

12. See the materialists on the Socialist Workers Party and Young Socialist Alliance in the Josephine Patrick Papers in Special Collections, University of Washington, Seattle, Wash. This political switch was around the time of Bulosan's death or just after, which coincided with the Khrushchev Revelations. It appears that Patrick was reunited with her husband, who also became a Trotskyist.

13. Carlos Bulosan, "Theseus," *Carlos Bulosan and His Poetry: A Biography and Anthology*, ed. Susan Evangelista (Seattle: University of Washington Press, 1985), 71–72.

14. Bulosan, *The Cry and the Dedication* (Philadelphia: Temple University Press, 1995), 54.

15. Ibid., 82.

16. A. E. Housman, "The Laws of God, the Laws of Man," in *Collected Poems* (New York: Henry Holt, 1965), 111.

17. Michael Lowy, "The Current of Critical Irrealism," in *Adventures in Realism*, ed. Matthew Beaumont (Oxford: Blackwell, 2007), 193–206.

18. The term "Late Modernism" is frequently used to refer to postwar painting in dialogue with postmodernism, but it was recently employed by Robert Genter to indicate a stage in literary modernism in *Late Modernism: Art, Culture, and Politics in Cold War America* (Philadelphia: University of Pennsylvania Press, 2010).

19. Ellison would seem to be a part of the phenomenon of Communist literary modernism up to the moment of publication of *Invisible Man*, which was changed

significantly by himself and his editors. For contrasting perspectives on how to read Ellison at this moment, see Barbara Foley, *Wrestling with the Left: The Making of Ralph Ellison's "Invisible Man"* (Durham, N.C.: Duke University Press, 2010), and Nathaniel Mills, "Ragged Figures: The *Lumpenproletariat* in Nelson Algren and Ralph Ellison" (diss., University of Michigan, 2011).

20. The expulsion is discussed in Wald, *Trinity of Passion: The Literary Left and the Antifascist Crusade* (Chapel Hill: University of North Carolina Press, 2007), 174–75. See the fictionalized version of the marriage and Bransten's suicide in Christina Stead's *I'm Dying Laughing* (New York: Henry Holt, 1986). Several searing letters from Bransten can be found in the Samuel Ornitz Papers, State Historical Society of Wisconsin, Madison, especially 3 August 1951 and 17 January 1952.

21. For details, I am grateful for two emails from Thomas Bransten, 13 May and 17 May 2010.

22. This led to some controversy about statements that he made to Allen Weinstein when interviewed for *Perjury: The Hiss-Chambers Case* (New York: Knopf, 1978). See http://www.thenation.com/article/allen-weinsteins-docudrama.

23. Milton Stern, phone interview with the author, 4 August 2009. Stern, a U.S. literary scholar, met Lieber in Poland and remained close to him during his years in the United States.

24. Ben Maddow, *Let Truth Be the Prejudice: W. Eugene Smith: His Life and Photographs* (San Francisco: Aperture Books, 1985).

25. See Victor Navasky, *Naming Names* (New York: Hill and Wang, 1980), 75, and Patrick McGilligan, *Backstory 2: Interviews with Screenwriters of the 1940s and 1950s* (Berkeley: University of California Press, 1997), 160.

26. See the letters from Guy Endore to Francis Faragogh, 11 March 1957, and to David Zablodowsky, 28 March 1957, in Endore Papers. Other information comes from Bobby Lees, interview with the author, Los Angeles, June 1992, and Tiba Willner, interview with the author, Ojai, Calif., 10 July 1990.

27. Mieczyslaw Brahmer et al., eds., *Studies in Language and Literature in Honor of Margaret Schlauch* (New York: Russell and Russell, 1965).

28. Milton Stern, phone interview with the author, 4 August 2009. The most complete information about Schlauch appears in Christine M. Rose, "Margaret Schlauch (1898–1986)," in *Women Medievalists and the Academy*, ed. Jane Chance (Madison: University of Wisconsin Press, 2005), 523–39.

29. The quip was reported by Alyse Conrad, interview with the author, Detroit, Mich., 7 November 1990. Details of Conrad's career are in "Autobiography of Earl Conrad," Earl Conrad Papers, Local History Collection, Cayuga Community College, Auburn, N.Y.

30. Milton Halpern, phone interview with the author, 8 November 1997; letter from Ben Field to Betty Ann Burch, 22 September 1972, quoted in Betty Ann Burch, "The Assimilation Experience of Five White Ethnic Novelists in the Twentieth Century" (diss., University of Minnesota, 1973), 102; and Eve Merriam, *Something about the Author* (Detroit: Gale Research Corporation, 1985), 73:153–59. If one was a staff mem-

ber of various publications, or in a Writers Unit, one may not have attended regular branch meetings, but there is much evidence that these three were ideologically committed Communists for substantial periods during the 1930s, 1940s, and early 1950s. For Seaver, see his superficial *So Far, So Good: Recollections of a Life in Publishing* (New York: Lawrence and Hill, 1985).

31. A. B. Magil to the author, 4 September 1991.

32. Milton Meltzer, interview the author, New York City, 6 May 1994.

33. Ira Wallach, interview with the author, New York City, 19 May 1994. The quotation is from Phillip L. Berman, *The Courage to Grow Old* (New York: Ballantine, 1989), 156–57.

34. For information on River, I am grateful to Robert Hethmon for showing me the FBI file he obtained on River, and to Dorothy River for a phone interview on 8 October 1990. Information on Michel's problem-filled life and tragic death is available in Damon Knight, *The Futurians* (New York: John Day, 1977), especially 157–69.

35. Information on Edward Newhouse comes from a phone interview with the author, 9 March 1999. The outstanding source for information on Newhouse is Billy Ben Smith, *The Literary Career of Proletarian Novelist and "New Yorker" Short Story Writer Edward Newhouse* (Lewiston, N.Y.: Edwin Mellen Press, 2001).

36. Fred Whitehead to the author, 13 May 1991.

37. See the file on Whittaker Chambers in the Endore Papers, especially the following: "Open Letter to Whittaker Chambers," 25 August 1952; letters to and from Elinor Kirstein, February 1954; and Endore to Cary McWilliams, 3 March 1954.

38. The various drafts and other related materials are in the Endore Papers. See especially his 28 June 1958 letter to Richard Arens.

39. Guy Endore, "Autobiographical Notes," Endore Papers, UCLA.

40. Paul Ricoeur et al., *Memory, History, Forgetting*, trans. Kathleen Blamey and David Pellauer (Chicago: University of Chicago Press, 2004), 430.

A NOTE ON METHODOLOGY

1. Walter Benjamin, "Theoretics of Knowledge, Theory of Progress," *Philosophical Forum* 15, nos. 1–2 (Fall–Winter 1983–84): 24.

2. Stefan Müller-Doohm, *Adorno: A Biography* (Cambridge, U.K.: Polity Press, 2005), xii.

3. Thomas McGrath, "McGrath on McGrath," *North Dakota Quarterly* 50, no. 4 (Fall 1982): 25.

4. A sound overview of the period can be found in Stephen J. Whitfield, *The Culture of the Cold War* (Baltimore: Johns Hopkins University Press, 1991). Some of the scholarly volumes on U.S. culture of the era (not specifically the Communist presence) since the late twentieth century include Arne Axelsson, *Restrained Response: American Novels of the Cold War and Korea, 1945–1962* (Westport, Conn.: Greenwood Press, 1990); Michael Barson, *"Better Dead Than Red!"* (New York: Diane Publishing Company, 1992); Jackie Byars, *All That Hollywood Allows: Re-reading Gender in 1950s Melo-*

drama (Chapel Hill: University of North Carolina Press, 1991); Virginia Carmichael, *Framing History: The Rosenberg Story and the Cold War* (Minneapolis: University of Minnesota Press, 1993); James Campbell, *Exiled in Paris: Richard Wright, James Baldwin, Samuel Beckett, and Others on the Left Bank* (New York: Scribner, 1995); Kevin J. Fernlund, ed., *The Cold War American West, 1945–1989* (Albuquerque: University of New Mexico Press, 1998); Joel Foreman, ed., *The Other Fifties: Interrogating Midcentury American Icons* (Urbana: University of Illinois Press, 1997); Woody Haut, *Pulp Culture: Hardboiled Fiction and the Cold War* (New York: Serpent's Tale, 1995); Margot A. Henriksen, *Dr. Strangelove's America: Society and Culture in the Atomic Age* (Berkeley: University of California Press, 1997); Daniel Horowitz, *Betty Friedan and the Making of the Feminine Mystique: The American Left, the Cold War, and Modern Feminism* (Amherst: University of Massachusetts Press, 2001); Fred Inglis, *The Cruel Peace: Everyday Life and the Cold War* (New York: Basic Books, 1991); Peter J. Kuznick and James Gilbert, eds., *Rethinking Cold War Culture* (Washington, D.C.: Smithsonian Books, 2001); Karal Ann Marling, *As Seen on TV: The Visual Culture of Everyday Life in the 1950s* (Cambridge, Mass.: Harvard University Press, 1994); Larry May, ed., *Recasting America: Culture and Politics in the Age of Cold War* (Chicago: University of Chicago Press, 1988); Melanie McAlister, *Epic Encounters: Culture, Media and U.S. Interests in the Middle East, 1945–2000* (Berkeley: University of California Press, 2001); Leerom Medovoi, *Rebels: Youth Culture and the Cold War Origins of Identity* (Durham, N.C.: Duke University Press, 2005); Joanne Meyerowitz, ed., *Not June Cleaver: Women and Gender in Postwar America, 1945–1960* (Philadelphia: Temple University Press, 1994); Alan Nadel, *Containment Culture* (Durham, N.C.: Duke University Press, 1995); Lisle A. Rose, *The Cold War Comes to Main Street: America in 1950* (Lawrence: University Press of Kansas, 1999); Andrew Ross, *No Respect: Intellectuals and Popular Culture* (London: Routledge, 1989); David Savran, *Communists, Cowboys, and Queers: The Politics of Masculinity in the Work of Arthur Miller and Tennessee Williams* (Minneapolis: University of Minnesota Press, 1992); Nora Sayer, *Running Time: Films of the Cold War* (New York: Doubleday, 1982); Thomas Hill Schaub, *American Fiction in the Cold War* (Madison: University of Wisconsin Press, 1991); Tobin Siebers, *Cold War Criticism and the Politics of Skepticism* (New York: Oxford University Press, 1993); and Penny Von Eschen, *Race against Empire: Black Americans and Anti-Colonialism, 1937–1957* (Ithaca, N.Y.: Cornell University Press, 1997).

5. For a brief argument on behalf of the contemporary, humane values of Marxism in contrast to the hypocritical blind spots of Western "democracy," see Terry Eagleton, "In Praise of Marx," *Chronicle Review*, 10 April 2011, available at http://chronicle.com/article/In-Praise-of-Marx/127027. *American Night* rejects the notion that Stalinism is a totalitarian double of Nazi Germany, especially in the areas of economy and ideology, but the Soviet Union under Stalin is referred to as a "police state" to underscore that the degree of political repression was enormous. For a compelling elaboration of differences between Nazism and Stalinism, see Enzo Traverso, "The New Anti-Communism: Rereading the Twentieth Century," in *History and Revolution: Refuting Revisionism*, ed. Mike Haynes and Jim Wolfreys (London: Verso, 2007), 138–55.

6. The Latin phrase translates as "hidden God" and has been used by many theologians and philosophers; Theodor Adorno famously discussed the notion in relation to Kafka in *Prisms* (Cambridge: MIT Press, 1983), 269.

7. This is the subtitle of Hobsbawm's book *The Age of Extremes* (New York: Pantheon, 1994).

8. See the meticulous study by Gerald Meyer, *Vito Marcantonio, Radical Politician, 1902-1954* (Albany: State University Press of New York, 1989), especially 53-86.

9. Trumbo stated:

> The blacklist was a time of evil, and no one on either side who survived it came through untouched by evil. Caught in a situation that had passed beyond the control of mere individuals, each person reacted as his nature, his needs, his convictions, and his particular circumstances compelled him to. There was bad faith and good, honesty and dishonesty, courage and cowardice, selflessness and opportunism, wisdom and stupidity, good and bad on both sides. When you who are in your 40s or younger look back with curiosity on that dark time, as I think occasionally you should, it will do no good to search for villains or heroes or saints or devils because there were none; there were only victims. Some suffered less than others, some grew and some diminished, but in the final tally we were all victims because almost without exception each of us felt compelled to say things he did not want to say, to do things that he did not want to do, to deliver and receive wounds he truly did not want to exchange. That is why none of us—right, left, or center—emerged from that long nightmare without sin.

The quotation can be found at http://www.imdb.com/name/nm0874308/bio.

10. This famous quotation appears in many places, but the original source is Thurber's 18 February 1939 *New Yorker* piece, "The Scotty Who Knew Too Much."

11. See "The Novelists' International" in Michael Denning, *Culture in the Age of Three Worlds* (London: Verso, 2004), 51-72.

ACKNOWLEDGMENTS

1. An endnote cannot provide a full bibliography, but the following are some recent book-length works especially influential in developing the argument of *American Night*, in addition to those already cited in preceding notes: Edith Anderson, *Love and Exile: An American's Memoir of Life in Divided Berlin* (Hanover, N.H.: Steerforth Press, 1999); Paul Buhle, *Radical Hollywood: The Untold Story behind America's Favorite Movies* (New York: New Press, 2002) and *Hide in Plain Sight: The Hollywood Blacklistees in Film and Television, 1950-2002* (New York: Palgrave Macmillan, 2004); Kevin Gaines, *African Americans in Ghana: Black Expatriates and the Civil Rights Era* (Chapel Hill: University of North Carolina Press, 2007); Julia Mickenberg, *Learning from the Left: Children's Literature, the Cold War, and Radical Politics in the United States* (New York: Oxford University Press, 2005); Bill Millen, *Afro Orientalism* (Minneapolis: University of Minnesota Press, 2004); Nikhil Pal Singh, *Black Is a Country:*

Race and the Unfinished Struggle for Democracy (Cambridge, Mass.: Harvard University Press, 2005); Judith E. Smith, *Visions of Belonging: Family Stories, Popular Culture, and Postwar Democracy, 1940–1960* (New York: Columbia University Press, 2004); and Chris Vials, *Realism for the Masses: Aesthetics, Popular Front Pluralism, and U.S. Culture, 1935–1947* (Amherst: University of Massachusetts Press, 2009).

2. The absence of a sustained discussion of gay and lesbian Left writers in any literature convinced me to develop a chapter tracing their history. Among the topics promised in my earlier volumes but now temporarily deferred are those about the literary criticism of blacklisted Communist professors, the cultural contributions of *Science & Society*, radical science fiction, and the significance of the experimental trend within left-wing theater. Moreover, for reasons of space and structure, I had to eliminate from the final version of *American Night* some draft chapters about writers such as Michael Blankfort, Phillip Bonosky, Olga Cabral, Stefan Heym, Alvaro Cardona-Hine, Grace Lumpkin, Warren Miller, James Neugass, William Gardner Smith, Janet Stevenson, Philip Stevenson, Helen Yglesias, Jose Yglesias, and others. My hope is that this material will appear in other venues.

Acknowledgments

American Night holds fast to the chronological span and major themes projected at the start of this multivolume venture. It brings to a close three decades of the literary Left depicted as a conduit of political struggle passing through phases significantly marked by romantic utopianism, antifascism, and resistance to domestic repression. Earlier volumes may be consulted for the procedures followed in these pages regarding the use of political terminology and identifying tags and dates, as well as for a "Chronology of the Mid-Twentieth-Century Cultural Left" (found in *Exiles from a Future Time*, pp. 327–29), which situates the establishment of Communist publications and organizations along with background events—the Moscow Trials, the Hitler-Stalin Pact, the Prague Trials. Much of the research conducted for the first two books is also the basis for the third. The acknowledgments sections of the earlier volumes provide a fuller understanding of source materials. They also identify the institutions (academic as well as other networks) that have sustained my research and the individuals who inspired my literary and political thinking.

Yet some changes in plans must also be disclosed. Since I began research, there has occurred a welcome outpouring in scholarship about specific areas of the postwar Left that addresses topics of direct concern to my own work. This impressive body of writing (only some of which is cited in the endnote that follows) includes academic volumes, memoirs, anthologies, dissertations, and key essays about the continuity between the Communist legacy and the emergence of the Black Arts movement and other forms of ethnic nationalism; the impact of the Popular Front tradition in mass culture and children's literature; the intersection of the Left and pulp fiction; the attendance of the Left in Cold War poetry; the omnipresence of radical connections to film and television; the Cold War "diaspora" of political refugees abroad; and even books specifically about writers' resistance to the Cold War.[1] In light of these advances, my own effort to craft a story both original and cogent has induced me to omit or curtail a few of the topics promised in earlier volumes and to add new ones.[2] Here I must apologize to many individuals who provided me with materials that I was not able to use, and especially in regard to writers who were targeted for analysis but ended up being mentioned only in passing. I acquired far more information than could be inserted within a limited number of pages, although I plan to employ some of this material in projects to come.

A scholar working in a complicated and controversial area such as the Left in the Cold War must take preventive measures to counter one's natural tendency to draw the conclusions that one wants to draw. *American Night* rests in the first instance on original primary research. When oral history is involved, there is always a risk of naively falling susceptible to those veterans who recount their stories in a compelling and assured manner, although nearly all such narratives are populated by at least a few self-serving or score-settling vignettes. Even the vast amount of letters and manuscripts one finds in archives can be selectively preserved and tweaked by authors (and sometimes further pruned by family members), hiding as much as is revealed. In navigating these sources, the researcher mostly designs his or her own controls for accuracy by reading widely, opening oneself to opposing points of view, noting where informants are few, and cross-checking information. But what finally prevents scholars in the humanities from massaging data to spin their work in a way that tells a prettier or uglier story than they really should are the hard questions posed by others.

These interrogations come from the quantity and diversity of the informed people interviewed in the primary research, colleagues in the field who reach other conclusions that they make known in print, independent-minded readers of the drafts of the manuscript who query and complain, students in classes who are especially valued when they speak up to inject doubt or dissent, and participants in conference sessions and seminars where the early versions of work are presented. I have been fortunate in finding challenging interlocutors at every turn. Several individuals were kind enough to read over chapters-in-progress on subjects about which they had unusual expertise: Peter Drucker, Konstantina Mary Karageorgos, Aaron Lecklider, Elisabeth Petry, Marlon Ross, and Alexander Saxton. Others went beyond the call of duty in reading unwieldy drafts of the book in its entirety: Howard Brick, Angela Dillard, Lawrence Goldstein, Patrick Quinn, Paula Rabinowitz, and James Smethurst. None of these individuals, nor anyone else who was interviewed or who rendered assistance, is in any way liable for the opinions or judgments expressed in this book.

Parts of this manuscript were given as papers at the national conventions of the Modern Languages Association in 2006 and the American Studies Association in 2009. Other portions were presented at events organized by the Left Forum in New York City, Stanford University's Humanities Center, the Department of English of the University of Wisconsin, the College of Liberal Arts and Sciences of the University of Indiana at South Bend, and the Department of English of the University of Michigan. An overview of the project, "Late Antifascism: Moral Certainty and the Cold War Cultural Left," was delivered by myself as the inaugural lecture of the H. Chandler Davis Collegiate Professorship at the University of Michigan in September 2011. Dr. Davis, whose name I selected for the professorship, is a distinguished mathematician and science fiction writer whose political history resembles that of the protagonists of *American Night*. Davis had asserted his First Amendment rights during the McCarthy era, only to be fired from the University of Michigan in 1954, blacklisted in U.S. academe, and imprisoned in 1960 for contempt of Congress. Davis traveled from his home in Canada, where he is professor emeritus at the University of Toronto, to Ann Arbor to be present at the event, an act of kindness making this a highpoint of my university career.

The following participated in interviews providing information used in this book: Irving Adler, Nathan Adler, David Alman, Herbert Aptheker, William Ash, Sanora Babb, Ben Barzman, Norma Barzman, Michael Blankfort, Philip Bonosky, Sandy Boyer, Zev Braun, Lloyd Brown, Oscar Brown Jr., Ben Burns, Olga Cabral, Angus Cameron, Alvaro Cardona-Hine, Frances Chaney, Alysse Conrad, Chandler Davis, Joe Doyle, F. W. Dupee, Mary Elting, Michel Fabre, Howard Fast, Julius Fast, Vincent Ferrini, Lawrence Fixel, Franklin Folsom, Gene Frumkin, Sender Garlin, Allen Ginsberg, Rosalyn Goldfield, Ernest Goodman, Marcia Endore Goodman, Horace Gregory, Louis Harap, Gertrude Hayes, Dorothy Healey, Milton Howard, David Ignatow, Stretch Jacobs, Charles Keller, Stetson Kennedy, Aaron Kramer, Ring Lardner Jr., Bobby Lees, Meridel Le Sueur, Ernie Lieberman, Judy Lowenfels, A. B. Magil, Jerre Mangione, Paule Marshall, Carl Marzani, Alfred Maund, Alice McGrath, Thomas McGrath, Milton Meltzer, Archibald Motley Jr., Edward Newhouse, Richard Nickson, Estelle Gershgoren Novak, Tillie Olsen, Myra Page, Grace Paley, Ted Pierce, Abraham Polonsky, Carl Rakosi, Abe Ravitz, Naomi Replansky, Dorothy River, Lillian Robinson, Sam Ross, Norman Rosten, Walter Roth, Annette T. Rubinstein, Eva Russo, Robert Ryley, John Sanford, Alexander Saxton, Junius Scales, Morris U. Schappes, Wilma Shore, Janet Sillen, Mary Smith, Maynard Solomon, Elaine Sorel, Joyce Sparer, Milton Stern, Janet Stevenson, Sterling Stuckey, Alan Trachtenberg, Ira Wallach, Frederika Westbrook, Tiba Willner, John A. Williams, Sarah Wright, Helen Yglesias, Jose Yglesias, and Marya Zaturenska.

Others shared information through correspondence: Joe Allen, Edward Bland, Thomas Bransten, Larry Ceplair, Peter Cohen, Brett Dakin, Philip Deery, John Durham, Peter Filrado, Robert Forrey, Frank Fried, Robert Friend, Estelle Fuchs, Sid Gershgoren, Marvin Gettleman, Richard Gibson, David Gilden, Jarius Gilden, Michael Goldfield, Rick Halpern, Benjamin Harris, Raphael Hayes, John Earl Haynes, Mike Hecht, George Hitchcock, Roger Horowitz, Fred Jerome, Joe Kaye, Laura Kramer, David Laibman, Andrew Lee, Richard L. Levenson, Tim Libretti, Ben Maddow, William Maxwell, Jack Mearns, Gerald Meyer, Julia Mickenberg, Bill Mullen, Michael Munk, Robert Nedelkoff, Roxanna Newman, Bryan Palmer, Elisabeth Petry, Michael Price, Greg Robinson, Lillian Robinson, Lester Rodney, David Roessell, E. San Juan Jr., Ellen Schrecker, Mimi Schwartz, Irwin Silber, Billy B. Smith, Mark Solomon, Edward Sorel, Constance Webb, James Weschler, Debra White, Fred Whitehead, Doug Wixson, Kent Worcester, and Milton Zaslow.

I am grateful to people who offered various kinds of assistance: Paul Anderson, Benjamin Balthaser, Graham Barnfield, Sara Blair, Paul Buhle, Jeff Cabusao, Alex Chis, Bruce Conforth, Manan Desai, Brian Dolinar, Sarah Ehlers, Geoff Eley, Samuel

Farber, Diane Feeley, Al Filreis, David Finkel, Barbara Foley, Jonathan Freedman, Kevin Gaines, Emma Garrett, Dan Georgakas, Andrew Hemingway, Julie Herrada, Robert Hethmon, Jessi Holler, Gerald Horne, Anita Israel, Maurice Isserman, Mary Janzen, Gene Jarrett, Robert Kauffman, Joshua Kupetz, Paul Lauter, Paul Levitt, Ralph Levitt, Robbie Lieberman, Grant Mandarino, Kathleen Manwaring, Brian Matzke, Kathlene McDonald, Miriam Meisler, Richard Meisler, James Miller, Nathaniel Mills, Bill Mullen, Cary Nelson, Rachel Peterson, Christopher Phelps, Phil Pochoda, Ellen Poteet, Joe Ramsay, Rachel Rubin, Nancy Shawcross, Judith Smith, Brian Thill, Zaragosa Vargas, Chris Vials, Penny Von Eschen, Sarah Wald, Mary Helen Washington, Susan Weissman, Joel Wendland, James Weschler, and John Woodford.

I cite materials from the following libraries and institutional collections, and I am grateful for assistance and in some instances for permission to quote from letters and manuscripts: Beinecke Library, Yale University; Butler Library, Columbia University; Charles Patterson Van Pelt Library, University of Pennsylvania; FBI Reading Room in Washington, D.C.; Harry Ransom Research Center, University of Texas; Homer Babbidge Library, Storrs, Connecticut; John Hay Library, Brown University; Labadie Collection, University of Michigan; Library of Congress, Washington, D.C.; Longfellow National Historic Site in Cambridge, Massachusetts; Princeton University Manuscript Library; Schomburg Center for the Study of Black Culture; Sterling Library, Yale University; Tamiment Library, New York University; University of California, Los Angeles, Research Library; University of Washington Library; State Historical Society of Wisconsin; Research Library, University of Wisconsin; Special Collections, University of Mississippi; George Arents Research Library, Syracuse University; and Newberry Library, Chicago. I am also grateful to a number of literary executors for permission to quote. The staff at the University of North Carolina Press has once more provided capable support and assistance, including Paul Betz, Julie Bush, Beth Lassister, Susan Garrett, Sian Hunter, Mark Simpson-Vos, Zachary Read, and Kate Torrey.

This book would have taken far longer to complete without the generous support of the University of Michigan, which awarded me research funds accompanying the H. Chandler Davis Collegiate Professorship in 2007, a Rackham Research Partnership in the summer of 2009, and a University of Michigan Humanities Fellowship in Winter 2010. Indispensable was a one-year Research Fellowship from the National Endowment for the Humanities for 2011–12.

A few additional debts: Kathryn Shanley invited me to spend an evening talking to Thomas McGrath in 1983, a conversation that planted the seeds for much of a project that crystallized in later decades. Patrick Quinn arranged for me to interview friends and relatives of Willard Motley throughout the 1990s, allowing me to obtain firsthand information of a hidden life. Veteran writers of post–World War II literary Communism—Alexander Saxton, Abraham Polonsky, Aaron Kramer, John Sanford, and so many others—spent hours in unforgettable private discussion about the very fiction and poetry that are vital to *American Night*. Annette T. Rubinstein, my redoubtable colleague at *Science and Society* for over a decade, provided many of the photographs and other materials indispensable to this study. My wife, Angela, has been a loving and generous partner in life beyond all imaginings, and her parents, Marilynn and Paul Dillard, exemplars of affection and devotion. For much of the past decade, Angela and my daughters, Hannah and Sarah, have endured my passion for parsing the enigmas of Marxist culture, time and again putting my needs first. This book is dedicated to Angela.

Index

Aaron, Daniel, *Writers on the Left*, 315
Abbe, George, 383 (n. 80)
Abraham Lincoln Battalion, 7; Brigade, 1, 3, 174, 283
Abraham Lincoln School, 211
Adler, Irving, 293
Adler, Nathan, 31, 32, 331 (nn. 30, 38), 333 (n. 61)
Adorno, Theodor, xiv, xvi, 41, 85, 238, 246, 295, 296, 298, 319, 384 (n. 3), 385 (n. 6), 387 (n. 2), 389 (n. 6)
African American writers on the Left, xviii, 11, 13, 117, 150–249, 274, 276, 277, 292, 294, 307, 311, 313, 356 (n. 4)
Alexander, Sidney, 68
Algren, Nelson (b. Nelson Abraham), 36, 88, 93, 162, 164, 208, 210, 215, 359 (n. 28); *The Man with the Golden Arm*, 89
Allen, Joe, 369 (n. 108), 370 (n. 132)
Alman, David, 220, 222, 372 (n. 17)
American Dialog, 275
American Writers Congress, 56, 141, 327, 337 (n. 18)
American Youth Congress, 73
American Youth for Democracy (AYD), 143, 198, 210, 340 (n. 93)
Amter, Israel, 166, 358 (n. 26)
Anderson, Edith, 169, 389 (n. 1)

Andrews, Dorothy ("Drews"), 203, 211, 369 (n. 104), 370 (n. 128)
Anti-Communism, 11, 102, 235, 356 (n. 4), 388 (n. 5)
Antifascism, and late antifascism, xv, xviii, 1–21, 59, 61, 70, 87, 97, 103, 151, 187, 216, 223, 229, 251, 253, 267, 271, 272, 287, 288, 290, 297, 304, 316, 317, 328 (n. 26)
Anti-Semitism, 13, 52, 172, 222, 233, 239, 242, 247, 305, 326 (n. 2)
Appel, Benjamin, 220
Aptheker, Herbert, 174, 185, 248, 267, 293
Arendt, Hannah, 184, 218, 364 (n. 35), 371 (n. 6)
Arnow, Harriette (b. Harriette Louisa Simpson), 109; *The Dollmaker*, 116, 320
Art Front, 75, 340 (n. 80)
Arts, Sciences and Professions (ASP, also called National Council of the Arts, Sciences and Professions), 10, 78, 79, 86, 139, 212, 327 (n. 19), 341 (n. 4); and Independent Citizens Committee for the Arts, Sciences and Professions, 86, 139
Arvin, Newton, 60, 68, 130, 134, 351 (n. 50), 353 (n. 67)

Asimov, Isaac, 88
Atomic bomb, 15, 43, 72, 191, 352 (n. 62)
Atwood, Margaret, 295
Auden, W. H., 57, 129, 255, 281, 282, 284, 348 (n. 15)
Avant-garde, 25, 30, 45, 104, 149, 241, 254, 255, 271, 272, 287, 288, 292, 378 (n. 15)

Baldwin, James, 78, 129, 131, 132, 133, 150, 201, 204, 209, 350 (n. 43), 351 (nn. 55, 57), 352 (nn. 60, 62, 63)
Barzman, Ben, 144, 146, 148
Barzman, Norma (b. Norma Levor), 145, 146, 147, 148, 149, 355 (n. 109), 356 (n. 112)
Beal, Fred, 142, 355 (n. 106)
Beecher, John, 383 (n. 80)
Bell, Thomas (b. Adalbert Thomas Belejcak), 51, 55, 59; *In the Midst of Life*, 59; *Out of the Furnace*, 51, 55; *Till I Come Back to You*, 59; *There Comes a Time*, 88
Bellow, Saul, 20, 21, 22, 23, 24, 26, 27, 28, 34, 44, 45, 216, 217, 329 (n. 2), 335 (n. 89); *The Adventures of Augie March*, 45, 217; *Dangling Man*, 22; *The Victim*, 45
Belzer, Sophie, 130
Benjamin, Walter, 217, 319, 371 (n. 3), 387 (n. 1)
Bentley, Elizabeth, 217, 218
Berger, Art, 384
Bergman, Alexander F. (b. Alexander Frankel), 36, 255, 334 (nn. 67, 68); *They Look Like Men*, 379 (n. 16)
Berkeley, Martin, 314
Berman, Lionel, 305
Bernstein, Joseph, 72
Bernstein, Leonard, 119, 138, 347 (n. 10), 354 (n. 88)
Berryman, John, 383 (n. 80)
Bessie, Alvah, 58, 337 (n. 22)

Bezzerides, A. I., 311
Bigsby, Christopher, 371 (n. 2)
Birobidzhan, 222, 235
Bisexuals. *See* Homosexuality and Communist writers
Black Arts Movement, 152, 292, 383 (n. 81)
Blacklist, xvii, 34, 58, 59, 200, 224, 225, 254, 260, 265, 292, 306, 311, 314, 315, 323, 328 (n. 21), 384 (n. 86), 385 (n. 1), 389 (n. 9), 390 (n. 2)
Blake, William J. (b. William Blech), 96, 216
Bland, Alden, 172
Bland, Edward, 164, 172
Bland, Edward, Jr., 172, 360 (n. 49)
Blankfort, Michael, 220, 310–11, 390 (n. 2)
Blau, Milton (also known as Eric Blau), 264, 380 (n. 34)
Blitzstein, Marc (b. Marcus Samuel Blitzstein), 119, 120, 278
Bodenheim, Maxwell (b. Maxwell Bodenheimer), 250, 252, 254, 377 (n. 1)
Bonosky, Phillip, 79, 89, 94, 313, 342 (n. 10), 390 (n. 2); *Burning Valley*, 89, 342 (n. 10); *The Magic Fern*, 89
Bowles, Jane (b. Jane Sydney Auer), 109, 120, 122, 129
Bowles, Paul, 45, 89, 120, 128, 129, 177, 303, 350 (nn. 44, 45)
Boyer, Richard, 11, 328 (n. 21)
Bragin, Moe. *See* Field, Ben
Branch, William, 153
Brand, Millen, 373, 383 (n. 80)
Bransten, Louise (b. Louise Rosenberg; also known as Louise Berman), 66, 305
Bransten, Richard (pseud. Bruce Minton), 66, 72, 304–5
Braun, Zev, 202, 213, 369 (n. 101), 370 (n. 113)

Braymer, Nan (b. Nan Apotheker), 278, 279
Brecht, Bertolt, 77, 262, 281, 360 (n. 40)
Brewster, Dorothy, 121, 122
Bright, John, 210
Brinig, Myron, 128, 350 (n. 42)
Brooks, Gwendolyn, 88, 155, 172
Brooks, Van Wyck, 68, 74
Browder, Earl, and Browderism, 20, 54, 58, 68, 69, 103, 129, 132, 152, 198, 305, 313, 327 (n. 14), 328 (n. 35), 338 (n. 24), 382 (n. 64)
Brown, Frank London, 153
Brown, Lloyd, 89, 91, 93, 152, 342 (n. 10), 372 (n. 19)
Buck, Pearl S. (pseud. John Sedges), 108, 124
Budenz, Louis, 217, 118, 247
Buhle, Paul, 13, 226, 327 (n. 17), 328 (n. 26), 371 (n. 8), 372 (n. 21), 373 (n. 35), 389 (n. 1)
Bulosan, Carlos, 298, 299, 300, 305, 385 (n. 8); *America is in the Heart*, 88; *The Cry and the Dedication*, 298–305
Burgum, Edwin Berry ("Berry"), 60, 63, 66, 67, 130, 351 (n. 53)
Burke, Fielding. *See* Dargan, Olive Tilford
Burke, Kenneth, 60, 331 (n. 36)
Burns, Ben (b. Benjamin Bernstein), 174, 361 (n. 53)
Burroughs, Margaret, 167
Bush, Lawrence, 293

Cabral, Olga, 288, 380 (n. 4), 390 (n. 2)
Caldwell, Erskine, 68, 306
California Quarterly, 256, 266, 379 (n. 24)
Calmer, Alan (b. Abraham Klein), 68
Cameron, Angus, 79, 254
Cameron and Kahn Associates, 254
Camus, Albert, 161, 162, 163

Canon, literary, xv, 20, 22, 44, 304, 328 (n. 29)
Cantwell, Robert, 35, 92, 142, 355 (n. 105)
Capote, Truman, 129, 130, 300, 351 (n. 50)
Cardona-Hine, Alvaro, 78, 268, 269, 383 (n. 80), 390 (n. 2)
Carse, Robert, 88
Caspary, Vera, 103, 109–16, 195; *Bedelia*, 345 (n. 42); *Laura*, 109–16, 345 (nn. 46, 48); *Music in the Street*, 110; *The Secrets of Grown-Ups*, 111, 345 (n. 41); *Stranger Than Truth*, 114; *Thicker Than Water*, 110; *The White Girl*, 110, 345 (n. 43)
Cerf, Bennett, 22, 329 (n. 2), 330 (n. 18), 332 (nn. 44, 48), 333 (n. 62)
Chambers, Whittaker, 129, 178, 189, 191, 217, 247, 305, 310, 314, 332, 356 (n. 58), 386 (n. 22), 387 (n. 37)
Cheever, John, 128, 129, 136, 239, 350 (n. 47), 353 (n. 77)
Chicago Defender, 175, 206, 307, 360 (n. 46), 361 (n. 58)
Childress, Alice, 153, 313
China/Chinese Revolution, 86, 108, 227, 272, 321, 382 (n. 65)
Citadel Press, 73, 77, 108
Clark, Eleanor, 175, 335 (n. 84), 344 (n. 34)
Clark, John Henrik, 153
Clark, Katerina, 336 (n. 2)
Clipper, 54, 337 (n. 15)
Coastlines, 256, 266, 269
Coates, Robert, 88
Cohen, Lester, 87, 89; *Coming Home*, 87, 89
Cohen, Lizabeth, 325 (n. 5), 331 (n. 13)
Cold War and McCarthyism, xi, xiii, xiv, xvi, xvii, 7, 10, 17, 19, 26, 34, 35, 45, 53, 60, 68, 84–88, 98, 102, 103, 120, 125, 129, 130, 151, 154, 155, 158, 160, 163, 176, 179, 192, 215, 217, 219, 224, 230, 232,

245, 247, 248, 249, 254, 269, 270, 288, 292, 296, 297, 299, 304, 309, 310, 311, 320, 322–25, 342 (n. 11), 347 (n. 13), 350 (n. 45), 351 (n. 49), 379 (n. 23), 383 (n. 81)
Collins, Richard, 53
Collins, Wilkie, 23, 111, 346 (n. 43)
Colonialism and anticolonialism, xii, xvii, 13, 15, 152, 153, 227, 303, 313, 340
Comintern (Communist International, Third International), 36, 66, 137, 256, 371 (n. 10)
Committee for the Negro in the Arts (CNA), 10, 86, 153
Communist International. *See* Comintern
Communist Literary Modernism, xiii, xvi, 44, 45, 47, 84, 88, 98, 124, 127, 204, 221, 223, 224, 271, 293, 294, 297, 298, 302, 303, 304, 316, 317, 386 (n. 19)
Communist Party (USA), xvii, 7, 9–12, 17, 19, 20, 31, 33–37, 47, 49, 52–74 passim, 77, 81, 82, 86, 87, 88, 90, 95–105 passim, 108, 110, 111, 117–34 passim, 137, 139, 142, 144, 147, 150–68 passim, 171–76, 198, 200, 211, 212, 221–42 passim, 250, 255–61, 265, 267, 268, 271, 275–85 passim, 292, 293, 297, 300, 301, 304, 305, 307, 308, 310, 312, 314, 325, 328, 329, 332, 333, 337, 341, 344, 346, 348, 350, 357 (n. 4), 361 (n. 45), 365 (n. 33), 374 (n. 53), 377 (n. 1), 378 (n. 16), 381 (n. 64), 382 (n. 65), 383 (n. 82), 385 (n. 8)
Conforth, Bruce, 366 (n. 63)
Congress of Industrial Organizations (CIO), 20
Conrad, Earl (b. Earl Cohen), 307, 308, 386 (n. 29)
Conroy, Jack, 65, 210, 370 (n. 126)
Consumers' Republic, 21, 28, 38, 42, 43, 45, 85, 88, 99, 102, 103, 109, 110, 118, 150, 153, 217, 239, 267, 296, 298, 316

Contemporary Reader, 78
Contemporary Writers, 222
Copland, Aaron, 119
Corwin, Norman, 130
Coser, Lewis, 337 (n. 19)
Council on African Affairs, 153, 328 (n. 29)
Cowley, Malcolm, 69, 139, 140
Cowley, Peggy (b. Marguerite Frances Baird), 139–40
Cross Section, 88
Cruse, Harold, 368 (n. 95)
Cultural and Scientific Conference for World Peace (also known as Waldorf Peace Conference), 10, 55, 59, 320
Cultural Division of Communist Party, 86, 341 (n. 3)
Culture war(s), xii, xvi, xvii, 7, 22, 26, 27, 42, 43, 296; Cultural Cold War, xvii, 325 (n. 6)
Cunningham, William, 129

Dahlberg, Edward, 24,
Daily Worker, 2, 11, 33, 35, 36, 51, 54, 60, 61, 62, 63, 70, 72, 75, 80, 96, 127, 128, 166, 168, 173, 175, 181, 254, 256, 257, 271, 274, 276, 277, 279, 307, 310, 311, 349 (n. 56)
Damon, Anna, 174–75, 361 (n. 57)
Dana, Henry Wadsworth Longfellow ("Harry"), 134–39, 353 (nn. 68, 69, 70), 354 (n. 87)
Dargan, Olive Tilford (pseud. Fielding Burke), 89, 103, 108
Davidman, Joy (b. Helen Joy Davidman), 220, 252, 334 (n. 67), 379 (n. 16)
Davidson, Richard, 383 (n. 80)
Davis, Benjamin, Jr., 172, 272, 277
Davis, Frank Marshall, 152
De Beauvoir, Simone, 82, 162, 163, 357 (n. 15), 359 (n. 28), 360 (n. 40)
Decision Magazine, 124

Denning, Michael, xvii, 19, 20
Dennis, Eugene, 174, 339 (n. 71)
Dickstein, Morris, 335 (n. 89)
Di Donato, Pietro, 313
Dmytryk, Edward, 222
Döblin, Alfred, 215
Doctorow, E. L., 294, 329 (n. 45)
Dodd, Bella, 362
Dodd, Martha, 121, 348 (n. 17)
Dodson, Owen, 201
Doolittle, Kenneth Waldron, 30, 335 (n. 88)
Dos Passos, John, 100, 106, 139, 141, 142
Dostoyevsky, Fyodor, 45, 97, 156, 162, 290
Double V, 15
Dreiser, Theodore, 54, 98, 141, 155, 156
Du Bois, Shirley Graham, 153, 313
Du Bois, W. E. B., 153, 185; *The Black Flame*, 208
Dunham, Barrows, 150
Dupee, F. W., 66, 67, 331 (n. 36), 338 (n. 49)
Duranty, Walter, 113, 345 (n. 46)
Durem, Ray, 383 (n. 80)
Dynamo, 30, 254, 287, 320

Eley, Geoff, *Forging Democracy*, 325 (n. 2), 328 (n. 25)
Elhers, Sarah, 359 (n. 32), 375 (n. 55)
Ellison, Ralph, 10, 88, 151, 155, 165, 168, 172, 174, 175, 177, 311, 356 (n. 10), 385 (n. 19); *Invisible Man*, 151, 153, 154, 162, 238, 304
Elting, Mary (also known as Mary Folsom), 133, 176
Eluard, Paul, 132
Endore, Guy (b. Samuel Goldstein), 313, 314, 315, 316, 372 (n. 18), 387 (n. 26); *King of Paris*, 314; *Satan's Saint*, 314–15; *Synanon*, 315; *Voltaire! Voltaire!*, 314; *Werewolf of Paris*, 314
Engstrand, Stuart, 89, 129, 130, 131, 164; *Beyond the Forest*, 131; *Husband in the House*, 131; *More Deaths Than One*, 131; *The Sling and the Arrow*, 89, 130–31; *Son of the Giant*, 135
Espionage, Communist, xviii, 6, 17, 19, 129, 158, 178, 305, 352 (n. 62)
Espiritu, Augusto Fauni, 385 (n. 8)
Evslin, Bernard, 132
Existentialism, xiv, 38, 45, 87, 89, 101, 103, 125, 155, 156, 159, 161, 162, 229, 262, 303, 357, 397

Fabre, Michel, 352 (n. 61), 357 (n. 11), 358 (n. 14), 360 (n. 43)
Fagan, Ruth, 250
Falstein, Louis, 220
Farrell, James T., 29, 175
Fascism (esp. Nazism), xvii, 2, 13–17, 37, 97, 105, 108, 132, 137, 145, 151, 186, 188, 221, 222, 243, 264, 354 (n. 99), 356 (n. 3), 364 (n. 7), 388 (n. 5)
Fast, Howard, 2–4, 7, 11, 15, 16, 56, 78, 88, 89, 96, 101, 102, 129, 219, 257, 336 (n. 5), 338 (n. 16); "Epitaph for Sidney," 2, 3, 7, 12, 13, 16, 19, 21, 326 (n. 2)
Fast, Julius, 89
Fearing, Kenneth, xiv, xvi, 23–48, 49, 65, 82, 83, 85, 86, 87, 96, 98, 100, 101, 102, 103, 106, 140, 169, 255, 295, 296, 302, 319, 330 (n. 9), 332 (n. 30), 333 (n. 43), 334 (n. 67), 335 (n. 75); *Angel Arms*, 33, 34; *The Big Clock*, xiv, 33–48 passim, 85, 86, 88, 103, 115, 295, 320, 329 (n. 3), 335 (n. 84); *Clark Gifford's Body*, 23, 34, 37, 329 (n. 2); *Collected Poems*, 34; *The Crozart Story*, 25, 29, 30; *Dagger of the Mind*, 24, 25, 47, 169; *The Generous Heart*, 25; *The Hospital*, 22, 35, 46; *The Loneliest Girl in the World*, 25; *New and Selected Poems*, 27; *Poems*, 24–32
Federal Arts Project, 35, 38, 167

Federal Bureau of Investigation (FBI), 17, 105, 117, 206, 210, 211, 285, 304, 311, 342 (n. 6), 369 (n. 104), 370 (n. 132)
Federal Writers Project, 27, 31, 35, 124, 130, 141, 362 (n. 5)
Fellig, Arthur (pseud. Weegee), 154, 183, 184, 364 (n. 25)
Fellow traveler, 9, 10, 33, 111, 133, 134, 135, 198, 212, 226, 242, 246, 307, 335 (n. 84), 360 (n. 47); definition of, 10
Ferrini, Vincent, 266, 380 (n. 35), 383 (n. 80)
Fiedler, Leslie, 201, 368 (n. 98)
Field, Ben (b. Moe Bragin), 220, 307, 386 (n. 30)
Film and Photo League, 78, 184, 306, 364 (n. 32)
Filreis, Alan, 347–48 (n. 13), 383 (n. 81)
Finnegan, Robert (also known as Mike Quin, b. Paul William Ryan), 88
Fixel, Lawrence, 383 (n. 80)
Flexner, Eleanor, 121, 348 (n. 18)
Flynn, Elizabeth Gurley, 348 (n. 16), 379 (n. 25)
Foley, Barbara, 151, 336 (n. 3), 343 (n. 14), 356 (n. 2), 386 (n. 19)
Folsom, Franklin, 175, 337 (18), 351 (n. 51), 361 (n. 60)
Forrey, Robert, 61
Foster, William Z., 33, 152, 275, 326 (n. 13), 327 (n. 14)
Franco, Francisco, 2, 7, 160. *See also* Fascism; Spain and Spanish Civil War
Frank, Waldo, 327 (n. 13)
Frankfurt School, xvi, 295, 385 (n. 6)
Freedom, 153
Freedomways, 153, 256, 257, 313, 350 (n. 43)
Freeman, Harry, 35
Freeman, Joseph, 35, 60, 68, 333 (nn. 5, 7)
Freiheit, 235
Freud, Sigmund, and Freudianism, 40, 79, 100, 131, 173, 174, 195, 228, 229, 241, 264, 266, 278, 352 (n. 56), 360 (n. 51), 375 (n. 58)
Friday, 351 (n. 49)
Friend, Robert, 285–87, 383 (n. 73)
Frumkin, Gene, 78, 269, 379 (n. 26), 383 (n. 80)
Funaroff, Sol (pseud. Charles Henry Newman), 32, 254, 331 (n. 38), 333 (n. 61)

Gaines, Kevin, 390 (n. 1)
Ganz, Earl, 350 (n. 41)
Garlin, Sender, 35, 73
Garrett, Emma, 365 (nn. 42, 43)
Gastonia strike, 89, 342 (n. 9), 355 (n. 106)
Gays and literary Left. *See* Homosexuality and Communist writers
Gellhorn, Martha, 107; *Liana*, 108; *A Stricken Field*, 108; *Wine of Astonishment*, 108
Gender. *See* Homosexuality and Communist writers; Masculinity; Women writers and the Left
Gershgoren, Estelle, 384 (n. 80)
Gershgoren, Sid (pseud. Herschel Horn), 79, 384 (n. 80)
Gibson, Lydia, 168
Gibson, Richard, 150
Gibson, William, 88, 373 (n. 27)
Gilden, Bert, 219, 220, 222, 223, 225, 232, 294, 298, 303, 346, 373 (n. 30)
Gilden, Katya, 219, 220, 222, 223, 225, 232, 294, 298, 303, 346, 372 (n. 11), 373 (n. 30)
Gilden, K. B.: *Between the Hills and the Sea*, 220, 222, 230–38 passim, 246, 347 (n. 6), 374 (n. 33); *Hurry Sundown*, 220, 231, 233, 234
Giles, Barbara, 78, 81, 94, 343 (n. 17); *The Gentle Bush*, 88
Gilkes, Lillian Barnard, 121, 122

Gilyard, Keith, 356 (n. 5)
Ginsberg, Allen, 216, 274
Gleason, Leverett, 130, 351 (n. 49)
Glenn, Charles, 52, 54, 55, 336 (n. 11), 337 (nn. 16, 18)
Gold, Michael (b. Itzok Granich), 56, 58, 60, 68, 74, 79, 337 (n. 18); *Jews without Money*, 216, 221
Goldberg, Itche, 371 (n. 8)
Goldfrank, Helen (pseud. Helen Kay), 129
Goldstein, Laurence, 378 (n. 15)
Gonzalez, Marcial, 337 (n. 22)
Goodheart, Eugene, 219, 371 (n. 10)
Gordimer, Nadine, 293
Gordon, Caroline, 344 (n. 35)
Gordon, Don, 266, 288, 289, 384 (n. 83)
Gordon, Eric A., 347 (n. 7)
Gordon, Eugene, 138
Gorky, Maxim, 93, 290
Gourfain, Edward, 167, 359 (n. 30)
Gourfain, Joyce, 166, 167, 168, 359 (nn. 30, 32)
Graham, Shirley, 153, 313
Great Depression, xi, xviii, 3, 7, 8, 9, 12, 14, 22, 23, 26, 27, 28, 30, 31, 32, 42, 43, 44, 45, 46, 48, 49, 50, 92, 93, 102, 103, 104, 106, 107, 108, 109, 110, 112, 117, 118, 126, 129, 140, 146, 150, 157, 159, 167, 186, 201, 221, 226, 229, 243, 252, 271, 273, 282, 283, 285, 286, 293, 311, 320, 322
Grebanier, Bernard, 282, 283, 382 (n.63)
Gregory, Horace, 25, 29, 31, 33, 34, 68, 120, 124, 142, 254, 332 (n. 49), 347 (n. 12)
Gresham, William Lindsay, 89, 378 (n. 16)
Griffin, Farah Jasmine, 366 (n. 69)
Guy, Rosa, 153, 313

Haas, Miriam (also known as Mimi Schwartz), 77, 83, 340 (n. 76), 341 (n. 103)

Haidt, Jonathan, 13, 14, 328 (n. 31)
Hall, Stuart, 15, 329 (n. 37)
Halper, Albert, 32, 33, 306
Hammett, Dashiell, 10, 24, 140, 177, 321
Hansberry, Lorraine, 10, 120, 121, 153, 198, 201; *A Raisin in the Sun*, 293
Harari, Hananiah, 16
Harburg, E. Y. ("Yip"), 335 (n. 110)
Hardwick, Elizabeth, 109, 344
Harlem Quarterly, 153
Harlem Writers Club, 153, 368 (n. 95)
Harlem Writers Guild, 153, 368 (n. 95)
Harris, Benjamin, 373 (n. 28)
Hay, Harry (pseud. Eann McDonald), 120, 346 (n. 5), 347 (n. 7)
Hayden, Robert (b. Asa Bundy Sheffey), 88, 201, 311, 383
Hayes, Alfred, 36, 88, 89, 254, 255, 342 (n. 10)
Hayes, Raphael, 255, 334 (n. 67), 378 (n. 17)
Haynes, John Earl, 341 (n. 2)
Hays, Lee, 119, 279, 347 (n. 8), 381 (n. 59)
Healey, Dorothy, 18, 329 (n. 42)
Hegel, Georg Wilhelm Friedrich, 45, 102, 225, 295, 296, 358 (n. 17)
Hellman, Lillian, 11, 35, 294, 320, 326 (n. 7)
Hemingway, Andrew, 335 (n. 2), 341 (n. 4)
Hemingway, Ernest, 89, 100, 106, 139, 141, 231
Herald, Leon Serabian, 28, 34, 332 (n. 49)
Herald, John, 332 (n. 49)
Herbst, Josephine, 103–8, 115, 123, 124, 125; *The Executioner Waits*, 106; *Hunter of Doves*, 107; *Money for Love*, 106; *Nothing is Sacred*, 106; *Pity is Not Enough*, 106; *Rope of Gold*, 106; *Satan's Sergeants*, 106, 343 (n. 30); *Somewhere the Tempest Fell*, 88, 105, 107, 108, 343 (n. 28)

Herndon, Angelo, 174, 175
Hernton, Calvin, 274
Herrick, William, 220
Herrmann, Gina, 372 (n. 13)
Heterodoxy Club, 191, 365 (n. 41)
Hethmon, Robert, 387 (n. 34)
Heym, Stefan (b. Helmut Flieg), 89, 90, 164, 311, 390 (n. 2)
Hickman, James, 212, 370 (n. 132)
Hicks, Granville, 51, 60, 65, 67, 68, 72, 138, 139, 151, 351 (n. 50), 354 (n. 87)
Highsmith, Patricia (b. Mary Patricia Plangman), 60, 122, 338 (n. 29), 349 (n. 18)
Himes, Chester, 88, 150, 151, 152, 154, 155, 163, 165, 177, 178, 201, 208, 356 (n. 1), 359 (n. 28)
Hitchcock, George, 78, 383 (n. 80)
Hitler, Adolf, 12, 14, 57, 222, 328. See also Fascism; Hitler-Stalin Pact
Hitler-Stalin Pact, 9, 14, 36, 51, 54, 56, 57, 67, 70, 97, 105, 111, 128, 147, 151, 169, 173, 255, 342 (n. 6), 345 (n. 36), 351 (n. 50), 356 (n. 3)
Hoberek, Andrew, 374 (n. 43)
Hobsbawm, Eric, 322, 389 (n. 7)
Hobson, Laura Z., 109
Hollywood and the Left, 6, 34, 52, 53, 55, 59, 144, 145, 146, 147, 222, 226, 228, 306, 314, 320
Hollywood Quarterly, 226
Hollywood Ten, 222, 228, 320, 337 (n. 16)
Hollywood Writers Clinic, 144
Hollywood Writers School, 147
Homosexuality and Communist writers, 57, 117–49, 150, 201–15, 281–91
Horne, Gerald, 337 (n. 16), 394
House Committee on Un-American Activities (HUAC), 6, 52, 55, 59, 144, 224, 225, 228, 230, 231, 232, 266, 268, 306, 308 (n. 21), 351 (n. 49), 373 (n. 30), 384 (n. 86)

Howard, Milton (b. Milton Halpern), 307, 386 (n. 30)
Howe, Irving, 337 (n. 19)
Huggins, Roy, 88, 314
Hughes, Langston, 43, 153, 174, 201, 252, 253, 288, 292, 321, 352
Hull, Helen, 187, 191, 366 (n. 68)
Humboldt, Charles (pseud. Clarence Weinstock), xvi, 60, 61, 75–83, 257, 265, 266, 267, 268, 340 (n. 80), 341 (nn. 103, 104), 381 (nn. 41, 42)
Hungarian Revolt (1956), 245, 246, 375, 376 (n. 59)
Hutchins, Grace, 348 (n. 16)
Hutner, Gordon, 344 (n. 34)
Hyman, Stanley Edgar, 60, 338 (n. 33)

Ignatow, David, 288, 383 (n. 80), 384 (n. 82)
Imperialism (Western), xiii, 15, 159, 274
Industrial Workers of the World (IWW), 2, 260, 361 (n. 45)
International brigades. See Abraham Lincoln Battalion
International Labor Defense (ILD), 43, 137, 264
International Literature, 373 (n. 33)
International Publishers, 69, 86, 141, 264, 265, 326 (n. 13)
International Workers Order, 360 (n. 45), 371 (n. 10)
Isserman, Maurice, 325 (n. 3), 329 (n. 42)

James, C. L. R., 150, 156, 170, 179, 356 (n. 6), 360 (n. 43), 361 (n. 56), 362 (n. 2)
James, Daniel (pseuds. Danny Santiago, Daniel Hyatt), 58, 59, 335 (n. 84), 348 (n. 21)
Jameson, Fredric, 293
Jeffers, Lance, 153
Jefferson School of Social Science, 228
Jerome, V. J. (b. Isaac Jerome Romaine),

54, 61, 62, 70, 71, 72, 73, 75, 83, 119, 152, 257, 339 (n. 64), 341 (n. 3)
Jewish Currents, 257, 372 (n. 18)
Jewish Life, 2, 3, 4, 221, 222, 326 (n. 2), 372 (nn. 14, 15)
Jews and Literary Communism, xvi, xvii, 1, 2, 3, 18, 19, 27, 29, 30, 60, 61, 72, 75, 108, 109, 119, 128, 142, 145, 154, 156, 165, 166, 168, 172, 173, 174, 201, 216–49, 251, 256, 257, 286, 295, 298, 313, 326 (n. 2), 331 (n. 30), 371 (nn. 3, 10), 372 (n. 14)
John Reed Club, 31, 32, 35, 124, 128, 130, 137, 141, 173, 175, 307, 327, 331 (n. 35)
Johns, Orrick, 140
Johnson, Hank, 171, 172, 360 (nn. 45, 46)
Johnson, Josephine, 147

Kahn, Albert, 120, 129, 254
Kahn, Arthur, 120, 347 (n. 11)
Kahn, Gordon, 220
Kallman, Chester, 283, 284, 285, 378 (n. 17)
Karageorgos, Konstantina, 357 (n. 15), 359 (nn. 27, 35, 38), 365 (n. 42)
Karsavina, Jean, 220
Kaufman, Bob (b. Robert Garnell Kaufman), 201
Kay, Helen (b. Helen Goldfrank), 129
Keeler, Harry Stephen, 25
Kelley, Robin D. G., xv, 325 (n. 4)
Kennedy, Stetson, 89
Kerouac, Jack, 217
Khrushchev Revelations, xv, 17, 61, 77, 78, 235, 256, 257, 274, 325 (n. 2), 385 (n. 12)
Killens, John Oliver, 153, 155, 198, 293, 313, 356 (n. 5), 398 (n. 95)
Kirstein, Lincoln, 119, 347 (n. 10)
Klehr, Harvey, 341 (n. 2)
Kline, Herb, 169
Korean War, 37, 211, 246, 247, 248, 376 (n. 62)

Kornbluth, Cyril, 88
Kraditor, Eileen, 339 (n. 68)
Kramer, Aaron, 250–56, 257, 260, 264, 270, 281, 378 (nn. 12, 17), 378–79 (n. 22)
Kranz, Sheldon, 284, 382 (n. 67)
Kreymborg, Alfred, 250, 252, 254, 377 (n. 2)
Kronenberger, Louis, 142, 355 (n. 105)
Kundera, Milan, 293
Kunitz, Joshua, 336 (n. 7)
Kurtz, Aaron, 288–89
Kutcher, James, 212, 370 (n. 133)
Kutulas, Judy, 327 (n. 16)

Labor Youth League, 153, 198
Lafargue Clinic, 173
Laibman, David, 382 (n. 65)
Lamont, Corliss, 138, 139, 354 (n. 86)
Landon, Edward, 35, 335 (n. 55)
Langer, Elinor, 343 (n. 27)
Lanham, Edwin, 89
Lardner, Ring, Jr., 228, 293
Larkin, Katherine, 348 (n. 13)
Larkin, Margaret (also known as Margaret Maltz), 348 (n. 13)
Lattimer, Margery, 28, 29, 35, 331 (n. 31), 332 (n. 49)
Laurents, Arthur, 119, 347 (n. 9)
Lawrence, D. H., 162, 190, 272
Lawson, John Howard, 52, 53, 54, 55, 56, 111, 228, 265, 266
League of American Writers, 31, 36, 56, 59, 69, 124, 130, 132, 140, 147, 175, 212
Lees, Robert ("Bobby"), 315, 386 (n. 26)
Lenin, V. I., 8, 68, 101, 132, 142, 146, 152, 290, 293, 296, 317
Leonard, William Ellery, 28
Lerner, Gerda, 73, 220, 310
Lerner, Tillie. *See* Olsen, Tillie
Lesbians. *See* Homosexuality and Communist writers
Lessing, Doris, 38, 293

Le Sueur, Meridel, 35, 89, 107, 116, 292, 333 (n. 66), 352 (n. 59)
Levenson, Lew, 127, 128, 129, 349 (n. 36), 349–50 (n. 38)
Levin, Dan, 220
Levitt, Paul, 234, 394
Liberals and liberalism, xvii, 8, 9, 10, 12, 13, 14, 33, 45, 59, 84, 86, 102, 103, 151, 152, 156, 159, 160, 176, 185, 198, 219, 261, 297, 309, 311, 317, 321, 325 (n. 6), 327 (n. 16), 352 (n. 50)
Libretti, Timothy, 373 (n. 35)
Lieber, Maxim, 239, 305, 307, 333 (n. 52), 386 (n. 23)
Lieberman, Robbie, 341 (n. 5)
Lipton, Lawrence, 130, 164, 157
Litvinov, Maxim, 54, 113
Litwack, Leo, 294
Locke, Alain, 201
Lonergan, Wayne, murder committed by, 40
Lorde, Audre, 121, 153, 199, 201, 313 (n. 80)
Lowenfels, Lillian (b. Lillian Apotheker), 271, 272, 278, 279, 280
Lowenfels, Walter, 271–81, 336 (n. 7), 381 (nn. 50, 58, 59)
Löwy, Michael, 385 (n. 17)
Luce, Henry, 26, 39, 44, 334 (n. 75)
Lukács, Georg, 78, 233, 236, 262, 373 (n. 35)
Lumpkin, Grace, 103, 114, 310, 390
Lurie, Nan, 35, 333 (n. 56)

Maas, Willard, 120, 347 (n. 13)
MacDonald, Dwight, 241, 347 (n. 13)
Maddow, Ben (pseud. David Wolfe), 254, 290, 306, 323
Magil, A. B. (b. Abraham Bernard Magil), 35, 266, 267, 307, 380 (n. 42)
Mailer, Norman, 10, 78, 88, 89, 154, 216, 217, 320

Mainstream, 16, 60, 69, 72, 77, 78, 79, 80, 82, 257, 269, 275, 333 (n. 58)
Major, Clarence, 274
Malamud, Bernard, 216, 217
Maltz, Albert, 20, 61, 68, 72, 73, 80, 132, 210, 228, 347 (n. 13), 364 (n. 33)
Maltz, Margaret (also known as Margaret Larkin), 348 (n. 13)
Mangione, Jerre (pseuds. Mario Michele, Jay Gerlando), 32, 141, 132, 143, 354 (n. 92), 362 (n. 5)
Manhoff, Arnold (pseud. Joel Carpenter), 58, 59, 337 (n. 22)
Mann, Thomas, 198, 200, 233
Marcantonio, Vito, 323, 389 (n. 8)
Marshall, Paule (b. Valena Pauline Burke), 152, 153, 198, 199, 368 (n. 97)
Marzani, Carl, 78, 79
Marx, Karl, and Marxism, xii, xiii, xvii, 8, 14, 15, 24, 25, 27, 30, 32, 33, 37, 45, 46, 50, 61, 63, 64, 65, 70, 71, 73, 74, 78, 79, 80, 83–88, 93, 98, 100–102, 113, 126, 127, 130, 132, 133, 134, 144, 146, 151, 152, 159, 163, 179, 184, 185, 197, 210, 211, 216, 220, 223, 225, 228, 250, 261, 264, 270, 280, 292, 293, 296, 301, 303, 310, 315, 316, 317, 319, 321
Masculinity, 40, 41, 113, 131, 133, 141, 143, 144, 181, 191, 202, 215, 240, 260, 350 (n. 46)
Masses & Mainstream, 16, 17, 35, 61, 62, 69, 71, 73, 78, 91, 181, 229, 256, 257, 266, 267, 333 (n. 58)
Massie Trial/Affair, 196, 197, 368 (nn. 89, 91)
Matthiessen, F. O., 134, 335 (n. 84)
Maund, Alfred, 89, 342 (n. 11)
Mayfield, Julian, 153, 313
McCarthy, Mary, 67, 241, 335
McCarthyism. *See* Cold War and McCarthyism

McCullers, Carson, 88, 87, 109, 124, 128, 129, 169, 344, 350, 351, 358 (n. 24)
McGrath, Alice, 258, 265, 266, 379 (n. 26), 380 (nn. 38, 39)
McGrath, Thomas ("Tom"), xii, xiii, 75, 78, 79, 80, 88, 256–71, 281, 291, 296, 303, 319, 379 (nn. 23, 25, 28), 380 (nn. 40, 45)
McKenney, Ruth, 304, 344, 358 (n. 26)
Meidman, Dhimah, 166, 167, 168, 169, 359 (nn. 34, 35)
Meltzer, Milton, 309, 387 (n. 32)
Meltzer, Rachel, 31, 35, 335 (n. 55)
Melville, Herman, 104, 179, 362 (nn. 2, 4)
Merriam, Eve (b. Eva Moscowitz), 307, 386 (n. 30)
Meyer, Gerald, 389 (n. 8)
Meyers, Bert, 268
Michel, John B., 88, 311, 287 (n. 34)
Miller, Arthur (pseud. Matt Wayne), 10, 41, 88, 132, 216, 219, 222, 320, 371 (n. 2), 372 (n. 15)
Miller, Warren, 21, 293, 313, 390
Millet, Martha, 252, 383
Mills, Nathaniel, 330 (n. 9), 386 (n. 19)
Milosz, Czeslaw, 70
Milton, Joyce, 329 (n. 44)
Minor, Robert, 139, 168, 174, 359 (n. 44)
Minton, Bruce. *See* Bransten, Richard
Minus, Marian, 164, 202, 358 (n. 20)
Mitchell, Loften, 153
Mitford, Jessica, 310
Mizener, Arthur, 59, 388 (n. 27)
Modern Age Publishers, 311
Modernism. *See* Communist Literary Modernism
Moral certainty, 7, 12, 13, 14, 15, 16, 224, 235, 291, 295, 298, 301, 306, 317, 392, 397
Morgan, Stacey I., 369 (n. 105)
Morris, Edita, 344

Morton, Brian, 293
Moscow Purge Trials, 13, 15, 36, 47, 67, 113, 331 (n. 61)
Motley, Archibald, I, 205
Motley, Archibald, II, 203, 205, 207
Motley, Archibald, III, 203, 269 (n. 109)
Motley, Willard, 88, 150, 152, 165, 201–15, 369 (nn. 104, 105, 107); *Knock on Any Door*, 88, 202, 203, 205, 207, 210, 215, 369 (n. 104); *Let No Man Write My Epitaph*, 203, 205, 206, 207, 209; *Let Noon Be Fair*, 203, 206, 207, 213, 214, 215; *We Fished All Night*, 150, 165, 203, 209, 210, 211, 215, 369
Myers, Henry, 144–49, 355 (nn. 108, 111); *Our Lives Have Just Begun*, 148; *The Signorina*, 146; *The Utmost Island*, 146; *The Winner of World War III*, 148

National Council of the Arts, Sciences and Professions (NCASP). *See* Arts, Sciences and Professions
National Guardian, 77, 252
National Negro Congress, 171, 360 (n. 45)
National Student League, 64
Naturalism, 96, 197, 203, 233, 236, 302
Navasky, Victor, 386 (n. 25)
Nazis. *See* Fascism
Nearing, Scott, 35, 278, 333 (n. 52)
Neel, Alice, 29, 30, 35, 38, 43, 355 (nn. 85, 88)
Negro Quarterly, 174
Nekola, Charlotte, 344 (n. 33)
Nelson, Cary, 378 (n. 19), 384 (n. 81)
Neruda, Pablo, 69, 75, 280
Neugass, James, 94, 95, 342 (n. 16); *Rain of Ashes*, 94, 96
New Africa, 153
New Century Publishers, 86
New Deal, 6, 9, 10, 11, 19, 26, 37, 42,

44, 47, 58, 152, 227, 297, 315. *See also* Roosevelt, Franklin D.
Newhouse, Edward (b. Ede Ujhazi), 68, 220, 312, 351, 387 (n. 35)
New Leader, 127, 131, 152, 352 (n. 63)
New Masses, 16, 28, 30, 34–37, 51, 52, 54, 58–61, 65–69, 71, 76, 77, 78, 91, 96, 97, 124, 126, 128, 131–34, 139, 141, 144, 174, 177, 181, 255, 261, 265, 304, 307, 309, 311
New Theater, 168, 169, 353 (n. 82), 359 (n. 35)
New Writing Foundation, 340
Norse, Harold (b. Harold Rosen, also known as Harold Albaum), 282, 284, 348 (n. 15), 379 (n. 17), 382 (n. 64)
North, Joseph (b. Joseph Soifer), 139, 276, 339 (n. 66)

Objectivism, 288
O'Casey, Sean, 281
O'Connor, Flannery, 20
Offord, Carl Ruthaven, 181, 362 (n. 5)
Olsen, Tillie (b. Tillie Lerner), 30, 107, 216, 292, 293
Oppen, George, 268, 282, 287, 341 (n. 64)
Ornitz, Samuel, 222, 306, 314, 385 (n. 19); *Bride of the Sabbath*, 222; *Haunch, Paunch and Jowl*, 222
O'Sheel, Shamus (b. James Shields), 251, 252, 253, 254, 377 (n. 2)

Page, Myra (b. Dorothy Page Gary, also known as Dorothy Markey), 103, 108, 345 (n. 40); *Daughter of the Hills*, 108, 117
Paley, Grace, 216
Partisan Review, 31, 33, 36, 63, 67, 68, 80, 127, 132, 141, 152, 175, 262, 335 (n. 84)
Patrick, Josephine, 301, 385 (nn. 9, 12)
Patterson, Louise, 43
Paull, Irene, 116, 383 (n. 80)
People's art, poetry, culture, 49, 58, 79, 85, 96, 251, 253, 254, 255, 271, 274, 276, 284, 287, 288, 290
People's Daily World and *People's World*, 52, 53, 54, 346 (n. 2), 385 (n. 11)
People's Songs, 86, 341 (n. 5)
People's Voice, 181, 183, 197, 262 (n. 5), 364 (n. 26)
Peters, Paul (b. Harbor Allen), 120, 347 (n. 13)
Peterson, Rachel, 365 (n. 38)
Petry, Ann (b. Anne Lane), xii, 85, 88, 150, 152, 153, 165, 179–200, 242, 296, 298, 318, 319, 366 (n. 66); *Country Place*, 363 (n. 13); *The Narrows*, 178, 179–200, 221, 362 (n. 3); *The Street*, 88, 155, 182, 344
Petry, George David, 181, 182, 362 (n. 5)
Phelps, Christopher, 346 (n. 3)
Phillips, William (b. William Litvinsky), 33, 63, 65, 67, 332 (n. 41)
Pierce, Theodore ("Ted"), 202, 203, 204, 212, 369 (nn. 99, 109)
Pillin, William, 383 (n. 80)
Pitts, Rebecca, 121, 123–27, 169, 348 (nn. 20, 21, 24), 349 (n. 25)
PM, 183
Poems for Workers, 254
Pohl, Frederik, 88
Polonsky, Abraham Lincoln, 82, 184, 220, 223, 225–30, 298, 303, 319, 372 (n. 20); *The World Above*, 220, 223, 225–30
Poplar, Ellen (b. Frieda Poplowitz, also known as Ellen Wright), 162, 166, 167, 172, 358 (n. 27)
Popular Front, xvi, xviii, 4, 8, 9, 10, 12, 13, 14, 15, 20, 33, 51, 54, 56, 58, 60, 61, 67, 93, 124, 141, 148, 151, 224, 240, 255, 261, 292, 300, 302, 314, 322, 326, 327 (n. 16), 336 (n. 7), 337 (n. 18), 356 (n. 4)
Porter, Katherine Anne, 107, 124
Potok, Chaim, 294

Powell, Dawn, 344 (n. 34)
Progressive/Progressivism, xi, 3–14, 17, 19, 24, 33, 36, 42, 50, 51, 52, 58, 59, 66, 74, 79, 104, 112, 120, 121, 142, 150, 157, 166, 189, 194, 197, 199, 201, 207, 210, 212, 216, 231, 251, 253, 278, 297, 317, 323, 338 (n. 22)
Progressive Labor Party, 268
Progressive Party, 33, 59, 120, 198, 210, 211, 213, 232. *See also* Wallace, Henry
Proletarian culture, xv, 8, 9, 24, 35, 50–116, 128, 129, 130, 140, 141, 143, 145, 158, 179, 203, 235, 236, 254, 255, 260, 263, 264, 286, 287, 288, 311, 324, 336 (nn. 3, 7)
Proletarian novel, 49–59, 65, 108, 130, 131, 143, 336 (n. 3)
Proletarian poetry, 250–91 passim
Promethean Review, 79
Pulp literature, 24, 30, 34, 88, 130, 140, 162, 196, 264, 265, 344, 349 (n. 36)

Rabinowitz, Paula, 344 (n. 33), 358 (nn. 17, 23), 362 (n. 5), 363 (n. 14), 368 (n. 85)
Racism, 13, 14, 15, 27, 57, 71, 153, 166, 172, 176, 184, 185, 208, 209, 213, 296, 303, 321, 368
Radosh, Ronald, 329 (n. 44), 337 (n. 16)
Rahv, Philip (b. Ivan Greenberg), 65, 67, 335 (n. 84), 336 (n. 3)
Rakosi, Carl (also known as Callman Rawley), 29, 32, 34, 282, 288, 331 (n. 40), 332 (n. 49)
Rand, Ayn, 344 (n. 34)
Randall, Dudley, 383 (n. 80)
Reader's Scope, 129, 130
Redding, Arthur, 326 (n. 7), 350 (n. 45)
Red Scare. *See* Cold War and McCarthyism
Reed, Ishmael, 274
Reed, John, 138, 139
Regionalism (radical), 49, 89, 92, 220

Rella, Ettor (pseud. John Condell), 79, 383 (n. 80)
Replansky, Naomi, 121, 123, 165, 169, 268, 359 (n. 40), 383 (n. 80)
Rexroth, Kenneth, 81, 82, 274
Ribuffo, Leo, 328 (n. 34)
Ricoeur, Paul, 316, 325 (n. 1)
Rideout, Walter, 341 (n. 1)
Riggs, Lynn, 118, 119
River, W. L. ("Les"), 28, 29, 33, 54, 311, 332 (n. 47); *Death of a Young Man*, 28–29
Robbins, Jerome (b. Jerome Wilson Rabinowitz), 119
Roberts, Marguerite (also known as Marguerite Sanford, "Maggie"), 118, 124
Robeson, Paul, 138, 153, 179, 191, 232, 363 (n. 14), 365 (n. 47)
Robinson, Mabel Louise, 187, 190, 191, 365 (n. 42)
Rodney, Lester, 349 (n. 38)
Rolfe, Edwin (b. Solomon Fishman), 254, 257, 266, 288
Rollins, William, Jr. (pseud. Stacy O'Conner), 140–44, 145, 148, 149, 354 (nn. 91, 99), 355 (n. 106); *Murder at Cypress Hall*, 140; *The Obelisk*, 140; *The Ring and the Lamp*, 140; *The Shadow Before*, 140, 141, 142; *The Wall of Men*, 140
Roosevelt, Eleanor, 73, 350 (n. 46), 367 (n. 74)
Roosevelt, Franklin D., 33, 58, 146, 194, 280
Root, E. Merrill, 310
Rosenberg, Julius and Ethel, trial of, 17, 18, 19, 250, 329 (nn. 44, 45), 361 (n. 51)
Ross, Harry, 34
Ross, Sam (b. Samuel Rosen), 89, 90, 164, 220
Rosten, Norman, 220, 252, 253, 261, 378 (n. 12), 383 (n. 80)

Roth, Henry, 29, 56, 67, 221, 320
Roth, Philip, 216, 241
Rousset, David, 158, 159, 357 (n. 10)
Rowley, Hazel, 162, 163, 351 (n. 51), 357 (n. 16), 358 (n. 27), 359 (n. 34)
Rubinstein, Annette T., 75, 78, 80, 81, 82, 121, 327 (n. 15)
Rukeyser, Muriel, 68, 124, 126, 254, 282, 287, 320
Russian Revolution, 16, 82, 139, 160, 185, 201
Ryley, Robert, 331 (n. 31), 333 (n. 66)

Sacco and Vanzetti trial, 136
Sackler, Arthur, 307
Salinger, J. D., 20, 21, 216
Salt of the Earth, 321
Sandoz, Mari, 108
Sanford, John (b. Julian Shapiro), 84, 96, 118, 119, 219, 220, 223, 224, 225, 230, 238, 270, 293, 298, 303, 315, 346 (n. 6), 372 (n. 19)
San Juan, E., Jr., 385 (n. 7)
Sartre, Jean-Paul, 96, 126, 158, 160, 162, 173
Sax, Saville, 132, 352 (n. 62)
Scales, Irving Junius, 117, 346 (n. 2), 382 (n. 64)
Schappes, Morris, 21, 326 (n. 2)
Schlauch, Margaret, 60, 66, 121, 306, 386 (n. 28)
Schmidt, James Norman (pseud. James Norman), 89
Schneider, Isidor, 60, 61, 66, 78, 132, 174
Schneir, Miriam, 329 (n. 44)
Schneir, Walter, 329 (n. 44)
Schreiber, Rebecca, 370 (n. 139)
Schulberg, Budd, 51–56, 59, 89, 323, 336 (n. 11), 337 (n. 16); *On the Waterfront*, 59; *What Makes Sammy Run*, 51–55, 221
Science & Society, 60, 396, 394

Science fiction, 88, 267, 293, 311, 317, 362 (n. 1), 390 (n. 2)
Scottsboro case, 43, 193, 174, 279, 308
Seaver, Edwin, 55, 88, 307, 338 (n. 15), 387 (n. 30)
Seid, Ruth. *See* Sinclair, Jo
Shanley, Kathryn, 394
Shapiro, Karl, 216
Shaw, Irwin (b. Irwin Shamforoff), 89, 285
Shechner, Mark, 335 (n. 89)
Siegel, Eli, 255, 284, 382 (n. 69)
Sigal, Clancy (b. Clarence Sigal), 293
Silber, Irwin, 119, 341 (n. 3), 347 (n. 8)
Sillen, Janet (b. Janet Feder), 62–74 passim, 338 (n. 36)
Sillen, Samuel (pseud. Walter Ralston), xvi, 52, 54, 56, 59, 60, 61, 62–74, 84, 174, 257, 267
Sinclair, Jo (b. Ruth Seid), 84, 121, 219, 224, 225, 238–49, 298, 303, 315, 319, 373 (n. 38), 374 (n. 47); *Anna Teller*, 223, 238–49, 374 (nn. 53, 54), 375 (nn. 58, 59), 376 (nn. 62, 65, 66); *The Changelings*, 244, 374 (n. 50), 375 (n. 53); *Wasteland*, 88, 108, 221
Sing Out!, 119
Sklar, George, 89
Slade, Caroline, 344
Slochower, Harry, 60, 198, 199, 200
Smethurst, James, 383 (n. 81)
Smith, Billy Ben, 387 (n. 35)
Smith, Lillian, 109
Smith, Lucy, 277, 383
Smith, Ray, 132, 352 (n. 59)
Smith, William Gardner, 89, 150, 153, 390 (n. 2)
Smith Act, 15, 18, 173, 257, 271, 339 (n. 71)
Socialist Party, 66, 132
Socialist Realism, 7, 9, 49, 50, 55, 75, 92, 233, 276, 336

Socialist Workers Party (SWP), 127, 212, 301, 385 (n. 12). *See also* Trotsky, Leon, and Trotskyism
Social Realism, 9, 27, 35, 45, 49, 84, 94, 97, 98, 155, 215, 226, 239, 284, 292, 300, 303, 369 (n. 105)
Sollors, Werner, 371 (n. 9)
Southern Negro Youth Congress, 213
South Side Writers Group, 164
Soviet Russia Today (later called *New World Review*), 141, 284, 354 (n. 99)
Spain and Spanish Civil War, xi, 2, 3, 7, 12, 15, 36, 101, 211, 242, 247, 261, 283, 288, 333 (n. 61), 343 (n. 28)
Stafford, Jean, 109
Stalin, Joseph, and Stalinism, xiii, xv, 12, 12–17, 20, 31, 55, 60, 65, 66, 67, 70, 72, 98, 102, 103, 105, 115, 132, 151, 152, 160, 191, 194, 217, 218, 224, 233, 235, 239, 245, 255, 268, 270, 274, 292, 293, 296, 305, 306, 315, 321, 328 (n. 33), 356 (n. 4), 388 (n. 5)
Starrett, Vincent, 24
Stead, Christina, 107, 386 (n. 20)
Steinbeck, John, xiv, 36, 51, 56, 57, 67, 68, 69, 78, 92, 130, 169
Steiner, Stan (pseud. Mike Newberry), 79, 80, 340 (n. 93)
Sterling, Dorothy, 310
Stern, Milton, 386 (nn. 23, 28)
Stern, Philip Van Doren, 130
Stevenson, Janet (b. Janet Alantis Marshall), 266, 311, 390 (n. 2)
Stevenson, Philip (pseud. Lars Lawrence), 89, 94, 266, 312, 343 (n. 15)
Strong, Anna Louise, 64, 338 (n. 39)
Stuart, John (pseud. for Jacob Vinocur), 139, 304
Suhl, Yuri, 220
Surrealism, xvii, 22, 35, 78, 127, 132, 154, 162, 262, 271, 275, 281
Synanon, xviii, 315,

TASS (Telegraphic Agency of the Soviet Union), 34, 35
Tax, Meredith, 293
Third Period of Communism, 60, 168, 255, 261, 314
Thompson, Jim, 88, 168, 253, 261, 314
Timberman, Elizabeth ("Timmy"), 77
Tito, Marshal Josip Broz, 17
Traverso, Enzo, 388 (n. 5)
Trilling, Diana, 335 (n. 84), 344 (n. 34), 361 (n. 52)
Trilling, Lionel, 70
Trotsky, Leon, and Trotskyism, 15, 36, 45, 65, 69, 132, 150, 156, 158, 160, 161, 169, 175, 210, 212, 264, 294, 301, 327 (n. 18), 347 (n. 12), 352 (n. 63), 357 (n. 10), 385 (n. 12)
Truman, Nelson, 313
Truman, Harry, 6, 19, 317
Trumbo, Dalton, 228, 323
Tyler, Parker, 127, 349 (n. 35), 352 (n. 63)

Uris, Leon, 216, 317 (n. 2)
USSR (former Soviet Union). *See* Russian Revolution; Stalin, Joseph, and Stalinism

Vargas Llossa, Mario, 293
Venture, 79
Von Eschen, Penny, 328 (n. 29)
Vorse, Mary Heaton, 103, 108, 345 (n. 37), 355 (n. 106)

Walker, Margaret, 164, 293, 358 (n. 20)
Wallace, Henry, 10, 33, 59, 198, 210
Wallach, Ira (pseud. Ted Tinsley), 310, 387 (n. 33)
Walton, Eda Lou, 66
Ward, Douglas Turner (b. Roosevelt Ward), 153, 198
Ward, Theodore, 152, 153, 164, 358 (n. 20)
Webb, Constance, 170

Weegee. *See* Fellig, Arthur
Welty, Eudora, 109, 344 (n. 34)
Wertham, Fredric, 154, 173, 351 (n. 490), 360 (n. 51), 361 (n. 51)
Wesson, Neil, 383
West, Dorothy, 137, 164, 201, 344
White, David McElvey, 283, 382 (n. 64)
White, Debra, 348 (n. 20)
Whitfield, Stephen, 387 (n. 4)
Whitman, Walt, 8, 24, 69, 70, 74, 254, 262, 273, 278, 282
Wiegman, Robyn, 368 (n. 98)
Wilhelm, Gale, 128
Williams, John A., 294, 359 (n. 28)
Wilson, Edmund, 142, 182, 355 (n. 83), 362 (n. 10)
Wilson, Mitchell, 225
Wilson, T. C., 120, 347 (n. 12)
Winter, Ella, 129
Winternitz, Mary, 129
Wixson, Douglas, 370 (n. 126)
Wolfe, David. *See* Maddow, Ben
Wollheim, Donald, 88
Women writers and the Left, xvi, 103–16, 179, 200, 238–49, 344 (nn. 33, 34)
Woollcott, Alexander, 112, 113, 345 (n. 46)
Workers Poetry. *See* Proletarian poetry
Works Progress Administration (WPA), 26, 34, 38, 44, 75, 124, 129, 181, 240, 242, 244, 249, 350 (n. 39), 374 (n. 53), 377 (n. 1)
Wright, Richard, xiv, 29, 57, 88, 93, 124, 140, 150–78, 179, 187, 200, 293, 298, 303, 319, 348 (n. 24), 356 (nn. 1, 4), 357 (n. 12), 357–58 (n. 17); *Native Son*, 150, 162, 348 (n. 24); *The Outsider*, 151, 152, 153, 154, 155, 156, 163–78, 357 (n. 15), 359 (n. 43)
Wright, Sarah, 277, 313

Yaddo, 124, 130
Yglesias, Helen (b. Helen Bassine), 220, 293, 373 (n. 30), 390 (n. 2)
Yglesias, Jose, 84, 293, 313
Yiddish writing and Communism, 221, 256, 278, 288, 371 (n. 10), 378 (n. 17)
Young, Murray, 282, 382 (n. 65)
Young Communist League (YCL), 1, 21, 60, 63, 198, 328 (n. 24)
Young Labor Poets, 255, 283

Zaturenska, Marya, 31, 32, 331 (n. 28), 347 (n. 12)
Zhdanov, Andrei, and Zhdanovism, 7, 9, 58, 79, 83, 215, 217
Zugsmith, Leane, 103, 108, 345 (n. 38)
Zukofsky, Louis, 287

www.ingramcontent.com/pod-product-compliance
Lightning Source LLC
Chambersburg PA
CBHW021114300426
44113CB00006B/143